York Deeds Volume 3

You are holding a reproduction of an original work that is in the public domain in the United States of America, and possibly other countries. You may freely copy and distribute this work as no entity (individual or corporate) has a copyright on the body of the work. This book may contain prior copyright references, and library stamps (as most of these works were scanned from library copies). These have been scanned and retained as part of the historical artifact.

This book may have occasional imperfections such as missing or blurred pages, poor pictures, errant marks, etc. that were either part of the original artifact, or were introduced by the scanning process. We believe this work is culturally important, and despite the imperfections, have elected to bring it back into print as part of our continuing commitment to the preservation of printed works worldwide. We appreciate your understanding of the imperfections in the preservation process, and hope you enjoy this valuable book.

YORK DEEDS.

BOOK III.

PORTLAND:
JOHN T. HULL AND B. THURSTON & CO.
1888.

PRINTED BY B THURSTON & COMPANY.

CONTENTS.

Preface	Pages	5—14
Register's Certificate	Page	15
Errata	Page	16
York Deeds	Folios	1—139
Index	Pages	1—157
I. Grantors	Pages	2— 57
II Grantees	Pages	58—115
III. Other Persons	Pages	116—127
IV. Places	Pages	128—135
V. General	Pages	136—157

PREFACE.

THE manuscript from which the following records are copied, is marked on the inside of the cover, "The third Book of Records of Deeds &c in the County of Yorke." The inscription is in the handwriting of Edward Rishworth, who was recorder during the entire period while the book was in use, from July 12, 1676, to Jan. 29, 1684. The volume is well preserved, though some of the pages are worn. The folio number 75 was accidentally omitted in numbering the leaves, but no part of the record is missing. The marginal notes by Joseph Hammond, giving the names of grantors and grantees, end at folio 46. Hammond, who was recorder from 1695 until 1710, made these notes to facilitate his examination of the records, which had often been duplicated in the early volumes. He became satisfied at this point, it appears, that a better method was needed, and so changed his plan and constructed the brief indexes which served the same purpose. Hammond himself makes two records in this book, both supplementary to documents recorded by Rishworth — in 1698, John Archdale's acknowledgment of a grant made by him in 1665, as agent for the younger Gorges; and in 1702, the testimony of a witness to a deed executed in 1680[1] In both cases he signs as register instead of recorder. The title was changed in 1697 The words recorder and clerk are used as equivalents in the colonial laws of Massachusetts, and this usage continued under the provincial charter until 1697, when it was provided by law that the clerk of the inferior court of pleas in each county should also be "the register of deeds and conveyances." In 1715 the register was made an independent officer, to be elected for a term of five years by the freeholders of his county.[2]

Two important public events mark the eight years from 1676 to 1684 — first, the Indian war known as King Philip's war;

[1] Infra, fol. 100, 90
[2] Charters and Laws of Massachusetts Bay (Boston 1814 Colony laws c Province laws, c 48, 114

and second, the sale of Maine to Massachusetts and the subsequent reorganization of the provincial government.

The first Indian war began, in Maine, in September, 1675, and ended with the peace concluded at Casco, April 12, 1678. Many traces of the struggle remain among these records of peaceful buying and selling.

Under the laws of Massachusetts, a committee of militia was appointed in each town to provide for the general safety, and every man above the age of sixteen, unless disabled or otherwise exempt, was enrolled for military service. The committee was also authorized, on receiving proper instructions, to impress as many men as might be needed, for expeditions against the enemy.[1] Francis Small and John Tomson relate in this volume, that they were impressed to hunt Indians in the Ossipee country, in 1676, and Tomson describes a memorable scene. He was sitting at breakfast, he says, with his comrade, Tristram Harris, up in the woods above Salmon Falls, and took occasion to ask what would become of Harris's estate, in case he should be taken off. Harris, being a solitary man, without wife or family, answered that he intended his estate for William Smyth's children, whenever he should be taken out of this life, which happened not long afterward.[2]

In August, 1676, the Indians burned Hammond's fort at Nequasset, and Clarke and Lake's fort at Arrowsic. Hammond and Lake were both killed, and the settlers on the Kennebec, taking warning by their fate, fled to the westward. A month later James Middleton, having arrived at the Great Island (now Newcastle) in Piscataqua river, sold the tract on the Kennebec called Small Point, to William Gowen of Kittery.[3] Edward Camers, who had been living on Purchase's island, in the Kennebec river, just below Merrymeeting bay, and opposite to Hammond's fort, sold the property to Samuel Lynde of Boston, whose name it still bears.[4]

Major William Phillips retreated from Saco to Boston, and never returned. Major Phillips was the successor to the Vines patent on the right bank of the Saco river, and had procured from Mogghegon, the sagamore of the Saco, a grant of the terri-

[1] Ibid, Colony laws, c 70   [2] Infra, fol 16   [3] Infra, fol 67

[4] Infra, fol 80 The description, "lying with the Widow Elizabeth Hammond's lands easterly," shows conclusively that Hammond's fort was not on Arrowsic, as stated by Sullivan

tory between the Kennebunk and Saco rivers, as far inland as Salmon Falls on the Saco; from another sagamore a giant extending his possessions on the Saco up to the Little Ossipee river; and from Fluellen, sagamore of Cape Porpoise (now Mousam) river, a tract extending from the upper line of Wells to Berwick on the west, and to the Little Ossipee on the north excepting the township (now Lyman) previously sold by Fluellen, and acquired by Harlakenden Symonds. These Indian deeds covered the towns now known as Sanford, Alfred, Waterborough, Hollis, Dayton, Biddeford, and Kennebunkport; they were confirmed by the younger Gorges in 1670; but the rights of settlers prevailed against the Indian titles, and indeed were recognized by Phillips himself.

In June, 1676, Major Phillips conveyed to his sons Samuel and William Phillips, his sons-in-law John Alden and Robert Lord, and to Edward Sprague of London, with whom he had business dealings, the southwest half of the township of Cape Porpoise, between Batson's river and Kennebunk river[1] The claims of these grantees lay dormant for more than half a century. For a long time, during the Indian wars, the town was deserted, but was reincorporated in 1719 and named Arundel.[2] In 1731, the Phillips claim was revived, but was easily and finally defeated.

Three days after making the conveyance just described, Major Phillips conveyed nineteen thousand acres to nineteen persons, in a tract laid out for a township eight miles square, above Wells, and southwest of Coxhall, now Lyman.[3] This was the beginning of the town of Sanford. The grantees were two sons and five daughters of Major Phillips by his wife Bridget, her four children by a former marriage with John Sanford, two sons-in-law, and six others. They were to take up a thousand acres apiece in the most convenient place for settling a town, as a majority of them should direct, but without detriment to the rights of former residents, if any should return to their abandoned dwellings within seven years. Their joint holdings amounted to nearly half of the township. The remainder passed by Mrs Phillips's will in 1698, to Peleg Sanford, her eldest son by her former marriage.[4] In 1734, or about that time, the proprietors under these titles organized a plantation called Phillipstown, which in 1768 became the town of Sanford.

[1] Infra, fol. . [2] The name was changed to Kennebunkport in 1-41. Infra fol 5
[4] History of York County, 368.

On the 25th of September, 1676, the settlement at Cape Neddick, in York, was destroyed by the savages, and about forty persons were slain or carried away into captivity. It was here that Peter Weare lived, but he and his family escaped. He sold a portion of his lands near Cape Neddick in 1683,[1] but still retained about two hundred acres at the time of his death in 1692. He was "lately deceased" Nov 1, 1692, when his widow filed an inventory of his estate, valued at £231[2]

Mrs. Ann Godfrey accuses Weare of negligence while he was recorder[3] She says she directed him to record her deed conveying two acres of marsh, a part of her farm in York, to William Moore; but learning that no record of the transaction was made, she is compelled to execute a new conveyance to perfect Moore's title. The history of the farm is interesting It was originally a tract of twenty acres, between York river and Braveboat harbor, granted to George Burdett, who was minister at Agamenticus from 1636 until 1640[4] In 1640 Mrs. Godfrey, then Mrs. Ann Messant, was Burdett's housekeeper, and on the 18th of March, he borrowed from her £112, giving security on six steers, three cows and his farm, for repayment by the last of March, 1641.[5] But on the 8th of the next September, Burdett was indicted "for a man of ill name and fame, infamous for incontinency," and heavily fined for his misdemeanors.[6] He was a ruined man, and his housekeeper became anxious about her money. Burdett gave her what purported to be a deed of the farm, but when she showed the document to Richard Vines, he discovered that the minister had neither dated nor signed it. Thereupon Mrs. Messant again importuned her slippery debtor, and he, in haste to be gone, finally authorized Edward Johnson, as his attorney, to deliver legal possession of the land to her.[7] Edward Godfrey was one of the magistrates who tried Burdett, and the fact that he afterward married Mrs. Messant, shows that her reputation did not suffer by reason of her residence with the profligate clergyman After Godfrey's departure for England, in 1655, she continued to reside on her farm, which she finally conveyed in 1667, being then again a widow, to her daughter Alice, wife of Nicholas Shapleigh, receiving in return Shapleigh's bond for an annuity of £20 during her life.[8]

[1] Infra, fol 132   [2] 5 York Deeds.   [3] Infra, fol 86   [4] 4 York Deeds, 46
[5] 4 Yo   [6] "   [7]   [8] fol 116
[9] 2 10

PREFACE. 9

The war ended in April, 1678, but a month before, on the 13th of March, Ferdinando Gorges had conveyed the province of Maine to John Usher, the agent of Massachusetts, who in turn executed a conveyance to the governor and company of Massachusetts Bay.[1] The two indentures were read to the general court of Massachusetts on the 2d of October, 1678, and were then delivered to the secretary, in a black box, for safe keeping. On the same day, the court desired the governor and council to take order for the government and disposal of the province, by sale or otherwise.[2] It was known that the King was much displeased by the purchase of Maine. It was known also that the crown lawyers had reported in May, that the misdemeanors of the Massachusetts company were sufficient to vacate their charter. The authority to sell the province, was probably intended to sanction a conveyance to the king, if in the judgment of the governor and council that step should become necessary.

In May, 1679. magistrates were appointed for York county as usual.[3] It was not until Feb. 4, 1680, that the general court took courage to reconstruct the government of the province and requested and empowered the council to appoint a president, justices of the peace, and other officers required by the Gorges patent.[4] The council thereupon appointed Thomas Danforth president, with eight resident justices — Bryan Pendleton, Charles Frost, Francis Hooke, John Davis, Joshua Scottow, Samuel Wheelwright, John Wincoll, and Edward Rishworth. Assistants Samuel Nowell and Nathaniel Saltonstall were appointed commissioners to aid President Danforth in settling the new government, which was inaugurated at York, March 17, 1680.[5] Pendleton was appointed deputy president, Hooke treasurer of the province, Frost commandant of the militia, and Rishworth secretary and recorder. The justices constituted a provincial council, and a general assembly was composed of the president and

---

[1] Both documents are printed in 2 Maine Hist Coll 257 Palfrey (3 New England, 312) and Williamson (1 Maine, 461), both give the year 1677, but the correct date is March 13, 1677-8 Gorges, in this conveyance expressly reserves the Indian grants confirmed or supposed to be confirmed, to Major Phillips in 1670, in favor of Nathaniel Phillips, the Major's son, by his second wife, Susanna Stanley, Bridget Sanford's predecessor Nathaniel was a merchant of Boston, whose business took him to England from time to time, and it would appear that he had procured this confirmation in his own name instead of his father's Compare 2 York Deeds, 169, 174, and fol 3 infra.

[2] 5 Mass Records, 183, 187   [3] Ibid 217   [4] Ibid 258

[5] Williamson (1 Maine, 563) appears to be in doubt about this date It is confirmed, however, by Hutchinson, who says (1 Mass 296) Danforth repaired to Maine "towards the end of 1679," (i e., 1679-80) and conclusively by the signatures of Francis Hooke, March 24, 1680, and Edward Rishworth March 31, 1680, as "justices of the peace" See fol 64, infra.

council with deputies elected by the towns. The deputy president, with the assistance of other justices, was empowered to hold courts from which an appeal lay to the president in council. The report of President Danforth and the other gentlemen employed in settling the government, was received at Boston on the 11th of June, 1680, and approved.[1]

The eastern settlements in Maine had been abandoned during the Indian war, but the inhabitants were now returning to their ruined homes. At the first general assembly, held at York, March 30, 1680, the towns of Cape Porpoise, Scarborough and Falmouth were not represented, though Walter Gendall appeared for Falmouth, but having no certificate of election, could not take his seat.[2] In September, President Danforth with his associates, Messrs Nowell and Saltonstall, visited Falmouth and held a court there On this occasion he made proclamation, that a new plantation, to be established on the northerly shore of Casco bay, should be named North Yarmouth.[3] It is said that Sir Ferdinando Gorges had granted a township between the Wescustogo (now Royall's) river and the mouth of the Bunganoc in Maquoit bay,[4] but no municipal government had been set up there. On the contrary, John Redding recites, in a deed recorded in this volume,[5] that he derived his title to a tract on the Harraseket river from a grant by the selectmen of Casco Bay, and names as one of the selectmen when the grant was made, Richard Bray, who bought half of Cousins island in 1651.[6] But Casco Bay, before 1658, was the name of the plantation which afterward became Falmouth,[7] and the northeastern boundary of Falmouth was the famous "Massachusetts line," which cut off, it appears, a considerable part of the territory belonging to Casco or Casco Bay, while George Cleve was agent there for Gorges, and afterward for Rigby Falmouth having now been re-organized, there was a desire for a new township beyond, and the general court at Boston, on the 11th of June, 1680, granted a township five miles square, on the east side of the Wescustogo

---

[1] 5 Mass Records 280 It was perhaps from these "commissioners," associated with Danforth, that John Bray received the order on the provincial treasurer for £3, acknowledged on fol 103, infra

[2] Willis's Portland, 225

[3] To distinguish it from Yarmouth on Cape Cod So the town of York is sometimes called East York, to distinguish it from the New York on Manhattan island See fol 81, infra

[4] Sullivan's Maine, 183   [5] Fol 53

[6] Infra

[7] 1 Yor

river, and two islands adjacent (probably Cousins and Littlejohn's), on condition that twenty or thirty families, and an able minister, should be settled there within two years[1] This was the town which President Danforth named North Yarmouth. He also added thereto the waste lands lying between the grant of the general court and the town of Falmouth, and an island called New Damariscove, now Haskell's island, near the southeastern point of Harpswell Neck.[2]

On the 19th of October, 1680, the President wrote from Boston to Deputy President Pendleton, or Justice John Davis, at York, directing them, or either of them, to summon a court to hear a complaint by Edward Randolph against one Nicolls, master of a ketch which had been seized in Maine for trading contrary to the acts of trade[3] Randolph had arrived in this country in December, 1679, commissioned as collector, surveyor and searcher for New England, to see that these odious laws were enforced. The navigation laws at that time prohibited any colonial commerce, save with English ports and in English vessels. Duties were required even on certain commodities carried from one plantation to another,[4] and the complaint against Nicolls was probably for neglect of this requirement. But the whole population resented these proceedings, and the juries quite regularly found against the "searcher." President Danforth therefore prudently ordered that Mr Randolph, on exhibiting his libel, should deposit £10 to cover costs of court, the remainder, if any, to be returned to the prosecutor after the trial

On the 11th of May, 1681, Danforth was re-appointed, and was formally authorized to confirm, under his official seal and signature, the rightful possessions of landholders in Maine.[5] The rule governing contested cases was laid down by the general court in 1674, the "eldest grant" was to be confirmed.[6] New grants were to be made by the general court and certified by the president An illustration of this practice is found in the grant recorded in this volume,[7] of sixty acres apiece and a mill privi-

---

[1] 5 Mass Records, 267   [2] 2 Maine Hist Coll 172. Wheeler's Brunswick, &c, 85

[3] Infra, fol 84 Pendleton died not long afterward His will was proved in April 1681 (Sargent's Maine Wills 61), and Davis succeeded him as deputy president

[4] 3 Palfrey's New England, 279. In May, 1634, Secretary Rawson wrote from Boston to Governor Cranfield, of New Hampshire, reporting complaints of customs improperly collected on the Piscataqua, from vessels carrying lumber from point to point on the Maine side of the river   5 Mass Records, 444

[5] 5 Mass Records, 306   [6] Infra fol 97   Compare 1 York Deeds ₣ 26

[7] Fol 125. Willis Portland 233, ... Purpooduc

lege to George and John Ingersoll of Falmouth. This was in 1682. Massachusetts had agreed in October, 1681, that all streams and mill-sites in Maine should be exempt from rent, leaving this source of revenue to the province, which soon afterward laid a tax upon mills to provide for the maintenance of a garrison at Fort Loyal. It must be understood, therefore, that the rent of £5 a year required of the Ingersolls by Danforth, is not for the mill-site but for the privilege of cutting timber anywhere above the proposed saw mill.

In 1682 the general court granted Merriconeag Neck to Harvard college, and in 1684 the island of Sebascodegan was bestowed upon President Danforth and Commissioner Nowell, as full recompense for their service in settling the government of Maine; but neither grant took effect. Both tracts had been bought from the Indians by Nicholas Shapleigh in 1659 or 1660, and his heir, John Shapleigh, sold them in 1683 to Richard Wharton, through whom the title passed to the Pejepscot company.[1] In Shapleigh's conveyance, the name Pejepscot appears for the first time in this series of records. The head of Merriconeag Neck is bounded, Shapleigh says, by "the plains of Pejepscot."[2]

The Massachusetts charter was annulled June 18, 1684; but Danforth's administration in Maine continued until May, 1686, when Joseph Dudley received his commission from King James II, and assumed the government of Maine, New Hampshire, Massachusetts, and the King's Province in the Narraganset country.

In a conveyance made in 1643 by Governor Thomas Gorges, and recorded in this volume, we find Saco described as "in the county of Surrey." Three of the names which Sir Ferdinando Gorges bestowed upon the eight bailiwicks or counties into which he divided his province, have now been discovered — Devon, Somerset and Surrey.[3]

Two conveyances by John Archdale, in October, 1665, show that he tarried in Maine after the Gorges government was dissolved, in June of that year, by the royal commissioners; and that he continued to act as the proprietor's agent in disposing of the lands[4]

[1] Wheeler's Brunswick, &c., 17.
[3] Inf
[2] Infra, fol. 128.

PREFACE.   13

In 1666, Thomas Mayhew, of Martin's Vineyard, sold one of the Elizabeth islands, on the Plymouth coast, to Peter Oliver of Boston. In 1682 the conveyance was recorded in Maine. This appears to have been done because the grantor was in fact a citizen of Maine, Martin's (or Martha's) Vineyard being the "Isle of Capawock, near Cape Cod," conveyed to Sir Ferdinando Gorges by the royal charter of 1639.[1]

The upper division of the town of Kittery, previously the parish of Unity, becomes in this volume the parish of Berwick, and sometimes the town of Berwick, though the town was not incorporated under that name until 1713. The name Berwick first occurs in 1681;[2] but a division of the town, for certain purposes, had been made ten years before. It is recorded here[3] that the selectmen and inhabitants of the parish of Unity, on the 13th of April, 1671, granted sixty acres of land to Alexander Cooper, and as many more to George Gray, "by virtue of a general act of the town, made the 24th of June last past." The general act still stands on the Kittery records, under the date, June 24, 1670·

> Voted and concluded that ye Selectmen this day chosen as above shall have full power to dispose of lands in ye Severall parts of this town, that is to say, the Selectmen that live in upper devision of ye town when they Intend to grant any land shall give Legall Notice to ye Inhabitants of that part of ye town, both of ye time and place of their meeting to ye purpose that soe who please to se what grants are made may be present, and what grants are soe made by ye sd Selectmen shall stand firm and good, and alsoe ye Selectmen that live in the lower Devision of ye town have the same power of granting lands for granting land there, giving like Notice to ye Inhabitants of that part of ye town.[4]

This explains the confirmation by "the selectmen of the town of Berwick, alias Newgewanac,"[5] in 1683, of the grants of the town of Kittery to Richard and George Leader, and to their successors, Richard, Eliakim and William Hutchinson, for the accommodation of their saw mills on the Asabumbeduc river. The old Leader mill, blacksmith's shop and other property there, were appraised in 1669 at £493.[6] In 1679 the Hutchinson mill

---
[1] Infra, fol 114 In the act of 1692, for establishing courts of justice (Charters and Laws of Mass. Bay Province Laws, c. 5), it is ordained that sessions of the peace shall be held "upon the Island of Capawock, alias Martha's Vineyard," and on the island of Nantucket, which is doubtless the "Isle of Nautican," also granted to Gorges in the charter of 1639. See Macy's Nantucket, 4, where it appears that Thomas Mayhew, senior, acquired his title to Nantucket from Richard Vines, steward to Sir Ferdinando Gorges

[2] Infra, fol 130.   [3] Infra, fol 22

[4] Certified copy, kindly furnished by D. M Shapleigh, town clerk of Kittery.

[5] Infra, fol. 133   [6] 2 York Deeds, 69

was known as the "great works saw mill," and the stream is now the Great Works river.

The Indian grant to Thomas Webber and John Parker's subsequent conveyance to his sister, Mary Webber, are the titles under which a large part of the town of Phipsburg is now held. They are recorded in this volume.

The manner in which the records have been transcribed and printed, is explained in the preface to the first book. An explanation of the contractions in the text will be found in the same place

H. W. RICHARDSON.

REGISTER'S CERTIFICATE.

State of Maine.

COUNTY OF YORK, ss:

This may certify that the following printed volume is a true copy of the third book of records of the Registry of Deeds for this County; that I have read and compared the same with the original records; and that all accidental variations that have been detected are noted in the table of errata on the following page.

Attest:

Justin M. Leavitt
Register of Deeds for York County.

ERRATA.

☞ The sign — is used below, when the line indicated is numbered backward from the end of the folio

Fol.					
4	line 44	*after*	proportions	*omit*	&
7	18	*for*	1674	*read*	1676
7		52 *before*	Pendleton	*repeat*	Bryan
9	57	*for*	bee	*read*	hee
9	—20	"	Hillon	"	Hilton
14	69	"	or	"	of
15	62	"	S	"	H S
15	73	*after*	South West	*insert*	&
17	75	"	yᵉ	"	intent of yᵉ
17		77 *erase*	houseing		
18	68	"	aforesd		
19	65	*after*	daughter	*insert*	the
22	—52	*for*	the	*read*	this
23	—53	*after*	with	*omit*	the
24	25	"	formerly	*insert*	was
25	4	"	with all	"	the
25	42	"	acres	"	of
25	49	"	on	"	the
25	—42	"	within	"	written
25	—15	"	vnder woods	"	waters
26	47	"	Act	"	&
30	—32	"	heyrs	"	Executors
32	—21	"	neede	"	soe
33	—17	"	or	"	his
34	—28	"	noe	"	other
35	—3	"	Bray	*omit*	&
41	37	*for*	Actually	*read*	mutually
43	30	"	Pʳsons	"	Pʳson
44	23	*after*	out	*omit*	all
44	—9	*for*	I	*read*	In
45	—27	*after*	by	*insert*	Mr
52	19	"	marke	"	of
57	4	*for*	my	*read*	any
57	—45	"	Redalds	"	Renalds
60	—47	*after*	joynturs	*insert*	Dowers
74	—68	*for*	Pishworth	*read*	Rishworth
74	—48	*after*	profetts	*insert*	&
95	—34	"	Walter	"	of
99	55	*for*	lawfully	*read*	lawfull
100	35	*after*	vpland	*insert*	begining

YORK DEEDS.

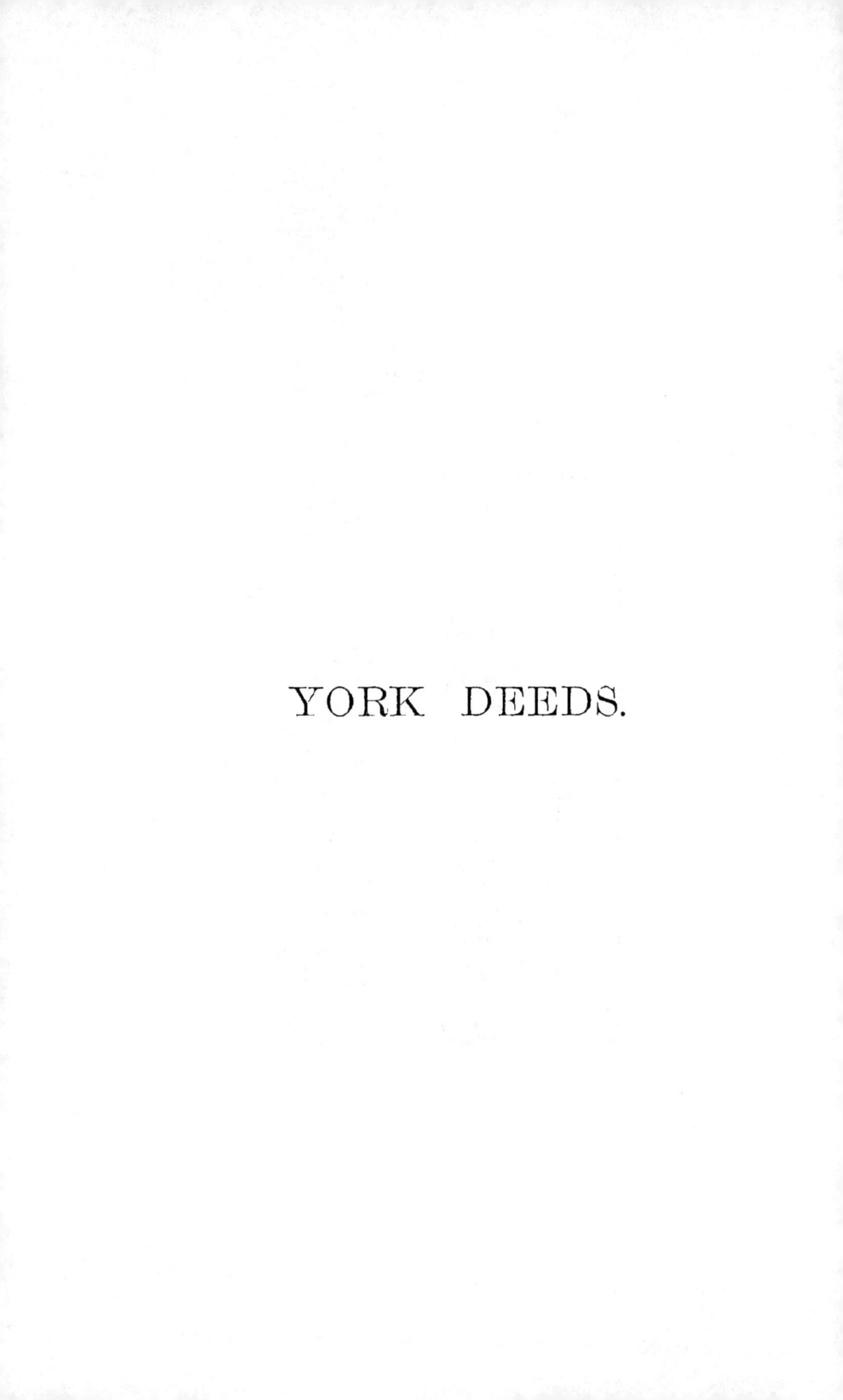

[1] To all Christian people, to whom these Prsents shall come, John Wincoll of Kittery, in the County of yorke, In New England, & Elizabeth his wife, & John Hull of Boston, in New England M^rchant, aforesayd, & Roger Playstead of Kittery aforesayd sends Greeteing, W^ras the Town of Kittery, on the fiueteenth day of Decemb^r sixteen hundred fiuety & nine, did giue & grant vnto the sayd John Wincoll, & his heyres for euer, all the accommodations of Tymber, from the Salmon ffalls & vpwards, on great Newgewanacke River, soe farc as the Town of Kittery goeth, & three Miles from the sayd River into the Woods, soe fare as It is in the Precincts of the sayd Kittery, as by the sd grant amply appeareth, & W^ras the sayd John Wincoll hath

J^no Wincol
Rog Plaisted
J^no Hull
To
Geo & John
Broughton

since y^t tyme bujlt & Erected Two saw Mills, & made dams, flumes, & all other necessary Twoles, & Vtensills, with Runing Geares, for the same, & that the sayd John Wincoll for the better secureing of seuerall debts wch hee the sayd John Wincoll by him selfe, & by Mr Tho: Broughton of Boston hath for ye Cairijng an end of the sayd Mills, for seuerall years past, mayd to Capt Thomas Clarke the sayd John Hull, & Capt Tho: Lake, as alsoe some severall hundred of pounds wch hath long since beene due to George & Jo^hn Broughton sonnes of the sayd aboue mentioned Thoms Broughton, for there getting of Loggs & ct, And the sayd John Hull, & Roger Playstead, haueing become bound, & by their bound^s bearcing date the sixt of Aprill 1671 more amply doth & may appeare/

Now know all men by these Presents that ye sayd John Wincoll, Roger Playstead & John Hull, for & in Consideration abouesayd, & that ye sayd Geor: & John Broughton may noe longer suffer discoragem^ts, by being out of soe Considerable somes, on whom much dependance is for the better

Book III, Fol. 1.

Managem{t} of the Mills, for Certajne yeas agreed vpon Wee the sayd John Wincoll, Roger Playstead, & John Hull, in whome, or some one or all of them, rests the true right & propriety of the aboue mentioned two saw Mills, dwelling house, out houses, & Lands they are vpon, & are Adioyneing doth app'rteyne, Haue absolutely given granted barganed, sould, alliened Enfeoffed, Assigned set ouer, & Confirmed & by these p{s}ents doth absolutely fully & Clearly giue grant bargane sell aleine Assigue set ouer & Confirme vnto the sayd Geo: & John Broughton, & thejr heyres & Assigns for euer, all that our & euery of our Right title Interest, Clayme & demand, that Wee or either of us now haue heretofore had, or hereafter may haue in one Cleare fourth part of the two Sall Mills, with all thejre running Geares, Vtinsills, Flumes, Bownes water, & water Courses, with the dwelling house out houses, & all the Lands as aboue, & in the originall grants aboue mentioned, is declared, with all the Tymber trees standing or lyng & being on the same, with all & all manner of Lybertys, privilidges, & appurtenances, as to one Cleare fourth part of, & into the whoole aboue mentioned given & granted/ To haue & to hould, to them the sayd George & John Broughton, thejr heyres & Assignes for ever, from the day & date hereof, one absolute Cleare & distinct forth part of the aboue mentioned two saw Mills, with y{r} running Geares, Vtensills, flewms, Bownes River water, Water Courses, dwelling house, & out houses, with the Lands on which they stand, & all other the aboue mentioned Lands, Tymber, trees, & all & all manner of other the lybertys priuiledges, & appurtenances thereto in any kind or wise vsed, belonging or app'tayneing, & to them & thejr severall heyres vsses benefitts & behoofes for euer, & the sayd John Wincoll, Roger Playstead, & John Hull for them selues thejr & euery of thejr heyres, executors Administrators & Assignes, doe Covenant promiss & grant to & with the sayd George Broughton & John Broughton, thejre respectiue hevires, & Assignes, that they the sayd John Win-

BOOK III, FOL. 1.

coll Roger Playstead, & John Hull, or some one or all of them, haue in them selues good right full pouer & authority the aboue granted Premisses, to sell Assigne & Assure, & that the same & euery part and Prcell there of, are free & Cleare with thejr priuiledges and appurtenances of and from all former & other Gyfts grants sayles Leases, Morgages Joynturs Judgm^ts Wills Intayles, executions, & all other Incomberances of what nature & kind soeuer, had made done acknowledged, Committed or suffered to bee done, or Committed by them or either of them, thejr or either of thejr heyres, executors or Assignes, whereby the sayd George Broughton, & John Broughton thejr respectiue heyres or Assignes shall or may any way bee molested, Ineuicted or erected, out of the Cleare fourth part as aboue is mentioned & granted, in all the sayd Mills houses Lands Rivers trees & other appurtenances/

In witness where of the sayd John Wincoll, Roger Playstead, John Hull, haue herevnto set thejr hands & Seales, with the Consent & full approbation of the aboue mentioned Thomas Broughton the father, this foure & Twenteth day of Septemb^r one thousand six hundred seaventy three. 1673

Signed sealed & Deliverd   John Wincoll (his seale)
   by Roger Playstead, &   Roger Playstead/ (his seale)
   John Hull the day & yeare   John Hull (his seale)
   aboue written in P'sence of Josua Scottow/
   William Needum/   Edw: Rawson/

Signed sealed & Delivered by John Wincoll the
   thyrteenth day of June, In the yeare of our
   Lord one thousand six hundred seaventy & six
   in the p'sence of us/

   Jabez ffox/   Capt John Wincoll P'sonally appeare-
   Richard Hartupp/   ing acknowledged this Instrument
                            to bee his Act & Deede July 5th
                            1676   before mee
                                William Stowton Assistant

Book III, Fol. 1, 2.

Boston 15th May : 1676 :

William Needum & Edw: Rawson sworne say, haueing subscribed thejr name with Josua Scottow, as witnesses to this Deede, did on the day of the date of this Deede aboue written, see the sayd Roger Playstead deceased, & Mr John Hull then to signe seale & Deliver the same as thejr Act & Deede, to ye vss y^rin expressed, the day & yeare aboue written before us/   John Pynchon } Assist^{ts}
Capt Josua Scottow made oath   Edw: Tyng
as a witness to this Instrum^t
July: 5th 1676 · before mee
     William Stowton/

A true Coppy of this Instrum^t aboue written, with those severall Attests relateing y^rvnto, transcribed out of the Origmall, & y^rwith Compared, this 12th day of July 1676
            p Edw · Rishworth ReCor

[2] The Depositions of Mr Edw: Johnson, & Robert Knights aged about 60 odd years/

Testimony of Edwd Johnson & Robt Knight For Hen Norton

These Deponents being sworne, do affirme, that Mr Richard Vines neare Twenty years past or there abouts, gave unto Mr Henery Norton as his proper right all & euery part of those shpps, & Parcells of Meddow lying along the River of yorke on the South West side thereof, begining at a Redd oake on the Westermost side of the ould Mill Cricke, & Ending at y^t foure Acers of Meddow, wch was formerly sould by Robert Knight, & now is in the possession of Edw: Rishworth/ & further sayth not/ August: 16th 62 :

Taken vpon oath before mee Edw: Rishworth Assote .

A true Coppy of these depositions transcribed out of the Originall, & y^rwith Compared this 11th July 1676 .
            p Edw . Rishworth ReCor :

Book III, Fol. 2.

Robt Jordan To his Son Robt

To all Christean people, to whom this Deede of Gyft or Instrument in writeing shall come, I Robert Jordan Senjo^r, & Sarah Jordan my wife both of Richmans Ysland, In the Easterne parts of New England, Clarke, send Greeteing, in our Lord God euerlasting Know yee that Wee Robert & Sarah Jordan, as well for & in Consideration of the Naturall affection W^{ch} Wee haue & doe beare, vnto our beloued son Robert Jordan Junjo^r, Planter, vs here vnto at this Prsent sepetially moueing, as alsoe Considering the many labours, & great Industry, Prformed by our sayd son In & about our sundrey imployments In New England, aforesayd, haue given & granted, & by these Prsents doe giue grant & Confirme, fully, freely, & absolutely vnto our sayd son Robert Jordan Junjo^r, one Certajn Tract or Prcell of Land, Commanly Called or known by the name of Cape Elizabeth, In the Easterne parts of New England aforesayd, bounded with a small Gutt or streame of Water Running into the sea, out of a small Marsh lijng behind the Long Sands, to the Westward, & soe to runne vp into the Mayn Land in a Streight Lyne to the Pond Commanly called the Great Pond/ Provided & It is hereby Intended, & appoynted that the sd Robert Jordan Junjo^r, our son, his heyres executors Administrators Or Assignes, shall at noe tyme or tyms hereafter Interfere, take away, Molest or deminish any part or Prcell of the sayd Marsh, or vpland that lyeth between the sayd Marsh, & the sayd Great Pond, to the sayd streight lyne to pass as aforesayd Northwards, & soe to runne down vpon the sayd Pond to the sea, takeing vnto the sayd Premisses, Mentioned one little Ysland seituate on the East side of the sayd Pond, togeathr with all the Marshes on both sid^s, of a Cricke runneing out of the sayd Pond into the sea at Aylewife Coue, as alsoe not to Intrench vpon the Mayne vpland or Playns there vnto Adiacent aboue the extent of Twenty measured pooles, always reseruing, granting giueing & allowing vnto his brother John Jordan of Richmand^s Y-land,

Book III, Fol 2.

afoesd, or vnto his Assigns, or Prsons Concerned with him, Convenjent Ingres, regress & Egress fully & freely at all tyms & seasons to the sayd Aylewifes Coue, & there & thence to procure fetch & carry away bayt for his or thejr fishing vses at tearms & tyms seasonable: To haue & to hould, all & singular the sayd given & granted Premisses, togeather with all the priuiledges, Accommodations, profetts, appurtenances, & Convenjences there of, as aboue bounded, mentioned, or Intended, vnto the sayd Robert Jordan Jujor, his heyres executors Administrators or Assignes for euer, freely, & quietly without any matter of Challenge, Clayme, or demand of us, the sayd Robert Jordan Senjor, or Saraih my wife, or of any other Prson or Prsons whatsoeuer, in my name, or by my Cause And I the sayd Robert Jordan Senior, & Sarah my wife, all & singular the aforesayd Land, with all things in or on the same, vnto our son Robert Jordan Junjor, his heyres executors Administrators & Assignes, against all people doe warrant, & for ever defend, by these Prsents, hereby makeing voyd, revoakeing, with drawing & disanullg all former agreement Trusts Instruments of writeing, promisses & pouer whatsoeuer, Wch Wee the sayd Robert, & Saraih Jordan haue at any tyme or Tymes heretofore reposed made & put two, or in any Prson or Prsons whsoeuer concerneing this abouesd part or any other part of my Patten/ Witness our hands & seals with out fraude, this twenty ninth day of Febru: In the yeare of our Lord one thousand six hundred seaventy & fiue, And In the Twenty seauenth yeare of the Reigne of our Soueraign Lord King Charles the secund/   Robert Jordan (his seale)
Signed, sealed & deliuered in   marke S of
Presence of Elyas Styleman/   Saraih Jordan/ (her seale)
Nathall Fryer/

    Great Ysland. J day of March 167⅔ Mr Robert Jordan, Senjor, & Saraih his wife, Came before mee & acknowledged this Instrument to bee thejr free Act & Deede/

            Elyas Styleman Commissior/

BOOK III, FOL. 2.

A true Coppy of this Instrument transcribed out of the Originall & there with Compared this 27th of July 1676
       p Edw : Rishworth ReCor :

The Deposition of Tymothy Sarden aged about 50 years/

Sardens Evidence

Being examined, maketh oath, that ye last spring of the yeare, being in discourse with Dygory Jefferys, about an Heffer that was lost, hee heard the sayd Jefferys say, that hee had sould the sayd Heffer soe lost in the Woods to Richard Roe dead or ahue, for tenn shillings, for wch to the knowledg of the sayd Deponent, Ric: Roe payd Dygory fiue days worke/ & further sayth not/

Dated July 25 · 76 · Taken vpon oath before mee
       Edw : Rishworth Assote/

The Deposition of Margery Bray aged about 16 years/

Margery Bray's Testimony

Being at Dygory Jefferys house the last spring, shee heard the sayd Dygory & Richd Roe, in some discourse about an heffer, yt Dygory Jefferys had lost in the woods, & did thinke as hee sayd, hee should never see her againe, wrvpon Ric: Roe sayd I would venter to buy her If I had money/ Dygory replyed yt hee should haue ye Heffer as shee was in ye woods for tenn shillings, wrvpon Ric Roe sayd hee would giue him fiue days worke for her, wrvpon they mayd a bargan for the sayd Heffer/ & further sayth not/ Dated July : 25 : 76 : Taken vpon oath before mee at this Prsent date/
       Edw : Rishworth Assote :

A true Coppy of these testimonys aboue written transcribed out of the Originall, & there with Compared this 27th day of July : 76 : p Edw : Rishworth ReCor .

BOOK III, FOL. 3.

[3] This Indenture made, between Thomas Cowell, & Elizabeth his wife, of Kittery in the Province of Mayn, in New England on the one party, & William Hubbard Esqr of Ipswich, in the Massatusetts Colony of New England aforesayd, On the other Party, Witnesseth, that the sayd Thomas & Elizabeth his wife, for & in Consideration of Eighty pounds, in good M'chtable provission in hand payd vnto ye sayd Elizabeth formerly Widdow & Relict of William Seely Mariner, of ye Ysles of shoales, but now wife of the sayd Thomas Cowell, haue freely given granted, bargained & sould, Enfeoffed, & Confirmed & doe by these

Cowell
To
Hubbard

Prsents freely give grant bargan sell Infeoff and Confirme, vnto the sayd William the dwelling house, where in the sayd Thomas & Elizabeth now dwells, with a Prcell of Land there vnto belonging, Where on the sayd house standeth, scitnate in the sayd Kittery, with in the province of Mayn, aforesayd Entring in of the Mouth of Crooked Layn, being one Moyety of a Necke of Land (all but two Acers granted to Thomas Trickie) bounded on the South by the River of Pischataqua, on the East North East, & North West by Spruse Crecke, on the west by a logg fence, from the land of Thomas Tricky, togeather with grantums Y-land, in the sayd spruse Cricke formerly belonging to Hugh Gunnisson of the sayd Kittery & by him granted to William Rogers, & William Seely for Tearme of Yeares, but since sould Infleoffed & Confirmed to them by Saraih late Widdow & Administratrix, or Execcutrix of the sayd Gunnisson, as appears by a deed made vnder the hand & seale of the said Saraih Relict of Gunisson aforesayd, being done July the Twenteth, in the yeare sixteen hundred & sixty in Referrence y^r vnto being had, that hee the sayd Hubbard shall haue, hould possess & Imoy the sayd house & one Moeity of the sayd Necke of Land, with all the priviledges & appurtenances therevnto belonging (saueing Francis Trickys two Acers) to him his heyres, execcutors, Administrators, & Assignes, for euer, to haue hould possess . . . . Promisses, as his

& thejr proper right & Inheritance for euer, without any lett hinderance Molestation or trouble, from the sayd Thoms & Elizabeth, or any of thejr heyres or Assignes, Claymeing any Title interest demand or right, to any of the sayd barganed Premisses, or any part there of, or from any other P'son whatsoeuer/ The sayd Thomas & Elizabeth hereby further Ingageing, Covenanting & promissing to & with the sayd William & his heyres & Assignes, that they are the true & rightfull owners, & possessors of the aforesayd barganed Premisses in fee symple, at the tyme of makeing this sayd Indenture/ provided always, that If the aboue named Thomas & Elizabeth, or thejr heyres or Assignes, doe truely and lawfully pay or Cause to bee payd to the sayd William his heyres or Assignes the some of Eighty pounds, with in the space of foure years in foure æquall payments in M'chan'ble fish at the Ysles of shoals, or in other Current pay of æquivolent nature, that then this Prsent writeing to bee voyd & of none affect, otherwise to remajne in full force & vertue/ In witness w'rof the sayd Partys aboue named haue here vnto set there hands & seales this sixteenth of June/ In the years of our Lord one thousand six hundred & seaventy fiue/   Thomas Cowell ($_{\text{seale}}^{\text{his}}$)
Signed Sealed & Delivered   Elizabeth Cowell ($_{\text{seale}}^{\text{her}}$)

In y^e Prsence of us/ Thomas Cowell this day came be-
Sarah Tricky/ fore mee, & did own & ac-
Saraih Parrott knowledg this Instrum^t aboue
her ℞ marke written, w'vnto his own &
  wifes name are afixed to bee
  his free Act & Deede, this 24th
  of y^e fifth M° 1676 :

Mrs Seely, the aboue sayd   Edw · Rishworth Assote :
Morgage, is to satisfy what
is due from your selfe to my
sonn John Hubbard, as well
as to my selfe/ Witness my
hand this 5th of July 1676 :
    William Hubbard/

BOOK III, FOL. 3.

A True Coppy of this Instrument aboue written transcribed out of the originall & of ye postscript vnderwritten, & Compared with ye Originall this 27th day of July 1676/
p Edw Rishworth ReCor/

To all Christean people, to whome this Prsent deed or writeing shall Come, Majo^r William Phillips late of Sacoe In the Jurisdiction Regall of the Province of Mayne, alias Yorke shyre, in New England, & now resedient in Boston in New England aforesayd, In the Colony of the Massatusetts, sendeth Greeteing &c · Know yee that I the sayd William Phillips, for diverse good Causes & Considerations mee y^{r}vnto moueing, & espetially for the some of one hundred & Twenty pounds payd at London in the kingdome of England, to my sonn Natha^{ll} Phillips, & for Twenty pounds more to bee payd by Edw : Spragg in Bishopsgate in London Packer, to the sayd Majo^r Phillips or his order, & for sixty pounds payd by Robert Lord of London Marmer, for ye Accop^t of the sayd Edward, to mee the sayd Phillips, & for full & valewable Consideration in hand received of my sonn in law Robert Lord for his own Piticular, & for ye like full & valewable consideration received of my sun in law John Allden of Boston in New England aforesayd Marmer, whereof & where with, I the sayd William Phillips do acknowledg my selfe fully satisfyd Contented & payd, & there of, & euery part & Prcell there of, doe for my selfe my executors, Administrators & Assigns, fully whooly clearely & absolutely acquit exonerate, release, & discharge the sayd Edw · Spragg, Robert Lord, & John Allden & all & euery one of there heyres, executors, Administrators for euer, by these Prsents, And for the naturall Loue, & tender affection wch I beare to my two sonns Sam^{ll} . & William Phillips, Haue giver granted bargained sould aliend Enfeoffed & Con-

*Phillps
To
Spragg
Lord
Allden &
Phillps's*

firmed, And by these Prsents do giue grant bargane sell, Infeoff & Confirme fully Clearly & absolutely vnto the sayd Edw: Spragg, Robert Lord, John Allden, Samll Phillips & Will Phillips, theire & euery one of theire heyres, executors, Administrators, & Assigns, such parts, & Prcells, & proportions of Land as are here vnder mentioned, & Nominated being parts of a Tract of Land, scituate lying & being between Kenebunke River & Batsons River (being soe Called, commanly, or known) W^ch sayd Tract of Land is by Estimation foure Miles, & more by the sea side, that is to say from River, [4] to River, & is to extend, reach & runne vp eight Miles into the Land, & which sayd Tract or Prcell of Land is scituate lying & being with in the province of Mayne, alias Yorke shyre, & was purchased by mee the sayd William Phillips of an Indean Sagamore Comanly known to the English people about that part of the Countrey by the name of Mogheggine, with other Land thereto adioyneing, as by the Deeds vnder his hand & seale may amply & fully appeare, relation being had therevnto, & W^ch are vpon ReCord in the publique office of the Province of Mayne, alias Yorke shyre/ & the true Coppys there of at any tyme to bee taken out wth the aforesd Mogghegin was formerly the true Indean Owner, proprietor & possessor of the sayd Tract of Land, with a greater quantity y^rto adioyneing, & which sd purchase thus by mee the sayd William Phillps, obtayned & bought of the sayd Sagamore Moghiggin hath been since Confirmed in the kingdome of England by Fardinando Gorges Esqr, the true & right heyre & successor of Sr Fardinando Gorges Kni^tt the Lord Proprietor of the sayd Province of Mayn, als Yorke Shyre, as by the Pattent vnder the great seale of England, granted by the kings Majesty, to the sayd Sr Fardind· Gorges his heyres executors or Assignes, may more at Large appeare, or by the true transcripts or Coppys there of: And which sayd Tract or Prcell of Land, soe allotted & appoynted out by mee the sd Will: Phillips is bounded by the se . .. the

South East, the Yslands lijng between the Mouths of the two Rivers, of Kennibunke & Batsons, to bee always Reckoned & Accompt^d to bee belonging vnto the Land aboue mentioned & Included there in, & is alsoe bounded by the two Riveis, one to the North East, & the other to ye South West or poynting y^{r}abouts, & soe to extend & runne vp eight Miles with in the Land, & there to crosse with a head lyne at the end of the sayd eight Miles, right vp from the sea side, fiom one River to the other, which Prscribed bounds are to bee the Lymitts, & extent of the aforesd Tract or Prcell of Land, & to bee deuided amongst the fore named Prsons after this manner, vidz^t to Edw : Spragg aforesd, one quarter & halfe quarter, that is to say three eight paits to my sonn in law Robert Lord, one quartei oi fourth part, & to my sonn in Law John Allden, one eight part, to my sonns Samll & William Phillips one quarter or fourth part, that is to say one eighth part to each of them/ & thus the whoole is deuided amongst them according to these propoitions, & & to all & euery one of thejr heyres executors, Administrators, or Assignes/ And that ye sayd Edward Spragg, Robert Lord, John Allden, Samll Phillips, & Willia~ Phillips thejr & euery one of thejr heyres, executors Administiatois or Assignes, shall haue thejr Conveniences for house lotts, Arrable Land, woodland, pasture, & Meddow Land, but not to take vp theie paits & pportions as is hereby given granted barganed sould ahend Infeoffed & Confirmd without the Consent of the rest of the partys Concerned in the whoole parcell of Land or the Majo^r part of them, thejr heyres, executors, or Assignes, for that the true meaneing & intent of these Prsents, is that noe man shall haue the Choyse, & best of ye sd paicell of Land, & others to haue the worke, & that the sayd Edw : Spragg, Robert Lord, John Allden, Samll Phillips, & Willia~ Phillips, thejr & euery one of thejr heyres, executors, administrators oi Assignes shall haue hould possess, & Inioy the sayd paits Prcells & proportions of Lands afore mentioned & expressed, according to ye true

Intent & meaning of this Deede, of gyft, grant, bargan & sayle, with all woods vnder Woods Tymber Trees mines quarrys, Rivers & water Courses, with all rights, priuiledges, & aduantag^s of fishing fowling hawking hunting, within the lymitts & bounds of the sayd Tract of Land of the sea bordering there vpon, & the Yslands in the sea Adiaycent, as aforesayd, & in both the Rivers, aboue mentioned from side to side, or the breadth of each of the Rivers, & with all & singular other benefitts profetts Convenjences or appurtenances, vnto the aforesayd Tract or Prcell of Land belonging, or in any wise, app^{r}tayneing for euer more, togeather with all such originall Deedes or other wriitengs as are relateing to the sayd Lands so given granted barganed & sould as aforesayd, either Intyre, or in Conjunction with other Lands adiacent, or bordering there vpon, or the true transcripts or coppys thereof, to ye onely proper vss benefitt & behoofe of them the sd Edw: Spragg, Robert Lord John Allden, Samell & William Phillips, thejr & euery one of thejr heyres, executors Administrators & Assigns, from the tyme of the delivery & Insealeing of these Prsents, for ever, & for the true Prformance hereof, I bind my selfe my heyres executors Administrators & Assignes to secure Indemnity & defend the sd Lands, soe given granted barganed & sould to the sd Edw. Spragg Rob. Lord John Allden Samll & Will Phillips thejr heyrs, executors administrators or Assigns, from all or former gyfts, grants barganes sayles Morgages or any Incomberances w^{t}soeuer, to any Prson or Prsons whomsoeuer, claymeing, deriveing or Challenging any pouer right, title, or Interest, to the sayd Lands or to any part there of from by or vnder mee the sayd William Phillips, & more ouer that ye sayd Lands, & euery part & Prcell thereof, are at the Ensealeing & delivery of these Prsents, cleare & free from all Prsons whomsoeuer, & soe from tyme to tyme, shall bee freely clearly & absolutely belonging & app^{r}tayneing to ye aforsd Edw: Spragg, Robert Lord, John Allden, Samll Phillps, & William Phillips, & to euery one of thejr heyres, executors, administrators, & Assignes for euer, as aforesayd/ In witness whereof I the aforesayd William Phillips, haue here vnto set my hand & seale, the twelfth day of June in the yeare of our Lord, one thousand six hundred seaventy & six, & In the Twenty eighth yeare of the Reigne, of our Soveraigne Lord Charles the secund, by the Grace of god, King of England Scotland France & Ireland Defend^r of the faith, &c·

Signed sealed & Delivered/   William Phillips ($^{his}_{seale}$)
    in the Prsence of/   William Phillips owned this to bee
    William Hudson/   his Act & Deede, d : 13 : M^{o}th :
    William Lusherland   4 : 76 : before mee/
                                 William Hawthorne Assist^t

A true Coppy of this Instrum^t transcribed out of the originall & there with Compared this 26th day of August 1676   p Edw : Rishworth ReCor :

[5] To all Christean people to whome this p̃sent deed or writeing shall come, Majo^r William Phillips late of Sacoe, In the Jurisdiction Regall of the Province of Mayn alias Yorke shyre in New England, & now rescident in Boston, in New England atoresayd, sendeth Greeting &c Know yee that I the sayd William Phillips for diverse good Causes, & Considerations mee y^{r}vnto moueing, & espetially for the loue & tender affection which I beare vnto my children, &

Major Phillips To his Sons Sam & Wm Phillips & his Daughters Field Thurston Lord & Allden Zech Gyllum

children of my now beloued wife vidz^t Samuell Phillips my Elldest sonn, & William Phillips my youngest sonn, Mary fejld my Elldest daughter, Martha Thurston my second daughter, Rebeccah Lord my thrid daughter, Elizabeth Allden my fourth daughter, Zachary Gillum my sonn in law & Saraih Turner my youngest daughter, Elephell Stratton daughter of Bridget my now beloued wife, Peleg Santford her Elldest sonn, John San-

Book III, Fol. 5.

his Daugh^r Turner
Eliph^{ll} Stretton Sanford's
Lord, Jolliffe Woodmansy Hutchinson Atkinson Santford Hudson

ford her secund sonn, & Elysha Sanford her third son, as alsoe for due & valewable Considerations by mee in hand received, of Robert Lord of London Ma^rin^r my son in law, of John Jolliffe of Boston afore sayd, M^rcha^t of John Woodmansy of Boston M^tcha^t of Elysha Hutchinson of Boston M^tcha^t of Theoder Atkinson of Boston feltmaker, of John Santford of Boston writeing schoolemaister, of William Hudson of Boston vintner, w^rof & where with I the sayd William Phillips doe acknowledg my selfe fully & wholly satistyd, contented & payd, & there of, & euery part & Prcell there of, doe fully clearly & absolutely acquitt, exonerate release, & discharge the sayd Robert Lord, John Jolliffe John Woodmansy, Elisha Hutchinson Theoder Atkinson, John Sanford & William Hudson, & all & euery one of thejr heyres, executors administrators for euer, by these Prsents, haue given granted barganed sould, alined, Enfeoffed & Confirmed, & by these p̄sents doe fully wholly clearely & absolutely giue grant bargan sell alliene Enfeoffe & Confirme vnto the sayd Robert Lord, & Rebeccha his wife, Two thousand Acers of Land being part of a Tract of Land formerly purchased by mee the sayd William Phillips Senjo^r aforesd, of an Indean Sagamore, Commanly known to ye English people, in & about that part of the Country by the name of Hluellme, formerly the true Indean Proprietor, Owner & possesso^r, of the sayd Tract of Land, as alsoe of a great quantity there vnto Adioyneing, wch alsoe is purchased by mee the sayd Willia: Phillips of the aforesd Sagamore, as by the Deeds vnder his hand may appeare, relation being had therevnto/ And which sd Purchase is since Confirmed by Fardind^o Gorges Esqr, the heyre & successo^r of Sr Fardinando Gorges Kn^{tt} the Ld Proprietor of the whoole province of Mayn, alias Yorke shyr as by the sayd Pattent vnd^r the great seale of England granted to him by the kings most excellent Majesty, may more at large appeare, & wch was soe done & Confirmed in the kingdome of England, & w^{ch}

sayd Land is scituate lijng & being in the sayd Province of
Mayn, alias yorke shyre/ the whoole Tract hereby appoynted
out by mee Willam Phillips to bee eight Miles square, & to
bee for a Townshipp ljng on the Westermost side of Kennebunke River, & eight Miles from the sea & Adioyneing to
ye Ysland head of the Townshipp of Wells, & soe to bee as
aforesayd eight Miles square, the wch sayd Land to bee disposed as followeth, to Samell Phillips my sonn one thousand
Acers, to Willam Phillips my sonn one thousand Acers, to
my aforesd daughters, Mary, Martha, Elizabeth, & Sarah
each of them one thousand Aacers, to Zachary Gyllum one
thousand Acers, to Peleg Santford John Sanford & Elisha
Sanford, each of them one thousand acers, to Eliphell Stratton one thousand acers, vnto the sayd John Jolliffe, John
Woodmancy, Elisha Hutchinson, Theoder Atkinson, John
Sanford & Willam Hudson, each of them one thousand
Acers of the aforesayd Tract of Land, to bee taken vpon the
most convenjent place for ye settleing a Town, & In order to
y^t way of Improuem^t euery one of the Pisons afoiesd, thejr
heyrs executors administrators or Assignes to haue propor-
tionable parts for house lotts, and arable Land, wood land, &
Meddow Land, but none to take vp y^r proportions hereby
granted & sould without the Consent of the partys aboue
named thejr heyres or Assigns or the Major part of them,
that soe the Intent of settleing a Town may not bee frus-
trated: All wch sayd Gyfts & purchases being summed vp
doth Amount to Nineteen Thousand Acers of Land, & is
neare one halfe of the Land of eight Miles square soe set out
for a Township, & the rest of the Land to bee still remajneing to mee Willia^m Phillips for my further disposall: To
haue & to hould the sayd Tracts & proportions of Land, as
is hereby given & granted, with all the woods vnderwoods,
Tymber Trees Mines quarrys, Rivers & water Courses, with
all rights priuiledges & aduantages of fishing fowling Hauk-
ing hunting with in ye limitts of ye sd Tract of Land, with

all & singular conveniences pfetts & aduantages whatsoeuer vnto yᵉ same belonging, or in any manner of wise app'tayneing, togeather with such originall Deeds or writeings as are Conceineing the sayd barganed Premisses, Intyre or togeather with other Lands adiacent, or the true transcripts or Coppys of them to him the sayd Samll Phillips, & to all & euery one of them the sd Grantees, & purchasers, & euery one of there heyres executors Administrators, or Assignes to yʳ onely proper vss, benefitt & behoofe from yᵉ tyme of the Ensealeing, & deliuery of these Presents, for euer/ & for the true Pformance here of I bind my selfe my heyres, executors & Administrators to secure, Indemnify, & Defend the Lands by mee soe given & granted, from all other & former Gyfts, grants, sayles, Morgages, or Incomberances whatsoeuer, to or by any Prsons whomsoeuer, Claymeing, dernieing, or Challengeing any right Title or Interest to the sayd Lands, from by or vnder mee the sayd Williā Phillips, & that the sd Lands, & euery part & Picell there of, are at this tyme Cleare & free, & soe from tyme to tyme shall bee clearly freely & absolutely belonging to the sayd Samll Phillips, & to euery of the aforesayd Grantees, & purchasers yʳ heyres executors Administrators & assignes for euer, as aforesayd/ In witness whereof I haue here vnto set my hand & seale, this fineteenth day of June in the yeare of our Lord, one thousand six hundred seaventy six, in the Twenty eight yeare of the Reign of our Soueraign Ld Charles: 2und, of England, Scotland, France, & Ireland, King, Defendʳ of the faith &c · prouided & always It is to bee vnderstood yᵗ notwithstanding wᵗsoeuer is given or granted or to whomsoeuer these psents are Confirmed in & by this bill of sayle, shall not any ways weaken or indemnify yᵉ Titles or Interests of any psons rights or pprietys wᶜʰ they formerly possessed & Improued either by Tillage, or Commandg, In Case they do

Book III, Fol. 5, 6.

returne to yʳ dwellings, with in the Tearme of seaven years from yᵉ date hereof/   William Phillips (his seale),
Signed sealed & Deliuered/
   in the pʳsence of us/

Ephraim Sauage	William Phillps owned this to bee
Joseph Tapping/	his Act & Deede. 8 : 5th Mᵒ 76 .
	before mee Willaᵐ Hawthorne
	Assistant .

A true Coppy of this Instrument aboue written, transcribed out of the originall, & there with Compared, this 30th day of August 1676 : p Edw . Rishworth ReCor .

[6]   To all Christean people, to whom this Prsent Deede of Gyft shall come, Thomas Broughton of Boston in the County of Suffocke, in the Colony of the Massatusetts Mʳchant sendeth Greeteing · Know yee that the sayd Thomas Broughton for diverse good Causes & considerations him

Broughton
To
Willett
Successor of
Cole

moueing, hath given granted barganed sould aliend Enfeotted & Confirmed, & by these Prsents doe fully freely Clearly & absolutely give grant bargan sell aliene enfeoff & Confirme vnto Jacob Willett Citizen of London Mʳchant & successor

vnto Peter Coole of London Mʳchant deceased, one third part of all that Tract of Land which was granted vnto him by the Select men of the Town of Kittery, in Pischataqua River in New England, aforesd, the fourteenth day of Octobʳ 1651 & Confirmed to him at a Town Meeteing held at Kittery aforesayd the one & Twenteth day of Octobʳ Anno . Domᵒ 1651 . the which Tract of Land is known by the name of Sturgeon Cricke swamp, & alsoe one third part of all the vpland, lying & being scituate betwixt the River that goeth vp to Dover & the sayd Cricke, & the sames scituate neare the head of the sayd Cricke, & one third part of all the vpland lijng beyond Sturgeon Crick swampe, being bounded on the

Book III, Fol. 6.

North side thereof, by a fresh Riverlett that runnes into a Coue Called the vpper Mast coue, by sturgeon Cricke on the south side, by the River that runnes vp to Dover at ye Westerly end, & by the Land belonging to the farmes at the head of the sayd Cricke, at the Easterly end togeather with all ye lybertys priuiledges profetts & appurtenanees belonging or any wise appertayneing, To haue & to hould to him the sayd Willett his heyres & Assignes for euer, to the soole & proper vss & behoofe, benefitt & aduantage of him the sayd Jacob Willett, his heyres executors administrators & Assignes for euer / And the sayd Thomas Broughton for him selfe his heyres executors administrators doth couenant promiss & grant to & with the sayd Jacob Willet his heyres executors Administrators & Assigns that hee the sayd Broughton hath in him selfe full pouer & good right to the Premisses, to giue grant Convey & Confirme to him the sayd Jacob Willet his heyres & Assignes in manner as aforesayd, & that the aboue granted Premisses are at the sealing & deliuery of these presents, free & cleare acquitted & discharged of and from all & all manner of former & other gyfts grants bargans sayles leases Morgages Joynters, Dowers Judgm^{ts} Executions forfiturs seizurs, titles troubles alienations and Incumberances whatsoeuer, had made done or suffered to bee done by him the sayd Tho: Broughton or by any other pson or Prsons from by or vnder him / And that the sayd Jacob willett his heyres executors & Assigns shall & may for euer hereafter peaceably and quietly haue hould vss occupy possess & Imoy all and singular the afore given & granted Premisses, with out the lett trouble hinderance, Molestation or disturbance, of him the sayd Thomas Broughton his heyres executors Administrators or Assignes, or of any other Prson or Prsons claymeing or to clayme a right thereto, by vertue of any Act or thing had made or done by his or thejr Assent, consent aduise, or procurement / And Mary the wife of the sayd Tho: Broughton In testimony of her free Assent to this Prsent deede of gyft doth hereby

BOOK III, FOL. 6.

surrender vp all her Interest of thirds, or otherwise in or to the aboue granted Premisses, to him the sayd Jacob Willet his heyres executors & Assignes for euer/ And the sayd Thomas & Mary doe alsoe Couenant, & promiss at any tyme hereafter to doe any further Act or Acts that may bee for the better Confirmeing of the Prmisses according to the true Intent of these Prsents, as may bee Adiudged to bee necessary or expedient, In witness where of the sayd Thomas & Mary haue here vnto sett there hands & Seales this foure & Twenteth day of August 1676. One third part of a lot Called Stephen Greenums Lott is Included in the Deede of gyft aboue written & given by Thomas Broughton & his wife to Mr Willet his heyres & assignes as firmely as the Premisses, hereby aboue given & granted this done before sealeing/   Thomas Broughton (his seale)
Signed sealed & Delivered in the
  Prsence of Thomas Kemble/
  Dauid Copp/   Thomas Broughton hath acknowledged
                    this to bee his Act & Deede this 26th
                    of August 1676: before mee
                          Tho Clarke Assistt

A true Coppy of this Instrument transcribed out of the originall & there with Compared this 30th ot August 1676.
                  p Edw · Rishworth ReCor ·

Let all men know by these Prsents, that I John Greene of the Towne of Kittery, in the River of Pschataqua Senior,
          for diuerse good causes & Considerations him
Jno Green   there vnto moueing, haue freely given & granted
To
Thoms Abbot   & by these Prsents doe absolutely & freely giue
          & grant & haue freely given & granted for euer,
vnto Thomas Abbet & Elizabeth his now wife, & daughter of John Greene, thejr heyres executors, Administrators & As-

signes, the best & biggest part of Twenty acers of Land, which Land was given vnto the sayd John Greene by the Townsmen of Kittery, in the yeare one thousand six hundred finety & six, & beginneth not at the water side, but at a Certen stumpe an oaken stumpe a little below an hill of Rox. which is between the new dwelling house of the sayd John Greene, & the house of Peter Grant, & the lyne to runne into the woods, as the rest of the sayd John Greens lott lyeth, or is bounded, & is to bee sixteen rodd in breadth, from the place aboue sayd, and soe to runn to ye end, Excepting out of ye sd grant one rodd of Land in breadth all along for a high way if it bee required, all which lands with all the woods, & Tymber & Tymber Trees, with other the appurtenances profetts & priuiledges w'soeuer, with in or to the same belonging, with free Egress & regress of passage or carrage in all or any part of the sayd John Greenes Land hereby granted where there is wayes for his or any of there proper vss or Occasion, as they shall haue neede there of, I doe hereby to, & with the full & free Consent of my wife Julian Greene freely & absolutely giue the sayd lands as afore expressed, vnto the sayd Thomas Abbut & Elizabeth his wife, the heyres executors administrators or Assignes to haue & to hould the sayd Lands with all the benefitts, profetts & priuiledges as aboue expressed, as his & their own proper priviledg, right & Interest for euer, with out the lett, hinderance trouble or Molestation, or putting of him the sayd John Greene his heyres executors Administrators or Assignes or of any other Prson or Prsones from by or vnd^r mee, the sayd John Green w'soeuer lawfully Claymeing or from by or under my wife Juliā [7] or either of us, in witness here of, I with my wife Julian Greene, haue here

Book III, Fol. 7.

vnto sett our hands & seales this twenteth day of May one thousand six hundred sixty & eight 1668 ·

Sealed & Delivered   John Greene (his seale)
   in the Presence of us/   The marke of
   Andrew Searle/   Julyan Green (her seal)
   James Emery/ witnesses/
   Jonathan Nayson   John Green Senjo^r, & Julyan his
   his marke /   wife did acknowledg this In-
                             strum^t aboue written to bee y^r
                             Act & Deed this nineteenth
                             day of March, one thousand
                             six hundred seaventy fiue, be-
                             fore mee Roger Playstead
                                         Assote/

A true Coppy of this Instrument transcribed & Compared with the originall this Secund day of Septemb^r 1674.

                 p Edw: Rishworth ReCor

To all Christean people to whom these Prsents shall come, William Phillips of Sacoe in the County ot Yorke shyre, or province ot Mayn in New England, & Bridget his wife send Greeteing/ Know yee y^t Wee ye sayd William Phillips & Bridget Phillips, haueing in the yeare of our Lord one thousand six hundred sixty & three, signed sealed & Delivered a Deed being for a Certajn Tract or Prcell of Land, lying vpon the same River, & alsoe for one eighth Part of a Mine lying & being vp in the Countrey aboue Sacoe River, & the sayd deed being for want of some punctilioes in Law, Judged not fully æffectuall according to Law vidz^t for want of acknowledgm^t by the Granters to ye Grantees, & want of warranty of the Granters to bee thejr iust rights, & in thejr

Maj^r
Phillips
To
Gyllum
&
Turner

lawfull pouer to dispose off· Therefore know all P'sons to whom these p'sents shall come, or may bee here in now or hereafter Conceined, that Wee the sayd Wilham & Bridget Phillips, for diverse good Causes & considerations us there vnto moueing, haue giuen granted aliend Enfeoffed & Confirmed & by these Presents do giue grant aliene, Enfeoff & Confirme vnto o^r Loueing sons in Law, Zachary Gyllum & Ephraim Turner, the aforesd Prcell of Land mentioned in the Deede, dated as abouesayd, & Recorded in the ReCords of the County of Yorke shyre, or province of Mayn in New England vidz^t A certen Prcell or peece of Land as in the sayd Deede is expressed, lijng & being scituate, on the South West side of Sacoe River, & bounded by the sayd River on the North East by a lott, commanly Called, & known by the name of Ly-combs lott, now the Land of William Hutchinson, on the North West side, & from ye sayd Land of the sd Hutchinson (with this Addition to ye grant aforesayd) runneing ouer Wests brooke home to ye Land of Major Bryan Pendleton South Easterly, from low water marke, of Sacoe River aforesd, running between the two aforesd boundarys of Hutchinsons & Pendletons, including Wests brooke into ye Country vntill the full & iust quantity of fiue hundred acers bee measured from low water marke of Sacoe River between the sayd boundarys of Pendleton & Hutchinson, to them o^r sayd sonns in law, Zachariah Gyllum & Ephram Turner, thejr heyres executors Administrators & Assignes, To haue & to hould the sayd Tract of Land, with all the Tymber Woods, or Trees, there vpon growing or standing, or y^t vnto any ways app^rtayneing, or belonging, togeather with one eight part of a Mine, lijng & being vp in the Countrey aboue Sacoe River, in which Major Tho: Clarke, Mr Edw. Tyng, Senjo^r, Mr John Hull & my selfe & others are partners, togeather with one eighth part of all the Lands, woods, trees, & priuiledges there vnto belonging, or any wise app^rtayneing, to them our sayd

sonns in Law, Zachary Gyllum, & Epraim Turner, & for
warranty of the aboue granted Premisses, Wee the sayd
William & Bridget Phillips, do for selues heyres executors,
Administrators & Assignes wariant, that Wee the sayd William & Bridgett Phillips, are the true & right owners of the
aboue sayd Premisses, & haue in our selues good rightfull,
pouer, & lawfull authority to grant & dispose of the same,
at our pleasures, & doe for our selues heyres executors
Administrators & Assignes, firmely by these Presents warrant, to the aboue sayd Zachary Gyllum & Ephraim Turner,
their heyres executors Administrators & Assignes, the
aboue sayd Premisses, to hould Occupy & Inioy, & for them
theire heyres, executors, Administrators & Assignes, to bee
held Occupied, & Inioyed for ever/ And at all tyme &
tymes hereafter shall remaine, Continew & abide vnto y^e
sayd Zachary Gyllum & Ephraim Turner, their heyres executors Administrators, & Assignes, freely clearly acquitted,
exonerated, discharged, or otherwise from tyme to tyme, &
at all tymes hereafter defended, & keept Harmlesse, of &
from all manner of former grants, barganes, sayles gyfts,
Leases, Morgages, Joytures, wills Judg^{ts} extents, executions, Dowris, & all other Incomberances whatsoeuer, had
made done, acknowledged, or Committed to bee done, by us
William or Bridget Phillips, w^{by} the sayd Zachary Gyllum
& Epharim Turner, their heyres executors Administrators
& Assignes, shall or may bee lawfully Euicted out of possession there of or any part there of, & further Wee the
sayd William & Bridget Phillips for o^r selues heyres, executors, Administrators, & Assignes, doe Couenant with &
promiss to the sayd zachary Gyllum & Ephraim Turner,
their hevres executors Administrators & Assignes, that the
sayd William Phillips & Bridget our heyres Exectors
Administrators & Assignes, shall and will from tyme to
tyme, & at all tymes on the reasonable request of the sayd
zachary Gyllum & Ephraim Turner their hevres executors
Administrators or Assignes, Prformed doe or cause to bee

Book III, Fol 7, 8.

Prformed & done any such further Act or Acts for a more full & Pifect Convayance, & Assurance of the aboue granted Premisses, according to ye laws of this Jurisdiction, as Wee the sayd William & Bridget Phillips, shall bee there vnto Advised, or required/ In witness where of, Wee have herevnto set our hands & seales, this eigth day of July in the yeare of our Lord one thousand six hundred seaventy six/ 1676:   William Phillips (his seale)
Signed sealed & delivered   Bridget Phillips (her marke)
 in the Prsence of/   William Phillips owned this
 Ephraim Savage/   to bee his Act & Deede,
 Joseph Tapping/   & Bridget his wife freely
          vp her right before mee
          William Hawthorne Assistant/

 A true Coppy of this Instrument or Deed of sayle, transcribed out of the originall & there with Compared this 4th Day of Septe^br 1676   p Edw: Rishworth ReCor·

[8] To all Christean people to whom these Prsents shall Come/ william Phillips of Sacoe in the County of yorke shyre, or province of Mayn in New England, & Bridget his wife sends Greeteing/ Know yee y^t Wee the sayd William & Bridgett Phillips, for diverse good Causes & Considerations us y^rvnto moueing, more espetially for ye loue & affection, Wee beare vnto o^r sonn in law Ephraim Turner, haue given granted aliend Enfeoffed, & Confirmed, & by these Prsents, do give grant aliene Enfeoff & Confirme vnto our aforesd sonn in law Ephraim Turner his heyres executors

Maj^r Phillips
To Turner

Administrators & Assignes for ever, a Certen Prcell or Tract of Land, ljng or being in the aforesd County of Yorke shyre, or the province of Mayn, in New England, South Westwardly from Sacoe River, & to the Northward of the Town of Winter Harbour, from whence the sayd Sacoe River takes his Inlett & is butted & bounded, on the North East side with a Tract of Land running from Sacoe River, South westwardly, between the Land of William Hutchinson, formerly Called or known by the name of Lyscombs lott. & bounded by it North Westwardly, & the land of Major Bryan Pendleton on the South East side of West brooke, running from the Land of Will Hutchinsons, home to ye Land of Major Bryan Pendletons, ouer Wests brooke, & bounded by the sayd Land South Eastwardly, vp into the Country, vntill fiue hundred acers bee expired Including Wests brooke granted in a Deede dated before the date here of, vnto our Loueing sonns in Law, Zachary Gyllum & Ephraim Turner, this gyft grant alienment & Confirment vnto our sayd sonn in law Ephraim Turner takeing its begining at the South Westerly end, of the aforesayd fiue hundred acers of Land granted as aforesayd vnto our sonn in Laws Zachariah Gyllum & Ephraim Turner & being bounded on the North Eastwardly side by the Land granted as aforesayd, to zachary Gyllum & Ephraim Turner, & runneing as aforesayd, from Sacoe River, between the Land of William Hutchinson on the North West side, & by the Land of Major Pendleton, ouer West brooke on ye South Easterly side & runneing between the two boundarys South Westwardly foure Miles from Sacoe River, Includeing the Land Granted as aforesayd, to our sonns zachary Gyllum & Ephraim Turner, to bee within the sayd foure Miles from Sacoe River North Westwardly vp into the Countrey, wch from the sayd River soe Running, & bounded between the Lands of Pendleton & Hutchinson aforesayd/ Which sayd Tract of Land butted & bounded as aforesayd, by the Land of zachary Gyllum & Ephraim Turner, North Eastwardly granted to them thejr heyres executors Administrators & Assignes by us, & William Hutchinson on ye North West side & from thence Running ouer Wests brooke home to Major Pendletons Land South Eastwardly: Wee the sayd William & Bridget Phillips, doe giue grant bargane aliene Enfeoff & Confirme vnto Ephraim Turner our Loueing son in law, his heyres executors Administrators & Assignes, & by these Prsents doe fully giue grant alliene Enfeoff & Confirme, the aforesayd Tract of Land, bounded by the Land of zachary Gyllum & Ephraim Turner North Eastwardly, the Land of William Hutchinson Northwestwardly, & the Land of Major Bryan Pendleton South Eastwardly, & South Westwardly on the Southwestwardly, or South Eastwardly of West brooke togeather with all y* Woods trees there vpon or there vnto belonging, or any wise app'tayneing, or belonging to him the sayd Ephraim Turner, his heyres executors Administrators & Assignes, for ever, the sayd Land being butted & bounded as aforesayd, & doe hereby promiss & Ingage, that Wee the sayd William & Bridget Phillips are the true and right proper owners there of, & euery part there of, & haue in our selues full pouer, & lawfull authority to dispose of the same, at our pleasuis & doe for our selues, heyres, executors, Administrators & Assignes firmely by these Prsents, to the aboue sayd Ephraim Turner, his heyres, executors Administrators, & Assignes, the aboue sayd Tract or Prcell of Land, runneing from ye Land granted as aforesayd, vnto zachary Gyllum & Ephraim Turner, & bounded by the same North Eastwardly, & the Land of William Hutchinson North Westwardly, & ye Land of Major Bryan Pendleton on the other side of West brooke, South Eastwardly, or South Westwardly to the extent of my Pattent, from Sacoo River vp into ye Country as aforesayd, includeing the fiue hundred acers granted zachary Gyllum & Ephraim Turner aforesd, this grant takeing its begining from that & is accompted foure hundred Acers more or less, W^{ch} I giue to my sayd sonn in law Ephraim Turner, to haue hould occupy & Inioy, & by him His heyres executors administrators & Assignes, to bee held Occupyed & Inioyed from the day of the date here of for ever, freely & Clearely acquitted, exonerated discharged, or otherwise from tyme to tyme, & at all tymes well & sufficiently defended & keept harmeless from all manner of

BOOK III, FOL. 8.

former & other barganes sayles gyfts grants, leases, Morgages Joyntuis, wills Judgmts, extents, executions, Dowrys, & all other Incumberances whatsoeuer, had made done acknowledged or Comītted, by us William Phillips, & Bridget Phillips, wby the sayd Ephraim Turner his heyres or Assignes shall or may bee lawfully Evicted out of the possession there of, or any partt there of/ And further Wee the sayd William & Bridget Phillips, for our selues our heyres executors Administrators, or Assignes, do Covenant with, & promiss to the sayd Ephraim Turner, his heyres executors Administrators & Assignes, that Wee ye sd William & Bridgett Phillips or heyres executors, administrators, & Assignes, shall & will from tyme to tyme & all tyms here after, on the Reasonable request of the sayd Ephraim Turner his heyres executors Administrators or Assigns, Prforme & doe, or Cause to bee Priormed & done, any such further Action, or Actions, for a more full & Prfect Conuayance & Assurance, of the aboue granted Premisses, according to the Laws of this Jurisdiction, as Wee the sayd William & Bridget Phillips, shall bee hereuuto aduised, & required/ In witness wof Wee haue hereuuto sett our hands & seales, this eight day of July in the yeare of our Lord, one thousand six hundred seaventy & six/ 1676 ·

Signed sealed & Deliverd   Willi: Phillips (his seal)
in ye Prsence of/   Bridget Phillips (her seal)
Ephraim Savage/   William Phillips owneth this to bee
Joseph Tapping/   his Act & Deede/ his wife owned
                      this to bee her free Consent before
                      mee Will Hawthorne Assist
                      : 8 : 5 : 76 ,

A true Coppy of this Instrument transcribed & Compared with the originall this 5th Septembr 1676 · 76 ·

                        p Edw. Rishworth ReCor .

BOOK III, FOL 9.

[9] At a Towne Meeteing held In yorke May first 1674/
At the same tyme It was granted vnto John
Yorke   Hoy by the Inhabitants of the sayd Town of
To
Jn⁰ Hoye   yorke, hee should haue a Lott of vpland of
thyrty Acers, vpon the North East side of Cap¹
John Daveses Lott, which is neare the way wch goeth vnto
Newgewanacke/ Taken out of the ReCords of the Town of
yorke the 18th day of Novemb^r 1674. Peter Weare

A true Coppy of this grant transcribed   Clericus/
& Compared with the originall this 30th of Decemb^r 76
p Edw Rishworth ReCor :

These Pr̃sents testify that I John Craford late of Newgewanacke, In the County of yorke, yeamon, for & in Consideration of Twenty thousand foote of M^{r}chtable pine boards,
secured by bill by Thoms Holms of the same place yeoman,
hath bargaued sould Infeoffed Conveighed, aliened, assignd,
& set ouer vnto him the sayd Thomas Holms, & by & with
the Consent of Elizabeth my wife, doe bargane sell Infeoffe,
Corvay aliene, assigne & sett ouer vnto him the sayd Thomas
Holms, his heyres executors, Administrators & Assignes, all
that my house barne, with what other out houseing is on my
Lands at Newgewanacke, togeather with a Certen Tract of
            Land, on part whereof the sayd houseing stand-
Crafford   eth, Contayneing fourty Acers, begining on the
To
Holmes   East End of Mr Thomas Broughtons Land, on
            the South side of ye dyrty swampe, & soe to
Wells path, which sayd Tract of Land was part of a grant of
the Town of Kittery vnto mee, as by the sayd Town ReCord,
due relation being had more at large appeareth, with all the
priuiledges, & appurtenances, Tymber, & Tymber trees,
woods, & vnderwoods there on & there vnto belonging, &
app^{r}tayneing/

BOOK III, FOL. 9.

To haue & to hould, the sayd house barne out houseing, Tract of Land woods vnderwoods, Tymber & Tymber trees. with all the priviledges & appurtenances there vnto belonging or in any wise app'tayneing, vnto him the sd Thomas Holms his heyres executors, Administrators & Assignes for euer, to & for his & there soole & own vss & benefitt & behoofe, & to & for noe other vss, purpose or intent whatsoeuer/ And the sayd John Craford for him selfe his heyres, executors & Administrators, doth Covenant, & promiss to & with him the sayd Thomas Holms his heyres executors Administrators & Assignes, & every of them, that at p̱sent & before the Insealeing here of, hee standeth ceased & possessed of the sayd Tract of Land, & houseing thereon in a good Estate of fee symple. And the sayd John Craford for him selfe, his heyres, executors, & Administrators doth Covenant & promiss, to & with him the sayd Thomas Holms, his heyres executors, Administrators & Assignes, & to & with every of them, that If there shall want of fourty Acers of Land, the sayd John Crafford will abate Thomas Holms Twenty shillings for every Acer there wanteth, to bee deducted out of the payment for the Premisses, & the sayd John Craford, for him selfe his heyres executors & Administrators, doth further Covenant & promiss to & with him the sayd Thomas Holms, his heyres, executors, administrators, or Assigns, & to & with every of them that hee will at all tyms hereafter defend the Tytle y'rof, freely acquitted & discharged of & from all former bargans, Contracts, sayles, Judgm'ts executions Dowers, Title of Dowers, or any other Incomberance, Act or Acts, done or suffered to bee done, by mee or any other by from vnder mee. In witness w'r of I haue hereunto set my hand & seale/ Dated on the great Ysland in Pischataq̱ River this 27'th day of Octob'r Anno Dom̄ one thousand six hundred seaventy six & in y'e Twenty eight yeare of the Reign of our Soveraigne Lord

Book III, Fol. 9.

Charles the secund, King of England, Scotland France & Ireland Defend{r} of the faith, 1676

Signed sealed & Deliver'd   John Crafford (his seale)
  In y{e} p̱sence of us/   Elizabeth Craford (her seale)
Rich{d} Abbott   her marke *E*

his marke *RA*   John Craford & Elizabeth his wife,
                 appeared before mee & owned, the
Elizabeth Abbot   aboue written Deede of sayle, to bee
her marke *EA*   thejr free Act & Deede/ alsoe Rich{d}
Edw. Taylour   Abbet, & Elizabeth Abbett ownd y{r}
                 hands to It, as witnesses this 8th
his marke   day of Decemb{r} 1676 :
                     John Wincoll Assotiate/

Ric: Stylemā. secretary

A true Coppy of this Instrum{t} transcribed out of the originall, & there with Compared this 13th day of Janvary 1676:
                p Edw Rishworth ReCor.

Kat Hilton
To her Son
Treworgy

These Presents testify that I Katterne Hilton of Ecceter, In the County of Norfocke, Widdow, for diverse good causes & Considerations mee y{r}vnto moueing, espetially In consideration of my motherly loueing affections w{ch} I beare vnto my Loueing sonn Samll: Trueworgye, of Portsmouth In Pischataqua River Marriner, doe freely fully & absolutely give, & grant vnto my loueing sonn Samuell Treuworgye of Portsmouth aforesayd, all that my necke or Tract of Land, scituate aboue Sturgeon Cricke in the Townshipp of Kittery in Pischataqua River, formerly Called Tomsons Poynt, now Called or known by the name of Treworgys poynt, lijng between Two Crickes, with all the Tymber, & Tymber Trees, & vnderwood there on, w{ch} Necke or Tract of Land I bought of Mr Rowles the Indean, togeather with all the priuilidges & appurtenances there vnto belonging, or ir any

Book III, Fol. 9, 10.

wise app'rtayneing; To haue & to hould the sayd Necke or Tract of Land vnto him the sayd Samll Treworgye, his heyres executors, Administrators & Assignes for euer, to & for his & there own proper vss, benefitt & behoofe, & to & for noe other vss intent or purpose w'soeuer, peaceably & quietly to haue occupy possess & Inioy, from the day of the date hereof for euer/ In witness where of I haue here vnto set my hand & seale/ Dated in Ecceter aforesayd, this secund day of Novemb', Anno Dom one thousand six hundred seaventy & foure, & in the Twenty sixt yeare of the Reign of our Soveraign Lord Charles the secund, King of England Scotland France & Ireland, Defend' of the faith &c, 1674:
Signed Sealed, & Deliuered in
the Presence of John Gillman/ Kattrein Hillon K (her seale) H
Moses Mavericke/

     Cap' John Gillman appeared before mee vpon the 11th of July 1676 · & testi-fy'd vpon oath y' hee saw Mis Kat-trein Hilton, sign seale & Deluer this writeing as her Act & Deede, to w'ch hee subscribed as a witness with Moses Mavericke a witness/ sworne the 11th of July 1676. before mee Samll Dawlton Comiss'o'

A true Coppy of this Instrument transcribed, & Com-pared with the originall this 16th day of January 1676
     p Edw Rishworth ReCor.

Treworgy   These Prsents testify, that I Samell Treworgye
To
Rich   of Portsmouth, In Pischataqua River Marinei, for & in the Consideration of the some of forty fiue pounds, of current pay of New England to mee in hand payd, before the Ensealing & Deliuery here of, by Richard Rich of Douer [10] In Pischataqua River, Mariner, the Recei⟨...⟩ elfe to

bee there with fully satisfyd, Contented & payd & doe hereby for mee my heyres, executors, & Administrators, & for euery of them, exonerate, discharge release & acquit him the sayd Richd Rich his heyres executors, Administrators & Assignes of & from the sayd some, & of euery part & Prcell & penny thereof, haue given, granted, barganed sould, aliend Enfeofd Convayed & Confirmed, & by these Prsents, do by & with the Consent of Darcas my wife, giue grant bargan sell aliene Enfeoffe, Convay, and Confirme vnto the sayd Richard Rich, his heyres, executors, Administrators & Assignes, all that my Necke or Tract of Land, scituate aboue Sturgeon Cricke In the Town shipp of Kittery In Pischataqua River aforesayd fformerly Called Tomsoms poynt, now Called or known by the name of Trueworgys poynt, lying between two Cricks Contayneing by Estimation fiuety Acers bee It more or lesse, togeather with all the Tymber & Tymber Trees, & vnderwoods there on wch Necke or Tract of Land my Mother Mis Katterin Hilton, bought of Mr Rowls the Indean while shee was my fathers Mr James Treworgys Widdow/ To haue and to hould, the sayd Necke or Tract of Land, with all the priuiledges & appurtenances there vnto belonging or app^{r}tayneing, vnto him the sd Richard Rich. & to his heyres executors Administrators or Assigns for euer, to and for his, & thejr own proper vsse benefitt & behoofe, & to & for noe other vsse Intent or purpose whatsoeuer/ And the sayd Samuell Trueworgy for himselfe, his heyres executors & Administrators, & for euery of them doth Couenant promiss, & grant to & with him the sayd Richd Rich, his heyres executors Administrators or Assignes, & to & with euery of them by these Prsents, that at Present & before the Ensealeing here of, hee standeth seazed & possessed of the sayd Necke or Tract of Land, In a good Estate of fee symple: And further the sayd Samell Trueworgye, for him selfe his heyres, executors & Administrators, & for euery of them doth Covenant promisse, and grant to & with him the sayd Richd Rich, his heyres, executors Administrators &

Assignes, & to and with euery of them, that hee will at all tymes defend the Title there of, vnto him the sayd Richard Rich his heyres, executors Administrators or Assignes, against all Prsons Claymeing any right title or Interest there vnto, by from or vnder mee/ In witness where of I haue here vnto set my hand & seale this sixth day of Noveb[r] Anno: Dom̄ one thousand six hundred seaventy foure, & In the Twenty sixt yeare of y[e] Reign of our Soveraign Lord Charles the second, King of England Scotland France & Ireland Defend[r] of the faith 1674

Signed sealed & Deluered/   Samell Trueworgy (his seal)
In y[e] psence of   The marke of ⓑ
Phillip Cromewell/   Darcas Treworgy/ (her seal)
Joseph Hodgsden/

Great Ysland the 9th of Novemb[r] 1674: Mr Samll Treworgye & Darcas his wife, came & acknowledged this Instrum[t] to bee y[r] free Act & Deede, & shee at y[e] same tyme rendred vp her thirds & right of Dowry/

        before mee Elyas Stylemā: Commissio[r]/

A true of this Instrument, with the acknowledgment aboue written transcribed out of the originall & there with Compared this 16: of Janvary 1676 · p Edw · Rishworth ReCor·

Indian Rowles To Kat Treworgy

Know all men by these Prsents, that I Mr Rowles Indean, Sagamore Resident In Pischataqua, haue given & granted vnto Katterine Trueworgy, my Poynt of Land Commanly known by the name of Tomsons Poynt, An ould Corne ground which I the sayd Mr Rowls haue formerly made vss of, & Improued/ And by these Prsents doe absolutely & freely give, & grant from my selfe my heyres or assignes, & from all other Prsons w[t]soever vnto Mis Katterine Trueworgy, her heyres & Assignes foreuermore & for an In Consideration of two bottles of Lyquo[r] to mee In hand payd; The Poynt of Land

Book III, Fol. 10.

with the Improved ground there on, I doe Ingage my selfe that ye sayd Katterine shall peaceably, & quietly Inioy the same/ witness my hand this 3d of Octob^r 1651 :

Signed & Delivered/   The marke of Maister Sagamore
In the Prsence of/
Nic. Shapleigh/   Rowles/
Humphrey Chadborne/

A true Coppy of this Instrument transcribed out of the originall this 16th day of Janvary 1676 · p Edw : Rishworth
                         ReCor

Barrett
To
Littlefield

To all Christean people whome this may Concerne/ Know yee that I John Barrett of Wells, In the County of yorke In New England Planter for diverse good causes & Considerations mee y^{r}vnto moueing, & more espetially for & In Consideration of a valewable some of six pounds already to mee in hand payd by ffran : Littlefejld of the afore sayd Town, & County In New England, Planter from mee my heyres, executors Administrators, & Assignes. doe Covenant bargajne Sell Assigne Infeoffe & Confirme, & by these Prsents haue bargained sould, & Confirmed a Certen Prcell of sault Marsh, scituateing & being in the Town of Wells, bounded vidz^t the lower end butting vpon the greate River, wch runnes from the Mill, & Joyneing to a small Prcell of Marsh of the aforesd Fran : Littletejlds, & soe Compassd round with a small Cricke, which Marsh Contaynes, about two Acers bee It more or lesse, to him the sd Fran : Littlefejld his heyres executors, Administrators & Assigns, to ha . & to hould & peaceably to Inioy for ever, with all the priuiledges, & Convenjences there vnto belonging. And doe by these Prsents Covenant bargane & promiss, that I will make good mantayn & defend the sd Title from any Prson or Prsons, not withstanding any

Book III, Fol. 10, 11.

Claym or Pretence w'soeuer, either from by or vnder mee: for the reall & true Prformance here of I the sd John Barrett doe bind my selfe, my heyres executors Administrators & Assignes, to the aforesd Francis Littlefejld his heyres, executors, Administrators & Assigns in the pœnall some of Twenty pounds of Lawfull money of New England, w'rvnto I haue subscribed my hand & seale this Twelth day of Aprill in the yeare of o'r Lord Anno Dom one thousand six hundred seaventy fiue, & In the seaven & twentheth yeare of the Reigne of o'r Soveraign Lord Charls the 2und, by the grace of god, of England Scotland France & Ireland King, Defend'r of the faith &c .   John barrett (his seale)

| Signed sealed & Deluerd in the p̱sence of us/ Jonathan Hammond/ James Littlefejld/ | John Barrett of wells appeared before mee this 26th day of Janva: 1676: & acknowledg'd this Instrume' aboue written, to bee his free Act & Deede/ |

Edw : Rishworth Assote

A true coppy of this Instrument aboue written transcribed, & with the Originall Compared this 29th day of Janvary: 1676.   p Edw . Rishworth ReCor .

[11] Bee It known vnto all men by these Prsents, that I Thomas Everell of the Town of Wells, In the County of Yorke In New England, for my selfe, my heyres executors, Administrators, & Assignes, for a valewable some of Twenty pounds with other pay already received, in hand haue Covenanted barganed sould & Assignd, & made over, & by these Prsents doe grant sell aliene & make over, vnto Francis Littlefejld Senjo'r of Wells in the County aforesd, Two

Averall to Littlefield   hundred Acers of vpland & tenn Acers of fresh Meddow, Lijng & being in the Town shipe of Wells, at a place Commanly Called Mary Land, ... Meddow begining at a little pitch pine tree marked Closs by the Meddow side, & a Maple Tree growing aganst It in the River, at the lower end of Fran: Littlefejlds Junjo^{rs} Meddow, & soe to runne eight scoore pooles down to the River on both sides, which is tenn Acers ye vpland to begine at the aforesd marked pine tree, at the vpper end of the sayd Meddow, & soe to runne eight scoore pooles by the Meddow, & soe along from the Meddow Westward, as It is bounded by marked trees, till two hundred Acers bee Compleated, with all the appurtenances & Commoditys there to belonging, to him the sayd Fran. Littlefejld Senjo^r, his heyres, executors, Administrators & Assignes, to haue & to hould for ever/ And by these Prsents doe Ingage to make good the sayd Tytle to ye sayd Littlefejld his heyres or Assignes from by or vnder mee or any other/ And the sayd Littlefejld is to discharge all such rents, or acknowledgm^{ts} as here after may bee demanded, by any Legall propriato^r, w^{r}vnto I haue set my hand & seale this Twenty thyrd day of Febru. In the yeare of our Lord Anno Dom: one Thousand six hundred seaventy three/ seaventy foure/   Thomas Averall (his seale)

Sealed signed & Deliuer̃d/   Thomas Averall appeared this
 In the p̃sence of us/   first of Aprill 1674: & did
 Joseph Bolls/   acknowledg this Instrument
 John Cloyse his   to bee his free Act & Deede,
 marke ⨍   according to ye Teno^r there
        of here in expressed, before
        mee Bryan Pendleton
                Assote

vera Copia of this Instrum^t aboue written, transcribed, & compared with the originall this 29th day of Janvary 1676.
        p Edw Rishworth ReCor:

Book III, Fol 11.

Ashly To
Fran Littlefield

Bee It known vnto all men by these Prsents, that I william Ashly of Wells, In the County of Yorke & Colony of the Massatusetts in New England, In Consideration of a peece of sault Marsh, Called & tearmed & Named by the name of Six Acer Marsh, that Fran: Littlefejld Senjo[r] of the Town aforesd, hath barganed with mee for, vnto mee sould, & the w[ch] hee hath alienated as p a writeing of the same date with this Instrum[t] will appeare more fully with which I confess my selfe to bee fully satisfyd contented & payd, haue barganed & sould & by these Prsents doe fully clearly & absolutely bargan & sell vnto the sayd Fran Littlefejld a Preell of Marsh sault & fresh, being & lijng in & by Wells great Marsh being formerly the Marsh of John Wadleigh Senjo[r], & bounded as followeth, that is to say, with y[e] sea wall on the South East side & Mr Safull wheelewrights on y[e] South West side & with a ditch on y[e] North East side, on the North West side, with y[e] Marsh of the aforesd Fran: Littlefejld Senio[r], to haue & to hould the sayd Tract of Marsh vnto the sayd Francis Littlefejld Senio[r], him his heyres executors Administrators & Assignes, to his & y[r] proper vss & behoofes for euer. And I the sayd will: Ashly my heyres executors Administrators the aforesd Tract of Land, vnto y[e] aforesd Fran· Littlefejld Senjo[r] his executors Administrators shall & will from any other Prson or Prsons, by from or vnder us, warrant acquit & for euer defend/ In witness w[rof] I haue here set to my hand & seale, this fourth day of Aprill one thousand six hundred seaventy two, with y[e] Consent of my wife Elizabeth Ashly/

Signed sealed & Delivered
in the prsence of us/
Sheth Fletcher/
James Pendleton/

William Ashlys marke (his seale)

Elizabeth Ashlys marke E (her seale)

This Instrum[t] acknowledged the day & yeare aboue written, to bee y[r] Act & Deede before us

Book III, Fol. 11.

A True Coppy of this Instrum^t aboue written tianscribed & Compared with the originall this 2und day of Febru · 1676:
p Edw: Rishworth ReCor:

Hamond
To
Averell

Bee It known vnto all men by these Prsents that I Jonathan Hamonds in the Town of Wells in the County of yorke In New England, for my selfe my heyres, executors Administratois & Assignes, for a valewable sume of Twenty pounds already received in hand h . . . Covenanted barganed sould assigned & made ouer, & by these Prsents doe grant sell Assig . . & make ouer vnto Thomas Everell of the Town of wells in the County aforesd, Two hundred Acers of vpland & tenn Acers of fresh Meddow, ljng & being In the Townshipe of Wells, at a place Commanly Called Maryland, bounded as followeth, the Meddow begining at a little pitch pine tree, marked Closse by the Meddow side, & a Maple tree growing against It, in the River, at the lower end of Francis Littlefejlds Meddow Junjo^r, & soe to runne eight scoore poole down the River on both sides, wch is tenn Acers, the vpland to begine at ye aforesd Marked pine tree at the vpper end of the sayd Meddow, & soe to runne eight scoore pools by the Meddow, & soe along from ye Meddow Westward, as It is bounded by marked trees till two hundred Acers bee Compleated: with all the appurtenances & Commoditys y^rvnt belonging, to him the sd Tho: Averell, his heyres executors, Administrators & Assignes, to ha . . & to hould for euer, & by these Prsents, doe Ingage to make good the sayd Title to ye sd Everell from any, either from by or vnder mee, & the sd Tho: Everell is to discharge all su . . Rents or acknowledgem^{ts} as may here after bee demanded by any Legall proprietor, w^rvnto I haue set my hand & seale, this Two &

BOOK III, FOL. 11.

twenteth day of Octob[r] In y[e] yeai of our Lord Anno Dom: 1671 :   Jonathan Hammonds (his seale)
Signed sealed & Deliverd In the
 Prsence of us/
 James Gooch/
 Israell Harding/

Bee It known vnto all men, that I Thomas Everell Aforesd, doe Assign & make ouer this Deede, & the right & Title of the Land Meddow, & app[r]tenances here in expressd, vnto Fran · Littlefejld Senjo[r] of wells, or to his heyrs executoi s or Assigns this 23[th] of Febru 73 · 74. witness my hand
 Witnesses   Thomas Everell
 Joseph Bolls/   Tho · Everell appeared before mee this
 John Cloyse   26[th] day of Janvary 1676 · & acknowl-
 his maike/ ☧   edged this Assigne[t] of all those Lands
                 with in written to bee his free Act &
                 Deede, with y[e] Consent of his wife/
                 Edw : Rishworth Assofe ·
A true coppy or Coppys of the Deede aboue written made p Jonathan Hammonds & Tho Everell, & of the sd Everells Assignem[t] y[r]of vnto Fran Littlefejld Senjo[r] of Wells transcribed out of the originall & v[r]with Compared this 2und of Febru: 1676: p Edw · Rishworth Re . . .

Cloice
To
Manning

Bee It known vnto all men by these Prsents, that I John Cloyce of the Town of Wells in the County of Yorke in New England, doe for my selfe my heyres, executors Administrators & Assigns, Covenant bargan sell Assigne & make ouer, & from mee my heyres & Assignes haue given granted barganed sould, & by these Prsents doe Confirme vnto John Manning of the aforesd Town & County, six Acers of fresh Meddow, ljng & being at a place Comanly Called Totnucke,

BOOK III, FOL. 11, 12.

In the Townshipp of Wells, the Meddow lying in th . . .
Prcells, about a quarter of a mile from Tho : Everells house,
& haueing an Oake tree ma.ked against each Prcell of
Meddow/ I say to him his heyres executors, Administrators
Assignes, to haue & to hould & peaceably Inioy for euer :
& doe by these Prsents further I . gage to Defend & make
good the sd Title to the abouesd Manning & his heyres
for eu . against any Prson or Prsons whomsoeuer, shall lay
any clame or Interest there vnto, for wch Meddow I doe p
these p̃sents acknowledg I haue received full satisfaction
already, & doe for euer after the Assignem^t here of, disclame
any Title or Interest to the sayd Meddow : In witness w^rvnto
I haue subscribed my hand & seale this 23 : day of Febru .
1673 :   John Cloyce his ($^{his}_{seale}$)
Signed sealed & Deliuer̃d   marke 𝚪
  In y^e Prsence of us/   John Cloyce came before mee this
  Jonathan Hamõnds/   26th day of Janva : 1676 : &
  . . . . . Littlefejld   Elizabeth his wife & did both
                             acknowledg this Instrum^t aboue
                             written to bee there free Act &
                             Deede,
                                 Edw . Rishworth Assot̃c/
vera Copia transcribed & Compared with the originall this
2cund day of F . bru : 1676 · p Edw : Rishworth ReCor ·

---

[12]   These Prsents doe witness that I John Playce now
liueing at yorke, formerly of Cascoe bay, for diuerse Con-
                  siderations y^rvnto Moueing, doe hereby putt my
. . Pluice puts sonn Richd Playce out as an apprentice to serue
his son
     Wood   Ric · Wood of yorke (being now about 8 years
                  of age) vntill the sd boy come to ye full age of
Twenty one years from the date here of, & y^t hee shall
Prforme true & honest seeruice, vnto him the sd Richd
wood his Maister according to the best of his ability, In all
such lawfull Imploymts as his Maister shall set him about, &

BOOK III, FOL. 12.

shall not any ways destroy his Maisters goods, nor suffer Damage to come vpon them by wasting or Imbesselling of them any ways to his disaduantage, but shall Prforme true faithfull & honest sceruice vnto his sayd Maister & Dame his Maisters wife, vntill the full tyme of the sd Ric Playce bee expired/

In Consideration of the Pformance w^r of, the sd Ric: Playce his sceruice truely pformed vnto Ric. Wood his Maister, the sayd wood doth hereby promiss &
Wood Covenat y^t in any Convenjent tyme, w^n John
To Playce father vnto ye sd Ric^d his sonn shall
Playce require or desire It that Ric. Wood his Maister, shall make him the sd John Playce, in the behalfe of his sonn Ric: Playce the sd woods servant a Legall Deed of sayle of Twenty Acers of Land wch now hee doth Covenant & promiss in the behalfe of himselfe & his wife to giue him, & by the sd Instrum^t Confirme vnto him, & In the meane tyme to pronide for Ric: thejr servant aforesd meate drinke apparell washing & Lodging as is fit for a servant to haue, & according to y^r best abilitys, to doe y^r best Indeauo^rs to teach him to reade & Write, provided hee bee Capable y^rof. & at ye end of his tyme to pronide & sujte him with such double apparell with other necessarys as the law in such Cases requirs/ It is likewise to bee vnderstood that Ric. Playce shall serue his apprentishipe with his maister & Dame, or the Longest surviuer of them, but both djing before his tyme bee expired, then ye sd Ric: Playce is to haue his Lyberty & bee a free man/ In witness w^r of Wee haue herevnto set our hands & seals, this 5th day of Octob^r 1676 ·

Sign'd sealed & Delivered   John Playce his
 in the p^sence of/   marke 𝒢 (his seale)
 Edw Rishworth/
 Arther Bragdon/   Ric Wood   (his seale)

A true Coppy of this Instrum^t transcribed & Compared with ye Originall this 3d day of Febru 1676:
        Rishworth R Cor:

Book III, Fol. 12.

Know all men by these P̃sents, that I Samson Anger of
Yorke fisherman, In Consideration of the some of fiue pounds
in hand payd by Ric: Wood, the receipt w^rof I

<small>Angier
To
Wood</small>

doe acknowledg, & am there with fully satisfyd
contented & payd, haue barganed & sould, & doe
by these p̃sents bargan sell aliene set ouer &
Confirme vnto the sayd Ricd wood his heyres executors,
Administrators & Assignes, a Certen tract of vpland Contayneing the full quantity of fourty Acers, being a lot of
Land granted & giuen mee by the Town, & layd out vnto
mee the sayd Samson Anger by Peter Weare & John Twysden, in the behalfe of the Town of yorke, ljing & being on
the North side of the Ledg of Rocks, at the hither end of
the long sands, ljing by the sea side, in the way to Cape
Nuttucke, being a Necke of vpland, wch deuides the barbary
Marsh into two parts, wch lot is Twenty fiue pooles in
breadth, & is bounded & marked sixteen scoore pooles in
length vpon a North West Lyne backe into ye Countrey, &
ye fore part there of butting vpon the sea Wall/ wch Tract
of vpland as bounded togeather with all the profetts Im̃un-
itys priuiledges & appurtenances there vnto belonging or
any ways app^rtayneing, to haue & to hould the aboue barganed Premisses, from mee Samson Anger my heyres executors Administrators & Assigns to him the sayd Richd
Wood, his heyres executors Administrators & Assigns for
euer, & I the sayd Samson Anger doe further Covenant &
promisse to & with the sayd Richd Wood, that I haue true
& good right to dispose of the sayd land, & that ye same is
free & cleare from all former Gyfts, grants bargans sayles
titles & Incomberances w^tsoeuer, had made done by him the
sayd Anger, or any other Prson or Prsons by his procurem^t
& the sayd Samson Anger doth further promiss for him selfe,
his heyres executors & Assigns to & with the sd Wood his
heyres, executors & Assigns to defend & saue harmeless
the Title & Interest there of aganst all pson or Prsons w^tso-

Book III, Fol. 12.

euer Pretending or laijng any Claime there vnto from by or
vnder mee/ In witness w'of I the sayd Samson Anger haue
set here vnto my hand & Seale this 25th day of Febru 1674 :
Signed sealed & Delivered/   Samson Anger
  In the Prsence of   his marke ◉ (his seale)
  Testes William Partridg/   Samson Anger doth acknowl-
            edg this Instrum^t to bee his
            Act & Deede this first of
            March 1674 : before mee
            Edw . Rishworth Assote/
  A true Coppy of this Instrum^t transcribed, & Compared
with the originall this 3d day of Febru · 1676
        p Edw : Rishworth ReCor :

Witnesseth these Prsents, that I william Johnson Inhabitant In yorke in New England. In Consideration of foure
pounds finteeen shillings in hand already payd

Johnson
To Wood

mee by Richard Wood, now Inhabitant In yorke
do bargan agree & grant, & Confirme & set ouer
vnto ye aboue sd Wood his heyres executors Administrators
or Assigns from mee my heyres executors administrators Or
Assignes a Certen Tract of vpland with all the Conveniences
there vnto belonging, Contayning thyrty Acers of Land w'on
now hee hath lately set his house, the sd Land lyeth as you
goe to Cape Nuttacke, & is bounded & lyeth between Nath'll
Prebles Lot, & was the Lot of Samson Anger/ Further I
the sayd Johnson do set ouer all the priuiledges & appurtenances y^{r}vnto belonging vnto him the sayd Wood, his heyres
executors Administrators Or Assign . for euer/ to haue &
to hould the sayd Land as aboue expres'd, from mee my
heyres executors Administrators Or Assignes for euer/ In

Book III, Fol. 12.

witness w^rof I haue here vnto afixed my hand & Seale this first day of March 167¾   William Johnson
Signed sealed & Delueř'd   his marke 〤 (his seal)
In y^e βsence of/
William Partridge/   William Johnson & Hannah Johnson his wife doe own this Instrum^t to bee y^r Act & Deede, this first of March, 1674 before mee
                   Edw: Rishworth Assote/

A true Coppy of this Instrum^t transcribed, & Compared with the originall this 5th of Febru · 1676 ·
                   p Edw: Rishworth ReCor

Pearces Bond To Bray

Know all men by these Prsents y^t I Joseph Pearce shippwright, lineing in the Town of Kittery in the County of Yorke Shyre, doe acknowledg my selfe to ow & Justly to bee Indebted vnto John Bray shipwright lineing in the same Town of Kittery, the full some of Twenty six pounds, In good M^rchantable pay to his content, & for the Prformance here of, I bind mee my selfe my goods, my heyrs executors Administrators & Assignes firmely by these βsents/ In witness hereof I haue here vnto set my hand this thyrty day of Janvary In the yeare of o^r Lord one thousand six hundred seaventy six in the 30: day of Janvary

Signed & Deliveied in the   Joseph Pearce/
   βsence of us/   Tymothy Cardon, & Stephen Reed
   The marke of   both Witnesses to this bill doe
   Tymothy Cardon/   Attest vpon y^r oaths, that this is
   Stephen Reed/   ye Act & deede of Joseph Pearce
& y^t they were both βsent & see ye sd Jos. Pearce deliver his gunne in o^r Marster Joⁿ Brays hands in lew of the rest of those goods of Pearces wch hee left in o^r Maisters possession, to giue him possession of the whool which hee left in his

Book III, Fol. 12, 13.

hands, vntill Jos. Pearces returned againe into the Countrey for his security, & vntill hee had mayd o^r Maister John Bray satisfaction for his debt of Twenty six pounds Contayned in ye bill aboue written

Taken vpon oath this first of Febru: 76 before mee
         Edw: Risworth Assote

A true Coppy of this bill with the witnesses Attested, transcribed & Compared with ye originall this 5th of Febru. 76. p Edw: Rishworth ReCor/

[13] Know all men by these Prsents, that I Richard Wood of Yorke In the County of Yorke Planter, for sev-

Wood
To Jos
Preble

erall Causes & Considerations mee there vnto moueing & more espetially for a valewable some of fiue pounds 6^s In silver, & the rest In M^rchantble boards & staues six pounds, to mee already payd, by Joseph Preble of the aforesayd Towne of Yorke, wch with I am fully Contented & satisfyd: Doe here by giue grant bargan sell alhene, Enfeoff & Confirme, & haue here by given granted sould alien'd Enfeoffed & Confirmed, vnto the aforesd Joseph Preble of Yorke, from mee Richd Wood my heyres, executors, Administratois & Assignes, vnto the sayd Joseph Preble his heyres executors Administrators & Assigns, Certen & Severall Tracts & Prcells of Lands vidz^t as followeth/

A certen Tract & Prcell of vpland, Contayneing the quantity of fourty Acers of Land, sould vnto mee by Samson Anger of Yorke, lijng on the North side of ye Ledg of Rocks, Abutting vpon the sea wall neare the long sands, In the way to Cape Nuttacke Abbutted & bounded, as appeareth by a Deed signed & sealed by the sayd Anger beareing Date the 25th of Febru: 1674·

As alsoe a Certen Tract of vpland, bought of Willia͠ Johnson, Contayneing ye quantity of Thyrty Acers of vpland, where now I the sayd Richd Wood haue lately bujlt a small Tenement, ljng ye way to Cape Nuttacke, bounded between Samson Angers & Nath^ll Piebles Lands, as by a Deede appeareth beareing Date May first 167¾ As alsoe another Tract & Prcell of vpland, Contayneing the quantity of Twenty Acers of vpland be it more or less, ljng or being vpon, or neare vnto the Marsh Called the barbary Marsh, being Twenty rod or pooles in breadth, ljng next Adiacent vnto the Land which I bought of Samson Anger, being on the North side of It, & also about the quantity of three acers of pond Marsh more or less, wch I bought of Henc: Donell, ljng neare vnto my house wch severall Tracts & Prcells of vpland & Meddow, being ninety Acers of vpland in the whoole, & three Acers of Marsh, as aboue bounded & expressd, according to y^r severall Deeds, with all the profetts, Imunitys priuiledges, & appurtenances there vnto belonging, or in any wise app^rtayneing, to haue & to hould from mee my heyres, executors, Administrators & Assignes, vnto ye sayd Joseph Preble his heyres, executors, Administrators & Assignes for ever, And I the sayd Richd Wood doe further Couenant & promiss to & with the sayd Joseph Preble, that the abouesayd Tracts & Prcells of Lands & Meddow, are free & Cleare from all other bargains sayles titles Morgages, & Incumberances whatsoever, & shall warrant & Defend the same from all other barganes, gyfts, sayles, from all manner of Prsons whatsoeuer, from by or vnder mee, or any others by my procurement/ In witness where of I haue here vnto afixed my hand & seale, this one & Twenty day of Aprill one Thousand six hundred seaventy & seaven/ Anno: Dom̄: 1677.

Signed sealed & Delivered/   Richd Wood (his seale)
  In the Prsence of   Richd Wood & Dorothy his wife,
  Edw · Rishworth/   doe acknowledg this Instrum^t
                      aboue written to bee y^r Act &
                        Deed, this 23th of Aprill 1677:
                        before mee
                              Edw Rishworth Assote

BOOK III, FOL. 13.

A true Coppy of this Instrument aboue written, transcribed & Compared with the Originall, this 26th of Aprill 1677 :   p Edw · Rishworth ReCor :

Know all men by these Prsents, that I Roger Hill haue agreed with Joseph Cross my brother in Law, about the portion that was due to my wife, & I the sayd Hill haue made a full agreement concerneing my wifes portion, wrof I haue received part, & the remajndr to bee payd as Wee doe agree, as witness here vnto I haue sett my hand, 1677 : one thousand six hundred seventy seaven, March, 30th day/   Roger Hill

Hill
To
Cross

Testes, witness/   vera Copia of this bill transcribed, &
Joseph Storer   Compared with the originall this 4th
Hene : Wakefejld   day of June : 1677.
his marke h   p Edw · Rishworth ReCor :

These Prsents witnesseth, that I Peter Weare Senjor, of Yorke, doe ow & stand Indebted vnto Mr George Pearson of Boston, for & In the behalfe of Fran : Littlefejld of Wells, the Just some of eight pounds in Mrchtable pine boards at Twenty shillings p Thousand, at some Convenjent Landing place at Yorke, or Cape Nuttacke, or Wells, at or before the last of Novebr next Insewing the day & date here of, & for the true Prformance there of I haue Caused this bill to bee made in the behalfe of a debt due from the County of Yorke vnto the sd Littlefejld, as witness my hand, May 3 : 1675 :
Witness Fran . Littlefejld/   Peter Weare Treasr

Weares
Bill to Pearson

Fran Littlefejld of Wells appeared before us, & attested that hee was prsent & see Peter Weare sett two his hand, & Delive͡rd It to Geo . Pearson, & set to his hand, as witness this 17 · Octobr 1675 :
              Samll Wheelewright/
                                              Commissiors

BOOK III, FOL. 13.

A true Coppy transcribed out of the originall this 23:
June: 77: p Edw: Rishworth ReCor:

    Phillip Swadden aged seauenty three years or y^rabouts,
testifyeth & sayth, that about thyrty eight or thyrty nine
yeares since, liueing then at pischataqua do pos-
<small>Swaddens
Test for
Frost</small> itiuely know, y^t Mr Thomas Wannerton gaue to
Nicholas Frost a Prcell of Land vp in Pischata-
qua River, now known by the name of Kittery
which pcell of Land was bounded, on the East with a little
Coue, Joyneing to the Fort Poynt, on the South West on
the River, on the North West Notherly, with a great stumpe
called the Mantilltree stumpe; which is about the Middle of
the Lane, wch Joynes to ye Land which Majo^r Nicho: Shapleigh now possesseth, & soe runneing into ye woods, as fare
backe as the sayd Wannertons Land went, which Tract of
Land Mr Thomas Wannerton, gaue to the sayd Nicholas
Frost to come to bee his Neighbo^r/ & further sayth not/
  Taken vpon oath August 27: 1673:
        before Edw · Tyng Assista^t
A true Coppy transcribed out of the originall this 5th of
July: 77: p Edw: Rishworth ReCor:

    Oliue Playstead Widdow Administratrix, & William &
James Playstead Administrators vnto the Estate
<small>Plaisted's
Acc^{ts} Ball^d
with
Hutchinson</small> of Mr Rog^r Playstead, her husband, & there
father deceased, do own that all Accopts w^{ch}
hitherto haue been between o^r deceased husband
& father, & Mr Eliakime Hutchinson, In the behalfe of him
selfe & his brother Mr William Hutchinson are now made
vp & fully ballanced from the begining of the world to this
Prsent date, wch by the Totall ballance there remaines due

Book III, Fol. 13, 14.

Eighty six thousand fiue hundred foote of M^rchantble pine boards vnto Mr Eliakime Hutchinson, & one hundred & twenty thousand foote of M^rchantble pine boards vnto the sayd will: Hutchinson aforesd, being for the rent of the Mills at Newgewanacke, both the aboue named quantitys of boards to bee deliuered vnto Eliakime & Willia: Hutchinson, or either of them or there Assigns, at Pipe staue poynt at Newgewanacke, In the ballanceing w^rof all former rents to this day, haue been & are Included, & fully discharged, & this wee own to bee o^r Act & Deed, vidz^t Oline & William Playstead, before mee this seauenteenth day of August, 1676.

       Edw: Rishworth Assote

A true Coppy of this ballance transcribed & Compared with the originall this: 17 · July. 1677 ·

       p Edw: Rishworth ReCor:

[14]   (March, 2 · 73 . 74)

Layd out & measured vnto John Green Senjo^r, his grant of Land Contayneing sixty acers neare Yorke pond, being two hundred & fourty pooles in Length North East & by East, & 40 poole in breadth North West & by Nore with Addition of fourty pooles in Length, & Twenty pooles in breadth at North East end of Peter Grants Land to make vp ye Coplement the sayd land being bounded with Peter Grants Land South East, & in part South West, & the rest of the sayd Land is bounded with the Comoues/   John Wincoll

Jno Green (margin)

      Roger Playstead Surv^rs

    Febru: 20: 1671:

Alsoe layd out vnto John Green Senjo^r, his Addition of sixty Rod in Length, at the head of his house Lott, at the East end, Contayneing fiueteen Acers, being fourty rodds in breadth

Green (margin)

       John Wincoll Surv^r

Book III, Fol 14.

A true Coppy of these two grants aboue written, transcribed out of the originall & y^{r}with Compared this 21th day of August : 77 : p Edw : Rishworth ReCor :

Know all men by these Prsents, that I James Emery Inhabitant in the Town of Kittery, haue sould vnto Peter Grant Scotchman, all that Messuage & Tract of Land I bought of John Lamb, & stands vpon record, beareing date 24th of Aprill 1654 : & which Tract of Lands I haue a bill of sayle for from John Lamb, wch I doe hereby Ingage to deliver to the sayd Peter Grant his heyres, & Assignes for euer, for & in Consideration of Twenty three pounds, & tenn shillings, Well & truely payd in hand, & by mee received, all which tract of Land & Tymber, for bujlding or fenceing y^{r}vpon, or other wise, I doe hereby fully & freely resigne & set ouer vnto Peter Grant his heyres, & his Assigns for euer without any Euiction, expultion or molestation, of mee my heyres or Assignes for euer/ In witness vnto the treuth here of I haue here vnto set my hand this 21th day of October 1659 :

Emery To Grant

Sealed & deliuered in the
Prsence of us/
Humphrey Chadborne/
Geo : Gray

James Emery/
The marke of ⋂
Elizabeth Emery/

James Emery & Elizabeth his wife acknowledged this Instrum^t aboue written to bee y^r Act & deede before mee this 18th of August (77)
Edw . Rishworth Assote :

Kittery To Lamb

Granted by the Select Townsmen for Kittery, vnto John Lamb his heyres or Assigns for euer Twenty Acers of Meddow, or soe much swamp that may make Meddow/ It being & lijng on the North East side of a brooke w^r there is a bridg Called

Book III, Fol. 14.

by ye name of William Loues bridg, & lijng in the way to a Marsh of Humfrey Chadbornes & Mr Broughtons/

A true Coppy taken the 25th of Nov͡b 1662 : p mee Humphrey Chadborne Town Clarke/

vera Copia, of the Instrume^t aboue written made to Peter Grant, & of the Tonn Grant vnd^r written made vnto John Lamb, & by James Emery sould vnto ye sd Grant, transcribed & Compared with ye originall this 21th of August 1677 : p Edw : Rishworth ReCor :

Emery
To
Grant

Know all men by these Prsents, that I James Emery Inhabitant in the Town of Kittery with Elizabeth my wife, haue for diuerse good Causes, & valewable Consideiations vs moueing there vnto, & for fiue pounds fiueteen shillings in hand payd, & by mee receiued, haue sould vnto Peter Grant the one halfe of tenn Acers of Meddow, wch was granted mee by the Town of Kittery, as may & doth appeare vpon ReCord, in the Town booke or Kittery pa . 19 : beareing date the fiueteenth day of Octob^r 1656 , all which tenn Acers of Marsh hath been by mee Improved in part by mowing what is mowable of It, & It lyeth with in sight of a great pond, com͞anly called by the name of yorke pond/ The one halfe of wch tenn acers of Marsh as is aboue specified, & lijng at that end next Yorke pond, I doe & haue sould vnto Peter Grant his heyres, executors Administrators & Assigns for euer, they peaceably to Imoy the same with out any Eviction or expultion of mee my heyres or Assignes for euer/ & In witness of the treuth hereof, I with my wife Elizabeth haue here vnto sett our

Book III, Fol. 14.

hands the sixth day of March in the yeare of o{{r}} Lord, one thousand six hundred sixtty & two/

Sealed & Delivered   James Emery/ (his seale)
in p{{s}}ence of us/   The marke of ⟨mark⟩
Humphrey Chadborne/   Elizabeth Emery
Wilha : Spenser

    James Emery & Elizabeth his wife acknowledged this Instrument aboue written to bee y{{r}} Act & Deed, before mee this 18{{th}} day of August · 1677 : Edw : Rishworth ReCor :

A true Coppy of his Instrum{{t}} transcribed, & Compared with the Originall, this 22{{th}} day of August 1677 ·

    before mee Edw : Rishworth ReCor :

    To all Christean people, to whom these Prsents shall come Richard Abbet of Portsmouth In the County of Douer &

Abbett
To
Holms

Portsmouth Now in y{{e}} Massatusetts Colony in New England black smyth, & Elizabeth his wife sends greeteing · Now know yee that I Richd Abbet & Elizabeth my wife for diverse good Causes & Considerations vs here vnto moueing more espetially for & in consideration of the some of fourty pounds of Current money of New England in hand Received of Tho : Holms of Kittery, in the Couty of Yorke shyre, & Colony aforesd, Yeamon, before the signeing & sealeing hereof, w{{r}}with Wee acknowledg our selues fully satisfyd, Contented & payd, & of euery part & Prcell there of, doe acquit exonerate, & discharge, the sayd Thomas Holms his heyres & Assigns for euer. Haue given granted, barganed sould alien'd, Enfeoffed, & Confirmed, & by these Prsents do absolutely giue grant bargane, sell alliene Enfeoff & Confirme vnto y{{e}} aforesd Thomas Holms, his heyres executors Administrators, & assignes, a Certen Tract of Land Neare vnto Quamphegine falls in the Town of Kittery, with the dwelling house & out houses &

fences, the Land being by Estimation thirty Acers bee It more or lesse, being bounded as followeth, vidz^t begining at a little brooke on the North side of the Fort Hill, & on the Eastward side, with seuerall marked trees vnto the upper end of Mr Thomas Broughtons Corne fejld, vnto a little fresh swampy brooke or spring, wch is the head & vtmost bounds of the sayd Tract of Land/ alsoe three Acers of swampy Meddow, Commanly Called by the name of blakeburry Marsh, being bounded by the Comanes, & two Acers of Meddow at the little River bounded with the Comons & one Acer of Meddow ljing on the North side of Mr Wills his Marsh, & a grant of fifety acers of Land, granted by the Town of Kittery to mee the sayd Richd Abbet, with all the appurtenances & priuiledges thereunto belonging, of w^t nature & kind soeuer; To haue & to hould vnto him the sayd Thomas Holms his heyres executors Administrators & Assignes for euer, all & euery of the seuerall Tracts of Land, dwelling house & out houses, with all the app^{r}tenances w'soeuer/ & I the sayd Richd Abbet, & Elizabeth my wife do couenant promiss & grant to & with ye sd Tho. Holms, [15] that they haue in them selues good right, full pouer, & Lawfull authority, the seuerall tracts of Land, & Meddow with the dwelling house, & out houses & all the priuiledges there vnto belonging, to sell & dispose of, & that ye same & euery part & parcell there of are free & cleare, & freely & clearly acquitted exonerated & discharged of & from all, & all manner of former gyfts, grants Leases Morgages Wills Intayles Judgments, executions, pouer of thirds, & all other incomberances, of what nature & kind soeuer, had made done Committed, or suffered to bee done or Committed, whereby the sayd Thomas Holms, his heyres executors Administrators or assignes may any ways bee Molested Euicted or Eiected out of the aboue mentioned tracts of Land or houses, or any part or Picell there of, by any Prson or Prsons w'soeuer, haueing clameing or Pretending to haue, or Clavm any Legall right title or Interest, of, in or to the

Premisses, or any part or Parcell there of · And the sayd Richd Abbet & Elizabeth his wife, doth for them selues there heyres, executors Administrators & Assignes, Covenant, promiss, & grant, to & with the sayd Tho: Holms, his heyres executors, Administrators, & Assignes, the severall Tracts of Land, & Meddow & houses aboue mentioned, with all thejr priuiledges & app^rtenances, aboue mentioned, with all y^r priuiledges & app^rtenances there vnto belonging of w^t nature & kind soeuer, aboue mentioned to warrant & for euer defend by these psents/ In witness whereof the sayd Richard Abbet & Elizabeth his wife haue here vnto sett there hands & seales, this thirty first day of May in the yeare of our Lord, one thousand six hundred seaventy & seaven/ 1677:

Signed sealed & Delivered/
In Prsence of us/
George Broughton/
Thomas Abbott/
William Spencer/

Richd Abbet
his marke R A (his seale)

Elizabeth Abbet
her marke E A (her seale)

Richd Abbet, & his wife Elizabeth came & acknowledged the aboue Instrument to bee thejr Act & deed, & the sayd Elizabeth doth freely resigne vp her 3d^s of the aboue mentioned houses & Lands to Thomas Holms, his heyres executors & Administrators for euer/ June. j: 77: before mee Richd Martyne Comissio^r

A true Coppy of this Instrument aboue written, transcribed, & Compared with the originall, this 22th day of August 1677: p Edw Rishworth ReCor:

Book III, Fol. 15.

Simpson's Bond To Ross

This bill bindeth mee Henery Symson Liueing in Yorke, who is alsoe in New England, doth bind my selfe heyres executors or Assignes to pay or Cause to bee payd vnto Roger Rosse hueing in Boston his heyres executors or assignes, the full & iust some of fiue thousand good M^rchantable redd oake pipe staues, to bee deliuered to Roger Rosse at Braue boate Harbour at ye bridg Landing place at or before/ It is here to bee vnderstood y^t fiue thousand of good Red oake pipe staues at or before the last of March next Ensewing, the Date here of/ Dated the 25th of August . 75 : Witness my hand/ Henery Symson

Nathaniell Maysterson/
Humfrey Spencer
his marke/ S

his marke /S/

A true Coppy transcribed, & Compared with ye originall, of this bill aboue written, this 27 : of August, 77 : p Edw · Rishworth ReCor · this bill satisfyd this 8 August 1679 : as
Attests Edw . Rishworth ReCor

March 4th 1673 74 ·

Peter Grant

Measured & layd out to Peter Grant, a hundred & twenty Acers of Land neare Yorke pond, on the West side of It/ Two hundred & twenty pooles in Length East & by North, & fiuety acers more on the North of James Emerys Land by his Marsh, two hundred poole in Length South West. by West & fourty pooles in breadth, as by the marked trees : And his Addition to his house Lot the breadth of fourty pooles, & sixty poole in Length layd out, Contayneth finieteen Acers/

A true Coppy transcribed
out of ye originall this
13th day of Sep^br 1677 :
p Edw : Rishworth ReCor :

John Wincoll
Royer Playstead } Suruyrs

BOOK III, FOL. 15.

Everett
To
Wentworth

Know all men by these P'sents that I Isacke Everest, with & by the free Consent of Joanna Everest my wife, do vpon good & valewable Considerations there vnto mee Moueing, & more espetially for the some of fourty pounds to mee In hand already payd, where with I am fully contented & satisfyd, giue grant bargan sell & Confirme, vnto John Wentworth of Cutchechah formerly now of the Town of Yorke, & by these P'sents haue given granted barganed & Confirmed from mee my heyres executors Administrators & Assignes vnto the sayd John Wentworth his heyres executors administrators & Assignes for euer, a certen Tract or lott of vpland, Contayneing the full quantity & proportion of fiueteen Acers of Land, w'on I haue bujlt a small house or Teneme' & fenced in about ye quantity of three or 4 Acers of the sayd vpland, which I haue broaken vp & planted, lijng & being vpon the North East side of the path, wch goeth from the Town of Yorke vnto the house of Henc: Sayword, Contayneing the breadth of Twenty two pooles & an halfe, bounded on the East side with a Lott of Sargeant John Twisdens, & on the West side with Lewis Beanes Lott, & soe to runne backe into the Countrey vpon a North and by East Lyne, vntill fiueteen Acers bee fully Compleated/ And alsoe another Tract of Land Contayneing the quantity of Twenty Acers of vpland as an Addition there vnto, given & granted vnto mee by the Select men of the Town of yorke, begining at the head of my home Lott, & soe to runne the full Length & breadth of the other fiueteen Acers Lott, as aboue mentioned, vntill Twenty Acers of Land bee expired; as by the sayd Town Grant doth & may appeare more fully/

To haue & to hould, the sayd Tracts of Lands & house as before mentioned with all the Tymber Woods, vnder Woods, & all other priuiledges, Immunitys & appurtenances there vnto belonging, or in any wise app'tayneing. I the sayd Isacke Everest, in the behalfe of my selfe, my heyres executors Administrators, & Assigns, do give grant & Con-

Book III, Fol. 15, 16.

firme vnto the sayd John Wentworth his heyres executors Administrators & Assignes for euer, & I ye sayd Isacke Everest, do Covenant & promiss y^t that the sayd house & Lands are free & Cleare, from all Clames Titles Troubles & Incomberances w^tsoeuer, [16] and that in the behalfe of my selfe, my heyres, executors, administrators & Assignes I will by these P^rsents defend, & saue harmeless the sayd John Wentworth his heyres & Assigns, from all Pr^son or Pr^sons whatsoeuer, Clameing or Pretending to Clame any right title or Interest, from, by, or vnder mee/ In witnesse w^rof Wee haue here vnto afixed our hands & seales this fifth day of Febru · one thousand six hundred seaventy fiue/

Signed sealed & deliver'd	Isacke Everest (his seale)
in the p^rsence of/	his marke ℓ
Edw : Rishworth	Joanna Everest
Hene . Sayword/	her marke ᘔ (her seale)

Isacke Everest & Joanna his his wife, do own this Instrume^t to bee their Act & deede before mee this 13th of March . 75

Edw Rishworth ReCor :
Rishworth Assote/

A true Coppy of this Instrume^t aboue written transcribed & Compared with the originall this 20th day of Septemb^r 1677 p

Received by mee ffran : Backus of Wells, of Joseph Cross of the sayd Town, Administrator vnto ye Estate of John Crosse Senjo^r my father in Law deceased, the Just some of fiuety two pounds, in Land Cattle, & househould stuffe in full satisfaction of all dues & demands for my wifes portion out of the sayd Estate/ I say received the some of 52 : 00 . 0 this 14 : d . of Janva · 1677 .   p mee Fran Backus/

Backus
Receipt To
Cross

ffran: Backus owneth this receipt to bee his Act & deed this: 17th of Septemb{r} 1677: before mee Edw Rishworth
Assote/

A true Coppy of this receipt transcribed & Compared with the Originall this 21th day of Septemb{r} 1677:
p Edw · Rishworth ReCor:

Mr John Paine/

Pain to McIntire

Sir/ I pray you bee pleased to satisfy vnto Mieu: Mackyntire the some of Twenty six pounds, on the Accopt of Yours to serue you/

Septemb{br} 26 : 64 :   Tho · Wiggin/

A true Coppy transcribed & Compared with the originall, this first of October, 77 : p Edw . Rishworth ReCor .

The Deposition of John Granger aged thyrty yeares or y{r} abouts/

Granger Test for Smiths Child{n}

This Deponent witnesseth, that hee haueing occasion to bee at Sturgeon Cricke about 8 or tenn days before Trustrum Harris was killed by the Indeans, y{t} on my comeing backe from Sturgeon Cricke towards the Euening, I Called in at Trustrum Harris his house to see how hee did, & found him y{r} at his house alone/ soe hee desired mee to sit down & take a pipe of Toba͞ · w{ch} accordingly I did, & in the tyme of y{t} wee were takeing o{f} Toba͞: hee was pleased to bee discoursing of his loanesome life, & dangerous condition, after w{ch} I was takeing my leaue of him, I being intended to Newgewanacke, but hee Intreated mee to stay w{th} him all night, w{ch} accordingly I did, soe wee walkeing in his fejld togeather, I asked him w{t} hee intended to doe with his Estate, in case hee should fall by the hands of his Enemys,

or otherwise come to his end/ hee answered mee & sayd
William Smyths children, sayd hee are children that haue
always loued mee & I loue them, & haue hitherto intended
for y^m w^soeuer I haue left at my decease, soe I purpose not
now to bee worse then my word, nor change my mind, but
w^soeuer Estate I haue they shall Inioy It after mee/ & further sayth not/

Taken vpon oath this 20th of June 77, before mee

                    John Wincoll Assote

vera Copia transcribed out of the originall y^s 10 : Octob^r 77
                    p Edw: Rishworth ReCor:

The Deposition of Mary Frost aged 21 years or y^rabouts/

I the Deponent being gathering Indean Corne, the last
Indean harvest in my husbands Corne fejld, I had with mee
in Company my brother Edw: Smale, & Trustrum Harris
for helpe. soe at Nowne w^n Wee satt down to

Mary Frost Test for W Smiths Children

dinner, I tooke occasion to aske of Trustrum
Harris if hee had made his will, & hee answered
Noe/ why sayd I to him, who doe you intend
shall haue Yo^r Estate shall ye Town haue It/ he answered &
sayd the Town shall neuer bee ye better for w^t I haue, for I
haue already intended It for them that shall haue It/ who
is It then sayd I, you haue Intended It for, shall William Smyths children haue It/ Trustrum answered & sayd,
It is very like y^t william smyths children may haue It/
& further sayth not/

Taken vpon oath this 16th day of June, 1677 : before mee
                  John Wincoll Assote:

A true Coppy transcribed & Compared with the originall
this 13th day, of Octob^r 1677: p Edw: Rishworth ReCor:

Book III, Fol. 16.

The Deposition of Joⁿ Forgison aged 22 yeares or y^r abouts/
Sayth, y^t being at ye house of Trustrum Harris, about 3 weekes before he was killed, I this Deponent did aske ye sayd Harris why hee did take soe much payns &

Forgison Test for Smiths Children

care, since hee had noe relation to leaue It to/ & hee did desire him to make him his heyre/ the sayd Harris made answere y^t If hee had Twise as much more as hee had, hee had heyres enough for It all I asked him who they were/ hee sayd y^t William Smyths Elldest sonn should haue his house; & home Lott after his decease, & the out Lot John Smyth ye second sonn should haue, & for w^t Cattle & other goods, hee had, should bee deuided amongst ye rest of the sayd Smyths children, after his funerall Charges were defrayed/ & further sayth not/ Taken vpon oath in Court this 11th of Septem^{br} 77 : as Attests Edw . Rishworth ReCor :

A true Coppy transcribed & Compared with ye Originall, this 13th Octob^r 1677 p Edw : Rishworth ReCor

The Deposition of Francis Smale Senjo^r aged fiuety years, or y^r abouts/

Small Test for Smiths Children

I this Deponent witness, that at the tyme y^t I was Impressed to goe vpon ye Countrys scervis to Ossaby, that Trustrum Harris was Impressed for ye same scervice, alsoe, soe I tooke occasion to aske ye sayd Trustrum how hee had disposed of his Estate in case hee should fall by ye hand of the Enemy, or otherwise come to his end/ hee answered mee & sayd that howsoeuer his end should Come, that William Smyths two Elldest sonns, namely Nicholas & John should haue all y^t hee had/ & wⁿ Wee Were onward o^r way at Newgewanacke I tooke occasion to aske him about ye same agayne/ hee answered mee then as he did before, y^t howsoeuer It should please god to bring him to his end, y^t Willi ·

Book III, Fol. 16, 17.

Smyths children should haue his Estate/ & further sayth not/ Taken vpon oath this 16: June, 1677: before mee John Wincoll Assote/

A true Coppy transcribed & Compared with y̆ᵉ originall y̆ˢ 13: Octobʳ 77:   p Edw: Rishworth Re: Cor·

The Deposition of John Tomson aged 22 years or yʳ abouts/

I this Deponent witness, yᵗ beimg Comanded by Capᵗ Frost last yeare to hunt yᵉ woods after the Enemy, yᵗ Trustrum Harris was one of yᵉ same Company alsoe, yᵉ sayd Trustrum & my selfe sitting at breakefast togeather vp in yᵉ woods aboue Salmon Falls, I tooke occasion to aske him who should bee yᵉ better for his Estate, in case hee should bee taken of by yᵉ Enemy, hee made answere & sayd, hee Intended his Estate for william smyths children, wⁿsoeuer hee should bee taken out of yˢ life   onely hee had something a greater loue for Nicholas then for yᵉ rest/ & further sayth not/ this yᵗ Trustrū: Harris spake to this Deponent was about a Twelue Moenth agone/

Tomson Test for Smiths Children

Taken vpon oath in Court yˢ 11th of Sepb̆ʳ: 77: p Edw· Rishworth ReCor·

vera Copia transcribed & Compared with yᵉ originall this 13· Octobʳ 1677: p Edw: Rishworth ReCor:

[17] Wee the Select men of Scarbrough do giue & grant & layd out vnto Henery Brookeing a Picell of vpland adioyneing to his Plantation, Eastward, from his house at a pine tree by the path, & soe runneing vp North & by West till hee Comes to the head of his vpper bounds E: S E· lijng North West & from his Westerne bounds to runne South down to yᵉ path West-...

Scarborough To Brookin

provided It bee noe bodys Legall right before/ Febru · 2 : 73 :
Witnessed by us/   John Tynny/
                                    Henery Williams
A true Coppy transcribed out of ye   Samll Oakemā
originall this 10th day of Decembr   Select men/
p 77 Edw · Rishworth ReCor :

Wee the Select men of Scarbrough do giue & grant to Hennery Brooking six Acers of Marsh adioyneing to beaver Cricke/ this Wee giue & grant to ye sayd Brookin. prouided It bee noe bodys legall Rights before/ witness or hands this 2nnd of Febru . 73 .

Ditto

A true Coppy of this grant tran-   John Tynny
scribed & Compared with the   Samll Oakemā
originall this 10th of Decembr :   Hene · Williams
77 : p Edw · Rishworth ReCor :   Select men

Articles of agreement made, Concluded & fully agreed vpon, between Major Nicholas Shapleigh. John Shapleigh, Jos . Hamonds, & William Spencer of the one Party, & Richard Otis & James Chadborne on ye other Party Witnesseth : That wᵃˢ the aboue named Nicho · Shapleigh John Shapleigh Jos . Hamonds, & william Spencer were by ye last Will, & testament of John Heard of Kittery, on Pischataqua River in New England, deceased, beareing date the 3d day of March, In the yeare of our Lord god one thousand six hundred seaventy & fiue Nominated, chosen & appoynted, with the aboue named James Chadborne, to bee his ouerseers in trust, so see the sayd will Prformed : Now Wee the sayd Nicholas Shapleigh, John Shapleigh, Jos : Hamonds & William Spencer aboue named, being the Major Part of the ouerseers of the sayd will, & Considering the Introcacy & mixture of the Estate of the sayd John Heard,

Shapleigh's Hamonds & Spencer & Otis & Chadburn Agreemts about Heards Estate

Book III, Fol 17

It being Intermixed with & amongst the Estate of James
Heard the sonn of John Heard who deceased without makeing any will: And Considering that many Inconvenjences
might arise in the deuideing of the sayd Estate. Doe by
these Prsents Assigne & make ouer all the right & ouerseei-
shipe of the last will & testament of the sayd John Heard
deceased, vnto the aboue named Richard Otis, who being the
now husband of Sarah, the Relict or Widdow of James
Heard & to the aboue named James Chadborne, & to both of
them Joyntly & haue fully for our parts haue authorized,
lyceneed, & Assignd the sayd Richd Otis, & James Chadborne to Act & doe all & euery thing or things, conceineing
the execution of the sayd Will, & testament, & shall not
Intermeddle with the Administration of any part of the
goods, Chattles, money debts, or other Estate of the sd Testament, without the Consent of the sayd Richd Otis, &
James Chadborne there heyres or executors but shall at all
tymes hereafter & from tyme to tyme Prmit* & suffer the
sayd Richd Otis, & James Chadborne their hevres, executors,
or Assigns, to Administer all such goods Chattles moneys
debts & Estate, as at the day of the date here of, bee in y^e
Custody of the sayd Nicho: Shapleigh, & the rest of the
ouerseers, or in the hands of any other Prson or Prsons w^{ch}
are to bee Administred according to ye Tenour & Intent of
the sayd will & testament. And the sd Richd Otis & James
Chadborne doe for them selues y^t heyres, executors, Administrators & Assignes, promisse & Ingage, that out of the
Moueables, the Estate of the sd John Heard, & James Heard
his sonn, that they will Administor & pay all the Just & due
debts, wch the sayd John Heard & James his sonn did ow
to any Prson or Prsons, & alsoe to satisfy all such Legacys,
as is by the Will & testament expressd & alsoe to take care
for ye Comfortable subsistance of Izbell Heard the Relict of
the sd John Heard, dureing her naturall life, & alsoe for the
Children of James Heard according to ye intent of ye sayd
will & testament : & alsoe to yeild vp the Estate of Lands, &

houseing vnto John Heard, the Grandchild of the sayd John Heard deceased, when hee shall Accomplish & Attayne to the age of Twenty one years, tenantable & sufficiently fenced, or as now It is, & in case of Mortality to whom soeuer It shall belong, according to the true Intent & Meaning of the sayd Will & Testament, & for the Pformance hereof, Wee the sayd Richard Otis, & James Chadborne doe bind our selues, our heyres executors & Administrators Joyntly and seuerally by these Prsents/

In witness where of Wee haue here vnto sett two our hands, & Seales this fifth day of Novembr In the yeare of or Lord one thousand six hundred seaventy seven/

Signed sealed & Deliuered   Nic: Shapleigh (his seal)
In the Prsence of/   John Shapleigh (his seale)
William Bickham/   Jos: Hammond (his seale)
Aylce Chadborne/   Wilhm. Spencer (his seale)
    The marke of
    Richd Otis/ 𝒰𝒪 (his seale)
    James Chadborne (his seale)

The settlement of the Estate of John Heard, & James as aboue is expressd by the agreement of the ouerseers & ye rest, is allowed & ratifyd by the Court provided yt Otis & Chadborne giue bond to ye satisfaction of this Court, to respond all Legall debts Legacys & reversions of the Estate to ye heyre Comeing to ye age of 21 years/ Signed in Court this 8th Novebr 1677: p Edw. Rishworth ReCor ·

A true Coppy of this Instrumt aboue written transcribed out ye originall & yrwith Compared this 8th day of Janva. 1677. p Edw: Rishworth ReCor:

Allard To Wainwright

Know all men by these βsents, that I Hugh Allard of the Ysels of Shoales fisherma· for an in Consideration of the some of seaventy pounds, in hand payd by Fran. Wanewright of Ipswich in the

BOOK III, FOL. 17, 18.

County of Essex M^rchant haue granted barganed & sould, & doe by these P^rsents clearly fully & absolutely grant bargane Confirme & sell vnto the sayd Fran: Wanewright all my right Title & Interest in & two my now dwelling & Land that is vpon ye Iles of shoales, togeather with all the priuiledges and appurtences, that doth any way app^rtayne, as alsoe my stage, & all other out houseing, & all my flakes & flake rowme, the flakes being in Number foure & a Trayne fatt · To haue & to hould, & quietly & peaceably to Inioy vnto him the sayd Fran: Wanewright, & his heyres executors Administrators & assignes for euer/ togeather with one fishing shallop, with all the appurtenances y^rvnto belonging, vidz^t Masts yards sayles ridging roade & Grappers oares bucketts, porredg pott & Compass, & ye sayd Hugh Allard doth by these P^rsents Covenant promiss & grant to & with the sayd Fran: Wanewright his heyres & Assignes to warrantize the sayle of the sayd dwelling house out housing stage, flakes, flake rowme Land shallop Masts yards sayls ridging roade Grapers bucketts oares porridg pott [18] & Compass, togeather with all the priuiledges & appurtenances, there vnto app^rtayneing or any wise belonging, to bee firme & good, free & freely discharged from all former Gyfts grants barganes sayles Morgages Dowers Judgm^{ts}, executions or any other Intanglements or Incomberances w^tsoeuer/ & that It shall bee Lawfull for the sayd Fran: Wanewright his heyres & Assigns hence forth & for euer, to haue vss occupy & possess & Inioy all the sayd house Land stage out houseing & shallop togeather with all the appurtenances, there vnto belonging & app^rtayneing, & without any Let hindrance Denyall interruption or Molestation, from mee the sd Hugh Allard my heyres executors, & euery of them for euer, or any P^rson or P^rsons makeing or Claymeing any right title or Interest there vnto, or any part y^rof for euer, always provided, that if the sayd Hugh Allard or his heyres or Assigns shall well & truely Content satisfy & pay or cause to bee payd vnto ye sayd Wanewright or his heyres Or

Book III, Fol. 18.

Assignes the full some of seaventy pounds, in Current M^rchantable dry Cod fish at or before the first day of July next vpon ye Ylses of shoales, at the Current shipping price, that shall bee vpon Marble head, then this Prsent Instrument to bee voyd & of none æffect, or else to stand & bee in full force & vertue, as witness my hand & seale this seventh day of Decemb^r In ye yeare of o^r Lord 1677

Signed sealed & Deliver'd   Hugh Allard (his seale)
   In p^rsence of us/   Hugh Allard acknowledged this
   John Wanewright/   writeing to bee his Act & deede,
   Nathaⁿ Tucker/   before mee Decemb^r 7 · 1677 :
                        Daniell Denison/

A true Coppy of this Instrument transcribed out of ye originall & y^rwith Compared this 2^d of Febru : 1677 :

           p Edw . Rishworth ReCor .

Morrell
To
Conley

Lett all men know by these Prsents, that w^ras Nicholas Hodgsden of the Town of Kittery, & County of Yorke, husbandman, & Elizabeth his now wife, by y^r deed beareing date the 3d day of December in the yeare of our Lord one thousand six hundred seaventy & foure, 1674 . did for & in Consideration of that tender affection that they bore vnto John Morrall & Sarah his wife, daughter of the sd Nicho . Hodgsden, to y^r children as alsoe in referrence & full satisfaction of the sd Saraihs Marriage portion, Giue grant alienate Enfeoff & Confirme vnd^r hand & seale, & acknowledged before authority, all that Tract of Land ljng & being in Kittery, by Estimation seaven Acres of Land wch was formerly part of the homestall, or farme of the sd Nicho · Hodgsdens, on wch Land the sayd Joⁿ Morrell hath bujlt an house & barne, & now dwelleth in It, To haue & to hould the sayd Land vnto him the sayd John Morrall his heyres or Assigns for ever, by & vnd^r diverse Covenants & reservations in the sd Deede

Book III, Fol. 18.

Mentioned & Comprized, & the bounds y^r of in the sd deed expressed, at Large & alsoe, was that the Town of Kittery at severall Legall Town Meeteings did giue & grant vnto the sayd John Morrall three severall Lotts or Tracts of Land, at severall Town Meeteings the one a grant of fourty Acers given & granted vnto him the sd Morrall by the Town of Kittery which grant beareth date the Twenty fourth day of ye eight Moenth Anno: 1668 another the secund grant is the Tenn Acres of swampe, granted ye sixteenth day of the Ninth Moenth, Anno 1668: And the 3d is a grant of Twenty Acers of Land Joyneing to his former Grant of 40 Acers granted vnto him by ye sd Town Decemb^r 13 Ann: 1669 all which Lotts or Tracts of Land being three in Number adioyneing & Compact togeather bounded on the South or y^rabouts by lands sometyms Peter Wittums & now purchased & in the possession of Nicho Hodgsden aforesd, & on the West with other ye Lands of the sd Nicho · Hodgsden aforesd, & on the North, & on the North Nore East, & by the North East & Nore, or y^r abouts, by the Lands of Ohne Playstead Widdow, Called birch poynt, & partly by birch Poynt brooke, & alsoe bounded by severall marked trees, at the laijng out all wch grants or Tracts of Land is now in the possession of him the sayd John Morrall, Now known yee that ye sd John Morrall being soe Legally seazed & possessed of the sd houses barne & Lott of Land, by vertue of a Deed as aforesd of the sayd Nicho: Hodgsden, & of the last recited three grants of Land from the Town of Kittery being compact as aforesd, for & in Consideration that Abra Conley of Kittery in the County aforesd, hath given granted & by his Deed of sayle vnder his hand & seale, clearly & absolutely from the Considerations y^r in expressed sould, alienated Infeoffed & Confirmed vnto him the sayd John Morrall, his heyres executors Administrrtors & Assignes all y^t Lott or Tract of Land Comanly known or Called by the name of Coole Harbour, wch the sd Conley purchased Lately of James Emery, of Kittery, wch Deed of sayle for the Convayance & Confirmation of the sayd Tract of Land beareth date the Twenty seaventh day of July in the Twenty eight yeare of ye Reigne of our Soueraign Lord king Charles the secund In ye yeare of our Lord god 1676 : & is granted vnto ye sayd Morrall, for ye vss benefitt & behoofe of him the sayd Morrall, his heyres executors Administrators & Assignes, & for noe other vss Intent or purpose, hath & by these Prsents, doth demise, grant, bargan, sell, aliene, Enfeoff, Convay, release, Deliuer, & for euer Confirme to him the sayd Abra · Conley his heyres executors Administrators & Assignes all the sayd houses & barnes, & the aforesd seaven Acers of Land with y^r & euery of there appurtenances, & all the profetts priuiledges, Emoluments & Comoditys y^{r}to belonging, or in any wise app^{r}tayneing wch hee the sayd John Moriall his heyres executors, Administrators or Assignes now haue or out to haue by vertue of ye former recited Deed given vnto him by the sayd Nicho · Hodgsden ; And alsoe all them three Grants or Lotts of Land given & granted vnto him by the Town of Kittery as aforesd togeather with all the profitts priuiledges & appurtenances there vnto belonging or in any wise out to belong vnto them or either of them of the sayd grants/ To haue & to hould the sayd houses barne & seaven Acers of Land, bee It more or lesse, Three Lotts & all & singular the aforesd Premisses with there & euery of thejre app^{r}tenances, vnto him the sayd Abra . Conley, his heyres executors Administrators & Assignes, from the day of the Date here of for euer, freed acquitted or otherwise sufficiently saued & keept harmeless of & from all other form grants bargans sayles Gyfts leases Joynters Dowrys, Title of Dowrys, pouer of thirds, & from all other Troubles & Incomberances w^{t}soeuer had made or suffered to bee made & [19] done by the sayd John Morrall or Saraih his wife, & alsoe against any other Pison or Pisons w^{t}soeuer Lawfully Clameimg the former recited Prmisses, or any part or Prcell there of, And that ye sayd John Morrall shall deliver vp vnto the sd Abra : Conley, all Deeds grants

BOOK III, FOL. 19.

or writeings that hee out to deliver wch doe Concerne any of the sayd Prmisses, or any part y^r of, & alsoe the sayd Morrall shall get the returne of the survayers that Layd out the aforesd three Lotts of Land to bee returned & Recorded into the Towne booke of Kittery, & give the sd Conley a Coppy of It, & all to bee done at ye pper Cost & Charge of the sayd John Morrell, & alsoe know yee that the aforesd Sarah haue given her full Consent vnto it, as may appeare by her hand & seale, for the full Confirmation hereof/ In witness hereof here the sayd John Morrall & Saraih his wife, haue here vnto set there hands & seals, even the Twenty eight day of July, In the Twenty eight yeare of the Reign of o^r Soveraigne Ld Charles the secund of England Scotland France & Ireland King, Anno Dom͠ 1676

Sealed & Delivered/   John Morrall (his seale)
In ye Prsence of us/   Saraih Morrell
Andrew Searle/   her marke H
James Emery/
Miles Tomson/   John Morrall & Saraih his wife doe acknowledg this Instrument to bee y^r free Act & deed this 18th Janva: 77. before mee Edw Rishworth
                                                                     Assote

A true Coppy of this Instrument transcribed & Compared with the originall this 12th day of Febru 1677:
                           p Edw: Rishworth ReCor:

Let all men know by these Prsents, that w^as James Emery & Elizabeth his now wife by thejr deede of sayle beareing date the Twenty seaventh day of Novemb^r one thousand six hundred seaventy & three, & in the fiue & twenteth yeare of the Reigne of our soveraigne Ld King Charles, the secund, did demise grant & Clearely & absolutely abounte bargan sell & Confirme vnto Abra: Conley,

Book III, Fol. 19.

Conley
To
Morrell

his heyres executors Administrators & Assignes all that Lot or Tract of Land Comanly called or known by the name of Coole Harbour, lijng with in the Town of Kittery, vpon the Lot or Tract of Land, Anthony Emery father of the afore sayd James Emery sometyms heretofore dwelt & inhabited, & is bounded as by the sayd Deede is expressed, with all the profetts priuiledges & app'tenances y'vnto belonging, or in any wise app'tayneing, & for good & valewable Considerations in the sayd recited deede is mentioned: All wch bounds priuiledges & appurtenances, & Considerations as by the sd recited deede fully & more at large it doth & may appeare/

Now know yee that the sayd Abraham Conley for diverse good Causes & Considerations, & espetially for & in Consideration that John Morrall of Kittery in the County of Yorke brickelayer, & Sarah his now wife, haue by a deed vnd^r thejr hands & seals, made ouer delivered & Confirmed, or otherwise doe hereby Covenant Imediatly to make ouer deliver & Confirme for them thejr heyres executors & Administrators vnto the abouesd Abra Conley of Kittery his heyres executors Administrators & Assigns, for euer, all that house & houseing, with all that Land being by Estimation seaven Acers bee It more or less belonging vnto the sayd Houseing Lijng in the Town of Kittery, & was given him by his father in Law Nicho Hodgsden as the Marrage portion hee gaue to the sayd Morrall, with his daughter now wife of the sayd Morrall, & alsoe for & in Consideration that the sayd John Morrall & Sarah his wife doth hereby Covenant imediately vpon the Insealeing here of to make ouer all y^r right & Title that they haue or ought to haue in thejr Lotts of Land granted vnto ye sayd Morrell by the Towne of Kittery Contayneing in the whoole seaventy Acers, bee It more or less, as by the sd Town grants doth & may appeare, & to Confirme it vnto the sayd Abra Conley his heyres & Assignes for euer/ Haue given granted barganed & sould, & by these

Psents do demise grant bargan sell aliene Infeoff Convay release dehuer & Confirme vnto the sd John Morrell all y^t lot or Tract of Land Called Coole Harbour aforesayd/ To haue & to hould the sayd Tract of Land Orchard Meddow vpland woods vnderwoods waters water Courses ways paths & all other profetts privilledges & Comoditys with theire & euery of thejr appurtenances vnto him the sayd John Morrell his heyres executors Administrators & Assigns from & Immediately after ye day & Date here of for euer, In as large & ample manner to all Constructions as hee ye sayd Abra. Conley can or may Estate ye same by vertue of the aforesayd Deede or by any other deed grant or writeing that doth or may any wise Concerne the sayd Lot or Tract of Land, & the sayd Abraham Conley doth further Covenant to & with the sayd John Morrell to deliver vp vncancelled vnto the sayd Morrell or his Assignes, vpon demand made to him the sayd Conley by the sayd Morrell, the sayd Deede Namely James Emreys deede & all other Deeds grants Manuscripts or, other writeings y^t doth concerne the same, & the sayd Abra: Conley, for him selfe his heyres executors Administrators & Assig^s doth couenant hereby to & with the sayd John Morrell his heyres executors Administrators & Assigns to & with euery of them, that hee the sayd John Morrell his hevrs executors Administrators & Assigns & euery of them shall & may from tyme to tyme & at all tyms hereafter vnder the Couenant & Condition herein expressed quietly & peaceably haue hould Occupy possess Inioy the sayd Tract of Land called Coole Harbour with the appurtenances vnto his & thejr own proper vss benefit, & behoofe, for euer, without the Lawfull Lett sujte vexation Molestation, disturbance denyall or putting out of him the sayd Abra: Conley his heyres executors Administrators or assigns or of any other Pson Lawfully Clameing, & alsoe acquitted, & is agreed & otherwise keept harmeless of & from all manner of former gyfts grants leases Joyntuis Dowers pouer thirds or other Titles w'soener, excepting & reserueing vnto him the sayd Abra · Conley his Assigns that plott of Land wch is now layd out & bounded, It being by Estimation Two Acers of Land bee it more or less on wch Land Hene: Kirke hath bujlt a dwelling house on It/ In witness here of the sayd Abra Conley hath here vnto set his hand & seale euen the twenty seaventh day of July in the Twenty eighth yeare of ye Reigne of o^r Soueraigine Lord Charles ye secund, of England Scotland France & Ireland King, Anno : Dom. 1676

Sealed signed & Delivered/
  In the Pr̄sence of us/
  Andrew Searle/
  James Emrey/ } witnesses/
  Miles Tomson

The marke of ⤫ (his seale)
Abra : Conley/

         Abra : Conley owned this Instrum^t
         aboue written to bee his free Act
         & Deede this 18th day of Janva :
         1677 : before mee
               Edw : Rishworth Assote :

A true Coppy of this Instrument transcribed out of the originall & y^{r}with Compared this 13th day of Febru : 1677 :
               p Edw . Rishworth ReCor .

[20] Bee It known vnto all men by these Prsents, that I James Emery with the free Consent of my wife Elizabeth Emery for & in Consideration of the Just some of Thyrty fiue pounds, in hand before the Insealeing & delivery hereof well & truely payd, the receipt w^{r}of I the sayd James Emery doe hereby acknowledg, & thereof & of euery part & Prcell there of, doe acquitt & discharge Abra : Conley of Sturgeon Cricke in the Township of Kittery, his heyres executors & Administrators, & every of them by these Prsents for euer/

Emery
To
Conley

Haue given granted barganed & sould, & by these Prsents, doe give grant bargan sell aliene Infeoff Convay release deliver & Confirme, vnto the sayd Abra: Conley his heyres executors

BOOK III, FOL. 20.

Administrators & assignes for euer, all that Tract peece or
Prcell of Land scituate & lijng & being at Kittery at a Poynt
Comanly Called Coole Harbour Poynt, formerly in the possession of Anthony Emery, his father & now since in the
possession of James Emery aforesd. sonn vnto the sayd
Anthony Emery, runneing in breadth next vnto the River
side about sixty three pooles, & backeward behind ye fejld,
runneing backe about one hundred & twenty pooles, being
part of a Lott of Land formerly granted to his father Anthony
Emery, wch ranne backeward about one hundred & twenty
pooles from the way behind the sd fejld vpon an East lyne
&c · onely tenn Apple trees the sayd James Emery reserveth
the propriety to bee his own to remoue & take vp & dispose
of as hee seeth cause, which Land aforesd with all the trees
woods vnderwoods Comanes Easements, profetts Comoditys
Aduantages Emoluments Hærıdaments & app'tenances w^{so}-
euer, & alsoe all the Claime right title vss possession reuer-
tion remajnd^r & demand of mee ye sd James Emery & Elizabeth my wife, of in & vnto the sayd Prcell of Land, & euery
part & Prcell thereof with y^r & euery of y^r app'tenances vnto
the sayd Abra. Conley his heyres & Assigns for euer, to &
for the sd proper vss & behoofe of the sayd Conley his
heyres executors & assignes, for ever · & for noe other vss
intent or purpose whatsoeuer / & the sayd James Emery &
Elizabeth his wife for them selues their heyres executors
Administrators & Assignes, & for all & euery of them doth
Covenant promiss & grant to & with the sayd Abra · Conley
his heyres & Assigns & to & euery of them p these Prsents
that ye sayd Abra · Conley his heyrs & Assignes & euery of
them shall & may Lawfully from tyme to tyme & at all tyms
hereafter quietly & peaceably haue hould vss occupy & Imoy,
to his & y^r own proper vss & behoofe all & singular the
before hereby granted & bargaıned Prmisses, & euery part &
Prcell there of with the app'tenances freed acquitted & discharged or otherwise sufficiently saved & keept harmeless of
& fro . . . . s gyfts

grants Leases Joynters dowers & title of Dowers, & from all other Titles, Troubles, incumberances whatsoeuer had made suffered to bee done, or hereafter to bee had, made Committed, or suffered to bee done by the sayd James Emery or Elizabeth his wife thejr heyrs executors or Assignes or any other Prson or Prsons whatsoeuer, lawfully Clameing from, by or vnd' him her them, or any of them, & further that the sayd James Emery will resigne & freely deliver vp all writeings, & Convayances deeds or euidences, which hee or the sayd Elizabeth hath in his or her hands Concerneing the Prmisses, fayrely written, & vncanselled/ In witness where of wee the sayd James Emery & Elizabeth Emery haue set two our hands, & seals, this twenty seaventh day of Novem'b'r, one thousand six hundred seaventy three 1673. In the fiue & twenteth yeare of our soueraigne Lord Charles the second of England Scotland France & Ireland King, Anno Dom : 1673 : James Emery (his seale)
Signed sealed & Deliverd Elizabeth Emery (her seale)
in the Prsence of us/ her Marke ꝗ
Richard Cutt
Josua Moody This Instrument acknowledged by the abouesd James Emery & his wife to bee y'r volentary Act & Deed this nineteenth of May 1674, the sayd Emery alsoe owned to haue received the trees reserved in the bill of sayle/ before mee Richard Walden

Commissio'r'/

A true Coppy of this bill of sayle aboue written transcribed & Compared with the originall this 14th day of Febru : 1677 : p Edw. Rishworth ReCor :

Book III, Fol. 20.

March 20 : 1655 :

Kittery
To
Lamb

Granted by the Select Townsmen for Kittery vnto John Lamb his heyres Or Assignes for euer, Twenty Acers of Meddow or soe much swamp that may make Meddow/ It being & lijng on the North side of a brooke Where y^r is a bridg Called by ye name of William Loues bridg, & lijng in the way to a March of Humfrey Chadbornes, & Mr Broughtons/

A true Coppy p me Humphrey Chadborne Town Clarke/

The 15th day of July : 1656 ·

Lotted & layd out by the Select Townsmen for Kittery vnto John Lamb his heyres Or Assignes for euer a lott of Land formerly granted & next Adioyneing vnto John Greens Lott, the breadth of the sayd Lott is by the water side fourty poole, & the Length Two hundred poole, & fourty pooles at the head line, as doth appeare by severall Marked trees/

A true Coppy p mee Humphrey Chadborne Town Clarke/

A true Coppy or Coppys of these two grants aboue written transcribed out of the originall & y^r with Compared this 14th of Febru. 1677 : p Edw. Rishworth ReCor.

Duston
To
Cutt

These Presents testify, that Wee Thomas Dustone & Elizabeth Dustone of Portsmouth doe hereby bargane sell alleine Assigne & set ouer vnto Mr John Cutt of Portsmouth M^{r}chant all that our Messuage or Tenement with all the Land y^{r}to belonging on Kittery side, now In ye possession Or Occupation of Richd Downe, with all o^r Land on that side vnto ye sayd John Cutt his executors Administrators & Assignes to haue & to hould the sd Messuage or Teneme^t &c · as aboue sayd for euer, vntill the some of seaventeen pounds 17^s, & 11d bee payd vnto ye sayd Jo^n Cutt/ & the sayd John Cutt, is to

haue & receive the Rent of Richd Downe & all the profetts yʳ of Ariseing & accrewing as & to his own vss, vntill the aforesd Debt bee payd & Wee do hereby Ingage oʳ selues our Executors Administrators & Assignes to make good yᵉ Title yᵗof vnto yᵉ sayd John Cutt, & to defend the Title yʳ of aganst all Prso . . wᵗsoeuer/ In witness wʳof wee haue here vnto set oʳ hands & seales, this 2nnd day of March 1659-60/   Thomas Duston (his Seale)
Sealed & Deliverd in yᵉ p̄sence of } Elizabeth Dustone
Dauid Wheeler/ Joⁿ CuttJunjoʳ } her marke ⊥ (her Seale)
Richd Stylemā: Scriviſi/

vera Copia transcribed & Compared with the originall this 7th of March 1677, p Edw: Rishworth ReCor:

[21] These Presents witnesseth, yᵗ wʳas I Elizabeth Duiston, Widdow of Thomas Duiston deceased late of Kittery, do acknowledg to haue sould vnto John
Widow Duston Cutt the houses & Lands on Kittery side, all
To
Cutt   that did belong to my husband deceased. for yᵉ valew of fourty pounds Sterlg: in hand received: as p an obligation of yᵉ sayle yʳof under my hand & seale Dated yᵉ 10ᵗʰ of Octobʳ 62 as may more fully appeare & doe acknowledg to haue deliverd John Cutt, both turfte & Twigg vpon the Land, as for him Lawfully & quietly to Inioy as hee own proper Estate, for him selfe his heyres executors Administrators & assignes for euer/ & for his soe Inioijng there of, & to make good the sayle yʳof as Lawfull, I bind mee my heyres, executors Administrators, in the some of sixty pounds Sterling to John Cutt, that hee as aforesd shall quietly Inioy It, for him his heyres executors administrators or Assigns, with out any Molestation from mee, or any for mee or my heyres executors or administrators, & to this as a reall obligation, I haue here vnto set my

Book III, Fol. 21.

hand & seal this 19th of March 1662 : 63 . & in the 14th yeare of our soueraigne Lord King Charles the secund/

        Elizabeth Durston (her scale)

Assigned & sealed & Deliv- her marke
ered in yᵉ psence of us/
Edw. Melleher/   Elizabeth Durston Widdow
The marke of ⌒ Aquilla/ did acknowledge this to
     Chase/ bee her Act & Deede, be-
         fore mee yˢ 19th of March
         1662 . as abouesayd/
           Tho: Wiggin/

A true Coppy of this Instrumᵗ transcribed, & Compared with yᵉ originall this 9th day of March 1677 :

      p Edw . Rishworth ReCor .

    Decembʳ 15th 1674 .

Measured & Layd out to Thomas Abbett sixty acers of
    Land being a grant made to him the 13th of
Thomas
Abbett Decembʳ 1669 : by yorke path, & alsoe fiuety
    Acers more being an Addition to yᵉ former
Grant granted to him the 13th day of Aprill 1671 : In all an hundred & Tenn Acers, runneing a mile in Length from the brow of the Rocky Hill at Slutts Corner, East South East to John Taylours Marsh, & fiuety six poole in breadth bounded on the North with Mr Fox his Land on the East with John Taylors Marsh, & Coman Land, & the South & West with Coman Land/ This was Layd out by Mr Roger Playstead & my selfe, as aboue/ John Wincoll Surveyeʳ

A true Coppy transcribed & compared with the originall this 9th of March 1677 · p Edw: Rishworth ReCor ·

BOOK III, FOL. 21.

Decemb^r 16 : 1674 :

Abbett
Measured & layd out vnto Thomas Abbett Thyrty one Acers of Land on the North West side of John Greens 60 Acres bounded with the sayd Greens sayd Land on ye South East, It being 128 pooles in Length, South West & by West, by the sayd Greens Lyne, the two Ends & the North West side are bounded with Lands yet in Coman, It being part of his fiuety acres granted Aprill 13th 1671 ·   John Wincoll Surveg^{hr}

vera Copia transcribed this 9th first, 77 : p Edw : Rishworth ReCor :

Abbett
Measured & Layd out vnto Thomas Abbett nineteen Acres of Land, at the head of his Addition to his house Lott bounded on the West with his own Land, & the Land of John Green Senjo^r, & on the South with Comanes, at the Head of Daniell Goodings Land, & on the East with the Comans, at the Craggy Hills, & on ye North with Ric : Naysons Lyne, as p the marked trees, It being part of the fiuety Acers granted Aprill 13th 1671 ·

John Wincoll Surveig^{hr}

A true Coppy of this grant transcribed, & Compared with the originall this 9th day of March 1677 :

p Edw : Rishworth ReCor :

·

To all Christean people, to whom these Prsents shall come/ John Crafford now of Portsmouth in the County of Douer & Portsmouth, now in the Massatusetts Jurisdiction in New England, & Elizabeth his wife sends Greeteing : Now know all men by these Prsents, that I the aboue mentioned John Crafford & Elizabeth my wife, for diverse good Causes & Considerations, us moueing there vnto, more espetially for

Book III, Fol 21

& in Consideration of the some ot eight thousand foote of
M^rchtable pine boards in hand received of Joseph
Barnard of Water Town, in the County of Middlesex, & Colony aforesayd, where with wee
acknowledg our selues fully satisfyd Contented
& payd & there of & of euery part. & P^rcell there of doe
acquitt, & for euer discharge the sayd Joseph Barnard, his
heyres & Assignes by these P^rsents ; haue absolutely given
granted, barganed, sould aliened, Infeoffed, & Confirmed, &
by these P^rsents do absolutely giue grant bargane sell aliene
Infleoff, & Confirme, vnto the aboue named Joseph Barnard
his heyres executors administrators, & Assignes, a peece, or
P^rcell of Land in the Town of Kittery, being by estimation
about Twenty Acers bee it more or less, being bounded as
followeth, vidz^t by the high way that goeth to Wells on y^e
South East End ot It, & by the Land that Isacke Botts
bought of the sayd Crafford on the South West & by the
Land of Mrs Oliue Playstead, Widdow, & the Durty
Swampe, on the North West, & the North East side of It,
with all the wood & Tymber that is either standing, or ling,
vpon the aboue sayd Land, & all the app^rtenances, & priuiledges y^rto belonging, or any wise app^rtayneing, of what
nature & kind soeuer To haue & to hould, the aboue men-
tioned peece or P^rcell of Land to him the sayd Joseph
Barnard his heyres & Assignes for euer, & to their onely
proper vss, benefitt, & behoofe for euer. & the sayd John
Crafford & Elizabeth his wife, for them selues, there heyres,
& Assignes, do Couenant, promiss & grant to & with the
sayd Joseph Barnard his heyres & Assignes, that they the
sayd John Crafford & Elizabeth his wife, haue in them selues
good right, full pouer, & Lawfull authority, the aboue given
& granted p^rmisses, to sell & dispose off, & that the same &
euery part & P^rcell there of are free, & Cleare, & freely &
clearely acquitted, exonerated, & discharged, of & from all
& all manner of former gyfts grants Leases, Morgages,
Wills Entayls Judgm^{ts} executions poner of thyrds & other

Crafford
To
Barnard

BOOK III, FOL 21, 22.

Incomberances, of what nature, & kind soeuer, had made, done, acknowledged Committed, or suffered to bee done, or Committed w^rby the sayd Joseph Barnard his heyres, or Assignes, shall or may any ways bee Molested, Euicted, or Erected out of the aboue granted Prmisses, or any part or Prcell there of, by any Prsone or Prsons whatsoeuer, haueing Claymeing, or Prtending to haue or Clame any Legall right, title, or Interest, clame, or demand of, in, or two the aboue granted Premises, & the sayd John Craflord & Elizabeth his wife, do for them selues, there heyres, executors, Administrators, & Assignes, Couenant promiss, & grant, to & with the sayd Joseph Barnard his heyres & Assignes the aboue granted peece, or Prcell of Land to warrant & for euer defend by these presents, In witness whereof the sayd John Craflord [22] & Elizabeth his wife, haue here vnto sett y^r hands, & seales, this Twenteth day of Octob^r In y^e yeare of o^r Lord one thousand six hundred seaventy & six, 1676 · John Crafford ($\substack{his\\seale}$)
Signed sealed & Deliuered/

In Prsence of us/ Great Ysland this 15th of May : 77 :
John Willkines/ John Crafford acknowledged this
Edw · Rawson/ Instrument to bee his Act, &
Joseph Beames Deed, & Elizabeth his wife ren-
his marke ⅅ dered vp her thyrds, & right of
Dowry at the same tyme, in the
Premisses/ before mee
Elyas Styleman : Commissio^r/

A true Coppy of this Instrument transcribed, & Compared with the Originall this 16th day of March 167$\frac{7}{8}$
p Edw : Rishworth ReCor :

Neale
To
Cooper

Know all men by these Prsents, that I John Neale in the Town of Kittery, in the County of Yorke, or province of Mayne do bargan sell, and by these Prsents do Confirme, vnto Allexand^r Cooper of the Town aforesayd, In y^e aforesayd County, or

province, of Mayne his heyres or Assignes all my right &
Title of a Prcell of Land contayneing about Twenty fiue
Acers be It more or less, ljing & being vpon the North East
side of Pischataqua River, being one halfe of a Tract of
Land wch I the sayd John Neale bought of Allexand^r Maxwell of the Town of Yorke, the sayd fiue & twenty Acers
of Land, being on the South side of the sayd Tract of Land,
with fiue Acers of Marsh ground, ljing & being neare a
place Commanly Called by the name of Whittes Marsh, For
& in consideration of Tenn pounds, Sterlg · to mee the sayd
John Neale in hand payd, by the sayd Allexand^r Cooper, &
furthermore, I the sayd John Neale doe hereby bind my
selfe my heyres & Assignes for ever, to beare the sayd
Allexand^r Cooper his heyres, & Assignes for euer, harmeless
from any Cause or Causes, for from, or by mee my heyres,
or assignes for euer, & for the Prformance of the Contents
of this bill of sayle, I haue here vnto set my hand this 7th
M^o 9th In ye Yeare of our Lord 1662 :

Sealed & Deliverd in the Prsence   John Neale his

of us/ James Heard/   marke ∓ (his seale)

Peter Grant his Marke ℞

A true Coppy of this Instrumet transcribed & Compared
with the originall this 14th of March 167½ ·

                     p Edw Rishworth ReCor :

             The : 15th day of July 1656 :

Lotted & Layd out by the Select Townsmen for Kittery,
vnto Allexand^r Maxell his heyres or assignes for

Kittery To Maxwell   euer, a lott of Land on the North side of James
Warrens lott, & Joyneing vnto It, fourty poole
In breadth by the water side, & tow hundred
poole in Length, & the head lyne of the sayd Lott, sixteen
poole broad, as doth & may appeare by severall marked
trees . . . . p^r us Humphrey Chadburn

                     Town Clarke/

BOOK III, FOL. 22.

This is a true Coppy taken out of ye Town booke pa · j : this 25 : of March 71 . by mee Charles Frost Cle^rs

A true Coppy transcribed & Compared with ye transcript aboue written this 14th March 167⅜ p Edw : Rishworth
                                                    ReCor :

Kittery
To
Cooper

At a Meeteing of the Selectmen, togeather with the Inhabitants of the parish of Vnity, In this Town of Kittery, this 13th day of Aprill 1671 · appoynted for the granting of Lands by vertue of a Generall Act of the Town made the 24th of June Last past, Granted vnto Allexand^r Cooper sixty Acers of Land/

This is a true Coppy taken the 4th of March 167½ by mee
                                    Charles Frost Cle^rs

To Gray

At ye same meeteing granted George Gray sixty Acers of Land/ As Attests
                                    Charles Frost Cle^rs/

A true Coppy of this grant transcribed & Compared this 14th March : 77 · p Edw : Rishworth ReCor :

March 6 : 1671 : 72 :

Kittery
To Cooper

Allexander Coopers Grant of sixty Acers was layd out on the East side of William Spencers Land, by Willcocks pond, Two hundred Rodds in Length, North & South & finety rodds In breadth East & West, being bounded on the South, with the brooke y^t runnes out of Willcocks pond/ the high way is to bee six rodds broad/   John Wincoll
                                    Tho : Wills

A true Coppy transcribed & Compared with ye originall the 14th March, 167⅜ p Edw · Rishworth ReCor

BOOK III, FOL. 22.

Decemb{r} 19{th} 1674:

Kittery
To
Cooper

Allexand{r} Coopers Addition of Land, layd out at the North end of his Lott, Neare Whittes Marsh, being sixty poole in Length, North & South, & finety pools in breadth, East & West, Contayneing eighteen Acers & three quarters of Land/

p us John Wincoll }
Roger Playstead   } Surveg{rs}

A true Coppy of this Addition as aboue bounded transcribed out of the originall & y{r} with Compared this 14th March 167⅝ p Edw · Rishworth Re · Cor ·

Know all men by these Prsents, that I James Grant of Yorke in the County of Yorke Planter, for seveerall good Causes & Considerations y{r} vnto mee moueing, & more espetially for the some of fiue pounds in hand received by mee of John Pearce of y{e} sayd Town, Planter, w{r} with I doe acknowledg my selfe to bee fully Contented, & satisfyd, doe hereby Giue grant, bargan sell aliene & Confirme, & haue hereby given granted bargained, sould, aliend & Confirmed, from mee my heyres, executors, Administrators, & Assignes, vnto the aforesd John Pearce, his hevies executors, Administrators & Assigns the full & Just quantity of Tenn Acers of vpland, lying & being vpon that Necke of Land, commanly called Mr Gorges Necke, between the New Mill Crieke, & basse Coue, & more Piticularly, between the Lotts of Nathall Maysterson, & John Pearces Land; To haue & to hould, the aboue sayd Tenn Acers of Land, with all the profetts priuiledges, Immunitys & all other app{r}tenances there vnto belonging, or in any wise app{r}tayneing frō me my heyres, executors administrators, & Assigns, vnto y{e} sayd John Pearce his heyres executors administrators, & Assignes for ever, for his, & tl   l James

Grant
To
Pearce

Book III, Fol. 22, 23.

Grant doe further promiss & Couenant, that yᵗ aforesd Tract of Land is free & Cleare, from all other barganes, sayles, Gyfts, titles, Clames, or Intcrests, & doe & hereby shall warrant & defend, the Title & Interest yʳof, from all other Clames, & Incomberances wᵗsoeuer, intending of Pretending any right, or Title from by or vnder mee, or any other by my procuremeᵗ In witness wʳof I haue herevnto afixed my hand, & scale, this 16th day of March 167¼   James Grant (ʰⁱˢ ˢᶜᵃˡᵉ)
Signed sealed, & Delivered   his marke ⌒

In yᵉ p̃sence of/
Edw Rishworth/   James Grant acknowledged this
Arther Came his   Instrumeᵗ to bee his free Act
Marke/   & Deede, this 16th of March
                                167¼ before mee
                                       Edw: Rishworth Assoʳe/
A true Coppy of this Instrument transcribed, & with yᵉ originall Compared this 23ᵗʰ day of March 167¼
                              p Edw: Rishworth ReCor.

[23] Received by mee Edw: Johnson the some of fiueteen pounds, of John Pearce of Yorke fisherman, which fineteen pounds the sayd Pearce stood Ingaged
Johnsons's
Recᵗ To Pearce to pay mee by a bill vnder his hand, wᶜʰ some by these p̃sents, I do acknowledg the receipt of, in full satisfaction of all debts, dues & Demands from yᵉ sayd John Pearce vnto mee, from the begining of the world vnto yᵉ date hereof/ I say received the Just some of fineteen pounds this 14th of June 1670:

Signed in the Presence of   p mee Edw: Johnson/
Edw: Rishworth/   A true Coppy of this bill tran-
Tho. Traffton his   scribed, & compared with the
marke T   originall this 24th of March 167¼
                                  p Edw. Rishworth ReCor

• BOOK III, FOL. 23.

This Indenture made this Twenty ninth day of May 1660 : between Robine Hoode alias Rawmegon, Ter-
rumpquine, Wesomonascoe, Sagamores, & Scaw-
que, & Abumhamen Indeans, on the one Prty,
& Tho : Webber on the other party witnesseth,
That Wee ye aboue sayd Roben Hoode, alias Rawmegon, Terrumquine, Wesomonasco, Sagamores, & Wee the rest of the Indeans aboue sayd, haue given granted, & Delivered ouer, & by these Prsents doe give grant & deliver ouer, & for euer alinene, & quitt Clame from our selues o^r heyres executors administrators & Assignes vnto ye sd Tho : Webber his heyres executors & Assigns all y^t Tract of Land, lijng on the Westerne side of Kenebecke River, ouer against part of Arousicke Island, the vpper part y^rof begining at a Poynt on the lower side of a Cone before the house y^t was William Cocks, & soe to runne downward by the water side, to ye vpper part of an Ysland, comanly known & Called by the name of Cheefe Ysland, & to runne into the Woods three Miles, with all ye woods, vnderwoods, Meddows, with in the sayd Tract of Land, & all fishing fowling haukeing huntmg &c : with all other priviledges there to belonging : To haue & to hould to him the sayd Thomas Webber, his heyrs executors Administrators & Assignes the aboue sayd Tract of Land, with all the pruiledges aboue sayd for ever, with out any Molestation or future demand w^tsoeuer/ And doe here by bind o^r selues our heyres, executors, Administrators & Assigns for euer any more from this day forward to make any more Clame challenge or Prtence of Title to the aboue sayd Tract of Land, & to mantayne this grant, against all other Clames titles Challenges or Interests w^tsoeuer/ In witness w^rof Wee the aboue sayd Sagamors, & Wee the rest

Robin Hood
& other Indians
To
Tho Webber

Book III, Fol. 23.

of the Indeans abouesd haue here vnto sett oʳ hands & seales the day & yeare aboue written/

Sealed signed & deliverd
In yᵉ Pʳsence of us/
Robert Goutch
Allexandʳ Thwayt/
John Devine
Allexandʳ ffrissell/
John Goutch/

The marke of Robine Hoode/ (his seale)

The marke of Terrumquine (his seall)

The marke of Weesomonascoe (his seale)

The marke of Squawquee (his seale)

The marke of Abumhamen/ (his seale)

A true Coppy of this Instrumᵗ transcribed, & Compared with the originall this 13th day of May 1678:
p Edw: Rishworth ReCor:

Parker to hĩr Sister Webber

I John Parker doe in the behalfe of my selfe my heyres executors & Assignes Convay & make ouer vnto my sister Mary Webber, all my right title & Interest, of a Tract of Land lijng in Kenebecke River bounded vpon the Southward side, by a fretchett or brooke, that is the bounds of Sylvanus Davis, & soe according to the bounds of the sayd Davis his Land to goe vpon a streight lyne to Cascoe, bounded vpon the Northward side by Winniganse Cricke, wᶜʰ by these Pʳsents I doe Confirme/ as witness my hand, this third of June 1661:

Signed & Delivered
in yᵉ p̃sence of/
Thomas Kemble/
Nicholas Renallds/
Silvanus Davis/

John Parker

& his wifes marke
marke
vera Copia transcribed & Compared with the originall this 13th of May 1678.
p Edw: Rishworth ReCor:

Book III, Fol. 23.

York
To
Donnell

vpon the request of Thomas Donell, wee whose names are vnderwritten, hath layd out & bounded a Certen Prcell of vpland given & granted vnto him by the Inhabitants of the Town of yorke vpwards of eight years w{ch} sayd Land lyeth on the South side of the sayd yorke River, & is bounded on the Eastward with the the bounds of the Land of Andrew Everest, & soe to runne along by the River side Westward, Thyrty & six pooles or pearch vnto the lott of vpland formerly granted & layd out vnto Arther Bragdon Senjo{r}, & soe runneth backewards vpon a South West lyne, vnto a certen small brooke Comanly Called & known by the name of Rogers Coue brooke, w{ch} sayd Lott of Land layd out vnto y{e} sayd Donell Contayneth about fourty fiue Acers more or lesse, p   Peter Weare Senjo{r}

(Janv : 7th 1677)   Hene Donell his

marke H𝔇

Job Allcocke/

A true Coppy of this Instrum{t} transcribed, & Compared with the originall this 14th of May : 1678.

p Edw Rishworth ReCor :

Davess
Penwill
&
Bray

Articles of agreement between Cap{t} John Davess, & John Penwill, with Mr John Bray Know all whom It may Concerne, that y{e} sayd John Davess & John Penwill haue fully barganed & agreed with Mr John Bray shipe wright, for y{e} Erecting & buylding of a vessell burthen Eighty Tunns vpwards, not vnder, & the Dementions as followeth, to say finety foote p keyle, & by beame seaventeen toote, & In howle nine foote/ & for the Tunns that the sayd vessell amonts vnto, the sayd Davess & Penwill to pay y{e} sayd Bray Three pounds fiue shillings p Tunns, to bee payd as followeth, to say one quarter money price the other three quarters in p{rice} C[...] to say fish, provission, & Barbadoes goods, & Inglish goods, but money the quarter If it can bee produced, or goods æquivolent. The sd Bray is to allow vnto Davess & Penwill foure pounds for Tarr & Ocum/ The sayd vessell to haue Two Decks, & to bee in proportion to Mr Robert Elliotts vessell (Joyners worke excepted) But y^e sayd Bray to fitt the sayd vessell, with Masts, yards, Boate all to a Cleate The sayd Davess & Penwill, & Bray, in witness here vnto haue Interchangeably sett two y^r hands & seals this 29th day of Janvary 1673 · the lower Decke noe further then the Hatch way/

Testes   John Davess ($^{his}_{seale}$)

                     John Penwill ($^{his}_{seal}$)

These articles of agreement owned by Capt John Davess, & Mr John Penwill to bee y^r Act & deede, vnto John Bray shipe wright before mee this 29th of Janvary 73   Edw: Rishworth Assote

A true Coppy transcribed. & Compared with y^e originall, this 23^d May, 1677 ·   p Edw. Rishworth ReCor ·

Davess's Bond to Bray

     Know all men by these Prsents, whom It may Concern, that I John Davess of yorke In New England resident do ingage my selfe, my heyres executors & Assigns to make satisfaction vnto Mr John Bray or his Assigns for the bujlding of the shipp Called the John, & Aylce, being in length by the keele finety six foote, & the beame eighteen foote, & depth in whowle nine foote Two Inches, & further [24] If the sayd Bray haue done more, then this Covenant, then the sayd Davess is to make him satisfaction, if not then the sayd Bray is to make satis-

Book III, Fol. 24.

tion to the sayd Davess, or his Assignes, as witness my hand
this 24th of Novemb^r 1675 :   John Davess/
Witness/
    the marke of   Tymothy Scarden & Stephen Reed,
    Tymothy **T** Sarden/   doe Attest vpon thejr oaths, that
    Stephen Reed   this Ingagem^t aboue written is the
                            Act & Deed of John Davess,
                            before mee this 4th of March, 75 .
                            Edw · Rishworth Assote :
vera Copia of this Ingagement aboue written, transcribed,
& Compared with the Originall this 23 : of May 1678 :
                      p Edw . Rishworth ReCor :

    These P'sents doe witness, that I Arther Bragdon Senjo^r
of the Town of yorke Planter, on good Consideration vnto
                mee moueing, doe sell giue grant my soole right
Bragdon   & Interest of a Certen P^rcell of vpLand & Marsh
To
Moulton   here in specifyd, vnto Thom^s Mowlton of the
                sayd Town, his heyres & Assignes for euer,
vidz^t A Certen P^rcell or Tract of Marsh, comanly Called &
known by the name of Gallows poyn^t Contayning by Estimation the quantity of three acres more or less, lijng neare
to that dwelling house wch formerly the sayd Mowltons, &
since by him sould vnto Allexand^r Maxell & butting vpon
the same Land, w^rot one part of that house standeth, towards
the North East, & with the River towards the South South
East, as alsoe y^t peece or Coue of Marsh, wch lyeth next
below the aforesayd peece of Marsh, lijng next Adioyning
vnto the Land of Mr Roger Garde, towards the South East,
& butteth to ye River towards the South/ I the sayd Bragdon do alsoe sell vnto the sayd Mowlton, all y^t poynt or
Tract of vplond, wch lyeth between the two aforesd peeces
of Marsh butting to the River, & from the head lyne into the

Countrey/ It is to begine at a great Marked Whitte oake, standing neare to the head of the fiist peece of Marsh Called Gallows poynt, on the North East side of the sayd Marsh, at wᶜh tree the sayd Mowlton is to begine, & from thence vpon a streight lyne, vnto the head or Easterne end of yᵉ aforesd peece of Marsh called Gallows poynt, & from thence vpon a streight lyne vnto yᵉ head of yᵉ secund Prcell of Marsh aboue specifyd, & from thence down along the South East side of the sayd Marsh, to a marked pine tree by the River side/ all wᶜh Prcells of Land aboue specifyd, I haue given & sould, by giveing possession vnto Tho : Mowlton haue Confirmed, with all the priuiledges, & appurtenances thereto belonging vnto the aforenamed Mowlton to his heyres & Assignes for ever : In Consideration of wᶜh Lands soe sould, as aboue mentioned, I Arther Bragdon do acknowledg my selfe to haue received full satisfaction of Tho : Mowlton for yᵉ same/ Witness my hand & seale this 29th of July 1661 · Arther Bragdon (ʰⁱˢ ₛₑₐₗ)

Signed sealed & Delivered/ his marke A B
in the Prsence of/
Hene : Doncill his Arther Bragdon, & Mary his wife
marke H D do acknowledg this Instrument
Tho : Curtis/ aboue written, to bee yʳ free Act
& Deede, this 10ᵗʰ Apill 1678 :
before mee Edw Rishworth
Assotiate .

A true Coppy of this Instrument transcribed, & Compared with the originall this 24ᵗʰ of May 1678,
p Edw : Rishworth ReCor :

These Prsents witnesseth, that I John Twisden of the Town of Yorke, In the County of Yorke Planter, for diverse

Book III, Fol. 24.

Twisden
To
Jn⁰ Preble

Considerations y'vnto mee moueing, & more espetially for the some of sixteen pounds, to mee In hand payd by John Preble of the Town aforesd, bricke layer, w'rwith I am payd, & y'r with am fully Contented & satisfyd, as by these P'sents I doe own & acknowledg: doe hereby giue grant bargan Enfeoff aliene & Confirme, vnto John Preble aforesd, his heyrs executors, Administrators, & assignes, from mee my heyres executors Administrators & Assignes, a Certen Tract or Pr'cell of vpLand Contayneing the quantity of Eight Acres of Land, ljing between the Land of the shoemaker, & the Land of James Sharpe w'ron hee hath now bujlded an house, & the Land w'ron the shoemakers house now standeth, being thyrty pooles in breadth, runneing backe vpon a North & by East lyne till eight acres bee expired, six Acers w'rof Lijng aboue the patch, & two Acres of Swampe lyeth below the path, between the Lotts of Phillip Addams & Benja: Johnson, & haue hereby given granted barganed sould Enfeoff'd aliend & Confirmd, the sayd Prcell of Land as aboue bounded, with all the profetts priuiledges Lybertys Immunitys, & all other app'ritenances y'rvnto belonging, or any wise app'rtayneing, to the Land aforesd, vnto the sayd John Preble his heyres, & Assigns for euer · To haue & to hould the sayd Eight Acres of Land as aboue expressed, with all the priuiledges y'rto belonging from mee the aforesd Twisden my heyres executors or Assignes, vnto the sayd John Preble, his heyrs executors & Assigns for euer & further I doe Conenant, & agree to & with the sayd Preble, that y'e Land aforesayd is free & Cleare from all Clames, Titles, Interests, & incomberances w'soeuer, & I doe by these P'sents Ingage my selfe my heyres & Assigns to defend the Title & Interest there of, vnto the sayd John Preble & his heyrs from all P'rsons w'soeuer, Clameing or Prtending any Clame from, by, or vnd'r mee & from James

Book III, Fol. 24.

Sharpe in Prticular/ In witness w^rof I haue here vnto set my hand & seale, this sixth day of May 1678 : John Twisden (his seale)
The fenceing lyng next the high way

John Twisden Ingageth not in this sayle/

John Twisden ownes this Instrument aboue written, to bee his Act & Deede before mee this 18th of May 1678: Edw ; Rishworth Assote/

A true Coppy of this Instrume^t transcribed, & Compared with the originall this 25th of May 1678 :

p Edw · Rishworth ReCor

Morgan's Bond To Bray

Know all men by these Prsents, y^t I Francis Morgan Liueing in the Town of Kittery in the County of yorke shyre, do acknowledge my selfe to ow & Justly to bee Indebted vnto John Bray shipewright hueing in the Town of Kittery in the same County ot yorke shyre, the full some of Eleven pounds & 8^s shillings in staues, Macharell, or fish or boards, to him the sayd John Bray his heyres, executors, Administrators or assignes/ in witwise w^rof I haue here vnto set my hand this first day of Aprill 1677 . ffrancis Morgan

Witness/
The marke of FC
Johanna Couch
John Pott/

A true Coppy of this bill transcribed & Compared with ye originall this 11th of June 1678 ·

p Edw . Rishworth ReCor :

Trafton To Couch

Know all men by these Prsents, y^t I Thomas Traffton of the Town of Yorke, In the County of Yorke fisherma͡ . do for severall good Considerations there vnto mee moueing, & more espetially for ye some of eight pounds tenn shillings, in silver to mee in hand payd by Joseph Coutch of the Town of Kittery shipewri... a with I am fully Contented & sac... here by giu grant bargan sell alliene & Confirme & Isau hereby

given, granted, sould aliend & Confirm'd from mee the sayd
Traffton, my heyres executors Administrators & Assignes,
vnto the sayd Joseph Coutch his heyres executors administrators & Assigns for euer, a Certen Tract Coue or Prcell of
Marsh Land Contayning the full quantity of Two Acres of
Marsh scituate & lyng neare & Adioyneing to the bounds of
Christopher Michells out side Marsh, w'of not Contayneing
the full [25] quantity, I the sayd Traffton do stand ingaged
to make It up full Two Acres of Marsh/ To haue & to hould
the aforesd Tract of Meddow as bounded & aboue expressd,
with all profetts priuiledges & Imunitys, & all other app'tenances y'vnto belonging, or any wise app'tayneing, from mee
mine heyrs Administratots & assigns for euer, for his & there
soole proper vss & benefitt/

And I the sayd Traffton, do further promiss & Covenant,
that the aforesd Tract & Prcell of Marsh, is free & cleare
from all other bargines sayles Titles Morgages & Incomberances w'soeuer, & do & shall warrant & Defend the same
from all other Prson or Prsons w'soeuer, Clamejng or p̃tend-
ing any Clame of Title or Interest from by or vnd' mee, or
any other by my procurement · In testimony w'of, I haue
here vnto afixed my hand & seale this 15th day of June:
1678 .   Thomas Traffton (his seale)
                his marke T

Thomas Traffton doth acknowledg this Instrume' aboue
written to bee his Act & Deed this 15th of June 1678 :
                before mee Edw: Rishworth Assot͠e:
A true Coppy of this Instrument transcribed, & with yͤ
originall Compared this nineteenth day of June 1678 ·
                p Edw: Rishworth ReCor:

York
To
Frost

wee whose names are here vnderwritten haue
given granted to John Frost ffisherman tenn
Ackers of vpland lying vpon that Necke of
Land Where Wilham Moore & Richard Whitte

Lineth, w{ch} tenn Acres of vpland begines at the Westerne poynt of Yorke Harbours Mouth, & soe by the River side to the bounds of Ric: Whittes Land witness our hands this 12th day of Octob{r} 1663: W{ch} vpland is to bee but Twenty pooles by the water side, butting from Richd Whitts Land, & soe backewards vntill the tenn Acres bee fully Compleated, w{ch} Land is granted with all the right that Wee haue y{r}in, & If not Improued in one yeare after y{e} Deluery here of, It falls to y{e} Town agajne/ by us whose names are vnder written/

                                      Fran: Rayns
A true Coppy transcribed, & Compared Jo{n} Allcocke/
with y{e} originall this 21{th} of June 1678: The marke of
    p Edw: Rishworth ReCor: Robert R knight

                                        Jo{n} Twisden/

York To Frost

W{as} there was a Certen Tract of finety acres vpland given vnto John Frost lijng on the other side of Yorke bridg, by the Select men of the Town of Yorke, vpon the eighteenth day of Janva. 1669: for the further Compleating & full filling of the sd Grant, Wee whose names are here vnderwritten doe bound out the sd finety Acres of Land, on the further side of the sd Bridg as followeth, begining at a Whitte oake marked on Nothern side of a small brooke, neare halfe a mile in distance from y{e} bridg runneing South South West, finety pooles in breadth, from the sd Tree to a pitch pine that is marked, & eight scoore poole backe into the Countrey, vpon a West North West Lyne, till finety acres bee Compleated/

Decemb{r} 15 · 1670 ·   John Davess Edw: Rishworth
A true Coppy of this Jo{n} Alleocke Edw: Johnson/
Grant transcribed &   Mathew Austine/ Select men
Compared with y{e} orig- of y{e} Town of yorke/
inall 21: of June 1678:
p Edw: Rishworth
      ReCor:

Book III, Fol 25

This Deed made 12th of August 1673 ·

Knight
To
R Young

Know yee that I Robert Knight of Yorke, for diverse good Considerations y^rvnto mee moueing, doe giue grant, & by these p̄sents Confirme, vnto my Grandchild Rowland Young Junjo^r, foure Acres of vpland, lijng & being between my fence of my own fejld, & a spring that is by a lott of Land, that formerly was Edw Starts by the Riuer side, & soe backe from the river to a swampe, the quantity that doth Contayne in that place bee It what It will, either foure Acres more or lesse, with all the priuiledges there vnto belonging vnto the sayd Rowland, & his heyres for euer, & likewise I the sayd Robert Knight doe giue & grant, & by these Prsents Confirme, vnto the sayd Rowland Young, & to his heyres for euer, two small peeces of Marsh, lijng & being between my Marsh & his father Rowland Youngs Senjo^r/ In witness vnto the treuth here of, I haue set my hand & seale the day & yeare aboue written/   Robert Knight (his seale)

Signed & sealed in the
Prsence of us/   his marke R
John Twisden/
Joane young
his marke ⅃
Mary young her
marke K

Joⁿ Twisden aged about 54 years doth Attest vpon his oath that y^t Instrume^t within written w^rvnto his hand stands as a witness was the Act & Deede of Robert Knight to Rowland Young Junjo^r/ Taken vpon oath before mee 24th of June 1678
            Edw Rishworth Assote.

Mary young alias Mowlton doth Attest vpon her oath that this Instrum^t within, w^rvnto her name stands as a witness, was the Act & Deed of her Grandfather Robert Knight vnto her brother Rowland Young Junjo^r · Taken upon oath before mee this 24th of June 78 · p Edw · Rishworth Assote :

A true Coppy of this Instrume^t transcribed, & Compared with the originall this 24th June 1678.
            p Edw : Rishworth ReCor

Book III, Fol. 25, 26.

Lord
To
Abbett &
Nayson

Lett all men know by these P̄sents, that I Nathan Lawd Senjoʳ of the Town of Kittery in the County of Yorke, & province of Mayn husbandman, togeather with Martha his wife, & by & with her full & free Consent & mutuall agreement, for & in consideration of the full, & whoole some of fiuety pounds Current & Mʳchatble pay of New England In hand payd, by Thomas Abbett, & Jonathā Nayson, vnto the sayd Nathan Lord, or his Assignes, before the sealing & delivery of these P̄sents, doth grant bargane, & sell, alienate, Infeoff & Confirme, vnto them the sayd Thomas Abbett, & Jonathan Nayson, & by these P̄sents haue Clearly granted, barganed, sould, alienated, Infeoffed & Confirmed, vnto them the sayd Abbet & Nayson, all yᵗ Marsh lijng & being at a place Called Sturgeon Cricke in the Town of Kittery aforesayd, commanly Called or known by the name of Abra : Conleys Marsh, being by estimation tenn Acres, bee It more or less, & It is bounded, & lyeth betwixt Mr Nicho : Shapleighs Marsh, & a certen swampe adioyneing · & som . other part of It, lyeth along by the sayd Mr Shapleighs Marsh, & the sd swamp togeather with all the woods, vnder woods, water Courses Emoluments, priuiledges & appurtenances, now within fence or all that is not fenced, that now is, or heretofore hath been accom̄pted, Abraham Conlys Marsh, & all that euer heretofore was Esteemed Reckoned, Accōpted or vsed or deemed as any part, or Prcell of of the sayd Marsh either by lott or quiett or peaceable possession, & seasme, in the sayd Abra Conlys former possession : To haue & to hould the sayd Marsh togeather with the appurtenances, & priuiledges there vnto belonging, or in any wise app̄'tayneing, vnto them the sayd Tho : Abbett, & Jonathan Nayson, there heyrs executors, Administrators, Or Assignes for euer, In as large & ample mañer to all Constructions, Intents, & purposes, as I the sayd Nathan Lord can or may Estate the same, & I the sd Nathan Lord, & Martha my wife for [**26**] oʳ selues our heyres, executors Administrators & Assignes, & for euery &

either of them, do covenant promiss & agree to & with the
sayd Thomas Abbett, & Jonathan Nayson, & either of them,
thejr heyres, executors Administrators, & Assignes, to &
with every & either of them that the sd Tho: Abbett & Jonathan Nayson or either of them thejr heyrs executors
administrators Or Assignes, or any or either of them shall
from tyme to tyme & at all tyms hereafter quietly & peaceably hould, occupy possess, & Inioy the sd Marsh, Called
Conleys Marsh, with all the priuiledges, & appurtenances,
Emoluments, & pfetts, & Comoditys y^rof, with out the lawfull, let, Molestation, sujte in law, eviction, or Eiection, or
disturbance of mee the sayd Nathan Lord Martha my wife,
or of any other Prson, or Prsons w'soeuer, lawfully Clameing, the sayd Marsh, or any part or Picell thereof, & further
I the sayd Nathan Lord for mee my heyres, executors
Administrators & Assignes do promiss Couenant & agree, to
& with Tho. Abett & Jonathan Nayson y^r heyres executors
Admministors & Assig͞ns to & with every of them to free, &
discharge, or otherwise saue & keepe harmeless, them the
sayd Tho. Abbett, & Jonathan Nayson, & either of y^m they
thejr heyres, executors, Administrators, & Assigns, of &
from all former gyfts, grants sayles, Judgm^ts executions sujtes
in law, poner of thirds, given, granted had, made or Committed, or suffered to bee had made, done or Committed, or
omitted, by him the sayd Nathan Lord, or Abra: Conley, or
either of them, thejr heyrs, executors, Administrators or
Assigns or either of them, before the date of these Prsents,
in reference to the sayd Marsh or any part there of, & for
the Consideration of ffiuety pounds as aboue sayd, I the
sayd Nathan Lord, do acknowledg the receipt y^rof, & y^rof
do acquitt y^m the sayd Tho: Abbett, & Jonathan Nayson, &
either & euery of them, thejr heyres, executors, Administrators, & Assigns for euer, in witness w'of Wee the sayd
Nathan Lord, & Martha my wife, haue here vnto set our
hands, & Seals, euen the Twenty eight day of June, in the
yeat of the Reigne of o^r soueraigne Lord, Charles, the

Book III, Fol. 26.

secund by the Grace of God, of England, Scotland, France, & Ireland, King, Defend^r of ye faith, the Thyrteth Anno· Dom̃: 1678 :

Sealed signed & acknowledged in the Prsence of us subscribed/ Henery Child/ the marke of & Andrew Seaile Witnesses/

The marke Nathan + Lord (his seal)
Martha Lord the marke of (A) (her seale)
Jabez H Jenkines

  Acknowledged by Nathan Lord to bee his Act Deed 3 · 5 : 78 · before mee Tho : Damforth Assista^t

Possession & Seasin, of the Marsh within written, was Delivered with y^s deed by delivery of one Twigg, & one Turffe in the name & lew of the whoole Marsh with in written/ Delivered by Nathan Lord, & Martha his wife in the name & Lew of the whoole Marsh with in written, & this was done the Twenty eight day of June in the yeare. 1678, the date of the within Deed, & Delivered vnto Thomas Abbett, & Jonathan Nayson in the Prsence of the witnesses, with in written/

Hene : Child/
Jabez Jinkines/
Andrew Seaile
Witnesses/

A true Coppy of this Deed aboue written, with seasine & possession given, transcribed & Compared with the originall this 9th day of July : 1678 :
p Edw. Rishworth ReCor :

Lord To
Abbett &
Nayson

Lett all men know by these Prsents, that I Nathan Lord of the Town of Kittery In the County of Yorke, & province of Mayn husbandmā : & Martha my now wife for & In consideration of the full some of Tenn pounds Current pay In New England, in hand payd vnto the sayd Nathan Lord by the hands of Thom^s Abbett & Jonathan Nayson, before the Insealeing hereof, w^{r}of, & where with I the sayd Nathan Lord, do

here by acknowledg my selfe fully satisfyd, & payd, &
there of, & of euery Part & Prcell there of, doe acknowledg
my selfe fully satisfyd & payd, & acquitt them the sayd Tho :
Abbett, & Jonathan Nayson thejr heyres executors, Administrators, & Assignes for euer · haue given grantd alienated,
barganed & sould, & by these Prsents doe giue, grant,
alienate, bargan & sell, Confirme & Infeoff vnto the sayd
Thomas Abbett, & Jonathan Nayson all that Tract of Land,
with the appurtenances lijng & being at Sturgeon Cricke
being by Estimation fourty Acres, or there abouts, wch was
granted to Abra . Conley, & Layd out by the Select men of
The Town of Kittery, & is adioyneing vnto that Marsh
Called & known by the name of Abra · Conleys great Marsh,
on the South side of the Cricke, excepting & reseruing out
of this Prsent grant, & sayle of all that plott of Land, y^t
Peter Wittum Senjo^r of Sturgeon Cricke did heretofore purchase, of the sayd Abra · Conley, deceased/ to haue & to
hould the sayd fourty Acres of Land (except before excepted) with all the Woods, vnder woods, waters, water
Comses, priuiledges, & appurtenances, thereof, & there
vnto belonging, or in any wise app^{r}tayneing, from the date
of these Prsents for euer : in as large & ample manner to all
Constru . tions, as I the sayd Nathan Lord can or may sell, &
Estate the same & noe otherwise/ & I the sayd Nathan Lord,
do Covenant & promiss to & with them the sayd Tho :
Abbett, & Jonathan Nayson, for my selfe Martha my wife,
& my heyres executors Administrators, & Assigns, that them
the sayd Abbett, & Nayson, thejr heyres executors Administrators & Assignes, shall from tyme to tyme, & at all
tymes hereafter, haue, hould Occupy, possess & Injoy the
sayd fourty Acres of Land (except before excepted) with
out the let, sujte, or Molestation of mee the sayd Nathan
Lord, Martha my wife, or any or either of mine, or o^r
heyres, executors Administrators or Assignes, & Noe further
warrant/ In witness where of, Wee the sayd Nathan Lord,

Book III, Fol. 26, 27.

& Martha my wife haue here vnto set my hand, & scale Even the Twenty Eight day of June Anno: Dom: 1678:

Hene: Child/
The marke of
Jabez Jenkines
Andrew Searle
Witnesses/

The marke of
Nathan Lord/ ✝ (his seal)
The marke of
Martha Lord (Ⓐ) (her seale)

acknowledged by Nathan Lord to bee his Act & Deed 3 . 5 78 : before Tho : Damforth Assistat

Possession & seasine of the within written fourty Acres of vpland was deliuered, by the with in written Nathan Lord, & Martha his wife, by the deliuery of a Twigg & Turffe in lew, & In the name of the whoole fourty Acres de-[27] livered in the same Land vpon the Twenty eighth day of June: 1678: in the Pisence of the with in written witnesses, vnto Thomas Abbett & Jonathan Nayson with in written/

Hene: Child/
Jabez Jinkines
Andrew Scale/

A true Coppy of this Instrument with in written, transcribed out of the originall, & there with Compared this 9th day M°th 5 : 1678 :

p Edw . Rishworth RcCoi .

To all people to whom this Prsent deed shall Come/ Know yee that I Antipas Mavericke, now residing with in the Town shipe of Ecceter, in New England for & In Consideration that Major Nicho : Shapleigh of Kittery in New England Mrchant, hath & hereby doth for him selfe his heyres, executors Administrators & & Assignes, exonerate acquitt & fully discharge him the sayd Antipas Mautericke his heyres executors Administrators & Assignes, from all bills, bonds, Reckonings, Accopts, Debtts, & demands, wsoeuer, that haue passed & been between him the sd Nicholas Shapleigh, & the

Maverick
To
Shapleigh

Book III, Fol. 27.

sayd Antipas Mavericke, from the beginning of the world to the day of the date of these P'sents, & for other Consideration him there vnto moueing, hee the sayd Antipas Mauericke, hath & hereby doth fully clearely & absolutely Give grant bargan sell aliene Infeoff Convay & Confirme, vnto him the sayd Nicho. Shapleigh, his heyres, & Assignes for euer, a peece & Prcell of Land lijng & being next Adioyneing to the Land formerly possessed by Willia: Ellingham deceased, & Contayneing thirty Acres of Land more then what was formerly possessed by the sayd Ellingham, about an Acre of Land that lyeth on the South East side of the sayd dwelling house, & next Adioyneing y'vnto, with a small spott of Marsh, being part of the sayd Thyrty Acres, the w'h thirty Acres of Land is bounded by a Cricke, or Coue lijng neare ye Land of Edw Hays deceased, on the North West side by the Land of Antipas Mauericke, on the South East side & Rangeth backe from the South East Corner of the sd Ellinghams fence, as It now stands, vpon an East North East lyne, & by the side of the aforesd Cricke, vpon a paralell lyne into the Woods vntill the sayd Thyrty Acres from the sd fence, bee fully extended, togeather with the lyberty & pruiledg of Cutting Wood vpon the Comon & all other lybertys, pruiledges, & profetts w'soeuer, to the sayd Land & Marsh belonging or in any wise app'tayneing; To haue & to hould, to him the sd Nicholas Shapleigh his heyres & Assigns for euer, to the soole & proper vss & behoofe benefitt, & Advantage of him the sd Nicho Shapleigh his heyres, executors Administrators & Assignes from hence forth for euer And the sd Antipas Mauericke for him selfe his heyres, executors, & Administrators, doth Covenant promiss, & grant to & with the sayd Nicho Shapleigh, his heyres executors, Administrators, & Assignes, y^t hee the sd Mauericke for ye Consideration aboue specity d, doth Clerely & absolutely remiss, release, & for euer quitt Clame, all his right, title, Interest propriety Clame, & demand of in Or vnto all the houseing Land Marsh or any other ye lybertys or pri

Willia͞. Ellingham deceased & of in or vnto any part, or
Prcell y'of vpon any Accomp' or p̄tence w'soeuer, And y'
hee the sayd Nicho · Shapleigh, his heyres executors &
Assignes, shall & may bee for ever hereafter, peaceably &
quietly haue hould occupy possess & Inioy the same to his
& there soole & proper vses, & behoofs togeather, with the
aboue granted thirty Acres of Land, soe butting & bounding
as abouesd, without the lawfull lett, trouble hinderance,
molestation, disturbance of him the sd Antipas Mavericke,
his heyres, executors or Assignes, or of any other Prson from
by, or vnder him, & free & Clea . . acquitted & dischargcd
of, & from all former, & other Gyfts, Grants, barganes, sayls
leases, Morgages, forfeturs, seazures, titles, troubles, alienations,
& Incomberances w'soeuer, had, made, or done, or
suffered to bee done by him by him the sd Antipas Mavericke,
or by any other Prsons from by or vnd͛ him, by vertue
of any act or thing had made or done or suffered to bee done
by his Assent, Consent advise or procurement, And against
him selfe, & every other Prson Clameing a Right to the
afore barganed Prmisses, vnto him the sayd Nicho. Shapleigh
his heyrs & Assigns the same shall warrant & for euer
Defend by these · And y' hee the sayd Antipas Mavericke,
at any tyme hereafter vpon the reasonable request, or
demand of him the sayd Nicho · Shapleigh his heyres &
Assigns shall & will doe & Prforme any Act or thing, that
may bee for the better Confirmeing & sure makeing the
p̄misses to him the sayd Nicho : Shapleigh his heyrs &
Assigns, according to yͤ true Intent of these Prsents, In
witness w͛of the sayd Antipas Mavericke hath here vnto set
his hand & seale this sixteenth day of June Anno Dom͞: one
thousand six hundred seaventy & Eight, Annoq, Regni Regis
Carolus secundj Angliæ, &c .

Signed sealed & Deliver̄d   Antipas Mauericke (his seale)
    In the Prsence of us/   Thomas Kemble appeared the
    Mary Bennicke/   sixth day of July 1678 . &
    Thomas K͞ ͞ ͞ ͞ /   m ͞ ͞ ͞ ͞ ͞ ͞ Antipas
        Mavericke ͞ ͞ ͞ ͞ le, &

Book III, Fol. 27, 28.

Deliuer the Deed aboue written as his Act & Deede, & subscribed his name as a witness there vnto/ Sworne before mee John Gyllmā. Commissio^r/

Mary Bennicke made oath to the same aboue written the same day as witness y^r vnto/ before mee John Gillman Commisso^r

A true Coppy of this Instrume^t transcribed, & Compared with the originall this 10th day of July 1678:

     p Edw · Rishworth ReCor.

    This Indenture made the forth day of Febru · In the yeare of o^r Lord God, one thousand six hundred sixty

Nayson
To
Lord

& foure, between Richd Nayson of Newgewanacke in the County of Yorke Planter, of the one party, & Nathell Lord of the same place Planter, on the other part Witnesseth that the sayd Richd Nayson for & in Consideration of an horse, of Culler sorrell, with a white starr in the forehead, which the sayd Nathell Lawd hath delivered vnto the sayd Richd Nayson, before the Insealeing, & delivery of these P^r sents, the receipt w^rof the sayd Richard Nayson doth here by acknowledg, & there of acquit, the sayd Nat̄ll Lord his executors, & administrators for euer · Hath & p these p̄sents doth sell, & hath sould vnto the sayd Nathaniell Lord, all that Plott of Land, It being by estimation, Nine Acres or y^rabouts, & is adioyneing vnto C ten Lands of the sd Nathell Lords, wch hath been & now is in the possession of ye sayd Lord, on the Sovth, or y^r abouts, & runnes along by the head of the secund swampe on the South East, & ouer the brooke, & on the West & North, the bounds [28] are bounded by a marked tree of redd oake, & on the North & by East, directly from Richd Naysons Barne, It is bounded with Certen marked trees, marked with two letters **R** & **N**, & is part of a great Piecell of Land granted vnto the sayd Richd Nayson by y^e grant of the Town of

Kittery/ To haue & to hould the sayd Land, & P\rmises, with y\e appurtenencys, vnto the sayd Nat͠ll Lord his heyres, executors Administrators or Assigns, from the day of the date here of for euer/ & the sayd Richd Nayson for him selfe his executors administrators & Assignes, & for euery of them, doth hereby promiss Covenant & grant, that hee the sayd Natha͠ll Lord his heyres, executors Administrators & Assignes, shall quietly, & peaceably haue hould Occupy, possess, & Inioy the sd P\rmisses in as large & ample manner, as hee the sayd Ric Nason his wife & heyres can or may grant, or Estate the same, freed, & discharged against all Prson or Prsons that shall lawfully Clame the sayd Land, or part y\rof (excepting the high Lord of y\e prouince) or the proprieto\r from by or vnd\r him the sayd Ric · Nason, or vnd\r his Estate or Title/ In witness whereof, I the sayd Richd Nason, & Saraih my now wife, haue here vnto set our hands, & seals, euen the day & yeare aboue written/

Sealed signed & Deliuerd/   The marke of Richd ($^{his}_{seale}$)
 In the Prsence of us   Nason/ O
 Andrew Searle   } witnesses/   ($^{her}_{seale}$)
 Samell Trueworgye

      Richd Nason doth acknowledg this
      Instrum\t aboue written to bee
      his Act & Deed/ Taken in Court
      this : 5th July . 76 :
        p Edw . Rishworth ReCor
A true Coppy of this Instrum\t transcribed, & Compared with the originall this 18th of July 1678 :
        p Edw : Rishworth ReCor :

To all Christean people vnto whome this Prsent Deede of sayle shall come, Jo\n Paine of Boston in the Massatusetts Colony of New England, M\rchant sendeth Greeteing &c: Know yee that the sayd John Paine for & in Con d ation

Book III, Fol 28

of the some of Twenty nine pounds tenn shillings money,
current of New England, to him in hand at the sealing hereof
Well & truely payd, by John Whitte of the sayd Boston
Joyner, & Robert Brȳsdon of the same Boston M^rchant the
receipt where of the sayd John Payne, doth
hereby own, & acknowledg, & hath therefore
given granted barganed sould aliend Assigned,
Enfeoffed & Confirmed, & by these Prsents doth
fully Clearely, & absolutely give grant bargane
sell alliene Assigne Enfeoff, & Confirme vnto the
sayd Robert Brinsdon, & John Whitte thejre heyres, executors,
& Assignes for euer, a certen quantity of Lands
vidz^t: eight hundred Acres at least, scituate lijng & being
nigh the Town-shipe of Wells, & Cape Porpus that is to say
on the North side there of, the which is a part of a great
Prcell of Land vidz^t about foure or six Miles square, & to
bee layd as nigh to the sea, & Cape Porpus River, as may
bee with Convenicney for thejr aduantage, with all & singular
the Rights, Royaltys, benefitts profetts, easements,
Woods, vnderwoods priuiledges, & appurtenances thereto
belonging, or in any measure app^rtayneing The which sayd
great Prcell of Lands, which was formerly sould by Sosowen,
the father, & Confirmed by Illewellen the sonn, both Sagamores,
vnto Peter Turbett, John Sanders, & John Bush, &
by them sould vnto Hayrlackendyne Symonds, vidz^t Two
thyrds of the sayd Great Parcell, And all Deeds, Eudences,
& writings, which Concerne the sayd barganed P^rmisses
onely, & otherwise Coppys of such Deeds &c as do Concerne
the same, with other things to deliver vp for the further
Confirmation thereof/

To haue & to hould the sayd Prcell of Land spetifyed as
aforesayd, with all & singular the rights Royaltys, benefitts
profetts, easements, woods vnder woods, priuiledges & appurtenances
thereto belonging, or in any measure app^rtayneing
them & euery of them vnto the sayd John Whitte, & Robert
Bryn   onely &

<small>J^no Payne
To
Brinsdon
&
White
White</small>

proper vss, behoofe, & benefitt of them the sayd Robert
Brimsdon & John Whitte, thejre heyres & Assignes for
euer; And the sayd John Payne for him selfe, his heyres,
executors, & Administrators doth Covenant & grant, & by
these Pr'sents do affirme to & with, the sayd Robert Brimsdon & John Whitte, thejre heyres & Assignes in manner &
forme following vidz't that hee the sayd John Payne, at the
tyme of the Grant bargane & sayle of the P'misses, & vntill
deliuery of the sayd John Whitte & Robert Brimsdon to the
vss of them thejr heyres, & Assignes for euer, was Lawfully
seized to his own vss of in & to the P'misses, in good profet
& absolute Estate of Inheritance in fee-symple, & hath in
him selfe, full pouer, & good right, & Lawfull authority, the
P'misses to giue grant, bargane, sell & Assure as aforesayd,
And that the sayd John Whitte & Robert Brimsdon thejr
heyres, & Assigns, & euery of them, shall and henceforth
for euer, lawfully & peaceably, & quietly haue, hould Occupy
possess & Inioy the sayd bargane, priuiledges & appurtenances, free & Cleare, & Clearely acquitted, and discharged
of & from all & singular other gyts, grants, barganes, sayles,
leases, Intayls, Morgages, Judgm'ts forfetures, seazures,
Dowers, & all other Acts & Incomberances whatsoeuer, had
made, done, or suffered to bee done, by the sayd John
Payne, his heyrs, executors, Administrators, Or assignes, or
any other P'son or person or p'r'sons whatsoeuer, Clameing,
or P'rtending to Clame, or demand any Estate right, title,
or Interest of in, or to the P'misses, or any part or Prcell
there of, for from by or vnder him or them or either of
them: Whereby the sayd Robert Brimsdon, or John Whitte,
thejr, or either of thejr heyres or Assignes, shall or may bee
expullsed, or euicted, out of the possession thereof, or any
part or Prcell thereof at any tyme hereafter, And that the
sayd John Payne, his heyres, executors, & Administrators,
the sayd barganed Prmisses vnto the sayd John Whitte, &
Robert Brimsdon, thejr & either of thejr heyres, & Assignes

against them selues, & all & euery other Prson, & Prsons whatsoeuer, as aforesayd, Claimeing, or to Clajme any Estate, right, Title Interest, or demand of in Or to the same, shall & will warrant & for euer Defend by these Prsents/ And that the sayd John Payne, his heyres, executors, and Administrators, vpon all reasonable Demãnds, shall, & will Prforme & do or cause to bee Prformed, or done, any such further Act, or Acts, thing & things, whither by acknowledgm^t of these Prsents, or leuery & seazine of the sayd barganed Prmisses, given, or In any other kind, that shall or [29] may bee for the more full Compleateing, Confirmeing, & sure makeing of the Prmisses vnto the sayd Robert Brimesdon & John Whitte thejr heyrs & Assigns for euer, according to the true Intent here of, & Laws Established/ In witness where of the sayd John Payn hath here vnto put his hand, & fixed his seale the fiue & Twenteth day of Octob^r Anno Dom̃ one thousand six hundred seauenty & three/ Regni Regis Charolj secundj, xxv/

Signed sealed & Deliuered/ John Paine (his seale)
In ye Prsence of us/   This was acknowledged by the
Danjell Stoone/   sayd John Pajne to bee his
Willia͂ Howard/   Act, & Deede, vpon the 8th
                       day of Janvary · 1673 : before
                       mee/ Sam̃ell Symonds/
                                    Dep^t Gouer/

A True Coppy of this Instrum^t or Deede aboue written transcribed, & with the originall Compard this 30th day of July 1678 ·   p Edw : Rishworth ReCor :

To all Christean people, to whom this p̃sent Deede of Sayle shall come, John Paine of Boston in the Massatusetts Colony of New England M^rchant sendeth Greeting &c : Know yee that the sayd John Pajne for & in Consideration

Book III, Fol. 29.

Paine
To
Brimsdon
&
Stone

of a valewable some of money, & current pay of New England, to him in hand before the scaleing hereof, Well & truely payd by Danjell Stone of Boston aforesd Chyergeon, & Robert Brimsdon of the same Boston M^rchant the receipt where of the sayd John Paine doth hereby own, & acknowledg &c· Hath therefore given granted barganed sould ahend Assignd, Enfeoffed, & Confirmed, And by these P^rsents doth fully clearly & absolutely, doth giue grant bargane sell aliene Assigne Enfeoffe, & Confirme, vnto the sayd Robert Brimesdon, & Daniell Stoone thejr heyres & Assignes for euer Jo^yntly, a P^rcell of Land vidz^t the Moeity of three hundred Acres, that is to say one hundred & fiuety Acres thereof, in an æquall devision, the whoole scituate lijng & being in the County of yorke shyre, in New England, in the Townshipe of Wells, about foure Miles distances from the sayd Town, lyng & being vpon the Edg of a great swampe, on the Easterly end thereof, by a great playne, & soe rumening vpon the Ridg of y^t sayd Playne towards the North East, & then to turne towards the North West, vntill the sd Three hundred acres bee expired, & fully made vp, & alsoe all that peece, or Prcell of Marsh, by the heath, & alsoe halfe that Marsh on ye South West, Next Adioyneing there vnto, which Marsh is bounded by marked trees, And alsoe all & singular the Rights, profetts, easements, priuledges & appurtenances thereto belonging &c: To haue & to hould the Moeity of, & in the sayd three hundred Acres of Land, & the two Marshes spetifyd as aboue sayd, formerly layd out by the measurers of Wells, & sometyms app^rtayneing vnto Nicholas Coole, & with all & singular the rights, profetts, easements, priui- & appurtenances, thereto belonging, or in any measure appertayncing, them & euery of them, the Moeity thereof vnto the sayd Daniell Stone, & Robert Brimsdon Joyntly thejr heyres & Assignes, to thejr soole onely & proper vse behoofe & benefitt of them the sayd Robert Brimesdon & Daniell Stone, thejr heyre & Assigns for euer And the sayd

John Paine his heyres executors, & Administrators doth Covenā^t & grant, & by these Prsents affirme, to & with the sayd Daniell stoone, & Robert Brimsdon their heyres, & Assignes in manner & forme following, vidz^t that hee the sayd John Paine, at the tyme of the grant bargane & sale of the P^rmisses & vntill the delivery here of, to the sayd Daniell Stoone, & Robert Brimsdon, to the vss of them their heyres & Assignes for ever ; was Lawfully seized to his own vsse, of in & to the P^rmisses, in a good Prfect & absolute Estate of Inheritance in fee symple, & hath in his selfe, full pouer, good right, & Lawfull authority the P^rmisses to giue grant bargane sell, & Assure as aforesayd.

And that the sayd Daniell Stoone, & Robert Brimesdon, their heyrs & Assigns & euery of them, shall & may hence forth for euer, lawfully peaceably & quietly haue hould occupy possess & Inioy, the sayd barganed P^rmisses, with the priuiledges & appurtenances free, & Cleare & clearly acquitted & discharged of, & from all & singular other Gyfts, Grants, bargans sales Leases, Intayles, Assignem^{ts} Morgages, Judgm^{ts} forfetuis seazurs, Dowers, or any other Acts, or Incomberances w^tsoeuer, had made done or suffered to bee done by the sayd John Pajne his heyrs executors, Administrators or Assignes, or any other Prson, or Prsons whatsoeuer Clajmeing, or P^rtending to Clajme or demand any Estate right or Title, or Interest of, in & two the P^rmisses, or any part there of, w^tby the sayd Robert Brimsdon, & Daniell Stoone their heyrs, & Assignes, shall or may bee expullsed, or euicted out of the possession there of, or any part, or Prcell there of, at any tyme hereafter / & that ye sayd John Payne, his heyrs executors & Administrators, the sayd barganed P^rmisses, vnto the sayd Daniell Stoone & Robert Brimsdon their heyres & Assigns against them selues, & all & euery person & Prsons whatsoeuer, as aforesayd Clameing, or to Claime any Estate right title Interest, or demand of in or two the same, shall & will warrant, & for euer defend by these Presents. And that the sayd John

Paine his heyres, his executors, or Administrators, vpon all reasonable demands, shall & will Prforme & doe, or Cause to bee Prformd & done, any such further act or Acts, thing, & things, whither by acknowledgm⁺ of this p⁺sent Deed, or livery & seizine of the sayd bargand Prmisses, given or in any other kind, that shall or may bee for the more full Compleating, Confirmeing & sure makeing of the pmises vnto the [30] sayd Daniell Stoone, & Robert Brimsdon, thejr heyres, & Assigns for ever, according to the true intent hereof, & Laws Established: In witness whereof, the sayd John Paine haue here vnto put his hand & seale Dated Decemb⁺ the Tenth Anno Dom: one thousand six hundred seaventy & three Annoq̃ Regnj Regis Carolj Secundj xxv/
Signed sealed & Delivered/   John Paine (his seale)
In P⁺sence of us/   This was acknowledged by the sayd
Anthony Checkley/   John Payne, to bee his Act &
William Howard/   Deed, vpon the 8th day of January 1673: before mee
                     Samll Symonds Depty Gou͠er/

A true Coppy of this Instrument transcribed Out of the originall & there with Compared this 31th of July: 1678.
             p Edw: Rishworth ReCor:

Rishworth To Trafton

Know all men by these Prsents, that I Edw: Rishworth of Yorke in the County of Yorke ReCor. for severall causes & good Considerations there vnto mee moueing & more espetially for a valewable some of eight thousand good M⁺chable red oake pipe staues to mee In hand already payd, w⁺with I am fully Contented & satisfyd, by Thomas Trafton of yorke Planter, do hereby giue grant bargan sell aliene & Confirme, & haue hereby given granted bargained sould aliend, & Confirmed, from mee the sayd Rishworth my heyres, executors, Administrators & Assigns vnto the sayd Tho: Traffton his heyres

Book III, Fol. 30.

executors Administrators & Assigns for euer a Certen Tract, Coue or P'cell of Meddow Land lying & being neare to the head of that Cricke Called the ould Mill Cricke, Contayneing the quantity of three Acres & an halfe or foure Acres of Marsh, bee It more or less, being vpon the Westerne side of the North West branch of the said Cricke, w^r sometyms Jere · Mowlton bujlt his logg house, when hee logged for Henery Sayword; To hould & to haue the sayd Tract ot Meddow Land, as aboue bounded, with all the profetts, priuiledges, Imunitys & all other appurtenances there vnto belonging, or in any wise app'tayneing, from mee my heyres executors Administrators & Assigns, vnto the sayd Tho Traffton his heyres, executors Administrators & Assigns for euer, for his & their soole proper vss & benefitt/ And I ye sayd Edw: Rishworth do further promiss & Couenant that the aforesd Tract & Prcell ot Marsh is free & Cleare, from all other bargans, sayles Titles, & Incomberances w^hsoeuer, & doe & shall warrant, & defend the same from all other Prson or Prsons whatsoeuer, clameing or P'tending any Clame of title or Interest from by or und^r mee, or any other by my procurement/ In testimony w^rof, I haue here vnto afixed my hand & seale, this 15th day of June, 1678 ·

        Edw. Rishworth (his seale)

Signed sealed & Deliuered   This Instrume^t acknowledged by
 In the P^rsence of/   Edw Rishworth & Susannah
 Joseph Coutch/   his wife, to bee their Act &
 Mathew Austine Senjo^r   Deed this ₁ August. 1678:
 his marke ᴍᴍ   before mee Samell Wheelewright
           Assōte/

A true Coppy of this Instrument transcribed, & Compared with the originall this 2. day of August 1678:
      p Edw: Rishworth ReCor.

BOOK III, FOL 30.

Know all men by these P̃sents, that I Micu :͏ Mackeintyre, now rescident in the Town of Yorke Planter, & In the County of Yorke, alias Province of Mayne, haue for diverse Considerations there vnto mee moueing, & more espetially, for the valewable some of Twenty pounds tenn shillings, by mee In hand received of Tho : Traffton of the Town afoiesayd ffisherm̃ w^rwith I do acknowledg my selfe, to bee fully payd, contented, & satisfyd, do hereby give grant bargan sell aliene Enfeoff & Confirme, & haue hereby given granted bar-

<small>McIntire
To
Trafton</small>

ganed sould aliend Enfeoffed & Confirmd from mee my heyres, executors, Administratois & Assignes, for ever, vnto the aforesayd Tho : Traffton his heyies executors Administrators & Assignes for ever, a Certen Tract or Prcell of vpland, with some small bitts or skirts of Marsh adioyneing there vnto ; Contayneing the quantity of about fourty Acres bee It more or lesse lijng & being along by the water side, on the South West side of Yorke River the bounds there of lijng from ye South West side of the Mouth of that Cricke Called by the name of the ould Mill Cricke, & soe along by the river side runneing vnto a Certen Gully or small brooke. that Emptys It selfe into the River, It being the deuideing bounds between the sayd Land, & the Land of Thomas Beeson, now in the possession of Edw . Rishworth, & soe to runne backe vntill the sayd quantity of Land aboue specifyd, bee Compleated, Which Land was formerly in the possession of Robert Knights Edw : Rishworth, John Pearce, John Cirmihill, & James Grant, & by the sayd Grant sould vnto mee the sayd Micu :͏ Mackeintyre aboue specifyd ; To haue & to hould, the sayd Tract or quantity of Land, as aboue expressed, with all the profetts, priuiledges, lybertys, Imunitys, & all other appurtenances, y^rvnto belonging, or in any wise app^rtayneing, from mee my heyres, executors, Administrators & Assignes vnto the sayd Thomas Traffton, his heyis Administrators & Assig . . for euer/ & I the sayd

Mackeyntyre, do Covenant, & promiss to with the sd Traffton that the sayd Land is free & Cleare, from all Clames, titles, Interests, Dowers, or Titles of Dowers, or other Incomberances w'soeuer, & do warrant & defend the Interest, & title there of, from all Prson, or Prsons w'soeuer, Clameing or P'tending any Clame or Title there vnto, from, by, or vnd' mee, or in any wise by my procurement/ In witness w'vnto, I haue here vnto afixed my hand & seale, by & with the Consent of my wife, this 21th day of July 1678:

Signed sealed & Deliver'd   Micu: Mackyntyre (his seale)

   In the Prsence of/   Micu: Mackintyre, doth acknowledg
   Edw: Rishworth   this aboue Instrument to bee his
   Will: Symonds/   Act & Deed this first of August
                             1678 · before mee
                             Samll Wheelewright Assote

A true Coppy of this Instrume' transcribed, & with the originall Compared this 2und of August: 1678 ·

                         p Edw: Rishworth ReCor ·

                 I Thomas Deane doe relinquish all my right
Deane's   title Interest and demand of in & to the Estate
Discharge
  To   with in granted, & euery part there of haueing
                 receiued full satisfaction, and do desire the
ReCord may bee discharged, there of/

  Boston August: 2: 1678.   Tho: Deane/
Witness   Acknowledged by Mr Thomas Deane to
  Isa: Addington/   bee his Act & Deed, 2: August ·
                      1678: before mee Edw: Tyng
                                       Assist:

A true Coppy of this discharge transcribed out of the originall & there with Compared this 29th of August: 78:

                         p Edw: Rishworth ReCor:

[31]   Septemb^r 28 : 1661 :

Received of Nicholas Ope servant to Mr Abra : Brown, a
fishing shallop with a Majne sale, a peece of a
Road about thyrty fathome, & a grapnell for y^e
vsse of Majo^r Nicho : Shapleigh/ I say received
a shallop & other app^{r}tenances/

White's Rec^t To Brown

Signed in ye P^{r}sence of/   p mee Richd Whitte his

Edw · Rishworth/   marke/ ⊕

John Davess/   Mr Edw : Rishworth, & Capt John
Davess gaue oath that they saw
Ric : Whitte, signe & Deliver the
aboue written receipt to ye vss of
Majo^r Nicho : Shapleigh, & y^t
thejr hands are to It as witnesses/
Sworne in Court Novemb^r 20 :
1678 . p order John Wincoll/

A true Coppy of this receipt transcribed, & Compared
with the originall, this 6th day of Decemb^r 78 :

                 p Edw : Rishworth ReCor :

Kirke To Morrell

Know all men by these p̄sents, that I Hene : Kirke of
Portsmouth, in the County of Portsmouth &
Douer Currier, for and in Consideration of the
some of Twenty two pounds of Current money
of New England in hand, before the Ensealeing
& Delivery of these P^{r}sents, well & truely payd, the receipt
w^{r}of the sayd kirke acknowledgeth, & him selfe to bee fully
satisfyd, Content & payd, & y^{r}of & of euery part Prcell &
penny there of, doth acquit exonerate & dischaige, John Morrall of Kittery in ye County of yorke, Mason, his heyres executors Administrators & Assignes, & euery of them by these
Prsents : As alsoe for good Causes & Considerations, him
ye sayd Kirke y^{r}vnto espetially moueing : Haue given
granted bargaued & sould aliened Enfeoffed released & Con-

firmed, & by these P^rsents, doth give grant bargane & sell aliene Enfeofe release & Confirme, vnto the sayd Morrall his heyres executors Administrators & Assignes, a peece of Land ljng & being in Kittery, Contayeing two Acres More or less, Joyning to ye Lott wch was formerly Anthony Emerys, Called by the name of Could harbour poynt, & after sould by him to his sonn James Emery, as appeareth by a bill of sayle, & since sould to Abra: Conley within which Land is sd two Acres, which was given to the sayd Kirke by Abra. Conley as alsoe a house which the sayd Kirke bujlt vpon the sayd Land, togeather with all profetts benefitts, & advantages to & with in the sayd boundary belonging and app^rtayneing To haue & to hould the before hereby granted & barganed P^rmisses, and euery part & P^rcell thereof, vnto the sayd Morrall his heyres executors administrators & Assignes for euer and the sayd Kirke for him selfe, his heyrs executors Administrators & Assigns doth Covenant promiss & grant to & with the sayd Morrall his heyres executors Administrators & Assignes, & to & with euery of them by these presents, that all & singular the sayd P^rmisses, with all the profetts benefitts and aduantages, in and by these p^rsents, given granted barganed & sould and euery part and P^rcell there of, at the tyme of the delivery & Ensealeing of these P^rsents, are & bee, & bee & at all tymes hereafter shall bee remajne & Continew Clearely, acquitted, exonerated, discharged, and keept harmeless of & from all and all manner of former & other barganes, sayles gyfts grants leases charges Dowers, titles troubles or Incomberances whatsoeuer made Comitted suffered done, or to bee made Committed, suffered or done by the sayd Kirke, his heyrs executors administrators or assignes, or by any of them, or by any other P^rson or P^rsons whatsoeuer, by his or there means, Acts titles Consents or procurement, as alsoe to keepe him harmeless from Nathall Lawd, his heyrs executors, Administrators or assigns/ as witness my hand

Book III, Fol. 31.

and seale, this thirteenth of Octob{r} one thousand six hundred
seaventy eight/   Henery Kirke his (his seale)
Signed sealed & delivered   seale
   In the P{r}sence of/
   John Partridge/   Henery Kirke & Ruth his wife came
   John Barsham/   & acknowledged the aboue Instru-
                    ment to bee there Act & Deede, &
                    shee freely rend{rd} vp her thirds of
                    Dowry In the aboue mentioned
                    P{r}misses, to the sayd John Morrall
                    Octob{r} 14 . 1678 : before mee
                         Richd Martyne Comissio{r}
A true Coppy of this Instrume{t} transcribed out of the
originall & y{r}with Compared this 7th day of Decemb{r} 1678 .
                  p Edw : Rishworth ReCor

     Lett all men know by these P{r}sents, that I Nicholas
Hodgsden of the Town of Kittery, & County of yorke &
Province of Mayne husbandmā . as Well for & in Considera-
              tion of the full some of one & thyrty pounds of
Hodsden   Current pay in New England, payd, & secured
To Son
Hodsden   to bee payd by Bennonj Hodgsden my sonn, vnto
              mee the sayd Nicholas Hogd{s}en my heyres, exec-
utors Administrators or Assignes, as by severall obligations
vnder the hand of the sayd Benoni It doth & may more
playnly & at large appeare, as alsoe that the sayd Benony
hath Covenanted to find & provide sufficient & Convenjent
meate, & drinke for Elizabeth my now wife, dureing her
naturall Life, And alsoe to pay her six pounds yearly dureing her Life, If shee happen to survive, & out liue mee the
sayd Niccolas Hodgsden, as by another Deed vnder his hand,
& seale It doth & may more at Large appeare, As alsoe for
& in Consideration that the sayd Bennony shall liue & dwell
on my farme with mee, soe that with gods blessing on his

BOOK III, FOL. 31, 32.

Endeauors, hee Mannageing & Improueing the sayd Farme, with mee dureing my Life, with that stocke of goods that now is, or hereafter may bee on the sayd Farme which I now liue & dwell vpon, both I & my wife togeather, with him the sayd Beñony & his family, may haue sufficient & Convenjent foode, & Rayment with other Convenjent necessarys, both as Well in sickeness as in health dureing my Life out of the produce of the sayd Farme, if It may bee by Improuement & Laboureing on it produced out of It, as by other Covenants for y{:t} purpose, given made sealed & Confirmed, as alsoe for diverse other good Causes, and Considerations mee the sayd Nichols Hodgsden espetially moueing; Haue given granted barganed sould & Confirmed, And by these p{:s}ents [32] do giue grant bargan sell & Confirme, vnto the sayd Bennony Hodgsden, his heyrs executors, Administrators & Assignes, all that my Mansion, or dwelling house or houses, and all barnes bujldings structurs, & ædifices now standing on, or belonging vnto the sayd ffarme, with all Oarchards, Gardens, Meddows, Marshes vpland & Tillage Land, either with in fence or with out, with all Woods vnderwoods waters, Water Courses and profetts, Emoluments priuiledges and Commoditys, with there & euery of there appurtenances, all which I heretofore purchased of one John Wincoll, & is lijng & being in Kittery, in the County of Yorke, & Province of Mayne, contayneing by aestimation fourty Acres bee It more or less, and alsoe fiuety six Acres of Land, long since granted vnto mee by the Town of Kittery aforesayd, with the app{:r}teances, profetts easements, & Commoditys there of, lijng & adioyneing vnto my home farme aforesayd, And lyeth adioyneing & butting vpon the aforesayd Land & farme, on the East or there abouts, the house farme or Lands aforesayd are butting on or bounded, with the great River of Pischataqua, or at least a branch thereof on the West, or y{:r}abouts, & with a fresh brooke on y{:e} North or there abouts, which brooke deuides between my Lands aforesayd, & on Leef{:t} Playsteads Lands late deceased; And

on the East with Certen Marked trees & on the South or
there abouts, with the Lands of one Miles Tomson · All w^ch
houses, Oarchards, Gardens, & other the afore recited P^rm-
isses, are my owne proper Estate, and haue full pouer to
sell & Estate the same, and is now scituate Lijng & being in
Kittery aforesayd, in the County of yorke, & Province of
Mayne aforesayd. Excepting out of this P^rsent grant bargane
& sayle one Little Tract of Land given and granted heretofore vnto Jo^n Morrall & Sarah his now wife which is my
daughter, & formerly was part of the home farme, It being
by Estimation seaven Acres or there abouts, on which Tract
of Land, as It is now layd & bounded out, the sayd John
Morrall hath bujlt a dwelling house, & barne & other structurs, And was formerly a part of that home farme, Which I
purchased of John Wincoll aforesayd, to haue & to hould,
all the fore granted & fore sayd P^rmisses (except before
excepted) with there & euery of there app^rteaces, Namely y^t
farme purchased of the sayd John Wincoll, as alsoe the
other forementioned Lott of Land, granted by the Town as
aforesayd, & euery part & P^rcell thereof from & Immediately after the death & decease of mee the sayd Nicho:
Hodgsden for euer, in as Large & ample manner to all Constructions intents and purposes as I the sayd Nicho: Hodgsden can or may grant sell Convay or Estate the same vnto
him the sayd Bennony Hodgsden, his heyres or executors
Administrators & Assignes for ever, the Tearme to comence
& begine as aforesayd, from & Imediately after my decease,
and to enter on the sayd P^rmises now at the sealeing hereof,
for the Improuement of it with mee for the best advantage,
& I the sayd Nicho: Hodgsden for mee my heyres executors,
Administrators, & Assignes, & for euery of them, do Covenant promiss & agree to & with the sd Bennony my sayd
sonn his heyres executors administrators & Assignes, to &
with either & euery of them by these p̃sents, that ye sayd
Bennony Hodgsden my sonn, his heyres executors Administrators & Assignes, & either & every of them. vnder the

Book III, Fol. 32.

Covenant Clawses promisses, exceptions & conditions herein mentioned, & Incerted, shall or may from tyme to tyme & at all tymes hereafter, dureing the sayd Tearme quietly & peaceably haue hould occupy possess, & Imoy all the aboue & the afore recited P'misses, with thejr & euery of thejre appurtenances, without the Lawfull lett sujte trouble Molestation disturbance denyall or putting out of mee the sayd Nicho: Hodgsden, my wife heyres executors, Administrators or Assignes, or any other Prson or Prsons w'soeuer, Lawfully Cameing the sayd Estate, or p'misses or any part y'of, from by or vnder mee, or vnder my Estats or Title. And that I the sayd Nicholas Hodgsden for mee my heyrs executors, & Administrators, do Covenant to & with the sayd Bennony my sonn, that vpon reasonable request, made vnto mee, by the sayd Bennony or his Assignes, will & shall do any further Act, or acts, thing or things, as shall bee devised by him, or his knowing Counsell in the Law, at any tyme hereafter, for the better Confirmcing & Legall Assureing the sayd Estate & P'misses, vnto him the sayd Bennony his heyres, executors, Administrators & Assignes for euer, If neede require; In witness here of I haue Caused this my bill or Deed of sayle in revoakabe, & Interchangeable to bee mayd, And haue here vnto set my hand, & seale, even the Two & twenteth day of October In the yeare of the Raigne of o' soueraigne Lord, Charles the secund by the Grace of god, of England, Scotland, France, & Ireland, King Defend' of the faith, the Thyrteth Anno Dom · 1678 : &c :

Sealed, signed, acknowledged   The Marke of ⨉ (his seale)
& Deliuered, in the Prsence
of us witnesses here vnder-   Nicholas Hodgsden
written/

Andrew Searle/   } witnesses/
Richard Walden Junjo' }

                     Nicholas Hodgsden acknowledged this
                     Writeing, to bee his Act & Deed,
                     this 29th of Octob' 1678 before
                     R..... W.... Com'ssio'/

Book III, Fol. 32, 33.

vera Copia of this Deede or Instrument aboue written, transcribed out of the originall & there with Compared this 24th day of December 1678 : As Attests

       Edw : Rishworth ReCor ·

[33] Whereas Wee whose handes are here subscribed, Were Impoured Administratrs for ye ordering & disposeing of the Estate of our father John Frost lately deceased, W^{r}by Wee stand obleigd both by civill & naturall obligations to take effectuall Care, for the most Comfortable & Convenjent Mantenance of o^r Mother Ross Frost, that lyeth in or pouers to do & for ye distribution of the sd Estate æqually to whom It doth of right belong, that by Pformance there of all future differences may bee Issewed amongst us, relateing to ye P^{r}misses ; Wee do here declare o^r selues to bee agreed, & do mutually Consent That Edw: Rishworth ReCor. & Capt John Davess, shall haue full pouer & hereby are Impoured, to heare settle & determine all matters of differences w^{t}soeuer touching y^t Estate, & all Prsons w^{t}soeuer y^{r}in Concern'd, who shall haue full pouer to settle o^r Mother where they Judg most Convenient, with such a part of the Estate more or less for her Comfortable Mantenance, as neare as may bee, to her satisfaction, & w^{t}soeuer o^r sayd arbitrators shall see good to do in the P^{r}mises, in any kind y^{r}in Wee do Consent & agree in a bond of one hundred & sixty pounds, each to other vpon forfiture y^{r}of, y^{r}with to bee fully satifyd, as witness our hands this : 14th day of Novemb^r 1678 .

Jno Frosts Estate settl^d

      p order & Consent of John Frost/

Ross Frost freely Con- Allexand^r Maxell his marke Z
sents to this agreeme^t Phillip Frost his marke P F
Witness her hand/
Ross Frost her
  marke

Book III, Fol. 33.

A true Coppy of this bond transcribed, & with y*e* originall Compared this 28*th* day of Decemb*r* 1678 :
p Edw · Rishworth ReCor :

Wee the appoynted arbitrators within written, haueing Considered the P*r*misses, according to the pouer Committed vnto us, do determine as followeth ; That Phillp Frost shall hence forward take aeffectuall care for y*e* mantenance of his Mother Ross Frost, with meate drinke & Cloathing, & such other necessarys, as are fitt & needfull for her Comfortable Liueing, dureing the Continewance of her natu-

Frost's Estate

rall life. vpon Consideratin there of Wee do mutually agree, that the sayd Phillp Frost, shall haue & Imoy as his own proper right all y*t* Estate of Cattle & all other Moueables, vidz*t* household-stuffe, Cattle, stanes, debts belonging to y*e* Estate, formerly belonging to his father John Frost deceased, & to haue the vss of the Marsh soe long as his mother liueth. It being always to bee vnderstood, that y*e* Land at Brickesome stands free to bee deuided amongst y*m* according to Law, & in Case that sayd Phillp should dy before his Mother, then this Estate remajnes good for his Mothers Mantenance Whilst shee liueth/ & farther y*e* sd Phillp Frost is to pay out of the Estate in his hands eight pounds · 14*s* in debts, onely hee is to receiue of his brother John Frost, in a debt due to y*e* Estate one pound seauen shillings & 6*d* this is o*r* determination/ witness o*r* hands this 26 : Decemb*r* 78 : Which we agree shall bee ReCorded, & Phillp Frost to pay for y*e* doeing of It/ Edw · Rishworth
John Davess/

vera Copia of this Conclusion aboue written, signed vnder o*r* own hands, transcribed & with y*e* originall Compared this 28th day of Decemb*r* 1678 :   p Edw : Rishworth ReCor .

Book III, Fol. 33.

Know all men by these P^rsents, that I Daniell Epps, of Ipswich in ye County of Essex Gentle: haue sett or Lett, or in Case sould vnto Henery Sayword of yorke, in the County of yorke shyre Mill wright, the three ffarmes which I bought of Gooch, Austine Mussy, vpland & Meddow, on both sides of Cape Porpus River, commanly soe Called, which in the Township of Wells in the County of Yorke shyre, as alsoe such a part of my purchase, that I bought of John & Robert Wadleigh of Wells as lyeth between the aforesayd Cape Porpus River, & Kenebunke River. Now It is sett or Lett, & in Case sould vpon the Conditions following, vizt The sayd Sayword is to pay the three next Insewing years, the first payment to bee in the yeare 1671: by the last of May eight thousand of M^rchantble boards to bee Delivered at such a wharffe in Boston as I shall appoynt, & so the next two yeares the like Numb^r of boards by the yeare which is for ye rent of the Land, & then if the aforesd Sayword

Epps & Sayword

shall pay or cause to bee payd one hundred pounds Ster^lg at Boston in M^rchantble boards at fiuety shillings p thousand, then the sayd Sayword is to haue one third part of the aforesd 8000^M of boards to bee deducted, out of the rent; And in case the next Yeare following, hee shall pay one hundred pounds Ster^lg more at Boston in M^rchantble boards at fiuety shillings p thousand, then is another third part of the rent (being 8000^M of boards to bee alsoe taken off; And if the sixt yeare wch will bee in . 76 : by the last of May the sayd Sayword shall pay one hundred pound Ster^lg more, in M^rchable boards at Boston at fiuety shillings p thousand, then ye aforesd Prcells of Lands to bee the sayd Saywords, his heyrs executors Administrators & Assignes for him & them to haue & to hould, peaceably & quietly to Imoy, with all ye rights titles primledges according as they are expressed by the severall deeds made by the sundry Prsons before mentioned vnto mee Daniell Epps; And in case of non payment of the rents or principle or both, then y sd Lands shall bee returned to

the sayd Daniell Epps his heyres, executors & assignes, &
the sayd Sayword shall pay vnto the sd Epps, or his Assigns,
double the sume of the rents due the whoole six yeares, in
which tyme It shall bee free to him the sd Sayword either
to make the purchase or to pay añuall rents, all any or
either of which rents or somes are to bee payd at any wharf
in Boston w^r the sayd Epps or Assignes shall appoynt. &
for the true P^rformance of the aforesd Covenant & bargane
Wee the aforesayd Daniell Epps, & Hen: Sayword do bind
o^r selues o^r heyrs, executors administrators & Assignes
w^rvnto wee haue sett o^r hands & seales, this twelfth of July
1670.   Daniell Epps (his seale)
Subscribed sealed & Delivered/   Hene: Sayword (his seale)
  in the P^rsence of us/
John Hale, Daniell Epps Junjo^r/
  A true Coppy of this Instrumet aboue written transcribed
& with ye originall Compared this 4th day of Janvary 1678 ·
                              p Edw: Rishworth ReCor:

These P^rsents testify, that I Robert Iordan Senjo^r, late of
Spurwinke, & now of Portsmouth in Pischataqua River
Presbito^r Administrator to the Estate of Mr John Winter
deceased, by & with the Consent of Sarah my wife out of
my naturall affection vnto my sonn John Jordan, & alsoe for
[34] & in consideration of a Legacy of tenn pounds sterling,
due vnto the sayd John by the Testament of his Grandfather,
John Winter deceased, togeather with diverse other Concer-
ments, him the sayd Robert therevnto moueing, doe by these
P^rsents giue grant bargan aliene appropriate Infeoffe Confirme, Assign & set ouer vnto the sayd John Jordan his
heyres executors Administrators or assigns, all my right
Title & Interest, in of & vnto the Ysland commanly called
Richmans Ysland scituate & ljing in the sea, off & aganst &

BOOK III, FOL. 34.

Jordan
Winter's
Adminr
To his
Son Jordan

between the Mouth of Spurwinke River, & Cape Elizabeth togeather with the houses Stage, & bujlding therevpon togeather with three hundred Acres of vpLand next adioyneing & lijng on a square on the West side of the Marsh, as alsoe a Prcell of Marsh scituate & lijng on the Mayne, next with in the Long sands Northward, from the sayd Ysland, togeather with all the wood, vnder wood, Tymber & Tymber trees wch are or hereafter shall bee growing on the sayd Land or any part y^{r}of togeather with all priuiledges, profetts, & imunitys therevnto belonging, or that may y^r & thence arise & accrew: To haue and to hould the sayd Ysland houses, stages, & bujldings, Marsh & vplands, to him the sd John his heyres, executors, Administrators or Assignes, to his & there own proper vss benefitt & behoofe, & to & for noe other vss for euer: provided always & Notwithstanding this p̄sent deed in case the sayd John or his heyres &c: shall at any tyme hereafter bee molested outed, or any way disceized of the whoole or any part of the sd Ysland, Marsh or vpland aboue P^{r}mised by any of y^r heyrs executors or administrators of the late Worshp^{ll} Robert Trelany of Plymouth M^{r}chant deceased · then the sayd Robert Jordan doth by these P^{r}sents in Lew y^{r}of giue grant appropriate & Confirme one Moeity or full halfe of all such some or somes of Money, as shall appeare to bee due to ye aboue sayd John Winter & Robert Jordan by assignem^t & delegation, & shall bee recouered from them or any of them, vpon the payment of wch somes to bee by them made the sayd Robert Jordan & his heyres by Act & Conclusion of Law stand obleidged to deliver vnto them or any of them the Interest of nine parts of the sd Ysland &c & not otherwise: In witness w^{r}of the sayd Robert Jordan hath here vnto set his hand & seale/ Dated in Portsmouth aforesd this Twenty fifth day of Janv: Anno Dom̃: one thousand six hundred seaventy seaven, & in the Twenty ninth yeare of the Reign of our Soveraign

Book III, Fol. 34.

Lᵈ Charles the secund, king of England Scotland, France, & Ireland Defendʳ of the faith/

Signed sealed & Deliverd in the ꝑsence of us/ Christian Hoskines/ William Hoskings his Marke W H Richard Stylemā .

By mee Robert Jordan (ₛ꜀ₐₗₑ ʰⁱˢ) pʳsbiter/ Signum Saraih Jordan/ ∫ (ₛ꜀ₐₗₑ ʰᵉʳ)

Great Ysland 20ᵗʰ of Janv: 1678.

Mr Robert Jordan Presbiter, & Saraih Jordan acknowledged this Instrumᵗ to bee yʳ free Act & deed, onely they at yᵉ signeing & sealeing reserued two boats rowme, & priuiledges of keepeing of sheepe, for yʳ longest liuer of them for thejr & either of yʳ own liuelyhood, & was Consented vnto by John Jordan before mee Elyas Stylemā :

Commissioʳ/

William Hoskings, & Christian Hoskines in the ꝑsence of the Lord, testify yᵗ this Instrument was signed & sealed by Mr Robert Jordan & Saraih Jordan as there free Act & Deed, & that at yᵉ signeing & Delivery the sayd Robert & Sarah did except & reserue two boats Rowm & yᵉ keepeing of sheepe, for yʳ own Liuelyhood, dureing both & yᵉ longest liuer life & lites on Richmans Ysland/ this before mee Elyas Stylmā Commissioʳ/

A true Coppy of this Instrumeᵗ with in written transcribed, & Compared with the originall the 24ᵗʰ of Janvary 1678

p Edw Rishworth ReCor :

These Pʳsents testify, that whereas there is an Intent of Marage between mee John John Jordan late of Richmans Ysland in Spurwinke River ffishermā · & now reseident in Portsmouth, in Pischataqua River, & Elizabeth Styleman of Portsmouth in Pischataqua River, do in Consideration thereof

Book III, Fol. 34.

Jordan
To his Spouse
Styleman

give grant, bargane aliene appropriate, Enfeoff Confirme Assigne, & set ouer vnto her the sayd Elizabeth Styleman, her heyres lawfully begot of her by mee all my right Title & Interest in & vnto Richmans Ysland in spurwinke River with all the houses Stages & bujlding there vpon with a P^rcell of Marsh, scituate & lijng with in the Long sand Northward from the sayd Ysland, as alsoe three hundred acres of vpland, next adioyneing & lijng in a square, on the West side of the sayd Marsh, with all the woods vnderwoods Tymber, & Tymber trees, which are or hereafter shall bee growing on the sayd Land or any part y^rof, togeather with all the priuiledges profetts, & Imunitys there vnto belonging, in as full & ample manner as they are mine, by vertue of a Deed this day signed vnto mee by my father Mr Robert Jordan late of Spurwinke, & now of Portsmouth aforesd/ To haue and to hould all the aboue mentioned P^rmises, & every part y^rof to her, & the heyres of her body by mee lawfully begotten, & to her heyres executors & Administrators for euer; but If It shall happen that the sayd John shall dy & depart this naturall Life before the sayd Elizabeth, then I the sd John do hereby fully frely & absolutely give grant Enfeoff aliene Confirme, Assigne & sett ouer vnto her the sayd Elizabeth (although I haue noe Issew by her) all ye aboue demised p^rmisses, with euery part & P^rcell there of, & to her heyrs executors administrators or Assigns, to & for her & there own proper vss, benefitt & behoofe for euer: & to & for noe vss & Intent whatsoeuer/ In witness whereof I haue here vnto set my hand & seale/ Dated in Portsmouth afo^rsd this Twenty fifth day of Janvary 1677: one thousand six hundred seaventy & seaven/ And in the Twenty ninth yeare of the Reigin of o^r Soueraign Lord Charles the secund king of Eng-

land, Scotland, France & Ireland Defend[r] of the faith &c:
1677   John Jordan (his seale)
Witness Christen Hoskins/

William Hoskines his
marke
Rich[d] Styleman/

Great Ysland 20th of Janvary 1678:
William Hoskines & Christian Hoskines the witnesses came & testifyd in the P[r]sence of god before whom they were that they saw John Jordan signe seale & deliver this Instrument as their free Act & Deed, before mee

               Elyas Styleman Comisso[r]

vera Copia of this Instrument aboue written transcribed out of the originall, & there with Compared this 26th day of Janvary 1678.   p Edw Rishworth ReCor:

Anger
To
Pullman

These p̃resents do testify that I Samson Anger of Yorke, in the County of yorke shjre planter, for severall good Causes & Considerations there vnto mee moueing, & more espetially for the some of Twenty six pounds to mee in hand payd by John Pullman of yorke afores[d] ffisherman, wherewith I am fully Contented & satisfyd, do hereby sell give grant allience Enfeof [35] and Confirme from mee my heyrs executors, Administrators & Assigns, vnto the s[d] John Pulman his heyrs executors Administrators & assignes, & haue hereby giuen granted, aliend Enfeoffed & Confirmed, vnto the sayd John Pullman, his heyres executors Administrators & Assignes for ever, a Certen Tract or P[r]cell vpland, & Meddow Land or sault Marsh, ljing & being on the South West side of yorke River, ljing & being bounded on the South, by the Land or fence of Henery Donells, on the West on the Marsh of Jesper Pullmans, on the North West on the Marsh of

Mr Edw: Johnsons, & on the North East by the River, Contayneing the quantity of tenn Acres of vpland & Marsh being more or less, ljng & being bounded as aboue expressed · To haue and to hould the sayd tract or quantity of vpland & Marsh, with all the priviledges lybertys Imunitys, & all other appurtenaces y^rvnto belonging, from mee the sayd Samson Anger with the Consent of my wife Saraih, my heyres executors Administrators & Assignes, vnto the sd John Pullmā aforesd, his heyres executors Administrators & Assignes, for euer, & further I ye sd Samson Anger do Covenant & agree with the sayd John Pullman, that the vpland & Marsh is free & Cleare from all Titles Troubles Morgages, alienations Clames, & all other Incomberances whatsoeuer, & that hee the sd Samson Anger in the behalfe of him selfe, his heyrs executors administrators & Assignes, will warrant & defend the same from all Pison or Prsons y^t shall Clame any title or Clame from by or vnder him his heyrs Administrators & Assigns for ever: as witness my hand & seale w^rvnto I haue afixed the same this Twenty sixt day of Octob^r one thousand six hundred serventy eight Anno Dom̄: 1678 in the Thyrteth yeare of the Reign of o^r Soveraigne Ld the King, Charles the secund, of England Scotland France & Ireland Defend^r of ye faith &c ·

Signed sealed & Deliver'd   Samson Anger
    in the P^rsence of/   his marke (his seale)
    Job Allcocke
    Edw · Wollcocke/   Saraih Anger
    John Brawn   her marke (her seale)
    his marke

possession given by Turff & Twigg the day & yeare aboue written, before us, Job Allcocke/ Edw: Wollcocke/ John Brawn

    his marke

Samson Anger & his wife Saraih, acknowledged this Instrume^t to bee thejr Act & Deed, this 18th of Noveb^r 1678: before mee Samll Wheelewright Assote

Book III, Fol. 35.

A true Coppy of, this Instrument transcribed, & Compared with the originall this 26: day of Janva: 1678:
p Edw: Rishworth ReCor·

To all Christean people to whom this P{rs}ent Deed shall Come/ Richard Bray now in Boston in New England, but formerly of Cascoe Bay in the province of Mayn Talour, & Rebella his wife send Greeting; Know yee that the sayd Richd Bray with the free & full Consent of his sayd wife, for & in Consideration of the some of eighty pounds, in Current money of New England, to him at & before thensealing & deliuery here of by George Pearson of Boston aforesayd M{r}chant Well & truely payd, the receipt Whereof, hee the sayd Richard Bray doth hereby acknowledg, and himselfe there with to bee fully satisfyd & Contented and there from and from euery part and Prcell thereof, for him selfe his heyres executors, & Administrators, do exonerate & acquitt, & fully discharge him the sayd George Pearson, his heyrs executors Administrators & Assignes for euer, by these P{rs}ents hath given granted barganed sould, aliend Enfeoff'd, Convayd & Confirmed, vnto the sayd George Pearson his heyrs & Assignes, & doth hereby fully freely Clerely & absolutely give grant bargajne sell Alliene Enfeoffe Convay, & Confirme vnto him & them the one halfe part of all that Ysland scituate in Casco Bay aforesd w{ch} hee formerly bought of John Cossons, then of Cascoe Bay aforesd, Commonly known by the name of Cussons his Ysland, with one halfe part of an Ysland Adioyneing to the sayd Cossons his Ysland, Called & known by the name of Long Ysland, with fiue Acres of sault Marsh bee It more or less, on the Mayne lijng on the West end of the Great Marsh, to the end of a Cricke or Landing place, where the aboue sayd John Cossons Landed his Hay in Chu... ... ... R... ... C... ... B... ... ... To haue and

Bray
To
Pearson

BOOK III, FOL. 35.

to hould the one halfe of both the abouesayd Yslands, with all the Marsh there vnto belonging, togeather with the sayd fiue Acres of Marsh on the Mayne with all other the houseing, Woods vnd'woods Mines, Mineralls, profetts, priuiledges, and appurtenances, to ye halfe of both the aforesd Yslands, belonging or any wise app^{r}tayneing, & all the Estate Right title Interest propriety, Clame possession that they the sayd Richd Bray Or Rebella his wife or either of them now haue or formerly had, in or to the aforebarganed P^{r}misses, or any part thereof, to him the sayd Geo: Pearson, his heyrs executors Administrators & Assigns for euer, to his & y^r soole & proper vss & behoofe, from hence forth for euer. And ye sayd Richard Bray, for him selfe, his heyrs, executors, & Administrators, doth Covenant promiss & grant to & with the sayd Geo. Pearson his heyres executors Administrators & Assignes, that hee the sayd Richd Bray is the right & proper owner of the aboue barganed P^{r}mises, & hath in him selfe full poner good right, & lawfull authority to bargane sell aliene & Convay the same, vnto him the sayd Geo: Pearson his heyres, executors, & Assigns in manner as aforesd And that the afore barganed P^{r}misses, & app^{r}tenances are at the sealeing & Delivery of these P^{r}sents, free & Cleare, & Clerely acquitted & discharged, of & from all manner of Gyfts, Grants bargans sales, Leases Morgages Wills, Intales Rents reversions, titles, troubles, alienations, & Incomberances whatsoeuer had, made or done, or suffered to bee done by him the sayd Richd Bray, or Rabellah his wife or either of them, or of any other P^{r}son from by or vnder them, or either of them And that hee the sayd Geo: Pearson his heyrs & Assignes shall & may for ever hereafter quietly & peaceably possess the same & all & every part thereof, with out the Lett trouble hinderance, or disturbance of him the sayd Bray or Rabella his wife, there heyrs or Assigns or any other Prson Clameing a Right there to, or any part there of from by or vnd^r either of them: And the Prmisses vnto him the sayd George Pearson his heyrs &

assigns, shall agaynst them selues, & euery other prson lawfully Claimeing a Right thereto, warrant & for euer defend by these Prsents: & the sayd Rebella Bray doth alsoe here by freely surrender vp vnto the sayd George Pearson his heyrs & Assigs all her Right of thirds of in & to the afore barganed Prmisses, & euery part there of/ And that hee the sayd Richd Bray & & Rebella his wife shall at any tyme here after vpon the reasonable request & demand of the sayd George Pearson his heyres, & Assigns do any further [36] Act that may bee for the better secureing, & sure makeing of the Prmisses, vnto him or them, according to the true Intent & Meaneing of these Presents/ In witness wrof the sayd Richd Bray & Rebellah his wife haue here vnto set theire hands & Seales. the first day of Janvary Anno Dom: one thousand six hundred seaventy & Eight, 1678

Signed sealed & delivered
  in the Prsence of   Richard Bray)(his (his seal)
John Brown his   make

Marke B   Rebella Bray   X   her (her seale)
Thomas Kemble/   marke

      Richard Bray acknowledged this Instrumet to bee his Act & Deede this first day of Janva: 1678. before mee Edw. Tyng Assistt

A true Coppy of this Instrumet transcribed, & with the originall Compared this 20th day of Febru. 1678:
                        p Edw: Rishworth ReCor·

To all Christean people, to whom this Psent Deed shall Come, Richard Bray of Boston formerly of Cascoe, with in the province of Mayn In New England Taylor, & Rebella his wife send Greeteing/ Know yee that the sayd Bray with the free & full Consent of his sayd wife, for & in Consideration of the   T   C   of New

Book III, Fol. 36.

Bray
To
Pearson

England to him by George Pearson of Boston aforesayd M^rchant Well & truly payd, at & before the sealing & deliuery here of, the receipt whereof hee the sayd Richard Bray doth hereby acknowledg & him selfe there with to bee fully satisfyd & Contented, & there from & from euery part there of for him selfe his heyrs executors & Administrators, doth hereby exonerate acquit & fully discharge, the sayd George Pearson his heyrs executors Administrators & Assignes for euer, by these P^rsents, hath & hereby doth fully freely clearely, & absolutely giue grant, bargane Sell aliene Infeoff Convay & Confirme vnto the the sayd Geo. Pearson his heyres & Assignes all that his plantation, houseing Lands both vpland & Meddow lijng & being scituate in Cascoe bay aforesayd, within the province of Mayne, & was formerly the Land of Thomas Drake Deceased, the wch the sayd Bray bought of the sayd Drake, & is scituate lijng & being between the Plantation of Richard Carter in Cascoe Bay on the one side, & the Pantation of John Mayne on the other side there of, & Contayneth sixty Acres of Land bee It more or less, & alsoe all the arable Land houseing bartys out houseing woods vnderwoods tymber & tymber trees Meddows Oarchards Gardens & all other profetts, priuiledges Lybertys, easements & all other ye appurtenances to the P^rmisses belonging, or in any wise app^rtayning To haue & to hould to him the sayd Geo. Pearson, his heyres executors Administrators & Assignes for euer, to his & there soole and proper vss, & behoofe, from hence forth & for euer/ And the sayd Richard Bray & Rebella his wife, for them selues there heyrs executors & Administrators, do couenant promiss & grant to and with the sayd George Pearson, his heyres executors administrators & Assignes, that they the sayd Richard & Rebella, are the true & proper owners of the aboue barganed P^rmisses, & haue in them selues full pouer. good right & Lawfull authority, the premisses to bargane Sell Convay & Confirme to him the sayd Geo: Pearson his

heyrs & Assignes in manner as aforesd And that at the sayd
P^rmises and appurtenances, are at the sealeing & deliuery
here of free & Cleare acquitted & discharged of & from all &
all mañer of former & other Gyfts Grants bargans sales
Leases Morgages Joynters Dowrys, Judgm^ts executions,
wills Intayls forfeturs seazurs titles troubles, and all other
Acts alienations & Incomberances whatsoeuer, had made or
done or suffered to bee done by either of them or by any
other Prson from by or vnder them/ And that ye sayd
George Pearson shall and may for euer hereafter peaceably
and quietly haue hould, vss occupy possess. & Inioy all &
singular the afore barganed premisses, and appurtenances,
with out the Lett trouble hinderance Molestation or disturbance, of them the sayd Richd Bray or Rebecca his wife, or
either of their heyrs executors or Assigns, or any other
P^rson Clameing a Right there vnto, or any part there of,
from by or vnd^r them; And the P^rmisses agajnst them selues
& euery other P^rson Lawfully Clameing a Right y^rto, vnto
him the sayd Geo. Pearson, his heyrs executors & Assignes,
shall warrant & for euer Defend by these p^rsents, And
Rebella, ye wife of the sayd Richard, doth here by fully &
freely surrender vp all her Right of thirds of in & vnto the
sayd barganed P^rmisses, vnto him the sayd Geo: Pearson his
heyrs & Assigns for euer, by these P^rsents, And the sayd
Richard Bray & Rebella his wife doe further Covenant &
promiss, that at any tyme hereafter, vpon the reasonable
request & Demand of the sayd Geo: Pearson to do any further Act or thing, that may bee for the better secureing of
the P^rmisses, to him & his according to the true Intent &
meaning of these P^rsents/ In witness w^rof they haue here
vnto sett y^r hands & seales the first day of Janvary Anno
Dom̄: one thousand six hundred seaventy eight/

Signed sealed & Deliverd   Richard Bray
  in the P^rsence of us/   his marke 🌕 (his seale)
  John Brown
   his 𝔅 Marke   Rebella Bray her
  Thom... ......   🜉 (her seale)

Book III, Fol. 36, 37.

   Richard Bray did acknowledg this Instrumeᵗ to bee his Act & Deed this first day of January 1678 before mee
        Edw : Tyng Assistant/
 A true Coppy of this Instrumeᵗ or Deede aboue written transcribed out out of the originall & there with Compared this 21th day of Februa : 1678 : as Attests
       Edw : Rishworth ReCor .

[37] Know all men by these Pʷsents that I John Cussons of Cascoe Bay Planter, do acknowledg to haue barganed & sould vnto Richd Bray & Sabella his wife one halfe of my Ysland wʳon I now liue, & the one halfe of the Ysland Adioyneing to It, & the one halfe of the Twenty Acres of Marsh ground, & the one halfe of fourty Acres of vpland lijng in the River of Cusquissacke wᶜh Ysland Marsh & vpland I the aforesayd John Cussons haue formerly received a deede Attested vndʳ Mr Cleeus his hand, & written down in the Court booke, for yᵉ Consideration of fiue & twenty pounds Sterlg to bee payd vnto mee the aforesd John Cussons in manner & forme following · that is to say to pay eight pound Sterlg & a noble between this being the 21ᵗʰ of ffebru : in the yeare of oʳ Lord 1650 & the 21th of Febru : In yeare of our Lord 1651 : & eight pounds Sterlg & a Noble the 21ᵗʰ of Febru : in yeare of oʳ Ld 1652 . & eight pounds stertg & a Noble the 21ᵗʰ of Febru : in the yeare of oʳ Ld 1653 . all wᶜh payments to bee made the one halfe in money, or beaver at Money price, & the other halfe in beife or porke at price Current/ & further It is agreed vpon that the aforenamed Richd Bray shall pay the aforesd John Cussons for the one halfe of yᵉ fence of the New fejld, & to pay the one halfe of the Rent to yᵉ Ld propriator, & the one halfe of all rates & taxes wᵗsoeuer, shall bee layd vpon the sd Ysland & further It is agreed vpon that yᵉ

Cossons & Bray

BOOK III, FOL. 37.

afore named John Cussons & Richd Bray shall not Pr'iudice one the other by vnd'trade with the Heathen, nor to detayne the oues Drs of the heathen from the other/ w'rvnto wee the aforenamed John Cussons & Richd Bray haue Interchange- bly set o'r hands this 21th of Febru : I say in the yeare of our Lord 1650 :   John Cossons his marke
Witness/
  Henery Webb   Richard Bray his
  John Payne/   marke

John Cossons hee owned that hee
had received satisfaction, & this
to bee his hand hee owned
  Geo : Pearson/
& before mee Mary Whitte/

A true Coppy of this Instrume't transcribed, & with the originall Compared this 22th of ffebru : 1678 :
  p Edw : Rishworth ReCor :

These p'sents Testify that I George Burrin of Yorke In y'e County of Yorke shyre in New England, for &
Burrin
To
Shapleigh
In Consideration of Twenty pounds sterling to mee in hand payd, by Majo'r Nicho Shapleigh of Kittery in the County aforesd, to full Content & satisfaction, haue given granted barganed sould, Infleoffed and Confirmed, & do by these P'rsents for my selfe my heyrs exe- cutors & Administrators giue grant bargan sell Infeoff & Confirme vnto the aforesd Majo'r Nicholas Shapleigh all my right title & Interest in a Certen Tract or P'rcell of Land, scituate & lying in the Town shipp of Yorke aforesd, on the Easterne side of Braueboate Harbour, It being the Land on w'ch my dwelling house now standeth, & Contayneth twenty Acres more or less, & is bounded round about with the Land of y'e sd Majo'r Nicho Shapleigh, & now by mee the sd Geo · Burrin sould vnto the sd Majo'r Nic : Shapleigh ; To haue &

to hould the abouesd Tract of Land, with the ædifices appurtenances & priuiledges y'rvnto belonging, To him the sayd Nicho: Shapleigh, his heyrs executors Administrators & Assigns for euer/ & for Confirmation of y'e treuth hereof, I the aforesd Geo: Burrin haue here vnto set my hand & seale this thyrteth day of Novemb'r Anno: Dom: one thousand six hundred seaventy eight/

Signed sealed & Deluer'd
in y'e p̄sence of us/
Ephraim Crocket/

his marke F̶

Dygory Jefferys his marke

Geo: Burrin his
marke ⁊ (his seale)

This Deed of sayle was acknowledged by y'e aboue named Geo: Burrin to bee his Act & Deede, this 30th day of Novb'r 1678: before mee John Wincoll
Assot̄e

A true Coppy of y's Deed transcribed & Compared w'th y'e originall y'e 27: ffebru: 1678: p Edw· Rishworth ReCor:

This Deed made the 10th of May 1653: Witnesseth that I Edward Godfrey, do giue grant Infeoffe & Confirme, vnto Phillip Addams his heyrs & Assignes for euer, one P'cell of Land where hee hath bujlt butting North East on the seituat mens swampe halfe way South East on the Land sometyms his fathers Now John Parkers, south West to the path Leading to Mr Gorges, & North West soe fare as the sd Edw· Godfreys first deuident is butting, on the Lauds layd out for Hene: Symson/ to haue & to hould the sayd Lands, from the sayd Edw· Godfrey his heyrs Assignes &

Godfrey
To
Addams

Assotiats, vnto the sd Phillip Addams & his heyrs for euer/ yeilding & paijng vnto the sd Edw: & his heyres & assigns yearly for acknowledgm't one days worke of a man at 6 days war .ing/ In witness the sayd Edw: Godfrey, hath here to put his hand & seale this day aboue sayd/

Sealed & Delivered   p mee Edw: Godfrey ($^{his}_{seale}$)
   in y^e P^rsence of us/   A true Coppy of this Instrume^t
   The marke of   aboue written transcribed, &
   Henery Donell HD   Compared with y^e originall this
   John Dauies   27th of ffebru: 1678.
                     p Edw: Rishworth ReCo^r:

This Deed made the 16th of August 1655/ witnesseth y^t w^as there was formerly granted by mee Edw: Godfrey, a Certen Tract of Land vnto Willia͂ Moore & Phillip Addams, on the West branch of the River of Agamenticus,

Godfrey To Adams

to Contayn in the whoole 80 Acres, & since Confirmed by the Commissio^rs Mr William Woster Mr John Brocke, & Mr Volentine Hill, Now this P^rsent writeing witnesseth, that I the sayd Edw: Godfrey do Confirme vnto Phillip Addams his heyres & Assigns for euer the Moiety of the sayd 80 Acres being 40 acres the bounds of ye sd 80 Acres North to ye Cricke, Com͂anly Called Mr Hulls Cricke, & soe fourty rod or poole by the wood side South West or Westwardly, & soe into the vpland North West, till the sayd eighty acres bee accomplished: they ye sayd William Moore & Phillip Addams to agree for the deuideing as they shall thinke meete/ to haue & to hould to them & y^r heyrs for euer: which warrantee from him the sd Edw: Godfred aganst him & his heyr. The sayd Phillip Addams his heyrs & Assigns Yeilding & paijng vnto the sd Edw: Godfrey his heyrs & Assignes such acknowledgm^t as is vsuall/ In witness w^rof the sayd Edw: Godfrey hath hither to put his hand & seale the day aboue written/ alsoe the Moeyty of the Marsh given him & William Moore at Mr Prebles Cricke/ p mee Edward Godfrey (his seale)

Signed sealed & Deluerd A true Coppy of this Instrume^t
In the P^rsence of/   abouewritten, transcribed &
Henery Norton/   with the originall Compared
The marke of   this 28th day of ffebru · 1678 :
                         as Attests Edw : Rishworth
Richd Burgess *RB*   ReCor .

The last Will & Testament of Robert Knight of Yorke/

Knights Will

Concerneing the small Estate left by the prouidence of god vnto mee/ I doe bequeath & dispose of as followeth/ Inp^rs fiue Acres of Marsh bounded West & by south, on the one side, & West & by North on the other side, vpland butting on the Land of Thomas Beeson, & soe backe vnto the swampe vntill It come to a P^rcell of Land of Mr Samll Mauericks, with an house & barne on the sayd Land, of Robert Knights, alsoe two Cows & a bull all wch as aboue expressed, alsoe w^tsoeuer else shall bee found to mee belonging, on or in [38] the sayd house land or barne, I do whoolely & for euer bequeath, vnto my sonn Richd Knight hueing in Boston, & to his Assignes for euer/ In witness of all which as aboue written, I haue here vnto sett my hand & seale this 23d day of June 1676 :

Owned & Delivered   The marke of
 In the P^rsence of
 Nicholas Willmott/   Robert ⨯ Knight (Locus Sigilli)
 his marke *P*
 John Tucker/   Nicholas Willmott & william Barthol-
 William Bartholmew/ mew, the first & 3d witness to this
                      Instrument P^rsonally appeared before
                      Edw : Tyng & Jos : Dudley

Esq^rs Assist^s August 24: 1676 · &
made oath they subscribed ye names
there vnto, as witnesses & was
P^rsent w^n Robert Knight did signe
seale & publish the same as a decla-
ration of his mind Concerneing the
disposall of his Estate, & y^t w^n hee
soe did, hee was of a sound disposeing mind, as Attests Is^a Addington
Cler^s

This is a true Coppy on fyle of the originall, with the
ReCords of the County Court of Suffocke, as Attests
Is^a Addington Cler^s

A true Coppy of this will within written with Attests
y^rvnto, transcribed & Compared this 28th day of Febru. 1678.
p Edw · Rishworth ReCor:

Knight
To
Young

Know all men by these P^rsents that I Richd Knight of
Boston, haue barganed sould sett ouer & Delivered all the houseing Marsh & vplands, with w^t
else is specifyd with in this will make mention
with in written, wch did belong vnto my father
Robert Knight deceased, & according as his last will & tes-
tame^t makes mention, hath sould the same vnto my brother
Rowland young, for and in ye Consideration of the iust some
of Eighty six pounds tenn shillings to mee in hand payd,
before the assigneing & setting ouer the same, & doe hereby
bind mee my heyres executors Administrators & Assignes
firmely vnto the sayd young his heyrs executors Administrators & Assignes, to his & there peaceable Inioijng euery

part & P^rcell there of/ In testimony there of I haue here
vnto set my hand this 15th day of Febru : 1677 ·
Signed & Delivered   Richard Knight
  in the P^rsence of/   Mr Weare & John Twisden doe Attest
  Peter Weare Senjo^r   vpon thejre oaths, that this Assigne-
  Job Allcocke/   m^t was the Act & Deede of Richd
  John Twisden/   Knight to Rowland Young taken
  Abra : Preble   vpon oath this 27th of Febru : 1678 :
          before vs
         Edw : Rishworth
         John Davess   Commissio^rs

A true Coppy of this Assignem^t transcribed & Compared
with the originall this 28th of ffebru · 1678 :
       p Edw . Rishworth ReCor :

To all Christan people to whom this P^rsent Writeing
shall Come ; I Anthony Emery of Kittery in the province of
      Mayn, in new England & ffrancis my wife, send
A Emery   Greeting/ Know yee that I ye aforesd Anthony
To
James Emery   Emery, & Francis my wife, for & in Considera-
      tion of one hundred & finety pounds, in hand
payd & by mee Received, Haue given granted Covenanted
Enfeff'd barganed sould & made over, & by these p̄sents do
giue grant Couen^t Enfeoff, bargn sell Confirme & make ouer,
vnto my sonn James Emery of the abouesd Town, & Province, my house & all my Land scituate lijng & being at
Could Harbōr, In Kittery in the Province of Mayn abouesd
with an hundred Acres of vpland Lijng vpon ye South side
of Sturgeon Cricke with barren Marsh lijng with in the
aboue sayd Cricke, & the little Marsh lijng aboue Nicholas
ffrosts, with a P^rcell of vpland adioyneing y^rvnto, alsoe a
P^rcell of Meddow with in a Coue where Daniell Forgissons
Lott is, with a Prcell of vpland In the head of Mast Cricke,
with a Prcell of Meddow adioyneing there vnto, with all &

singular the houseing barne Garden oarchards Commans, profetts priviledges fences wood Tymber appurtenances & Hæredtaments belonging, or in any wise app'rtayning there vnto/ To haue and to hould, all the aboue sayd P'rmises from the day of the Date hereof, to the proper vss & behoofe of the aboue sayd James Emery, his heyrs, executors or Assigns for euer, & I the aboue named Anthony Emery, & Frances my wife do Couenant promiss & agree to & with o'r sonn James Emery aforesayd, to warrantize the sayle of all & every part of the aboue sayd P'rmisses, that o'r sd sonn James Emery shall both hee is heyrs executors & Assigns from tyme to tyme & at all tyms, for ever, hereafter haue hould vss occupy possess, & Inioy all the aboue sayd P'rmisses, with out any lett hinderance Molestation, or Interruption of mee, the aboue Named Anthony Emery or ffrancis my wife, our heyrs executors or Assignes, or any other P'rson or P'rsons w'tsoeuer, Lawfully Clameing in by or from, or vnder us, or any or either of us our heyrs executors or Assigns further for & in Consideration of the satisfaction aboue specifyd, I sell & make ouer vnto my sayd sonn James Emery, severall Cattle & goods belonging to househould according as they are mentioned in a sedule Or Writeing vnd'r both our hands/ In witness where of I the aboue named Anthony Emery, & Fran'c my wife haue set our hands, & seals this Twelth day of May, In the yeare of our Ld one thousand six hundred & sixty

Signed sealed & Deliuered/   The marke **A** of (his seale)
   in y'e P'rsence of us/   Anthony Emry/
   John Emery Senjo'r   The marke of
   John Emery Junjo'r/
                                         Frances Emry/ (her seale)

John Emery Senjo'r, & John Emery Jujo'r vpon thejr oaths testifyd this Deed was sealed & Deliuered in there P'rsence by Anthony & frances Emery/ Taken before mee this 30'th of June 1660: Dañll Denison/

Book III, Fol. 38, 39.

A true Coppy of this Instrument transcribed, & Compared with ye originall this 14th of March 1678 :
p Edw : Rishworth ReCor .

J Emery

A lott layd out of fiuety acres, to James Emery, on the South side of Daniell Gooddings Lott, bounded with the same Lyne according to order fourty eight 1odd by the water side/ Novemb^r 1 : 1654 :

A true Coppy transcribed out of ye originall
as Attests Edw Rishworth ReCor ·

[39]   first Novemb^r 1654 :

Kittery
To A Emery

A Lott of Land Layd out to Anthony Emery, at his dwelling one hundred & twenty pooles backe from the way behind his fejld, that now is on an East Lyne, & from the head of the sayd East lyne to goe North by Certen Marked trees vntill It is the same breadth, as It is at ye water side, & from thence to goe West to a Certen Coue, between the sayd Anthony Emery & Henery Pounding/   The mark of
                                                    O
vera Copia transcribed & Compared with   Richd Nasone
the originall this this 14 : March 1678 :
p Edw . Rishworth ReCor .

Know all men by these P^rsents, that I Thomas Cowell of Kittery, In the County of Yorke shyre alias Province of Mayne, haue & do with the Consent of Elizabeth my wife late Widdow & Administratrix of William Seely deceased, this 3d day of January 1678 for & in Consideration of

Book III, Fol. 39.

Twenty pounds Current pay of New England already received of Abell Porter of Boston in New England aforesd, w^rwith I do acknowledg my selfe fully satisfyd & payd, & do hereby exonerate acquit & discharge, the sayd Abell Porter of euery part & P'cell there of, for which I haue given granted bargained sould Enfeoffed & Confirmed,

Cowell
To
Porter

& do by these p̃sents for my heyrs executors & Administrators giue grant bargan sell Enfeoff & Confirme unto ye aforesayd Abell Porter one Messuage or Lot or tenement scituate & being in the Town of Kittery aforesd, & butting against spruse Cricke, on the West side there of being a Lot granted vnto Wilha: Seely deceased, Contayneing twenty fiue Acres by measure, more or less, & It is bounded on the North West side by the Land of Mis Mary Cutt, deuided by a North East & South West lyne, from spruse Cricke on ye North East End, to another small Cricke at the South west end there of, & on the South West side by the Lands of William Scriuine, deuided by an East North East Lyne of fiuety foure pooles in Length, & then South East & by East lyne of tenn pools, & from thence an East lyne down to spruse Cricke aforesd, Twenty fiue Acres of Land, as It was granted by the Town of Kittery, vnto William Seely aforesd, & layd out & measured by Capt John Wincoll the 25th day of May 1678 · the same to haue & to hould all ye aboue bargained Prmises, with all the priuiledges, app'rtenances thereto belonging, or in any wise singularly app'rtayneing, to him the sayd Abell Porter his heyrs & Assigns for euer, the same to warrant, & Defend against any Prson or Prsons w'soeuer, makeing any Clame thereto or to any part there of, or P'cell y'of, & for Confirmation of the treuth here of I the aforesd Thomas Cowell, wth Elizabeth my wife haue set both o^r hands & seales, & haue given possession to ye sayd Abell Porter by Turffe & Twigg, for him his heyrs or Assigns, to Injoy the same for euer, from

the fourth day of Janv : in the yeare of oʳ Lord one thousand
six hundred seaventy eight :

Signed sealed & Deliver'd   Thomas Cowell/ (his seal)
  in the ꝑsence of us/   Elizabeth Cowell (her seal)
  & possession giuen/   March 5 : 167⅞ Mr Robert Elliot &
  Robert Elliot/   William Scriuine the winesses
  Willia͞ : Scrivine/   came and made oath yᵗ they saw
  Richd Cutt/   Tho : Cowell, & Elizabeth Cow-
                       ell signe yˢ Instrumᵗ as yʳ free
                       Act & deed before mee
                       Elyas Stylema͞ : Commissioʳ

A true Coppy of yˢ Instrumᵗ transcribed & Compared with
yᵉ originall this 14 . March 1678 .
                       p Edw : Rishworth Re :Cor ·

The testimony of Richard Row aged about fourty yeares,
testifys this that in the latter part of yᵉ yeare of our Ld one
thousand six hundred seaventy six that Jos : Pearce hueing
then in kittery came to mee Richard Row hueing in Kittery
& John Andrews both of us togeather, & desired

R. Row's
Test for
Margʳʸ Bray

of us very earnestly, beging of us both to take
notice of his words, that after his deccase, wⁿ
all his debts was payd, that yᵉ remajndʳ of his
Estate hee freely gaue vnto Margery Bray daughter to John
Bray of Kittery, shippwright, & further begging very Earnestly of this Deponeᵗ that hee would not forget It, that shee
might not bee Cheated of It/ & further sayd this shall bee
my last will & testameᵗ

  Taken vpon oath by Richd Row the first of Octobʳ 1678
            before mee Elyas Stylema͞ : Commissioʳ/

Book III, Fol. 39.

Samson Whitt aged 23 years Testifyeth/
That when Joseph Pearce went last to sea, the sayd Pearce desired this Deponent & John Andrews to take notice that hee gaue vnto Margery Bray his whoole Estate after his decease, his debts being first payd, & sayd y' should bee his last Will & testament/

Whitt D°

Taken vpon oath by Samson Whitte this 14th of Novebr 1678, before mee John Wincoll Assotiate

Andrews D°

John Andrews aged 26 years testifyd vpon oath to the treuth of both the testimonys of Richd Row & Samson Whitte written on the other side this paper/

Sworne this 4th day of Decembr 1678:
before mee John Wincoll Assote/

A true Coppy of these three testimonys aboue written transcribed out of thejr originalls, & y'with Compared this 15th · d : of March 1678 · p Edw : Rishworth ReCor :

To all people to whom these P'sents shall Come, Henery Sayword of Yorke in the County of Yorke shyre alias Prouince of Mayn In New England Millwright, sendeth Greeteing/ Know yee that I the sayd Henery Sayword, for & In Consideration of the some of one hundred thyrty fiue pounds seauenteen shillings, & foure peence, Lawfull money of New England to mee In hand by John Leverett Esqr of Boston in New England aforesd, well & truely payd, the receipt where of I do acknowledg & there of, & of euery part & P'cell there of, do clerely acquitt, dischaige, the sd John Leverett, his executors Administrators & assignes by these p'sents, Haue barganed & sould, giuen, granted, Assignd Enfeoffed & Confirmed, And do hereby bargan sell give grant Enfeoff &

Sayword
To
Leverett

Confirme, vnto the sayd John Leverett his heyrs executors Administrators & Assigns for euer; One third part of my saw Mill, & Grist Mill, lijng & being scituate, In the Town of Yorke aforesayd, with one 3d part of all Towles, materialls, & Implements there vnto belonging, And one third part of all Tymber, & Lands there vnto belonging, And one third part of all rights of Comanidg, there vnto belonging, the sayd Land being by Estimation about six hundred Acres in the whoole. belonging to the sayd Mill, bounded with ye River to the Westward, & extending to ye vtmost bounds of the sayd Town, or how euer otherwise bounded, or reputed to bee bounded.

To haue & to hould, the afore barganed, one full third part of the sayd saw Mill & Grist Mill, togeather with one full third part of all & singular the Towls, Materialls, Implements, Tymber, Lands, Comanages with all other Lybertys & priuiledges there vnto belonging, or in any manner & wise app^rtayning, with the benefitts profetts & Aduantages there to bee [10] had made or raysed, to him the sayd John Leverett, his heyres, executors, Administrators & Assignes, to his & theire onely proper vss, & benefitt & behoofe for euer/ & I the sayd Henery Sayword do for mee my heyres executors & Administrators, Covenant promiss & grant to & with the sayd John Leverett, his heyrs executors Administrators, & Assignes that I the sayd Henery Sayword, am before the Ensealeing & deliuery here of the true & proper owner of the afore barganed Estate, & haue in my selfe full pouer, & Legall right & authority to sell, & Confirme the same vnto the sayd John Leverett as aforesayd, & that not onely the afore barganed P^rmisses, & euery part & Prcell there of, are free & Cleare from all other & former bargans, sales gyfts grants Titles, Morgages, charges, or Incomberances whatsoeuer, but alsoe shall & will at all tyme & tymes, warrant Mantayn, & Defend the same, & euery part & Prcell y^rof, against all & euery Prson or Prsons whatsoeuer, any ways Clameing or demanding the same; or any part or Prcell there of/ And shall & will at any tyme hereafter, on the

BOOK III, FOL. 40.

request & Demand of the sayd John Leverett his heyrs executors Administrators & Assignes, giue & pass any further or ample Assurance, & Confirmation of the Prmisses, as in Law or æquity Can bee deuised or required, & shall & will giue quiett, & peaceable possession of the sayd barganed P'misses, & every part, & Pr'cell there of, vnto the sayd John Leverett his heyrs, executors Administrators, or Assignes, prouided always any thing in y^s Deede Notwithstanding: It is further agreed & Concluded on, by & between the aboue mentioned Prtys, that If the aboue named Henery Sayword his heyrs executors, or Administrators, shall Well & truely pay, or Cause to bee payd, vnto the aboue named John Leverett, his heyrs executors Administrators or Assigns the full & Just some of one hundred thyrty fiue pounds seaventeen shillings & foure peence, in good M^rchantable saw Mill pine boards, square Edgd, full Inch thicke, or in good M^rchatble planke to bee Deliuered in Boston, at the same price they are then sould for money, or that hee shall worke out the whoole, or some part there of, in the way of his Calling, Which the sayd Leverett shall desire, the one moeity of the sayd some to bee payd, & Delivered in spetie, & place afore-sayd, at or before the first day of Septemb^r Which shall bee Anno. Dom: 1674/ the other Moeity to bee Deliver'd as aforesayd, at or before the first day of Septem^{br} wch shall Anno Dom: 1675: then this Deede & euery Clawse there in, to bee voyd, to all Intents & purposes in the law w'soeuer, otherwise to bee, & stand in full force, pouer, & vertue: In witness where of I the sd Henery Sayword, haue here vnto put my hand & seale, this third day of Septemb^r Anno. Dom. Anno Dom: 1673: one thousand six hundred seaventy three/   Henry Sayword (Locus Sigilli)
Signed sealed & Delivered,

   In the P'sence of us/   This Instrument was acknowl-
   James Oliver   edged by Hene: Sayword as
   Isaac Addington/   his Act & Deed, Septemb^r 3:
                                1673 before Edw Tynge
                                         Assist

vera Copia of this Instrum^t transcribed, & with the originall Compared, this 27th of March : 1679 :

p Edw : Rishworth ReCor

Margerett Thatcher, Daughter to Mr Henery Webb late of Boston in New England deceased, & Jonathan Carwine & Elizabeth his wife, & Sampson Sheath & Mehitabell his wife, grand children to ye sayd deceased Webb, Executrixes to ye Estate of the sayd Webb deceased, Enter thejr Cawtion against granting Administration vpon, or any Inventoring of one third part of the saw Mill & all other Mills y^r vnto app^{r}tayneing, or in any ways belonging, Comanly Called yorke Mills, as alsoe of one third part of the Land at Mill Cricke, & all other Lands grants & priuiledg^s in any ways app^{r}tayneing to the sayd yorke Mills, & alsoe of one third part of the dwelling house, barne & all out houses, & other Improuemts whatsoeuer, vpon that Land (all lately in the Occupation of Henery Sayword of yorke deceased) as any part of the Estate of Henery aforesd deceased/ all the afore mentioned one third part, being part of the reall & proper Estate of the aforesd Webb deceased, & neuer alienated nor any ways Convayd by the aforesayd Webb, vnto the aforesd Sayword/

Webbs Heirs y^r Caution about Saywords Mills

A true Coppy of this Cawtion transcribed out of the originall & y^r with Compard this 28th day of March 1679 :

p Edw : Rishworth ReCor :

Jonathan Corwin, & Elizabeth his wife, Administratrix to ye Estate of Robert Gibbs late of Boston in New England

Book III, Fol. 40.

Gibbs's Exec.^r Caution about Saywords Estate

deceased, Enter y^r Cawtion against granting Administ vpon or any Inventoring of the saw Mill at Cape Porpus River ffalls, with all vtellenses & appurtenances there vnto belonging;

Alsoe three hundred Acres of Land on the East side of Cape Porpus River, next Adioyneing to ye aforesd Saw Mill, by grant from the Town of Wells, with all other Grants & priuiledges, for Cutting of Tymber for ye vss & benefitt of the sayd Mill, as any part of the Estate of Henery Sayword late of yorke deceased/ all the afore mentioned Prmisses, with all other bujldings & Improuements vpon ye sayd Land being long since forfeted vnto ye aforesayd Robert Gibbs, & now in the possession of the aforesayd Jonathan Carwin according to Law/

A true Coppy of this Cawtion transcribed out of the originall, & y^r with Compared this 28th day of March 1679 :
p Edw : Rushworth ReCor :

Clarks Caution D^{us}

Thomas Clarke Esqr, Enters his Cawtion against granting Administration vpon, or any Inventoring of two thirds parts of the Saw Mill, & all other Mills thereto app^rtayneing, or in any ways belonging, Comanly Called yorke Mills/ Alsoe of two thirds parts of the Land at Mill Cricke & all other Lands Grants & priuiledges in any ways app^rtayneing to the sayd Yorke Mills, & alsoe of Two third parts of the dwelling house, barne & all out houses & other Improuements w^tsoeuer, vpon y^t Land all lately in the Occupation of Hene : Sayword of Yorke deceased, as any part of the Estate of Henery Sayword deceased; All the afore mentioned two third parts, being the reall & proper Estate of the aforesd Thom^s Clarke Esqr & neuer alienated nor Convayd by ye aforesayd Clarke, vnto y^eaforesd Sayword/

Book III, Fol. 40, 41.

vera Copia of this Cawtion transcribed out of y̐ originall, & yͬ with Compared this 28th day of March 1679.
p Edw · Rishworth ReCor:

At a Town Meeteing, Wee the Select men of Scarbrough, do giue & grant to John ffoxwell a P͌cell of Marsh lijng between the Marsh, that was bought by Nathan Bedford, from Mr Isacke Walker, & Andrew Brown his Marsh, wͨh March lyeth on the Northern side of y̐ River open to ye Plantation Called Phippenys/ It being in quantity about six Acres, prouided It bee noe mans Legall right afore/

Scarboro'
To
Foxwell

A true Coppy of this grant transcribed out of the originall & yͬ with Compared, this 28th of March 1679:
p Edw: Rishworth ReCor:

Richd Foxwell/
John Tynny/
Samll oakemā.
Hene: Williams
Select men/

[41] Know all men by these P͌sents, that I Jane Bray, now in Boston formerly of Cascoe Bay in New England, widdow, the relict of Samll Bray, sonn of Richd Bray now in Boston aforesayd Taylour, Do acknowledg to haue received of Mr Geo: Pearson of Boston aforesayd, M͌chant full satisfaction by a valewable some payd by him vnto mee for my Interest in an Ysland scituate in Cascoe bay aforesayd, Comanly Called & known by the name of Cossons his Ysland, & yͬfore for my selfe heyres executors, Administrators, & Assignes, do surrend͌ vp vnto him the sd George Pearson his heyres, executors, & Assigns all my right, title, & Interest In the sayd Ysland, & all the priuiledges, profetts, & ap͌tenances there vnto belonging, to haue & to hould to him the

Jane Bray
To
Pearson

Book III, Fol. 41.

sayd George Pearson his heyrs & Assigns for euer, & do & shall for euer remiss release, & for euer acquitt, clame to haue any right or Interest in the sayd Ysland, or any part thereof/ In witness where of I the sayd Jane Bray haue here vnto set my hand, & seale, this eight day of Janvary Anno Dom͠: one thousand six hundred seaventy eight/

Signed sealed & Deliverd
in the P^rsence of us/
Richard Stower/
Edw: Payn/

Jane Bray (her seale)
her Marke

Richd Stower appeared before mee this 27th of flebru: 1678: & affirmeth y^t hee was P^rsent & see Jane Bray, seale, & signe this Instrume^t & Deliuerd It as her Act & Deede, & was P^rsent Wm Edw: Paine set to his hand with my selfe as Witnesses/
Symon Broadstreete D: Goũer
Edw: Tynge Assista^t

A true Coppy of this Instrume^t transcribed out of the originall, & there with Compared this 28th of March 1679:
p Edw: Rishworth ReCor:

Articles, Covenants, & Conditions of agreement, Covenanted, Conditioned & Actually agreed on the ninth Day of December in the yeare of o^r Ld God sixteen hundred seauenty & eight, by & between, Nicho: Hodgsden of ye Town of Kittery in the prouince of Mayn husbandman of the one Party, & Bennonj Hodgsden sonn of ye sd Nicholas of the same Town, & province husbandman, of the other party now as followeth &c: 1678:

<small>N Hodsdon & his son Benoni</small>

Inprimis Inp^{rs} the sayd Nicholas Hodgsden for him selfe, his heyrs executors & Administrators, for either & euery of them doth Covenant, to & with the sayd Bennony his sunn

BOOK III, FOL. 41.

his heyres, executors, & Assignes, & to & with euery of them by these P'sents, that hee the sayd Bennony his heyrs executors or Assignes, shall from tyme to tyme & at all tyms hereafter, dureing the . . rall lite of the say Nicho: Hodgsden, haue, hould, vss Mannure, & Inioy peaceably and quietly in partnership togeather with his sayd father all that Farme y^t hee the sayd Nicholas now, & for severall yeares late past hath and now doth possess, & dwell on togeather, with all that halfendeale of the houses, either, dwelling houses, or other houses, as barnes, stables, or other structures, now already bujlt or to bee bujlt on the sayd farme, for the vssfull, & necessary Mannagem^t of the sd Farme togeather, with all Lands, Meddows, Oarchards, Marshes, Gardens, & all the priuiledges, & appurtenances there vnto belonging, or in any wise app'tayneing, with out any deuission of Lands, or houses, but In partneishipp, & according to the Conditions in these Insewing Articles mentioned: And for that very Consideration in partnershipp to hould It, dureing the Naturall life of the sayd Nicholas/

Item The sayd Nicholas doth hereby Couenant and acknowledg, that all the Neate Cattle, Labour, horses, or other horse kind, swine, Hoggs, tame fowles, or any other liueing Creaturs, that are now liueing, pastureing or feedeing on the sayd farme, either heretofore belonging to ye sayd Nicholas, or Bennonj, are now at the sealeing hereof, the one halfe the sayd Nicho: his goods, & the other halfe the sayd Bennonys in Comman with out any devission, excepting or reseruation, here after Mentioned, & reserved/

Item the sayd Bennonj doth Covenant, & promiss his father Nicholas aforesayd, that hee shall & will to the best of his knowledg, & ability manure the sayd farme, & Cattle for the best Aduantage, dureing the sayd Tearm in partnershipp, & all Charges, seruants wages, taxes, & prouissions for ye family to bee payd out of the produce of the fruits, which shall arise of the sayd farme, with & by gods blessing on

Book III, Fol. 41.

thejr Indeauours, dureing the sayd tearme And If any ouerplus do remajne, of the Increase, & produce that shall arise out of the same, more then shall bee spent in the famly, & other Charges It is mutually agreed & Covenanted, by & between the sayd partys to these Pʳsents, that It shall bee æqually deuided between them at euery years end/

Item It is Mutnally agreed, & Covenanted on, by & between the Partys to these Pʳsents that all such Cloath whither Woll, Cotton, or Linnng that shall bee spunn & made to Cloath in the house the sayd Nicholas to haue the one halfe for his famaly & the sayd Bennonj to haue the other halfe/ And what shall bee bought for Cloathing or any vss (except victualls) to bee payd for at each Partys own proper Cost, & out of thejr own halfendeale not Impouerishing the stocke, & If one of these partys shall fit to buy, & the other haue noe Occasion, then what one party shall bestow, the other may take soe much goods out of the Comman stocke, æquivolent to yᵗ some soe bestowed, for his own vss, & noe expence to bee made to Impouerish, or lessen the sayd stocke, but that a full stocke of Cattle, & other quicke, & moueable goods bee still keept on the sayd farme dureing the sayd Tearme (with out any Wasting Imbesselling or decaijng the sayd Stocke) as the hay, & ffodder, that shall arise on the sayd farm will winter, keepe & Mantayn (except It bee by Consent of both partys, to these Pʳsents, none to bee put off, sould, given, or disposed off, but by mutuall Consent of both partys to these Pʳsents/

Item The sayd Nicholas doth reserue, & It is mutnally Covenanted, & agreed on by & between the sayd Nicholas, & the sayd Beñonj, that yᵉ sayd Nicholas shall at any tyme take off the abouesayd stocke, Two oxen, or young steeres, & two Cows for his own vss, & to bestow them where . . pleaseth, & yet to take the produe of the halfe neuertheless: And at the end of the Tearme the day of death, & decease of the sayd Nicholas, the whoole stocke to bee, & remajne to the sayd Benony, or his Assignes; togeather with all moueables on the sayd farme, as his own proper goods/

Item The sayd Nicholas doth further Covenant, to & with the sayd Bennonj, that after the death, & decease of the sayd Nicholas, all the Implements of husbandry and furniture, of what sort soeuer, either Iron Towles, or Wodden Instrumts, or Implements, vtensills, Casske table boards, stowles, & his greatest Iron pott, & his Andirons, & spitt, with some dishes, & spoones, & the pot hookes, & Tramells all which are now in the farme, or house or which shall bee then besid' the sayd Bennonjs own goods, to bee whooly the sayd Bennonys his heyres, or Assigns, which I the sayd Nicholas doth Covenant, to leaue to him, for his better Incoragment/

[12] Item The sayd Nicholas doth further Covenant, with the sayd Bennoj, for his better Incoragem't that If the sayd Nicholas do happen to dy, before that the tyme of the apprentishipp of that apprentise William Wadleigh, bee expired, that then hee shall serue out the remaynd' of his Covenant, and Indenture with the sayd Bennonj, Bennonj P'formeing the sayd Nicholas Conditions to the sayd William Apprentice/ & that y'e sayd Bennonj shall not bee Molested, disturbed, or putt out by the sayd Nicholas, nor by any other P'son or persons by his meanes, procurement, or allowance/ And for the true P'formance here of, the partys to these P'sents, do bind them selues in one hundred pounds Sterling, each to other, to bee payd on default or breach of any, or all these Covenants, by the Party offending, neglecting, or refuseing, to y'e party obseruening, fullfilling, & P'formeing/ In witness hereof the partys to these P'sents

Book III, Fol. 42.

haue sett thejre hands, & Seales, euen the day & yeare first aboue written/
Sealed, & Delivered in the P^rsence of us/
The marke of Nathan Lord
Jujo^r ⊖
The marke of Hannah Curtis/
Andrew Searle/

The marke of Nicholas Hodgsden H (Locus Sigill)
Bennonje Hodgsden (Locus Sigill)

The aboue written Nicholas Hodgsden & Bennoj Hodgsden, Acknowledged the aboue written articles, of agreeme^t to bee there Act, & Deede, this 12th day of Febru. 1678. before mee John Wincoll Assot̃e

vera Copia of these Covenants & Articles of Agreem^t aboue written transcribed out of the Originall & y^r with Compared this 31th day of March 1679

p Edw. Rishworth Re Cor:

To all Christian people, to whome this P^rsent writeing may Come: Know yee y^t I Clement Hardy of Winter Harbour in New England fishermã: for a valewable Consideration of money to mee in hand payd, before the signeing & Delivery hereof, haue barganed & sould, & by these P^rsents, do bargan & sell vnto John Praesbery of Sacoe in New England shoemaker, a Tract of Land Contayneing finety Acres of vpland with the Marsh y^rvnto belonging, lying on the North East side of Sacoe River, being bounded by two fresh water Gutts, that runnes into Sacoe River, & was formerly known & Called by the name of Page his plantation, the wch plantation I do Ingage to bee free of any Claime w^tsoeuer, from any P^rson or P^rsons, & shall & will make the same good for one whoole yeare & a day, according to the Laws of Oller-

Hardy
To
Prasberry

oune, vnto the sayd Presbery his heyrs, executors Administrators & Assigns & for the true P'formance of the P'misses, I bind my selfe my heyrs executors Administrators & Assigns, In the pœnulty of fourty pounds Sterlg : that ye sd tract of Land shall bee for the soole & proper vss & behalfe of ye sayd Presbery, his heyrs executors, Administrators & Assigns for euer · In witness w^rof I haue here vnto set my hand & seale, in winter Harbour, this 24th d : of June In the yeare of o^r Ld one thousand six hundred & seaventy/
Signed sealed & Deliuered/   Clement Hardy (Locus Sigilli)

  In the P'sence of us/
  Judeth Gibbons her marke ✍

William Bonightō his   Judeth Gibbons made oath the 4th
    marke ✝   of June 1670 : that shee was
                         P'sent & a Witness, w^n Cleme
                         Hardy signed sealed & Deliued
                         this aboue written Instrume^t as
                         his Act & Deed vnto Jo^n Pres-
                         bery before mee
                               Fran · Neale Assotiate
vera Copia of this Instrume^t aboue written transcribed & Compared with the originall this 3d day of Aprill 1679 :
                     p Edward Rishworth ReCor

  Bee It known vnto all men by these P'sents, that I Ralph Blasedell of Sawlsbury, In the County of Norfocke, Taylour, haue sould vnto Robert Knight Mason, from mee

Bleasdall   the sayd Ralph my heyres executors Administra-
  To
Knight   tors & Assigns, to the sd Robert his heyres,
              executors Administrators & Assigns, one dwell-
ing house being scituated in Agamenticus, in the Province of Mayn In New England, with all Lands, as vplands, Meddows, gardens, fences, Tymber, Comanage & all app'rtenances whatsoeur, there vnto belonging to the said Robert

Book III, Fol. 42.

to haue & to hould, & peaceably to Inioy, to him the sayd Robert his heyrs, executors Administrators & Assigns for euer/ In witness here vnto the sayd Ralph doth sett two his hand & seale, this 22th of July (1642)
In Prsence of us/   Ralph Bleasdall (his seale)
Joseph Miller/
Richd Bullgar/

A true Coppy of this Instrumt transcribed & Compared with the originall, this 11th day of Aprill 1679 :
       p Edw : Rishworth ReCor :

To all Christean people to whom this Prsent deed of sale shall Come/ John Howell late of Bla ͞ Poynt, in New England, & now resident in Boston in New England bla ͞ Smyth/ & prudence his wife send greeteing/ know yee that the sayd John Howell, & prudence his wife, for & in Consideration of the some of Tenn pounds, of Lawfull money of New England, to them in hand at & before the Ensealeing & delivery of these Prsents, by John Morton of Boston aforesayd Carter, well & truely payd, the receipt they do hereby acknowledg, & them selues there with fully satisfyd & Contented, & there of, & of euery part, & part & Prcell thereof, do acquitt, exonerate, & dischaage, the sayd John Morton his heyres, executors, & Administrators for euer by these Prsents : Haue given, granted barganed sould, alien'd, Enfeoffed, & Confirmed, & by these Prsents do fully Clearly & absolutely give grant bargan, sell, aliene, Enfeoff, & Confirme, vnto the sayd John Morton his heyres, & Assigns for euer, all that there peece, or Prcell of Land scituate lyng & being with in the Town shipp of Bla ͞ Poynt aforesayd, in or neare vnto a place there Comanly Called or known by the name of Dunston, being an house lott Contayning by Estimation one hundred Acres bee the same more or less, where of foure or fiue Acres there of

<small>Howel
To
Morton</small>

is sault Marsh Meddow, and six Acres there of or there abouts, is fresh Meddow, being butted and bounded South, Eastwardly, by blacke Poynt River, South Westwardly, by Comman Lands North Westwardly, by the Land of Elyas Oakeman, & North Eastwardly by bla? Poynt River: Togeather with all fences, trees, woods, vnder Woods, swamps, Meddows, Marshes, Rivers rights Commonages Comoditys, profetts, prmiledges & appurtenances, whatsoeuer, to the sd peece or P^rcell of Land belonging, or in any wise app^rtayneing, and als . all Deeds wrightings & euidences, w^tsoeuer touching, or Concerneing the same P^rmisses, onely or onely any part, or P^rcell y^rof. To haue & to hould, the sayd peece or P^rcell of Land, butted & bounded as aforesayd, with all other the aboue granted P^rmises vnto the sayd John Morton his heyres, & Asignes, & to the onely proper vss benefitt & behoofe, of the sayd Morton his heyrs, & Assignes for euer/ And the sayd John Howell & prudence his wife, for them selues, there heyrs executors & administrators, do hereby promiss Covenant & grant, to & with the sayd John Morton his heyres, & Assigns, that at the tyme of the Inscaleing here of, they [**43**] the sayd John Howell & Prudence his wife, are the true soole & Lawfull owners of all the afore barganed P^rmisses, and are lawfully seized of, and in the same, and euery part there of in there own proper right/ And that they haue in them selues full pouer good right, & Lawfull authority, to grant, sell, Convay & Assure the same vnto the sayd John Morton, his heyres & Assignes, as a good P^rfect & absolute Estate of Inheritance in fee symple, without any manner of Condition, reversion, or Lymitation whatsoeuer, so as to alter Change, defeate, or make voyd the same: And that the sayd John Morton, his heyrs, & Assigns shall & may by force & vertue of these P^rsents, from tyme to tyme & at all tyms for euer hereafter, Lawfully quietly and peaceably haue, hould, vse, occupy, possess, & Inioy the aboue granted P^rmisses with there app^rtenances, & euery part & parcell there of free, & Cleare, and Clearly acquitted,

Book III, Fol. 43.

& discharged, of & from all & all manner of former & other gyfts, grants, bargans sales Leases, Morgages Joynters Dowers, Judgm^ts, executions Intayles, forfeturs, & of & from all other titles troubles charges, & Incomberances w^tsoeuer, had made, Committed done or suffered to bee done, by they the sayd John Howell or Prudence his wife, or either of them or either of thejr heyres, or Assignes at any tyme, or tyms before the Ensealeing hereof: And further that they the sayd John Howell, & Prudence his wife thejr heyrs, executors, & Administrators shall & will from tyme to tyme, and at all tyms for euer hereafter, warrant & Defend the aboue granted P^rmisses with there app^rtenances, & euery part & P^rcell there of, vnto the sayd John Morton his heyres, executors, Administrators & Assigns, against all P^rsons & P^rsons whatsoeuer, any ways lawfully Claimeing or demanding the same, or any part there of/ In witness where of the sayd John Howell, & Prudence his wife, haue here vnto sett thejre hands, and seales the thyrteenth day of February Anno Dom̄ one thousand six hundred seaventy & eight, & in the Thyrty first yeare of the Reign of our Soueraigne Lord Charles the secund, King of England &c:
Signed sealed & Delivered
   in y^r P^rsence of us/ John
   Howard Secr̄ty
   Eliazer Moody serv^t

      There is Legall possession given by John Howell of all his right and possession in that Plantation to John Morton, Aprill 15th in the yeare of o^r L^d 1679:

      Andrew Brown ff   John Howell (his seale)
      witness, my hand   Prudence Howell (her seale)
      Nicho: Edgscome   her P marke

vera Copia, of this Instrum^t transcribed out of the Originall, & y^r with Compared this 14th day of May 1679:
               p Edw. Rishworth ReCor:

Book III. Fol. 43.

March 4th 1673:

Measured & layd out vnto James Emery Senjo[r] his Grant of sixty rodds in length into y[e] woods from the end of his house Lott, being fourty pooles in breadth, the sayd Grant beareth date the thyrteenth day of December. 1669·

Kittery
To
James Emery

Alsoe his grant of fiuety Acres of Land at his Marsh at Yorke pond, beareing date Dēmber 13: 1669:

Alsoe his grant of sixty acres of Land by his Meddow at Yorke pond beareing date Aprill 13th 1671·

Alsoe his grant of fourty Acres more beareing date 13th of of Aprill 1671· Layd out as followeth, vidz[t]

2 Measured & Layd out vnto James Emery Senjo[r] fiuety Acres of Land on the North West side of the Marsh at yorke Pond, two hundred pools in Length South West & by West, & fourty six pooles in breadth, & bounded with Peter Grant on the North, & Edw. Hays on the West, as by the marked trees, allowance being given for the high ways/

3ly Alsoe layd out unto the sayd James Emery, fourty & fiue Acres of Land on the South side of the sayd Marsh, two hundred & twenty pooles in Length, West & by Nore, from a Marked tree, neare the Falls of a little brooke y[t] runnes out of yorke pond, & thirty three pooles in breadth, bounded on the West with Edw· Hayes, & on y[e] South with Edw· Waymoths Land/

4ly Layd out to the sayd James Emery, twenty nine Acres of Land, at the head of his home Lott, a hundred & thirteen pools in Length, East & West & fourty poole in breadth North & South, bounded at y[e] East End with Rocky Hills/

5 Alsoe lade out vnto the sayd Emery Twenty six Acres of Land, by the vpper end of his house Lott, on the South side a hundred & six pooles in length East & West, & fourty poole in breadth, North & South/

BOOK III, FOL. 43, 44.

ffoure of the aboue sayd P'cells of Land, Were layd
out by Mr Playstead & my selfe, & the last layd
out this 11th day of March 167¾

p me John Wincoll Surv^r

A true Coppy of the severall grants aboue written, transcribed out of the originall & y^r with Compared this 15th of May 1679 ·   p Edw Rishworth ReCor:

Bartholmew Gydney of Salem, in the behalfe of him selfe his heyrs executors &c: Enters his Caution against granting Administration vpon, or any Inventoreing of one halfe of the Saw Mill, & all other Mills there vnto belonging, & all the appurtenances there vnto app'rtayneing, Called by the name of Cascoe Mills, & alsoe one halfe of all the Lands, grants of Tymber, & all other accomodations belonging vnto the sayd Mills, at Cascoe afores^d, & one halfe of any houses or other Improuements made vpon ye sayd Lands, all lately in the Occupation of Hene. Sayword of Yorke deceased; All the before Mentioned Estate being the reall & proper Estate of Bartholmew Gydney, & neuer alienated, nor Convayed by the aforesd Gydney/ Dated 16: June/ 79: vnto ye sayd Sayword/

vera Copia of this Caution transcribed out of the originall & there with Compared this 23 · of June 1679 ·

p Edw: Rishworth ReCor:

[11]   June 12. 1679.

Symon Lyde of Boston M^rchant in the behalfe of him selfe & his heyrs, Enters Cawtion against the granting Administration vpon, or any Inventoreng of one halfe of

Lyde s Caution about Mousum M

the saw Mill or Mills, & all other app'rtenances y^rvnto belonging, Called by ye name of Mowsum Mills one within the Towneshipp of Wells, &

alsoe the one halfe of all the Lands Grants of Tymber & other Accomodations, whither obtayned by purchase from any P^rson or by Grants either from ye Town of Wells or from ye Genell Court of ye Massatusetts, belonging to ye sd Mills, at Mowsum neare ye River of Cape Porpus, as aforesd, & one halfe of any houses or other Improuem^ts made, vpon the sayd Lands, all lately in ye occupation of Henery Saward deceased, all ye afore mentioned P^rmisses, being the Estate really & Legally falln into his hands, by or vpon ye forfeture of a Morgage beareing Date 2 : Sep̃ber 1673 : wch by the aforesd Symon Lynde were neuer alienated nor Convayd by him to ye sd Hen · Sayword June : 26 : 1678 ·

 vera Copia of this Cawtion & Compared this 22 : of June : 79 :   p Edw · Rishworth ReCor :

W^ras Wee whose names are here vnderwritten, by the request of Nathan Lawd Senjo^r, haue layd out all that P^rcell or Tract of Land, which Abraham Conley sould vnto Nicholas Frost, It being in Length Two hundred Twenty eight Rodd, And in breadth seaventy one Rodd, besid^s the six Acres at ye Ceaders, Which Land Joynes vnto John Hords Lyne, as may appeare by severall marked trees It being one hundred & six Acers of Land/ The Corner bounds neare the Cricke, are foure beach trees, vpon a square from John Hords Land, standing in the Westward Lyne of Nicho : Frost Land/ It being seaventy one pooles in breadth, from John Hords Land/   Christopher Banefejld/
Attest   James Emery/
 the marke of
 Richd ◯ Nasone/ A true Coppy transcribed, & Compared with the originall this 28 : June, 79

     p Edw : Rishworth ReCor :

Land laid out y^t Conley sold to Frost at Lords Request

BOOK III, FOL. 44.

:16: June: 1679:

Bartholmew Gydney of Salem, In the beLalfe of him selfe & his heyres Enters Caution against the granting Administration vpon, or any Invenorting of one halfe of the Saw Mill or Mills, & all other Mills & app^rtenances y^rvnto belonging, Called by the name of Cascoe Mills, & alsoe one halfe of all the Lands grants of Tymber & other accomodations belonging to the say'd Mills, at Cascoe aforesd, & one halfe of any houses or other Improuements made vpon the say'd Lands, all lately in the occupation of Hene. Sayword deceased/ all the before mentioned P^rmisses, being the estate really falln into his hands by or vpon the forfituie of a Morgage beareing date 14th Octob^r 74. wch by the aforesd Bartholomew Gydney were neuer alienated nor Convay'd by him vnto ye say'd Hene. Sayword/

<small>Gydney's Caution about Sacoe Mills</small>

A true Coppy of this Caution transcribed & Compared with the originall this first day of July 1679:

p Edw Rishworth ReCor:

This Indenture made the Twenty sixt day of Aprill In the nineteenth yeare of the Reigne of our most gratious Soueraigne Lord Charles by the Grace of god of England Scotland France & Ireland King Defender of the faith &c: between Thomas Withers Inhabitant in the Town of Kittery In the province of Mayne In New England on the one Party, & John Ball of the same place on the other party/

<small>Withers To Ball</small>

Witnesseth that the say'd Thomas Withers for & in Consideration of the some of nine pounds seaven shillings of Lawfull pay of New England by mee in hand received, before the signeing sealing & Delivery here of, of John Ball, haue for diverse good Causes mee y^rvnto espetially moueing, bargained, sould Infeoff'd & by these P^rsents do bargan sell Enfeoff & Confirme vnto the aboue mentioned John Ball, his heyres executors administrators & Assignes for euer, the quantity of twelue acres of vpLand lijng & being in spruce Cricke, within spruse Cricke, within the Town of Kittery aforesayd, at a place Comanly Called & known by the name of Eagle poynt, being butted & bounded on the East side, with a P^rcell of Marsh Joyneing to the Mayne Cricke, Called Eagle poynt Northwardly, & on the North side with a Cricke that goeth in West, & from y^t Cricke Twenty foure Rodd East South East, & Eighty Rodds West South West/ the whoole is Twelue Acres/

To haue, & to hould, all the sayd P^rmisses, to him the sayd John Ball his heyres, executors, Administrators, & Assignes for euer, from mee the sd Thom^s Withers my heyres, executors, & Administrators for euer: And furthermore, I the abouesd Thom^s withers, do ratify, & Confirme all the abonesd P^rmisses vnto the aboue sayd John Ball his heyrs & Assigns for euer, of & from all manner of P^rson or P^rsons w^tsoeuer, that may P^rtend any Title, or Clame two or Interest in any of the P^rmisses, by vertue of any Deed of Sayle, or gyft or otherwise from him the sayd withers, or any other in his behalfe, vnto ye sayd John Ball or any other in his behalfe, paijng vnto the sayd Thomas Withers, his heyrs executors Administrators & Assigns for euer, three days worke Annually, as an acknowledgment of It being Legally demanded/ In witness w^rof I haue here vnto sett my hand & seale/ Dated in Kittery abouesd, the Day & yeare first aboue written/ 1667.   Thomas Withers ($_{seale}^{his}$)

Signed sealed &
   Deliuered in   y^e 3 days worke y^t Jo^n Ball was
   the P^rsence of us   to pay yearly, to Tho : withers
   Witness William Palmer/ mentioned on y^e other side,
   John Amerideth/   was excepted against y^e sd
                                   Jo^n Ball & allowed of by y^e
                                   sd withers, & from hence
                                   forth standeth voyd & of
                                   none affect/

Book III, Fol. 44, 45.

vera Copia transcribed, & Compared with the originall this 5th of July 1679 p Edw : Rishworth ReCor :

At a meeteing of the Select men the 5th of the 8 Mo 1671 : being P'sent Capt Wincoll Robert Mendum, Christean Ramacke, John Bray/ & Charles Frost/

Kittery
To
Ball

Granted to John Ball tenn Acres of Land, Joyneing to his Land In Spruce Cricke, on the head of his Land, prouided It bee free from former Grants of the Town/

This is a true Coppy taken out of the Town Booke of Kittery this 25th of Novemb' 1678 :

p mee Charles Frost Clers

vera Copia transcribed & Compared with the originall this 5th of July 1679 p Edw Rishworth ReCor :

Robt Jordans
Will

In the name of god Amen, I Robert Jordan Senjor Gentlem̃ : formerly of Spurwinke, & now resident on the Great Ysland in the Townshipe of Portsmouth, I New England, being weake of body, but of sound & P'fect Memory praysed bee God/

Do make ordayne & declare this P'sent writeing, to bee & remajne my last vndoubted will, & Testament in manner & forme ffollowing/

Imp'rs I Bequeath my soule to god, hopeing by the meritts of Christ my Sanjor to Inioy Eternall life, & my body to ye earth to bee decently buried, & what temporall things I am blessed with, all by ye prouidence of [45] almighty God, I giue & bequeath as followeth/

Item I do hereby ratify allow & Confirme two Deeds or writeings Which formerly I made & gaue vnder my hand & Seale one to my Elldest sonn John Jordan, & another to

BOOK III, FOL. 45.

my secund sonn Robert Jordan, according to the Contents y^rin exprest/

Item I giue & grant to my wife Sarah Jordan now Liueing the ould Plantation at Spurwinke, Contayne-
To his Wife   ing one thousand Acres bee It more or less,
begining w^r the Grant belonging to my sonn John Jordan
doth end, & Ending where the Lott bequeathed by this my
Will to my 3d sonn Domimicus Jordan doth begine, & soe
along the high way vntill you come to the greate pond, for
& dureing the Tearme of her naturall life/ The reversion &
Inher'ance y^rof to bee & reamine vnto my youngest sonn
Jeremiah Jordan, his heyres & successors for euer, as his
part & portion/

Item I giue & bequeath vnto my sayd wife Sarah Jordan,
one other farme Called Nonsuch, Contayneing two thousand
Acres bee It more or less, for & dureing her
D^o   naturall life, & for ye more strict obleighing my
childrens duty to her, my will is that shee wholly & absolutely dispose the succession & Inheritance there of, to
either or any of my sonns they, or thejr or any of thejr
heyres or Issew Lawfully by them or any of them begotten
for ever/

Item I giue & bequeath vnto my sonn Dominicus Jordan
one thousand Acres of Land. at Spurwinke to
To Domimicus   begine where the aboue sd ould Plantation End-
eth, as hee shall make Choyce of, to bee layd out by the
ouerseers hereafter Nominated/

Item I Giue & bequeath vnto my sonn Jedediah Jordan,
one thousand Acres of my Land at Spurwinke
To Jedediah   aforesayd, to bee chosen by him out of my Land
not disposed before, to bee to the vss of him & his heyres
for ever/

Item I giue & bequeath vnto my sonn Samuell Jordan by
Reason of his posterity, Choyse of Eleaven hun-
To Sam^{ll}   dred Acres of Land of my sayd Land at Spur-
winke, to bee to the vss of him, & his heyres for ever, &

whatsoeuer part or Prcell of Land remajnes not bequeathed nor giuen of my sayd Lands, at Spurwinke by any or all of the aboue resited & expressed articles, I do hereby giue, & bequeath the same, being vpland, vnto my sonns aboue named, to bee deuided & æqually allotted amongst them/

Item My will is that my Meddow bordering along by the River Spurwinke bee æqually deuided to each portion of the aboue given Land nearest & most Convenjently Adioyning, to each Prcell or portion as is aboue disposed/

Item I giue & bequeath vnto my foure youngest sonns, Namly Dominicus Jedediah Samuell & Jeremiah Jordan to each of them one feather bedd, & bowlsters/

<small>To ye 4 Young-est Sons</small>

Item I make & ordayne my sayd wife Sarah, & my two sonns, John & Robert Jordan, to bee my Joynt executors/

Item I make & hereby ordayne Major Nicho Shapleigh of Kittery Mr Nathl ffryer, & Mr William Bickham Mrchants, to bee oneerseers & to end all differences in any matters ariseing, by means of my not fully expressing my selfe in this my last will & testament between My Legatees, & the executors here of, & to settle all things according to thejre best Judgments, & nearest Intent of this my will, that noe further or future differences may arise/

Lastly/ My will & Intent is, that each & euer of my afore mentioned sonns, there heyrs & successors, shall haue & Imoy, all & singular the aforesayd specifyd Grants, Gyfts, & Legacys, & If any or either of them want Naturall Issew, that then that Legacy shall redown & bee æqually deuided amongst the rest/

Great Y-Iand 28th of January 1678: Mr Robert Jordan Senjor acknowledged this with in written, to bee his last will & testament & was at the same tyme of a sound mind, & Prfect Memory but haueing lost the vse of his hands, Could not signe & seale the same/ & owned alsoe Mr Nathll Fryer to bee one of his onerseers who is Interlynd aboue/ This owned

Book III, Fol. 45, 46.

This will was exhibited in Court July · j : 79 : by Nath͡ll Fryer vnder the Attestation Annexed, & is allowed & ordered to bee ReCorded   Jos : Dudley Ass͡ist͡t

vera Copia of this Will & Testament aboue written transcribed & Compared with originall this 7th day of July one thousand six hundred seaventy nine, & p y͡e County Court allowed, as Attests Edw Rishworth Re Cor/

Emery
To
Robinson

These P͡rsents Testify that I James Emery of Kittery in Pischataqua Riuer Planter, for & In Consideration of finety one pounds in hand payd by Stephen Robinson of Oyster River Carpenter, the receipt w͡rof the sd James Emery hereby acknowledgeth, & of every part & P͡rcell there of doth exonerate release & discharge, the sayd Stephen Robinson his executors, Administrators & Assignes, hath barganed sould alienanted Assignd & sett ouer, And by these P͡rsents doth bargane sell alliene Assigne & sett ouer vnto the sayd Stephen Robinson, all that dwelling house with about finety Acres of vpland bee It more or less, lately the house & Land of Robert Waymouth, of Kittery Deceased; being forty three Pole in bredth scituate, ljing, & being neare ffranks ffort, between the Land of Richard Rogers, & Richd Greene Senjo͡r/ which sayd house & Land, Robert Waymouth bought of John Greene/ To haue & to hould, the sayd house & Land, to him the sayd Stephen Robinson, his executors, Administrators & Assignes for euer/ And the sayd James Emery doth hereby promiss to defend the Title [46] there of, vnto him the sayd Stephen Robinson, his executors, Administrators & Assignes, against all P͡rsons w͡hsoeuer, Claymeing any right title or Interest there vnto/ In witness w͡rof the sayd James Emery hath here vnto sett his hand & seale/ Dated in Portsmouth In Pischataq͡ River The fourth day of December one

Book III, Fol. 46.

thousand six hundred sixty three, & in the finteenth yeare of the Reign of o' Soueraign Ld Charles the secund, King of England, Scotland, France, & Ireland Defend' of the faith &c: 1663:   James Emery/
Signed sealed & Deliverd/
  with the Consent of my wife
  Elizabeth, In y̆ ꝑsence of/
  John Johnson his marke ⊢┼┤
  John Taylo' his marke 𝔱

Richd Stylemā Seer^tv   This Deede was Acknowledged by James Emery this 4th of Decemb' 1663 : before mee
                         Bryan Pendleton Comissio'/
vera Copia transcribed, & Compared with the Originall this 9th day of July 1679   p Edw: Rishworth ReCor.

Robinson
To
Hāmond

To all Christean people, to whome these ꝑsents shall come/ Stephen Robinson of Oyster River In Pischataq̊ sends Greeteing; Know yee y^t I Stephen Robinson, for diverse good Causes, & Considerations mee moueing, there vnto more espetially, for & in Consideration of the some of fourty pounds, in Current Money of New England in hand Receiued, of Joseph Hamonds of Kittery In New England where with I acknowledg my selfe to bee fully satisfyd, Contented, & payd, & of euery part, & P^rcell there of, do hereby acquitt, exonarate, & discharge the sayd Joseph Hammond, & his heyrs for euer, & do hereby sell, Assigne & set ouer vnto Joseph Hāmond of Kittery, his heyrs, executors, Administrators, & Assigns for euer all that fincty acres of Land, bee It more, or less, as It is expressed In the with written Deede of Sayle, to bee to him the sayd Jos. Hāmond, & his heyrs executors, Administrators & Assigns for euer/ In witness w'of the sayd Stephen Robinson, hath heivnto set his hand,

Book III. Fol. 46.

& Seale, this fifth day of Aprill, one thousand six hundred
Seaventy Nine/   Stephen Robinson
Signed, sealed, & Delivered In
  the p'sence of us/   Stephen Robinson Came & acknowl-
  George Broughton/   edged, the aboue Assignem't to bee
  Geo:e Jaffaray/   his free Act & Deed, Aprill 28
        1679 : before mee
         Richd Martyn Com̃isio'
vera Copia transcribed, & with the Originall Compared
this 9th day of July 1679 . p Edw : Rishworth ReCor :

     Kittery 4th M^{o}th 166$\frac{8}{9}$/
Kittery   Granted vnto Stephen Robinson, eighteen
To
Robinson   Acres of vpland, lijng Next behind his own
    Land, w'r hee now dwelleth, prouided It bee not
already granted, or possessed, by any other P'son/
      p mee James Heard Town Clarke/
A true Coppy transcribed & Compared this 9th day of
July 79 : p Edw : Rishworth ReCor :

    I Stephen Robinson do by these P'sents As-
Robinson   signe, & make ouer to Joseph Hamonds & his
To
Hamond   heyres for euer, my full Interest right, & Title,
    to the with in written Grant of Eighteen Acres
of vpland/ witness my hand this fifth of Aprill 1679 :
Testes/   Stephen Robinson/
  Geo Jaffray/   Stephen Robinson Came & acknowledged,
  Geo : Broughton   the aboue assignem't to bee his free Act
       & Deed, 28 Aprill, 1679 : before mee
        Richd Martyn Com̃isso'/
A true Coppy transcribed & Compared this 9th July 79 :
      p Edw . Rishworth ReCor :

BOOK III, FOL. 46.

To all Christean people, That I Abra: Collines of Wells, In the County of yorke shyre Planter, & Pœby my wife, for & In Consideration of ffourty pounds In Moneys to us well made, contented, & payd, by Wilham Sawyear of Wells In the County of Yorke Shyre yeamon, the receipt where of, Wee doe acknowledg by these P^{r}sents: & do for o^r selues, o^r heyrs, executors, Admistrators & Assignes, for euer, quitt & discharge, the sayd Wilham Saywyer, his heyrs executors, Administrators, & assignes y^{r}of, & from euery part, & P^{r}cell thereof, haue given, granted, bargained, & sould vnto the aboue named William Sawyer, his heyrs executors Administrators & Assignes, a parcell of vpland & Meddow, being by æstimation ninety three Acres, of vpland bee It more, or less, & Tenn Acres of sault Marsh Meddow, all lijng in the Town of Wells, being butted, & bounded, vidz^t on the South side p by ye Land of Mary Smyths Land, & on the North side, by the Land of Thomas Wells, being foureteenne pooles wide, or In breadth, with Tenn Acers of vpland at ye Lower end, at the Easterly side, bee It more or less/ & Tenn Acres of sault Marsh Meddow, lijng at the South East End of the Long poynt, with all priuiledges of the Comanes y^{r}vnto belonging, with all ye Land with in fence, & all trees, woods, vnderwoods, mines, mineralls, priuiledges & app^{r}tenances therevnto belonging/ & the Abouesayd Abra Collines & Pœby his wife, do acknowledg that they are ye true & Lawfull owners of the same, & haue full pouer to sell & dispose of ye same/ And y^t It is free & cleare, of all Morgages, Dowers, Titles, Troubles, & Incomberances whatsoeuer: And do warrant ye abouesayd vpland, & Meddow, vnto ye aboue named Willia^m Sawyer, his heyres, executors, administrators, & Assignes for euer against mee my heyrs, executors & Administrators, & any P^{r}son or P^{r}sons w^{t}soeuer from by or vnder mee, Laijng any Clajme, right, Title, or Interest y^{r}vnto by the P^{r}misses. & the aboue sd Abra: Collines, & Phebe his wife, do promiss to vp all writeings Concerneing the same, & vpon

Book III, Fol. 46, 47.

reasonable demand, to make & Seale to any other Instrument for the more Confirmeing of the aboue named Title, Interest, or priuiledg, vnto the Land & Meddow aboue mentioned/ In witness where of Wee haue here vnto sett our hands & Seales, this Twenty sixth day of March, one thousand six hundred seaventy & nine/ 1679 : In the one & Thyrtyeth yeare of our Soueraign Lord Charles King of England Scottland &c : Abraham Collines ($^{his}_{seal}$)

[47] Signed sealed & Deliuered his marke ✗

    In the p̄sence of Phebe Collines/ ($^{her}_{seale}$)

    Jane ℒ Coole

her marke/ Abraham Collines & Phebe his wife
George Pearson/ appeared before mee, & acknowledged this Instrument to bee there Act & Deede/ 26 : 1 M°
1674 Samell Wheelewright
             Assote/

vera Copia of this Instrument with in written transcribed & Compared with the originall this 11th day of July 1679 :
        p Edw · Rishworth ReCor :

To all Christean people to whome these P̄sents shall come/ Dinis Downing of Kittery in the County of yorke In New England bla͠: smyth. send Greeteing/ now know yee that I Dinnis Downeing, for diverse good Causes mee there vnto moueing, more espetially for & in Consideration of the some of tenn pounds in hand received of Joane Dyamont, the Relict or widdow, of William Dyamont of Kittery, lately deceased, w͇ᵗʰ with I acknowledg my selfe to bee fully satisfy'd Contented, & pay'd, & of euery part & P͇ᵣcell thereof do hereby acquit, exonerate, & discharge, the say'd Joane Dyamont her heyrs executors, Administrators & Assigns for euer : Haue given granted sould Aliend Infeoffed & Con-

Book III, Fol. 47.

firmed, And by these P^rsents, do absolutely giue grant sell Alliene Infeoffe & Confirme vnto the aforesayd Joane Dyamont, her heyres, executors, & Assigns for euer, all that Tenn Acres of Land, which was granted to mee by the Town of Kittery, lately possessed by William Dyamont deceased ; To haue & to hould the aboue given and granted, P^rmisses, with all the priuiledges & appurtenances there vnto belonging, or in any ways app^rtayneing to the sayd Joane Dyamont, her heyrs executors, Administrators & Assigns for euer, as thejr own, from mee the sayd Dinis Downing, my heyrs executors Administrators & Assigns with out any Molestation, lett, or hinderance, by mee the sayd Dinis Downing, or any other by from or vnd^r mee, by any Claime or P^rtence whatsoeuer/ In witness w^rof I haue here vnto sett my hand & seale this one & Twenteth day of June, In the yeare of our Lord God, one thousand six hundred seaventy & Nine, & In the Two & thyrteth yeare of the Reign of o^r soueraign L^d, Charles secund, by the Grace of god of England, Scotland, France & Ireland, King, Defend^r of the faith 1679

The marke of

Signed sealed & Delivered/
In the p^sence of us/
John Dyament/
Joseph Hammonds/

Dinnis *D D* Downeing/ (his seale)
Josua Downeing/
The marke of *P*
Patience Downeing/

Great Ysland the 21th of June 1679 ·

Josua Downing in the behalfe of him selfe & patience his wife, & Atturney to Dennis Downeing, Came & acknowledged the aboue Instrum^t to bee his free Act & Deed before mee/

Elyas Styleman Comissio^r

A true Coppy of this Instrum^t transcribed out of the Originall, & there with Compared this 11th day of July 1679.

p Edw: Rishworth ReCor:

Book III, Fol. 47.

Wʳᵃˢ John Wincoll, & Roger Playstead both of Kittery, in the County of yorke, & John Hull of Boston in New England, did by yᵉ deed of sayle dated the Twenty fourth day of Septembʳ sixteen hundred seaventy & three, Sell & make ouer to George & John Broughton, the sonns of Thomas Broughton, one fourth part of the two Salmon Falls Saw Mills, with one fourth part of the runneing geares, & of all vtensills belonging to them, as alsoe a like fourth part of all Tymber Grants & Accomodations belonging to them, with the like fourth part of all the Land, dwelling houses, out houses, with all priuiledges appʳtayneing to the sayd part, to them & their heyres for euer, as may more amply appeare by the sd Deed refereence yʳvnto being had, It being Entred into the 3d booke of ReCords for the County of Yorke pa: j: 12ᵗʰ day 1676 · Now know all men by these Pʳsents that I John Broughton beforesd, by vertue of the Deed abouesd, being the right owner of one eighth part of all the abouesd saw Mills, togeather with one eigth part of all the Pʳticulars expressed to belong vnto them, & haueing full pouer & Just right in my selfe to alienate the same eigth and euery part yʳof; I the sayd John Broughton for good & valewable Considerations, mee there vnto moueing, espetially In Consideration of fourty & one pounds, & tenn shillings in Moneys, which some years past, I stoode & still do stand indebted to Capᵗ John Hull of Boston, & alsoe in Consideration of finety pounds in Moneys, which the sd Hull stands security for mee to Zachary Long of Charles Town Marriner; I say on the Considerations aforesd, I the sd John Broughton haue absolutely given granted, barganed, & sould, aliend, Inffeoffed & Confirmed, & by these Pʳsents do absolutely fully & Clearely giue grant bargan sell aliene Enfeoff assign set ouer & Confirme, vnto the sd Capᵗ John Hull his heyres & Assigns for euer, all that my one eigth part in the saw Mills Tymber Grant, or wʰsoeuer else pʳticularizd belongeth to them, to haue & to hould to him the sayd John Hull, his heyres & Assignes for euer, all the aboue granted Pʳmisses,

Book III, Fol. 47.

whither one eight part of the sd Mills, with Land they stand on, or w'soeuer else belongs to the sd eight part, & the sd John Broughton for him selfe & his heyres executors & Assigns doth Couena^t promiss, & grant two & with the sd John Hull his heyrs & Assigns, that hee the sd Jo^n Broghton hath in himselfe good right & full power, & Lawfull authority, the aboue granted P^{r}misses to sell & Assigne & Assure, & y^t ye same & euery Parcell thereof, is free & Clea . from all other & former Incomberances w^{t}soeuer made done, or suffered to bee done by him or any other vnd^r him, w^{r}by the sd John Hull his heyrs executors or assignes may bee any ways Evicted molested or eiected out of the sd eight part of the sd Saw Mills, or any of the P^{r}misses to ye sd eight part belonging, prouided always & the true Intent & meaneing of the Deed abouesd is y^t If the sd John Broughton his heyres executors or Administrators, shall Well & truely pay vnto ye sd John Hull his heyres executors Administrators or Assignes, the debt of fourty one pounds tenn shillings in Moneys current of New England, & shall farther pay to Zachary Long euery 22th day of Decemb^r foure pounds Anually for six years to come to & fiuety pounds in monys alsoe to ye sd Long, at ye end of ye sd six years, then this Deed to bee voyd & of none effect, otherwise to abide & bee for euer in force & full vertue/ Witness my hand & seale this 7th day of June 1679 :   John Broughton (his Seal)
Signed Seale & Delue^{r}d/

in the P^{r}sence of/   Jo^n Broughton acknowledgd the
John Wincoll/   aboue written Instrum^t with his
Richd Hartopp/   hand & seal to it, to bee his Act
                    & Deed y^s 7th day of June 1679 :
                    before mee Jo^n Wincoll Asso$\overline{\text{te}}$

vera Copia of this Instrume^t transcribed & Compared with y^e originall y^s 25th day of July 1679 :
                    p Edw . Rishworth ReCor ·

[48) To all Christean people, to whome these P'sents shall come/ John Crafford of Kittery, in the County ot yorke shyre, now in the Massatusetts Jurisdiction, in New England, & Elizabeth his wife, send Greeteing, now know yee, that I the aboue mentioned John Crafford, & Elizabeth my wife, for diverse good Causes, & Considerations us hereunto moueing, more espetially for & in Consideration of sixty Acres of Land, received before the signeing & sealeing hereof of Isacke Botts, as may by a deed of Sayle beareing date with these P'sents, more amply appeare, w'with Wee do acknowledg o' selues fully satisfyd, Contented, & payd, & there of & of euery part & P'cell y'of, do acquitt, & for euer dischaige the sayd Isacke Botts, his heyrs & Assigns by these P'sents: Haue absolutety given granted, burganed, sould, aliend, Enfeoffed & Confirmd & by these P'seuts do absolutely giue, grant, bargan, sell, alliene, Enfeoff, & Confirme vnto the aboue named Isacke Botts, a peece or P'cell of Land by measure Twenty Acres with all the wood, & Tymber, that is either standing or lijng vpon the afore-d Land, & all the app'rtenances, & priuiledges thereto belonging, or in any ways appertayneing of w't Nature & kind soeuer, the sd Land being bounded as followeth, vidz't with the highway to the dirty swampe, on the South East End of It, & with y'e Land of Mr Tho. Broughton on the South West side of it, & with the salmon ffall brooke on the North West End, & with Jo'n Craffords Land, on the North East side of It, It being fourty pooles wide on the South East end, & seaventy seaven pooles in length on the South West side, & fourty eight pools wide on the North West end, & sixty eight pooles in length on the North East side/ To haue & to hould aforementioned peece, or P'rcell of Land with all the Wood Tymber & all the appurtenances & priuiledges, y't to belonging, or any ways app'tayneing, to him y'e sayd Isacke Botts, his heyrs & Assignes for euer; & to his onely proper vss, benefitt & behoofe for euer: & the sd John Crafford & Elizabeth his wife, for them selues their heyrs & Assigns do

BOOK III, FOL. 48.

Covenant promiss & grant, to & with the sd Isacke Bott his heyrs & Assigns that the sayd John Crafford & Elizabeth his wife, haue in them selues good right full pouer & lawfull authority, the aboue given, & granted P^rmisses to sell & dispose off, & y^t the same & every part & P^rcell y^rof, are free & Cleare, & freely & Clearely acquitted, exonerated & dischargd of & from all & all manner of former Gyfts, grants, leases, Morgages, wills Intayls Judgmts, executions, pouer of thirds, & all other Incomberances, of w^t nature & kind soeuer, had made done, acknowledged, Committed or suffered to bee done, or comitted, w^rby the sd Isacke Bott his heyrs or assignes, shall or may bee any ways Molested, Euicted, or ejected out of the aboue granted P^rmisses, or any part, or P^rcell thereof, by any P^rson or P^rsons w^tsoeuer, haueing Claymeing, or P^rtending to haue, or Clayme any Legall right, title Interest Clayme, or demand of in & tow the aboue granted P^rmises · & the sayd John Crafford & Elizabeth his wife, do for them selues thejr heyres executors, Administrators, & Assigns, Couenant & promiss, & grant to & with the sayd Isacke Bott, his heyrs, & Assignes, the aboue given & granted peece or P^rcell of Land, with all the priuiledges & appurtenances y^rto belonging, or or any ways app^rtayneing, to warrant & for euer defend p these P^rsents/ In witness w^rof the sayd John Crafford, & Elizabeth his wife, haue here vnto sett thejr hands & seales, the Twenty third day of March, in the yeare of o^r Ld one thousand six hundred seauenty foure, seauenty & fiue, & In y^e Twenty seauenth yeare of the Reign of o^r soueraign Ld Charles the 2cnd of England, Scottland, France, & Ireland, King, Defend^r of the faith/   John Crafford ($^{his}_{seale}$)

Signed sealed & Deliuered   The marke of $\cancel{E}$
  in the P^rsence of us/   Elizabeth Crafford ($^{her}_{seale}$)
  Christopher Banfejld/
  William Gowein/   The aboue sd John Crafford & Elzabeth his wife, appeard before mee this 23d day of March,

Book III, Fol. 48.

167⅜ & did acknowledg the aboue
written Instrume^t to bee y^e Act,
& Deede/

John Wincoll Assotiate/

A true Coppy of this Instrume^t aboue written transcribed out of the originall & there with Compared this 26th day of July 1679: p Edw: Rishworth ReCor:

To all Christean people, to whom these P^{r}sents shall Come/ Moses Spencer Administrator to the Estate of Isacke Botts, & Marrjed to Elizabeth Botts widdow of Isack Botts Deceased, being of Kittery in the County of yorke shyre, now in the Massatusetts Jurisdiction, in New England, & Elizabeth his wife send Greeteing: Now know yee, that I the aboue mentioned Moses Spencer, Administrator to the Estate of Isack Botts, & Elizabeth my wife, for diverse good Causes & Considerations vs here vnto moueing, more espetially for & In Consideration of the some of Twenty three pounds, in hand payd & secured to bee payd before ye signeing, & sealeing hereof, by Walter Alline of Kittery In the County & Coloney aforesd, where with wee acknowledg our selues fully satisfyd Contented & payd, & there of, & of euery part & P^{r}cell there of, do acquitt, & for euer discharge, the sayd Walter Alline, his heyrs & Assigns for euer, by these P^{r}sents, Haue absolutely given granted barganed sould aliend Enfeoffed & Confirmed, & by these P^{r}sents, do absolutely giue grant barganc sell aliene Enfeoff & Confirme vnto the aboue named Walter Alline, a peece or P^{r}cell of Land by measure Twenty Acres, with the dwelling house wood & Tymber, that is either standing or lying vpon the aforesayd Land, & all ye app^{r}tenances & priuiledges thereto belonging, or in any way appertayneing of what nature & kind soener the sayd Land being bounded as followeth, vidz^t with the high way to the Dyrty swampe, on the South East end of it,

& with the Land of Mr Thomas Broughton on the South West side, & with Salmon Falls brooke on the North West End, with ye Land of Joseph Barnard, on the North East side of it, It being fourty pooles wide On the South East end, & seauenty seauen pooles in Length, on the South West side, & fourty eight pooles wide on the North West End, & sixty eight pooles in Length on the North East side/

To haue & to hould, the aboue mentioned peece or P^rcell of Land, with the house wood Tymber, & all the appurtenances, & priuiledges there to belonging, or in any ways app^rtayneing, to him the sayd walter Alline his heyres & Assignes for euer, & to his onely proper vss, benefitt & behoofe for euer, & the sayd Moses Spencer & Elizabeth his wife do for them selues thejr heyres, & Assignes, Covenant promiss, & grant to & with the sayd Walter Alline, his heyrs & Assignes, that they the sayd Moses Spencer & Elizabeth his wife, haue in them selues good right, full power, & Lawfull authority, the aboue given & granted P^rmises, to sell & dispose of, & that ye same & euery part, & parcell y^rof are free & Cleare, & freely & Clearely acquitted exonerated & discharged, from all & all manner of former Gyfts, grants, leases, Morgages, wills Intayls Judgments, executions pouer of thirds, & all other incomberances of what nature & kind soeuer, had made done acknowledged Committed, or suffered to bee done or committed wth by the sayd Walter [49] Alline his heyres or Assignes shall or may any way, bee Molested in, evicted, or Ejected out of the aboue granted P^rmisses, or any part or P^rcell thereof, by any P^rson or P^rsones w^tsoeuer, haueing Clameing or P^rtending to haue or Clayme any Legall right title Interest, Clayme or demand of, in or to the aboue granted P^rmisses, & the sayd Moses Spencer Administrator to the Estate of Isacke Botts & Elizabeth his wife do for them selues thejr heyres, executors Administrators & Assignes, Couenant promiss & grant, to & with the sayd Walter Alline, his heyres executors Administrators & Assignes, the abo.. with the house & all the priuiledges & appurtenances thereto belong-ing, or in any ways app'tayneing to warrant & for euer Defend by these P'sents/ In witness where of the sayd Moses Spencer, & Elizabeth his wife haue here vnto sett thejr hands & seals, this Twenty fifth day of July in the yeare of our Lord one thousand six hundred seaventy nine, & In the Thyrty secund yeare of the Reign of our Soueraign Lord Charles the secund of England Scottland France & Ireland King, Defend' of the faith/

Signed sealed & Deliver'd
In the P'sence of us/
Geo. Broughton
Will · Playstead/
James Playstead/

The marke of
Moses M Spencer (his seale)

Elizabeth Spencer (her seale)

This Instrument acknowledged by Moses Spencer to bee his Act & Deede before mee this 25th of July 1679 : Edw: Rishworth

Assot͠e

vera Copia transcribed, & with the Originall Compared this 29th of July 1679 : p Edw: Rishworth ReCor :

To all Christean people to whom these P'sents shall Come, John Broughton of Kittery In the County of Yorke shyre, now in the Massatusetts Jurisdiction in New England Gentlem͠ : & Abigayle his wife, send Greeteing, where as John Broughton & his brother Geo: Broughton did formerly buy a P'cell of Land being by Estimation three Acres of Mr Roger Playstead Senjo', they being Joynt partners in the sayd purchase, as may appeare by the sayd Playsteads deed, of Sayle beareing date the eighteenth day of Aprill one thousand seauenty & one, reference thereto being had, & since y' they haue bujlt a dwelling house & barne there on/ now know yee that I the aboue sayd John Broughton, & Abigayle my wife, for diverse good Causes & Cons'l ations us there vnto moueing, especially for & In Consideration of the some of six thousand & fiue hundred foote of M^rchtable pine boards, & fiue pounds tenn shillings in Monys of New Eng^ld in hand received of my brother Geo: Broughton, before the signeing & sealeing here of, where with wee do acknowledg our selues fully satisfyd Contented & payd, & do hereby acquitt exonerate, & discharge the sayd Geo: Broughton from euery part & P^rcell there of, by these P^rsents, haue absolutely giuen granted barganed sólld alliened Inffeoffed & Confirmed, & do by these P^rsents absolutely giue grant bargane sell allienc Infeoffe & Confirme vnto the sayd Geo: Broughton the sayd Moeity of the sayd P^rcell of Land which they Joyntly bought of the sayd Playstead, being by Estimation about Three Acres bee It more or less, being next to ye Salmon Fall Mills, & is butted & bounded as followeth vidz^t on the South West side of it with ye high way that goeth down to the Salmon Fall Mills on the East End with the Countrey high way, being in breadth at the Easterly End Eighty & one foote to a Marked poast, & from thence to runne down towards the River, to the vpper end of the Logg fence, & from thence to runne down by the Logg fence to the Salmon falls River, the Westerly end thereof being bounded with the sayd River: To haue & to hould, the sayd his Moeity, of the sayd purchased Land, in partnershipe of the sayd Playstead, with the like Moeity of all the buildings since bujlt thereon, to him the sayd George Broughton his heyres & Assignes for euer, & to y^r onely proper vsse, benefitt, & behoofe for euer/ & the sayd John Broughton & Abigayle his wife, for them selues there heyres executors & Administrators, do Covenant promiss, & Grant to & with the sayd Geo: Broughton, his heyrs executors Administrators & Assigns that they the sayd John Broughton & Abigayle his wife, haue in them selues good right, full pouer, & Lawfull Athority, the aboue given & Granted P^rmisses, to sell, & dispose off: & that the sayd Moeity, & euery part y^rof is free & Cleare, & freely & Clearly acquitted,

exonerated, & discharged, of & from all manner of former Gyfts, grants leases Morgages, wills Intayles Judgments executions, pouer of thirds, & all other of Incomberances of w^t nature & kind soeuer, had made done acknowledged, Committed or suffered to bee done, whereby the sayd George Broughton, his heyres, executors Administrators & Assignes shall, or any ways bee Molested in, Euicted or eiected, out of the aboue barganed P^rmisses, or any part y^rof by any P^rsone or P^rsones, whatsoeuer, haueing Clayīng, or P^rtending to haue or Clayme, any Legall Right title Interest Clayme or Demand of In or two the aboue granted Moeity/ & the sayd John Broughton & Abigayle his wife, do for them selues there heyrs executors Administrators & Couenant promiss & grant to & with the sayd Geo: Broughton his heyres executors Administrators & Assignes the aboue granted Moeity, of Land & houses to warrant & Defend by these P^rsents/ In witness where of [**50**] the sayd John Broughton, & Abigayle Broughton his wife haue here vnto sett thejr hands & Seales, this twenty fourth day of Octob^r In the yeare of our Lord one thousand six hundred seaventy eight, & In the Thyrty first yeare of the Reign of our Soueraigne Lord Charles the 2und (IIth) of England, Scottland France & Ireland King, Defend^r of the faith/   John Broughton (his seale)
Signed Sealed & Deliuer'd   Abigall Broughton (her seale)
In ye P^rsence of/
Thomas Broughton/   John Broughton & Abigall his wife,
Benjã: Barnard/   appeared before mee this nineteenth day of July 1679: & did acknowledg the aboue written deed of sayle, to bee thejre free Act & Deede/
                  John Wincoll Assotiate

A true Coppy of this Instrument transcribed, & with the originall Compared this 29th day of July 1679:
                p Edw: Rishworth ReCor:

Book III, Fol. 50.

Know all men by these P^rsents, that I Edw: Rishworth of yorke ReCo^r : do own & acknowledg my selfe to bee Indebted vnto Mr John Cutt of Portsmouth M^rchant the Just some of seauenty one pounds 19^s & 4d/ fiue pounds w^rof to bee payd in siluer & the remajnd^r being 66·19·4d, In good M^rchatble pay of New England at Current prises, for fiue pounds in siluer borrowed of him, & the remajnd^r for seuerall goods Recued of him according to ye aforesd valew/ for the security of the aforesd some & payment thereof vnto the sd Mr Cutt his heyres or assignes within the Tearme of three years, I the sd Rishworth in the behalfe of my selfe & assigns do by these P^rsents make ouer Morgage & Assign my soole right Title & Interest of my dwelling house y^t I now liue in, ljing ouer against that house wch Hene: Saywoid formerly liued, & his family now liueth in with 34 Acres of Land Adjoyneing to It, & finety Acres of Land more ljing & being on the South West, or Westermost side of yorke bridg, with all the pasturs fejlds Gardens, Inclosurs & all the p^rviledgs & appurtenances y^rto belonging, vnto the sd John Cutt his heyrs & assignes for euer/

The Condition of this obligation Morgage & alienation is such that If the sd Rishworth do pay or Cause to bee payd vnto Mr Jo^n Cutt his heyrs & Assignes the Just some of seauenty one pounds 19s 4d, with in three years tyme from ye date hereof, then this obligation to bee voyd, & of none effect, otherwise to stand In full force pouer & vertue/ I do alsoe make ouer vpon the same obligation & Morgage, that foure Acres of Land, ljing next to Leefe^t Allcocks in yorke, prouided always I reserue pouer to sell It, & make payment of w^t I sell It for to Mr Cutts, & I y^rby pouer to make a sufficient deede of sayle, for the P^rmisses, as witness my hand & seale this 22th day of July 1679· w^ras It is sayd in the Eleauenth lyne onely my selfe & Assignes It is to bee vnderstood, & is Included my heyrs executors or Administrators, w^rvnto I haue afixed my hand & seale, the day &

Book III, Fol. 50.

yeare aboue written/ these Lands aboue written are free from all Incomberances w'soeuer/
Signed sealed & Deliuer'd   Edw: Rishworth (Locus Sigilli)
   In the P'sence of/   Edw: Rishworth came before mee
   Thomas Wills/   & acknowledged this Instrument
   Anthony Nutter/   to bee his Act & Deed this 9th of
   James Levitt/   August 1679:
                         John Wincoll Assotiate.
vera Copia of this Morgage aboue written transcribed out the originall & y'with Compared this 10th day of August 1679:   p Edw: Rishworth ReCor:

Know all men by these P'sents, that I Andrew Everest of Yorke, In the County of Yorke Planter, with the free Consent of my wife Barbery Everest, upon seuerall good Causes & Considerations y'vnto mee espetially moueing, & more espetially for the Just some of sixteen pounds to mee In hand payd by Jeremiah Mowlton of the Town atoresd, where with I own my selfe to bee fully Contented & satisfyd, Do hereby sell giue grant aliene bargan Enfeoff & Confirme from mee my heyrs executors Administrators & Assignes, vnto the sayd Jere: Mowlton his heyrs executors, & Assignes, & haue hereby sould giuen granted aliend barganed Enfeoffed & Confirmed vnto the aforesd Jere: Mowlton, his heyrs executors Administratots & Assigns for euer. A Certen Tract of sault Marsh or Meddow Land, Contayneing by Estimation the quantity of three Acres of Marsh lijng, & being vpon the North West branch of the River of yorke the vpper part there of on the Westermost side of the River goeing to Yorke bridg, bounded on the Northermost part there of, by & next Adioyneing to John Twisdens Marsh, & on the Southermost part extending in Certen P'cells on both sides of the branch of that Cricke, & comes downeward, to the bounds of Mr Edw: Johns   & Abra

Book III, Fol. 50.

Prebles Marshes, vntill the extent of three Acres of Marsh bee Compleated, bee they more or less/ To haue & to hould the sd Tract & quantity of Marsh bee It more or less, as aboue bounded & expressed, with all the Lyber̃tys, priuiledges, Immunitys profetts, Commody%, & all other appurtenances there vnto belonging, or in any wise app'tayneing, from mee the sd Andrew Everest, & my wife Barbnry my heyrs executors Administrators & Assigns, vnto the aforesd Jere. Mowlton his heyrs executors Administrators & Assigns for euer/

And further I the sd Andrew Euerest, do further Couenant & agree with the sd Jere: Mowlton, that the abouesd Marsh is free, & cleare from all titles troubles, Morgages Dowers, alienations, Clayms & all other Incomberances w'soeuer, & the sd Andrew Euerest in the behalfe of him selfe his heyrs executors Administrators, & Assigns, doe warrant, & will defend the same from all P^{r}son & P^{r}sones w'soeuer, that shall make any Clajme to any title Interest or Cajme from by vnder him or them, or by his meanes, or y^r procurement, vnto the sd Jere: Mowlton his heyrs, & Assigns for euer/ In witnes w'of Wee haue herevnto afixed our hands & Seales, this twenteth eight day of Aprill one thousand six hundred seaventy nine, In the one & thirteth yeare of our Soueraign Ld the King, Charles the secund, of England Scotland France & Ireland King, fidej Defensoris, 1679:

Signed sealed & Deliver'd   Andrew Everest ($^{his}_{seale}$)
in the P'sence of   Barbury Everest ($^{her}_{seale}$)
Edw. Rishworth/
Mary Whitte   her marke

     Andrew Everest, & his wife Barbury, owneth this aboue written to bee y^r Act & Deed, this 15th day of July · 79: before mee Edw: Rishworth Assotiate

vera Copia of this Deed transcribed & Compared with y^e originall this 6th of August 79 · p Edw: Rishworth ReCor:

BOOK III, FOL. 51.

[51] Know all men by these P^rsents that I Allexand^r Maxell of yorke, in the County of Yorke Planter, for diverse good Causes, & Consideration there vnto mee moueing, & more espetially for that Naturall affection wch I do beare vnto my beloued brother in Law, John Frost now of the Ysles of shoales fishermā: vpon wch Considerations for the same I do y^t with alone do acknowledg my selfe to bee fully contented & satisfyd do hereby giue grant bargan sell bequeath Assigne make ouer, & Confirme, & haue hereby freely & absolutely given granted barganed sould, bequeathed Assignd, make ouer & Confirmed from mee, my heyres, executors, Administrators or Assigns vnto the sayd John Frost his heyrs executors, Administrators & Assignes, for euer, vidz^t a Certen Tract or quantity of Land, lying & being with in ye P^rcincts of the Town of Yorke, at a Certen place thereof called commanly by the name of Scotland. Adioyneing to a part of my Land, at the vpper end of my pasture, next the way, rangeing along vpon the North East side of a P^rcell of Land which I haue lately taken in, & planted, Contayneing Twenty pooles in breadth, begining at a bla͞: Stumpe about 3 or foure foote of the South East Corner of a small frame, wch the aforesayd John Frost hath lately Erected, & bujlt vpon the sayd Land, & so to runn backe into the woods, vpon the same Lyne that my own Land runneth vpon vntill eight scoore pooles, or soe fare as my owne Land shall further extend, in Length to bee fully Compleated · To haue & to hould the sd Tract or P^rcell of Land, as aboue bounded, with all the rights Lybertys priuilidgs & Imunitys of Tymber, fyre wood, or any other app^rtenances belonging y^r vnto, vnto the sd John Frost his heyrs, & Assigns for euer, prouided always It is to bee vnderstood that John Frost is to Come, & him selfe, & family & hee to Improue the same with in the Tearme of Two years/ & further ye sd Allexand^r Maxell doth reserue, soe much lyberty for him selfe as to sell some trees or Tymber vpon the aforesd Land sometyms (if hee haue Occasion) vp^n which

BOOK III, FOL. 51.

Conditions before excepted, him selfe with the free Consent of his wife Annas Maxell stand hereby Ingaged to warrant & Defend the Title & Interest of the P'misses from all P'son or P'sons w'soeuer clajmeing any right title Interest by from or vnd' mee/ In witness w'of Wee haue set two o' hands & seales, this 2cund day of Novemb' 1678 :

Signed sealed & Deliverd/ Allexand' Maxell
in the P'sence of his marke ⚹ (his seale)
Edw : Rishworth/ Annas Maxell
Arthur Bragdon/
  her marke ⊘ (her seal)

A true Coppy of this Instrum' transcribed, & Compared with the Originall, this 7th of August : 79 :

p Edw : Rishworth ReCor :

Bee It known vnto all men by these P'sents, that I John Whitte Panter haue sould vnto Anthony Emery a house & fejld & all that is belonging to the sayd John Whitte, & the Great barian Marsh, hjng in Sturgeon Cricke, & y° little Marsh that lyeth vpon y° right hand/ & another Marsh w°h is Called Hereges Marsh, on the same side for the some of seaven pounds, Sterlg : to bee payd at Michelmass next, finety shillings, & the next Michalmass Ensewing finety shillings & the last payment fourty shillings/ Dated 15th of Novemb' 1648 & herevnto I putt my hand/

Witnesses/ John Whitte
Daniell Dauis/ his marke ⋈
Renald Jenkins,

his marke ⚹ vera Copia transcribed & Compared
  this 13th August 1679.
  p Edw · Rishworth ReCor :

BOOK III, FOL. 46.

Received the 11th of Novemb^r 1650 · the some of fiue pounds Sterling, in part of payment of this Couenant/ I say Received by mee/   The marke of John Whitte
A true Receipt transcribed & Compared
  with the originall this 12th, of August   ΛΛ
  1679 : p Edw · Rishworth ReCor ·

Know all men by these Presents, that I George Lidden of Kittery, Seaman in Pischataqua Riuer, for a valewable consideration in hand payd, and acknowledged, & my selfe to bee fully satisfyd, Contented, & payd, and doe hereby for mee my heyres, executors, Administrators, & Assigns, & from euery of them for ever, fully & absolutely acquitt, discharge, Edward Clarke his heyres executors Administrators, or Assignes of euery part & P^rcell there of, haue giuen granted bargained & sould, aliend Infeoffed released deliuered, & Confirmed, & do by these Prsents, giue grant bargan, & sell aliene Infeoffe release deliver, & Confirme, vnto the sayd Clarke, his heyrs executors Administrators, & Assignes, the one halfe of a Town Grant of Twenty Acres of Land, the whoole grant of Twenty Acres lying & being In Kittery In Crooked Lane, between the Land of John Ameridath, & Francis Tricky, and the now bargained halfe between the sayd George Lyddens now dwelling house & Francis Trickys with some Much Orchard fence as Commeth with in the sayd halfe, as alsoe all benefitts, profetts, priuiledges, and aduantages whatsoeuer, to & with in the sayd boundary/

To haue & to hould the sayd Land vnto the sayd Clarke, his heyrs executors, Administrators & assigns for euer, and the sayd Lidden for him selfe, his heyrs executors, administrators, & Assignes, & for euery of them doth Couenant & promiss, to & with the sayd Clarke his heyres executors administrators & Assignes, to & with every of them by these Prsents, that all & singular the sayd [52] Premisses, with all profetts & Aduantages, hereby giuen, granted & sould & euery part, & part & Prcell there of, at the tyme of the Insealeing & deliuery of these Presents, are & bee, & at all tymes here after shall bee, and Continew Cleanely acquitted exonerated & discharged, & keept harmeless of & from all & all manner of other barganes, sales, gyfts, grants troubles, or incomberances whatsoeuer, made Committed, suffered or done, or to bee made Committed suffered or done by the sayd Geo: Lidden, his heyrs executors, administrators or assignes, or by any of them, or by any other Prson or Prsons Clajmeing from by or vnder him, them or any of them/ In witness whereof I the sayd Lydden haue put hand & Seale here vnto this Twenty seavēth of Decembr 1672: one thousand six hundred seaventy two/

<table>
<tr><td>The marke of ⚡
John Bugg/</td><td>George Lydden (Locus Sigilli)
Sarah Lydden (her Seale)</td></tr>
<tr><td>The marke ⟊
William Wells/</td><td>her marke ⚡
Georg Lydden Came & acknowledged this aboue Instrument to bee his Act & Deede, this 12th of March 167⅞ before mee Richard Martyne Comissior</td></tr>
</table>

Sarah Lydden Came & did freely surrender her right of Dowry, to the 3d part of the Land aboue expressed vnto Mary Clarke her heyrs & Assigns for euer/ Septembr 13: 1677 before mee Richd Martyne Commissior/

A true Coppy of this Instrument transcribed, & with the originall Compared this 18th of August 1679:

p Edw. Rishworth ReCor:

Book III, Fol. 52.

These Presents shall Ingage mee Saraih Letton, Atturney to my husband George Litten, to acquitt Mary Clarke Widdow & relict of Edw: Clarke deceased, from a bill that my husband had of the sayd Edw. Clarke for foure pounds, for which the sayd bill I haue received full satisfaction of the sd Mary Clarke: I say I do fully acquitt & discharge sayd Mary her heyrs, executors Administrators, & Assignes for euer, as witness my hand this: 13th of Septemb^r 1677:

 Saraih Letton acknowledge the   The marke of
  aboue accquittance to bee her   Saraih Letton G L
  Act & Deede Septemb^r 13:
  1677· before mee
   Richd Martyn Commissio^r/
vera Copia transcribed, & Compared with the ye originall this 19th of August 1679:   p Edw Rishworth R:Cor:

Witness these P^rsents, that I Job Allcocke of Yorke Leefte^t for severall Consideration y^rvnto mee moueing, & more especially for the summe of fourty three pounds already in hand payd mee by Joseph Penwill of Yorke In the County of York Marner, do by these P^rsents giue grant Assigne make ouer & Confirme, vnto the sayd Penwill, my soole right title & Interest, of my house, with halfe the Comanidg belonging y^rvnto, runneing backe into the Woods vpon a North East Lyne, next Adioyneing to the house & Land of Edw: Rishworths, formerly sould vnto him the sd Rishworth by my father John Allcocke, as alsoe Three scoore ffootes of Land squaie Liing & being right before the sayd house, adioyneing to the Northermost side of the fejld of Edw: Rishworth that Lyeth next to Goodwife Dixons Lott, with the garden plott, lijng on the North side of the sayd house, & likewise free & P^rpetuall Lyberty (with out any Interruption) of a Continall passage by Egress &

regress through my Land for fetching of water, prouided
the sayd Penwill see meete to digg a Well at or neare the
River side/ all which houseing Lands Comaniges, with all yᵉ
pruiledges & appurtenances as aboue expressd, app'tayneing & belonging therevnto, I the sayd Allcocke haue given
granted, barganed & sould from mee my heyres executors,
Administrators & Assignes to haue & to hould the same
from all Clajms Titles & Incomberances w'soeuer vnto the
aforesd Jos. Penwill his heyrs & Assigns for euer/ In testimony w'of I haue here vnto afixed my hand & seale, this
sixt day of Janv: 1670:   Job Allcocke (Locu-/sigilli)
Signed sealed & Deliverd   This Instrumᵗ acknowledged p
   in the P'sence of/   Leefᵗ Job Allcocke to bee his
   Edw. Rishworth/   Act & Deede before mee Edw:
   Abra · Browne/   Rishworth Assote/ Sepbr: first
                              1679:

A true Coppy of this Instrumenᵗ transcribed, & Compared
with the Originall, this 28ᵗʰ day of August 1679:
                                   p Edw: Rishworth ReCor:

To all Christean people to whom this p͂sent writeing shall
Come, I Richard Bray of Westquatogoe in the province of
Mayne Planter, send Greteing In our Ld God Euerlasting,
Know yee, that I the sd Richd Bray as well for & In Consideration of the naturall affection, & fatherly Loue, which I
haue & do beare vnto my Well beloued sonn John Bray, as
alsoe for diverse other good Causes, & Codsiderations mee
at this P'sent espetially moueing, haue given, & Granted, &
by these P'sents do absolutely giue grant & Confirme vnto
the sayd John Bray, & to the heyrs of his body Lawfully
begotten, one halfe of all that halfe Ysland, or Yslands, I
Richd haue form͂ly bought of John Cossons, & by yᵉ sayd
Cossons bought of Mr Richd Vines as by a Deede made

vnder the sayd Vines his hand beareing date the eight of Aprill 1645 more Largely will appeare, which Ysland or Yslands, the sd John Cussons likewise bought of M{r} Geo: Cleeues as p a deede vnd{r} his hand beareing date the 22{th} of June one thousand six hundred fourty seaven, will appeare which Ysland or Yslands is Comanly Called & known by the name of Hogg Yland or Cussons his Ysland, lijng and being in midst of Cascoe Bay/ I say I Richd Bray, do by these P{r}sents absolutely giue grant, and Confirme [53] vnto my beloved son one quarter of the afore mentioned Ysland or Yslands vidz{t} one halfe of that halfe I bought of the afore mentioned John Cossons as p a deede vnder the sayd Cossons his hand, beareing date the fourth day of May 1669: more Largely will appeare, togeather with all Lands Marshes Woods vnderwoods Royaltys, of Haukeing hunting fishing & fowleing, & all other priuiledges of w{t} nature soeuer, to the quarter or halfe Moeity doth belong or any wise app{r}tayne/

To haue & to hould the afore mentioned quarter, or halfe Moietie, of the aforementioned Ysland or Yslands as aforesayd, to the aforesayd John Bray, and the heyrs of his body Lawfully begotten for ever, and to his and there own proper vsses, there of & there with to do, & vsse at their Will & pleasure, with out any manner of Challenge, Clayme, or demand of mee Ric Bray, or of any other P{r}son or P{r}sons, by my means Cause Consent or procurement always provided the aforesayd John Bray is not to sell aliene dispose of any manner of ways directly or indirectly of the aforementioned P{r}misses, or any part y{r}of, otherwise then is aboue expressed, vidz{t} for his own vsse, & the heyres of his body Lawfully begotten, and If it should soe happen, that the aforesayd John Bray should dy without Issew Lawfully begotten, then the aforementioned Premisses is to fall to my sonn & his brother Nathan{ll} Bray and his heyres/ And in witness of the treuth of the aboue written P{r}misses, I Rich-

Book III, Fol. 53.

ard Bray haue here vnto set my hand & seale this 24th day of Decembr 1669

Signed Sealed & Deliver'd Richard Bray (Locus Sigilli)
In ye p̄sence of/ witness his marke
William Haines
James Layne Jujor/ William Hajnes aforementioned hath taken his oath before mee, that hee saw Ric: Bray signe seale & Deliver this Deed as his Act this 25th day of August: 79: & yt James Lane was then P̄sent/
Edw: Tyng Assistant:

vera Copia of this Instrumet transcribed & Compared with the originall this 4th of Septebr 1679: p Edw: Rishworth ReCor·

This Indenture made & Conenanted & agreed vpon, between Edw: Stephens now rescident in Boston in New England Taylor & Edw: Budd of Boston Carver, Witnesseth, that the aboues'd Edw: Stephens, hath for a valewable some of money sould & by these P̄sents, do sell make ouer, & Confirme his plantation of vpland, ljing vpon Harricissecke his house or houses, the aforesd Plantation beginning at a mark'd tree on the North side of the River, & ending at the Mouth of the Gutt on the West side, ljing between John Holmans Land, on ye North side, & Thomas Joans his Land on the West side, with fiue Acres of Marsh or ther abouts, ljing with in the Mouth of the westerne Arme in the Easterne Cricke, vnto the aboue sd Edw: Budd his heyrs executors Administrators & Assigns for euer/ to haue & to hould: And further the aboue sayd Edw: Stephens, for him selfe his heyres executors Administrators & Assigns, doth hereby declare that hee hath sould & by these P̄sents doth sell make ouer Establish & Confirme, all the abouesd Lands,

BOOK III, FOL. 53.

house or houses & Meddows, with all thejr priuiledges & appurtenances y^t to them & every part of them is belonging vnto the abouesd Budds, his heyrs executors, administrators & Assignes for euer, warranting & defending vnto the sayd Pity, or partys that hee or they shall haue quiet & peaceable Inioyme^t of the abouesd P^rmisses, with all the priuiledges there vnto belonging with out any Molestation, by any P^rson or P^rsons what soeuer, from by or vnd^r mee, & for the Confirmation here of, the aboue sd Edw · Stephens haue set two his hand & fixed his seale, this twelfth day of March In the yeare of our L^d one thousand six hundred seaventy eight/

Signed sealed & Deliver'd   The marke of   ⌐√   (Locus Sigilli)

    In the P^rsence of us/   Edw : Stephens
    Testes the marke of   This Instrument acknowledged
    Richd Bray ⊗   by Edward Stephens as his Act
    Isacke Cossons/   & Deede March 12th 1678 :
    Samell Mattocks   79 : before mee
    Job Tookie/   Edw : Tyng Assist^t

    vera Copia Transcribed out of the originall, & y^rwith Compared, this 5th of Septemb^r 1679 :
                 p Edw : Rishworth ReCor .

This Indenture made Couenanted, & agreed vpon, between John Redding now rescident In Waymouth in New England Seaman, & Edward Budd of Boston Carver, Witnesseth/ that the abouesd John Redding haue for valewable Considerations In hand received, sould, & by these P^rsents doth sell, make ouer, & Confirme that whoole Tract of his Land lijng in Cascoe Bay, vnto the abouesayd Budd his heyres, executors, Administrators & Assigns, lijng & being bounded by Henery Sickett his River, vpon the West side of the sayd River, which was given vnto the sd Redding by the Select men of the Town of Cascoe Bay, which Tract of Land Contayneth sixty Acres, or there abouts, togeather with all priuiledges, there vnto belonging, being bounded on the North side with a Little River, & on the West side, w'th a Coue, & the other part is bounded with Marked trees/ & that this Tract of Land thus bounded aboue mentioned, was given to the sd John Redding as aboue sayd, may appeare, by the testimony of Richd Bray who was then a Select man In the Town of Cascoe bay, & of Edw. Stephens of the same town/ with a Prcell of Meddow Contayneing fiue Acres, three of it sault Marsh, & two of it vpland, ljng on the West side of Westgostuggo River, & Northwest by the Falls, & bounded westwardly by the Coman Lands, & Eastwardly by the Meddow of Ellner Redding/ to haue & to hould for euer/ & further the aboue sayd John Redding, for him selfe his heyres, executors, administrators, & Assigns, doth hereby declare that hee hath sould, & by these P'sents doth sell, make ouer, establish & Confirme, all the aboue sayd Lands Meddows with all y'r priuiledges, & app'rtenances that to them, & euery part of y'm is belonging, unto the sayd Budd, his heyrs executors administrators & Assigns [54] for euer, warranting & defending vnto the sd party or party's, that hee or they, shall haue quiet & peaceable Inioyment of y'e aboue sd P'rmisses, with all the priuiledges there vnto belonging, with out any Molestation, by any P'rson or P'rsons w'tsoeuer, from by or vnd'r mee, & for the confirmation here of, the abouesd John Redding hath sett to his hand

& fixed his seale, the eighteenth day of February in the yeare of o^r Lord one thousand six hundred seaventy & eight/
Signed sealed & Delive-   The maike of
 red in ye P^{r}sence of us/   John Redding ✗ (Locus Sigilli)
 Isacke Cussons
 Sam̃ll Mattocks/   This Instrument was acknowledged by John Redding to bee his Act & Deede this eighteenth of Febru : 1678 : before mee
   Symon Bradstreet Dep^t Goue^r
A true Coppy of this Instrument transcribed & Compared with the originall this 5th day of Septemb^r 1679 ·
   p Edw · Rishworth ReCor .

Know all men that I Daniell Goodin Senio^r of Kittery in the County of Yorke shyre, In the Massachusetts Colony In New England Planter for, & In Consideration of the naturall Loue & affection that I beare vnto my sonn Daniell Goodin, & for his more Comfortable subsistance now in the world, haue by these P^{r}sents, for my selfe my heyrs executors, & Administrators, them & euery of them, freely given granted alienated, & Confirmed vnto my sd sonn Daniell Goodin, a Certen P^{r}cell of Land Scituate & lijng in the Town of Kittery aforesd, on wch the sayd Goodin formerly built a small dwelling house, in which John Ross liued, & now Daniell Stoone liueth in, & is bounded with the fowling Marsh by the River on the West, & the Land of Daniell Stoone & James Emery on the South, the Land belonging to my selfe, on the East, & the Land of John Greene Senjo^r on the North, It being part of a Grant made to mee by the Town of Kittery, & now by mee the sd Daniell Goodin Senjo^r freely passed ouer & given, with all & singular the app^{r}tenances, & priuiledg^s y^{r}vnto belonging, Contayneing in the whoole by Estimation Twenty Acres more or less/ to haue & to hould to him the sayd Daniell Junjo^r my sonn his heyres executors Administrators & Assignes for euer, with out any molestation Lett or hinderance, of mee the sayd Daniell Goodin Senjo^r, my heyrs executors Administrators or Assignes, or any P^rson or persons vnd^r mee or any ofthem/ & for confirmation of the treuth here of, I the sd Dañll Goodin Senjo^r, haue here vnto set my hand & seale this foure & Twenteth day of May, In the yeare of o^r Ld one thousand six hundred seaventy nine/

Signed Sealed & Deluer'd   Dañll Goodin (Locus Sigilli)

   In the P^rsence of/
Thom^s Abbett/   Senjo^r his
Daniell Stone/   Daniell Goodin Senjo^r   marke
            acknowledged this aboue written Deed
            of Gyft to bee his free Act & Deed,
            y^s 24th of May 1679. before mee
            John Wincoll Assote :

vera Copia of the Instrume^t aboue written transcribed out of ye originall, & y^r with Compared this 27th day of Septemb^r 1679 :   p Edw. Rishworth ReCor.

Know all men by these P^rsents that I Daniell Goodin Senjo^r of Kittery in the County of Yorke shyre, In the Massatusetts Colony in New England Planter, for & In Consideration of Daniell Stone, of the same Town haueing married my daughter, & haueing severall children by her, & for ye naturall Loue I beare vnto my sayd daughter, & to her sayd husband, & all the sd Children, as a part of the Marrage portion of my daughter do by these P^rsents, for my selfe, my heyres executors, and Administrators, freely & absolutely giue grant aliene Infeoff & Confirm vnto the sd Daniell Stoone a P^rcell of Land, scituate & lijng in the Town of Kittery, & Contayneing fiue Acres more or less, as is bounded with ye River at high water marke, on the West, James Emerys Land on wch hee dwelleth, on the South, & the Land of Daniell Goodin Senjo^{r} on the East & on the North, It being part of a grant of Land formerly made by the Town of Kittery vnto mee the sd Daniell Goodin Senjo^{r} & now by mee the sayd Daniell Goodin Senjo^{r} freely passed ouer & given by this deede of Gyft vnto the sayd Daniell Stone To haue & to hould, with all the app^{r}tenances, & priuiledges w^{t}soeuer, there vnto belonging or in any wise app^{r}tayneing, to him the sayd Daniell Stoone, his heyres executors Administrators or Assignes for euer, the same to defend against all P^{r}sons w^{t}soeuer, makeing any Legall Clajme or Title thereto, or to any part or P^{t}cell there of, by from or vnd^{r} mee, my heyrs executors & Administrators for euer, & for Confirmation of the treuth here of I the sd Daniell Goodin Senjo^{r} haue here vnto set my hand & seale, the foure & Twenteth day of May, one thousand six hundred seaventy & nine/

Daniell Goodin Senjo^{r} his marke (Locus Sigilli)

Signed sealed & Deliuerd In ye P^{r}sence of/
Stephen Jenkines/
his marke
Daniell Gooding/

Daniell Goodin Senjo^{r} acknowledged y^{s} aboue written Deede of Gyft to bee his free Act & Deede, this 24th of May 1679. before mee John Wincoll
Assote.

A true Coppy of this Instrum^{t} transcribed, & with the originall Compared this 27th day of Septemb^{r} 1679:

p Edw. Rishworth ReCor:

Book III, Fol. 54, 55.

W̃as there is a difference arisen between John Hord & Abra · Conley both of Sturgeon Cricke, about the devision of a Certen Tract of Land, Joyntly granted vnto y̅e sd Hord & Conley, by y̅e Select men of y̅e Town of Kittery in the yeare 1652: Therefore Wee the sd John Hord & Abra: Conley, do for y̅e finall ending & determining of the abouesd difference Mutually make choyce of Richd Nason, James Emery Christopher Banefejld, & Nicho. Shapleigh as o̅r arbitrators, & Wee the abouesd John Hord & Abra: Conley, obleidg o̅r selues & o̅r heyrs each to other, In the pœnall some of one hundred pounds Sterlg: to stand to & abide, the award Judg̃t & arbiterment of the aboue named arbitratȯrs/ as witness o̅r hands & seales this 28th of y̅e 4th M̃o 1676:

Signed sealed & Deliver̅d in   John Hord (his seale)
  the P̃r̃sence of us/   The marke of

The marke of Peter Wittum/   Abra · Conley (his seale)
John Ross/ his marke

         Its y̅e day Consented to & agreed by Jȯn Hord & Abra: Conley y̅t y̅e lot of Land Joytly granted them shall bee æqually devided between y̅m, with y̅e Necke of Land bordering vpon Stephen Greenhams Lott/

A true Coppy of this agreem̃t   Jȯn Hord/
transcribed & Compared w̃th   the marke of
y̅e originall y̅s 27: Septemb̃r 79:   Abra: Conley
    p Edw. Rishworth ReCor:

[55] W̃as John Hord, & Abraham Conley both of Sturgion Creeke, now deceased made Choyce of the subscribers, as arbitrators for the Ending a difference then depending between the sd Hord & Conley, according to a bond given vnder there hands, & seales beiremg date 28th of 4th

Mo 1676 : Now Wee the arbitrators for the finall ending, & determining of the aforementioned difference, haue measured the breadth, & Length of the Land given us in charge æqually to bee devided, between the aforesd Hord & Conley, & find the iust breadth on & East & West Lyne, begining at a marked hemlocke tree, on the East side two hundred twenty eight pooles, vnto a little brooke or runne of water, on the North East side of Stephen Greenhams Lott, so called, vnto a Marked Ashen tree, formerly marked on foure sides, by the siruayer of ye Town, as Wee are Informed/ therefore Wee do Adiudg & award vnto the sayd John Hord one hundred & foureteen pooles, from the abouesd marked Hemlocke tree West vnto a certen small pine tree neare the Ceaders/ & to Abia · Conley from thence one hundred & fourteen poole more, West, vnto the fore mentioned marked Ash tree, with all the sayd Conleys Improued Lands, liyng & being with in the bounds & Lymitts of John Hord aforesd/ & Wee do alsoe declare that ye deuideing or middle Lyne runnes vpon the North Poynt by marked trees, vnto a stake driven down into the earth, on the Eastward side of the high way, neare vnto William Smyths fejld/ & that this is our full & finall determination, Wee haue herevnto set our hands & seales this 24th 4th M^o 1678 : In kittery/

A true Coppy transcribed & Nicho : Shapleigh (his seale)
Compared with the Origianll Ric · Nason by his (his seale)
this 29th Septr 1679 :   marke ◯
p Edw : Rishworth ReCor   James Emery (his seale)
                             Christopher Banefejld (his seale)

At a County Court houlden at yorke July first
(1679)
This Court doth order that John Evines of Douer, Mr Fran · Hooke, & Anthony Nutter, to bee a Committee vpon

BOOK III, FOL. 55.

the place to vew the Clajms survey the grounds, & finally to determine & settle thejr severall bounds, & make y^r returne y^{r}of to this Court/ Mr Fran · Hooke to appoynt tyme & place of Meeteing, & this to bee finished before the next Court of Assotiates for this County/ This order refers to settle the Land in difference between Nathan Lawde & Nicho · Frost, ljng at Sturgeon Creeke, wch formly was ould Conlys, relateing to ye Case In this Court between Richd Otis & the sd Frost/

vera Copia transcribed out of the ReCords this 29th September 79 ·   p Edw: Rishworth ReCor .

At Sturgeon Creeke the 10th of 7th 1679 .

In obedience to an order of Court held at yorke July 1 · 1679: Wee haue vewed the Clajmes vpon the place w^{ch}on ordered to settle the severall bounds of ye Lands in difference, between Nathan Lawd & Nicho Frost, & relateing to a Case in the sd Court, between Richd Otis & the sayd Frost & finding an obligation vnder the hands of John Hord, & Abra. Conley beareing date the 28th 4th 1676. W^{r}in they bind them selues & thejr heyres each to other, to stand to the determination & finall ending of the deuission of the sayd Land granted between them as doth appeare by the sd bond or obligation of the some of one hundred pounds, that Nicho · Shapleigh Ric Nason James Emery, & Christopher Banefejld being Chosen & appoynted by the sd obligation, who haue given thejr determination by an Instrume^t vnder thejre hands beareing date the 24th 4th 78: vnto wch determination & deuission Otis & Lawde, the survivers of the aboue Hord & Conley, do willingly accept of. Wee haue accordingly vewed thejre bounds & do Judg them to bee æquall/ & In reference to the Land in difference, between Nathan Lawde & Nicho: Frost, according to his Deede Wee haue layd It out as followeth, vidz^t from a little pine tree, being the South West Corner bound marke of John Heads

Land, neare to the place Called the Ceaders, from the sd tree North two hundred twenty & eight rodds, by the Land of Jo[n] Heard to a Stake neare the high way, Joyneing to the Land of William Smyth alias Gowine, from the sayd Stake West seaventy & one Rodds, to a small maple tree marked on foure sides, from the sd tree South Two hundred twenty eight Rodds, to fiue beach trees, growing neare togeather from the sd beach[s] East to the first tree, & the sd Tract being one hundred Acres, & vpward/ Alsoe layd out to the sd Frost, six Acres of Land with Allowance for the ould high way, & Landing place at the Seaders, the sd P[r]cell of Land as It is now within fence at the Seaders togeather: Two Acres of Land on the South West side, of his Land as it is bounded/ & this is o[r] finall end & determination according to order of Court/ as witness o[r] hands & Scales

vera Copia of this determination Francis Hooke (Loous/Sigilli)
transcribed & with the Originall John Evens (his/seale)
Compared this 29th Septemb[r] Anthony Nutter (his/seale)
1679 · p Edw. Rishworth ReCor:

Boston the 10th of June 1679:

Symon Lynde Entereth his Caution against the Inventorijng any of the Estate of Henery Saywod, of the Land & Meddows, w[ch] the sd Hene. Sayword deceased held or occupyed from or by the right of Mr Daniell Epps Senjo[r], which sd lands & Meddows were sould, vnto the sayd Symon Lynde by the sd Daniell Epps, vidz[t] the three farmes or P[r]cells of Lands & Meddows bought by the sd Epps, of Mr Gouch Austine, & Mussy on both sides of Cape Porpus River, as alsoe such a part of the purchase that the sd Mr Epps bought of John & Robert Wadleigh, of Wells as lyeth between the aforesd Cape Porpus River, & Kenebunke River, as by the Deed & ReCord there of may appeare;

Book III, Fol. 55, 56.

Alsoe the sd Symond Lynd Entreth his demand & Claime in & vnto. the halfe part of all the houseing, & Mills Called Mowsom Mills, being vpon or neare Cape Porpus River & the halfe part of all the Land & Meddows, grants & priuiledges for tymber &c. & benefitt in any wise y'vnto belonging, being by the sd Hene: Sayword deceased made ouer vnto the sayd Lynde by a deede of Morgage (in a Clawse w'of the sd Henery Sayword fully acknowledgeth the sd Lynde his right & propriety in & vnto the aboue mentioned Land & Meddows sould him by Mr Epps, & fully Assents thervnto) which aforesd Estate [**56**] by deede of Morgage from the sayd Sayword is forfejted to the sd Lynde; for default of payment of what hee the sd Hene Sayword iustly owed vnto the sayd Lynde, being fiue hundred pounds & vpwards, as may duely appeare vnd^r the sayd Saywords hand, & seale, & hath beene, & is alsoe hereby duely demanded from those that are or may bee Concerned in the sayd Hene: Saywords deceased his Estate/

To Mr Edw: Rishworth ReCor: Symon Lynde/
  for the County of Yorke shyre

In New England/   A true Coppy of this Cawtion transcribed & with the originall Compared this 29th day of Septemb^r 79. p Edw. Rishworth ReCor:

To his very Loueing frejnd, Samll
  Sayword liueing at yorke this Deluer/

Loueing & kind frejnd, my hærty Loue remembred vnto you, & my respects to your Ouncle & Aunt, & so vnto the Select men of the Town, with the rest of my Loueing frends for whose loues sake, I am obleigded to rend^r vnfayned & hærty thankefulness/ The Occasion of my P^{r}sent writeing is such, wch I take little pleasure in, or once Conceiud of, w^n I was last with you, which is to let you vnderstand y^t It is

best in my opinion for mee not to remoue to you: If I should goe thither seekeing to follow other Imploym^ts then my Trade, will not bee to my Comfort, neither redown to yor Contents/ & as for my Trade, for the sake of wch you were pleased Lyberrally to accom̅odate mee, God by his prouidence hath much vnfitted mee the same to follow by reason of an Impediment In my sight, wch doth Inforce mee in great part to leaue it off/ Now my reall desire is that Neither your selfe, nor any other P^rson should bee wronged, so I hope you Sam̅ll, & the rest of my frejnds there, will with such prudence Mannage affayrs there, that I may not bee two much damnifyd in the house/ I know not vnto whom to surrend^r It better then vnto yo^rselfe, & Dadiver. Yet It standing vpon the Land my much respect fiejnd Capt Davess gaue to mee vpon my settleing there, I thinke It most Convenjent to Conferr with him of this matter, whose Assistance & advise I question not will bee most aduantagious, both to you & alsoe to mee/ w^t Capt Davess his Accop^t Cometh to I purpose to giue in w^n hee comes to this Town/ I pray you ord^r the rest with as much discretion as may bee, for the Content of all men concerned herein, onely let mee not loos all/ so at P^rsent I rest yor Loueing fiejnd/
                                             John Knoulton

Aprill 5 : 75. one thing more I did forget/ Two fforks wch I delivered to Mis Sayword wch came to = 00 : 07 : 6 I alsoe left w^n I was there at Thom^s Symsons, one spade y^t Cost mee = 0 : 08 : 6 It one shouell 5^s 6^d, one Mattocke 8^s, these things I know in my worke = 13 6 were little the worse, take y^m yo^rselfe if you do good they cost me in good pay all 22^s/ Alsoe the nayls I sent about the house were Two thousand one hundred/ one Thousand 2^s 6^d p C the rest 1^s 4^d p C y^e Hinges 3^s 6^d /

vera Copia of this letter transcribed & Compared with y^e originall this 11th of Octob^r 79 : p Edw. Rishworth ReCor.

BOOK III, FOL. 56.

Know all men by these P^rsents that Wee Capt John Davess, & Sam^ll Sayword do here sell vnto John Parsons an house, that Jo^n Knoulton had bujlt for him here in Yorke/ Wee do Ingage vnto the sd John Parsons, for to get of the sayd Knoulton, or his Assigns a Legall & a Lawfull bill of sayle/ witness our hands, this in which Consideration wee are to receiue six & Twenty pounds/ Dated this fourteenth of March 1678 :   John Davess

  Sam^ll Sayword Came before mee this   Sam^ll Sayword/
  6th of Octob^r 79 : & owned this
  aboue written to bee his Act &
  Deed/ Edw · Rishworth Assote

Jo^n Davess owned ye same writeing according to his pouer giuen him p John Nowlton/

vera Copia transcribed & Compared with the originall this 12th of Octob^r 1679 :   p Edw : Rishworth ReCor :

W^ras I Sam^ll Sayword of Yorke, In the County of Yorke, received an order from John Knoulton of Ipswich beareing date the 5th of Aprill 1675 : with a request from him w^rby hee did Invest my selfe & Capt John Davess of ye Town afor^esd by his Counsell & Assistance y^rin to Joyne with mee according to o^r best discretion to make sale of his house at yorke to his best advantage, wch accordingly Wee attended & sould vnto John Parsons & accepted his bill, for payment y^rof to the valew of valew of Twenty six pounds, ingageing a Legall bill of sale vnto John Parsons who bought the sd house of us in the sayd Knoultons behalfe, haueing already payd a Considerable part of the sd Moneys, & stands lyable to pay the rest, & the sd Parsons being very solicitous with us by reason of his more then ordinary P^rsent occasions, according to o^r obligations to him vnd^r o^r hands, to giue him a Legall bill of sale in your behalfe, wch neither according to Law nor reason Wee Can fayrely deney/ The P'misses Considered/

Know all men by these P'sents, that Wee Samll Sayword & Joⁿ Davess, both Inhabitants of the Town of Yorke, vnder the Jurisdiction of the Colony of the Massatusetts, In new England, by the order & in the behalfe of Joⁿ Knoulton of Ipswich vnder the same Coloney, vpon good Considerations y^rvnto us moueing as are aboue expressed, & more espetially for, & in Consideration of the Just some of Twenty-six pounds to bee payd in shooes att current prises, already received & accepted, w^tby Wee do acknowledg o^r selues to bee fully Contented payd & satisfyd, & do for o^r selfes, in the behalfe of John Knoulton his heyrs executors Administrators & Assigns, for euer acquit, & discharge the aforesd John Parsons his heyrs executors, administrators, & Assignes, of whom Wee haue received the aforesd some from euery part & Prcell there of, Haue given granted barganed sould Enfeoffed, & Confirmed, & do hereby giue grant bargan sell Infeoff & Confirme, vnto the abouesd Joⁿ Parsons his heyres, executors administrators & Assigns, a Certen dwelling house formerly bujlt by the aforesd Knolton, with all the pruiledges & apprtenances y^rvnto belonging or in any wise app^rtayneing, lijng & being between the houses & Lands of Hen: Symson on the South East, & of Joⁿ Prebles on the North West side y^tof, to the sd Parsons his heyrs & Assigns for euer/ And the aforesd Samll Sayword & John Davess do acknowledg that the sd John Knoulton is the true & Lawfull owner of the sd house, & hath full pouer & authority to dispose there of, & that ye sd house is free & Cleare from all Clajms, morgages Dowers & Incomberances w^tsoeuer, & do hereby warrant the aforesd house, in the behalfe of the sd Joⁿ Knoulton, him selfe his heyrs executors, Administrators & Assignes, from any pson or P^rsons w^tsoeuer, Prtending any Clajme title or Interest there vnto, from by or vnder him, or any else by his procurement, & Wee the sayd Samuell Sayword & John Davess do furth^r

BOOK III, FOL. 56, 57.

Ingage in the behalfe of y[e] sd Knoulton [57] that If neede require, vpon all reasonable demands, that they according to y[r] obligation in his behalfe, shall & will P[r]forme or Cause the sayd Knoulton to do & P[r]forme my other Act or Acts, whither by acknowledgm[t] of these P[r]sents, or giueing liuery & seizein, for the better sure makeing, & Confirmeing of the P[r]misses, vnto the sd John Parsons & his Assigns for euer, according to y[e] true Intent & meaneing here of, & Laws here Established/ In testimony w[r]of Wee haue here vnto afixed our hands & seales, this fifth day of October 1679 :
Signed sealed & Deliverd   Samuell Sayword (Locus Sigilli)
In y[e] P[r]sence of   John Davess/ (His seale)
    Samuell Sayword & John Davess do acknowl-
      edg this Instrument to bee their Act &
      Deede, this 9th of October 1679 · before mee
         Edw · Rishworth Assofc/
A true Coppy transcribed, & with y[e] originall Compared this 12th d. of Octob[r] 1679 p Edw · Rishworth ReCor :

Wee whose names are vnder written, haue layd out vnto John Parsons a Tract of Land, from John Prebles bounds by the highway eleuen rodd, & North & by East, to a blacke burch marked foure square w[ch] is from the high way Eleaven scoore rodd North & by East, the w[ch] Land was formerly granted to the sd John Parsons by the Town, the w[ch] Land is layd out for Twelue Acres, less or more by us the Select men of the Town of Yorke, this 12th of March 1678 :
This aboue written was Entred   The marke of
  into the Town booke of Re-
  Cords this 29th of March   Hene . *HD* Donell/
  1679 : p mee Abra Preble   Job Alcocke/
  Town Clarke/   Nath[ll] Preble
vera Copia transcribed & with y[e] originall Compared this 12th of Octob[r] 1679 . p Edw . Rishworth ReCor ·

Book III, Fol. 57.

Capt John Davess/ this may satisfy you that whereas there was a bond made w'in you Were Ingagd with Mr Rishworth, I neuer Accepted of the bond, nor payd the money, this being all y^t is needefull from your frejnd Robert Elliet/
Great Ysland 2 Septemb^r 1679

vera Copia transcribed & Compard with ye originall this 17th of October 79 : p Edw. Rishworth ReCor :

This 12th day of Febru : in the yeare of our Lord 1674 : In Kenebunke this Deed of Gyft made by mee William Renalds Senjo^r vnto my sonn John Renalds/ Witnesseth these P^{r}sents that I William Renalds senjo^r in Kennebunke with the free Consent of my wife Aylce Renalds for diuerse good causes haue freely giuen to my sonn John Renalds all my whoole Estate, that the Lord hath given mee here vpon earth, that is to say all my Land, trees tymber Meddows houses, cattle or w'euer else to me belongeth, with all the appurtenances belonging to the same, in one kind or another to this sonn of mine, & to his vss for euer/ To haue & to hould keepe & possess, & Imploy for his & there proper vsse, and behoofe as the sayd John shall see meete for his profet in any wise, without any Contradiction of mee or any that belongeth to mee/ And on this Accop^t this our sonn John doth promiss to looke after us, that is to say his aged father & mother & mantayn them, in the best manner hee can vntill they both shall liue, or any one of them liue on the earth/ Seing my sonn doth accept of the same I William & Aylce my wife, haue freely given & alienated this 12th day aboue mentioned, free & full possession into the hands of our sonn all that is aboue mentioned, makeing Null all former Wills & barganes made by mee in this Case, y^t my sonn may not bee depriued of any thing, that hath been in my possession till this day; Onely this in case this our sonn should dy, While either of us William or Aylce doth liue, & doth not take some care in his life tyme, for ye comfortable subsistance dureing thejr liues as may appeare then all shall fall into the hands of William & Aylce as It was before/ this is my free Act as may appeare vnd^r o^r hands/   William Renalds his

Witness us/   marke (Locus Sigilli)
 John Daves/
 Richd Hickes/   Aylce Renalds her
  William Renalds Senjo^r Marke (her seale)
  owneth this Instrument
  aboue written as alsoe
  Aylce his wife ownes the
  same as thejr Act & Deede,
  this 12th of Aprill 1675 :
  before us Edw · Rishworth
  John Wincoll Assotiats/

The aboue written William Renalds, gaue vnto his sonn William Redalds tenn shillings, & vnto his sonn Job Renalds fiue shillings before the sealeing & deliuery of this Deede before us/ E · R   J . Wincoll Ass^{ts}

vera Copia of this Deed aboue written transcribed & Compared with the originall this 18th day of Novemb^r 1679 .
       p Edw : Rishworth ReCor ·

Know all men by these P^{r}sents y^t I Peter Turbet of Cape Porpus haue Couenanted barganed & sould vnto william Renalds of Kenebunke my house & ground, being Two hundred Acres of vpland, with all the Marsh y^{r}vnto belonging, lijng at Kenebunke neare vnto the aforesayd William Renalds, & that the aforesd Peter shall haue lyberty to take away his Corne y^t is now vpon ye ground in tyme Conuenjent. & here vnto I haue set my hand, this 2cund of July 1657:

        Peter Turbet P his marke
 Witness
William Scadlocke/
John Bush/   Saraih Turbet/ her Marke ϒ

  Acknowledged before Ezekell knights Jos: Bolls Commissio⁻

A true Coppy of this Instrument aboue written transcribed & Compared with the originall this 18th day of Novemb⁻ 79:   p Edw: Rishworth ReCor:

  Boston · 3d Septemb⁻ 1679: Neighbour Smyth/

I am troubled that you haue Occasion to send to mee about y⁻ I haue Endeauored to satisfy Justly, what you recouered of mee by Law, though in my own Conscience not iustly your right due/ & for as much as yo⁻ freind Geo: Pearson haueing been often with mee about the P⁻ticulars, how & w⁻h way I payd it, I haue sent you so fare as I Can remember at P⁻sent/ Norton Marshall of Agamenticus made John Readman of Hampton his Deputy/

I payd by M⁻s Gunnisson	16.00:00	All this at P⁻sent I
p Mr Thomas Rucke	02:12:00	Can well remember,
p Mr Richd Woddy	01:10:00	besid⁻ seuerall other
p Fran: Smyth	01:00:00	P⁻ticular somes, w⁻h
p a Rapire Delmer'd him at		at P⁻sent I Cannot
Hen Donells	00:10:00	find w⁻h I did pay
p one peyer of shooes at	0:05:00	to the abouesd John
	£21·17·00	Redmā as Marshalls

        Deputy by pouer of y⁻ execution

There was a tenn Acre Lott in the bounds of Lynn valewed at fifety shillings, which was the full ballance of the execution w⁻h Wee neuer yet receiued; To all the P⁻misses aboue [58] mentioned, I shall bee ready to bee deposed,

Book III, Fol. 58.

when Legally Called, as witness my hand the day & yeare aboue mentioned/   Joseph Armitage/
In ye P^rsence of us/
　Rebechah Thaythes
　her 𐂂 marke/
　George Pearson/

A true Coppy of this letter tran-scribed out of the Originall, & y^rwith Compared this 26th of Novemb^r 1679:
　p Edw: Rishworth RcCor:

Bee It known vnto all men by these P^rsents, that I Edmund Pickeard, of Northan neare Biddiford, In the County of Deavon in ould England, Mariner, ffor & in Con-sideration of one hundred thyrty & fiue pounds In hand payd, by Mr Nath^all Fryer of Pischataqua in New England, M^rchant where with I acknowledg my selfe to bee fully sat-isfyed, do bargane sell, alliene, Assigne, & sett ouer vnto the sayd Nat^ll ffryer, his heyrs, executors, & Assignes for euer, Two shallops with all things belonging vnto them, togeather with a Moreing Cable & Anker, and places of Moreing, where now the sayd Cable, & anker lyeth, at Smuttinose Ysland, on the Ysles of Shoals, as alsoe one Stage, & Stage Rowme, the Title & Interest there of, with flakes, & flake rowme, dwelling house & out housen, possessed & Improued by mee Edmund Pickard aforesayd, & my agent at Smutti-nose Ysland, with all the priuiledges & appurtenances there vnto belonging, & app^rtayneing/ All which P^rmisses I the sd Edmund Pickard do acknowledg, to bee barganed & sould vnto the sayd Fryer & his heyrs for euer: Which stage & flake rowme is scituate between the Stage of Walter Mathews, & the stage & flake Stephen fford, made uss of the last yeare, & the sayd flakerown is against the Meeteing house, at ye Ysland of Smuttinose/ And I the sd Edmund Pickeard, do hereby promiss, to defend the title of the before barganed premisses against all manner of P^rsons from

Book III, Fol. 58.

by or vnder mee, & here vnto I bind mee mine heyres, & executors/ In witness w{r}of I haue here vnto sett my hand & seale, this 13th day of July : 1661 :

Signed sealed & Deliver'd   Edmund Pickeard/ (Locus Sigilli)
In P{r}sence of/   Portsmouth N : E :
Thomas Broughton/   This Instrument aboue was ac-
Elyas Styleman/   knowledged by M{r} Edmud Pickeard to bee his Act & Deede this 13th of July 1661 : before mee Elyas Styleman
                       Commissio{r}/

A true Coppy of this Instrum{t} transcribed out of y{e} originall, & y{r}with Compared this 18th Decemb{r} 79 :
                 p Edw : Rishworth ReCor :

Know all men by these P{r}sents, that I Abraham Preble of the Town of yorke, In the County of yorke, vnder y{e} Coloney of the Jurisdiction of the Massatusetts, In New England Yeamon, for diverse good Causes, & Considerations y{r}vnto mee moueing, & more espetially for the Just some of fourty shillings In good Current pay to mee In hand payd, by John Stouer Senjo{r}, residemg In the Town aforesd, w{r}with I do acknowledg my selfe to bee fully payd, & there with to bee fully Contented & satisfyd, & do for my selfe my heyres executors, & Administrators, for euer acquit & discharge the sayd John Stouer, of whom I received the some aforesd from euery part & P{r}cell thereof, Haue given granted sould, Enfeoffed & Confirmd & do by these P{r}sents give grant sell Enfeoff & Confirme, vnto the aboue named John Stouer, as Assigne of John Laws appoynted by the last County Court, his heyres executors, Administrators & Assigns, a Certen Tract or parcell of ground or Land ljng on the South side of yorke River, formerly Called by the

BOOK III, FOL. 58.

name of Gorgeana, bounded from the Coue opposite to the house, formerly known by the name of Richard Ormesbys house, & the aforesd Coue, Called by the name of the little Coue, vp to y^t Land Called Eddy Poynt : & so backe into the Countrey South South West, vntill twelue Acres of Land bee fully ended & Compleated, there being a small stripp of Marsh about halfe an Acre bee It more or less. Included with in ye aforesayd bounds/

To haue & to hould the aboue named & bounded tract of Land, vpland & Meddow with all the profetts, priviledges Comans Immunitys, & Lybertys of wood Tymber & all other appurtenances belonging vnto the sayd Lands, or to them any ways app^rtajneing, from mee my heyrs executors Administrators & Assigns vnto the aforesd John Stover his heyrs executors administrators & Assigns for euer/ And further I the sd Abra Preble do Covenant & agree with the sd John Stover, y^t the Land aforesd, as fare as hee knows, is tree & Cleare from all Clames bargans sales Morgages, titles, & Incomberances w^tsoeuer, & do by these P^rsents warrant & Defend the same from mee my heyrs executors, Administrators & Assigns, vnto ye sd John Stover his heyrs executors, Administrators & Assigns for euer : from all P^rsons w^tsoeuer P^rtending any Clayme title or Interest by from or vnd^r mee, or any by my procurement/ In witness w^rvnto I haue here vnto afixed my hand & Seale, this twenty seauenth day of Septemb^r 1679   Abra : Preble ($^{Locus}_{Sigill}$)

Signed sealed & Deliverd,   Abra : Preble Came before mee
In the P^rsence of/   this 18th of Decemb^r 1679 &
   Edw · Rishworth/   owned this Instrument to bee
   Andrew Everest/   his Act & Deed
                         Edw Rishworth Assoate

vera Copia of this Instrume^t transcribed, & with y^e originall Compared this 19th of Decemb^r 1679

                 p Edw · Rishworth ReCor :

Wee whose names are here vnderwritten, being appoynted by the last County Court for Yorke Shyre, to run the Lynes between the Towns of Yorke & Kittery, did accordingly on the Two & Twenteth day of October, 1679 : begin at the head of braue boate Harbour, & from thence ran a Lyne North West a little Northwardly, to the station formerly appoynted at the head of Yorke Marshes, & fayrly marked the Trees in the whoole Lyne, & from the sayd station, at the head of the sayd Yorke Marshes, Wee rann a lyne North a little Westwardly, to the South East side of the pond, Called Yorke Pond, & accordingly marked the trees in the lyne, & from the end of the sayd Lyne at the sayd pond Wee rann a lyne North East & by North, vnto a certen spring iseing vnder a rocke on the North [**59**] East side of Totnucke Marshes, that is accompted the bounds between Wells & Kittery; These seuerall stations, being formerly agreed vpon by Commissioners of Seuerall Towns, appoynted & approued of, by former Courts/

vera Copia of this returne compared with the originall, & thence transcribed this 28th d : of Janvary 1679 · p Edw : Rishworth Re Cor .

John Wincoll
John Davess
Charles Frost
Abra . Preble/

Know all men by these P^rsents, that I John Barret of Wells, in the County of Yorke Planter, have barganed & sould vnto Jos : Boolls Senjo^r of Wells Gentle : three acres of Marsh, to haue & to hould, to him the sayd Jos . Boolls, his heyrs, executors, Administrators & Assigns for euer, being bounded as followeth, with Mr Boolls his Marsh on ye one side, & butting on Meribah Littlefejlds, on the Lower end, & Goodm. Austines Marsh on the Southward side, & soe runneing vp to Mr Wheelewrights vpland on the vppard end, for & In Consideration I do acknowledg my selfe to

BOOK III, FOL. 59.

bee fully satisfyd, Contented & payd/ in witness wrvnto I haue set to my hand & seale, this nineteenth day of September 1678: I Elizabeth wife vnto ye sayd
Signed sealed & Deliverd In   John Barret, do Consent
  Prsence of us/   vnto this deed, & do yeild
  Samell Wheelwright/   vp my right of Dowry/
  William Symonds/   John Barret (locus sigill)
  John Barret & Elizabeth his wife,   Elizabeth Barret
    did acknowledg this Instrument   her marke ✝
    to bee yr Act & Deede, before
    us this 19th of Septembr 1678:
Samll Wheelewright Assotes
Willia: Symonds

A true Coppy transcribed & Compared with the originall this 28th d. of Jany: 1679   p Edw: Rishworth ReCor:

To all people, to whome these Prsents shall Come, Peter Cloyce now resident In Salem In the County of Essex, formerly of Wells in the County of Yorke, In New England Yeamon, sendeth Greeting/ Know yee, that I the sd Peter Cloyce for diverse & sundrey Considerations there vnto mee moueing, espetially for & in Consideration of sixty fiue pounds to mee in hand payd, Or secured In the Law to bee payd, by william Frost of Salem aforesayd, Cordwinder, before the Insealeing of these Prsents which I do acknowledg, & there with my selfe fully satisfyd, & payd, Haue bargained & sould, & do by these Prsents absolutely & clearely bargain sell aliene Assign set ouer, & confirme vnto the sayd William Frost, his heyres executors Administrators & Assigns, All that my houseing both dwelling house, barne out houseing, with all these my Land, vpland pasture Meddow, & arable Land lijng in the Town shipp & lymitts of Wells aforesayd that is to say a Certen tract of Land, wch I formerly bought of Francis Littlefeild, lijng & being on the westermost side of that River called by the name of Webhannent River, at y⁰ falls whereon the sayd Francis hath built a saw Mill, & the full breadth of vpland Contayneing Thyrty foure pooles & an halfe, from a marked redd oake tree, at & neare vnto the bridg, next vnto the Lott of Fran : Littlefejld Senjoʳ on the Westermost side there of, & from thence thwart the sayd Land, the dwelling house standeth vpon ; & the sayd Peter Cloyce late lived in, & was forṁly built by mee the sayd Peter, vnto the bounds of that Land formerly Edmund Littletejlds deceased, goeing downward towards the sea South Eastwardly, to the fence a small distance below the high way, & soe to runne backe into the woods so fare in distance & Length, vpon the same lyne, as the lotts of yᵉ Town do extend, excepting the hill one the other side of the sayd River, to the runn against where the Milline standeth, reseruing one poole & an halfe vpward for an high way, for his the sayd Francis proper vss, In wᶜʰ bounds the small Pʳcell of Marsh ljng on the West side of Webhannett River is Included, & a Convenjent high way for Town & Countrey reserved &c : All aboue mentioned more fully appeareing in a deed, from the sd Francis Dated the 6th of Febru · 1673 · alsoe all my right In that two acres of Marsh formerly convayd to mee by ffrancis Littlefejld, & is bounded & expressed as by his Deed to mee beareing date the Twenty first day of May Anno Dom : 1672 : more fully & Largely appeareth, alsoe fiue Acres of Marsh with the vpland there to belonging, bee It more or less, being neare about the one halfe of that tenn Acres of Meddow formerly given mee by the Town of Wells, the one halfe being now barganed & sould with the vpland yʳto belonging, ljng in two stripps on both sides the River, haueing belonging thereto Tenn poole of vpland, ljng on either side soe fare as the sayd Meddow runnes, for convenjency of fenceing, & bounded vpward the River with that halfe I sould formerly to Thomas Baston, & runnes downeward to the River to the Meddow of Thomas Littlefejld, alsoe one hundred Acres of vpland formerly given

BOOK III, FOL. 59, 60.

mee by the Town of Wells, vpon Mary Land Playne so called, & bounded with some Land of Thom^s Littlefejlds to the North, & from the sayd Thomas Littlefejld It extends Southward finety pooles In breadth, & carrys the same breadth East & West, as to make vp the full of one hundred acres, with all my right Title & Interest that I haue, or ought to haue, at the tyme of the sealing of these P^{r}sents, in all the aforesd houseing or Lands with all Comanages profetts priuiledges & app^{r}tenances thereto belonging/

To haue & to hould all & singular the aboue granted, & barganed P^{r}misses, with euery part & P^{r}cell there of, with all the profitts priuiledges & appurtenances, to euery part & parcell therevnto belonging, with all my right title & Interest y^{r}in, vnto the sayd Willm̃. Frost his heyres & Assignes, to his & there owne proper vss benefitt & behoofe for euer/
[60] And I the sd Peter Cloyce do by these p^{r}sents, Covenant promiss for my selfe my heyres, executors & Administrators, to & with the sayd William Frost, his heyres executors & administrators & Assignes, that at & Immediately before the Insealeing of these P^{r}sents, was the true & Lawfull owner of all & singular the afore barganed P^{r}misses, & that I haue good right & lawfull authority in my own name to grant bargan & sell, & Convay ye same as aforesd, & that the sd william Frost his heyrs or Assigns, shall & may be vertue of these P^{r}sents, from tyme to tyme, & at all tyms for euer here after, Lawfully, peaceably & quietly, haue hould occupy & Inioy the aboue granted P^{r}misses, with thejr appurtenances, free & cleare & freely & clearely acquitted & discharged of from all manner of former gyfts, grants, bargans sayls, leases Morgages Joyntures, Dowers Judgm^{ts} executions, forfetures, troubles, & Incomberances w^{t}soener, had made done or suffered to bee done, by mee the sayd Peter Cloyce or my Assigns, at any tyme or tyms, before the sealeing & Deliuery of these P^{r}sents, & I ye sayd Peter Cloyce, my heyrs executors & Administrators, shall & will from . . . . grant &

Defend the aboue granted Pᵣmisses, with yʳ appurtenances, & euery part & Pʳcell yʳof/ And alsoe my wife Hannah doth freely yejld vp all her right title Dower & Interest yʳin vnto the sayd william Frost his heyrs & Assigns for euer, against all & euery Pson laijng Clame yʳto, or any part yʳof by from or vnder us, or either of oʳ heyrs executors or Administrators/ In witness wʳof I the sayd Peter Cloyce & Hannah my wife, haue set to our hands & Scales this seauenth day of April in the yeare of our Lord one thousand six hundred seaventy & nine, Annoq̣ Regni Regis Caroli secundj xxxi :

The signe of Peter
Signed sealed & Deliuerd   Cloyce 𝓟 (loens Sigilli)
  In the Psence of us/
  Hilliard veren Senjoʳ/   The marke of
  Hilliard veren Jujoʳ/   Hannah Cloyee H (her seule)
to yᵉ Deliuery of Peter Cloyce/

    Peter Cloyce owns this to bee his Act & Deede, & Hannah his wife fiely yejlded vp her 3ds 14 . 2cūd : 79 : before mee Witt . Hawthorne Assisᵗ

Entred in the Margent by Consent of both partys before signeing sealing Memorandum It is agreed vpon, & the true Intent & meaneing of these Pˢents, wᵗsoeuer may bee to yᵉ contrary expressd, that I the sd Peter Cloyce do sell onely, all my right & title that I now haue in the sd one hundred Acres vpon Mary Land Playne, & do noe furthʳ warrant yᵗ Pʳcell of Land/

vera Copia of this Instrument aboue written, with yᵉ postscript transcribed out of the originall, & there with Compared this 30th day of Janvary 1679, as Attests, Edw : Rishworth ReCor :

Know all men by these Pʳsents, that I william Frost, & Mary my wife, do assign all the Pʳmises mentioned In the with in Deed, vnto ffra Littlefejld of Wells, his heyrs executors administrators & assigns for euer/ And do hereby acknowl- edg full satisfaction, & payment received for the ··· of &

from which Wee our heyrs executors & Administrators, do for euer discharge & acquitt, the sd Fran: Littlefejld his heyres executors administrators & Assigns, & do further Ingage that all the sayd with in mentioned P'misses in the Deed, is now free & Cleare and for euer freely & Clearely acquitted, and dischaiged from all former gyfts grants barganes sales, forfiturs leases Morgages Joynturs Judgm^{ts} executions, troubles, & Incomberances w^tsoeuer; And Wee do lastly Ingage that Wee our heyres executors, & Administrators, and euery & all of them shall & Will from tyme to tyme, & all tyms for euer here after warrant & Defend all the within granted P'misses, with all y^r appurtenances & priuiledges, there vnto belonging, & euery part & Picell there of, to the sayd Fran: Littlefejld his heyrs executors administrators & Assigns, from all P'rsons whatsoeuer, laijng Clajme there vnto/ In witness whereof, wee haue here vnto sett our hands & seals this three & twenteth day of Decemb^r one thousand six hundred seaventy Nine 1679:

Signed sealed &	Willia: Frost (Locus Sigilli)
Deliuer'd In the	his marke W
P'sence of us/	The marke of
Ele. Hathorne/	Mary Frost ⊓ (her scale)
Nathall Cloyce/	William Frost & Mary his Wife owned the aboue writeing, to bee y^r Act & Deed, and freely Consented y^rvnto, before mee this 23th of Decemb^r 1679.

        Samll Wheelewright Assote

A true Coppy of Peter Cloyce his Deed to Will Frost, & of Will Frost his Assigne^t y^rof vnto Fran: Littlefeld of Wells, transcribed out of the originall, & y^rwith Compared this 31th day of Janv'ry 1679:

        p Edw: Rishworth ReCor:

BOOK III, FOL. 60, 61.

This Indenture or bill of sale made this eighteenth of Novemb^r in the yeare of our Lord god one thousand six hundred seaventy & eight, & In thirtoth yeare of the Reign of Charles the secund, of England Scotland France & Ireland King: Witnesseth that I John Twisden of Yorke In the County of Yorke Shyre, being appoynted Administrator by the County Court held at Wells the first Tuesday In July last past, of the Estate of Joseph Alleocke late of Kittery deceased, haue by vertue of an order of the sayd Court, bargained sould & Deliuered, & made ouer for a valewable consideration in hand Receiued vnto Mr Shuball Dumer of Yorke in the County of yorke shyre aforesd, the one halfe or moeity of the Necke of Land, Comanly & properly known by the name of Farmer Alleocks Necke, lijng in yorke aforesd neare the Rivers Mouth, as alsoe a Prcell of meddow or sault Marsh, contayneing foure Acres be It more or less, lijng & being on the Westerne branch of Yorke River, being formerly known by the name of Farmer Allcocks Marsh, all which Necke of Land & Marsh aforesd, I the sd John [61] Twisden haue sould alienated Confirmed & set over, & do by these P^r alienate & Confirme, the aboue sd halfe part or moeity of the aforesd Necke of Land & Marsh to him the sayd Shuball Dumer, to haue & to hould to him his heyres executors administrators & Assigns for euer, quietly & peaceably to inioy with out Let hinderance or Molestation, from mee John Twisden mine heyrs executors administrators & Assigns, & I do by these P^rsents warrant & confirme all the aboue sayd P^rmisses, from all P^rson or P^rsons w^tsoeuer, from by or through my meanes, or any vnder mee, & I the sd John Twisden do by these P^rsents alienate ratify & Confirme all the aboue sd P^rmisses with all the p^ruiledges & app^rtenances y^rvnto belonging, vnto the sd Shuball Dummer, to him his heyrs executors, administrators & Assigns for euer, to all which I the sd John Twisden do bind mee my heyrs executors Administrators & Assigns to

BOOK III, FOL. 61.

ratify & Confirme, w^rvnto I haue set my hand & seale, the day & yeare aboue written/

Signed sealed & Deluei̇d   John Twisden (Locus Sigilli)

In the P^rsence of,   This Instrument acknowledged by
Fran: Johnson/   Jo^n Twisden to bee his Act &
Mary Davess   Deede, & by this Court allowed &
her marke *ND*   Confirmed in Court, this 19th of
     Novemb^r 1678 · As Attests
      Edw · Rishworth ReCor.

vera Copia transcribed & compared with the originall this 17th of Febru 1679 :   p Edw Rishworth ReCor :

This Indenture made between Allexand^r Rigby of Rigby, In the County of Lancaster in the kingdome of England Esqr on the first Party, & William Ryall of Cascoe, in the Province of Lygonia in New England in America Gentle:̃ on the Secund Party, & George Cleeue & Michaell Mitton of Cascoe aforesd, Gentlemen vpon the third Party, Witnesseth that the sayd Allexander Rigby for diverse good causes & considerations him there vnto moueing. doth by these P^rsents, grant Infeoff & Confirme vnto the sayd William Ryall his heyres, & Assigns for ever, all that one Messuage or Mantion house, in Lygonja aforesd, wch hee the sayd William Ryall now Inhabiteth, & all gardens Courts & Curtillges there vnto belonging, & alsoe all that Parcell of Land now or late in the possession or occupation of the sayd William Ryall contemeing Thyrty Acres of Land or neare there abouts, & vsually occupied with the sayd Messuage, as therevnto belonging, and bounded in manner following, that is to say on the West & North sides thereof, with a Cricke & Crickes Mouth running on the backe side of ye sayd Messuage on the South side thereof, with the sea, & on the East side there of, with the Land of Arnold Alline, and all y^t Ysland called Ryalls Ysland Conteineing Twenty

Acres of Land or y^r abouts, & lijng before the sayd Messuage or Mansion house, & alsoe all y^t Necke or other P^rcell of conteinening Two hundred & finety Acres of Land bounded on the South side there of, with the River of Westgustuggoe, & on the North side with the River of Shushquisacke, the East end of which sayd last mentioned Parcell of Land, is about foure poole ouer, with all & singular Woods, vnderwoods, waters water Courses Mines Mineralls, & quarrys w^tsoeuer in and vpon the sayd Granted P^rmisses, To haue & to hould the sayd Messuage Lands Yslands & P^rmisses, before by these P^rsents mentioned to bee granted, with these & every of thejr app^rtenances, to the sayd William Ryall his heyrs & Assigns for euer, of the sayd Allexander Rigby his heyres & Assignes, in free & comon soccake doeing y^rfore fealty vnto the sd Allexander Rigby his heyrs & Assigns & Yeilding & paijng y^rforo yearely, vnto the sd Allexander Rigby his heyrs & Assigns for ever, soo many severall somes of one farthing of Lawfull money as there are severall acres of Land in the P^rmisses, before by these P^rsents mentioned, to bee granted in & vpon the first day of Aprill, and the first day of October yearly, by even & æquall P^rcells for all demands, by the sayd Allexander Rigby his heyres & Assigns, & If It shall happen the sd yearely Rent before by these P^rsents reserved vnto the sayd Allexand^r Rigby, his heyrs or assigns or any part there of to bee arreare & vnpayd at any day w^rin the same ought to bee payd, then & in such case, It shall bee Lawfull two & for the sayd Allexand^r Rigby, his heyrs & assigns into ye sd Messuage Lands & P^rmisses, or any part y^rof, to Enter & distreine, & the distress then & thejr found, to leade drive chase & carry away & the same to detayn & keepe, vntill such tyme or tyms as hee or they shall bee fully satisfyd Contented & payd. the sayd Annuall Rent & the arrears thereof, & the sd William Ryall his heyrs & Assigns, shall from hence forth pay vnto ye King of England, his heyrs & successors one fifth part of all the gould & silu^r Oare to bee had & found in & vpon

the sayd Land herein before mentioned to bee Granted, &
shall alsoe from henceforth yearely pay vnto the Counsell
established at Plymouth in the County of Deavon for the
Planting ruleing ordering & governing of New England
aforesd & thejr successors for euer, one pecke of the best
bread Corne, accompting two gallons after Winchester
Measure to euery pecke, for euery hundred acres of the sayd
Land before by these P^rsents granted/ And It is hereby
declared that ye Acres aboue mentioned are intended to bee
accompted after the Measure of fiue yards & an halfe to a
peaich, & eight scoore pearches in Length & one pearch in
breadth to euery acre, And It is hereby granted & agreed
by & between all the sayd Partys to these P^rsents y^t It shall
& may bee Lawfull to & for the sayd Allexand^r Rigby his
heyrs, & his Assigns & his & thejr substitutes, to survay &
measure the sayd Lands before by these P^rsents granted at
any tyme or tymes [62] hereafter to the intent that the
mettes bounds & Lymitts there may bee known & distin
guished the aforesayd yearely rents ascertajned, & Injury &
Wrong on all sides P^rvented/ and the sayd Allexander
Rigby doth hereby make ordayne Constitute, & In his place
put the sayd George Cleeue & Michaell Mitton his true &
Lawfull Atturneys Joyntly & Seveially to take possession
for him, & in his name in the sayd Messuage, Lands & P^rm-
isses before by these P^rsents mentioned to bee granted, &
after such possession taken & had, then for him & in his
name deliver full & peaceable possession & seizine vnto y^e
sayd William Ryall or to his certen Atturney in this behalfe
according to the tenour force forme & æffect of this P^rsent
Indenture there of made & what the sayd Atturneys or
either of them shall do in the P^rmisses the sayd Allexander
Rigby doth hereby ratify & Confirme the same/ And in
testimony hereof the sayd Partys haue to these P^rsents, to
the severall Parts thereof Interchangeable set thejr hands &

seales, this thirteenth day of Aprill in the yeare of o^r Lord
God, one thousand six hundred fourty six/

Sealed & Deliuered,   Allexander Rigby (Locus Sigilli)
  In the P^rsence of,
  Thomas Leigh/   vera Copia, of this Instrument aboue
  Allexand^r Rigby/   written transcribed out of the orig-
  Edw: Rigby/   inall, & there with Compared, this
  John Watson/   23th day of Febru. 1679:
          p Edw. Rishworth ReCor:

To all Christen people to whom this P^rsent writeing shall Come, I William Ryall Senjo^r of Westgostucko In the Province of Mayne Planter, send Greeteing In our Lord God Eeuerlasting/

Know yee that I the sayd William Ryall, as well for the naturall affection & fatherly loue, which I haue and do beare vnto my Well beloued Sonns, William Ryall, & John Ryall, as alsoe for other good Causes & Considerations hereafter mentioned, haue given granted & by these P^rsents, do absolutely give grant & Confirme vnto my afore mentioned sonns William Ryall and John Ryall all that Land & Marsh vpon or belonging to that Necke of Land lijng & being betwixt Wesgostucko River, & Chesquissicke River & vpon which my dwelling house now standeth, & is bounded as hereafter followeth, That is to say on the one side, with Chusquisset River & vp the sayd River, vnto the first Cricke in that River and on the other side with Westgotoggo River, & vp the sayd River to the hiest Marsh in that River, & so cross ye Land from the first Cricke (in Cusquisecke River) to the hyest Marsh In Westgotogoe River/ & after my decease the sayd Land & Marsh to bee æqually devided betwixt them as they can agree between them selues/ If not indifferent men chosen between them & William Ryall is to haue his first Choyce/ & so I say I William Ryall do hereby ... rely

Book III, Fol. 62.

give grant & Confirme vnto my afore mentioned sonns William & John & to y^r heyrs & Assigns for euer, all the afore mentioned Tract of Land & Marsh, with all the Lands Marshes woods Tymber, trees vnder woods fejlds houses, gardens & all other priuiledges profetts of what nature soe euer, is belonging, or any ways appertayneing to afore mentioned P'misses/ To haue & to hould to the onely vss & behoofe of the afore mentioned William Ryall, & John Ryall thejre heyrs & Assignes for euer, which is vpon these Considerations following/

1: ffirst the sayd William Ryall & John Ryall are to provide for mee and my wife Phœby, sufficient meate drinke & apparell tendance & Phisicke (if neede require) and all other necessarys meet & convenjent for people of our ages dureing our Naturall liues/

2: Secundly they are not to dispose nor any ways alienate ye premisses or any part thereof, dureing our naturall lifes/

3: Thirdly, In case the sayd William Ryall & John Ryall shall omitt there duty in prouiding for mee and my wife Phebie dureing our naturall lifes, as before is expressed, It shall bee in my pouer & at my will to resume & take the afore mentioned P'misses into my hand, & to bee at my disposall agajne/

And In witness of the treuth hereof, I William Ryall haue herevnto set my hand & seale this Twenty eight day of March one thousand six hundred seaventy three/ 1673.

Signed sealed & Deliuered, In   William Ryall (Locus Sigilli)

the P'sence of us/

ffrancis Neale/
Richard Bray/
his marke

A true Coppy of this Instrument aboue written transcribed out of the originall & therewith Compared this 23^d day of ffebru: (1679)

p Edw: Rishworth ReCor:

[63] Know all men by these P^rsents, that John Wentworth now of Yorke in the County of Yorke Planter, with & by the free Consent of my wife Marthah, do vpon good and valewable Considerations therevnto mee moueing, & more especially for the some of fourty pounds in good M^rchantble pay to mee In hand payd already where with I am fully Contented & satisfyd, do hereby giue grant bargan sell & Confirme vnto Isacke Parker of ye Town aforesd, Planter, And by these Prsents, haue given granted barganed sould & Confirmed from mee my heyrs executors administrators & Assigns, vnto the sayd Isacke Parker his heyrs, executors administrators & Assigns for euer, a Certen Tract or Lott of vpland, contajneing ye full quantity & proportion of fiueteen Acres of Land, w^ron I haue built a small house or Tenement, & fenced in some small part of it, which is or at least was, broaken vp & planted, lijng & being vpon the North East side of the path, wch goeth from the Town of Yorke vnto Henery Saywords house, Containeing the breadth of Twenty two Pools, & an halfe, bounded on the East side with a Lott of Sargeant John Twisdens, & on the West side with Lewis Beanes Lott, & soe to runne backe into the Countrey vpon a North & by East Lyne, vntill fineteen Acres bee fully Compleated; And alsoe another Tract of Land, Contajneing the quantity of Twenty acres of vpland as an Addition y^rvnto. given & granted vnto Isacke Everest form̅ly by the Town of yorke, by whom this Twenty Acres, & the other fiueteen Acres was sould to mee, by the aforesd Isacke Everest, which Twenty Acres begineth at the head of my home Lott, & so to runne ye full Length & breadth thereof backeward, vntill the full Twenty acres bee expired, as by the sayd Town grant doth more fully appear To haue & to hould, the sayd Tract of Land, & house as aboue mentioned, with all the Tymber, Woods vnd^r Woods, & all other profetts, priviledges & Immunitys y^rvnto belonging or any ways app^rtaineing I the sd John Wentworth from my selfe, my heyrs executors administrators & Assigns, do hereby

ratify grant & confirme to ye aforsd Isacke Parker his heyrs executors, administrators & Assigns for euer, & I the sd Wentworth do Covenant & promiss to & with the sayd Parker, that ye sd house & Lands are free & Cleare from all Claymes Trouble & Incomberances w^tsoener, & that in the behalfe of my selfe my heyrs executors, administrators & Assigns, will by these P^rsents defend & saue harmeless the sayd Isacke Parker, his heyrs & Assigns from all P^rsons w^tsoener, Clajmeing Or P^rtending to Claime any right Title or Interest, from by or vnder mee, or by my procureme^t In witness w^rof I haue here vnto afixed my hand & seale this 28th of August Anno: Dom͞ 1679.

Signed sealed & deliuered,   John Wentworth (Locus Sigilli)

In ye P^rsence of/
Mary Whitte/   his marke ʒ

    John Wentworth owneth this Instrum^t aboue written, to bee his Act & Deede, this 28th of August 1679: before mee Edw: Rishworth Assotiate/

A true Coppy of this Instrume^t transcribed, & with the originall Compared this 5th of March 16⅞

           p Edw · Rishworth ReCor:

Know all men by these P^rsents that John Green senjo^r & Julian his wife of Kittery In the County of Yorke shyre, or province of Mayne, in New England for diuerse good causes & Considerations, them moneing there vnto, espetially in Consideration of an Ingagem^t made by Thomas Abbet of the same Town, vnto the aforesd John Green Senjo^r, & Julian his sd wife, for y^r Comfortable mantenāce dureing the whoole tyme of y^r naturall lifes, as may more amply appeare by ye sayd Ingagem^t vnder the hand & seale of the sayd Thom^s Abbett & beareing date here with, haue absolutely given granted barganed sould Inffeoffed & Confirmed & do by these P^rsents for v---shues, their heyrs executors &

Book III, Fol. 63.

Administrators, giue grant bargan sell, Enfeoff & Confirme vnto yᵉ aforesd Thomˢ Abbett, one Messuage or Tenement scituate & being in the Town of Kittery aforesd, & is the homestall of the sd Green on which hee now liveth, contayneing one dwelling house out houseing, one oarchard pastures Corne fejlds & wood Lands by Estimation, about fiuety foure Acres more or less, as It is now bounded with the great River of Newgewanacke, on yᵉ West, & the Land of Daniell Goodine on the South, the Land of Joⁿ Searle on the East, & the Land of the aforesd Tho: Abbet, & of Peter Grant on the North, the aforesd P'cell of Land was formerly granted by the Town of Kittery to the sayd John Green, & now by the sd John Green & Julian his wife sould vnto the sayd Tho · Abbett/ To haue & to hould, all & singular the p͂misses, with all the appurtenances & priuiledges y'vnto belonging, or any wise appertayneing, to him yᵉ sayd Thomˢ Abbett his heyres executors, administrators or Assigns for euer/ & further yᵉ sd Joⁿ Green & his wife vpon yᵉ considerations aforesd, haue sould vnto yᵉ sᵈ Thomˢ Abbet yʳ P'sent stocke of Neate Cattle (excepting one Cow) wᶜʰ they keepe at yʳ own disposeing/ & alsoe the sd Abbet is to haue & Inioy, yᵉ halfe of the sayd Greens P'sent stocke of swine/ & for Confirmation of the treuth of all the P'misses the aforesd Joⁿ Green Senjoʳ & Julian his wife, haue here vnto set yʳ hands & seales the first day March in yᵉ yeare of oʳ Ld one thousand six hundred seaventy nine & eighty/

Signed sealed & Deliud   Joⁿ Green his
  in the p͂sence of us/
  Geo: Broughton/ Daniell   marke ⟂ (his seale)
  Stoon/ Ephraim Joy   Julian Green
  his marke ⟂   her marke ん (her seale)

    John Green Senjoʳ & Julian his wife, acknowledged this
    aboue written deede of sayle to bee yʳ free Act &
    Deed, this first of March 16⁷⁹⁄₈₀ John Wincoll
                                         Assotiate/
vera Copia transcribed & Compared 16: March 1⸱⸱⸱ : 80
                             p Edw: Rishworth ReCoʳ.

BOOK III, FOL. 64.

[64] 12th of Aprill · 1654/

Granted vnto Mr Richard Leader, by the Select Townsmen for Kittery all the pine trees vp the Little River soe fare as the bounds of yͤ Town Kittery goeth, for the accommodations of his Mill, onely excepting Tom Tinkers Swampe & the near swampe aboue It on yͤ East side of the little river, which swamps are granted & giuen to Humfrey Chadborne, & Thomˢ Spencer, & It is here to bee vnderstoode, yᵗ Mr Richd Leadʳ is to pay In Consideration of this his grant for Tymber vnto his Mill, fueteen pounds a yeare vnto yͤ Town of Kittery It being Demanded/

A true Coppy taken the 27th of Aprill, 1654/

        p mee Humphrey Chadborne Town Clař ·

A true Coppy transcribed, & Compared with yͤ originall this 27th of March 16⅝   p Edw. Rishworth ReCor ·

To all Christean people to whom these Pʳsents shall Come/ Richd Abbett of Kittery In the County of Yorke shyre, now in the Massatusetts Jurisdiction in New England & Elizabeth his wife, Send Greeteing : Know yee yᵗ I yͤ aboue mentioned Richd Abbett, & Elizabeth my wife for diverse good Causes & Considerations vs hereunto moueing, more espetially for & in Consideration of thyrty pounds, in Mʳchᵗble pine boards, at fourty fiue shillings p thousand already in hand received before yͤ signeing & sealeing hereof, of Thomas Parkes of Kittery, & in the County & Colony abovesd, wʳwith Wee acknowledg, oʳ selues fully satisfyd, Contented & payd, & yʳof & of euery part & Pʳcell yʳof, do acquitt & for euer discharge, the sd Tho Parkes his heyrs & Assigns by these Pʳsents haue absolutely given granted barganed sould aliened Infeoffed & Confirmed, & by these Pʳsents do absolutely giue grant, bargane sell alliene Infeoff & Confirme vnto yͤ aboue named Thomas Parkes, a peece & P· · · · · · · · · · · · · · · · · · · · es, lying neare a Certen place Comanly Called & known by the name of Post Wigwame, being one hundred & twenty pooles in Length, from Newgewanacke River North West, & by north, & In breadth finety & three Rodds and an halfe, North East & by East, & South West & by West, bounded on the South West with the Land of Phyneas Hull, & on the South East with the River, on the North East, with the Land of y² sd Richd Abbett, & on the North West with y² Comans, with foure pooles in breadth, at y² North West end of the sd Land, in lew of the high way, passing through it, with all the Woods & Tymber y⁴ is either standing or lijng vpon the Land aforesd, excepting the pine Tymber, belonging to Mʳ Leaders grant of Tymber/ To haue & to hould the aboue mentioned Lands, with all the Wood & Tymber standing & lijng vpon the sayd Lands, not excepted to him the sayd Thomas Parker, his heyrs & Assigns for euer, & to his & yʳ onely proper vss benefitt & behoofe, for euer, & the sd Richd Abbett, & Elizabeth his wife for yᵐ selues there heyrs & Assigns, do promiss Covenant & grant to & with y² sayd Thomˢ Parkes his heyrs & Assigns, that they y² sd Richd Abbet & Elizabeth his wife haue in yᵐ selues good right, full pouer & lawfull authority, the aboue given & granted Pʳmisses to sell & dispose of & that y² same & every part & Prcell yʳof are free & Cleare is free & cleare, & freely & clearely acquitted, & exonerated & discharged of & from all & all manner of former gyfts, grants Leases Morgages Wills Intales Judgmᵗˢ executions, pouer of thirds & all o-incomberances, of what nature soeuer, & kind, had made done acknowledged Committed or suffered to be done or Committed, wʳby the sayd Thomˢ Parkes or his Assigns, shall or may any ways bee Molested in euicted or Eiected out of the aboue granted Pʳmisses, or any part or Prcell there of, by any Pʳson or Pʳsons whatsoeuer, haueing clameing or Pʳtended to haue, or Clajme any Legall right or Title Interest Claime or demand, of in or to the aboue granted Pʳmisses. And the sayd Richd Abbet & Elizabeth his wife,

Book III, Fol. 64.

do for them selues there heyrs executors Administrators & Assigns Covenant & promiss, & grant to & with the sayd Thom⁵ Parkes, his heyrs & Assigns, the aboue given & granted peece Or Prcell of Land with all the priuiledg⁸ aboue mentioned vpon the sayd Lands, to warrant & for euer Defend by these P⁻ʳsents : In witness wʳof I the sd Richd Abbett, & Elizabeth my wife, haue here vnto sett oʳ hands & seales, this tenth day of Janva⁻ one thousand six hundred seaventy & fiue & in the twenty seaventh yeare of yᵉ reigne of our Soueraigne Lord Charles the secund of England Scotland France & Ireland King, Defendʳ of yᵉ faith/

 Tho Holms his   Richd Abbet his
 marke/   Humfrey   marke   (Locus Sigilli)
 Spencer his marke/   Elizabeth Abbet her
   his marke/   marke   (her seal)

   The aboue written Deed of sayl
   was acknowledged by the
   abouesd Richd Abbett & Elizabeth his wife, to bee yʳ Act
   & Deed this tenth of Janv :
   1675 : before mee John
   Wincoll Assotiate/

vera Copia of this Instrum⁺, transcribed, & Compared with the originall this 27ᵗʰ of March 1680 : p Edw : Rishworth ReCor :

These P⁻ʳsents Witness that I Abra⁻ Tillton of the Town of Wells Carpenter for a some of money to mee In hand payd, by William Gowine alias Smyth, of the Town of Kittery Carpenter, haue barganed & sould, & do by these P⁻ʳsents bargan sell & set ouer, vnto the sayd William his heyrs & Assigns all my right title & Interest, to a Prcell of Tymber l... growing

& being on the sd Conlys Land at Sturgeon Cricke wch was bought about foure years since/ as witness my hand this 3d of Aprill 1672.

Testes Peter Weare Senjo^r/   Abra Tillton his
   Peter Weare Junjo^t/   marke
   Charles Frost/

          Capt Charles Forst maketh oath y^t hee saw Abra: Tillton signe this Instrum^t as his Act & Deed/ 24th of March 1680. before mee Fran: Hooke Jus^ts pe:

Peter Weare Senjo^r maketh oath that hee as a witness to this bill doth Attest that this was y^e Act & Deed of Abra. Tillton who afixed his hand y^r\nto/ Taken before mee this 31th of March 1680/   Edw: Rishworth Just· pe

vera Copia transcribed & Compard 1: Aprill 80:
                p Edw: Rishworth ReCor:

The Deposition of Charles Frost aged 48 years, or there abouts/

Sayth, y^t in y^e yeare of o^r Ld 1667: or 1668: being in discourse with Abra. Conley who lived then at Sturgeon Cricke, the sd Conley tould mee the Depon^t that hee had sould vnto Abra. Tillton Carpen^r who y^n was rescident at ye aforesd Sturgeon Cricke, all ye building Tymber on ye sd Conleys Land, on the North side of Sturgeon Cricke aforesd Joyneing to Jo^n Hords Land, as alsoe If the sd Tillton had Occasion for eight or tenn Trees in his other Lott on the South side of ye Cricke, hee should haue them alsoe/ for wch tymber as abouesd, the sd Conley tould mee ye Deponent, that ye sd Tillton had payd him part of ye pay in money, & the rest was to bee in other pay/ Taken vpon oath this 24th of March 1680: before mee

                    Fran: Hooke Just pe:

A true Coppy transcribed & Compard Aprill 1:
                p Edw: Rishworth ReCor:

BOOK III, FOL. 65.

[65] The Deposition of Peter Wittum Junjor aged 22 years/

This Deponent maketh oath, that I haue severall tyms heard Abraham Conley declare that hee had sould buylding Tymber to Abra Tillton & alsoe heard yᵉ sd Conley say yᵗ If the sd Tillton Could not find Tymber enough for his turne on the North side of the sd Cricke, that then hee the sd Tillton should haue eight or tenn trees vpon his Lott on the South side of the Cricke/ Abra. Tillton did then dwell in Abra. Conlys house, & wrought vpon yᵉ aforesd Tymber/ This was in the yeare 67· or 1668· & further sayth not/ Taken vpon oath this 24ᵗʰ of March 16⁷⁹⁄₈₀: before mee Fran: Hooke Just pe.

vera Copia transcribed & Compared this j. March 1680
p Edw · Rishworth ReCor:

Wᵗas Sagamore Thomas Chabmoet of New-scossecke, by vertue of his last will & testament hath given & bequeathed, & for Certen good Causes & Considerations, him yʳvnto moueing, hath & by vertue hereof, doth freely & forever bequeath giue & grant vnto John Wadeigh of Wells, to him his heyrs & successors, & yᵗ for euer, of his own accord & with the Consent of his mother Romansco, to whom yᵉ sd Wadleigh hath given a Consideration, the Prmisses Considered, after yᵉ manner of a purchase, bargan, & sayle the sd Sagamore & his adhearents & sur-viuers, haue for yᵐselus & successors, Con-firmed & made sure vnto the sayd Wadleigh, & his successors, to bee Inherited Prsently after yᵉ death of yᵉ sd Sagamore, all yᵗ the sd Sagamors Lands, with his whoole right, Title, & Interest Called by yᵉ name of Nischassett, bounded . . . . as high as . . . . ntl the pfetts &

Robert Wadleigh appeared before mee, & testifyeth hee was Present & did see Romansco & Thomas Chabocko signe seale & Deliuer these Instruments as on both sides appeares to hee yᵗ art & De d & Sett too his hand as a witness | taken vpon oath yᵉ 8th of July 1680 Before mee Edw Gillman of yᵉ Councell 6 July 83 vera Copia, transcribed p Edw Rishworth ReCor

Book III, Fol. 65.

Comoditys & app'tenances, against all men to recouer & Defend/ witness his hand & seale/ Dated 18th of Octob' 1649 :

The Sagamores marke with his own hand/ (his seale)

Testes/ Philemon Pormot/
Stephen Batson his marke/
Robert Wadleigh/ William wardell

Sealed signed & Delineɼd   & they all affirme Cæsars
in the P'sence of us/   Consent to this/

12th of April 1680

Romanascoe her marke/

Sasogibowah his marke

Nell wife to Sagnawah

The Sagamors sister her marke/
vera Copia transcribed out of y'e originall

p Edw: Rishworth ReCor:

William Wardells Testimony/

See farther Proof of this Deed Pa. 77.

That this is y'e Act & Deed of Thomas Chabinnake the Sagamore of Wells/ Taken before mee: Jos: Bolls Commissio' the 25: of March: 57:

W'as Romanasco mother of y'e Sagamore of Thomas Chabinocke of Nimschasett of late deceased, & as appearth by his last will & testament. on the other side Contayned, & being Witness to y'e same, as her own hand y'vnd' subscribed, testifyeth showing her Consent vnto y'e sd Will as then, shee hath y'fore now vpon better aduisement & for further establishm' of the sayd Will according to y'e Intent y'rof, vnto the sd John Wadleigh his heyrs & Assigns as on the other side Contayned w'to reference bee had to Assign & set o... ... signs from hence forth alsoe. & for euer, all her ... le &

Book III, Fol. 65.

Interest, in the purchase & bequest of Land therein Contayned, that either formerly was, or since the Sagamores death is, or might become hers, in regard of her relation to him, vtterly rnownceing & disclameing the same, & euery part y^rof wth an acknowledgm^t of Tenn pounds Sterlg: wch shee & the sd Sagamore In his life tyme receiued, of the sd John Wadleigh, to full, satisfaction & Content, for the sd Land, & euery part y^rof, as on the other side Contayned, & w^tto referrence bee had, & further shee ye sayd Romanascho acknowledgeth her selfe to bee also fully requited & payd, by the sd John Wadleigh in her Constant recourse to his house, & severall Gyfts shee Continually receiveth to a greater valew then ye thing is worth as shee supposeth/ witness her hand & seale the 17th day of 8th M^o (1650)
Signed sealed & Deliuerd
 in ye P^rsence of/ Romanascoh her marke (her seale)

Philemon Pormott/ Jone Junkssquaw
Robert Wadleigh/
Sasagihuah marke her marke
Tho. Baston/
Will Coole his marke Junjo^r/

Philemon Pormott sworne Philemon Pormott testi-
alsoe before mee, Mr fyeth y^t hee was P^rs-
Dane being P^rsent. Oc- ent & did see both the
tob^r 29 79. writeings on both sid^s
Daniell Denisson/ of this paper signed
  sealed & delivered by the two
  severall Prtys y^t haue sd to
  haue done It, & y^t hee set to
  his hand as a witness, y^rvnto,
  18 Octob^r 1679 · sworn before
  mee Humfrey Dauie Assist

vera Copia transcribed & Compared with the originall this 12th of Aprill (1680)

William Coole whose name is subscribed as a witness to ye writeing, made oath the was Present & saw this writeing subscribed & deliuered, as also y^t on the other side subscribed by the Sagimore, before me, October 5 1681

Daniell Denison.

Book III, Fol. 65.

The Deposition of Stephen Batson of Cape Porpus/
Sworne sayth, y^t this Deed which John Wadleigh haue of the Sagamore Thomas Chabinacke & his Mother Romanasco Concerneing the Interest of all his Lands which the Deeds do express, hee being in his P^{r}fect Memory, did do, as his Act & Deede, & Assignd It to John Wadleigh & his heyrs for euer/ & further sayth not/

Taken vpon oath before mee this 6th of March 1658.
Ezek^{ll} Knights Comissio^r
vera Copia transcribed 12 : Aprill 1680 ·
p Edw : Rishworth ReCor :

31 : 3d M^o 1650/
John Wadlew tooke quiet & peaceable possession of ye P^{r}misses in y^s paper Contayned, as his Indean right, & y^{r}in Deliver'd vnto his sonn Robert Wadleigh as Joynt purchescer laying ye whoole Continent from Cape porpus Falls, & so by a streight lyne to Ogunquett & down to ye sea side of Lygonia & further assigns ye same as It shall be Inhabited to bee Lyable to all Comon Charges & rates, for ye Town of Preston, Nay^r Wells, & to this as in the same or like case requirs Wee the Witnesses being y^{r}to requested, haue subscribed o^r hands the day yeare aboue sd/   Philemō · Pormot

Philemon Pormot testifyeth vpon   Willā : Wardell
oath to ye treuth of this writeing,   his marke
& owned this to bee his hand/

Boston 18   Octob^r 1679 · before mee, Humfry Dauie Ass^t
Philemon Pormot sworne alsoe before mee, Mr Dauie being p̄sent   Octob^r 29 : 79 . Dan^{ll} Denisson/

vera Copia, transcribed out of the originalls of these testimonys aboue written this 12 · of Aprill 1680 . p Edw : Rishworth ReCor :

BOOK III, FOL. 66.

[66] The Deposition of John Allden aged 42 yeares or y'abouts/

This Deponent testifyeth & sayth, that being requested by Mr George Pearson of Boston to goe with him into the Town, likewise tould the sayd Deponent y' hee was goeing to pay Richd Bray formerly of Cascoe bay In the Province of Mayne, a some of Money for a Tract of Land that hee had purchased of the sayd Bray/ the sd Deponent went with him in Company of the sd Richard Bray, vnto the house of Cap' Wright, W' the sd Deponent see Mr Geo: Pearson tell out twenty nine pounds In money for the vss of the sayd Bray, & the sd Bray desired the sd Deponent to tell It after the sayd Pearson w'h hee did & alsoe see it delivered to y'e sd Ric: Bray w'ch money the sayd Bray put into a Capp, & Caryed away with him The money was payd some tyme in the winter in the yeire one thousand six hundred seaventy eight/ & further this Deponent sayth that hee heard Richd Bray say, y' he neuer gaue but one Deed to his sonn John Bray, & y' runne In this tenour, y' after the death of his sayd sonn John Bray, It was to returne to his brother Nath[ll] another son of the sd Richd Brays/ alsoe It is to bee vnderstood that the abouesd Deed of sayle, w'ch sayd Bray gaue to his sun John was in reference to part of an Ysland, lijng in Cascoe Bay Com'anly Called by the name of Cossons his Ysland/ & further sayth not/

Taken vpon oath 11th of y'e first M° 16$\frac{7}{8}$: before Anthony Stoddard Comisr

vera Copia transcribed out of y'e origall this 13th of April 1680. p Edw: Rishworth ReCor:

The Deposition of John Howman aged 35 years or y'abouts/

Testifyeth, that hee was by & see Geo: Pearson of Boston pay vnto Richd Bray formerly belonging to Cascoe bay nine pounds In money, wch was for part of an Ysland the sayd Geo. Pearson had formerly bought of sayd Bray lijng in Cascoe Bay, known by ye name of Cussons his Ysland/ this money was payd sometyme the winter one thousand six hundred seaventy eight/ & further sayth not/

Taken vpon oath the 11th of the first M^o 16⅞ · before mee Anthoy Staddard Comisi^r

vera Copia transcribed this 13th of Aprill 1680:

p Edw: Rishworth ReCor:

Thomas Kemble aged 58 years or y^rabouts. testifyeth y^t in ye begiñg of Janv · 1678: being desired by Mr Geo: Pearson to draw 2 deeds for Land that ye sd Pearson had before bought of Richd Bray sometyms before liuing in Cascoe Bay w^n I had drawn the sayd Deeds, I carrjed them at ye request of the sd Pearson, to ye house w^r then ye sayd Bray & his wife then liued, & before the sayd Bray & his wife would sign or seale them, they would needs haue them red to them, wch accordingly I did once or Twise, to the best of my remembrance at y^t tyme, wch they did likewise accept of & seale sign & Deliuer, & w^n they came to acknowledg them before Mr Tyng, a good part of them were red to them agajne. before hee did acknowledg the same. wch afterwards hee freely did/

Taken vpon oath the 5th of ye first M^o 16⅞ before mee
          Anthony Stoddard Comisso^r

vera Copia transcribed out of the origmall this 13th Aprill 1680   p Edw Rishworth ReCor

Know all men by these P^rsents, that that Wee Thomas Clarke, & Thomas Lake of Boston M^chant, haue bargained & sould, vnto John Clarke of Pischat... ...nd, formerly purchased of Christopher Lawson, lijng neare the mouth of Pischataq River, In Consideration of Thyrty pounds, to bee payd by him the sayd John Clarke by bond the receipt of Which, wee acknowledg o{r} selues fully satisfyd with. Do here by bargan, sell, alienate, Assigne, & set ouer, vnto the sd John Clarke the sayd Ysland, with all the Tymber vnderwoods, & all priuiledges there to belonging, to haue & to hould & peaceably Inioy by him & his heyres for ever/ And further Wee the sayd Thomas Clarke, & Thomas Lake, do fully Conenant grant & agree, to & with the sd John Clarke, to free & acquitt him from any Just Caime w{ts}oeuer made by any Prson or Prsons whomsoeuer, from any Act, or Acts done by us, warranting the sayd John Clarke against all former barganes, sales, leases, Morgages, Deeds or Ingagem{ts}, made by from or vnder vs/ To the true & Just P{r}formance of all & euery part of the Pr{r}misses. Wee firmely bind vs o{r} heyres executors Administrators & Assigns, by subscribing o{r} hands, & afixing o{r} seales, this 3d day of Aprill, In the yeare of o{r} Ld one thousand six hundred seaventy foure/

Signed sealed & Deliuered/ Tho: Clarke (Locus Sigilli)
 In the Presence of/   Tho. Lake (Locus Sigilli)
 John Wally/ This Instrum{t} was acknowledged by
 Joseph Farnum/ Thomas Clarke Esq{r}, & Cap{t}
        Thomas Lake, as thejr Act &
        Deed, this 3d of Aprill 1674.
        before mee Edw. Tyng Assist:

vera Copia of this Instrum{t} transcribed out of the originall & y{r}with Compared this 21th day of Aprill 1680:
      p Edw · Rishworth ReCor:

Know all men by these P{r}sents y{t} I John Parsons of yorke in the County or province of Mayn, Cordwinder, for & in Consideration of the full & Just some of fiuety pounds in good & Mrchble soole & vpper Leather in hand, & already payd mee, p william Vahan Esq*r*, liueing at Portsmouth Mrchant in the Province of New Ham Shyre, wthwith I do acknowledg my selfe to bee fully satisfyd Contented & payd, do by these Prsents sell giue grant Enfeoff, & Confirme, & haue hereby granted sould given Enfeoff & Confirmed, from mee my heyrs, executors, Administrators & Assignes, my soole right & Interest of my dwelling house, wch I bought of Capt Davess, & Samuell Sayword, both of yorke aforesd wth I now liue in, p order given vnto the sd John Davess & Sayword, as appeareth from John Nowlton of Ipswich Cordwinder, by a writeing vndr his hand vpon ReCord, beareing date Aprill 5th 1675. & by a fuithr obligation vnder the hands of John Davess & Samll Sayword to procure a suffitient bill of sayle, of & from ye sd John Nowlton aforesd, to make good yr sayle vnto the sayd John Parsons, as the law requireth, as by a record appeareth beareing date the fourteenth of March 1678 vnder both there hands, & do alsoe further giue grat & Confirme, from mee the sd John Parsons my heyrs & Assigns Twelue acres of vpland, on part of wch vpland my house now standeth [67] Wch Land was given vnto mee by the Town of Yorke, as by the Town Grant doth & may appeare, March 12th 1678 : with all other profetts priuiledges & Imunitys there vnto belonging, according to the boundarys there in expressed, vnto the sayd William Vahan, his heyrs executors, administrators & Assigns for euer · To haue & to hould the before granted Prmisses, as free & Cleare from all gyfts, grants, bargans sayles, & all or any other Incomberances wtsoeuer, from him the sd Jon Parsons, his heyrs & Assignes, vnto the aforesayd Will · Vahan his heyrs, executors, Administrators & Assignes for euer : without the lett denyall hinderance or Molestation of all Prson or Prsons wtsoeuer Clajmeing any right title, or Interest the sd John Parsons, his heyrs or Assignes or any Prson or Prsons by or vnder him, or ym or any by his or yr procurement, always provided, & is euer Intended, & truely

& really agreed vpon by & between the afore named Prtys, John Parsons & Willm̃ Vahan, & is the true Intent & meaneing of these Prmisses, that If the sd John Parsons shall well & duely pay, or Cause to bee payd vnto the sd William Vahan or his Assignes, at his dwelling house at Strawbury Banke in the Town of Portsmouth aforesd, the full & Just some of fincty pounds, the one halfe being Twenty fiue pounds in good dry or raw Neate hides, dry at 6^d p ^{lb} & raw at 3^d p ^{lb} & the other halfe being Twenty fiue pounds, in good Mrchtble shooes at Current prises as taken p Mrchants, or such other Mrchtble pay as the sd Vahan will accept of, dehvered in place as aforesd, & between this, & from the date of June last 1679 · will bee two years to the yeare June 1681: wthout frawde or delay, that then this Morgage, Deed, or obligation, to bee voyd, & of none æffect, otherwise, to stand in full pouer & vertue, to all Intents, & purposes wtsoeuer/ In witness wrof I haue here vnto afixed my hand & seale, this 20th day of March : 16$\frac{78}{79}$ In the 33th yeare of the Reign of our Soueraign Ld Charles the 2und, of England Scotland, ffrance & Ireland King Defendr of ye faith &c ·

Signed sealed & Delivered,   John Parsons ($_{Sigill}^{Locns}$)
In the Prsence of/   yorke March 20 . 79 :
Edw Rishworth   John Parsons acknowledged this
Jonᵃ Twisden/   Instrumt to bee his Act & Deed,
    before Tho . Damforth Prsident/

vera Copia of this Instrumet transcribed, & with ye Origmall Compared this 23th Aprill 1680

p Edw : Rishworth ReCor :

Wee whose names are vnderwritten haue layd out & bounded a Lott of vpland vnto Thomas Addams, vpon the South side of Yorke River, begining at the bound & marked tree, of Leeft Job Alcocke, vpon the South East, & is to

BOOK III, FOL. 67.

runne along p the River side fourty pooles, or pearch & soe runneth South West one hundred & fourty pearch, which maketh fourty Acres vnto ye sayd Addames, or his Assignes, according to that Interest, Wee haue in the sayd Land/ given vnder our hands this 9th of Octob^r 1678 :

vera Copia transcribed & Compared   Peter Weare
   with the originall this 23 : Aprill 1680 :   Job Allcocke
       p Edw . Rishworth ReCor :   Hene . Donell
                                             his marke

These P^{r}sents testify that I James Middleton late of Kennebecke yeamon, & now resedent on the Great Ysland In Pischataqua River, for diverse good Causes, & Considerations mee there vnto moueing, haue given granted Enfeoffed, confirmed, aheaned, Conveyed, assigned & set ouer, & by thes P^{r}sents do give grant, Enfeoff, Confirme alieane, assigne & set ouer vnto William Gowine alias Smyth of Kittery In Pischataq̄ River yeamon, all my right title & Interest, that I formerly had or now haue in any Lands, lijng vpon or adioyneing to Kennebecke River aforesd, vidz^t all y^t my Interest with Thomas Humfrys, as alsoe a Tract of Land y^r com̄anly Called & known by the name of small poynt, which I lately bought of Pattricke Denmarke, togeather with all & singular the priuiledges, & appurtenances to them or either of them, belonging, or in any wise app^{r}tayneing, To haue & to hould, both the sd Tracts or Prcells of Lands, as they haue beene formerly by mee, & the sd Tho : Humphreys, & Pattricke Denmarke vsed, & vnto his heyres executors Administrators & Assignes for ever, as his & y^r owne proper Estate, & benefit vsse, & behoofe, & to & for no other vss, intent or purpose w^{t}soeuer/ In witness w^{r}of, I haue here vnto set my hand & seale/ Dated on the Great Ysland in Pischataq̄ River, the sixteenth day of Septemb^r Anno Dom̄ : one thousand six hundred seaventy six, & in the Twenty

Book III, Fol. 67, 68.

eight yeare of the Reigne of oʳ soveraigne Lᵈ Charles the secvnd King of England Scotland France & Ireland Defendʳ of the faith, &c. (1676)

Signed sealed & delivered/   James Middleton (Locus Sigilli)
  In the Pʳsence of vs/   Great Ysland 18ᵗʰ July 1677 :
  Joseph Hodgsden/   James Middleton Came & acknowl-
  Ric: Styleman Secreᵗʸ   edged this Instrument to bee his
                                      Act & Deed, before mee
                                      Elyas Stylemā: Commissoʳ/

A true Coppy of this Instrument aboue written, transcribed, & with the originall Compared this 13th day of May · 1680   p Edw. Rishworth ReCor:

Wʳ as by order of the Honoʳᵈ County Court, houlden at Yorke, the 6ᵗʰ day of July 1675 : Major Ric: Walden, Edw: Rishworth, John Wincoll & Roger Playstead, were appoyted to heare & make a full Issew of all Controvereys Or differences between the relations of Nicho: Frost Junjoʳ lately deceased in Ireland, Concerneing the devission of the sd Frosts Estate, & the sd Major Ric Walden, Edw: Rishworth, John Wincoll, & Roger Playstead, vpon heareing of all then pleas, gane their determination vnder yʳ hands, August 11th : 1675/ [68] That the whoole Estate of the sayd Nicho · Frost Junjoʳ, should bee æqually deuided between all his surviueing brethren & sisters; This writeing witnesseth an agreement between William Gowine alias Smyth who married Elizabeth the sister of the sayd Nicho: Frost: Charles Frost for him selfe & for his brother John Frost & Joseph Hammonds who married Katterne, the sister of the sayd Nicho. Frost deceased That the aforesd William Gowine alias Smyth, shall receiue possess & Inioy to him his heyrs & Assignes for euer, sixty acres of that sixty fiue acres of Land lately belonging to the sayd ffrost deceased, & layd out by surgeon Cricke Mouth, on the South side of the sd Cricke, as it is bounded by an agreemeᵗ made the first

Book III, Fol. 68.

day of Septemb' one thousand six hundred seaventy two, between the sayd Frost deceased, & Phillip Benmore, wch sixty Acres of Land William Gowine alias Smyth shall take in full satisfaction, for all his Interest In all the Lands, the sd Nicho: Frost Junjo' dyed seized of, & the other fiue acres the sayd Gowine alias Smyth shall leaue out, at the East or eastermost End of the sd land butting vpon the aforesd Sturgeon Cricke, & runnieg from thence South by paralell Lynes, to ye Southwardmost part of the sd Land the sd fiue Acres of Land, with all the other Prcells of Land, lately belonging to the sayd Nicho: Frost deceased (excepting the aforesd sixty acres) shall remajne to ye soole Interest of the aforesd Charles Frost, John ffrost, & Jos. Hamonds, thejr heyres & Assignes for ever, to wch agreement the aforesd William Gowine alias Smyth, Charles Frost for him selfe & his bro^r John Frost & Joseph Hamonds haue set to y^r hands & seales this thirteenth day of Aprill: 1680:

Signed sealed and delivered,   Charles Frost (his seale)
   in the P^rsence of/   Jos Hamond (his seale)
   Mary Leighton   William Gowine
   John Wincoll/   alias Smyth (his seale)

     Charles Frost Jos: Hamond & William Gowine alias Smyth acknowledged the aboue written agreement to bee ye free act & deed, the 13th day of Aprill (1680) before mee John Wincoll Just^s pe·

A a true Coppy of this Instrume^t aboue written transcribed & Compared with the originall, this 16th of May 1680.   p Edw: Rishworth ReCor.

George Cleves to Hope Allen

     This Indenture made the one and thirtieth day of May in the yeare of o^r Lord one thousand six hundred & sixty, between George Cleeues of Falmouth in Cascoe bay in Yorke shyre New England Gentle: on the one part· & Hoope

Book III, Fol. 68.

Alline of Boston in Suffucke New England Currier, of the other part, Witnesseth that the sayd George Cleeue, for & in Consideration of a valewable some of money to him in hand payd before the scaleing & delivery hereof, as alsoe in Consideration of an annuall rent of eight shillings Sterlg p Anñ· at or before the Tenty Ninth day of Septemb^r in euery yeare from hence forth euen for euer, for all sceruices to bee payd by the sayd Hoope Alline his heyres & Assignes vnto the sayd George Cleeues, his heyrs executors administrators Or Assignes, hath granted barganed sould Enfeoffed & Confirmed, & by these P^{r}sents do grant bargan sell Enfeoff & Confirme, vnto the sayd Hope Allene his heyrs & Assignes, ffoure hundred Acres of Land, lijng togeather being part vpland, & part Medlow bounded with a River, Called Cascoe River, South East with the Lands of Ann Mittine, & James Andrews Westwardly, & so to runne down the River, towards the sea, ffoure hundred pool according to sixteen foote & an halfe to euery poole, & to runne into the Woods North West eight Scoore poole, vntill the sayd foure hundred Acres bee fully Compleated, with all ye Tymber woods & vnderwoods there standing, growing or being, with other ye appurtenances & priuiledges to the same belonging, or any ways appertayneing, which sayd Land is part of a greater quantity granted vnto the sayd Cleeues by Sir Fardinando Gorges, & afterwards Confirmed vnto him the sayd Cleeus by Barron Ridgby, to haue hould possess & Inioy all & euery the afore barganed P^{r}misses, with the appurtenances as before bounded, vnto the sayd Hope Alline his heyres & Assignes, to the onely proper vss, & behoofe, of the sayd Hope Alline, his heyis & Assigns for euer, provided & vpon Condition that hee the sd Hope Allen his heyres & Assignes, do pay or cause to bee payd the aforesayd yearly rent of eight shillings p Anñ. for all seruices, from hence forth by these p̃sents to bee due vnto the sayd Geo. Cleeues his heyres executors administrators & Assigns And the sayd Geo

tors, vpon Condition aforesayd, doth Covenant & grant to & with the sayd Hope Allen, his heyrs executors, Administrators & Assigns, by these presents, that the sayd barganed P'misses shall bee & Continew to bee the proper right and Inheritance of the sayd Hope Allen, his heyres & Assignes for euer, without any the lett, interruption, or euiction of him the sayd Geo: Cleeus his heyrs, or Assigns or any Claymeing any title Clayme or Interest to the same, or any part thereof, from or vnder him them or any of them, & alsoe vpon Condition as aforesd, shall & Will warrant & defend the same, against all 'Lawfull Clajmes of any other Prson or Prsons w'soeuer· It is further Covenanted Concluded & agreed vpon, by & between the sayd Hope Allen in ye behalfe of him selfe his heyrs & Assignes, on the one part, & ye sayd Geo: Cleeues, his heyrs executors, administrators & Assigns on the other part, that the sayd Geo: Cleeues his heyrs executors, Administrators & Assigns shall haue Lyberty, & hereby hath Lawfull pouer at any tyme hereafter to distrayne vpon any part of the afore barganed P'misses, for the aforesd Anuall rent & arrearages, there of in case of non payment, at day as aboue sayd/ In witness where of the sayd George Cleeues, hath here vnto put his hand & scale, the last day of May in the yeare of our Lord one thousand six hundred & sixty/

Signed sealed & deliverd   George Cleeues (Locus Sigilli)
in the P'sence of   This writeing on the other side was
[69] Robert Howard   acknowledgd by Mr Geo: Cleeues
Noto^s: publ^s to bee his Act & Deed, the eight
Benjamin Tyding   day of June 1661: before mee,
Nic: Bartlett   John Endecutt Gouer/

his ℬ marke

Possession & seizen was deliuered vnto Hope Allen of all

BOOK III, FOL. 69.

the Land mentiond in this deed, vpon the 3d day of June 1662 : in the p̄sence of the witnesses vnderwritten/

Testes Geo : Munoy/   by mee Geo · Cleeus/
The marke of Anthony Brackett/   Joanna Cleeues/

Geo : Lewis/   p her marke/

Allen To Bramhall

Know all men by these Presents, that I Edw : Allen of Douer In the County of Portsmouth & Douer, do Assigne ouer to George Bramhall his his heyrs & assignes the whoole right & title to ye within mentioned, excepting fincty Acres to Henery Kirke, as appeares by a deed of Gyft Witness my hand/

Testes/   Dated 13th Novēb^r 1678 .   Edw : Allen/
Hene . Kirke/   Edward Allen came & acknowledged
John Barsham/   the with in Assignement, to George
              Bramehall & Hene : kirke to bee his
              free Act & Deed . 13th of the ninth
              M^o 1678   before mee
                    Richd Martyn Comīsso^r/

vera Copia of this Instrument on the other side, & of the Assigm^t aboue written, transcribed out the originall, & y^r with Compared this 19th of May 1680 ·

          p Edw : Rishworth ReCor ·

To all Christean people, to whom this Instrument in writeing or deed of sayle shall come, I Robert Jordan, Junjo^r, sonn of Robert Jordan Senjo^r deceased, in tyms past liueing at Richmans Ysland in the Easterne parts of New England, send greeteing In o^r Ld God Everlasting ;

Know yee that I the sayd Robert Jordan Junjo^r for & in Consideration of the some of eighty pounds, to mee In hand payd & secured, to bee payd by Mr Nathell Fryer of the Towneship of Portsmouth In New England, aforesayd, M^rcha^t with which I do hereby acknowledg my selfe satisfyed, & fully Contented: haue given & granted, And by these P^rsents do give grant & Confirme fully freely & absolutely vnto the sd Natll ffryer Senjo^r his heyrs executors administrators & Assignes, the one halfe deale, Or halfe part of one Certen Tract or P^rcell of Land Comanly Called or known, by the name of Cape Elizabeth, In the Easterne parts of New England aforesayd, bounded with a small gutt, or streeme of Water runneing Into the sea out of a small Marsh liyng behind the Long Sands, to ye Westward, & so to runne vp into the Mayn Land in a streight lyne, to the pond, Comanly Called ye greate Pond: Provided, & it is hereby intended & appoyted, y^t sd Natll Fryer, his heyres executors Administrators Or Assignes, shall at no tyme or tymes hereafter, Interfere take away Molest or deminish any part or Prcell of the sayd Marsh or vpland, that lyeth between the sd Marsh & the sayd Great Pond, to the sayd streight lyne to pass as aforesayd, Northwards & so to runne down vpon the sayd Pond to the sea, takeing in to ye sd P^rmisses mentioned, one little Ysland Scituate, on the East side of the sayd Pond, togeather with the Marshes on both sides of a Cricke runneing out of the sayd pond, into the sea at Aylewife Coue, & alsoe not to Intrench vpon the Mayn vpland or plaines, there vnto Adiaycent, aboue the extent of Twenty Measured pooles, always reserveing, granting, giveing & allowing, vnto my brother John Jordan of Richmans Ysland aforesd, or to his Assigns or P^rsons Concerned with him Convenient Ingress, Egress & regress, fully & freely at all tymes & seasons to the sayd Aylewifes Coue, & there & thence to procure fetch & carry away baite for his or there fishing vses, at tyme & Tymes seasonable · To haue & to hould the sayd one halfe part of the sayd Tract of Land, togeath^r with ye priuiledges accomodations, profetts app^rtenances & Conveniences there of, vnto the sd Natll Fryer his heyrs executors administrators Or Assigns for ever freely

& quietly without any hinderance or Interrvption, as It was
granted & given to mee by my father Robert Jordan, & my
mother Sarah Jordan, as by a Deede of Gyft beareing date
the Twenty ninth day of Febru: In ye yeare of our L^d one
thousand six hundred seaventy & fiue, may & doth at Large
appeare: And More ouer Whereas my father Robert Jordan
did by his last will & testament giue & grant vnto mee
Robert Jordan & the rest of my brothers one certen Preell
of Marsh & Land scituate & being in spurwinke Riuer in the
Easterne parts of New England, aforesd to bee deuided in
æquall parts amongst us, as by the sayd will doth euidently
appeare, I Robert Jordan aforesd haue given & granted, & p
these P^{r}sents freely do giue grant & Confirme vnto Natha^{ll}
Fryer in manner & altogeather as the first granted P^{r}misses
aboue mentioned are the one halfe, or halfe & deale part of
the sayd Marsh & Land, In w^{t}soeuer place y^{r}of my Lot
shall bee after It bee deuided, And It is hereby intended
granted & mutually agreed on by mee the Vendor with the
Vendee that in the halfeing or the deuideing, any or all of
the aboue recited P^{r}misses there shall bee a iust Complyance
each with other y^t in quātity quality Conveniency, as much
as may bee o^r proportion may bee a like; And I the sayd
Robert Jordan for my selfe my heyres executors, & Administrators do hereby Covenant & Ingage to warrant & for
euer Defend, vnto ye sayd Natha^{ll} Fryer [70] all the
P^{r}misses mentioned in this writeing, togeather with the
priuiledges there of vnto the sayd Fryer his heyres, executors & Administrators & Assignes, peaceably & quietly &
without Interrvption to Inioy the same/ Witness my hand
& seale the foureteenth day of July in the yeare of o^r Lord
one thousand six hundred seaventy & Nine/

Signed sealed & deliuered   Robert Jordan (Locus Sigilli)
  In the P^{r}sence of us/   July . 16 . 1679 : Mr Robert Jordan
  Thomas Cobbett/   Came acknowledged this Instru-
  Nicho : Heskines/   me^t to bee his free Act & Deed
                                (omisio^r

BOOK III. FOL. 70.

vera Copia of this Instrument aboue written transcribed out of the originall, & y^r with Compared this 22th of May, 1680:   p Edw: Rishworth Re Cor

To all Christian people to whome this P^rsent writeing shall Come, health & peace in our Lord God Amen/

Know all men by these P^rsents, that I Humfrey Chadborne of Newgewanacke, haue for diverse good Causes, & valewable Considerations mee there vnto moueing sould vnto Mr Hateeuill Nutter, of Dover, all my Meddow, lijng on the East side of Pischataq̃ River, It lijng in two Parcells, as namely the one peece of Meddow, being Called by the name of Burcham Poynt/ the other peece lijng between Joⁿ Hords Marsh & his vpland vpon the Cricke, Called the blã Cricke, & this I do acknowledg to haue sould, & deliuered, all my right, & Title in the afore sayd Meddows to Mr Nutter, his heyres, & Assignes, to haue & to hould peaceably, without the least Molestation, of mee, my heyrs & Assigns for euer/ in witness to the treuth I haue here vnto set my hand this 15th day of May 1651/

Signed & Deliuered   Humfrey Chadborne/
in the P^rsence of/   vera Copia of this Instrument tran-
Nicho: Shapleigh/   scribed, & Compared wth ye orig-
                    inall this 22th of May (1680)
The marke of ⊃   p Edw: Rishworth ReCor:
George Rogers/

To all Christean people to whome these P^rsentt writeing shall Come, & appeare/ I John Roberts of the Town of Douer In the County of New Ham shyre In Pischataqua River, now vnder his Majestys most excellent Gouerm^{et} In New England, sendeth Greeteing, Know yee that I the sayd

BOOK III, FOL. 70.

John Roberts Senjo^r for diverse good Causes, & Considerations mee moueing there vnto but more espetially for the naturall Loue which I haue to my sonn John Roberts now lueing in the Town shipp of Doner aforesd, do giue & freely give vnto him his heyrs executors Administrators, & Assigns, a peece of Marsh Contayning three three Acres bee It more or less, It being a peece of Marsh wch my father Hatevill Nutter, hath fenced & Improued euer since the 28 day of July 1643 It now ljng & being in the Town shipp of Kittery. in the Province of Mayn Adioyneing vpon the fore River, aboue burch poynt, neare the Land of James Emery, & Danjell Gooding, which sayd Marsh is Comanly Called the fowling Marsh, wch sayd Marsh was Granted to Thomas Canny, by Mr Thom^s Gorges, In the right of Sir Fardinando Gorges, then proprieto^r of the Province of Mayne, wch sayd peeces of Marsh my father in Law Mr Hateuill Nutter bought of Thomas Conny, & afterwards hee Assignd It ouer to mee my heyrs & executors for euer, which in the ReCords of the province of Mayne will more largely appeare/ all wch sd peeces of Marsh with all priuiledges & appurtenances there vnto belonging, by vertue of an assignment given mee by my father Nutter, I do freely & Clearely giue It to my sonn John Roberts, to him & his heyres, & Assigns for euer, to haue & to hould the P^rmisses aforesayd, with the appurtenances thereto belonging; & for the true P^rformance of the aboue given P^rmisses, that my sonn may peaceably inioy them, with out any Molestation by mee, or through my meanes, Consent, or procurement, I haue here vnto set my hand & seale, this 20 Twenteth day of Aprill in the yeare of o^r Lord God, one thousand six hundred & eighty/

Signed sealed & Deliuer̃d   John Roberts Senjo^r ($^{Locus}_{Sigilli}$)

In y^e P^rsence of us/   John Roberts Senjo^r Acknowledge l
Thomas Austine/   this writeing to bee his Act &
Edw. Alline/   Deed, this 13th of May: 1680:
                           before mee Job Clements Cõssio^r

Book III, Fol. 70.

A true Coppy of this Instrument transcribed out of the originall & therewith Compared this 24th of May 1680
p Edw: Rishworth ReCor.

To all Christean people, to whom this P'fent writeing shall Come & appeare, I John Morrall of the Town shipp of Kittery in the Province of Mayne, now in the Massatusetts Jurisdiction in New England, sendeth greeteing; Know yee that the sd John Morrall, for diverse good Causes, & Considerations him moueing y'vnto, more especially, for & in Consideration of the some of nine pounds to him in hand payd before the sealeing & delivering of these P'sents, by Thomas Roberts, & Hateevill Roberts of the Town of Douer, in the County of New Ham shyre, w'of hee doth acknowledg him selfe satisfyd & payd, of euery P'cell & peeces there of, doth acquit & for euer discharge, the sd Thomas Roberts, & Hateeuill Roberts, there heyrs executors, & Administrators by these P'sents, hath absolutely given granted, barganed, aliend Inffeoffed Assignd & Confirmed & by these P'sents doth giue grant bargane sell aliene Enfeoff Assure & Confirme, vnto the sayd Tho: Roberts & Hateeuill Roberts a peeces of Marsh or Meddow lyng on the East side of Pischataq, River Comanly Called by the name of Burcham Poynt, w'ch was formerly Humfrey Chadborns, & afterwards Mr Hateeuill Nutters, which aforesayd peecs of Meddow, I bought of Mr Nutter, as shall appeare by a deed of sale giuen vnder his hand, all w'ch sayd peeces of Meddow, with all priuiledges & app'rtenances, y'vnto belonging, or app'rtayneing vnto the sayd Joⁿ Morrall, [71] shall bee for the soole & proper vss & benefitt of the sayd Thomas Roberts & Hateeuill Roberts, thejr heyres executors Administrators & Assigns for ever; To haue & to hould, the P^rmisses aforesd, & the sayd Joⁿ Morrall doth for him selfe his heyrs executors administrators, Covenant & Promiss to & with Thomas Roberts & Hateeuill Roberts, thejr heyrs executors & administrators & Assignes, that the sayd John Morrall hath in him selfe good right, full pouer, & Lawfull authority, to the aboue giuen & granted P^rmises to dispose off, & that the same & euery part & P^rcells y^rof, are free & Cleare, & freely & Clearely acquitted & discharged, of, & from all manner of former Gyfts & grants, sayles, Leases, Morgages Wills, Intayles Judgm^{ts} executions, pouer of thirds, & all other Incomberances of w^t nature or kind soeuer, had mayd done acknowedged or suffered to bee done, where by the sd Thomas Roberts, & Hateeuill Roberts, theire heyrs executors, Administrators or Assigns, shall or may any ways bee Molested in, or Eiected out of the aboue granted P^rmisses, or any part or P^rcell thereof, by any Prson or Prsons haueing Clajmeing, or Prtending to haue or Clajme any Legall right title Claime or demand, in or to the aboue granted P^rmises And the sayd John Morrall doth for him selfe his heyrs executors Administrators, Covenant & promiss to & with Thomas Roberts, & Hateeuill Roberts thejre heyrs executors Administrators & Assignes, to warrant & to mantayn & make good the same against all manner of P^rsons w^tsoeuer, from by or through him, or thejr means Consent P^rmission or procurement in witness hereof the sayd John Morrall hath here vnto set his hand & seale/ dated the thirteenth day of May,

The meaning of Tho. Roberts, & Hateeuill Roberts, are to bee vnderstood the sonns of Joⁿ Roberts now liueing in Douer this Prsent Date, this being writt before the sealing & Deliuery of these Prsents

Book III, Fol. 71.

In the yeare of o' Lord god one thousand six hundred & eighty/

Signed sealed & Deliver'd   John Morrall (his seal)
  in the P'sence of us/   John Morrall acknowledged this
  John Roberts Junjo'   writeing to bee his Act & Deed,
  Edw Allen/   the · 14th of May · 1680 . before
                      mee Job Clemments Comissio'

vera Copia of this Instrume' transcribed, & Compared with the originall, this 25th of May 1680 .

                    p Edw : Rishworth ReCor:

Know all men by these P'sents, that I Michaell Endle, late of the Yses of shoales fisherman, haue barganed sould, & by these P'sents do bargan & sell vnto William Oliver, & Richd Oliver of sd Yslands fishermen, my stage scituate & standing on smuttinose Ysland, one of the Y'les of shoales, & Joyneing to y'e stage of sd Olivers on the South West side, as alsoe eight flakes with the Rowme, & priuiledges belonging there vnto, all & euery of the before mentioned Stage, flakes rowme &c . I do acknowledg to haue sould to sd William & Richard Ohuer, with all my right Title & Interest y'rin . To them & to thejr heyres for euer, to haue hould & possess without any lett, hinderance or Molestation of mee, or any other Clajmeing by from or vnder mee/ Witness my hand & seale this ninth day of Decemb' 1678 :

Signed sealed & Delivered,   Michaell Endle his
  In P'sence of vs/
  Jeremiah Belcher Senjo'/   marke (his seale)
  Samuell Belcher/

           Michaell Endle came before mee this
           9th day of June 1680 : & owned this
           Instrument to bee his Act & Deed/
           Edw . Rishworth Just' pe :

Book III, Fol. 71.

vera Copia, of this Deed of Sayle abone written, transcribed out of yͦ originall & yͬwith Compared, this 12th day of June 1680. p Edw: Rishworth ReCor:

The testimonys of Andrew Dyamont aged about thyrty nine years, & of Michaell Endle aged about sixty years/

Being examined maketh oath, that do very Well remember yͭ Walter Mathews deceased, hath peaceably & quietly possessed that house, Wͨʰ now Mary Mathews his Widdow liueth in, & that house which now Jo͐ Martyne liueth in, let vnto him by the sayd Mary Mathews, with all the flake Rownes, lijng rownes, & a Garden plott with a store house rownes & Leane twoes & alsoe yͤ priuiledge of a Moreing place for two boates, lijng between smuttinose & Mallıgoe, with all other priuiledges belonging there vnto, for the full tearme of Twenty seaven or twenty eight yeares, & for the moreing place they remember, It was Twenty foure years or yͬ abouts & the Garding place Wee remember was possessed about eighteen yeais & further sayth not/ Dated June · 9th : 1680 : Taken vpon oath before mee

Edw: Rishworth Just · pe ·

vera Copia transcribed, & with originall Compared, this 12th J̄ue. 80: p Edw: Rishworth Just: pe ·

The Testimonys of William Oliver aged about 60 years, & of John Tetherly about fiuety yeares or there abouts/

Being examined maketh oath, that Walter Mathews Now deceased, did peaceably & quietly possess & Inioy, the same house which his widdow now liueth in, Mary Mathews, & yͭ house wͨʰ shee lett vnto John Martine wͨʰ hee liueth in, with all the flake rownes, lijng rownes, a garden plott, with a stoore house roumes & Leanetwos, with the priuiledg of a moreing place for two boats lijng between smuttinose, & Malligoe Yslands, with all other priuiledges belonging there vnto, for the full tearme of Twenty odd yeares or yr abouts/ & further sayth not/ Dated the 9th of June. 1680: Taken vpon oath before mee Edw Rishworth Just pe

A true Coppy of these depositions aboue written transcribed out of the originall, & yr with Compared this 12th of June 1680 : p Edw · Rishworth ReCor:

To all Christean people to whom these P'sents shall Come/ Greeteing, now know yee that I John Heard late of Gorgeana Carpenter, for diverse good Causes & Considerations mee herevnto moueing, for the some of Twelue pounds sterling or to the valew there of, by John Parker of Marble head in the Massatusetts bay Carpenter. In manner & forme following, that is to say/ the aforesd John Parker is to pay [72] or cause to bee payd vnto the sayd John Heard, his heyrs executors or Assignes the some of fiue pounds, at or vpon the nine & Twenteth of September in the yeare of our Lord god Anno 1649 next Insewing the date hereof, to bee payd in Money, or in good M'chr̄ble Corne or boards, at price then Current, alsoe the aforesd John Parker, is to pay or cause to bee payd vnto the sd John Heard his heyrs executors or Assigns, the some of fiue pounds more, In money Corne or boards, at price then Current, at or before the fiue & twenteth of Septembr 1650 · & afterwards the sayd John Parker is to pay or Cause to bee payd, vnto the aforesd John Heard his heyres executors or Assignes, the some of fourty shillings in money, or good Mercha'ble corne or boards, at the price then Current at or before the nine & Twenteth of Septembr next Insewing being in the yeare of or Ld god 1651: for which payment of the aforesd some &

BOOK III, FOL. 72.

somes, I the aforesd John Heard do by these P'sents giue grant bargane sell & Confirme for euer, all that my house & Land & all my vpland, Marsh Ground, with all the Woods or vnderwoods, belonging in Gorgeana aforesd, with all the whoole Estate right title Interest, propriety priuiledg & benefitt which I the sayd John Heard haue had or out to haue, with all & singular the p'misses & app'tenances, therevnto belonging, to haue & to hould vnto y'e sayd John Parker & to his heyres for ever/ Witness my hand this Twelfth of June 1648.   The Marke of John

Witness to these P'sents/
  Wee whose names are here   Heard
  vnder written/ Dated the
  twelth of June Anno: 1648.
John Allcocke/ Henery Norton/

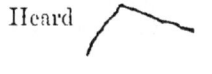

A true Coppy of this Deede transcribed out of the originall & therewith Compared this 14th of June 1680:
                p Edw: Rishworth ReCor

Wee the select men of the Town of yorke hath layd out vnto William Roanes vpon the North East side of the path, aboue bass Coue, which goeth to the Marsh, next to the Lott of Job Allcockes, & so runneth in breadth Twenty & fiue pooles, & In length foure scoore rodds or pooles, which is full Twelue Acres & an halfe/ Which Lott of Land is given by the Townsmen of Yorke, to the wife & children of the sayd William Roanes/ Septemb'r 21. 1666/

  This aboue written is a true Coppy   Peter Weare/
    taken out of the towne booke of   Jo'n Twisden/
    ReCords of yorke this first of
    June (80) p mee Abra Preble Town Clarke
vera Copia Transcribed & with y'e Towne records Compared this 18th June: 1680 ·   p Edw Rishworth ReCor:

Book III, Fol. 72.

Aprill: 22th 67.

Layd out to William Johnson thirty Acres of vpLand, tenn Acres w'of was granted vnto him before, lijng west, from the little high way bridg next adioyneing to John Twisdens Lott, Twenty seaven pooles to the bounds of Hen: Saywords Lott, & from thence North one hundred & Twenty pooles/

A true Coppy of y' grant transcribed & compared with the originall this 28th of June. 80:
p Edw: Rishworth ReCor:

John Davess
Hene · Donell
Hene: Sayword

To all people to whome these P'sents shall Come/ Know yee that Wee John Ryall sometyms of Cascoe, now liueing at yorke In ye Province of Mayne Planter, with the Consent of Elizabeth my wife, & Mehitabell Dod Which Elizabeth Dod now Ryall the wife of John Ryall & Mehitabell Dod being Legatees vnto whom a certen Legacy of an house & Lands were given them in æquall thirds between them selues & Mary Dod Now In England, by the last will & testament of their Grandfather, Mr Nicho: Davis deceased, beareing Date vpon record Aprill 27. 1667: as doth & may appeare/ The P'misses Considered, Wee the sd John Ryall, In the behalfe & with the free Consent of Elizabeth his wife, & Mehitabell Dod, now both of Yorke, do for severall Considerations there vnto us moueing, & more espetially for & in consideration of the some of Twelue pounds to us in hand payd, or secured by Law to bee payd to us or our Assigns by Samll Donell of sd yorke, w'with Wee acknowledg o' selues to bee fully payd Contented & satisfyd; by these P'sents do absolutely giue grant bargan sell Infeoff & Confirme, & haue hereby given granted barganed sould, Infeoffed & Confirmed absolutely from us o' heyres, executors, Administrators & Assigns all o^r right Title & Interest, Wee had haue or out to haue from the will of Nicho: Dauis our deceased Grandfather (being the two parts of the three parts giuen vnto ye s^d Mary Elizabeth & Mehitabell, the Marsh being left to respond the 3d part yet remajneing to bee disposed off) of a Certen Tract or P^rcell of Land, w^ron formerly the s^d Dauis hued, vntill his decease, Contayneing the quantity of three or foure Acres bee It more or less, the sunken Marsh Included y^rin, wch lyeth bounded on the North West Adioyneing to ye Land of John Brawn, & on the South West a small distance aboue the path, as Wee goe to the fferry, between the Southerne side of the Cricke & s^d path, & vpon the North East next vnto Hene: Donells Land vnto the aforesd Samll Donell his heyrs executors administrators & Assigns for euer/ To haue & to hould all & singular the aboue granted P^rmises, with euery part & P^rcell thereof, with all the Comonages, profetts, priuiledges, & appurtenances, to euery part y^runto belonging, with our right title & Interest, y^rin vnto the s^d Samll Donell his heyrs & Assigns, to his & y^r proper vss, & benefit & behoofe for euer/ And we s^d John Ryall & Mehitabell Dod, do further Covenant & promiss with & to ye s^d Samll Donell y^t wee the Granters & sellers here of, haue good right & lawfull authority in our own names to convay & dispose of the P^rmisses, as abouesd, & do by these P^sents further promiss & Ingage in the behalfe of o^r selues our heyrs administrators & Assigns, vnto ye s^d Samll Donell his heyrs executors Administrators & Assigns, y^t the s^d Land is free & Cleare from all grants gyfts leases Dowers, Morgages, & all Incomberances w^tsoeuer, & y^t Wee ye s^d John Ryall & Mehitabell Dod, In ye behalfe of our selues our heyres executors &c: will warrant & Defend the before recipted P^rmisses, & euery part & Parcell there of vnto the s^d Samll Donell his heyrs & Assigns aganst all P^sons whatsoeuer Clajmeing, or P^rtending any Clajme there vnto [73] by from or vnder vs,

BOOK III, FOL. 73.

or any others by our procurement/ In Witness w^r^vnto, Wee haue afixed our hands & seales, this 21th day of June, Anno Dom: 1680 :

Signed sealed & Deliver'd,
in the P^r^sence of
Mary White/

John Ryall his marke R (his seale)

Mehitabell Dod (her seale)

  John Ryall & Elizabeth his wife, & Mehitabell Dod, Came before mee this (7th of July 1680 :) & owned this Instrument aboue written to bee y^r^ Act & Deed, before mee

      Edw Rishworth Just pe :

vera Copia of this Instrumet transcribed out of ye originall, & y^r^ with Compared this 9th July : 1680 :

      p Edw : Rishworth ReCor :

These P^r^sent Indenturs do witness, that I Phillip ffrost, with the free Consent & approbation of Mathew my wife, of the Town of Yorke, in ye County of Yorke alias province of Mayne, Planter, do vpon good Considerations y^r^vnto vs moueing, dispose of & bind out my wifes sonn Jos : Raynkine, vnto ye Reverd Shuball Dumer Pastor of the Church of Yorke aforesd, to serue him & his wife Mr Lydea Dumer, as an Apprenice, for ye full Tearme of Twelue years from the Date hereof, & do further Covenant, & agree in ye behalfe of ye sd Ladd, y^t^ hee shall faithfully do & Piforme the place & trust of a servant, vnto his Maister Mr Dumer, & Mis Dumer, aforesd, In all such lawfull Imployments as his Maister or Mistress shall set him about, durcing ye whoole tyme of his seruice from wch hee shall not absent him selfe day or night, with out y^r^ Consent/ hee shall not Imbessell his Maisters tyme, or goods, nor giue Consent to those y^t^ shall, but shall in all things truely & faithfully behaue him selfe dureing ye tyme of his apprentishipp, as becometh an honest servant/

Book III, Fol. 73.

vpon which aforesd Considerations, the sd Mr Shuball Dumer doth Couenant & promiss, to & with yͤ sd Phillip ffrost, in the behalfe of Jos: Raynkine his sonn in Law, yᵗ hee will provide for him dureing yᵗ twelue yeares tyme, Meate, drinke, lodging & apparall, washing &c: & wᵗ is sufficient for a servant to haue of his Capacity & do his best Indeauour to teach him or cause him, to bee taught to write &c · read, Legably & audibly according to his Capacity, & at the expiration of his tyme, to double sujte him in apparell according to yͤ Law & Costome of Costome of yͤ Country/ In witness wʳvnto, wee haue herevnto, Interchangably set two oʳ hands & seales, the 4th day of March 16$\frac{79}{80}$

Signed sealed & Deliverd/   Phillip ffrost his
 in the Prsence of   marke P ff (his seale)
 Samll Wheelewright/
 Mary Whitte/   Shuball Dumer his (his seale)
        Phillip ffrost & Mathew his wife   seale
        & Mr Shuball Dummer do own this Instrumᵗ to
        bee yʳ Act & Deed, before mee this 5th March
        16$\frac{79}{80}$ Edw: Rishworth Assote/

A true Coppy of this Instrumᵉ aboue written transcribed & Compared with yͤ originall this 10th. July: 1680
                    p Edwᵈ: Rishworth ReCor:

Mr Shuball Dumer, doth before us Ingage, to deliuer a yeareling Heffer for the vss of his apprentise Jos: Raynkine vnto his father in Law Phillip ffrost, who before us stands bound by his promiss to keepe the sd Heffer for his sonn Joseph vnto the halfes vntill his Tyme bee expired, & then to returne the prinsiple & his halfe into his own possession/ Dated 5th of March 16$\frac{79}{80}$ Edw: Rishworth
    vera Copia of this postscript   Samull Wheelewright
    transcribed this 10th July: 80:   Assotiats/
        p Edw · Rishworth ReCor .

This Confirmation of a bill of sale, made this 12th of
August 1661 : & w'as I John Billine, with the Consent of
my Mother Elizabeth Tommass, did make sale of an house
& Land, as shall bee here after mentioned, which foresd
sayle was made by mee, John Billine, & my sd Mother in y^e
yeare of o^r Ld 1656 . on the eleaventh day of Octob^r & w'as
I was then in my mmority, & Could not make Legall sale of
the sd Land, for wch I was fully satisfyd, according to condition, by the partys y^t I sould It vnto, wch was namely to
Thomas Crockett, & Rice Tommass, I do now being of full
years Confirme the same/

Know all men by these P^rsents, y^t I John Billine of
Kittery in the County of Yorke, haue bargained & sould
vnto Thom^s Crocket, as is aboue expressd, an house & Land
with all ye Rights, titles & priuiledges, there vnto belonging,
my heyres, executors, Assigns, or Administrators, shall own
the sd sayle vnto his heyres, executors, or Assigns, the sd
sale is made for euer, to Inioy peaceably with out Molesta-
tion/ Which house & Land lyeth in the Town of Kittery, at
the place Comanly Called the Poynt, neare the Harbours
Mouth, a part of y^t necke of Land on which Majo^r Shapleighs stoore house stands on/ Which house & Land I had
possession of a Inheritance, after ye decease of my father,
John Billine Senjo^r, the former husband of my Mother the
abouesd Elizabeth Tomass, which house & Land I haue
really sould & Deliuered vnto Thomas Crocket as aboue
sayd, for & In Consideration of Twelue pounds already
payd vnto mee John Billine, at y^e first sale as is aboue
expressd, which was done according to Condition, six pounds
by Tho: Crokett, & six pounds by Rice Tomass/ In witness

w^rof I haue here vnto set my hand & seale, this twelueth day of August one thousand six hundred sixty : 1661

Signed sealed & Deliuered,   The marke of $\mathcal{UU}$ (his seale)
   in P^rsence of us/   John Billine
Jos . Davis/   John Billine Came this day & owned this
James Pheelps/   Instrum^t to bee his Act & Deed, 23th
Samll Davis/   June : 1680 : before mee mee
                      ffran : Hooke Just : pe .

vera Copia of this Instrume^t transcribed & with ye originall Compared this 13th of July   1680 ·

                        p Edw : Rishworth ReCor ·

ffurther, each of us do allow of the sajle of y^t Land formerly sould by our father vnto our brother Ephraim Crocket, onely hee is to allow vnto the Estate seauen pounds, mentioned in the Inventory into all which Wee do here vnto sett o^r hands, this day & yeare aboue written/

   The marke of Ann Crocket/
                      The marke of Ephraim Crocket
                      The marke of Hugh Crockett
[74] The marke of Joseph Crocket/
              Josua Crockett/

Acknowledged this 21th of July : 1679 : before mee ffran : Hooke Commission^r

A true Coppy of this Instrume^t transcribed, out of the originall & y^r with Compared this 13th of July, 1680 .

                     p Edw : Rishworth ReCor :

Book III. Fol. 74.

Witness these P^rsents, that I Hene. Donell of Yorke rescident in New England, haue bargained sould alienated, Infeoffed & Confirmd vnto Majo^r Thom^s Clarke of Boston, in New England a Certen P^icell of Marsh ljing & being on the North West branch of Yorke Marsh In New England, a little below the bridg, which Marsh I do alienate & Confirme, vnto ye sd Thomas Clarke of Boston, his heyres & Assignes forever, from mee my heyres or Assigns or any vnder mee, which I do acknowledg my selfe to bee fully satisfy & payd, for every part & Picell of the sd Marsh, ljing & being in the River of Yorke aboue sd, in the Province of Mayne/ Which Marsh is bounded as followeth, on the Lower side with Abra: Prebles Marsh, on the higher side with Andrew Everests, & William Freathys, which Marsh in quantity, is in Contents two or three Acres, or there abouts, more or less, which I do alienate, & Confirme to make good vnto Majo^r Thomas Clarke, his heyres or Assignes for euer from mee my heyres or Assignes, or any vnder mee/ Which Land is deliuered vnto Majo^r John Davess of Yorke, for ye vss of Maj^r Thom^s Clarke abouesd, & for the true P^rformance hereof, I haue here vnto sett my hand & seale, this 12th of July 1680:

Signed sealed & Delivered,   The marke of
 In the P^rsence of, us
 ffrancis Johnson/   Henery Donell ⟨HD⟩ (his seale)
 John Penwill/   Hene: Donell Came before mee this 12th of July 1680. & acknowledged the aboue instrumet to bee his Act & Deed,
         John Davess Jus^t pe:

A true Coppy of this aboue Instrumet transcribed & Compared with ye originall this 13th of July · 1680 ·
     p Edw. Rishworth ReCor ·

Book III, Fol. 74.

To all whome these P^rsents, shall Come greeteing/ Know yee y^t I Thomas Gorges Esqr Deputy Gou̅er, of the Province of Mayne, by vertue of Authority vnto mee given, from Sir Fardind^o Gorges K^t Ld Propriato^r of s^d Province for diverse good causes & Considerations, mee there vnto moueing, haue given granted bargained sould, Infeoffed & Confirmed, & by these P^rsents in the behalfe of s^d Sir Fardind^o Gorg^s do give, grant, bargan sell Infeoff & Confirme vnto John Smyth of Sacoe in the County of Surry Carpenter, his heyrs & Assigns, one hundred Acres of Land, & one Ysland seituate lyng & being at Cape Porpus in the s^d Province, the s^d Ysland ljng in Length from North East, to South West, and the s^d hundred acres of land ljng from the North East, at the end of the sayd Ysland 80 pooles to ye South west, & so vp into the Mayn Land on a North West Line, by all the breadth afores^d, till one hundred Acres bee Compleated, the s^d Ysland ljng South East from the sayd Land To haue & to hould the afores^d hundred acres of Land & Island, & all & singular ye P^rmises appurtenances, & every part, & Parcell thereof vnto the s^d John Smyth his heyres & Assigns for euer, to the onely vss & behoofe of the s^d John Smyth his heyrs & Assignes for euermore, Yeilding, & paijng for the P^rmisses vnto the s^d Sir Fardinando Gorges, his heyrs & Assignes, six shillings, & eight peece yearely, on the nine & Twenteth day of September/ And I the s^d Thomas Gorges, do by these P^rsents Constitute ordayne & appoynt ffrancis Robinson Gentle̅: my true & lawful Attunney (in my place & stead) in the name of ye s^d Sir ffardind^o Gorges, to enter into the s^d P^rmisses, or into any part or Parcell thereof, in the name of the whoole, & y^rof to take full & peaceable possession & seazin, & after such possession, & seisin so had & taken then for him & in his name, to deliver full & peaceable possession & seisin of the same Land, & P^rmisses, vnto the s^d John Smyth, his heyrs & Assignes, according to ye Teno^r æffect, & true meaneing of

these P'sents/ In witness w'of, I the sd Thomas Gorges, haue here vnto set my hand & seale this 18th of July 1643·
Sealed & deliver'd   Thomas Gorges
   In ye P'sence of/   Depty Gouer̃ (locus sigill)
   Bartholomew Barnett/   A true Coppy of this Instrument
   Roger Garde/   aboue written transcribed out
                      of the originall, & y^t with Com-
                      pared this 14th day of July
                      1680 :
                      p Edw : Rishworth ReCor.

I William Phillips of Sacoe in the Province of Mayn, in New England, by vertue of my pouer to & in this Instrument, with euery part, & P'cell of the Land here in mentioned, by means of a Deed of sale made ouer to mee of ye same by the aforesd Smyth, as by the sd Deed will more fully appeare, haue given granted, barganed, sould Assignd, & set ouer, & do by these P'sents give grant, bargane, sell, Assigne, & set ouer the same vnto Bryan Pendleton his heyrs, & Assignes to haue & to hould for euer, to his & thejr own proper vsse & behoofe, hereby freeing the sd Pendleton, his heyrs, & Assgnes for euer, from any Clajme, & Demand to the sd Land or any Instrum^t Concerneing it w^tsoeuer, that either my selfe, John Smyth, or either of us, haue or hath may or might, or any for us, or in o^r names should, or in any wise haue or Clajme of in, or two the same/ In witness where of for my selfe my heyrs, & Assigns I haue set my hand this 11th of Octob^r 1666.

I Bridget Phillips do hereby manifest   William Phillips
   my free & full Consent, vnto w^tso-
   euer my husband hath done, & doth
   do in relation to this Instrument/
                Bridgitt Philhps/

A true Coppy of this Assignem^t transcribed & Compared with the originall this 14th July 1680 :
                    p Edw : Rishworth ReCor :

Book III, Fol. 74.

To all Christean people to whom these P'sents shall Come/ Ambrose Boaden of Blã˙ Poynt alias Scarbrough, & Province of Mayne ffisherm͠a: sends Greeteing˙ Know yee that hee the sd Ambrose Boaden for & in Consideration of the some of thirty pounds, to him in hand already payd by Nathan Bedford of the Town of Blã: Poynt & Province aforesayd, ffisherman & Yeamon, W'with hee the sd Boaden doth acknowledg him selfe Satisfyd, & by vertue of these P'sents haue given granted sould ahend, & Confirmed, vnto the sd Bedford all my right, & title that I haue or ought to haue, by grant, possession or any other propriety w'soeuer, to one hundred & fiuety acres of Land & Meddow, lijng & Situateing on the North West side of the Mouth of Spurwinke River, with in the Township of Blã: Poynt, alias Scarbrough, W^r the sd Ambrose Boadens father did formerly possess, & Inhabite/ To haue & to hould, the sd one hundred & fiuety Acres togeather with all ye benefitts, priuiledges, profetts, & Imunitys, there of & thence ariseing, to the onely proper vss, & behoofe, of him the sd Bedford his heyrs & Assigns for euer, & the sd Boaden for him selfe, his heyres executors & Administrators, doth Covenant sell, & grant, to & with the sd Bedford his hevrs executors & Assigns, that hee the sd Bedford, the day of ye date hereof, is & standeth lawfully Seized, according to the Nationall Law of o^r soueraign Ld, the King of England &c˙ the full poner, good right & authority, to grant bargan, sell convay, & Assure the same in manner, & forme aforesd, & y^t hee the sd Bedford his heyres, executors & Assigns, & euery of them, shall & may for euer hereafter, peaceably & quietly haue, haue hould Occupy & Injoy the aforesd P'misses free, & cleare, & clearly acquitted, & discharged from all Legall Molestations, & Incomberances from any Prson or Prsons w'soeuer/ In Confirmation of which Premisses, the sd Ambrose Boaden, hath here vnto subscribed his hand, &

Book III, Fol. 74.

seale this Twenty ninth day of July in the yeare of our L{{d}}
one thousand six hundred seaventy nine/

  Ambrose Boadens wife did free- Ambross Boaden ($\binom{his}{seale}$)
   ly signe this aboue Instrume{{t}} The marke of
   in the P{{r}}sence of us, this 29th
   July . 79 :   Mary Boaden   ($\binom{her}{seale}$)

Signed sealed & Deliver'd Great Ysland 11th of August
In y{{e}} P{{r}}sence of us/ 1679 : Mr Nathell Fryer, &
Nathaell Fryer/   Robert Jordan, made oath y{{t}}
Robert Jordan/   they saw Ambrose Boaden, &
         Mary Boaden signe seale, &
         deliver the aboue Instrume{{t}}
         as y{{r}} Act & Deed before mee
         Elyas Styleman Commission{{r}}

A true Coppy of this Instrument aboue written, transcribed, & with the originall Compared this 16th of July :
1680 .   p Edw . Pishworth ReCor :

  To all Christean people to whome these P{{r}}sents shall
Come/ Mr Hene : Watts of the Town of Scarbrough, &
Province of Mayne fishmonger, Sendeth Greeteing ; Know
yee that the sd Hene . Watts, for & In Consideration of y{{e}}
some of sixty pounds to him in hand already payd, by
Nathan Bedford, of the Town of bla͠ : Poynt, & Province
aforesd, Yeaman, w{{r}}with hee the sd Watts doth acknowledg
him selfe satisfyd, & by vertue of these P{{r}}sents, haue given,
granted aliend, & Confirmed, vnto y{{e}} sd Bedford a P{{r}}cell of
Land contayneing one hundred Acres, with the Meddow
thereto lyng & belonging, scituate & lyng or in a place
Comanly Called Blew Poynt, within the Township of Bla͠ :
Poynt, alias Scarb{{r}}g{{h}} W{{r}} the sd Hene . Watts did formerly
possess, & Inhabitt, togeather with all his Westerne Marshes
excepting onely what Marsh is Contayned in another deed
of sd Wattes of Two hundred Acres : To haue & to hould,
the sd hundred acres & Marsh according to y{{e}} bounds

Book III, Fol. 74.

expressd, in a Deed of the sd wattes from Mr Geo : Cleeues, lijng as aforesd, lijng with the Westerne Marsh, togeather with all the benefitts, profetts, Emolum^{ts} thence ariseing, to the onely proper vss, & behoofe of him ye sd Bedford, his heyrs & Assigns for euer : And the sd Watts for him selfe & Assigns his heyrs, executors & Admistro^{rs} doth Couenant promiss & grant to & with ye sd Bedford his heyr executors that hee the sd Bedford the day of the date here of is, & standeth lawfully Seized, according to the Nationall Law of our soueraigin Ld the King of England &c · of the sd Premisses, & euery part thereof, in a good P^{r}fect, & absolute Estate of Inheritance, & hath in him selfe full pouer, good right, & authority to grant, bargan, sell, Convay, & Assure ye same in manner, & forme aforesd. & that hee the sd Bedford, his heyrs executors & Assignes, & every of them, shall & may for ever hereafter, peacably & quietly, haue hould, Occupy, & Inioy the aforesd P^{r}misses free & cleare. & freely acquitted, & discharged, from all Legall Molestations, & Incomberances, from any Prson, or Prsons w^{t}soeuer, togeather with all his right, & Interest, of a Parcell of Marsh scituateing & lijng or by a Certen place known, & Called by the name of Crooked Lane, on the Eastward side of the River/ In Confirmation of which P^{r}misses the sd Hene : Watts, hath here vnto subscribed his hand, & seale, this Twenty sixt day of June In y^e yeare of o^r Ld, one thousand six hundred, & Eighty, annoq$_\text{e}$ Regni Regis, Carolj secundj Angliæ, Scotiæ, et Hiberniæ Rex : xxx/

Signed sealed & Deliver'd in the Prsence of us/ Nathan^{ll} ffryer/ Nicholas Heskins/	p mee Henery Watts ($^{his}_{seale}$) Mr Henery Watts mentioned in this Deede, was P^{r}sent before mee, Walter Gyndall, & did signe seale, & deliver the same, and acknowledged all the articles thereof, to Nathan Bedford this 26 . June . 80 : before mee Walter Gyndall Commissio^r/

Book III, Fol. 74-76.

A true Coppy of this Instrument, transcribed out of yͤ originall & yͭ with Compared this 17th day of July 1680
       p Edw Rishworth ReCor:

Bee It known by these Pr̃sents, that I Geo: Cleenes Gentle: agent for Colonell Allexandr Rigby, Pr̃sident & proprietor of the province of Lygonia, do by authority derived from the Pr̃sident, give, grant, sell & Confirme vnto Michaell Mitton of Cascoe Gentle: & to his heyrs for euer, all that Poynt of Land in Cascoe Bay, lijng ouer the River, & butting against the now dwelling house of him the sayd Michaell Mitton, & from the sd house South westwardly, togeather with all yͤ Marsh ground adioyneing to yͤ sd poynt of Land, on both sides of the Cricke or sault water Gutt [76] from the sd poynt of Land, South westwardly, togeather with so much vpland, on the West side, of the sd Marsh & by the side of the River, as will make vp the Poynt of Land & Marsh ground one hundred acres w͗ch Land & Marsh ground is now & hath been for yͤ space of tenn years past, in the possession of yͤ sd Michell Mitton/ To haue & to hould all the sd demised Pr̃misses, to him the sd Michaell Mitton & his heyrs for euer of & from the sd Pr̃sident & his heyrs for euer, yeilding & paijng therefore yearely & euery yeare for euer, to the sd Allexandr Rigby, his heyrs & assignes, the yearly rent two shillings & six peence, vpon euery first day of Novembr euery yeare, for all seeruices, & demands, And If it shall happen, that the sd rent bee vnpayd, It shall bee always due for yͤ sd Proprietor, & his heyrs to Enter into any of the Pr̃misses, & to distrayne, & yͤ destres to detayne, & keepe, vntill the sd rent & all the arers bee payd, & this grant, is to bee Inrowled in the Provinciall Court of pleas, within one yeare, next after yͤ date here of, & in testimony here of, I haue here vnto set my hand, & seale, this first day of Janvary one thousand six hundred & fiuety/

Witness vs/   George Cleeue (his seale)
   Richd Bray   Attested by Mr Geo Cleeue this 9th
   his marke   day of May 1660: before us to bee
   Thomas Harlo   his Act, & Deed, by mee Robert Jor-
   his marke   dan Assotiate/ firan : Neale Comisso^r/
vera Copia of this Instrume^t transcribed out of the originall & y^r with Compared this 19th July · 1680 :

                  p Edw : Rishworth ReCor :

Mitten To Clarke   These P^rsents witnesseth, y^t I Elizabeth Mitton, late wife to Michaell Mitton deceased, in Consideration that Taddeous Clarke married my daughter Elizabeth, I do by these P^rsents, grant, giue, & make ouer, all my right Title & Interest in the Land with in mentioned vnto ye sd Taddeous Clarke his heyrs executors administrators & assigns from mee my heyrs executors administrators & Asigns to inioy for euer/ as witness my hand this first day of March 1662

Testes George Mumoy
   Peter Harvy/   Elizabeth Mitton/
                           marke/

vera Copia of this Assignem^t transcribed & Compared this 19th of July : 1680 · p Edw : Rishworth ReCor :

To all Christean people, to whome this P^rsent deed shall Come/ George ffelt Senjo^r of Cascoe bay In the Province of Mayne in New England Planter, sends Greete^r Know yee, that the sd Geo. ffelt Senjo^r, on the one part, & Walter Gyndall of Spurwinke Yeamon in the province of Mayn In New England as abouesd on the other part, Witnesseth, that ye sd George ffelt for the full some of six pounds, in monys

of New England, to him by Walter Gyndall well & truely
payd, at or before the sealeing & delivery hereof, the receipt
w'of, hee the sd Geo: ffelt Senjo' doth hereby acknowledg,
& him selfe there with to bee fully satisfyd, & contented, &
there from, & from euery part there of, for him selfe, his
heyrs executors administrators do hereby exonerate & acquit,
& fully discharge the sd walter Gyndall, his heyrs executors
& Assigns for euer, by these P'sents, Hath & hereby doth
fully freely clearely & absolutely, giue grant bargan sell
Alliene Infeoff, convay & Confirme, vnto the sayd Walter
Gyndall his heyrs executors, administrators & Assigns, One
hundred Acres of vpland lying & being on the Westward
side of Geo ffelts ould house in Cascoe bay about Eighty
rodd from sd house, begining at a three forked bla͞ Oake
tree neare the high way being marked on both sid^s, & so
down to ye water side and then to runne vpon a square vntill
the whoole hundred Acres bee fully Compleated, & accomplished with priuiledg & full propriety & benefitt of the
sea down to Low water marke breadth of his sd Tract of
Land, with foure Acres of fresh Meddow, lying about three
Miles from ffelts ould fejld, & two Acres of sault Meddow
at the head of the great Coue w^r Walter Gyndall pleaseth
to lay It out, with all other Meddows belonging to the hundred Acres of vpland, with all mines, Minneralls, Woods
vnderwoods, profetts priuiledges Lybertys, easements, & all
other the apputences to the Premisses belonging, or any
wise appertayneing, To haue & to hould, to him the sd
Walter Gyndall, his heyrs executors, administrators &
Assignes for euer, to his & thejr soole & proper vss & behoofe from hence forth & for euer/ And the sd Geo. ffelt
Senjo^r, for him selfe his heyrs executors Administrators, do
covenant promiss & grant, to & with the sayd Walter Gyndall
his heyrs, executors administrators & Assigns, that hee y^e
sayd George ffelt Senjo^r is the true & proper owner of the

aboue barganed P^rmisses, & haue in him selfe full pouer & good right, & lawfull athority the P^rmisses to bargan sell Convay & Confirme, vnto him the sd Walter Gyndall, his heyrs executors administrators, & Assigns, in manner as aforesd/ And that the sayd Premisses & appurtenances, are at the sealing & delivery here of, free & cleare acquitted & discharged, of & from all manner of former Gyfts, grants, bargans sales Leases, Morgages Joynters Dowers, Judgm^{ts}, executions, Wills, Intayls forfeturs ceazurs titles troubells, & all other Acts alienations & Incomberances whatsoeuer, had made or done, or suffered to bee done by mee, or any other Person from by or vnder mee, and that the sayd Walter Gyndall shall & may for euer here after peaceably & quietly, haue hould vss Occupy possess & Imoy all & singular the afore barganed P^rmisses, & appurtenances without the Lett, trouble hinderance, Molestation & disturbance of mee the sayd George ffelt Senjo^r, my heyrs executors, administrators Or Assignes, or any of them, or of any other Person Clajmeing a right thereto, or any part there of, from by or vnder him, And the Premisses against him selfe & & euery other Prson lawfully Clajmeing a right there to vnto the sd Walter Gyndall, his heyrs executors Administrators [77] & assigns, shall warrant & euer defend by these P^rsents, & the sd George ffelt Senjo^r do further covenant & promiss, that at any tyme here after, vpon the reasonable request & demand of the sd Walter Gyndall to do any further Act, or thing, that may bee for the better secureing of the P^rmisses to him & his, according to ye true Intent & meaneing of these P^rsents/ In witness whereof I haue here vnto set my hand & seale, this Twenty third day of June, in the yeare of o^r Ld one thousand six hundred & Eighty, & In the thyrty secound yeare of the Reign of our Soueraigne Ld Charles the secund, by the Grace of God of England Scotland &c: King, Defender of the faith/

Signed sealed & Delivered   George ffelt Senj[r] his (his seale)
  In the P[r]sence of/
  John Graues/ George Pearson/   marke

Isacke Davis his Mr Geo: Pearson Came before mee &
marke did Attest vpon his oath as a witness to y[s] Instrum[t] y[t] hee was
P[r]sent & saw Jo[n] Graues sign It as
a witness, & Geo · ffelt Senj[r] signe
seale & deliuer this sd aboue Instrume[t] as his Act & Deed
Taken vpon oath this 23th July ·
1680: before mee/
Edw: Rishworth Just pe:

A true Coppy of this Instrume[t] transcribed out of y[e] originall & y[r] with Compared this 23th of July 1680:
                p Edw: Rishworth ReCor:

Cap[t] Walter Barefoote Enters Cavtion against Mr John Jefford as haueing not any right to any Lands w[r]in the sd Barefoote is Concern'd at Sacoe haueing relinquished all former contracts therein, w[r]by y[e] Interest lyes sooly in the sd Barefoote, & John Sargeant is cawtioned not to pay the sd Gifford any more rent touching y[e] P[r]misses/
          23: July: 80: Edw: Rishworth ReCor:

      Robert Wadleigh appeareth before mee & tes-
The oath hath relation to Deed on ReCord pa. 65 tifys that hee was P[r]sent & did see Thomas Cabinnocke, & Romanascoe, signe seale & deliuer these Instruments as on both sid[s] appear-

Book III, Fol. 77.

eth, to bee thejr act & deed & set two his hand as a witness/
Swoine before mee this 8th of July · 1680 ·
   John Gillman of the Cousell of the Province
   of New Ham shire/
vera Copia of this oath as Attests this 23 . July 1680 :
       Edw : Rishworth ReCor

 Know all men by these Presents, that I Lewis Tucker
ffisherman, late of the Ysles of shoales, now of Pischataqua,
haue barganed sould, & by these P^rsents do bargan sell,
aliene & set ouer, all that my dwelling house on smuttinoss
Ysland, on the Yseles of Shoales vnto Roger Kelly of sd
Ysland, his heyrs executors, administrators & Assigns, for
euer, for a valewable Consideration in hand receiued namely,
by Tenn shillings money recciued my selfe, Thirteen pounds
tenn shillings pay'd for mee to Mr Rewben Hull, & full discharge of all debt, between sd Mr Kelly & my selfe, vnto
this day, I do y^rfore hereby acknowledg to hau sould sd Mr
Kelly, sayd house & garden, with all my right Title &
Interest, therein to him & his heyres &c : for euer, peaceably to Inioy the same, & do promiss to defend the Title
against all manner of P^rsons, claymeing from by or vnder
mee/ Witness my hand & seale, this fifth day of Aprill 1680 :
Signed sealed & Delivered/   Lewis Tucker (^{his}_{seale})
 In the P^rsence of/
 Samll Belcher   his marke
 John ffrost/   Lewis Tucker did acknowledg this In-
 his marke/   strument to bee his Act & Deed this
        23d of July 1680 ·
    before mee than : Hooke Just^s pe
vera Copia of this Deed transcribed out of the originall,
& there with Compared this 27th day of July 1680
       p Edw : Rishworth ReCor

Book III, Fol. 77.

Know all men by these Presents, y{t} I Bryan Pendleton of Sacoe in the Province of Mayne, in New England, for & in Consideration of the full & iust some of one hundred & sixty pounds, sterlg : in hand payd already vnto mee by Joseph Cross of Wells in the province abouesd, the receipt where of & euery part thereof I do acknowledg, & am there with satisfyd & do hereby acquitt, & discharge the sayd Joseph Cross, his heyres, executors Administrators, & Assignes, from euery part, & Parcell there of, haue given granted bargained, sould, Infeoffed, & Confirmed, & do hereby giue grant bargan sell Infeoff & Confirme vnto the afore-sd Joseph Cross, a Certen Parcell of Land scituate, & being, in the Town of Wells aforesayd, Contayneing foure hundred seaventy & foure Acres, of vpland & Marsh, as it is now bounded South East. with the River antiently Called Webhannett River, & on the South West, bounded with the Land of the sayd Joseph Cross, on the North East, bounded with y{e} Town Land appoynted for y{e} Ministrey, & on the North West bounded with the Comans, of which Parcell of Land, I the sayd Bryan Pendleton bought Two hundred Acres of Sheath Fletcher, as by his Deed bearcing date the Twenteth day of May one thousand six hundred sixty three, & a hundred & finety Acres of William Hammonds as by his Deed, dated May eleventh one thousand six hundred sixty one, & 124 Acres bought of Jo{n} West as by his Deed bearemg date Novb{r} 8th 1661 · & all lyng togeather in one Parcell, & bounded as aforesayd/ and now sould as aforesayd from mee the sayd Bryan Pendleton my heyres executors & Administrators, to y{e} sayd Joseph Cross/ To haue & to hould, all & singular the aboue bargained Premisses, with all & singular the appurtenances, & priuiledges thereto belonging, or in any wise app'tayneing, to him the sayd Joseph Cross his heyres, executors, Administrators, & Assigns for euer, the same to defend against any manner of Prson, or Persons makeing any lawfull Claime to the

Book III, Fol. 77, 78.

P'misses, or any part, or parcell there of, of by or from vnder mee, for Confirmation w'of, I the sayd Bryan Pendleton haue here vnto set my hand, & seale the third day of [78] July, in the yeare of our Lord one thousand six hundred & eighty/

Signed sealed & Delivered/   Bryan Pendleton (locus sigilli)
in the Presence of us/   Bryan Pendleton appeared be-
Mary Bolles her   fore mee this 3d day of July
marke NB   one thousand six hundred &
Joseph Bolles   eighty, & did freely acknowledg the aboue written
deed of sayle, to bee his
Act & Deed/
John Wincoll Just: peace/

vera Copia of this Instrument transcribed out of the originall & y'with Compared this 9th of August 1680·
           p Edw. Rishworth ReCor:

Know all men by these Presents, that I Abell Porter Junjo', of Boston, in New England hath & do, with the Consent of Hannah my wife, for & in Consideration of thyrty pounds according to agreement & the receipt w'of, I am well Assured of Michaell Endle, fisherman, at Pischataq in New England, w'with I do acknowledg him selfe to bee fully satisfyd, & payd, & do hereby exonerate acquit & discharge, the sayd Mihall Endle, of euery part, & Parcell thereof, for w'ch I haue giuen granted, barganed, Infeoffed, & Contirmed, & do by these P'sents giue grant grant for my selfe, my heyres, executors, & Administrators, sell Infeoff & Confirme, vnto the sd Michell Endell, one Messuage, or Lot of Land scituated, & being in the Town of Kittery neare the River of Pischataqua in New England, aforesd, & butting against Sprice Cricke on the west side there of, being a lot

BOOK III, FOL. 78.

granted to William Seely deceased, Contayneing twenty fiue Acres by measure, more or less, as It is bounded on the North West side, by the Land of Mis Mary Cutt, deuided by a North East & a south West lyne, from spruse Cricke on the North East End, to another small Cricke on the South west end thereof, & on the South West side of the Land of William Scriven, deuided by an East South East Lyne, of finety foure pooles in length, & then South East & by East Lyne of Tenn poole, & from thence an East lyne down to spruse Cricke aforesd, Twenty fiue Acres of Land as It was granted by the Town of Kittery vnto William Seely aforesd & layd out & Measured by Capt Wincoll May 25th 1678. The same to haue, & to hould all the aboue mentioned P^{r}misses, with all the priuiledges, & appurtenances thereto belonging, or any way app^{r}tayneing to him the sd Micall Endall, his heyrs, & Assigns for euer, the same to warrant, & Defend from any P^{r}son or persons makeing Clajme thereto, or to any part y^{r}of, & for Confirmation of the treuth hereof I the aforesd Abell Porter haue in behalfe of my selfe, & Hannah my wife, given possession vnto the aforesd Micall Endell for him selfe, & his heyrs for euer, in Consent w^{r}to & witness y^{r}of, I the sd Abell Porter with Hannah my wife, haue set both o^r hands, & seales, this Twenty secund day of March in the yeare of o^r Lord 16$\frac{78}{80}$

Signed, sealed   Abell Porter (his seale)
& deliuered for the vsse   Hannah Porter (her seale)
abouesd expressed before   Abell Porter, & Hannah his
William Sargant/   Wife, acknowledged this
Joseph Morse/   Instrument or writeing, to
            bee y^r Act & Deede, hand &
            seale in Boston 22th of
            March $\frac{79}{80}$ before
            Humphry Davie Assistant:

A true Coppy of this Instrument aboue written, transcribed out of y^e originall & there with Compared, this 10th day of August 1680

       p Edw. Rishworth ReCor:

Book III, Fol. 78.

This Indenture made the 7th of Aprill 1680: between Henery Symson of the Province of Mayne, haue sould elienated, Infeoffed & delivered, & by these P^rsents sell alienate, Infeoff & deliver vnto Edw: Johnson of Yorke in the province of Mayne, to him, his heyrs, executors & Assignes, for euer. a P^rcell of Land lijng & being in Yorke in the province of Mayne aforesd, that is to say, tenn Acres of Land bee It more or less, wch Land was purchased by my father Henery Symson of Mr Henery Norton, which sd land lymited & bounded In manner, & forme following, that is to say on the North East side bounded by the Cricke y^t is by the Meeteing house, on the South side bounded by the Land of Mr Edw Godfreys, on the North West side from ye bridg, & so along by the Land of John Parker Senjo^r, vnto a great pine tree, which is still standing & was the Antient bound at that Coner, & bounded on the South West on Thomas Donells Land, as also another Parcell of Land scituate & lijng in Yorke In ye Province of Mayn aforesd, that is to say foure or fiue Acres bee It more or less being lymited & bounded in manner & forme following, That is to say from a tree bridg at the head of a Coue, Comanly Called biss Coue, & so by the Coues side to the Land of Samll Bragdons, & so from thence along by ye side of ye sd Bagdons Land to the Coman path, that goeth from John Parkers Senjo^r & William Freathys, which sayd Tract of Land, I the sd Henery Symson do likewise sell, deliuer, & Confirme vnto the aboue Edw. Johnson to him & his heyrs for euer, onely I the sd Hene Symson do reserue for my selfe & heyrs & Assigns for euer, a free passage for a Cart way down to ye Coue for a sifficient Landing place, for hay or any other things, & I the abouesd Hene: Symson, do by these P^rsents, ratify & Confirme ye abouesd Parcells of Land, with all the priuiledges & Imunitys y^rvnto belonging, vnto the abouesd Edw Johnson, to him & his heyrs, for euer, for a valewable Consideration in hand Received, & I the sd Hene. Symson, do bind my selfe & heyres to mantayn the

BOOK III, FOL. 78, 79.

Lawfull sayle of It, being free from all intanglements of any kind, & to defend the sayle of them from any P^rson or P^rsons y^t may or shall hereafter lay any right, or Clajme to either of the sd P^rcells, vnto all which I the sd Hene. Symson, binds my selfe my heyrs executors, Administrators, & Assigns, as witness my hand & scale. the day & yeare aboue written/

Signed scaled & Deliuered,   Henery Symson ($_{seale}^{his}$)
In the P^rsence of vs/   his marke
Richard Bankes/

his marke,   Henery Symson made his acknowl-
              edgm^et that this is his Act &
Abraham Preble/   Deed, this seaueth of May 1680
               before mee Jo^n Davess Jus^t pc

A true Coppy of y^s Deed, transcribed & Compared wth the originall this 10th of August 1680.

                    p Edw · Rishworth ReCor :

Know all men by these P^rsents, that I Richd Whitte now of Braue boate Harbour, of the Town of Kittery, do for & in Consideration of Two hundred & tenn pounds Sterlg: already received in hand from Majo^r Nicho: Shapleigh, & Fran Hooke both of Kittery, do by these P^rsents for y^r security, Morgage, & make ouer vnto ye sd Majo^r Nicho: Shapleigh, & ffran · Hooke, thejr heyrs, executors, administrators or Assigns all [**79**] my right, title, & Interest of one dwelling house, & Land app^rtayneing to it, which I bought & purchased of Ephraim Crocket, lijng & scituateing at the head of braue boate harbour as may appearemore fully, by the sd Crocketts Deed, of sayle, now now in the hands of the sd Majo^r Shapleigh, & Hooke/ further, I do by these P^rsents, give grant, & make ouer vnto the sd Majo^r Shapleigh & Hooke, eighteen head of Cattle, y^t is to say, six

Book III, Fol. 79.

Cows, foure Steeres, foure heffers, & foure Calfes, as also thyrteen Hoggs, two horses, & one Mare all which, I do by these P^rsents make ouer, & alienate vnto the sd Majo^r Shapleigh & Hooke, vnto them y^r heyres, executors, administrators, & Assigns for euer, as thejr own proper Estate, without let, or Molestation, by mee my heyrs, executors or Administrators for ever/

The Condition of the abouesd obligation is such, that If the sd Richd Whitte, his heyrs executors, Administrators, shall Well, & truely pay or cause to bee payd vnto the sd Majo^r Shapleigh, & Fran: Hooke, the full some of Two hundred, & Tenn pounds aboue mentioned, in good M^rchtable pay, at or before ye last day of Aprill next Insewing, the date here of, then the abouesd obligation or Morgage, to bee voyd, & of none ælfect, or otherwise to stand in full pouer, force, & vertue, vnto all which I haue here vnto set my hand, & seale, this 29th of June 1679:

Signed sealed & Deliuered/   The marke of ⊗

In ye P^rsence of us/   Richd Whitte/ (his seale)

Shubeall Dumer/   Ri^chard Whitte acknowledged the aboue

Hannah Snell   written Instrume^t to bee his Act, &

her ℒ 𝛿 marke   Deed, this 2nnd of July 1679:

    before mee John Wincoll Asso^te:

Samson Whitte aged about 23 years, & James Wiggin Jujo^r aged about 21 years testifyd, that they saw Richd Whitte, deliver the Land expressed in ye aboue Instrum^t into ye hands of Mr Fran Hooke, by Twigg, & Turffe, & also saw the sd Whitte deliver the Cattle aboue expressed, into the hands of ye sd Hooke for his own vss, & for ye vss of Majo^r Nicho· Shapleigh, the 13th day of Septemb^r 1679:

Taken vpon oath this 17th of Septemb^r 1679. before mee
                       John Wincoll Asso^te

BOOK III, FOL. 79.

A true Coppy of this Morgage aboue written, with ye possession expressd, transcribed out of the originall & y^r with Compared y^s 10th of August : 1680 :

p Edw : Rishworth ReCor :

Bee It known vnto all men by these Presents, that I John Henderson now of Salem In the County of Essex, in New England ffisherman, for & in Consideration of the full, & iust some of Twenty pounds eighteen shillings & 7^d, Sterling which I do ow & stand Justly Indebted to William Down of Boston In the County of Suffocke, in New England aforesd M^{c}hant haue barganed & sould, & Do by these P^{r}sents, grant, bargane sell, aliene, Assigne set ouer & Confirme, unto the sayd William Down, his heyrs, executors, & Assigns a Certen Tract, & P^{r}cell of Land, Contayneing fourty Acres, bee It more or less, of vpland, & Meddow, scituate lijng & being, at or neare a place to the Eastward, Called Comanly Winter Harbour, lijng on the South West side of Sacoe River, bounded on the South East with some Land of Peter Hendersons, on which side there is a spring, as the bounds North West, by the Land of Humfrey Case, there being between them a small brooke, as the bounds North East by Sacoe River, & the Woods, & Coman Land to the South West/ To haue, & to hould, the sayd Parcell of Land, bee It more or less, both vpland & Meddow, with all the profetts, priuiledges, & appurtenances of what kind soeuer, is there to in any wise belonging, vnto the sayd Willm Down, his heyrs & Assigns, to his & thejr own proper vss, benefit, and behoofe for euer : And I the sayd John Henderson, for my selfe, my heyrs executors, & Administrators, do Covenant, promiss, & grant, to, & with ye sayd William Downe, his heyrs & Assignes, by these Presents, that ye sayd John Henderson haue good right, full pouer, & Lawfull authority, in my own name to grant, bargain & sell,

the aboue granted, & barganed Premisses, & euery part
there of, with all the priuiledgs, & appurtenances, there
vnto belonging vnto ye sayd William Downe, his heyrs, &
Assignes, for euer, And that the sd William Downe his heyrs,
& Assignes, shall & may at all tymes And from tyme to tyme
for euer hereafter peaceably, and quietly hould, haue, occupy
possess, & Inioy, all and singular the Premisses, in & by
these Presents, granted, barganed, & sould, with all the
priuiledges, & appurtenances, to the same, app'rtajneing or
in any ways belonging, without any lett, denjall, or disturbance, of mee the sayd John Henderson, my heyres executors, Administrators, or assignes, or any of them, or any
other Prson or Prsons w'soeuer Claimeing, or haueing lawfull right, title or Interest y'in or any part thereof, by from,
or vnder mee: Provided always, & It is the true Intent, &
meaneing of these Prsents, that If I the sayd John Henderson my heyres executors, Administrators, or Assignes, or
any in our name, or steade, do pay or Cause to bee payd vnto
ye sayd William Down his heyres & Assignes, the abouesd
some of Twenty pounds, Eighteen shillings, & seaven peence
in Current Money, of New England, or in good dry fish at
price Current, at or before the fourth day of Novemb^r in the
yeare of our Ld One thousand six hundred Eighty one, that
then this bargane & sale to bee voyd, & of none æffect,
otherwise, to stand in full pouer, force, & vertue/ In witness
whereof I the sd John Henderson, haue set to my hand, &
seale, this fourth day of November, In the yeare of o^r Lord
one thousand six hundred seaventy nine, Anno Regni Regis
Caroli Secundj Angliæ, thyrty one. xxxj:

Signed sealed & Deliuered,   John Henderson ($^{his}_{seale}$)
   in the Presence of us/   A true Coppy of this Instrument
   Hilliard Verin Senjo^r aboue written, transcribed out
   Edward Mowle/   of the originall & there with
                             Compared this 10th day of Sep-
                             tember 1680:
                             p Edw Rishworth ReCor:

BOOK III, FOL. 80.

[80] I Christopher Lawson of Kenebecke, now resedient in Boston In New England, do hereby affirme, that I bought the Ysland formerly Called Purchases, now Called Cameis Ysland of the Indean Sagamore Derumem, & his kindred which were then the owners of it, & I truely payd them for the same, & received a deed signed & delivered to mee by them, but lost the sd Deed in these late Troubles/ this Ysland lijng in Kenebecke River wch I had possession off, & afterwards I sould & Delivered the same vnto Edward Camer, who possessed, & Improued the same 14 or fiueteen years, till forced to Come away by the Indean Warr, & now hath sould & disposed the same, vnto Samell Lynde of Boston with the full Consent & approbation of mee the sd Christopher Lawson, who hath a ly or Morgage from ye sd Camer, vpon the same, but being now fully satisfyd & payd by the sd Samell Lynd do hereby fully ratify & allow, & Confirme vnto him the sd Samell Lynde, his heyrs & Assigns for euer, all the aforesd Yslands, with his rights, benefitts & appurtenances as It is sould & made ouer, & assigned, vnto him the sd Lynde, by the sd Cameis & his wifes Deed/

In witness w^rof I haue here vnto put my hand & seale, this Twenty seaueth day of Decemb^r 1677
Signed sealed & Delivered/   Christopher Lawson (his seale)
    In P^rsence of us/   Christopher Lawson acknowledgeth
    Edmund Ranger/   this Instrum^{tt} is his Act, & Deed,
    William Pajne/   before mee, Septem^{br} 10. 1680.
                                      John Hull Assista^t
vera Copia of this Instrume^t transcribed, & with ye originall Compard this 22th of Septemb^r 1680.
                     p Edw Rishworth ReCor

Know all men by these Presents, that I Edw: Camer formerly of Kenebecke & now of Boston, husbandman, & Mary my wife, for & in Consideration of nine pounds to u in hand

BOOK III, FOL. 80.

by Sam{ll} Lynde of Boston M^rchant In New England well & truely payd, the receipt w^rof wee do hereby acknowledg, & y^rof & of every part & P^rcell thereof, do fully acquit & discharge the sd Sam{ell} Lynde & his by these P^rsents, Haue & hereby do give, grant, bargain, sell, Assign, aliene, Infeoff, & Confirme, vnto ye sd Sam{ll} Lynde, his heyrs, executors, Administrators & Assignes for euer, all that our Ysland, formerly Called Purchases Ysland, & now by the name of Camers Ysland, togeather with the Land houseing Meddows trees & flatts to Low water Marke, togeather with all the priuiledges, & app^rtenances belonging, or in any wise app^rtayneing there vnto, scituate & lijng with the Widdow Elizabeth Ham{m}onds Lands, Eastwardly, & with the Plantation Called Wisqueg Westterly, & with Mene Meeteing Northwardly, & with the River Southwardly/ To haue & to hould, possess, & Injoy, all the afore barganed Yslands, Called Camers, togeather with all & singular the houseing fences Meddows, trees, flatts to low water marke, togeather with all the priuiledges, app^rtenances, & benefitts in any kind or nature belonging to ye same, or thence to bee had, made, or Raysed with out any exception, lymitation or reseruation, vnto him the sd Sam{ll} Lynde, his heyres, executors administrators & Assignes, & to his & there soole & onely vss, & behoofe for euer; And I the sayd Edw: Camer, & Mary my wife do for us our heyrs executors & administrators Covenant promiss & grant, & agree to & with the sayd Sam{ell} Linde his heyres executors, Administrators, & Assignes, by these P^rsents, in manner & forme following, To wit that I the sd Edward Camer & Mary my wife, are at & before the sealeing & delivery hereof the true & lawfull owners of the afore barganed P^rmisses, & haue in our selues full right & pouer to sell, alienate, & dispose the same vnto the sd Samuell Lyndes & his, as an Estate of Inheritance, in fee symple, & that the same & euery part, & Parcell there of are free & Cleare, from all other & further bargans sales, Gyfts, grants, alienations, Dowrys, titles, Claims, charges, demands, trōbles or Incomberances w'soeuer/ And shall & will warrant & Defend ye same, & euery part & Parcell there of vnto the sayd Samuell Lynde his heyres executors & Assignes for euer, against all P^rson or P^rsons, any ways lawfully Clajmeing or Demanding, the same or any part y^rof/ And also I the sd Edw · Camer, & Mary my wife, or our heyrs shall & will at all tyme or tymes, bee willing & ready to giue & pass more full & ample Assurance & Confirmation of the afore bargained Premisses, as in Law & equity Can bee demised, or required & hereby rendering & giueing vnto the sd Samell Lynde full possession seazine & deliuery, of the afore bargained P^rmisses/ In witness w^rof I the sayd Edw: Camer, & Mary my wife haue here vnto put o^r hands & seales this Twenty eight day of Decemb^r Anno one thousand six hundred seaventy & seaven, 1677:

Signed sealed & Deliverd   Edw. Camer (his scale)
in P^rsence of us/   his marke ⌐⌐
Edw: Ranger   Mary Camer
William Paine/   her marke ⌐⌐ (her seale)

This Deed was acknowledged by Edw: Camer & Mary his Wife this 29th of Decemb^r 1677: before mee

           Edw · Tyng Assista^t

A true Coppy of this Instrument transcribed & Compared with the originall this 22th Septemb^r 1680:

           p Edw. Rishworth ReCor ·

ffebru: 27. 1671:

William Spencers grant made In 1651: layd out as followeth, from a Markd tree, by the brooke y^t Comes out of Willcocks pond, through the Marsh, down to ye great swampe, belonging to Humfrey Chadborne, & Thomas Spencer, two hundred fiuety foure rodds North, to a great pine tree p the sd swampe side, & from thence to ye River finety foure rodds, North West, to a great pine stumpe, & from thence by the River side, one hundred & seaventy rodds, to a great Hemlocke Marked, & from thence vp to ye aforesd Marsh one hundred seaventy two rodds South East/

Thomas Spencers Lott of one hundred Acres layd out on the South West side of William Spencers Land, one hundred seaventy two Rodds long, & in breadth ninety three Rodds/

A true Coppy of the sd Two grants aboue written transcribed, by Capt Charles ffrost out of ye Towne booke & y^rwith Compared this 27th day of Septemb^r 1680

p Edw Rishworth ReCor

[81] Let all men know by these Prsents, that I William ffrethy, & Elizabeth ffrethy, wife of ye sayd William ffreathy, doth hereby acknowledg, & Confess, that as well for the naturall loue & affection, that I beare vnto my daughter Joane Holms, the wife of Thomas Holms & her children borne & to bee borne of her body, & for & in Consideration, that ye sd Thom^s Holms marjed by daughter Joane, as alsoe for diverse other good Causes, & Considerations haue & by these P^rsents, do giue, & grant, vnto Thomas Holms & Jone his wife, & his, or y^r heyrs executors administrators or Assignes, a Certen lott of land, or tract of Land, by Estimation Thyrty or fourty Acres bee It more or less, which is a part of y^t Land Which I sd William ffreathy, purchased from one Rice Howell & It is that tract of Land that sd Thomas Holms now dwelleth in, & hath set an house vpon, & It is bounded by the River of Yorke, in the Province of Mayn, on the South West or y^rabouts, & It is adioyneing to ye Land of one Edw. Start on the North West, & with the Land of Hene Sayword on the North East, or by the Comanes, & on the South East or y^rabouts by other Lands, all wch poynts of the Compass Wee do not grant Infallable,

but yᵉ same. or very neare, & bounded with marked trees on euery side, & end/ all which Tract of Land now lyeth in East Yorke in the piovince of Mayne, & is now in the possession of the sd Thomas Holms/ To haue & to hould the sd Tract of Land with all the appurtenances there vnto belonging, with all the profetts, piiuiledges, thereof with all woods, vndei woods, profetts Emoluments Meddows & Marshes waters & water Courses, if any bee there to belonging, from the day of the Date of these Presents, for euer; And also do giue, the sd Holms my sonn in Law full pouer to sell & dispose of the sd Land, for his best Aduantage provided always, hee do provide a better or so good Estate by Estimation for yᵉ Tearme of thejr liues as this is, or otherwise as his Occasion may bee, provided always that his wife giue consent vnto it, conceiving It, to bee for the good of shee & her children : And I the sd William ffreathy & Elizabeth my wife, & for mee, my heyrs, executors, & Administiators oi Assigns foi the full Confiimation hereof vnto the sd Thomas Holms, his heyrs or thejre heyrs executors, Administiators oi Assigns, do heieby warrant Assure & Confirme vnto him oi them, with out the lawfull lett Molestation Interruption, disturbance, lett, or denyall, of him the sd William ffreathy or Elizabeth his wife, or any other Prson or Prsons lawfully Clajmeing from by or vnder mee yᵉ sd William ffreathy, or Elizabeth my wife, my heyres executors, Administiators, or Assigns & against all other Prson or Prsons wᵗsoeuer, lawfully Clajmeing the sd Premisses, or any part or Prcell yʳof, heretofore granted/ In witness here of Wee the sd William ffieathy, & Elizaᵗʰ my wife haue here vnto set oʳ hands, & seals, in the yeare of oʳ Ld one

BOOK III, FOL. 81.

thousand six hundred seaventy & one, vpon the 10ᵗʰ day of
June 1671. The marke of
Signed sealed & deliuer'd William 2 ffieathy (locus sigilli)
In yᵉ Prsence of us/ The marke of Eliza-
Andrew Searle/ beth O•O ffieathy (her seale)
The marke of
William ⊃ oulted/ William ffieathy & Elizabeth his
Mary Sayword/ wife, acknowledged the aboue
wiitten Deed of gyft to bee yʳ
Act & Deed this eight day of
May, 1679. before mee
John Wincoll Assotiate/

A Tive Coppy of this Deed or Instrument aboue written,
transcribed out of the originall & there with Compaied this
27ᵗʰ day of October: 1680. p Edw Rishworth ReCoi:

Know yee all men by these Presents, that Wee Thomas
& Jajne Witheis, of Kitteiy in the County of Yoike in New
England for the Consideration of the some of Twenty seaven
pounds, & foure shillings, to us in hand payd, before the
Insealing here of. by John ffeanix of yᵉ same Town & place,
the receipt wʳof, wee acknowledg & own oʳ selues fully satisfyd, Wee do acknowledg to haue barganed & sould, aliend
assign'd & set ouei vnto the afoiesd John ffeanix his heyrs
executors administiatois Oi Assignes for euer a Prcell of
Land Contayneing fourty fiue Rodds, In bieadth by the
water side, & runnes backe into the Woods, vpon an East
lyne, foure scooie rods, this sd Land, lying & being on the
East side of spruse Cricke, in the Town ship of Kittery In
the County of yorke, wʳas the sd ffenix hath bujlt & possesd,
& is bounded on the West side, with spruse Cricke, on the
North side with a Coue on the south side with Marked trees,
adioyneing to Peter Lewis his Land, with all the appurten-

ances there vnto belongıng, to the onely vss & behoofe of the aforesayd John ffenix, his heyrs executors administrators & Assigns, for euer, from us Thomas & Jane Withers, our heyrs executors, Admınıstrators, & Assigns for euer, promissing y° sd ffenix these baı ganed P'mısses, aboue written to bee Cleare from all former Gyfts, grants. Morgages, sayls Infeoffs or troubles of any kind w'soeuer/ As witness o' hands & seals thıs tenth day of Aprill one thousand six hundred seaventy fiue/ since sealed, & delıveı ed In the Presence of vs/   Tho: Withers (his seale)

   Witness   The marke of

   Thomas Rice the marke of

      John Grejne   Jane Withers (her seal)

This Instrument aboue wrıtten was acknowledged by Thomas Withers to bee his Act & Deed this 10th of Aprill 1675 : Portsmouth   before mee Ric · Cutt Comissio'/

A true Coppy of this Instrument aboue written transcribed out of y° orıgınall, & yʳ with Compared this 2ᵈ day of Novembʳ 1680/   p Edw Rishworth ReCor.

Know yee all men by these Presents, that Wee John & Deborah ffeanıx, of Kıttery ın the County of Yorke In New England, for the Consideration of the some of Thyrty two pounds, by Peter Lewis of the Yslos of shoals in New England, wee do also own to haue barganed & sould Alıen'd or assigud, & set & sett ouer vnto the aforesd Peter Lewıs, hıs heyrs executoı s admıınıstrators or Assigns, foı euer a Parcell of Land, with a house vpon It, the sd Land Contayneing fourty & fiue Pooles ın breadth, by the water sıde & runnes backe ınto the Woods vpon an East lyne, foure scoore Rodds, thıs land lıjng & being on the East sıde of spruse Crıcke, ın the Town shıp of Kıttery in the County of Yorke, wʳon the sd Lewis is now in possessıon, and is bounded on the West sıde with spruce Cricke, & on the North side with a Coue, on the South side with marked trees, adioying to [82] former Land of the sd Peter Lewis, with all the appurtenances there vnto belonging, to the onely vss & behalfe of the aforesd Peter Lewis, his heyrs executors Administrators or Assigns, for euer, from us John & Deborah ffenix o^r heyrs executors administrators or Assigns for euer promissing this sd Peter Lewis these barganed Premisses aboue written to bee cleare from all former gyfts grants Morgages Infeffts, sales or troubles, in any kind w'soeuer, as witness our hands & seales, this twelfth day of Aprill in the yeare of our Lord one thousand six hundred seaventy fiue/ sealed signed & Delivered In

Presence of us Witness/   John ffenix ($_{seale}^{his}$)

Testes/   The marke of

Samell Wentworth/   Deborah R ffenix ($_{seale}^{her}$)

Joseph Beirye his

marke   Ŧ

: 13th of Aprill 1675   John ffenix & Deborah his wife owned the aboue Instrum^t to bee thejr free Act & Deed before mee Elyas Stylemā : Comissio^r/

A true Coppy of the aboue written Instrument transcribed & Compared with y^e originall this 3^d of Novemb^r 1680 ·

p Edw : Rishworth ReCor :

Know all men by these Presents, that I Majo^r William Phillips of Sacoe, in New England, for & in Consideration of Twenty pounds, to mee in hand payd by John Sargeant of Winter Habour before the Insealeing & deliuery of these P^rsents the receipt w^rof I do hereby acknowledg, & am y^rwith fully satisfyd, Contented & payd & from ye same do absoultly acquitt, & discharge the sd John Sargeant his heyrs executors & administrators, Haue given granted barganed sould Enfeoffed & Confirmed, & by these Presents, do giue grant bargan sell Enfeoff & confirme, vnto John Sargeant of Winter Habour, aforesd ffisherman, heyrs executors & Administrators, a Prcell of vpland lijng & being in Winter Harbour aforesd, being the Just quantity of Thyrty acres, bounded with Land of George Pearson Eastwardly, & with the Land of Ralph Trustrum Westwardly, & Ralph Trustrums brooke Southwardly, lijng & butting Northwardly, from the sayd brooke, betwixt the Land of sayd Geo: Pearson & Trustrum, vntill the full Complement of Thyrty Acres as aforesd bee expired To haue & to hould all the aforesd Prcell of vpland, with all all the Tymber & vnderwoods y^{r}vpon, & all other priuiledges & app^{r}tenances y^{r}vnto belonging, or any wise app^{r}teineing, to him the sayd John Sargeant his heyres, executors administrators & Assigns for euer, without any lett sujte denyall hinderance, or Molestation of mee ye sayd William Phillips, my heyrs executors, administrators or Assigns; And I the sd Wilha Phillips do hereby Couenant promiss & grant to & with sd John Sargeant, that I was before the sale of the P^{r}misses, & at the tyme there of was ye right & proper owner thereof, & that the same, was free & Cleare, & freely & clearely acquitted, & discharged, of & from all other former barganes sales Gyfts, grants Morgages leases, & all other Incomberances w^{t}soeuer; And I do hereby further Couenant promiss & Ingage for my selfe my heyrs executors & Administrators, to warrant & Defend the sayd Parcell of vpland, with all the priuiledges & appurtenances there vnto belonging, vnto him the sayd John Sargeant, his heyrs executors administrators & Assigns for euer. from all Prsons whatsoeuer laijng Clajme y^{r}vnto, or any part or Prcell there of, by from or vnder mee: In witness where of, I the sd William Phillips haue here vnto put my hand & seale this fifth day of July

Book III, Fol. 82.

Anno Dom͠: one thousand six hundred sixty nine, Annoq̨ Regni Regis Caroli Secundj xxxj/ William Phillips (Locus Sigilli)

Signed sealed &	The Land which Richard Randall
delivered in	bought of mee is excluded out
Prsence of/	of this Deed/

The marke of ℞ Ralph Trustrum/
Walter Mare
his marke 〽
Anthony Checkley/

A true Coppy of this Instrum͠t aboue written transcribed out of the originall, & there with Compared this 22th of Novembr 1680 :
p Edw : Rishworth ReCor

Know all men by these Presents yt I John Carter of Boston in New England Mariner, with the Consent of my wife Ann Carter for diverse good causes & considerations yrvnto moueing, doth bargan giue grant Enfeoff & Confirme & by this Prsent Deed hath barganed given granted Enfeoffed & Confirmed, vnto ffrancis Backeus of Wells husbandman, his heyrs executors, administrators & Assigns, one hundred & fourty Acres of Land with all the Meddow & Marsh there vnto belonging, scituate liing & being on the South side of the River of Sacoe, bouded on the South West with the brooke Called Smyths brooke, on the North East with Sacoe River, & a Necke of Land, Called the Church Poynt/ To haue & to hould for euer, with free lyberty for fishing & fowling according to the Costome of this Countrey, vnto the aboue named ffran : Backus his heyres executors, administrators & Assigns for euer, for the some of sixty eight pounds being already payd to ye aboue sd John Carter for the sd Premisses . And ye sd Jon Carter doth Covenant & promiss, for him selfe his heyrs & Assigns, shall peaceably hould & Injoy the aforesd Premisses, with euery Part, & Parcell yrof with out Lett or disturbance of

the s^d John Carter, his heyrs executors, Administrators &
Assigns, or any other P'son by his or thejr meanes or pro-
curement/ In witness w^rof, the aforesd Partys haue Inter-
changbly set to there hands & seals, this sixteenth day of
April, Anno Dom̄ 1680 :   John Carter (his seal)
Signed sealed   The marke
   & Deliuered in P'sence   of Ann Carter (her seal)
   of us/ Mary Pendleton/
   Job Tooseer/   John Carter & his wife appear-
                      ed this day before mee & acknowledged
                      this Instrum^t to bee y^r Act & Deed
                      before mee
                      Bryan Pendleton Dep^ty P^rsident
   It is agreed vpon by both Partys with in mentioned that
If ye sd ffran : Backus hath occasion to build a mill vpon y^e
brooke within mentioned, hee may build vpon both sid^s of y^e
sd Brooke, by the leaue of mee & my wife/
                                    John Carter/
   A true Coppy of the Deed aboue written, & postscript
vnder written, transcribed out of the originall & y^rwith
Compared y^s 23th of Noveb^r 1680 ·
               p Edw : Rishworth R . . . .

[83]   To all Christean people, to whome this Deed or
Instrument shall Come/ I Edw : Johnson of the Town of
Yorke, & Præcilla my wife, both rescident at Yorke In the
Province of Mayne, In New England Gentle : send greeteing ;
Know yee that Wee Edward & Præsilla Johnson, as well for
& in Consideration of the naturall æffection which Wee haue,
& do beare vnto our beloued daughter Deborah, whom o^r
loueing sonn in law John Harmon hath married, & from y^t
loue & affection which for her sake & for other Considerations of sd John Harmons Manifestations of his vnfayned

loue towards vs, by his great care & Industrey, in his frugall
Management of o^r Estate to best aduantage for o^r Comfortable subsistance, since hee Maried our daughter: Haue given
granted barganed sould, Enfeoffed & Confirmed, & by these
Presents, do giue grant bargane sell, Enfeoff & Confirme
fully freely & absolutely vnto our sd sonn in Law John
Harmon a Certen tract or Prcell of Land scituate & lijng in
Yorke In ye province aforesd, Contayneing the full quantity
of Tenn Acres of Land being more or less, which Land was
forrmly bought by Hene: Symson Senjo^r, deceased, of Mr
Henery Norton deceasd & since purchased of Henery Symson Junjo^r by mee ye sayd Johnson as p the deede appeareth
beareing date Aprill ye seauenth one thousand six hundred
& Eighty/ sayd Tenn Acres of Land being bounded in
Manner as followeth, that is to say, on the North East by
the Cricke, lijng opposite to ye meeteing house, on the South
East by ye Land of Mr Edw: Godfreys, on the North West
by the bridg, & so along by ye Land of John Parker Senjo^r
vnto a Great pine tree, which was the Antient bounds, still
standing, at the South Corner of the Land, being vpon
Thomas Donells Land/ On wch tenn Acres of Land since
my purchase y^toff, I haue bujlt a dwelling house w^t in I do
now liue/ I do also freely grant & giue, with the free Consent of Præsilla my wife, foure or fiue Acres of Wood Land,
be it more or less, being bounded at a tree bridg, at the head
of a Coue, Commanly Called by the name of bass Coue, as by
the Deed aforesd doth appeare/ And three Acres of Marsh
lijng vpon the River & sixty acres of vpland granted by the
Town to him; Which Lands aboue mentioned, with all the
houseing garden oarchard, pasture, fejlds, woods, vnderwoods, togeather with all & singular the privilidges, profetts,
& all manner of appurtenances w^tsoeuer, belonging y^rvnto,
with all the right I haue in Yorke from mee my heyres, executors, Administrators & Assigns, vnto the sd John Harmon
his heyres, executors, Administrators & Assigns, for euer.

Book III, Fol. 83.

To haue & to hould freely & quietly, with out any matter of Challenge Clajme or demand, of us the sd Edw: Johnson & Præcilla my wife, or any Prson or Prsons by or vnder us, or heyres executors Administrators & Asˢ for euer: And Wee do further Covenant & agree, with the sd John Harmon his heyres & Assigns, that yᵉ true meaneing & intent of these Prmisses, are & by them It is always intended & to bee vnderstood, that vpon Consideration there of that sayd John Harmon shall not any way with draw, but continew his filiall care and Industrey, to Mannage our Estate of Cattle, & what else wee haue according to the best of his skill, for oʳ comfortable lineing & subsistance, dureing the whoole tearme of our naturall lifes, according to what the valew & Capacity of such an Estate can rationally afford; And lastly I the sd Edward Johnson, do hereby Couenant & promiss, in the behalfe of my selfe, my wife my heyres executors & Administrators, to & with sd Joⁿ Harmō his heyrs executors administrators & Assignes, that yᵉ sd house & Lands are free & Cleare, from all gyfts grants, barguns leases, Dowers, Morgages Judgmᵗˢ & all other Incomberances whasoeuer, & do further promiss & Covenant, to warrant & defend the same, the right title & Interest there of from mee my heyrs executors, & from any Prson or Prsons vnder us, or from or by vs, or our meanes, or any others by our procurement/ In testimony of all & every of the abouesd Premisses, wee haue here vnto set oʳ hands & seales, this Eighteenth day of August one thousand six hundred & Eighty, in the Thyrty secund yeare of the Reigne of oʳ soueraign Ld, Charles the secund of England Scotland, France & Ireland King, Defendʳ of the faith &c: 1680:

Signed sealed & Deliuered,   Edw: Johnson (his seale)
    In Prsence of/   Præcilla Johnson (her seale)

And further the sd Edw· Johnson doth hereby Couenant & agree with the sd John Harmon, that wᵗ Interest & Title

I haue or shall Continew to haue, in Mr Edw: Godfreys Lands & Meddows wch hee left in my Costody, and possession when hee left this Countrey, hee the sd Harmon & his Assigns shall haue the free vss & benefit of them, vntill such tyme as Mr Edw: Godfrey or his lawfull heyrs shall Legally take them out of his hands, as Witness my hand at ye day & yeare aboue written/

 Edw: Rishworth/   Edw: Johnson/
 Abra: Preble/   Mr Edw: Johnson Came before mee this eighteenth day of Septem^br 1680 & owned this Instrum^t to John Harmon & this Postscript to bee his Act & Deed/
           Edw: Rishworth Just pe:

A true Coppy of this Instru-   Præcilla Johnson owned this
ment aboue written & this   Instrume^t to bee her Act
postscript vnd^rneath trans-   & Deede this 17th d of
cribed out of the originall   January 1680 : before mee/
& y^rwith Compared this   Edw: Rishworth Jus^t pe:
11th of Decemb^r 1680 ·
p Edw: Rishworth ReCor:

[84]   For Majo^r Bryan Pen-
  dleton & Majo^r Jo^n Davess   Boston, 19th : 8M^o 1680:
  or to eith^r of y^m at yorke/
  Gentle ~/

It is the request of Edw · Randolph Esqr, for ye Calling of a Court to Judg in a Case between him selfe, & one Mr Nicolls, the maister of a Ketch ceized with you, for tradeing Contrary to the Acts of Trade/ these are to order you on the sd Mr Randolphs exhibiteing his libell, & laijng down tenn pounds Caution, for paijng the Charge of ye trauell & disbursments for sd Courts Intertayneme^t you appoynt him a tyme for a spetiall Court, to meete & giue Judgm^t in sd Case, & order yor secretary to giue notice y^rof to ye Magestrates, & also tymely to send his warrants to ye Connstable of yorke, Kittery & Wells for sumoneing a Jury of meete Prsons to Attend the service of sd Court/ To the Jury you are to allow for y^r expenses 4^s p day, dureing the Courts sitting, & to ye Magestrates, & other officers for y^r trauell & expences according as ye Charge shall arise, & if any bee remajneing of ye tenn pounds, deliuer It backe agajne to Mr Randolph, Comitting you to ye guidance, & blessing of god almighty, I take leaue,

                               & am Gentle

vera Copia of this letter tran-   your fiejnd & servant/
   cribed & with originall Com-   Tho Danforth P^rsidet
   pared this 18th d : Decemb^r
   1680 : p Edw : Rishworth ReCor .

     Nicholas Coole aged fiuety two years or y^tabouts, & Ellner Redding aged fiuety fiue years or y^rabouts, testifyeth & sayth, y^t John Bray sonn to Richd Bray, & Rebella of Cas'coe Bay in the Province of Mayn in New England, was neuer Legally married to Ann Lane, daughter to James Lane with the Consent of his father, & mother, nor married by any Magestrate Just^s of peace Commissio^r, nor by any Minister, nor by any man Impour^d or authorized by any authority, nor by any Act done by the Inhabitants y^t liued there, or else w^r, but the sd John Bray liued with the abousd Ann Lane, by whom hee had a daughter, W^{ch} wee Judg was not according to Law or Justice/ & further sayth not/

     The Deponents further sayth, that ye abouesd John Bray, was neuer published to ye abouesd Ann Lane, according any law/ & further sayth not/

     All this to bee vnderstood According to y^r knowledg , who liued long by them & know how they came to liue as man & wife togeather/

Book III, Fol. 84.

Richard Bray also deposeth, y^t hee neuer gaue Consent y^t his sonn Bray, should Marry with ye sayd Ann Lane/

Taken vpon oath this 23th of Decemb^r 78: before mee Symon Bradstreete Depu . Gou͞r

A true Coppy transcribed, & with originall Compared this 21 : December : 1680 . p Edw · Rishworth Re · Cor :

Know all men by these Prsents, that I John Wentworth of Yorke in the Province of Mayne Planter, do for my selfe my heyres executors Administrators & Assignes, for a valewable Consideration, in full satisfaction already receiued in hand. haue barganed Covenanted & sould, Assigned & made ouer vnto Jo^n Harmon of Wells in the Province afoiesd, in New England Planter, to him his heyres executors Administrators & Assignes, a Certen tract of Land ljng & being in the Town of Wells, which Land Contayneth one hundred acres, Which the sd Wentworth had of Ezekell Knights, being Twenty pooles in breadth, butting vpon the high way next adioyneing vnto Mr Samll Wheelewrights Land, & so to runne backe into ye Countrey vntill one hundred Acres bee fully Compleated, the sd Land being bounded with ye Land of Nathell Maisters, on the West side, & with Land which was formerly ye Land of Isacke Cossons on the East side, with all the benefitts app^{r}tenances & priuiledges there vnto belonging ; To haue & to hould & peaceably to Inioy, or in any wise app^{r}tayneing with euery part & Parcell thereof as aboue expressed, vnto the sayd John Harmon his heyrs executors, administrators & Assigns for euer, for his & y^r proper vss & benefitt/ And I the sd John Wentworth doth further promiss & Covenant to & with ye sd John Harmon to haue lawfull right, & title, & pouer to dispose of ye sd Land aforesd, & that ye same & euery part y^{r}of, is free from all former & other barganes, Gyfts, grants, sales, titles

BOOK III, FOL. 84, 85.

& Incomberances w'soeuer, & y^t I will warrant, & defend the same, against all Prson & Persons w'soeuer, from by or vnder mee, or by my meanes or procurement/ In testimony w^r of I haue here vnto put my hand & seale, this 20th day of Octob^r 1680:

Signed in the P^r sence   John Wentworth
   of Peter Cloyce   his marke 𝒩 (his seale)
     his marke ⋎   Martha Wentworth
  John Wheelewright/   her marke ✗

John Wentworth & Martha his wife Came before mee & acknowledged this Instrument aboue written to bee y^r Act & Deed this 12th Noveb^r 1680:   Edw: Rishworth Just: pe:

A true Coppy of this Instrum^t transcribed & Compared with ye originall this 28th Decemb^r 1680

               p Edw: Rishworth ReCor.

This writeing witnesseth, that w^r as William Hooke of Agamenticus by his writeing vnder his hand beareing Date the fourteenth of Aprill one thousand six hundred & fourty, did Allejne & sell vnto Hene: Sympson of Agamenticus aforesd, his heyrs & Assigns for euer, all that Prcell Land Comanly Called the playne, lately fenced in by the sayd William Hooke, lijng neare the dwelling house of the sayd Henery Sympson, with all such priuiledg^s behind the sayd fejld as ye sd William Hooke then had, as by the aforesayd writeing more at large It doth & may appeare · Now this writeing further witnesseth, that the sayd Henery Symson for & in Consideration of the sume of fiueteen pounds Sterling: to him in hand payd or Assured to bee payd, by George Puddington of Agamenticus aforesayd, as also for diverse good Causes & Considerations, him there vnto moueing, hath given granted barganed [85] sould Infeoffed

Book III, Fol. 85.

& Confirmed, and by these Presents, doth for him and his heyres, giue grant bargan sell Enfeoff and Confirme vnto the aforesd George Puttington, his heyrs & Assigns, the aforesayd Parcell of Land, with the appurtenances (excepting two Acres of Land) on the East side of the sayd fejld, formerly granted by the sayd Henery Symson vnto Thomas ffooteman to bee taken in length from the Corner of ye fence next Adioyneing vnto a Certen house and yard lately bought by the sayd Henery Sympson of the sayd William Hooke, vnto that end of the fejld, next vnto the swampe, & so much in breadth as may Contayne the sayd Two Acres/ To haue & to hould, the aforesayd fejld with the app^{r}tenances, to the sayd George Puddington his heyrs & Assignes for euer, togeather also with the aforesd writeing, the sd George Puddington yejlding paijng Prformeing & doeing, for the Premisses, all such rents, Covenants & Conditions as the aforesd William Hooke his heyrs or Assigns, are by any Pattent or Pattents bound to yejld, pay P^{r}forme & Do. And ye sayd Henery Sympson doth for him selfe, his heyrs & Assigns, & for euery of them Covenant promiss, & grant to & with the sayd George Puddington his heyrs & Assigns, to & with euery of them by these Presents, y^t hee the sayd George Puddington his heyrs & Assignes, & every one of them shall & may from tyme to tyme, & at all tymes from tyme to tyme & at all tymes hereafter by & vnder ye rents, Couenants & Conditions before mentioned, peaceably & quietly, haue hould occupy possess, & Inioy, all the aforesd parcell of Land with ye appurtenances, with out the Lawfull let sujte trouble denyall eniction, or expulsion of the sayd Henery Symson his heyrs or Assigns of or by any other Prson or Persons whasoeuer lawfully Clajming the same, or any part thereof in by or vnder them, or any of them/ And that the sd Henery Sympson his heyrs & Assigns & euery of them, at the proper Costs & charges in law of y^e

Book III, Fol. 85.

sayd Geo: Puddington his heyres, & Assigns vpon reasonable request, in y^t behalfe, shall & will from tyme to tyme, & at all tyms hereafter do, make acknowledg execute & suffer or cause to bee done made acknowledged & suffered, all & euery such further & Lawfull & reasonable Act & Acts thing & things deuise & deuises in ye law for the further & better Assurance, & sure makeing of all & singular ye P^{r}mises before in these P^{r}sents specifyd, according to ye true intent & meaneing of this P^{r}sent Deed/ In witness w^{r}of I the sd Henery Sympson hath herevnto sett his hand & seale, the 15th day of Aprill, In ye hueteenth yeare of ye Reign of our Soveraign Lord king Charles Año Dom : 1640:
Signed sealed & Deliuered   The signe
  in ye P^{r}sence of us   of Henery /s/ Sympson (his seale)
  whose names are
here vnderwritten/ Geo: Burdett
Edw: Godfrey Roger Garde/
A true Coppy of this Instrum^{et} transcribed & Compared this 14th of Janv: 1680/

                 p Edw: Rishworth ReCor:

To all Christean people to whom these Presents shall Come/ Henery Sympson of Agamenticus sendeth greeteing in our Lord God Everlasting: Know yee that the sd Henery Sympson, for & in Consideration of the some of thyrty pounds Sterling, to him assured to bee payd by George Puddington of Agamenticus aforesd, at & before the Ensealing & delivery here of, as also for diverse good Causes & considerations valewable, him the sd Henery Symson there vnto espetially moueing, hath given granted barganed sould Enfeoffed & Confirmed, & by these P^{r}sents doth freely & absolutly giue grant bargan sell Enfeoff & Confirme, vnto the sayd George Puddington his heyres & Assigns all that his Planting fejld & other his Land, scituate, ljng, & being, between the Land of the sayd George Puddington, & the Land of Ralph of Ralph Blaysdell, lately bounded out in Agamenticus aforesayd, with all & singular the appurtenances, & euery part and Prcell there of, and also all Deeds euidences writeings, escripts and Mniments, which hee or any other Prson or Prsons to his vss hath or haue, concerneing the Prmisses or any part or Prcell y^{r}of, with all such priuiledges on the backe side of ye sayd Land, as other planters haue y^r & Inioy, To haue and to hould, the aforesd planting fejld, & all other the Premisses, with appurtenances, vnto ye sayd George Puddington, his heyrs & Assigns for euer, hee ye sayd George Puddington, his heyrs & Assigns, yeilding paijng Prformeing, & doing for the Premisses vnto ye Cheefe Lord or Lords of the fee all such rents, & sceruices as the sd Henery Symson his heyrs or Assigns out to yeild pay Prforme or do for the same; And the sd Henery Sympson doth for him selfe, his heyrs executors, Administratois & Assigns & for euery of them Couenant promiss & grant to & with the sd George Puddington, his heyrs & Assigns, & to & with euery of them by these Prsents, that hee the sayd Puddington his heyrs & Assigns & euery of them shall & may from tyme to tyme & at all tyms hereafter, peaceably & quietly hould haue, occupy, possess, & Inioy the aforesd Planting fejld, & all & singular other ye P^{r}misses, with the appurtenances & euery part & Prcell there of, with out the lawfull lett sujte Trouble Deniall euiction or expulsion, of the sd Henery Symson his heyres or Assigns, or of any other Prson or Prsons w^{t}soeuer lawfully Clajmeing the same or any part or Prcell thereof, in from by or vnder him, or any of them, freed & discharged of & from all other barganes, & sales, Joynters and Dowers, leases, Judgmts, executions, intrusions, & all other incomberances, & charges w'soener, they bee except the Rents & sceiuices of [86] the Cheefe Lord or Lds of the ffee, from hence forth to bee due & also that hee the sd Henery Symson shall & will, at all tymis here after vpon reasonable request, by the sd George Puddington his heyrs or Assigns to bee made seale & deliuer, to the sd Geo: Puddington his heyrs, one other Deed or parchment, agreeable virbatim to these P'rsents, & also shall & will do make, acknowledg execute & suffer, or cause to bee done made executed & suffered, all & euery such further & other lawfull & reasonable Act, & Acts, thing & things, devise & deuises, in the law, for the further, & better Assurance & sure makeing of & all & singular the Premisses, in these presents specifyd, at the proper Costs & Charges of the sayd George Puddington his heyres & Assigns/ In witness w'rof the sayd Henery Sympson hath here vnto set his hand & seale y'e Third day of March, In the seauenteenth yeare of our Soueraign Lord King Charles Anno Dom̃: one thousand six hundred fourty one: 1641:

Sealed signed & Deliuered/   The Marke of
In the Presence of us/   Henery Sympson /S/ (his seale)
Roger Garde/
John Allcocke/

vera Copia of this Instrument aboue written transcribed out of the originall & there with Compared this 16th of Janua: 1680: p Edw: Rishworth ReCor:

W'ras I Ann Godfrey, sometyms of Yorke, now of Kittery In the Prouince of Mayne In New England, did about 20 odd years agone, giue & grant vnto William Moore of Yorke aforesd, a small Tract or Parcell of Marsh lijng at Braue boat Harbour, Called by y'e name of sunken Marsh, Contaȳing about the quantity of two Acres of Marsh & Thatch, being about the middle of my farme, wch since I disposed of to Maj^or Nicho. Shapleigh, since which tyme sd Moore hath had the sd Marsh in occupation & possession & which I ordered Pet^r Weare to ReCord seuerall years agone; But vnderstanding nothing relateing to ye P^rmiss to bee found vpon ye ReCords, vpon ye request of sd William Moore, for ye Renewing & Confirmeing my former grant to him, I sd Ann Godfrey do by these P^ʳsents giue grant & Confirme that abouesd Parcell of sunken Marsh, as aboue bounded & express'd, with all the priuiledges y^rof. to ye sayd William Moore his heyrs & Assigns for euer/ In witness w^rof I haue here vnto sett my hand & Seale, this 5th day of Janv: 1680:

Testes Henery   marke
Donell his Marke H⸺D   Ann Godfrey her C (her seale)
John Puddington/   Mis Ann Godfrey Came before
                      mee this 6th of Janv: 1680:
                      & owned this Instrum^t to bee
                      her Act & Deed, Edw: Rish-
                      worth Just^s pe

A true Coppy of this Instrume^t transcribed & Compard with the originall this 26th of Janva: 1680/

                 p Edw Rishworth ReCor:

Know all men by these Presents, that I John Stover Senjo^r an Inhabitant in the Town of Yorke, do by these Presents obliedg, make ouer, all my house & Land & appurtenances w^ʳon now I liue vnto Thomas Lee, his heyrs or Assigns for euer · To haue & to hould from mee my heyres or Assignes for euer/ It being for ye valew of foure pounds thyrteen shillings & foure peence, money, wch I the sd Stouer are Indebted vnto the sd Thomas Lee/ & for the true payment hereof I the sd Stouer hath hereby made ouer my house & Land, & alienated to the sd Thomas Lee, his heyres or

BOOK III, FOL. 86.

Assigns for euer, from mee my heyrs or Assigns for euer to bee ye sd Lees, without any lett hinderance or Incomberances from mee or mine/

This Condition of this obligation such, that if the aboue sd John Stouer Senjo^r, shall pay or cause to bee payd vnto the sd Thomas Lee, or his order the some of foure pounds thirteen shillings & foure peence, in money or staues at money price, at or before the last of March next Insewing, the date hereof, then this obligation to bee voyd, & none æffect, or otherwise, to stand in full force & manner to all Intents & purposes, as witness my hand this 28th Janva : 1680 :

The staues to bee payd at some Convenjent Landing place in the River of Yorke

Testes/ Signed sealed &   John Stouer
deliuered in ye P^rsence of/
John Penwill/ Jos · Weden/   his marke ⊥

      Jo^n Stouer Senjo^r came before mee & did acknowledg this aboue written to bee his Act & Deed
      John Davess Just pe

vera Copia of this Instrume^t transcribed & Compared with ye originall this 29th of Janva · 1680 :

     p Edw : Rishworth ReCor .

At a generall Court held at Boston 16th October 1660 :

Wee whose names are vnderwritten, being appoynted by the Generall Court held at Boston the 18th of October 1659 : for to heare & determine Certen differences, wch Concerne Leef^t William Phillips, Mr Geo : Cleeue Mr Jo^n Bonighton, & Mr Rich^d ffoxwell, & to make returne y^rof vnto this Court; Wee accordingly haue Attended that scervice, returne as followeth/

BOOK III, FOL. 86, 87

Saco

That the Town of Sacoe shall haue belonging vnto it, all the Land lijng within the bounds hereafter mentioned, vidz^t from Winter Harbour to Sacoe River Mouth, & from thence vp along the sd River towards the Falls, as fare as the house of Ambrose Berry, & from thence a Lyne to runne on a square towards Cape Porpus, so fare as the bounds of the sd Town of Sacoe goeth, that way & so down the deuideing lyne betwixt Cape Porpus & Sacoe, vnto ye sea, & so along the sea vnto Winter Harbour reserving out of this Tract the sea Wall begining at a pound about halfe a Mile Southward from the Mill Com̄anly Called Ducke pond, & runneing from the sd Pond to the Mill, & from thence to ye Necke of Land on Which Roger Spencer liueth, with the Marshes adioyneing to the sea Wall, not exceeding fourty rodd broad from the sd Wall/ & also a Necke of Land Com̄anly Called Parkers Necke/ also finety Acres of Wood land, adioyneing to an allotment late in ye possession of Goodman Leighton, now in the possession of Leef^t Phillips/ also finety acres of Land lijng between Mr Hichcoks house & Sacoe river Mouth, W^r Leef^t Phillips shall make Choyse, of it in any Land not in lease, which afoersd Tract of Land so bounded, shall bee disposed of by the Townsmen of Sacoe, either for Com̄ans or otherwise as they shall see Cause/ [87] vnto wch disposall of the aforesd Tract, Leef^t William Phillips doth Consent, & all Contracts made by any of the possessors of any Lands within the Lymitts of the Pattent in Sacoe, which did belong vnto Mr Richd Vines with Leef^t Phillips is to stand good, & such possessors of Lands within the sd limitts, as haue not as yet Contracted for their Lands, that they do possess, are to pay the like proportions of rent which those do who haue alredy Contracted/ And all other Lands layd out within the limits of the before mentioned Pattent of Mr Vines, excepting that Necke of Land where Roger Spencer dwelleth, wch sd Necke is bounded with the end of the sea Wall next to it adioyneing to belong vnto Leef^t William Phillips/

BOOK III, FOL. 87.

In relation to the Complaynt of Mr John Bonighton, Wee find his Pattent is in Joynt to Mr Thomas Lewis, & the father of Bonighton, & y^t seuerall of those wch hee Complayns agaist had leaue from the aforesd Lewis or his successors, Wee y^{r}fore ord^r that a due divission bee made betwixt them, If it bee not already done, & then those that trespass on any of Mr Bonightons righs, hee may haue his remidy in a Course of Law, where we hope hee may haue Justice/

And as for the Complaynt of Mr Geo: Cleeues, W^n Wee were at Sacoe Attending ye Generall Courts before mentioned order, his writeings & euidences Were not present, y^{r}fore Wee Can make no certen returne y^{r}of, but Judg meete the Townsmen of ffalmouth bee ordered not to dispose of any lands, which are within the boundarys of the Pattents, or grants of the sd Mr Geo: Cleeus, vntill this Court take further order thejr in/

As to ye Complaynts of Mr Richard Foxwell, hee appeared not thejr to make any proofe thereof/ Dated 25th of 8th M^{oth} 1660: & signed by
          Humpfrey Atherton/
The Court approues of the returne of Tho: Sauage/
 these Commissio^{rs} & do order it   Tho: Clarke/
 shall bee a finall Isew of all matters
 in difference between the Partys
 y^{r}in mentioned, & the matters
 Contayned y^{r}in:

This is a true Coppy of the Courts order as Attests
        Edw: Rawson Secre^{ty}:

A true Coppy of this Instrument aboue written transcribed & Compared this first day of March 168$\frac{9}{?}$
     p Edw: Rishworth ReCor:

At a Generall Court houlden at Boston 18th of October 1659:

BOOK III, FOL. 87.

The Court haueing Considered the petitions of Mr George Cleeues, Mr John Bonighton, Mr Richd ffoxwell, & Mr William Phillips, Craueing the helpe of this Court for settleing thejr respectiue Interests, & possessions in the East parts of this Jurisdiction, Do Judg meete to order that y^r respectiue Cases, & Complaynts, for a finall Issew bee referred to Majo^r Humphrey Atherton, Capt Thomas Sauage, Capt Edw: Johnson, & Capt Thomas Clarke, or any three of them, who are hereby chosen, & Commissionated by this Court to heare & Determine the severall differences of ye sd Partys as in thejre Wisedoms they shall Judg most meete, hereby Impoureing the sd Committee to appoynt the tyme & place of y^r meeteing, as they shall Judg most Convenjent, all P^{r}sons Concerned therein, being hereby Injoyned to Attend the same; & to send for Partys & witnesses, & examine thejr seuerall Complaynts, according to Laws provided the Complajnants bee at ye charge of procureing the attendance, & satisfy the charges of ye Committee, & y^t returne bee made by the Comittee vnto y^e next Generall Court, after thejr determination/ This is a true Coppy of the Courts answere to y^e petition on the other side, As
     Attests Edw. Rawsone Sec^{ty}

A true Coppy of this order transcribed, & compared with the originall this first day of March 16$\frac{80}{81}$
    p Edw: Rishworth ReCor ·

At a Generall Court held at Boston 20th May: 1674:

The Court alloweth, & approveth of this returne, & declareth that the Elldest grant of Land in the County of Yorke shyre whither by Pattent, or grant from the Generall Court shall take place before any other, according to ye Consession made to them by the Generall Court in thejr reception into this goverment; It is further ordered that ye former

Book III, Fol. 87.

Comittee bee Impoured, & bound the Land of Richd ffoxwell & Ric. Cummines, & to heare Issew, & determine by three or more of y^m any difference that shall or may arise between them, & all Prsons y^rin Concern'd vpon blew Poynt, or the Westerne side of bla͠: Poynt River In the Town of Scarbrough/

 vera Copia transcribed & Compared this · j · March 16⅔
     p Edw: Rishworth ReCor

 These may Certify any whom It may Concerne, that I did grant vnto John Bush foure hundred Acres of Land, & Marsh ground lijng neare the little River, between Sacoe & Cape Porpus, as I was appoynted by vertue of Agency from Allexand^r Ridgby Esqr for ye yearely Rent of one farthing an Acre, Insevreing it to bee in the Province of Lygonia, & without the bounds of Sacoe Pattents, granted to Mr Vines & others, but I never did receiue any Rent, nor any other Composition for Mr Ridgby, nor my selfe for y^t to this day, being the 14th of May 1661: as Attesteth mee
       George Cleeue/
 vera Copia transcribed & Compared as Attests
       Edw: Rishworth ReCor:

 The Deposition of George Munjoy aged about 47 years, sworne sayth, that about the end of May, or begining of June last past, hee was desired by Major William Phillips to measure the length of foure Miles, begining neare to ye house of John Henderson on Sacoe River, & so to runne South West towards Cape Porpus, & to ye end of the foure Miles, to the best of my Judgm^t extended to a marked tree, a little to y^e Westward

Geo Munjoy's deposition

BOOK III, FOL. 87.

of a great Rocke that lyeth on the Sands goeing to Cape Porpus, from the little River/ Sworne the 9th of July 1674: befoie mee Tho: Clarke Assist^t
vera Copia transcribed & Compared this j: of March 16$\frac{89}{90}$
p Edw: Rishworth ReCor ·

Know all men by these Presents, that I Andrew Everest of the Town of Yorke in the Province of Mayne, in New England, do & haue sould vnto Thomas Everell of Wells with in the aforesd Province, a Certen Tract of vpland & Marsh Comanly Called & known by the name of Pond Marsh, & is in the way which goeth from Cape Nuttacke, to Wells, which sd vpland is bounded on the East, with a small brooke to ye westward, vnto a small brooke, which runneth into the sd Pond as is in breadth about 60 pooles, or pearches, which Land & Marsh Contayneth sixteen Acres, as also more added vnto the sd lott of Land, given by the Inhabitants of the Town of Yorke in quantity being fourty Acres, rangeing, & runeing out ye aforesd breadth of the whoole, which is fiuety & six Acres, of vpland & Marsh which sd Land & Marsh I the sd Everest, with the full & free Consent of my wife Barbary Everest, haue sould vnto ye sayd Everell for the full some of foureteen pounds of Current pay of New England, to mee in hand payd, before signeing sealeing & delivery hereof, for which Consideration I the sd Everest, do hereby bind mee my heyres, executors, administrators, & assignes, & espetially from hinderances, or any hinderance, or any Molestation in from or by my sonn Job Everest, vnto ye sayd Everell his heyres, executors Administrators & Assignes, shall peaceably Inioy all the sd Land, with all the Tymber & benefitt, the sd Land doth produce/ And that the sd Everell shall haue & to hould, the sd Lands peaceably from the aforesd Everest, his sayd heyres,

Book III, Fol. 87, 88.

executors, administrators & Assignes, [88] firmely according to the true meaneing, & intent here of, vnto which Wee haue here vnto set o[r] hands this 5th day of June, & in the yeare of our Lord one thousand six hundred & eighty 1680:

    Signed sealed & Deliv- Andrew Everest (his seale)
    ered/ In the P[r]sence of/ The marke of Barbary
    Peter Weare Senjo[r]/ Everest /*W* (her scale)
    John Bankes/

Andrew Everest & Barbery his wife, Came before mee the 23th of March: 1680: & acknowledged this Instrume[t] as thejr Act & Deed, before mee John Davess Just pe:

A true Coppy of this Instrume[t] transcribed, & Compared with the originall this 24th March 16⁸⁰⁄₈₁
       p Edw. Rishworth ReCor:

[Margin: Andrew Everst & his wife Barbary desired Peter Weare Senjo[r] in thejr behalfe to giue Tho. Everell possession of the Land with mentioned which was done the first of Octob[r] 1680. as Attests Peter Weare Senjo[r] John Smyth Senjo[r] his marke vera Copia Edw Rishworth ReCor.]

⊢⊣

Thomas Eeverell Enters Caution against any ReCord of Andrew Everests, or Deed of sayle of sd Everests house & land made or given by him to John Bankes or any other Prsone, to bee Entred into the ReCords of this Province of Mayne, till the sd Andrew Everest haue given sufficient security to Tho· Everell to make good that sayle of Land to him & his which Andrew Everest sould of his sonn Job Everests to the sd Thomas Everell/

This Caution transcribed out of the originall & y[r]with Compared this 25th March 1681: by Edw: Rishworth ReCor:

Book III, Fol. 88.

(May 6th 1680)

Wʳas Wee whose names are here subscribed, Were at a Generall Town meeteing appoynted by yᵉ Town of yorke, beareing Date August 25 : 1679 : to settle yᵉ bounds of severall Lands, between Silvester Stover & Jere : Sheeres, & to runne the diuideing line between them, according to oʳ best discretions as Wee shall Judg to bee most Convenjently sutable in reference to yᵉ places, & lijng of the sayd Lands : The Premisses Considered, vpon oʳ vewing of their seuerall bounds, do determine as followeth/

ffirst that the bounds which Wee adiudg to bee the most Certen bounds Wee do begine at Silvester Stovers Necke of Land Comanly Called the Stony Necke, being bounded on the South East side with the sea, & on the North East side by the Land the sd Stover bought of some ffishermen, & Now lieth vpon, & on the North west side lyeth from yᵉ head of yᵉ Cricke down to high water marke, next vnto the sd Stovers house on yᵉ North West, being the diuideing bounds between the sd Stouer & Jere : Sheeres, & so backe as the sd Stouers fence Now standeth, to a little Hill & a small Hemlocke tree, being the Eastermost Corner yʳof next Jere : Sheers his Land, adioyneing vnto fourty Acres of Land which the Town gaue vnto the aforesd Sheeres, & so to runne backeward vpon a West South West lyne, vnto that brooke yᵗ runneth into yᵉ sd Stouers Marsh at Cape Nuttacke Necke & emptieth It selfe into the sea at yᵉ short sands on yᵉ North East side of Cape Nuttacke Necke, which brooke is the bounds on the South West side/ all which Tract or Prcell of Land so bounded as aboue expressed, according to pouer diligated & given to us by the Town, do give & grant vnto Sylvester Stouer, his heyrs & Assignes for ever, Contayneing the quantity of one hundred Acres bee

Book III, Fol. 88.

It more or less/ In testimony w^r of Wee haue herevnto subscribed our hands/ Dated 15th of March 16⁸⁹/₉₀

         Edw : Rishworth
A true Coppy of this Instrume^t tran- John Davess
scribed, & with the originall Com- Abra : Preble/
pared this 26th March 1681 :
 p Edw : Rishworth ReCor :

These Presents testify, that I Digory Jefferys of Kittery, In the County of yorke Carpenter, by & with the Consent of Mary my wife, for & in Consideration of ninety pounds secured to mee, by John Moore of Starr Ysland Senjo^r fisherman, by & with the Consent of Mary my wife, do giue grant bargan sell, aliene Assign & set ouer vnto the sd John Moore Senjo^r, all that my two Necks or Yslands, scituate lijng & being in the Town shipp of Kittery, between John Bray & Roger Decaremg, with foure Acres of Land there vnto adioyneing, & all the houseing now standing vpon ye sayd Land, or any part thereof, with all the priuiledges & app^rtenances there vnto belonging or app^rtajneing : To haue and to hould the sayd Neckes of Land or yslands, with the foure Acres of Land & all the houseing now standing thereon to him the sayd John Moore, his heyrs executors, Administrators or Assignes, from the first day of May now next Insewing the date here of for ever/ And the sd Digory Jeffery, for him selfe his heyrs executors & Administrators, & for euery of them doth Couenant & promiss to and with him the sd John Moore, his heyrs executors Administrators, or Assignes, and to & with euery of them by these Presents, that at Present, & before the Ensealeing here of, hee standeth seized & possessed of the aboue demised premisses, in a good Estate of fee symple, & that hee hath not heretofore done nor suffered to bee done any

Act or thing, which may any way hinder or Impeach his the sayd John Moores right, title, or Interest vnto the aboue mentioned Premises, or any part thereof, & further the sd Dygory Jefferys, for him selfe his heyres, executors, & Administrators, & for euery of them doth Covenant & promiss to & with the sd John Moore his heyrs executors Administrators or Assignes, to deliver vp vnto him the sayd John Moore, his heyrs executors Administrators & Assignes, all such writeings Deeds & euidences, as any way concerne the Premises, or any part thereof, which hee now hath in his keepeing, or which hereafter may Come to his hands/ And further the sayd Dygory Jefferys for him selfe his heyrs executors & Administrators, & Assignes, & for euery of them, doth Covenant & promiss to & with the sayd John Moore his heyres executors & Administrators & Assigns & to & with euery of them, that hee will Defend the Title thereof vnto him the sayd John Moore, his heyres executors, Administrators & Assignes against all Prsons whatsoeuer (the Pattentees onely excepted) In Witness whereof I haue here vnto sett my hand & seale Dated In Portsmouth In Pischaqua River, this fifth day of June one thousand Anno Domi̅: six hundred sixty & nine [89] And in the one & Twenteth year of the Reigne of or Soueraigne Lord Charles the Secund, King of England Scotland ffrance and Ireland, Defender of the faith/ 1669:

Signed sealed & delivered/ Dygory Jefferys (his seale)
 In the Presence of us/ his Marke D
 Richard Styleman/ Mary Jefferys (her seale)
 Mary Styleman/ her marke M

Dygory Jefferys acknowledged this Instrument aboue written to bee his Act & Deede, this 24th of August (1680)
  before mee ffrancis Hooke Just pe:
vera Copia transcribed out of ye originall, & yr with Compared this 5th day of Aprill 1681:
   p Edw: Rishworth ReCor.

Book III, Fol. 89.

Know all men by these Prsents y^t I Andrew Everest of the Town of Yorke of the Province of Mayne In New England Planter, & Barbery my wife vpon good & valewable Considerations there vnto us Moueing, & more espically for & In Consideration of the full & Just some of seaven pounds tenn shillings, to mee already in hand payd, the payment where of I do hereby own & acknowledg, to haue received of Benja: Curtis of yorke aforesd, w^{r}with & of euery part & Parcell thereof, I do own my selfe to bee fully payd Content^d & satisfyd, & do in the behalfe of my selfe, my heyrs executors Administrators, & Assignes, acquit & discharge the sd Benjame Curtis his heyres executors administrators & Assignes for euer, of whom I received the aforesd some of 07 10 · 00, from euery part & Parcell there of, Haue given granted barganed sould, Enfeoffed & Confirmed, And do by these Presents give grant bargane sell Enfeoff & Confirme, from mee my heyres, executors, Administrators & Assigns, vnto the aboue named Benjamen Curtis his heyrs, executors, Administrators & Assigns, a Certen Prcell of vpland, Contayneing the quantity of fourty Acres of Land, lijng & being with in the Townshipp of Yorke vpon the North West branch of Yorke riuer On the West side of the sd branch, which sayd Lott of vpland is in breadth about Twenty fiue pools, the full breadth of my Marsh, on y^t side & so runne backeward vntill fourty Acres bee fully Compleated, according to a Town Grant beareing date May the tenth 1667 · with all the profetts priviledges and Imunitys, to haue and to hould, with Commans easements Tymber Tymber trees, and all other appurtenances y^{r}vnto any ways belonging or appetayneing, vnto the sayd Benjamen Curtis, his heyres executors, Administrators & Assignes for euer/ And the sayd Andrew Everest doth acknowledg him selfe to bee the true & lawfull owner of the aboue named Premisses, & hath of him selfe full right pouer & Authority, to bargan dispose off & make Sayle of the sd Land,

BOOK III, FOL. 89.

& that It is free and Cleare from all Morgages, Dowers titles troubles Judgments executions & all other Incomberances whatsoeuer/ And do further by these Prsents bind my selfe my heyres & Assignes to warrant and defend, the right and title of the aforesayd Land, from mee my heyres executors & assignes, vnto the aforenamed Benja͞. Curtis, his heyrs executors & Assignes for euer, from all or any Prson or Prsons w'soeuer, Clajmeing or Pretending any Clajme title or Interest there vnto, from by or vnder mee, or any other by my procurement/ In testimony whereof I the aforesayd Andrew Everest, haue here vnto afixed my hand & seale, In the Thyrty secund yeare of the Reigne of our Soueraign Ld Charles the Secund, of England, Scotland, ffrance & Ireland King fidej Defensoris, this Eighteenth day of March Anno Dom͞. one thousand six hundred & Eighty & eighty one/ 168?

Signed sealed & delivered/   Andrew Everest (locus/sigilli)
In the Presence of/

Ric · Hunnell his Marke   R

Andrew Everest acknowledgeth this Instrument to bee his Act & Deed, this eighteenth day of March 168? before mee

Barbury Euerest came before mee this 8th day of June 1681 & did acknowledg this Instrument to bee her free act & Deed—   Edw: Rishworth Just: pe:
Edw Rishworth Justis pe   A true Coppy of this Deed or Instrument aboue written transcribed out of the originall & there with Compared this 17th day of Aprill (1681) p Edw: Rishworth ReCor:

To all Christian people vnto whom this Deed or Instrument shall Come/ William Hammonds In the Town of Wells, In the Province of Mayne In New England Planter, sends greeting: Now know yee that I the sayd William Hamonds, vpon severall good Causes & Considerations, there vnto mee moueing, & more espetially for that Naturall loue,

& affection which I haue, & do beare vnto my beloued sonn Jonathan Hamonds, haue by these Presents given granted, barganed sould Enfeoffed & Confirmed & do hereby give grant bargan sell Enfeoff & Confirme, freely fully & absolutely vnto my aforesd sonn Jonathan Hamonds, from mee my heyres executors administrators and Assignes, my soole right Title & Interest of my whoole Estate of Lands, houses, Cattle, & Chattles, Moveables & vnmoueables with in doores & with out, & whatsoeuer doth of right doth any ways belong or app'tayne to my visible or Invisible Estate, lijng or being in the Town shipp of Wells or else where, vnto my aforesayd sonn Jonathan Hamonds his heyrs executors Administrators & Assignes for ever, & More Prticularly as followeth/

A Certen Tract or quantity of vpland Contayneing the quantity of ffoure hundred Acres of Land bee It more or less lijng between ye Land formerly of John Bates on the East side, & a Prcell of Land given by the Town to my sonn Jonathan Hamonds on the West side, with foureteen acres of Marsh butting on the front on the Sea Wall, Adioyneing to a Prcell of Marsh on the East formerly Thomas Mills his Marsh now in the Custody of John Cloyce, & to a Parcell of Marsh of Wilha~ [90] Ashleys on the West side thereof, as alsoe a parcell of vpland most part y^rof fenced in, lijng vpon the sea Wall at the East End of the sayd Marsh, aforesayd, Contayneing the quantity of foure or fiue Acres more or less with all the profetts, priuiledges Comanes Easements Imunitys, with all & singular the appurtenances y^rvnto any wise appertayneing; freely & quietly to haue & to hould, with out any matter of Challenge Clajme or demand, of mee the sd William Hamonds, or any Prson or Prsons from by or vnder mee, my heyres executors, administrators or Assignes for euer: Provided always It is to bee vnderstood. that I the sayd William Hamonds & Jonathan Hamonds my sonn in the behalfe of him selfe his heyres & Assigns haue agreed, & do mutually Covenant the one with each other, that vpon the Considerations given as aboue mentioned, by the sd Will: Hamonds, to his son Jonathan, that ye true & reall Meaneing of the Premisses, are fully intended, & so always to bee vnderstood, that ye sayd Jonathan Hamonds In the behalfe of him selfe, his heyrs & Assigns stands firmely obleig'd by these Psents to exercise his filiall Care, by his vtmost diligence skill & Industry to make the best provission hee is able, for the Comfortable subsistance of his parence, vidz^t William Hamonds his father, & his aged Mother, that now lyeth sicke, by his frugall management of the state aforesayd, for whose necessary & Comfortable Mantenance, hee is wholly to take care, dureing the full tearme of thejr naturall lifes, according to the valew & capacity of what such an Estate Can ordinarily & rationally produce, being Industriously & thriftily managed/ And further I the sayd William Hamonds, vpon my sonn Jonathan his Prformance of the Conditions aboue mentioned, do hereby covenant & promiss in the behalfe of my selfe my heyres, executors & Administrators to & with my sonn Jonathan Hamonds, his heyrs executors administrators, & Assignes, that the sd Estate of houses Lands & goods are free & Cleare, from all gyfts grants barganes, leases, Dowers Morgages Judgments and all other Incomberances whatsoeuer, and do likewise promiss & Covenant to warrant & defend the title & Interest of the Premisses, from mee my heyres executors, or from any Prson or Prsons vnder mee, or by mee, or my meanes or any other by my procurement/ In testimony of all & euery of the abouesd Premisses, I haue here vnto afixed my hand & seale this 23th day of March 168¾ In the thirty secund Yeare of the Reigne of o^r Soueraign Lord Charles the secund, of England, Scotland, France, & Ireland, King, ffidei Defenso^r 16$\frac{80}{81}$

Signed sealed & Delivered/   William Hammonds (locus sigilli)
In the Presence of/   Jonathan Hammōds (his seale)
Edw: Rishworth/   William & Jonathan Hammōd do
Samell Wheelewright/   own & acknowledg this Instrumet aboue written to bee y^r free act & Deed, each to other/ Taken before vs this 28th day of March: 1681
        Edw: Rishworth
        Samell Wheelewright   Just^s: pe:

A true Coppy of this Instrument aboue written transcribed & Compared with the originall this 16th day of Aprill 1681:   p Edw: Rishworth Re Cor.

Kittery in the County of Yorke/

This Deed made the 4th day of March 1675, between Thomas Withers on the one Party, & Thomas Ryce on the other Party, Witnesseth, that I Thomas Withers haue barganed, & sould vnto Thomas Ryce aforesd, a Tract of Land lijng & being in spruse Cricke, Contayneing of thirty two Acres of land with some Marshes Conveij^t begining at a Poynt Called ox Poynt, & so from the sd oxe Poynt from a Marked Hemlocke Tree one hundred & sixty rodd, on a north Nore West lyne, & on the South side by the sd Cricke, Thyrty & two Rodds, to a marked tree, & from thence one hundred & sixty rod on a Nore Nore West lyne, which in all do Contayne Thyrty & two Acres, with all the appurtenances y^{r}vnto belonging, or in any wise app^{r}tajneing there vnto, the aforesd Thomas Rice his heyres & Assignes for euer, from the sd Thomas Withers his heyres & Assignes/ To haue & to hould all the sayd Premisses, with whatsoeuer belongeth there vnto for ever more ; And further more I the sayd Thomas Withers do promiss & Ingage the aforesd Tract of Land to bee free & cleare from all former sayles morgages, barganes whatsoener/ And further more the sd Withers doth acknowledg him selfe to bee fully satisfyd, & payd for the aforesd Land, as Witness my hand & seale the day & yeare aboue written/ Thomas Withers (his seale.)

Mr Thomas Withers owneth this Instrument aboue written to Thomas Ryce to bee his free Act & Deed, this 4th day of March 1675 : before mee

Edw : Rishworth Assotiate/

A true Coppy of this Instrument aboue written transcribed & with originall Compared this 16th day of Aprill 1681 :
p Edw : Rishworth ReCor :

Know all men by these Prsents, that I Thomas Riice of Kittery In the County of yorke, for and In Consideration of ye some of Twenty two Pounds in Current pay in hand Received, before the Insealeing & delivery of these P'sents, the receipt where of sd Thomas Rice doth acknowledg him selte to bee fully satisfyd, & payd, & there of, & of euery part & penny there of doth acquit exonerate and discharge Richard Monson his heyrs executors, administrators and Assigns for euer; As also for diverse other good causes & Considerations, mee here vnto espetially moueing, haue given granted barganed & sould Enfeoffed & released Deliuered & Confirmed & by these Presents do give grant bargan & sell, Enfeoff release deliuer & Confirme vnto the sayd Richard Monson of Portsmouth, In the Province of New Hamshyre fisherman, his heyrs executors Administrators & assignes, a Tract of Land lijng & being in spruse Cricke, In ye Town of Kittery Contayneing thirty two Acres of vpLand, with some Marsh begining at a place Called ox poynt, & so from the·

sayd poynt, from a Marked & Hemlocke tree one hundred & sixty rod On a Nore Nore West lyne and on the South side by the sayd Cricke Thyrty two Rodds to marked tree, & from thence one hundred & sixty rod on a North Nore West lyne/ which in all do Contayne Thyrty & Two Acres with all there appurtenances there vnto belonging; To haue & to hould [**91**] the abouesd given & granted Premisses, togeather with all profetts priviledges & aduantages there vnto belonging to the sayd Richard Munson his heyres executors, Administrators & Assignes for ever: And sayd Thomas Rice for him selfe his heyres, executors, administrators & Assignes, doth Couenant promiss & grant to & with the sayd Richard Munson his heyres executors administrators or Assignes, that all & singular the aboue granted & barganed Premisses are and bee & at all tymes hereafter shall bee Continew & remajne clearely acquitted, exonerated, discharged & keept harmeless from all & all manner of former & other barganes Gyfts, grants leases Dowers, titles or Incomberances whatsoeuer, made Committed suffered or done, by sayd Thomas Ryce his heyres, executors, administrators & Assignes, or by any other person or Prsons whatsoeuer, Clajmeing from by or vnder him, them or any of them/ as witness my hand & seal herevnto this Twenty eight of June one thousand six hundred & eighty/

Signed sealed & Delivered   Thomas Rice (his seale)
  In Psence of vs Test^s: Mary Rice *M* (her seale)
  John ffennicke   her marke
  John Batsham/   Thomas Rice & Mary Rice his wife acknowledged this Instrument aboue written to bee thejr Act & Deed this 10th of July 1680, before mee
                            ffran Hooke Just pe:

[Margin note:] Kittery as Janry 12th 1701 | the within named John ffinnicke psonally Appearing before me ye Subscribr one of his Mats Justices of the Peace within ye County of York made oath that he was psent & did Se ye within named Thomas Rice give delivery and Seizen of ye psnt mentioned in the within written Deed unto ye within named Richard Monson & that Richard Monson Junr was psent at ye Same time

A true Copie of ye originall Testimony Transcribed & compared Janr 12, 1701
               Jos Hamond
       p Jos Hamond Registr

BOOK III, FOL. 91.

Aprill 16th one thousand six hundred eighty one, Wee whose names are here vnderwritten do testify that Thomas Rice did give before us possession of this Land that this aboue written Instrument speaketh off vnto Richard Munson Senjo^r, this 16th day of Aprill : 1681 :

         John ffennicke
A true Coppy of this Instrument   Richd Munson Jujo^r
aboue written, with the possession of y^t land y^rin mentioned given to Richd Munson Senjo^r, transcribed out ye originall & there with Compared this 20th day of Aprill 1681 :
        p Edw : Rishworth ReCor :

Know all men by these Presents, that I Samuell Symonds of Ipswich In ye County of Essex Gentle : haue assigned 250 acres, being part of the thousand Acres which I purchased of my son Hayrlacmden (It being no part of 500 Acres which I haue reserved to my selfe) backe agayne to my son Harlacmden, to Impoure him y^rby to Grant the sayd 250 Acres to my daughter Martha Symonds/ to haue & to hould the same to him, & his heyres & Assignes for euer/ Dated 17th of ye secund Moenth Called Aprill : 1661 .
This Assigment was signed,   Samuell Symonds (With a seale)
sealed & deliuered in the
P^rsence of us/   A true Coppy Compared with y^e
Samull Symonds Junjo^r/   originall this 29 of Aprill 1681 :
Daniell Epps/   p Edw : Rishworth ReCor/

Know all men by these Presents, that I Thomas Withers of Kittery In the prouince of Mayne, yeoman In Consideration of the Covenant & agreements, hereafter in these presents expressed, Haue given granted Assign'd barganed sould & Confirmed, & by these presents doe giue grant, assigne bargan sell & Confirme to Major Nicholas Shapleigh & John Shapleigh, both of Kittery aforesd Gentle: theire heyres & Assignes, all that peece of Land, lijng & being at Oake Poynt, in Spruse Cricke In Kittery, aforesayd, contameing so much In quantity as shall by the sd Major Nicholas Shapleigh bee thought convenient & necessary w^rvpon to Erect a Saw Mill or Mills; To haue and to hould the sayd p^rmises, togeather with lyberty to lay Convenjent qnantitys of Loggs & boards on the East side of ye sd Cricke, & also to fell & Cutt timber for the supply of such Saw Mill or Mills, & likewise the priuiledg^s of all ye sayd Cricke, & euery part there of, & also one thousand of pine Trees, which Were formerly granted to mee by a Kittery Town Grant, vnto ye sd Major Nicho: Shapleigh, & John Shapleigh thejr heyres & Assignes for euer; Prouided always, that I the sd Tho Withers, my executors & Administrators, shall & may haue, & take to my own & there vss, & behoofe the Moeity of all such Loggs as shall at any tyme hereafter by mee, & them bee brought to the saw Mill or Mills When Erected & sawn there; And I the sd Thomas Withers for my selfe my heyres executors Administrators do Couenant & promiss, to & with the sayd Major Shapleigh & John Shapleigh, there heyres executors, adnumstrators & Assignes, y^t I am rightfully & lawfully seized in fee symple of the sayd Premisses & do & will warrant ye sd p̄misses to the sayd Major Nicho Shapleigh, & John Shapleigh there heyres & Assignes, for from, & against mee my heyres & Assignes, & all other Prsons whatsoeuer/ In witness where of I haue here vnto set my hand & seale this 25 · March: 1681:

Sealed & deliuered   Thomas Withers (his seale)
  In the Presence of/   Mr Tho: Withers Came before mee
  Richd Chamberlajn   this Eleauenth day of May: 1681:
  Joseph Rayn/   & did own this Instrument aboue
  James Johnson/   written to bee his free Act &
  John Purrington/   Deede/
       Edw Rishworth Just pe:

BOOK III, FOL. 91, 92.

A true Coppy of this Instrument transcribed & Compared with originall this 21ᵗʰ May 1681 :
p Edw. Rishworth Re: Cor:

Was by the request of William Hutchinson & Humprey Chadbowrn, vnto Major Nicholas Shapleigh & Richard Nason, formerly Townes men of Kittery, for the bounding of Lands In the sd Town, & Wee the sd Prsons vpon Inquiry & examination of the bounds of some Lands formerly granted vnto Richard Leader, & Humfrey Chadbowrn Senjor now In the hands of the sd Hutchinson & Chadbowrn Junjor about the dividing Lyne between them, & finding such a deconnancy between the lyne mentioned In yᵉ ReCord & the bound trees marked, do by these prsents firmely settle, & agree with the Mutuall Consent of the sayd Hutchinson & Chadbowrne, to disanull & reverse all former bounds Prefixed by yᵉ ReCords. & do settle & Conclude the bounds, as by Poynts & Marked trees now runne & stated, to bee & remajne as perpetuall bounds, & bound Markes to them & thejr heyres for ever/

Which bounds so stated begmneth six pooles or rodds below Assabumbedicke falls at a marked tree by the River side there, & from thence runneing one hundred fourty eight rodds, North vnto a Whitte oake marked tree, with a W & H on the one side, & an H & C on the other side, & from thence to runne one hundred poole vpon a North East lyne about halfe a poynt Eastwardly, by a great ould white oake tree vnto a little pine tree, about three rodds below It, being the vtmost bounds vpon a North East poynt, & from the sayd small pine tree, neare the sd great Whitte Oake, at the foote of the White Hill so Called, vpon a South East & by south Lyne, by marked trees to runne down [92] to the riv⸺ ⸺ked, one

Book III, Fol. 92.

w'ot marked with **W H**, neare the place Called John Lambs Landing place where hee burned CharCoales, & so bounded by the river side to the Mills six Rodd, below the falls, which are the full & Compleat bounds, of the lands formerly granted to Richard Leader & Humfrey Chadbowrn, bounded between them on the North side of the river/ as witness our hands this eighteenth day of July one thousand six hundred seaventy three, 1673:

    vera Copia of this Instrume^t Nic: Shapleigh
    aboue written transcribed   Richd Nason his
    & Compared cum origine   marke **O**
    this 27th of May 1681   William Hutchinson
    p Edw: Rishworth ReCor·   Humphrey Chadborne/

To all christian people to whom this writeing may come: Know yee y^t I Thomas Williams late of Sacoe, in the Province of Mayne, now of Newgewnnacke in the Town of Kittery, in the Province of Mayn abouesd, for good Considerations mee moueing there vnto, espetially for the naturall loue & affection I beare vnto Lydea Playstead, the daughter of my daughter Lucretia Hitchcocke, late of Sacoe afores^d, haue passed ouer & given, alienated Infeoffed & Confirmed, & do & by these Presents, pass over giue grant aliene Infeoff & Confirme vnto the aforesd Lydea Playstead, wife to James Playstead of Newgewanacke In Kittery aforesd, a Certen Tract of Land scituate, & being in Saco aforesd, & butting vpon winter harbour, being part of my house lott in the sd Sacoe Contayneing twenty Acres, & being a iust third part of my sayd house lott, & is the Middle part of the sd lot, to lie the whoole Length of ye sd lott, from Winter Harbour into the Woods, to the vtmost end of It/ Which land I formerly bought of Mr Vines, & now given by mee vnto the sd Lydea Playsted togeather with the one halfe of my Marsh,

BOOK III, FOL. 92.

lijng in the sd Harbour/ Which halfe part is Esteemed to bee about foure acres, more or less; To haue & to hould the sayd Twenty Acres of Land, & the sd foure acres of Marsh, with all the app'tenances, priuiledges & Comoditys, w'soeuer there vnto belonging, or in any wise app'tayneing, to her the sd Lydea Playstead, to her heyres, executors, administrators & Assignes for euer, the same to seise vpon & possess, as aforesd Immediately after my death/ In witness w'rof I haue set too my hand & seale, this twelth day of Octob'r one thousand six hundred & eighty/

Signed sealed & Deliuered/   Thomas Williams (his seale)
in the Presence of us/   his ⌐ Marke
William Playstead/
Thomas Parker his   Thomas Williams owned the aboue
marke ✗   written deed of gyft, to bee his free Act, & Deed this 12th day of October 1680 · before mee
         John Wincoll Just pe

vera Copia, transcribed, Concordat cum origine, this 27th of May one thousand six hundred eighty one/
         p Edw: Rishworth Re: Cor:

These P'rsents witness, that Tymothy Collines now of Nubery, for & in Consideration of a valewable some of Money or Monys worth received, being full satisfaction to him the sd Tymothy Collines, haue giuen granted & sould, & by these Presents do give grant sell, Conhrme, & deliuer vnto Dunkum Stewart his heyres & Assigns for euer a tract of vpland, Meddow & Marsh, of about one hundred Acres, bee It more or less, scituate & lyng Eastward in the Province of Mayne, at or neare a place Called blew poynt, & also my right or title that I haue or may bee Cleared vp by the sd Stuart or his Assignes to bee my proper right,

Book III, Fol. 92.

desending to mee from my father Christopher Collines, or by purchase or otherwise, & in spetial the tract of Land my father Christopher Collines was possessed of In his life tyme at blew poynt bounded as followeth; By the sea, on the East, or the Easterly side & by land of the sd Gyles Barge, on the Westerly side, Nathan Bedfords Land on the North-wardly side, with all the Lands, Marshes, Meddows Improuements, priuiledges y^runto belonging; To haue & to hould vnto him the aforesd Stuart, his heyres & Assignes for euer, peaceably & quietly to Inioy vss & occupy to him & them, with out any let hinderance, Molestation, or Interruption of him the sd Tymothy Collines, his heyres, executors, or Assignes for euer/ for full Confirmation of the Premisses, & every part there of with all its app^rtenances, vnto the sd Dunkum Stuart his heyres & Assignes for ever, the sd Tymothy Collines hath put too his hand & Seale, this Twenty eight day of Decemb^r one thousand six hundred & Eighty/

Abigæyll Collines gave vp her right in this Land vnto the sd Stuart before the witnesses of this Deed/

The marke of (his seale) Timothy Collines/

Richard Dummer
Beniamen Boodridg
his marke/ B

Timothy Collines acknowledged the aboue written to bee his Act & Deed before mee ffebru. 15th 1680. Daniel Denison/

A true Coppy of this Deed transcribed, & with originall Compared this third day of June 1681:

p Edw · Rishworth Re: Cor:

July · 5th 1680 ·

Then measured & layd out to Mr Edw: Rishworth, his land given him in his father Wheelewrights will, by order of Mr Samuell Wheelerright & sayd Rishworth as followeth vidz^t: fiuety acres of vpland, begining at the lower end of John Cloyse his house lot, at a marked tree ninety two pooles East South East down to the Marsh, then bounded with the Marsh, till It comes neare to the ffalls of Ogunquet river & so vp to a tree marked, that is eighty foure poole, South South West, from the first Corner marked tree, Which is the sayd fiuety Acres of Land/

Also measured & layd out vnto sayd Rishworth, Twenty acers of Marsh as followeth, begining at the East end of a part of the sayd vpland vpon an East & by South lyne, till it come to a Certen cricke which deuides between the sd Marsh & James Littlefejlds, & runnes vpon the same East & by South lyne, excepting the seuerall poynts of Marsh made by the Crookeing of the sd Cricke, in which poynts there is two Acres of Marsh, with the aforesd East & by South Lyne, which sd lyne vpon that side next James Littlefejlds Marsh, is eighty fiue pooles in length to a river neare the sea Wall · And the breadth North & by East is thirty two pools & is bounded at that East end, with the sd river, & is on the North side next Mr Samll Wheelewrights Marsh bounded vpon a West & by north lyne, backe to the vpland, where It hath a Coue of Marsh extending so fare beyond the length of eighty two pooles, togeather with such another peece made at the sea Wall by the Crookeing of the River, that fully made vp the loss of Marsh by the pond or otherwise/   John Wincoll Survayer/

[93] Articles of agreement made & Concluded betweene Christopher Pecket of Muddy River on the one party, & Henery Williams of Boston on the party Witnesseth, that I the aforesd Christopher Pecket, do by thes presents bargan, sell, & Confirme to the sd Hene Williams, his heyres executors, administrators & Assignes, for ever, all my houses & land, liing & being in the Townshipe of Scarbrough, alias

Bla͠: Poynt, in the prouince of Mayn in new England, which houses & land is for & in Consideration of a debt of six pounds fiueteen shillings, y^t I ow to Hene: Wilhams/ as witness my hand & scale the eleuenth of June 1681:

The Condition of the aboue obligation is such, that If Waymouth Bickton of the aforesd place, pay to the sd Henery Williams six pounds fiuetenn shillings, in refuge fish vpon sight hereof, then ye aboue obligation is to voyd & of none æffect, otherwise It is to stand in full force pouer & vertue, as witness my hand & seale this eleventh day of June 1681.

Signed sealed & deliuered/   The marke of

in presence of vs/   Christopher Pecket   (his seale)

Richd Trewiss/

Nat̃ll Addams Jujo^r Christopher Pecket acknowledged this Instruent to bee his Act & Deede, June 11th: 81: before mee John Richards Asist^t

vera Copia of these Articles aboue written, transcribed & Compared with originall this 17th of June 1681·

                     p Edw: Rishworth ReCor:

Know all men by these presents, that I James Pendleton sometyme of Pischataqua, River, now resident In stoneington In new England for & in Consideration of the full quantity of Twenty thousand of M^{r}chantable redd oake pipe staues, by mee in hand received of William Vahan of Portsmouth on Pishataqua river in New England aforesd M^{r}chant, w^{r}with I acknowledg my selfe fully satisfyd, contented & payd, haue barganed & sould, & by these presents do bargan sell, alliene, Assigne & set ouer, Enfcoff Conuay release, deliuer & Confirme vnto William Vahan aforesd, all that my vpland, Marsh & yslands adioyneing, at Cape porpus, In the prouince of May a, cont͠ainm͠g t̃ree ...   Acers more or less, besid[s] yslands, are as followeth, vidz[t] one hundred acres of Land given, & granted by Thomas Gorges Esq[r], with one Ysland, as by a deed to John Smyth, beareing date the eighteenth of July 1643: With all the priuiledges & appurtenances there vnto belonging, & by another deede from sd Smyth, to to Majo[r] William Phillips, & from sd Phillips, to Majo[r] Bryan Pendleton/ also one hundred Acres of Land, given to the sd Bryan Pendleton, by the Town of Cape porpus, as by ReCords in the sd Towne booke, beareing date the first of Septem[br] 1672, may appeare with all the appurteances therevnto belonging/ also one hundred acres of Land, sd Pendleton bought of John Sanders, as by a deed bearing date the 6[th] of October, 1673: may appeare, with all priuiledges, & appurtenances there vnto belonging, & three small Yslands bought of the sd Bryan Pendleton, of one Gregory Jefferys as appeareth by a deed beareing date the twenty fifth of June 1658: with the app[r]tenances/ all which, the before hereby bargained Prmisses, with the app[r]tenances, were given to the aforesd James Pendleton, by the aforesd Bryan Pendleton, as may appeare by his last Will, & testament beareing date the 9th of August 1677: Recorded in the records of Yorke: with one small Island, bought by sd Bryan Pendleton, of Grace Bush, as p a deed beareing date the 24th of August 1670. To haue & to hould, & peaceably to Imoy, the before hereby bargained Premisses, with all the rights priuiledges, appurtenances, to all & euery part & Prcell there of, belonging or appertajneing, to him the sd William Vaughan his heyres executors, administrators, or Assignes for ever, to bee to thejr proper vsse benefitt & behoofe of the sd William Vaughan, his heyres, executors, administrators or assignes for ever, free, & Cleare, & freely Clearely acquitted, from all & all either Gyfts, grants, barganes sayles Morgages, dower, or title of Dower, by Hannah now wife of the sd James, or Ellner Relict of ye sd Bryan, or any other incomberances Whatsoeu[r] made had or done by the sd

Book III, Fol. 93.

James, or sd Bryan, or any other Prson, from by or vnder the sd Bryan, or James, the sd William Vaughan, onely paijng to the Ld Proprietor, such acknowledgmt If demanded, as sd James & his Prædecessors, are or were Ingaged to do/ furthermore, the sd James Pendleton doth promiss & Covenant to deliver vp vnto the sd Vaughan all writeings Concerning the Premisses, fayrely written & uncancelled, & that hee will make any further Assurance of the Prmises, if neede bee, as the sd Vaughan shall reasonably desire/ vnto all & euery the aforementioned Premisses, the sd James Pendleton to the Prformance, doth bind him selfe his heyres, executors, administrators, vnto the sd William Vahan his heyres executors Administrators & Assigns/ In witness wrof hath here vnto set his hand, & seale, the 13th day of June: 1681 & In the Thirty third yeare of the Reign of or Soveraigne Lord, Charles the secund, by the Grace of god, King of England, Scotland, France, & Ireland, Defendr of the faith/

Signed sealed & delivered in the Presence of/
Josua Moodey/ Robt Elliot/

James Pendleton (Locus Sigilli) Ellner Pendleton, & James Pendleton Came before mee, this one an twenteth day of June 1681 · & did acknowledg this Instrument aboue written, to bee yr free Act & Deed/ Edw: Rishworth Just pe ·

Possession & seazin of the Premisses with in written, given by Capt James Pendleton vnto Mr William Vaughton who received the possession thereof by Turffe & Twigg from him, this twenty first day of June 1681 . & this was done in the Presence of/ Capt James Pendleton owneth this possession thus given at Cape Porpus to
John Davies/
Pendleton ffletcher/ bee his Act & Deed, this 22cund day of June 1681 before mee
Edw . Rishworth Just pe:

Book III, Fol. 93.

vera Copia of the Deed aboue written, with the Deliuery of the Possession, & acknowledgm⁺ thereof, transcribed out of the originall, & y⁺ with Compared this 25ᵗʰ day of June 1681 :   p Edw : Rishworth ReCor/

These Presents testifyeth, that wᵃˢ Thomas Redding my deceased husband, did in the yeare of our Lord one thousand six hundred seauenty too, Morgage & make ouer vnto Mr John Sands, Shopp keeper, of Boston all his Land, & Plantation, as land, March, & for the some of Twenty pounds in money to him in hand, as reference to the sd Morgage, will appeare more largely ; I Ellner Redding widdow, to the sd Thomas Redding, did desire my loueing friend Mr James Andrews of Cascoe alias Falmouth, to take vp the sd Morgage, & pay the sd some of Twenty pounds to Mr John Sands, I ingageing to allow him fiue pounds for the vss of his Twenty for a yeare, & at yᵉ expiration of yᵉ yeare, I or mine was to pay to him, the aforesd Mr James Andrews, the aforesd twenty fiue pounds/ Which some of Twenty pounds Mr James Andrews hath payd ; Now know all men by these Presents, that I Ellner Redding, for the better security of him the sd James Andrews, do by these Presents, giue vnto the sd Mr James Andrews his heyres & Assigns all my right, title, & Interest, to two thirds of all yᵉ Land Marshes, or w'soever is mentioned in the aforesd Morgage, & haue given him possession of the sd too thirds, by Truff & twigg, always prouided, that if the aforesd twenty fiue pounds bee payd according to spetie, that is in money bee pd by mee or mine vnto the sd James Andrews, his heyres or Assignes, at or before the last of October next Insewing the Date here of, then Mr James Andrews is to redeliuer vnto mee, or mine, possession of the sd too thirds, with the Morgage & this Instrument : but if the Money bee not payd, then I say I Ellner Redding do acknowledg &

own, the afore mentioned too thirds, to bee absolutely & soulie James Andrews, his heyres or Assignes for euer, wholly emptijng my selfe, of all right Clajme or interest, to the sd too thirds, or any part y^rof, & onely one third to belong to mee & mine/ & In witness of the treuth here of I Ellner Redding, haue here vnto set my hand & seale, this 10th day of March, 167¾

Signed, sealed & deliuered, & posses- Ellner Redding (her seal)
sion giuen by turffe & Twigg in
Presence of us/   her marke
Fran: Neale in Presence of us/
James Lane his   his
marke John Mosean
     marke

  A true Coppy of this Instrument transcribed & Compared with ye originall
this 18th of July: 1681:
    p Edw: Rishworth ReCor:

[94] To all people, to whome these Presents shall Come/ Ellner Redding relict of Thomas Redding deceased, late of Cascoe bay in the County of yorke, in New England, sendeth Greeting Know yee y^t I the sd Ellner Redding, for & in Consideration of the some of fourty pounds, foure shillings & foure peence, which I haue in hand received of Mary Higginson, late ye Relique & executrix of Josua Atwater, late of Boston in New England deceased Merchant, & sd some was for the payment of my husbands Debts, & supply of my Present necessity, in the tyme of my distresse, & do acknowledg my selfe Justly indebted vnto ye sd Mary, the sayd some in money, have barganed, & sould, & do by these Presents, fully Clearely & absolutely grant, bargan sell alliene Infeoff & Confirme, vnto the sd Mary Atwater, as executrix afor^esd, alias Higginson, all ye housing &

BOOK III, FOL. 91.

Lands scituate, lijng & being vpon Westgotoggoe river, in Cascoe bay aforesd, Contayneing by Estimation two hundred Acres of vpland, being butted & bounded by the Land of James Lane Eastward, westward with the sd river, North & South with Crickes, as alsoe sixteene Acres of Meddow, bee the same more or less, being about one mile & an halfe, aboue the dwelling house, It lijng north west or there abouts, from the sd dwelling house James Laine haueing a peece of Meddow lijng below it/ also all my right title Interest vss Clajme & Demand, of in or to the same, or y^t of right may or out to belong, or appertajne to mee the sd Ellner, for tyme to come, togeather with all profetts, priuiledges, Commanages & appurtenances to the same belonging, in any manner or wise, or thence to bee had made or raysed/ And also all deeds, writeings, Euidences, touching, & Concerneing the same, or any part y^{r}of: To haue & to hould, the sd Parcell of Land, with all & euery of the rights, Members & appurtenances, vnto the sd Mary Atwater alias Higginson, as executrix aforesd, her heyrs & Assignes for ever/ And further the sd Ellner doth Couenant & promiss, for my selfe my heyres, executors, & Administrators, to & with the sd Mary her heyres & Assignes, that the barganed Premisses, & euery part y^{r}of, are free & Cleare, & freely & Clearely acquitted & discharged, of & from & from all manner of former, & other gyfts grants barganes, sayles leases, Joynters, Dowers, titles of Dowers, Judgments executions Intayles, forfitures, & of & from all other titles, troubles, charges, & Incomberances w'soeuer/ And also shall & will warrant & Defend the same against all & euery Person, & Prsons w'soeuer, any ways lawfully Clajmeing or demandmg the same, or any part or Prcell there of, & that ye sd Ellner Redding, at or vpon ye reasonable request of ye sd Mary executrix her heyres Or Assignes shall & will at all tyme & tymes bee ready & willmg, to giue & will giue to the sayd Mary Atwater, alias Higinson h r h ... A... ... and further & ample

Book III, Fol. 94.

assurance of all the aforesd barganed Premisses, as in law or æquity Can bee desired or required, piouided always, & It is neuer the less Concluded, & by & between the sd Partys to these Presents & it is the true Intent & meaneing y'of, that if the sd Ellner Redding her executois, administratois or Assignes or either, or any of them shall Well & truely pay, or Cause te bee payd vnto the sd Mary Atwater, alias Higginson executrix her executors, Administrators oi Assignes, the full & Just some of fouity pounds, foure shillings & foure peence, in lawfull money of New England, on or before the first day of May In the yeare of our Lord, one thousand six hundred eighty & one at ye now dwelling house of Mr John Higginson Senior at Salem, that then this Present deede of sale & Grant, euery Clawse & article y'in, Contained shall Cease, determ^e bee voyd, & of none æffect, any thing in these Presents Contajned to ye Contrary there of, in any wise notwithstanding, or other wise to remajne abide & stand, in full pouer foice & vertue/ In witness w^{r}of, I the sayd Ellner Redding haue here vnto sett my hand & seale, this twelfth day of Aprill In the yeare of our Lord, one thousand six hundred & eighty/

Signed, sealed & Deliveied/   The Maike of Ellner
   in the piesence of us/   Redding/ ☥ (her seale)
   Hilliaid Veien Senior   Ellner Redding owned this to bee
   Eleazar Gydney/   her Act & Deede, 12th 2cund
                              Moenth 1680 : befoie mee
                              Willa^m Hawthoine Assistant

A true Coppy of this Instrument transcribed, & with originall Compared this 18th day of July 1681 ·
                    ,   p Edw Rishworth ReCor

Know all men by these Presents, that Wee John Redding of Waymouth in the Coloney of the Massatusetts, in New England, John Taylor of Boston in New England afoiesd, & Joseph Donell of Cascoe Bay In New England, & Ruth his

Book III, Fol. 94.

wife, haue Surrendered, remitted, released, & quitt Clajmed: And by these Presents, do for our selues, & our respectiue heyres, executors, administrators & Assigns & for each & euery of vs, & them, fully freely, & absolutely surrender, remitt, release, & for euer quitt Clajme, vnto the with in named Mary Higginson, Relict, Widdow, & executrix, of the last will & testament of Josua Atwater, late of Boston aforesd M^{r}chant, dec̄d; and to her heyres & Assigns, into hers & there quiett & peaceable possession & Seizen. All o^r, & each & euery of o^r whoole Estate, right title Interest, Clajme property & Demand, w^{t}soeuer of in & to the with in mentioned Premisses, & euery part & parcell y^{r}of, with there & euery of there rights, Members, hereditaments, & appurtenances/ To haue & to hould all our & each, & euery of o^r whoole Estate, right title, Interest, Clajme property, & Demand, whatsoeuer, & every part y^{r}of, vnto the sd Mary Higginson, her heyres & Assigns for euer, with out any manner of reclajme, Challenge, & Demand, of vs the sd John Redding John Taylour Jos: Donell & Ruth his wife, or either or any of vs, or either or any of o^r heyres, executors, administrators or Assignes, vnder the Conditions & prouissions with in mentioned/ In witness w^{r}of the sd John Redding, John Taylo^r, & Joseph Donell & Ruth his wife, haue here vnto set y^r hands & seales, the nineteenth day of November, Anno Dom̄: 1680 .   John Redding ✝ (his seale)
                                                        his marke
Signed sealed & Deliuered/
  in Presence of vs/   John Redding who hath set his
  William Gyllbard/   name to this Instrument, did
  Eleazer Moody/   acknowledg It to bee his act &
  John Haward Jujo^r Secr^ets Deed, the 20th of Novemb^r
                                 1680: before

                                        Tho. Sauage Assista^t

A true Coppy of the further Confirmation of y^s Deed by ye Party aboue written, transcribed & Compared with the originall this 21th of July: 1681.

                    p Edw Ri-bworth ReCor:

Book III, Fol. 94.

<small>the Deed Entred in ye New booke of ReCords pa. 7.</small>
This may Certify all whom it may Concerne, that I am freely willing as I am one of the Select men for the Town of Kittery, for this Present yeare 73 : that Mr Thomas Withers shall haue & Imoy all that Land & Meddow wch is specifyd in this with in writteng as witness my hand/ this 20th of Janva : 1673 :   Roger Playstead/

I do freely Consent to w^t is aboue wrntten as I am one of the Select men for this Present yeare, 1673 : as witness my hand this 21th of Janv :   Charles Frost/
Christian Ranacke, his maike R   Robert Mendum, M
Fran : Hooke/   John Wincoll   Select men for the same yeare, do agree to y^t same aboue sayd/

A true Coppy transcribed & Compared with originall this 21th of July 1681 · p Edw : Rishworth ReCor

Know all men by these Presents that I James Gibbones of Sacoe in the Prouince of Mayne, with the Consent of Judeth my wife, in Consideration of a some of money to mee in hand payd, by Benjamē. Blackeman at Present rescident at bla͞ : Poynt, In the sd Prouince, the receipt w^rof I acknowledg by these Presents, & do here by for euer acquitt, exonerate & discharge him the sd Blackeman, his heyres executors & administrators, of all & euery part thereof. Haue giuen, granted, sould, alliend, Enfeofed & Confirmed, and by these Presents do giue grant bargan sell alliene Enfeoff & Confirme, vnto the sayd Benja͞ : Blackeman, his heyres executors, administrators & Assignes, a tract of Land lijng & being vpon Sacoe Riuer, on the Eastward most side against the falls of sd Riuer being Contayned in the Pattent of my deceased father, Mr Thomas Lewis, Contameing one hundred acres bee it more or less, butting & bounding westwardly, vpon the River & Falls of the River of

Sacoe, Southwardly vpon the little brooke, that [95] falls into the sayd riuer, between the lower ffalls, & dwelling that was Cap`t` Bonightons, Northwardly, extending it selfe aboue the sayd ffalls, to a small brooke, and Eastwardly extending it selfe, vntill the hundred acres bee out: To haue & to hould y`e` sd Land, with all its woods Tymbers waterings, riuers, priuiledges, & appurtenances, with all those rights & Conveniences, as my selfe do or might Inioy, or is mentioned to bee Inioyed, by my father in law Mr Thomas Lewice, as in his Pattent granted, may more amply appeare, in as ample manner, as hee did or might Inioy It, to him the sayd Blackeman, his heyres, executors, & Assignes for euer, by these Presents: And the sayd James Gibbones, & Judeth his wife, for themselues heyres, executors, and Administrators do Couenant promiss, and grant by these Presents, that at the tyme of y`e` Insealeing hereof, they are the true soole & lawfull proprietors, of the aboue barganed Premisses/ And that they are lawfully seized in, & of the same & all the priuiledges mentioned in there own proper right, & that they haue in themselues full pouer, & lawfull authority to sell grant, & Conuey the same to the sd Benjam: Blackeman, his heyres administrators & Assignes, as an absolute Inheritance, in fee symple, with out reuersion or Condition, to make voyd, & defeate the same · And that the sayd Benjamen Blackeman, his heyrs executors, administrators & Assignes, shall & may by uertue of these Presents, peaceably hould Occupy & Improue, at his own discretion y`e` Prmis`s` with all its priuiledges freely & Clearely discharged, from all manner of Gyfts grants bargans sales, leases, Morgages, Joyntures, Dowers, Judgments, forfeitures, & all other incomberances whatsoeuer/ And will from all Prsons laying Clajme thereto, for euer defend by these Presents, the sd Blackeman his heyres executors, administrators & Assignes/ In witness the sd James Gibbones, & Judeth his wife, haue sett too thejr hands & seales, for the Confirmation of all the aboue mentioned Premisses this tenth of Aprill In the yeare of o^r Lord, one thousand six hundred & eighty . 1680 :

Signed sealed & deliuered   The marke of
  in Presence of us/
  Phœnis Hull/   James   Gibbones/

  The   marke   The marke of
  of John Edgscome/   Judeth   Gibbons/

    James Gibbones this 25th of July : 1681 : acknowl-
    edged this to bee his Act & Deede, before mee
    Jo^n Dauess Depu^{ty} P^{t}side^t

vera Copia of this Instrument aboue written, transcribed out of the originall, & there with Compared this 27th day of July 1681 :   p Edw . Rishworth Re .Cor :

    To all Christian people , Know yee that Thomas Withers of Kittery in the County of yorke shyre, In New England, for & in Consideration of the some of three pounds, in English Goods already receiued of Edmund Hammon of the same town to full Content, & satisfaction : Hath given granted, barganed, sould, Enfeoffed, & Confirmed vnto the aforesd Edm : Hammon, a Certen parcell of Land lijng & being in the Town of Kittery, & on the East side of Spruse Cricke, & Contajneing too acres, & being sixteen pooles in breadth, North & South, & foureteen pooles long on the North side, & twenty eight pooles In length, on the South side, & is bounded on the West with spruse Cricke. in part, & part with ye sayd Withers his sault Marsh : & bounded on the South with ye land of the sd withers, and on the North with the land of John Hoole · To haue & to hould the aboue barganed two Acres of land, with all the appurtenances, & priuiledges there to belonging, to him the sd Edmūd Hammon, his heyres, executors, administrators, & Assigns for euer, against yᵉ sd Withers, his heyres, executors, administrators, or Assignes, freely & Clearely acquitted, from all former barganes, sales, gyfts, Morgages, Dowers, or titles of Dowers, Claimes or Interest, of any Pson wᵗsoeuer, & for Confirmation of the treuth here of, the aforesd Thomas Withers hath here vnto set his hand & seale, this third day of October in the yeare of oʳ Lord, one thousand six hundred seauenty nine/ and further the sd Withers doth reserue, vnto him selfe & his heyres for ever, a liberty, to set vp & Mantayne a fence Conveniently vpon the vpland, where it Joynes to the sd Withers his Sault Marsh/

Signed, Sealed, & Deliuered   Tho: Withers (ˡᵒᶜᵘˢ/ₛᵢgᵢₗₗᵢ)
  In the Presence of/   Thomas Withers acknowledged the
  Tho · Ryce/   aboue written Deede of Saile to
  John Wincoll/   bee his Act & Deed this 3d day
         of October 1679 : before
          John Wincoll Assotiate/

vera Copia of Deede as acknowledged transcribed, & with yᵉ originall Compared this 29th day of July 1681 :
      p Edw : Rishworth ReCor :

To all Christian people, to whome this Present Deede of Sale shall Come/ Bartholmew Gydeny of Salem, in the County of Essex, In the Colonev of the Massatusetts in New England Esqʳ, & Hannah his wife, send greeteing; Know yee yᵗ the sd Bartholmew Gydney, & Hannah his wife, for & in Consideration of the some of one hundred & fiuety pounds of Current money of New England, to them in hand at or before the Ensealing, & delivery of these Presents, by Walter Gyndall of Cascoe, in the prouince of Mayne in New England aforesd, yeoman, Well & truely payd the receipt wʳof, they do hereby acknowledg, & them

selues yͬwith fully satisfyd, & contented: & yͬof & of euery
part, & Parcell yͬof, do acquitt, exonerate & discharge the
sd walter Gyndall, his heyres, executors, administrators, &
Assigns & euery of them for euer by these Presents. Haue
given granted barganed sould aliened Enfeoffed & Confirmed,
& by these Presents, do fully freely, Cearely & absolutely,
giue grant, bargan, sell, aliene Enfeoff, & Confirme vnto the
sd Walter Gyndall his heyres, & Assignes for euer; All yᵗ
thejr Tract or Parcell of Land, Scituate, ljing, and being in
Casco aforesd, on the North sid. of the Bay there, the
ffront whereof next the sea, ljing with in the Town shipp of
North yarmouth, In new England aforesd, as the same land
was formerly granted by seuerall Indean Sagamores to
Thomas Stephens, of Kenebecke yeoman, as by Deede of
Sale vnder the hands & Seales of the sd Indean Sægamos,
beareing Date the nineteenth day of January 1673: reference
wͬvnto, being had more fully, & at large doth & may
appeare; And one Moeity yͬof was granted by the sd Steuens to the sd Gydney, as by a Deed of sale beareing date the
Twelph day of October, one thousand six hundred seauenty
foure, more fully may appeare, & the other Moeity yͬof,
was granted by the sd Steuens vnto Hene: Sayword, & by
him Morgaged unto the sd Bartholmew Gydney, & afterwards the same became forfited, into the hands of sd Gy-
ney, togeather with all & singular, the houses, out houses,
Edifices, bujldings, yards Gardens, orchards, Lands, Meddows, Marshes, Swamps, woods vnderwoods Trees, Rivers,
pounds, Dames, head wares, fishings, fowlings ways Eeas-
meᵗˢ waters water Courses, profetts, priuilidges rights,
lybertys, Commoditys, hærnditaments, & appurtenances
wˢoeuer, to the sd Tract or Parcell of Land belonging, [96]
or in any wise appertajneing: & also all deeds, writeings, &
euidences, wˢoeuer touching or Concerneing the Premisses,
onely, or onely any part, or Parcell yͬof: to haue & to hould,
the sd Tract, or Parcell of Land, scituate, ljing & being as
aforesayd, with all other the aboue granted Premisses, with

thejr appurtenances, & euery part, & parcell thereof, vnto
the sd Walter Gyndall, his heyres & Assignes, & to the
onely proper vss, benefit & behoofe of the sd Walter Gyndall, his heyres & Assigns for euer · And the sd Bartholmew
Gydney, & Hañah his wife, for them selues, thejr heyres,
executors, & Administrators, do hereby Couenant, promiss
& grant, to & with the sd Walter Gyndall, his heyres and
Assignes, in manner & forme following, that is to say, that
the sd Walter Gyndall, his heyres & Assignes, shall & may
by force, & vertue of these Presents, from tyme to tyme, &
at all tymes for euer, hereafter, lawfully & peaceably &
quietly haue, hould, vsse, occupy possess, & Inioy the
aboue granted Premisses, with their appurtenances, & euery
part & Parcell y'of, as good Prfect & absolute Estate, of
Inheritance, as fee symple, with out any manner of Condition, reuersion, or lymitation w'soeuer, so as to alter change,
defeate, or make voyd the same: free & Cleare, & Clearely
acquitted, & discharged of & from all former and other
Gyfts, Grants, barganes, sales, leases, Morgages, Joynters,
Dowers, Judgme^{ts} Executions Entayles, forfitures, & of &
from all other Titles, troubles, charges, & Incomberances
whatsoeuer, had made Committed, done or suffered to bee
done by them, the sd Bartholmew Gidney & Hannah his
wife or either of them thejr heyres, or Assignes at any tyme
or tymes before the Insealeing hereof, & further y^t ye sd
Bartholmew Gydney & Hannah his wife their heyres executors administrators & Assignes, shall and Will from tyme to
tyme, & at all tymes, for euer hereafter warrant & Defend
the aboue barganed tract & Parcell of Land, with all other
the aboue granted Premisses, with theire appurtenances, &
euery part thereof vnto the sayd Walter Gendall his heyres,
& Assignes against all and euery Prson, and Persons whatsoeuer, any waves lawfully Clajmeing or demanding the
same, or any part y^{r}of, by from or under the sd Bartholmew
Gydney and Hannah his wife or either of theire heyres or
Assignes/ In witness whereof the sayd Bartholmew Gedney,

Book III, Fol. 96.

& Hannah his wife, haue here unto sett theire hands & seales, the tweluth day of July Anno Dom̄ one thousand six hundred eighty and one/ Annoq̨ Regni Rex Carolj secundj, xxxiij/

Signed sealed & deliuered,   Bartholmew Gydney/ (locus sigilli)
   in the Presence of us, by ye This Instrnment was ac-
   with in Named Bartholmew   knowledged by the with
   Gedney/ John Hayword/   in named Bartholmew
   Elnazer Moody   Secr̄e^{ty} Gedney as his Act &
                                                   Deede in Boston this 12th
                                                   of July 1681 : before mee
                                                   Thomas Damforth
                                                                      P^{r}sident/

vera Copia of this Instrument aboue written, transcribed out of the originall, & there with Compared this 30th day of July 1681 :   p Edw : Rishworth ReCor :

Know all men by these Presents, y^t I Joseph Holmes, late of Cambridge, & now rescident at Casco haue barganed, & bought of Capt Josua Scottow of bla͞: Poynt, all his farme at Dunstance, bordering vpon Andrew Brown, or adioyne-ing to his Plantation, in Scarbrugh Contajneing too hundred Acres, more or lesse, for which I am to pay him, vidz^t the aboue sd Scottow, the some of one hundred & sixty pounds, at or before the first of May 1682 : one hundred pounds to bee payd In money, & sixty pounds in M^{r}chan^{tble} prouissions, or uictualls, at money price. all at Boston, as aboue to ye sd Scottow, or his order for secureing of which Bargan or Con-tract, the sd Joseph Holms maketh ouer all the Land hee bought, & now possesseth In Casco. from Mr Fran . Neale late there rescident/ the sd Holms reseruceing him selfe lib-erty to sell or dispose of it, paijng the money, or Moneys worth, to ye abouesd Capt Scottow, in part of payme^t for his farme as aboue , the sd Holms is now to enter . . . the

BOOK III, FOL. 96.

farme, not to bee aliend, or to putt away, from the sd Scottow, but to bee secured to him, vntill the whoole payment bee made, & then further Deeds are to bee made, of the relinquishing of all Scottows right, therein to the sd Joseph Holms, & all the ould Deeds to bee deluered up to him · To the Piformance of the Premisses, the sd Joseph Holms binds him selfe, his heyres, executors, administrators, vnto the sd Scottow his Heyres or Assignes/ In witness of the Premisses, the sd Joseph Holms, & Cap.t Josua Scottow, haue Interchangeably set y.r hands & seales/ made at Bla: Poynt this 16th of Aprill 1681:

Witness John Howell/   Joseph Holmes (his seale)
  Benjamen Pickering/   July 25th 1681 : Benjamen Pickering made oath, that hee saw Joseph Holmes signe Seale & deluer this Instrument aboue/ taken at Saco before mee
         John Dauess, Just: pe:

vera Copia of this Instrument aboue written transcribed, & Compared Cum origine, this 30th July 1681.
         p Edw. Rishworth Re: Cor:

Know all men by these Presents that I Arther Bragdon of Yorke, In the Prouince of Mayne Planter, & Lydea my wife, vpon good Considerations there vnto mee moueing, with the free Consent of my wife Lydea aforesd, & more espetially, for & in Consideration of the Just sume of sixteene pounds, in M.rchantable pay to mee in hand already payd, w.rwith I do acknowledge my selfe, to bee fully Contented & satisfyd, & do for my selfe my heyres, administrators, & Assignes for euer, acquit & discharge Phillip flrost now rescident at York aforesd, of euery part & parcell there of, of whom I haue received the afore mentioned sume, haue giuen granted, barg: by giue

BOOK III, FOL. 96, 97.

grant, bargan, sell Enfeoffe & Confirme vnto the aboue named Phillip ffrost, his heyres, executors, administrators & Assignes, a Certen Tract, or Parcell of vpland Contayneing the full quantity of twenty Acres, more or less, lijng & being, in the Town of Yorke, lijng between the Lotts formerly of Andrew Raynkine, now in the possession of Phillip ffrost, & of the aforesd Arther Bragdon (onely the Landing place accepted) which Arther Bragdon & his wife, are to haue a way vnto dureing their naturall lifes, which land is bounded as followeth ; Tenn pooles in breath along by the River side, between the lotts aboue mentioned, of Arther Bragdons & Frosts, & so to runn backe vpon the same Lyne that ye other lotts do, till they Come to Bass Coue riuer, To haue & to hould the aboue bounded tract or Parcell of Land, with all the profetts, priuiledges, of Tymber, Imunitys & all other app^{r}tenances y^{r}vnto belonging, or any wise appertayneing, from mee my heyres, executors, administrators & Assignes, vnto sayd Phillip Frost his heyres, executors, administrators & Assigns for euer, & further the sd Arther Bragdon doth Couenant, & agree with the sd Phillip ffrost, y^t the sd Land, is free & Cleare from all Morgages, Dowrys, titles, & Incomberances w^{t}soeuer, & do hereby warrant, & Defend the same, from mee my heyres executors administrators & Assignes, vnto the before named Phillip ffrost, his heyrs executors, administrators, & Assigns for euer, from all Prsons w^{t}sover Pretending any title, Claime or Interest there vnto, from by or vnder mee, or any by my procurement/ In witness w^{r}unto I haue with the free Consent of my wife Lydea, here [97] vnto afix my hand & seale, this 4th day of May 1680/

Signed sealed & deliuered   Arther Bragdon ($^{locus}_{sigilli}$)
   in the Presence of/   Arther Bragdon Came before mee
   Allexander Maxell   the 10th day of June 1681 : & his
   his marke   wife Lydea, who did both own
   James Grant his   & acknowledg this Instrument
   marke   aboue written to bee ther Act &
    Deede/ Ldw Rishworth Just pe:

Book III, Fol. 97.

A true Coppy of this Instrument aboue written, transcribed & Compared with y̦ originall, this 4th day of August 1681 : p Edw. Rishworth ReCor :

Know all men by these Presents, that I Job Allcocke of yorke In the County of yorke under the Jurisdiction of the Massatusetts in new England, Leefe‘ for seuerall good Causes & Considerations y‘vnto mee moueing, & more espetially, for the valewable some of eight eight pounds, payd unto mee by Abra · Parker of the Town of yorke afores̄d, In Current M‘chan‘ble Red oake pipe & Hodgsed staues, w‘with I am fully Contented & satisfyd, do by these P‘sents, giue, grant, bargan, aliene, Assign, sell, & Confirme, & haue hereby giuen granted, barganed, aliend, Assignd, sould, & Confirmed, from mee the sd Job Allcocke my heyrs executors, administrators, & Assigns vnto the afore named Abra · Parker his heyrs executors, administrators & Assigns for euer, a Certen tract or Prcell of Land Contayning the quantity of eighty Acres, bee It more or less, lijng & scituate on the South West side of yorke Riuer, adioyneing vnto Thomas Addams his Land, on the West side vnto Sam̄ll Bragdons land, on the East side, & so runneing along between the sd boundarys, on a due South West Course, vntill It runn vnto the bounds of Pischataq̄ To haue & to hould the afores̄d Tract or Parcell of upland, as aboue bounded, with all the woods, vnderwoods, trees, tymber trees, togeather with all other profetts, priuiledges lybertys, Com̄anages, & all other appurtenances y‘vnto belonging, or in any wise app‘tayneing, from mee my heyrs Administrators, & Assigns vnto the afore sd Abraham Parker, his heyres Administrators, executors, & Assigns for euer/ And the sd Job Allcoke doth further Couenant, & promiss to & with the sd Abra Parker, that y̦ afores̄d Parcell of Land is free & Cleare from all Laims &c Claims titles Interests,

Dowers or title of Dowers or any incomberances w'soeuer,
& do hereby promiss & stand Ingag'd to defend the same, &
the Interest y'rof, from all Pson, or Prsons w'soeuer. Pretending any title or Clajme y'rvnto, from by or under mee,
or in any wise by my procurement/ In testimony w'rof, I
haue here vnto afixed my hand & seale, this tenth day of
December · 1679 ·

Signed sealed & Delue'rd   Job Allcocke (his seale)
  In Presence of/   Leeftent Job Allcocke came before
  Arther Bragdon/   mee this 22th day of March 167$\frac{9}{80}$ &
  Nathall Preble/   doth acknowledg this Instrument
                          to bee his Act & Deede/ before mee
                               John Dauess Just pe ·

A true Coppy of this Instrument aboue written, transcribed out of the originall & there with Compared this 5th
day of August 1681 · p Edw · Rishworth ReCor ·

Granted vnto James Emery, by the Select Townes men
for Kittery, six Acres of vpland, the next Poynt below
Thomas Spinnys, & so to bee bounded with the next great
Coaue below/

A true Coppy taken the 16th day of March : 1653 :
                      p mee Humfrey Chadborne/
vera Copia of this Town order transcribed & with ye originall Compared, this 10th of August : 1681
                      p Edw Rishworth Re : Cor :

I underwritten, do Assigne & set ouer unto Samell
Fernald his heyres & Assignes for euer, all my right title &
Interest of the aboue sd Grant, to bee his proper right, as
really as euer It was mine, unto which I with the Consent of

BOOK III, FOL. 97.

my wife, do here unto set my hand, this secund day of
August, . 1681 :   James Emery

<small>The sale of this Entred in ye new booke of reCords pa 163</small>   James Emery, & Elizabeth   The E marke of
his wife, owned this In-   Elizabeth Emery
stiument to bee their Act
& Deed, this secund day of
August : 1681 : before mee
Fran : Hooke Just : pe :

A true Coppy of this Assignement transcribed out of the
originall & yr with Compared this 10th of August 1681 ·
   p Edw : Rishworth ReCor

This Indenture made the twelth day of December, in the
Twelth yeare of the Reigne of our soueraigne Lord Charles
by the Grace of God, king of England Scotland, ffrance &
Ireland, Defendr of the faith &c · between Sir Fardinando
Gorges of Ashton Phillips in the County of Somerset knight
of the one Party, & Arthure Champernoown of Darrington
in ye County of Deanon Esqr, of the other part, witnesseth,
that ye sayd Sir Fardinando Gorges, for & in Consideration
of the some of two shillings for euery one hundred Acres of
land, which are Imployed, or hereafter shall bee Imployed
either for wood pasture, meddow, or tillage, being part
Parcell or Members of one thousand Acres of Land hereafter
granted by these Presents, to the sd Arther Champernoown,
his heyres or Assignes, as also for diuerse other good
Causes & Considerations, him the sd Sir ffardinando Gorges,
hereunto espetially moueing ; Haue given, granted, barganed, sould, Infeoffed, & Confirmed, & by these Presents,
doth giue, grant, bargan, sell, Enfeoff, & Confirme unto the
sd Arthur Champernoown his heyres, & Assignes, all that
part, purpart & portion of Lands in America, parcells of
New England in a America, hereafter in these Prsents
discribed, & to bee discribed, by the lymitts, & bounds

thereof, that is to say, all that part, purpart, portion, & Necke of Land ljng vpon the East side of the Riuers Mouth of Pischataway alias Pischataquacke, & so along the sea side, Eastward, to y{e} mouth of the Riuer Called Braue boate Harbour, & so through, & along the sd Riuer, from the Enterance y{r}of, into the Riuer of Pischataway, alias Pischataquacke, afsd, in, & from thence agajne Southward, along the Riuer of Pischataway, alias Pischataquacke, aforesd, to the sea the whoole Contayneing by Estimation fiue hundred Acres of Land, of English measure or y{r}abouts, from hence forth to bee Called or knQwn by the name of Darrington/ As also fiue hundred acres more of Marsh land, ljng vpon the North East side of the sd Riuer, of Braue boate Harbour here after to bee known or Called by the name of Godmorrocke, to bee alotted out by Richd Vines Esq{r}, my Steward Generall of my land, the Marsh lijng not scatteringly, nor in length but round & square togeather, & not already possest or past. to any other Prson or Prsons by mee p any spetiall order under my hand & seale: All w{ch} P{r}misses now are, & hereafter shall bee deemed. reputed, & taken to bee part Prcells, & Members of the prouince of New Summersett, in New England aforesd: And also the sd Sir ffardinando Gorges, for the Consideration aforesd hath giuen granted, barganed, sould Enfeoffed & Confirmed, & by these Presents doth giue grant bargan, sell, Enfeoff & Confirme vnto the sd Arther Champernoown his heyres & Assignes, togeather with the sd portion of Lands & P{r}misses, all the soyles Grounds, woods & vnderwoods, Hauens, Porpts, Riuers, waters, lakes, fishings, Mines Miueralls as Well Royall Mines [98] of gould & siluer, as other Mines, and Mineralls, prætious stoones, quaryes, & all and singular other Commoditys, Jurisdictions, Royaltys, priuiledges, ffranttses, and Preheminences w{t}soeuer, with in the sd Tract of land & Premisses, or with in any part or Parcell thereof; Sauing, excepting & reseruing, onely out of this Prsent Grant. the fifth part of all the Oare, of gould & siluer found,

Book III, Fol. 98.

or to bee found in or upon the Premisses: or any part or Parcell thereof, due unto his Majesty, his heyres, & successors, and now or at any tyme reserved, or to bee reserued · To haue and to hould, all and singular the sd part, purpart, & portion of Lands and all other the Premisses here in mentioned, to bee barganed, sould, or granted, with thejr & euery of thejr appurtenances, unto the sayd Arther Champernoown his heyrs & Assignes, unto the onely proper vss and behoofe, of him the sd Arther Champernoown, his heyres & Assignes for euer, to bee houlden of the sd Sir ffardinando Gorges, and his heyres, Lord or Lords of the sd Prouince of New Summersett shyre, as of his, & there Mannor of   in fee & Comman Soccage, by ffealty onely, for all manner of seeruices, and the yearely rent of two shillings, the hundred for euery hundred Acres thereof, bee it in wood, pasture, Meddow, and tillage, wch shall from tyme, to tyme, bee Inclosed and remajne so, or Conuerted unto tillage, the same to bee leayed by destress, or otherwise, according to the Laws, & Costomes of the Realme of England, used and apponed, with in the same for teñants of like nature, and the sayd Sir ffardinando Gorges for him selfe his heyres, and Assigns, doth Couenant promiss, & grant, to & with the sayd Arther Campernowne, his heyres and Assignes, by these Presents that hee the sayd Sir ffardinando Gorges, his heyres, & Assignes, shall and Will from tyme to tyme and at all tyms hereafter, do, make, acknowledg, execute, and suffer or Cause to bee done, made, acknowledged, executed, and suffered all and euery such further, and other reasonable Act and Acts, thing and things, deuise, and deuises, in the Law, for the further & better Assurance, & sure makeing of all and singular the sayd lands, and other the sayd Premisses, and with there and euery of thejr appurtenances, unto the sayd Arther Champernoown, his heyers and Assignes, as by his his, and thejr Counsell, learned in the Laws, shall bee reasonably diuised   And   the   Sir ffardinando Gorges, hath Constituted, ordayned, & appoynted, and by these Presents doth Constitute, ordayne an appoynt, his trusty, and Well beloued Nephew ffrancis Champernoown Gentleman, one of the sonns of the sayd Arther Champernoown, and Richard Vines Esqr, his true and lawfull Atturney and Atturnys Joyntly, and in his Name, to Enter into the sayd lands, and other the sayd barganed Premisses, or into any part or Parcell thereof, in the name of the whoole, and there of to take full and peaceable possession, and seizin, and after such possession and seasin, so had and taken; Then for him, and in his name, to deliuer full and peaceable possession, and seasin of the same Lands, and Premisses, vnto ye sayd Arther Champernoown, his heyres, & Assignes, according to the Tenour &effect, and true meaneing of these Presents/ In witness whereof the sayd Partys, to the Present Indentures, Interchangeably haue set thejre hands & seales/ Dated the day & yeare first here in aboue written/ Annoq, Domi: 1636:

Sealed signed, & deliuered   Ar Champernown/
in the Presence of/   : 12th December: 1636:
Francis Rogers/   The Counterpart of Sir ffardinando
Richard Clarke/   Gorges lease to Arthure Champer-
Richd Battson/   nown Esqr, of one thousand Acres
John Winnington/   of Land, in New Sommerset In
     New England in America/

A true Coppy of this Instrument or Indenture aboue written transcribed out of the originall, & y^{r}with Compared this 12th day of August 1681: p Edw: Rishworth Re: Cor·

This Indenture made the foureteenth day of June, in the foureteenth yeare of the Reigne of our Soueraigne Lord Charles, by the grace of god, King of England Scotland ffrance, and Ireland, Defender of the ffaith, between Sir ffardinando Gorges, of Ashton Phillips, in the County of

BOOK III, FOL. 98.

Sommersett, Knight, on the one part And Arthur Champernoowne of Dartington, in the County of Deanon Esqr, of the other part: Witnesseth, that ye sayd Sir ffardinando Gorges, for and in Consideration of the some of two shillings, for euery one hundred Acres of Land which are Imployed, or here after shall bee Imployed, either for wood, pasture, Meddow, or tillage, being part, parcell, or Members of one thousand Acres of Land, bee It more, or less, hereafter granted, by these Presents to the sayd Arthur Champernoowne, his heyres and Assignes, as also for diuerse other good Causes, & Considerations, him the sd Sir Fardinando Gorges, here vnto espetially moueing, haue giuen, granted, barganed, sould, Enfeoffed, & Confirmed, And by these Presents, doth giue, grant, bargan, sell, Infeoff, & Confirme, vnto ye sayd Arthur Champernowne, his heyres, and Assignes, all that parte, purparte and portion of Lands, in America, parcell of New England in America, hereafter in these Presents discribed, and to bee discribed, by the lymitts, & bounds thereof, that is to say, all that part, purpart, portion, & Necke of Land, lying vpon ye East side of the Rivers Mouth of Pischataway, alias Pischataquake, and so alongst the sea side, Eastward to the Mouth of the River, Called Braueboate Harbour, and through, or along the sayd Riuer, to the Entrance there of, into ye Riuer of Pischataquay, alias Pischataquacke, aforesd, and from thence againe Southwards along the River of Pischataway, alias Pischataquacke as aforesd to ye sea/ the whoole Contajneing by æstimation, fiue hundred acres of Land, of English measure, bee It more or less, from hence forth to bee Called, or known, by the name of Dartington/ as also fiue hundred Acers more of Land, lying vpon the North East side of the sayd Riuer of Braueboate Harbour, hereafter to bee known or Called by the name of Godmorocke, to bee Lotted out by Richard Vines Esqr, my Stuard Generall, of my lands, for the tyme being, not scatteringly nor in length, but round, or square togeather, & not directly possest or prest to any other Prson or Persons by mee, or by my speciall order, under my hand and seale, all which Premisses now are, and hereafter shall bee, deemed reputed, & taken to bee parts, Parcells, and Members of the Prouince of New Sommersett, In New England aforesd, & also the sd Sir ffardinando Gorges [99] for the Considerations aforesayd, haue giuen, granted, barganed, sould, Enfeoff'd & Confirmed, and by these Presents, doth giue, grant, bargan, sell, Infeoff & Confirme, unto the sd Arthur Champernowne, his heyres & Assignes, togeather with sd Portion of lands, & Premisses, all the soyles, grounds, woods, & undewoods hauens, Ports, Riuers, waters, lakes, ffishings, Mines, and Mineralls as well Royall Mines of gould, & siluer, as other Mines, & Mineralls, prætious stoones, Quarrys, & all and singular other Comoditys, Jurisdictions, Royaltys priuiledges, ffrantisces, & Preheminences w'soeuer, with in the sd Tract of Land, & Premisses, or with in any part or Prcell thereof, saueing, excepting and reseruing only out of this present grant, the fifth part of all the oare of Gould & siluer, found or to bee found, in or vpon the Premisses, or any part or parcell there of, due vnto his Majesty his heyres & successors & now or at any tyme reserued or to bee reserued/ To haue & to hould, all & singular the sd part, purpart, & portion of land, & all other the Premisses, here in mentioned, to bee barganed sould, or granted with there & euery of y^r appurtenances, vnto the sd Arthur Champernowne, his heyres, & assignes, to the only proper vss, & behoofe of him the sayd Arthur Champernowne his heyers, & Assignes for ever, to bee houlden of the sd Sir ffardinando Gorges & his heyres Lord or Lords of the sd Prouince, of New Sommersett shyre, as of his or thejr manner of   In fee & Comman Soccage, by fealty only for all manner of sceruices, & the yearely rent of too shillings for the sayd part, purpart portion, & Necke of Land, Contajneing by Estimation fiue hundred acers, bee It more, or less/ And the yearely rent of two shillings the hundred for

Book III, Fol. 99.

every hundred Acers of the other land bee It Wood, pasture, Meddow or tillage, which shall from tyme to tyme, bee Inclosed, & remajne so, or Convirted vnto tillage; the same to bee leauied by distress, or otherwise according to y⁰ laws & Costomes of the Realme of England, vsed, & approued with in yᵉ same for teñants of the like nature; And the sd Sir ffardinando Gorges, for him selfe, his heyres, and Assignes, doth promiss, Couenant, & grant to & with the sd Arther Champernowne, his heyres, & Assigns by these Presents that hee the sd Sir ffardinando Gorges, his heyres, & Assigns, shall & will from tyme to tyme, & at all tymes, hereafter, do, make, acknowledg, execute, & suffer & Cause to bee done, made acknowledged, & executed, & suffered all & euery such further, & other reasonable Act, & Acts, thing, & things, deuise, & deuises in the Law, for the further, & better assurance, & sure makeing, of all and singular the sd Lands, & other Premisses, with yʳ & euery of thejr appurtences, vnto the sd Arthur Champernowne, his heyres & Assignes, as by his thejr Counsell learned in the Law, shall bee reasonably deuised, aduised or required: And lastly the sayd Sir ffardinando Gorges, hath Constituted, ordained, & appoynted, & by these Presents doth Constitute ordajne & appoyᵗ his trusty & well beloued Nephew, ffrancis Champernoowne Gentle͠: one of the sonns of the sd Arthur Champernowne, & the sd Richard Vines Esqʳ his true & lawfully Attuɪney, & Attuɪneys, ioyntly for him & in his name to enter into the sd Lands, & other the sayd barganed Premisses, or into any part or parcell there of, in the name of the whoole, & thereof to take full, & peaceable possession, & seisin & after such possession, & seisin, so had & taken, then for him and in his name to deliuer full & peaceable possession, & seisin of yᵉ same, Lands & Premisses, unto the sd Arther Champernowne his heyres, & Assigns according to the Tenour, ffect, & true meaneing of these Presents, in witness wʳof, these Partys to these Presentt Indentures, Interchangeably

Book III, Fol. 99.

haue set thejr hands & seales/ Dated the day & yeare first
aboue written, Annoq Dominj : 1638 :

sealed, & Delivered/   Ar · Champernowne/
in the Presence of/
Henery Dynham/   vera Copia of these Indentuis or
John Hart/   Instrument transcribed out of the
William Stachfejld/   originall, & there with Compared
                      this 13th day of August : 1681 :
                      p Edw : Rishworth Re : Cor .

This Indenture made the 20th Twenteth day of October in the scauenteenth yeare of the Reigne of our Soueraigne Lord Charles the secund, by the Grace of god, of England, Scotland, ffrance, & Ireland, King, Defendr of the faith &c : between Colonell John Archdeale of Wickeham In the County of Bucks Esqr, Agent unto ffardinando Gorges Esqr Lord of the Prouince of Mayne, in New England, on the one parte, And Capt Francis Champernowne of Kittery in the Prouince aforesayd Esqr of the other parte ; Witnesseth that ye sayd Colonell John Archdeale, for & in Consideration of the Intyre affection hee beareth unto the sayd ffrancis Champernowne, & for the Good & faithfull seruice by the sayd Francis Champernowne done for, and on the behalfe of the sd ffardinando Gorges, and for and in Consideration of the some of tenn pounds of lawfull pay of New England in hand before then sealeing & deliuery of these Presents, well & truely payd, the receipt wrof the sayd John Archdeale doth hereby acknowledg, & him selfe to bee fully satisfyd, Contented and payd, and thereof doth acquit, exonerate, and discharge the sayd Capt ffrancis Champernowne his heyres executors, & administrators, & euery of them for euer, by these Presents , Hath giuen, granted, barganed, and sould, aliend, Enfeoffed, Convayd, released, Assured, deliuered, & Confirmed, And by these presents doth giue grant bargan &

sell, alliene, Enfeoffe, Convaw, release, Assure, deliuer and Confirme unto the sayd ffrancis Champernowne, his heyres & Assignes, All that Tract, peece, or Prcell of vpland, scituate, lijng & being in Kittery in the sayd Prouince, between the land of Thomas Crockett, & an house formerly the sayd Capt Champernownes, & runnes vpon an East & by Nore Poynt, vp into the Woods there, & Contajnes by Estimation three hundred acers/ & also all and singular ways, paths, Passages, trees, woods, & vnderwoods, Comanes, Easements, profetts, Comoditys, aduantages, Emoluments, hæreriditaments, & appurtenances w'soeuer, unto the sd ffrancis Champernowne, his heyres & Assignes, for to haue, to hould the sd peece, parcell, or tract of land, & euery part and Parcell thereof, with all trees, woods, & vnderwoods, Commanes, Easements, profetts, Emoluments, hæreditances, & appurtenances w'soeuer, unto the sd Capt ffrancis Champernowne, his heyres, & Assignes for euer · And to & for no other vss intent & purpos . w'soeuer, yejlding, & paijng therefore yearly for euer, vnto the sd ffardinando Gorges his heyres & Assignes the yearely rent of one Cowple of Henns, at the ffeast of Easter, [100] onely if the same bee lawfully demanded/ In witness w^rof the Partys first aboue named, haue Interchangeably set theire Hands & Seales, the day & yeare first aboue written/ John Archdeale (Locus bigilli)

Sealed & Deliuered

in the Presence of/
Nic. Shapleigh/
Abra Corbett/

vera Copia of this Instrument transcribed, & Compared with the originall, this 14th day of August. 1681 :

Aprill 23th 1695 Colloⁿ John Archedale come before me & owned the aboue Instrum^t to be his Act & deed,
 Robt Elliot of ye Councill

p Edw: Rishworth Re: Cor:

This acknowledgm^t transcribed & compared May 20th 1698 p Jos Hamond Regist^r

Book III, Fol. 100.

At a meeteing of the Select men of Kittery this 17th day of July · 1666 :

Granted vnto Capt ffrancis Champernowne, fiue hundred Acres of Land, adioyneing to the house, where Capt Lockewood now liueth, Neare the lower end of the Town by the water side, that runneth towards Braue boate Harbour, to bee layd out by Mr Robert Cutt, Mr Withers, & Mr Mendum, to begin next Majo^r Shapleighs Land, & not two much breath by the water side, to the Preiudice of the Inhabitants towards Braue boate Harbour, to bee layd out with as much speede as may bee/

vera Copia of this Towne grant aboue written, transcribed out of the originall, & there with Compared, this 14th day of August : 1681 :
    p Edw : Rishworth ReCor/

John Wincoll/
Charles ffrost/
James Emery/
Richard Nason/
his O marke

July : 5th . 1680 :

Then measured & layd out unto Mr Edw : Rishworth, his land giuen him in his father Wheelewrights will, by order of Mr Samuell Wheelewright, & sayd Rishworth as followeth/ vidz^t fiuety Acres of vpland at the lower end of John Cloyse his house lott, at a marked tree, Ninety too poole East south East down to the Marsh, then bounded with the Marsh till It Come neare the falls of Ogunquet River, & so vp to the tree marked, that is eighty foure poole south south West, from the first Corner marked tree, which is the sd fiuety Acres of Land/

Also measured & layd out unto the sd Rishworth, Twenty Acres of Marsh as followeth/ begineing at the East end of a part of the sd vpland, vpon an east & bee South lyne, till It come to a Certen Cricke, which diuides between the sd Marsh & James Littlefields, & runnes vpon the sd East &

Book III, Fol. 100.

by South lyne (excepting the seuerall poynts of Marsh, made by y̆ᵉ Crookeing of the sd Cricke In which poynts yʳ is too Acres of Marsh, with out the aforesd East & by south lyne, which sd lne vpon yᵗ side next James Littlefejlds Marsh, is eighty fiue poole in Length, to ruer neare yᵉ sea Wall, & the breadth North & by East, is thirty too poole, & is bounded at that east end with yᵉ sayd Riuer, & is on the North side, next Mr Samuell Wheelewrights Marsh bounded, vpon a West & by North lyne, backe to the vpland wʳ It hath a Coue of Marsh, extending so fare beyond yᵉ length of Eighty too poole, togeather with such another peece, made at the sea Wall by yᵉ Crookeing of the Riuer, that fully makes vp the loss of Marsh by yᵉ pond or otherwise/   John Wincoll Suruajᵒʳ

Testes Samuell Wheelewright }
  John Cloyce his marke   } who helped to lay it out/

A true Coppy of this Instrument, or Suruay aboue written, transcribed out of yᵉ originall & there with Compared this secund day of Septemᵇʳ 1681 :

                    p Edw: Rishworth Re: Cor:

Know all men by these Presents, that I Job Allcocke of Yorke in the Prouince of Mayne in New England Planter, haue & in Consideration of a ualewable some payd mee in hand before the sealeing & Deliuery of these Presents wʳwith I Job Allcocke Do acknowledg my selfe to bee fully satisfyd & payd, to my Content & yʳfore I do firmely bargan & haue sould unto Syluester Stouer all the right & title that is mine of a quarter part of the Cape Necke, this quarter part of the Cape necke, with all the appurtenances yʳvnto belonging, I the sd Job Allcocke do acknowledg, to haue sould unto Syluester Stouer & to his heyres executors administrators & Assignes, to haue & to hould for euer, they or either of them quietly to posses the same with out Molestation, by

mee my heyres or Assignes, & against all & euery Prson, or
Persons lawfully Clajmeing from or under mee or any of
them shall & will warrant & for euer Defend, by these
Presents: And in witness w^r of I haue here vnto set my
hand & seale, this thirteenth day of Septemb^r one thousand
six hundred & eighty   Job Allcocke (his seale)
Sealed signed & Deliuered/   Dorothy Allcocke/
  in the Presence of us/
  Josua Downing/   Capt Job Allcocke, & Dorothy Allcocke
  Edw: Wollcott/   his wife Came before mee this 27th
         of September, 1680, & did acknowl-
         edg the aboue Instrument to bee y^r
         Act & deed/ acknowledged before
         mee/ John Dauess Just pe/
a true Coppy of this Instrument transcribed out of the
originall & y^r with Compared this 4th day of Septemb^r 1681:
       p Edw: Rishworth ReCor:

Know all men by these Presents, that I John Hord of
Cuttchecha, in the prouince of New Hampshire, in New
England Planter. In Consideration of a ualewable some payd
mee in hand before the sealeing & Deliuery of these Presents, w^r with I John Heard do acknowledg my selfe to bee
fully satisfyd & payd, to my Content, & y^r fore I do firmely
bargan, & haue sould vnto Syluester Stouer, all the right &
title that was mine of a quarter part of the Cape Necke, this
quarter part of Cape Nuttacke Necke, with all the appurtenances y^r unto belonging, I the sd John Heard do acknowledg
to haue sould vnto Silnester Stouer, his heyres executors, &
Assignes to haue & to hould for euer, they or either of them
quietly for to possess the same with out Molestation by mee
my heyres or Assignes, & against all & euery Person or
Persons, lawfully Clajmeing from or under mee, or any of
them, shall & will warrant, & for euer defend by these Pres-

Book III, Fol. 100, 101.

ents, & in witness here of I haue here unto set my hand & seale this 5th day of Nouember: 1680.

Signed, Sealed, & deliuered/   The marke of ⌐ (his seale)
in the Presence of us/   John Herd/
The marke of Hen · Symson/ H : H :
Henc : Towltwood   John Herd acknowledged this
A true Coppy of this Instru-   Deed to bee his Act, & his
ment transcribed out of the   wife surrendered vp her
originall, & y^r with Com-   right of Dowry in the same
pared, this 4th of Septem^{br} Necke of land this 5th day of
1681 : p Edw : Rishworth   Nouember 1680 : before mee
ReCor/   Richd Walden
                                             Deputy P^{r}sident
                                             New Hampshire/

To all Christian People, to whome this Present writeing shall Come, and appeare/ I Edward Alline of Douer, in the prouince of new Hampshyre, now vnder his Majestys imme- diate Gouerment, in New England sendeth Greeteing; know yee that sayd Edward Alline, for diuerse good causes & Considerations him moueing there unto & more espetially for and in Consideration of fiue new saddles, and one pilleon, to mee in hand delivered before the Insealeing of these Presents, by the hand of Andrew Marenell, now liueing in the same Town, and Prouince afor esd, Tanner the receipt whereof, I do acknowledg my selfe fully satisfyd & payd, & of euery pennys thereof, [101] doth acquit, and for euer discharge, the sayd Andrew Marenell, him his heyres, exec- utors, adminstrators, by these Presents, hath absolutely giuen granted, barganed sould aliend, Infeoffed, Assignd, & Confirmed, And by these Presents doth giue grant bargane sell, aliene, Infeoff, Assure, & Confirme, vnto the sayd Andrew Marenell, fiuety Acres of Land, lijng and being in Casco Bay . . . . to my father Hope Allene, from Mr George Cleeues, and afterwards to mee, before my fathers decease, whis is part of a greater quantity which in the ReCords of Yorke will more largely appeare/ Which Parcell of Land lyes in Casco in the Prouinces of Mayne In New England, the aboue sayd fiuety Acres, to runne fiuety rodds vpon Casco Riuer, and eight scoore rodds backewards, till the fiuety Acres bee accomplished, the whoole Tract Land, lijng and bounded, Neare James Andrews, and Ann Mitton, Which peece of Land I gaue to Henery Kirke, by deede of Gyft vpon Conditions, y^t hee was to Improue as y^r is mentioned, but for not Improueing according to his Deed of gyft, the sd Kirke hath forfited his right, & now returnes to mee the sd Alline: All which sd land with all priuiledges, & appurtenances y^{r}unto belonging, and app^{r}tayneing unto the sd Allen, shall bee for ye proper vsse & benefitt of the sd Andrew Marenell, his heyres, executors, administrators & Assigns for euer/ To haue & to hould the Premisses aforesd: And the sd Edw: Alline, doth for him selfe his heyres, executors, administrators, & Assignes, doth Couenant & promiss to & with the sd Andrew Marenell his heyres, executors, administrators & Assigns, that ye sd Edw: Alline, hath in him selfe, good right, full pouer, & lawfull Authority, to the aboue giuen, granted Premisses, to sell & dispose off, & y^t the same & euery part thereof, are freely & Clearely discharged of & from all manner of former Gyfts, grants, bargans sales leases Morgages wills Intales, Judgm^{ts} executions, & all other Incomberances of w^t nature & kind soeuer, had, made, suffered to bee done, w^{r}by ye sd Andr: Marenell his heyres, executors, administrators, or Assignes, shall or may any ways bee molested, or exirted out of ye aboue granted Premisses, by any Prson or Prsons haueing any legall right, title, or demand in or too any of ye aboue granted Premisses: And ye sd Edw: Alline doth for him selfe, heyres, executors, administrators, Couenant promiss to & with the sd Andrew Marenell his heyrs, executors, administrators & Assignes, to

Book III, Fol. 101.

mantajne & make good the same, as fare as my fathers bill of sale extends/ In witness hereunto, I haue set my hand & seale the fifthteen day of July in the yeare of o^r Lord god one thousand six hundred & eighty one/

Witness Signed sealed & Delivered/ Edward Allen (locus Sigilli)
in the Presence of us/   The marke (/\\) of
John Tuttle/   Saraih Allen/
Thomas Robertts/   Edw: Allen & his wife Came before mee, & acknowledged this Instrument to bee y^r free Act & Deed, before mee Dated 15th July 1681 · Job Cleamons of the Counsill of New Hampshyre/

A true Coppy of this Instrument aboue written, transcribed out of the originall, & there with Compared this 16th day of Septemb^r 1681 p Edw: Rishworth Re: Cor:

Bee It known unto all men whome It may Concerne, that I Mary Barret in the Town of Wells, In the County of yorke In New England, Widdow for diverse good causes & Consideration mee there unto mee moueing, do giue & grant, & by these Presents do Confirme, vnto my sonn John Barrett of the aforesd Town & County, his heyres executors administrators & Assignes, for euer: my now dwelling house with the out houseing, together with all my land & Meddow lijng & being in the Town of Wells, In any wise to mee Prtajneing, or belonging, with all the appurtenances & priuiledges y^{r}unto belonging, also I do giue unto my sonn John Barrett, all my house hould stuffe, both moueables & unmoueables, all which houses lands, Meddows goods I do freely giue to my sonn & his heyres for euer, w^{ru}nto I haue set my hand & seale, this fourteenth day of Sepb^r In the

yeare of our Lord, Anno Dom: one thousand six hundred & seauenty/
Signed sealed & Deliuered/
  In Presence of us/
Samell Austine/
Jonathan Hammond/

The marke of Mary Barrett (her seale)

This Deed or Instrument was owned & acknowledged before us the 14*th* day of Septemb*r* 1670 : & Legall possession giuen by Turffe & Twigg/
William Hammonds
Samll Austine/
Commission*rs*/

vera Copia of this Instrument aboue written, transcribed out of the Originall & y*r* with Compared, this 18*th* of Septemb*r* 1681 :
p Edw : Rishworth ReCor :

Dominicus Jordan his Clajme of Land, bequeathed by his father the late Mr Robert Jordan, & layd out accoiding to order/

ffiue hundred acres from the ould Plantation, along to a Cart path, to the great Pond down to the brooke, in a swamp runneing into Spurwinke Riuer, It being on the North West side of the sd path, & fiue hundred acres more, on the other side of the greate Marsh, goeing vp to a new Marsh, the land ljing in ffalmouth Town, & a Prcell of Meddow in deuission between us all/

Signed by mee Josuah Scottow
in behalfe of Dominicus Jordan

vera Copia transcribed & Compared with y*e* originall this 22*th* of Septemb*r* 1681 . p Edw : Rishworth Re : Cor .

Book III, Fol. 101, 102.

Aprill 16th 1663 :

Agreed the same day for her Interest in the Lands in the possession of Capt Thomas Sauage, that Capt Sauage, & his successors shall pay unto Mrs Hill, or her assignes, fiuety shillings a yeare, or after y^t rate dureing her life, from ye tyme of her husbands death, in Cloathing or prouission at prise Current, & for tyme to come to bee payd euery halfe yeare, indz^t on the 25th of March & on the 29th of Septem^br from tyme to tyme, & the 50^s a yeare payable by Capt sauage to Mrs Hill, was by agreement between Capt Sauage & Joseph Hill Attorney to Mrs Mary Hill, in our Presence, w^rvpon Wee made no deuission or setting forth of a third part thereof;

The sd Lands & houseing thereon to bee her security for the Performance of ye sd fiuety shillings a yeare, as is before expressed/ witness our hands the day & yeare before mentioned/   William Parkes/

Mr Joseph Hill, haueing heard these   William Stillson
too last perticulars redd, indz^t that con-   Thom. Lake/
cerneing Capt Tho. Sauage, & Capt
William Dauiss, concerneing the seuerall payments as is expressed in the seuerall articles to Mrs Mary Hill, doth on his oath testify to the treuth of the sd agreement/ Taken before mee 21th of July 1679 ·

     John Woodbridge Commissoner/

vera Copia of the agreement aboue written, & the testimony of Mr Jos: Hill transcribed out of the originall & Compared this 5th of October: 1681.

     p Edw: Rishworth ReCor:

[102] To all Christian people to whome this present writeing shall Come, & appeare/ Know yee that I John White of could Harbour on Kittery side in the County of

yorke now in the Massatusetts Jurisdiction, sendeth greeteing, Know yee that I John Whitte father unto Hannah Allene, wife of Robert Allen, for diuerse good Causes & Considerations, besid^s my naturall loue which I beare to my naturall Child Hannah Allen, do giue, & for euer giue unto Robert Allen & his wife, & his children wch shee now hath, by Robert Allen onely, more espetially after his decease, & my daughter Hannah, I do descigne & bequeath w^t I giue unto them, unto Francis Allen soun unto Robert Allen after my decease/ I do freely giue all my Estate to my soun & daughter, dureing there liues, & after thejr decease, I do order as is aboue expressed, to my grandsonn ffrancis, or the next Elldest Child if it please god to take him away, that shall succeede him in ages, that is to say my house & land, & all my land & houseing, wch I now haue in the Towne shipe of Kittery, & all my Cattle & kind of w^t nature souer, with all the Moueables, with in doores or with out, to bee for the soole & proper & sole vsse of my sonn & daughter dureing y^r liues, after my death, onely one heffer wch I now haue in being, to bee at my disposeing, before my death, & for all & euery thing after my death (excepting the Heffer I do freely giue unto my sonn & daughter Hannah Allen, & her heryrs for euer as is aboue expressd/ & for all other Children or Childrens Children, this my deed of gift shall Cut them from demanding any thing from my sonn & daughter or recouering any part of that which was my Estate or now in my possession, that is my sonns sons after my death, but they shall peaceably inioy them, & theire heyres for euer, but dureing my naturall life I will haue my being in & vpon the aboue expressed Estate, & after my death to bee theirs, how is aboue writting, in witness w^{r}vnto I haue set my hand &

seale this first of Nouember one thousand six hundred seauenty & eight/   The marke $\mathcal{M}$ of
Sealed signed & Deliuered   John Whight
  in the Presence of vs/   The aboue written John whight
  Witness Edw. Allen   acknowledged the aboue written
  The ✝✝ Marke of   deede of Gyft with his hand &
  Jabez Gynkens/   seale to it, to bee his act &
deede this 8th day of Febru:
1678. before mee
    John Wincoll Assotiate/

A true Coppy of this Deede aboue written transcribed, & with originall Compared this 11th day October 1681:
    p Edw · Rishworth Re: Cor ·

Know yee all men by these Presents that I Thoms Withers of Kittery, in the County of yorke husbandman, hath sould & deliuered vnto John Waters of the same Town or place fisherman a Tract or Picell of Land, lijng on the South side of Spruse Cricke, Containeing eight acres, being sixteen rodds in breadth by the water side, & runns backe into the woods vpon a West South West lyne vntill eight acres is accomplished, being bounded on ye East side with a Cricke of water called spruse Cricke, on the North side with a little Coue & Spring: on the south side, next adioyneing to Allexander Joanes his land, with all ye appurtenances y^{r}unto belonging, to the onely vse & behoofe of the aforesd John Waters his heyres, executors, administrators, or Assigns from mee the aforesd Thomas Withers my heyrs, executors, administrators or Assigns for euer: The aforesd John Waters paijng vnto the aforesd Thomas Withers, one pound & fiue shillings for an Acre, & so by Acre for the whoole eight Acres/ also I the aforesd Thomas Withers do promiss the aforesd barganed Premisses, to bee Cleare & free from all former gyfts grants, sales Incomberances of

any kind w'soeuer, as witness my hand this 13th day of May one thousand six hundred seauenty foure, this sd Land was sould to John Waters before his decease, in the yeare fiuety one, as witness my hand & seal this 23 : June 1676
Signed Sealed & Deliued/   Tho · Withers (his seal)
  in P'sence of us/   The aboue written Tho : Withers
  Tho : young/   acknowledged this Deed of Sayle
  Mary Rice/   to bee his free act & Deed ye
     15th d : June 1678 : before mee
     Jon : Wincoll Assote/
  A true Coppy of this Instrument transcribed & Compared with originall, this 11th day of Octobr 1681 :
      p Edw : Rishworth Re . Cor :

   Receiued by mee John Cut Senior of stiabury Banke, President of the prouince of New Hampshyre Esqr the full & iust some of tenn pounds in Current new England Silver, of Edw : Rishworth of yorke in the prouince of Mayne ReCor . & tenn pounds accepted by a bill made & giuen by Capt Job Allcocke to the sd Rishworth, or his Assignes, bereing date 26 · ffebr : 1680 · to bee payd vnto him or his Assignes, at or before the 14th of July next Insewing, 1681 : In consideration of which twenty pounds in siluer as aboue specifyd, wrof I the aforesd John Cutt, do own & acknowl- edge the receipt off, & do accept of the sd some payd in money in lew of 26b twenty six pounds hereby dischargeing & acquitting the sd Rishworth from so much due vnto mee of that seauenty too pounds in ordinary pay, as appeareth by his Morgage, as standing on record & by which payment yt foure acres of Land mentioned in the Close of ye sd record, is disingag'd, & fully cleared from mee or any of mine, to haue any interest yrin, by vertue of the Morgage aforesd/ I say receiued & accepted the some of Twenty pounds in Siluer this eight day of March 16 ,   the some

of Twenty six pounds in comman pay as aboue expressd, the fiue pounds in money borrowed of him being therein included/   John Cut/
Testes John ffletcher/
   John Cutt Junio^r

vera Copia of this receipt transcribed & Compared cum origine, this 12th day October : 1681 :
                                p Edw : Rishworth ReCor :

Wee John Wincoll, John Penwill, & Abraham Preble, being Chosen by mutuall Consent of James Gibbines, John Boughton, Phillip ffoxwell & John Harmon, heyres & proprietors of that Pattent land, granted to Mr Lewis, & Capt Richd Boughton as by theyre agreement obligatory beareing date the Twelth day of Nouember one thousand six hundred & eighty may appeare, for equally deuideing the sd Land between the sayd Proprietors, Wee accordingly on the 19th day of Septemb^r 1681 : Came & measured ye lower part next Sacoe riuer, one hundred fourty too pooles, North West from the foote Lyne, unto a certen small water runne Called Halys Gutt, being the Antient bound Marked between the aforesayd Boughton, or his father, & the sayd Gibbines, and from the sd Haleys, vpon a North East, & by north Lyne, unto the Middle lyne of the sayd Pattent, togeather with y^t Triangle peece of Land, lijng next Sacoe Riuer, & below ye North East, & South West lyne of the sd Pattent, which Contayns foure hundred Acres of Land, next the sea, all which is to belong vnto the sd James Gibbines for his first demission/

2ly ffrom the aforesd Halys Gutt, Wee mesured fiue hundred ninety & two poole North West unto a little brooke, and Marked tree, a little below Mr Blackemans Mill and from thence North East & bee North vnto the Middle lyne aforesayd/ Which is too Miles, and It belongs to the aforesayd John Bonighton, for his first deuission/

3ly Wee measured too Miles & fiuety poole North West from Thomas Rogers his garden by the sea in the aforesayd Middle lyne, & from the end of y^t sayd Too Miles & fiuety pooles, Two Miles North East, unto the lyne of the Pattent next blew Poynt, the aforesayd fiuety pooles aboue ye too Miles North West is in lew of the halfe of the aforesd Tryangle next of land next Sacoe Riuers Mouth, which is to belong vnto Phillip ffoxwell and John Harmon for thejr first deuission/

4ly Wee measured from the Northwest End of the aforesayd two Miles, & fiuety pooles, too Miles wanting fiuety pooles, North West in the aforesd Middle lyne unto a Maple tree which Wee Marked for a Corner tree, & from thence too Miles North East unto the outside lyne of the Pattent, to belong unto the aforesd James Gibbines for his secund deuission/

[103] 5ly The next deuition is to runne from the aforesd little brooke, & Marked tree below Mr Blackemans Mill in Saco Riuer three Miles & an halfe, & eighteen pooles North West, & from thence too Miles North East, vnto the Middle lyne of the Pattent and is to belong unto the aforesd James Gibbines for his third deuission/

6ly/ ffrom the North West end of the aforesd three Miles, & an halfe and eighteen pooles, John Bonighton is to runn North West too Miles & fourty eight pooles, next Sacoe Riuer, vnto the North west end of the Pattent, & from thence too Miles North East, along the head lyne of ye Pattent, unto the aforesayd Middle lyne for his secund deuission/

7ly The next deuition on the North East side of the sd Pattent is to begine at the North west end of the aforesd foure Miles in length already measured out, & to bee too Miles square square, & to belong unto the aforesayd Phillip ffoxwell, & John Harmon for thejr secund deuission/

Book III, Fol. 103.

8ly The last deuission of the North East side of the sd Pattent, is to begine at the North west end of the first too Miles square, & to bee also too Mile square to the head of the sd Pattent, & to belong vnto the aforesd James Gibbines, for his fourth deuition/

Witness of hands this 23. Septemb^r 1681:

      John Wincoll/
      John Penwill/
      Abra: Pieble/

Wee the with in mentioned heyres & proprietors, of the sd Pattent, do own the deuission made of sayd Pattent. by the abouesd John Wincoll, John Penwill, & Abraham Pieble, & to stand as now denided by them/ without any alteration to vs, & our heyres for euer/ witness our hands this 23th day of septem^{br} 1681:

James Gibbines, John Bonighton, John Harmon Came before mee this 23th of Septemb^r, 1681 & acknowledged this Instrument of writeing to bee there act & deede/ John Wincoll Just^s pea.

 James Gibbine s his marke ϛ
 John Bonighton his Marke/ ℘
 John Harmon his Marke ✝
 Phillip Foxwell/

Phillip ffoxwell Came before mee this 24th of Septemb^r 1681. & owned this Instrument to bee his free Act & Deede/

   Edw: Rishworth Just pc:

vera Copia of this Instrument aboue written, with acknowledgments under written, transcribed out of the originall & there Compared, this 14th day of October · 1681.

      p Edw · Rishworth ReCor ·

Witness this 29th September: 1681: then receiued vpon Accomp^t of the Treas^r of the prouince of Mayn, from the Commissioners of the Prouince for eight pounds. halfe of y^e

some to bee as money, the other halfe as current pay, being in full of all debts, dues & demands, w'soeuer from the sd Prouince/

Witness my hand the day aboue written   John Bray/

vera Copia of this receipt transcribed, & with originall Compared this 27th Octobr 1681 :

p Edw : Rishworth ReCor :

To all Christean people, to whome this writeing Indented shall Come greeteing/ Know yee that I Jane Waddocke, the wife of Henery Waddocke deceased, of Sacoe in the prouince of Mayne Widdow, haue by these Presents, for & in Consideration of the some of fourty pounds of Current pay of New England, in hand payd mee by Humfrey Scammon of the Town of Cape Porpus, the receipt where of I ye sd Jane Waddocke do hereby acknowledg & Confess, my selfe to bee there with fully satisfyd, Contented & payd, & do for mee my heyres, executors, administrators, & Assignes, for euer acquitt & discharge him the sd Humphrey Scammon, his heyres executors administrators & Assigns, of euery part parcell & penny there of, haue hereby absolutely barganed sould, aliend, Confirmed, Enfeoffed assigned & set ouer, & for euer do by these Presents, giue grant bargan sell, aliene Confirme Enfeoff assigne & set ouer unto the sd Humphrey Scammon, his heyres executors administrators & Assignes, Too hundred acres of Land scituate on the North side of Sacoe Riuer, begining at a brooke by a thorne tree, tending & runeing partly North & by East/ And likewise twenty Acres of sault Marsh lijng at Gowse fayre, prouided yr bee not measure of Land Enough at Gowse fayre, the sd Humphrey is to

Jane Waddocke Came before mee this 21th day of Octobr 1681 & did acknowledg this Instrument with in written to bee her Act & Deede | Edw Rishworth Jurt pe & did do'mer Humphrey Scamon possesion of the Premisses by Turffe & Twigg at this Present date, is Witness Edw Rishworth, John Harmon |

haue It with the Premisses before mentioned, with all priuiledges & appurtenances y'unto app'rtajneing or any ways belonging: And I the sd Jane Waddocke do Couenant promiss & grant for mee my executors & Assigns to warrant & defend unto the sd Humphrey Scammon his heyrs & Assigns the quiett & lawfull possession of the Premisses, here granted, against all men what soeuer/ witness my hand & seale this fourth day of December Anno: Dom̃: 1679:

Sealed & deliuered/   Jane Waddocke
   In Presence/   her Marke ⁀ (her seale)
Mathew Clarke
his marke M
John ꟻ ꞗ Boaden/
Margeret Wallis
her Marke ⁀
John Bowey/

These are to Certify before whom It may Concerne, that the sayle of the land on y'e other side was done with the Consents of the late Major Pendleton & my selfe, according to the order of the Generall Court March last 1680: witness my hand
     Josua Scottow Just pe:
Blacke Poynt 21th Octobr 1681:

A true Coppy of this grant transcribed out of the originall, & there with Compared this twenty seauenth day of October 1681: p Edw: Rishworth ReCor:

The Deposition of Nicholas Heskins aged about 45 years, & Fran· Tucker aged about 30 yeares/

That wee deponents testifyeth, & sayth that ye yeare of or Lord, one thousand six hundred seauenty & six, went from the great Ysland vp into Crooked lane to & into the house of Thomas Cowell, to demand a debt due to Mr Richd Bickeham & Company, of about twenty six pounds, wch debt was Contracted by will Seely deceased, & Elizabeth now wife of sd Thomas Cowell, shee sd Elizabeth being at yt tyme at home, Confessed to us the Deponents, that It was a due debt, & ·   ·   · Land for & in Consideration of y^t debt, shee would shew it him Presently, so Wee these too Deponents, & shee sd Elizabeth went togeather vp into spruse Cricke, to a Prcell of land, wch was William Seelys land deceased, & then shewd us the bounds of the Land, Namly to begin at Kirkes his land, & so vp by water side of Spruse Cricke, to ye Middle of a poynt of Land Called long poynt to a high pine tree on y^t poynt & so vp into the woods to Mr Robert Cutt his land, backe from ye water side to bee ye bounds; so shee gaue sd Fran: Tucker possession, linery & seizen by Turffe & Twigg, of & vpon the sd land, to bee & remajne to & for the uss of sd Richd Bickeham & Company, & to them & y^r heyres & Assignes for euer, John Turbet, John Renalds, William Renalds, & Edw Randall, being all Present w^n the possession was giuen: And further Wee these Deponents do both testify, that Thomas Cowell owned the Land to bee Richd Bickeham & Companys Land, & shee sd Elizabeth ordered the sd Nicolas Heskines to draw out a bill of sale of sd Land, according to the aboue mentioned bounds, all wch sd Thomas Cowell approued, & hee & his wife Elizabeth Cowell, agreed & ordered this Deponent Nicho: Heskins to draw a deed of sale for the sd Land, & shee in Prticular gaue mee the Coppy of the Town grant, [104] to draw the sd Deed by, & hee & his wife promissed in Presence of these deponents that they would signe y^{r}unto, w^{n}soeuer It were demanded, & y^t w^{as} the sd Town grant was made to William Seely deceased. so the sd Land It should bee Confirmed to the sd ffrancis Tucker, for the vsse of ye sd Richard Bickehum & Company, & in y^r behalfe, & y^t the abouesd Land, was to bee in full satisfaction for the abouesd debt/

Nicholas Heskins & ffrancis Tucker, Came before mee & made oath to the aboue written Deposition this Twenteth day of October 1681

    before mee Elyas Styleman Dep^{ty} P^{r}sident/
vera Copia transcribed, & with ye originall Compared this 31th day Octob^r (1681) p Edw: Rishworth ReCor

BOOK III, FOL 104.

The Deposition of John Renalds aged 30 yeares, or yr abouts
& John Turbet 30 years or there abouts/

Testifyeth, that being sometyme in ffebru: 1676: in
Spruse Cricke with John Turbet & William Renalds Cutting
of wood, in a Parcell of Land by leaue from ffran: Tucker
on a Prcell of land which was sd to haue been the Land of
Mr Will Seely, the sd ffran Tucker Nicho: Heskins & Mrs
Cowell, which was formerly wife to Will Seely deceased,
but now wife of Tho: Cowell, the sd Tucker demanded of sd
Mis Cowell deluery of ye sd land, so shee gaue him possession of sd Land, appoyting him his bounds, to begin from
Carles Land vp the Cricke, by the water side to a poynt
Called long Poynt, to a high pine tree on that Poynt; & vp
into the Woods vnto Mr Robert Cutt his land, so gaue him
possession luery & seasin, shee went off the land & left him
in possession, & Wee stayd & Cutt wood by Tuckers order
on the sd land, seuerall days after, & fetched It away, by
his leaue with out any Molestation, or being warned off, or
forbid to the Contrary by any Prson whatsoeuer/
October · 13: 1681.

Taken vpon   by John Renalds before mee
                    Elyas Stylemā Depty Prsidt:
John Turbet Came & made oath to the uerity of abouesd,
this 25: of Octobr 81: before mee ffrancis Hooke Just pe:
vera Copia transcribed & Compared this 31th Octobr 1681:
                    p Edw: Rishworth Re: Cor:

Wee vnderwritten being desired by Mis Elizabeth Seely
in the yeare 74: May (9th) to try the deuideing Lyne
between her land & Mr Robert Cutt his land, do find it to
runne by a fayre marked lyne, North East to spruse Cricke,

according to yᵉ grant, & former laijng out, as aboue men-
tioned/   Nathall ffryer   Select men/
first Decembʳ 1681 : transcribed John Wincoll
& Compared
    p Edw : Rishworth ReCor :

Know all men by these Presents that I John Moore now of the ysles of shoals by & with the Consent of my wife, for & in consideration of eighty pounds sterlg : which is to bee satisfyd to mee according to a bond giuen mee by Thomas Andrews, Anthony ffarley, & John Winslou Juniorʳ, of the aforesd Ysland wʳof, & wᵗʰwith I do acknowledg my selfe to bee fully satisfyd & Contented for a dwelling house & seauen flake rowmes, on the North west side of the house, as alsoe a stage & sault house, & a moreing place, togeather with the Mooreings that now do belong there vnto, & all the appurtenances yʳunto belonging or that euer did belong or appʳtajne unto mee, John Moore, which delling house land & other Matterialls, I do acknowledg to haue barganed sould & am hereby obleidgd to deliuer unto the abouesd Tho : Andrews, Anthony ffarley & John Winslou Junioʳ abouesd, at or before the first day of October next Insewing the date hereof, which houseing & Lands & Matterialls abouesd lyeth & is vpon starr ysland which is one of the Ysles of shoales, & is Joyneing to Mr John ffabmes, on the one side, & that which was formerly James Waymouths on the other side ; To haue & to hould the sd housen land & other Materialls abouesd with all the appʳtenances there vnto belonging, & made good to the abouesd Thomas Andrews, Anthony ffarley & John Wineslou, theji heyres executors administrators or Assignes, freely peaceably & quietly as yʳ own proper right for euer · with out any let or denyall of mee the sd John Moore, my heyres executors, or administrators, or any of us for euer/ & with warrantees against all people euer,

BOOK III, FOL. 104.

by these Presents/ In witness w^rof, I haue here unto set my hand & seale, this tenth day of Septemb^r Anno Dom : one thousand six hundred eighty & one/ 1681 :

Signed sealed & deliuered   John Moore (his seale)
in the P^rsence of us/   Margerett Moore/

The ⎰ marke of   John Moore & Margerett his wife
                       owned this Instrument to bee y^r
John Dale/   Act & Deed this 10th day of Sep-
Mary Hooke/   temb^r 1681. before mee
                         ffrancis Hooke Just pe :

A True Coppy of this Instrument aboue written, tran-scribed out of the originall & y^rwith Compared this 2 d: of Decemb^r 1681 : p Edw : Rishworth ReCor .

Know all men by these Presents, that I James Wiggines Senjo^r of the Town of Kittery, in the prouince of Mayne, for & in Consideration of Certen somes & other good pay in hand receiued, from Robert Elyett of Portsmouth in new England Mariner, do by these Presents alienate dispose, sell & make ouer to, for s^d Robert Elliott his heyres, executors administrators or Assignes, my full right interest & Title, & all & sundrey my goods & Chattell hereafter in these Pres-ents, exprest & now in my possession, nid_z^t foure Cows three steares, of three yeares ould a peece, foure yearelings, six Hoggs too horses & two Mares, to haue & to hould for him & his foresd^s for euer: for his & their proper vse & uses, & do further by these Presents oblidge my selfe my heyers executors, administrators to deliuer or cause to bee deliuered to the aforesd Robert Eliott or his foresds all sun-dreys, the goods & Chattles aboue written, on all demands, & do for my selfe & foresds warrant this my alienation, to stand in full force strength & uertue against all P^rsons w^tsoner, Clajmeing any right or title to the foresd Cattle, hoggs   true

Prformance of the Premisses, I do bind my selfe, my heyres & executors, in the some of fourty pounds Current money of New England/ Witness my hand at Portsmouth this 20th day of ffebru: 1678 167⅞   The marke ⱻ of James
                                        Wiggins Senior/
Great Ysland yᵉ 21ᵗʰ of ffebru: 1678.
James Wiggines Senjoʳ Came & acknowledged
   the aboue written to bee signed & deliuered
   by him as his Act & deede/ before mee
            Elyas Styleman Commissioʳ
A true Coppy of this Instrument aboue written transcribed & Compared with the originall the 3d d of December 1681
            p Edw: Rishworth ReCor:

[105] Know all men by these Presents, that I William ffeathy, now rescident in the Town of yorke In the Prouince of Mayne, in new England fisherman, with the free Consent of Elizabeth my wife, for diuerse good Causes & Considerations thereunto mee moueing, & more espesially out of that naturall affection & loue which I do beare vnto my beloued son, John ffeathy, now liueing in yᵉ towne & prouince aforesd, do hereby from my selfe my heyres executors administrators & Assignes, giue grant bargain sell bequeath aliene & Confirme, & by these Presents haue giuen granted, sould, bequeathend, aliend, & confirmed, vnto my aforesd son John ffeathy, his heyres, executors administrators & Assignes, my soole right & Interest of a Certen tract Pᵗcell, or portion of land, the full quantity being the one halfe of my homestall feild & lott, that I haue these many years possessed & occupied, & do now liue vpon & possess, being the full north part & halfe, of the North East side of the sd fejld Contayneing the one halfe of the full breadth of my sd lott, & runneing backewards into the woods in length, so fare as the bounds of my said lott extends   vpon

the same Considerations, giue & grant vnto my sd son John
ffreathy, after the decease of my selfe my wife & his Mother,
the other halfe being on South West part of my aforesd lott,
which I do now Improue, down to the water side, which
I now liue vpon, from mee my heyres executors administrators & assignes, to him the sd John Freathy, his
heyres, executors, administrators & Assignes for euer/
to haue & to hould & peaceably to inioy the sd tract of land
according as is aboue expressed the North East part y^rof
forth with, & the south West part or halfe y^rof, after mee &
my wifes decease, with all the priuiledges profetts, aduan-
tages, & Immunitys y^r vnto belonging or in any wise app^r-
taynting, vnto sd John Freathy, his heyres executors administrators & Assigns for euer/ And further I the sd William
Freathy do Coueñnt & promiss to with ye sd John Freathy
my son, that sd land is free & Cleare from all Clajmes, sales
morgages & incomberances w^tsoeuer, & do hereby Ingage to
warrant & Defend the right & title y^rof, vnto the sd John
Frethy his heyrs & Assigs, against all Prson, and Prsons
w^tsoeuer, Clajmeing any right from, by or under us,
or any way by o^r procurement/ In witness whereof wee
haue here unto afixed o^r hands & seales, the 31th day of
October, 1681 : in the 33th yeare of the Reigne of o^r Soueraigne Lord, Charles ye secund of England Scottland, &
France, & Ireland King, Anno Dom 1681 ·/

Signed sealed & deliuered/   William Freathy (his seale)
In the Presence of, us   his marke
Samell Freathy his marke/   Elizabeth Freathy (her seale)
    her marke
William Bray his marke WB

A true Coppy of this Instrument transcribed out of y^e
originall, & there with Compared this 11th day of Decemb^r
1681 · p Edw. Rishworth ReCor :

BOOK III, FOL. 105.

These Presents witnesseth, that I Thomas Mills of Wells, in the Prouince of Mayne in New England, for diuerse good Causes, & Considerations, there unto mee moueing, & more espetially in Consideration of that filiall portion which I intend to giue, & by these Presents do now giue grant & bequeath unto my beloued sonn in Law, Nathan[ll] Cloyce Now resendent in the aforsd Town & Prouince, a Certen Tract or quantity of Marsh or Meddow Land Contayneing the full one Moeity, or halfe of a part Parcell or portion of Meddow, formerly giuen & granted unto mee sd Thomas Mills, by my father Wadleigh deceased : lijng & being on the East side of Mr Wheelewrights Necke of Land bounded on the west side, next adioyneing to the Marsh of Thom[s] Littlefejlds, his Marsh, & on the East side with the Marsh of my son in law, his brother John Cloyce his Marsh or Meddow, which Tract of Meddow land, the sd Natha[ll] Cloyce. his heyres executors Administrators or Assignes, is to haue hould & peaceably to Inioy, from mee the sd Thomas Mills, my heyres, executors, administrators & Assignes, with all & singular the Premisses, & appertenances, any ways y[r]unto belonging, or app[r]tayneing, to the sd Nathan[ll] Cloyce his heyres & Assignes for euer/ & I do further Couenant & agree, that y[e] sd Meddow aboue mentioned, is free & Cleare from all bills obligations, Morgages, titles Dowers, & titles of Dowers, Judgm[ts] executions & all other Incomberances w[t]soeuer, & do further Ingage & Couenant, to warrantize & defend the Title y[r]of, against all Prsons w[t]soeuer Pretending any title from mee, or from any from by or under mee, or any by my pcurement/ In testimony w[r]of, I haue here unto afixed my hand & seale this seauenteenth day of Decemb[r] 1681. being the 33[th] yeare of the Reigne of o[r] soueraigne

BOOK III, FOL. 105.

Lord of England Scotland France & Ireland King, fidej Defensoris Anno Dom ‾ 1681 :

Signed sealed & deliuered/   Thomas Mills his
   In the Presence of/   marke ꝳ (his seale)
   Edw : Rishworth/
John Cloyce his marke   Thomas Mills Came before mee
      Ŧ   this 17th Day of December
                      1681 : & owned this Instru-
                      ment to bee his Act & Deede/
                      Edw . Rishworth Just : pe :

A true Coppy of this Instrument aboue written, transcribed, & Compared with the originall this 12th day of Janvary, 1681 · p Edw . Rishworth Re : Cor :

These Presents do witness, that I Thomas Mills of Wells, in the Prouince of Mayne, for good Causes & Considerations there unto mee moueing & more espetially in lew of that filiall portion, which I resolue to giue my beloued sonn in law, John Cloyce of Wells in the Prouince of Mayne, do giue grant & Confirme my soole right & Interest, of too Acres of sault Marsh lijng in Wells, at the lower end of my father Wadlows Marsh, ioyneing to the Town Marsh, butting vpon a little sea Wall ioyneing vpon Webb hannett Riuer, & further I do giue unto my aforesd sonn Cloyce one halfe of my Marsh at the Necke of Land, which I had of my father Wadleigh, being bounded on the East side, by Thom^s Littlefejlds Marsh & on the West side with John Cloyces, both which Prcells of Marsh lyeth on ye East side of Mr Wheelewrights Necke of Land ; To haue & to hould the sd tracts of Land, being Marsh as aboue specifyd, with all & singular the priuiledges & appurtenances, y'unto belonging, vnto him the sd John Cloyce, his heyres & Assignes for euer, without any Clajm or lett from mee, my heyres or Assignes, or any othe. lawfully Climing ⸺ from by or under mee, my

heyres, or Assignes/ In testimony w^{r}of I haue here unto
afixed my hand & seale, this 12th of July 1681 :
Signed, sealed, & deliuered/   Thomas Mills ($^{his}_{seale}$)
  in Presence of us/   This Instrument was acknowledged
  John Wheelewright/   by Tho : Mills to bee his Act &
  Wilham Frost/   Deed, this 12th of July (1681)
                    before mee Samll Wheelewright
                                  Just. pe.
vera Copia of this Instrument transcribed, & Compared
with the originall this 13th day of Janvary 1681 :
                    p Edw : Rishworth Re . Cor :

[106]   1680 This Indenture made ye secund day of ffeb-
ruary in ye thirty third yeare of the Reign of our Soueraign
Lord Charles the secund, by the grace of god of England,
Scotland ffrance & Ireland King, Defend^r of the faith, &c :
between James Chadborne of Kittery of ye Prouince of
Mayne of the one part, & Thomas Roads of the same Town
& Prouince Joyner of the other part ; Witnesseth, that
where as John Heard late of Sturgeon Cricke, in the Town
of Kittery in the Prouince of Mayn aforesd, deceased, did by
his last will & testament beareing date the third day of
March in the yeare of our Ld God 1675 : amongst other
things giue & bequeath, vnto his two Elldest Grand daughters Mary & Elizabeth Heard, the daughters of his late
deceased sunn James Heard a Certen lott or tract of Land
lijng & being in the Town of Kittery aforesayd Comanly
Called or known by ye name of Tomson Poynt, Contajneing
by Estimation sixty Acres, or there abouts bee It more or
less, as It was layd out & bounded by the sayd Town of
Kittery, with the appurtenances, as by the sd will, & testament & Town Grant more at large doth & may appeare :
Excepting to John Ross his house & land, for the Tearme of
his life which had thirty baylt & fenced &c &c h was

granted unto him the sayd Ross, by the Consent of the sayd
Testator/ Now Know yee, that since the sd Will & testament
made, & Confirmed in law & by law, that James Chadborne
Party to these Presents, did Mary with Elizabeth the youngest of them too sisters, or Legatees, & thereby is Intitled &
Inuested vnto the one Moeity part & purpotty, of the sayd
tract of Land so given, by his wifes Grandfather, John
Heard deceased, & doth hereby owne & acknowledg him
selfe the right owner there of at this Present, & hath full
power, togeather with his wife to sell, giue, sett, or otherwise to dispose of the same/

Now know yee, that I James Chadborne, Party to these
Presents being so Intitled Invested & possessed of the sd
Land & Premisses, haue & by these Presents do, with the
free will & Consent of my now wife Elizabeth, for & in Consideration of the some of thirty pounds of Lawfull pay in
New England vidzt in hand payd, or secured to bee payd
vnto mee my wife, my executors, administrators or Assignes
before the Insealeing hereof by the hands of Thomas Roads
his heyres, or Assigns, giue grant Enfeoff sell, and Confirme
unto him the sayd Thomas Roads, all that Moeity halfendeale
part, & purputy of yt lott or Tract of Land atoresd, with all
& euery of the appurtenances y'runto belonging or in any wise
app'rtajneing: To haue & to hould the Moiety, & halfendale
of the sayd sixty acres with the appurtenances, to him the
sd Thomas Roads his heyres & Assignes from the day
of the Date here of for euer/ & the sayd James Chadborne for him selfe his heyres executors, & administrators,
doth further promisse Couenant & grant to & with the sayd
Thomas Roads, his heyres, executors, administrators &
Assignes to and with euery of them, & either of them, that
hee sayd Thomas his heyres executors Administrators &
assignes, shall & may from tyme to tyme, & at all tyms
hereafter for euer quietly, and peaceably hould haue vss, &
possess the same, & euery part & Prcell there of, with out
the lawfull lett suite Molestation or trouble of him the

sayd James Chadborne & Elizabeth his wife, or thejre heyres, executors, administrators or Assigns or of any other Prson or Prsons whatsoeuer, lawfully Clajmeing the sd Moeity or halfendeale of the sayd Land & Premisses/

(The Proprietor or the high Lord of the soyle, & John Ross his Grant onely exepted) In witness here of the sayd James Chadborne Party to these Presents & Elizabeth his wife vnto this Indenture, interchangeably thejre hands & seales haue set euen the day & yeare first aboue written/ Anno Domi: 1680.

Sealed & Deliuered in   James Chadborne ($^{his}_{seale}$)
the Presence of us/   Elizabeth Chadborne/ ($^{her}_{seale}$)
The marke of John   James Chadborne & Elizabeth his
Breathy ✚   wife did acknowledg, this aboue
    written Instrument to bee thejre
Joane ✚ Neale   Act & Deede, this 5th of Septem^{br}
    1681 : before mee
her marke   Charles ffrost Just^s of pea :
Andrew Searle/

vera Copia of this Instrument aboue written transcribed out of the originall & y^{r}with Compared this 7th day of March 1681 : p Edw : Rishworth Re : Cor :

Know all men by these Presents, that I William Rogers of Kittery in the Prouince of Mayne, of the one Party, & Elihew Gullisson of the same place of ye other Party, haue agreed as followeth ; I the sd William Rogers for & in Consideration of the sume of thirty fiue pounds, in hand before ye sealeing & deliuery of these Presents, well & truely payd the receipt w^{r}of, the sd Rogers acknowledgeth, & him selfe to bee fully satisfyd, Contented & payd, & y^{r}of & of euery Prcell & penny y^{r}of, doth acquitt, exonerate, & discharge, the sd Elihew Gunisson his heyrs executors, administrators & Assignes, & euery of them for euer, by these Presents, as also for diuerse other good Causes & Considerations, mee the sd Rogers y`r`unto espetially moueing, haue given granted, barganed & sould, aliend, released, Enfeoffed deliuered & Confirmed & by these Presents, doth giue grant bargan & sell, alieane release, deliuer & Confirme, unto sd Elihew Gunnisson his heyres, & Assignes for euer, all that dwelling house y`t` I sd Rogers bujlt at the Mouth of Spruse Cricke, on the Westerne side of y`e` sd Cricke, togeather with halfe of y`e` whoole Necke of Land, adioyneing to the sd house, which Land is the Land which william Seely, & I y`e` sd Rogers formerly possessed, of Mr Hugh Gunnissons deceased, & now is in the possession of my selfe & Mistres Cowell, formerly the wife of William Seely/

To haue & to hould, the before hereby granted & barganed Premisses, & euery part & parcell thereof, with all y`e` appurtenances unto the sd Gunnisson, his heyres & Assigns for euer; And the sd William Rogers for him selfe, his heyres executors administrators, Assignes, doth Couenant promiss & grant, to & with sd Elihew Gunnisson, his heyres & Assignes, & to & with euery of them by these Presents, y`t` all & singular the sd Premisses, with all y`e` priuiledg`s` & appurtenances y`r`unto belonging, & in & by these Presents before given barganed & sould, & euery part & Parcell there of, from the tyme of the Ensealeing & deliuery of these Presents, are & bee & at all tymes hereafter, shall bee & remajne & Continew Clearely acquitted, exonarated, discharged and keept harmeless of & from all manner of former barganes, had made Committed suffered or done, or to bee had made Committed suffered or done by the sd Rogers, his heyres executors administrators or Assignes, or any of them or any other Person or Prsons whatsoeuer by his or thejre meanes also to [**107**] saue & keepe harmeless the sayd Gunnisson from all manner of former bargains whatsoeuer, made by mee the sayd Rogers, or any from by or under mee/ In witness whereof I haue here unto set my hand & seale, this

Book III, Fol. 107.

sixth day of May in the yeare of our Lord one thousand six hundred seauenty fiue/ 1675 : William Rogers (his seale)
Signed Sealed & deluerd

In Presence of us/ William Rogers acknowledged this
John Pickerin/ Instrument, to bee his Act &
Sam:ll Whidden/ Deede to Elihew Gunnisson this
24th day of Septembr 1680 : before mee ffrancis Hooke
Justs of pe :

Bee It remembered that vpon the day of the date of the bill of sayle with in written quiet & peaceable possession & seizin of the with in mentioned Premisses, was done & deliuered by the with in Mentioned Rogers, unto ye with in mentioned Gunnisson, as his ye sd Gunnissons proper right in the Presence of John Pickerine & Sam:ll Whidden/ John Pickerin/

A true Coppy of this Deed aboue written, transcribed out of ye originall, & there with Compared this 20th day of March 168½ p Edw · Rishworth ReCor :

Septembr 4th 1680 ·

Receiued then of Elihew Gunnisson full satisfaction for all debts, dues, Demands agreements, Contracts & all other thinges w:tsoeuer Therefore I Isaac Waldron, do hereby acquitt free & discharge the sd Gunison his heyres executors & administrators from all Damages w:tsoeuer hee hath done to mee or any of my heyres, executors, Administrators at any tyme heretofore, from the begining of the world to ye day first aboue written, as Attests my hand/

Testes Isaac Waldron
Sam:ll Wentworth/ 6th Septembr 1680. Mr Isaac Waldron acknowledged the aboue written to bee signed by him as his
John Pickerin/ Act & Deede, before mee
Elyas Styleman of the Councill/

Book III, Fol. 107.

vera Copia of this receipt aboue written transcribed, &
with originall Compard this 20th March 168¼
     p Edw : Rishworth ReCor :

Ann Crocket sayth y^t shee being severall tymes at y^e
house of Mr Hugh Gunnisson in his life tyme & neare his
death, the sd Gunnisson always Charged mee the Deponent
& my husband, that wee should not see the Too Gunnissons
wronged, of the necke of Land & & Ysland belonging to it,
Which hee the sd Gunnisson had set out to his too sonns in
law, Seely & Rogers for one & Twenty yeares, paijng to
him or his Assignes 10^s p yeare dureing the sd Tearme/ &
If it pleased god to take him away before the expiration of
ye sd lease, It was his will & determination It should returne
to ye too Gunnissons, for ye Lynns should neuer Inioy it,
for hee thought hee had done sufficiently for them already/
y^{r}fore hee desired mee & my husband oftentyms to discharge
o^r Consciences Concerneing it y^t so the two Gunnissons
might by no meanes bee Depriued of the Land abouesd but
that wee should bee ready w^n Called y^{r}unto to speake y^e
treuth for y^m, as hee wonld do for them if Called y^{r}unto :
the two Gunnissons aboue mentioned hee ment his too sonns
Joseph & Elihew/ & further sayth not/

 Taken vpon oath this 27th of Janvary 1679 : before mee
      ffrancis Hooke Comissio^r
vera Copia of this oath transcribed out of the originall &
y^{t}with Compared this 21th March 168¼
     p Edw : Rishworth ReCor :

To all whome these may Concerne/ Know yee that I
William Hooke of Sawlsbury, M^{r}chant, do couenant & grant
unto John ...

the one halfe of the Necke of land At Cape Nuttacke unto y^m & y^r heyers for euer with as full right & Interest, as I the sd William Hooke haue granted unto mee by my le^rs Pattent, which Necke of land is bounded from one sandy beach to ye other sandy beach & the sd John Allcocke & John Hord, do Couenant with ye sd William Hooke for to take in the whoole Necke of land, with the spring by the pond with a sufficient fence to keepe all manner of Cattle, & to Mantaine It with a sufficient fence, & vpon this Condition, to aforesd John Allcocke & John Hord are to haue one halfe of the sd Land to them & y^r heyres for ever; And It is further Couenanted betwixt ye aforesd partys, that ye Necke of Land bee for pasture & feedeing, & Cattle &c : & that If the sd William Hooke or his Assignes do not make uss of his part of ye sd Land, that It shall bee lawfull for ye sd John Allcocke & Jo^n Heard, to put in what stocke of Cattle they shall haue Occasion for, to make vss of, & y^t not any of us, at any tyme ouercharge It with Cattle/ In witness w^rof wee haue hereunto set o^r hands & seales, 16th day of July 1650/
Sealed signed & deliuered/   William Hooke (his seale)
In the presence of/   vera Copia of this Instrument tran-
Basill Parker/   scribed, & with the originall Com-
John Tayer/   pared this 22th of March 168½
               p Edw: Rishworth ReCor

To all whome these may Concerne/ Know yee y^t J William Hooke of Sawlesbury M^rchant, do Couenant & grant unto John Allcocke, & John Heard of Gorgeana Planters, ye one halfe of the Necke of Land at Cape Nuttacke unto them & y^r heyres for euer/ with as full right & Interest as I the sd William Hooke haue granted unto mee by my letters pattent, which necke of Land is bounded from one sandy beach to the other sandy beach/ & sd John Allcocke

BOOK III, FOL. 107.

& John Heard, do Couenant with the sd Willam Hooke to take in the whoole Necke of Land with ye spring by the pond with a sufficient fence, to keepe all manner of Cattle & to Mantaine it with a sufficient fence & vpon this Condition ye aforesd John Allcocke, & John Hord are to haue one halfe of ye sd Land to them & y^r heyres for euer And It is further Couenanted betwixt the aforesd Partys that ye necke of Land to bee for pasture & feedeing of Cattle &c: And y^t if the sd William Hooke or his Assigns do not make vss of his part of ye land, that It shall bee lawfull for sd John Allcocke & John Heard, to put in w^t stocke of Cattle they shall haue occasion for, to make vss off, & not any of us at any tyme to ouercharge it with Cattle/ In witness w^rof Wee haue here unto sett o^r hands & seales, the 16th day of July (1650) William Hooke (his seale)
Sealed signed & deliuered in P^rsence
of Basill Parker/   Mary ⟨⟩ Jewell marke/
John Harkers marke ℛ

Wee whose names are here subscribed, being Chosen & appoynted by ye heyrs & Children of Jo^n Allcocke deceased, for diuideing & Settleing sd Allcocks Estate, amongst them selues as appeareth by an agreement under thejr hands, beareing date Octob^r 29 · 75: which in the generall wee haue Prformed & done, onely since the Prformance w^rof Wee find too distinct debts due from ye Estate aforesd, to Mr Shuball Dumer, vidz^t 33s to Mr Dumers salery y^t same yeare John Allcocke deceased, & Twenty shillings to bee payd by Leef^t Job Allcocke, wch fiuety three shillings Leef^t Allcocke satisfijng to Mr Dumer, for security of his satisfaction & repayment, Wee do by these Presents according to pouer Committed to us, Convay unto him & Interest him in the propriety of yᵉ land lijng at yᵉ Cape Necke, according to this Deed with in written/ ffebru: 18ᵗʰ 1679:

I underwritten do Assigne & make ouer all yᵉ right title & Interest of this with in written Instrument unto Siluester Stouer, to his heyres & Assigns for euer/ witness my hand March: 4ᵗʰ 16⅞⁰⁄₈₀

                    Edw: Rishworth
                    Abra: Preble/
                    John Twisden/

before mee Samˡˡ Wheelewright Asṡōte/

Leefᵗ Allcocke acknowledgeth this to bee his Act & deede, the 4ᵗʰ March: ⅞⁰⁄₈₀ before mee Samˡˡ Wheelewright

                                    Assotiate

A true Coppy of this Deed abone written, with the post script & Leefᵗ Allcocks assignᵗ under written, transcribed, & there with Compared this 22ᵗʰ day of March 168½

                    p Edw: Rishworth ReCor.

[108] To all Christian people to whom these Presents may Come; Know yee yᵗ wᵃs there is a Contract of Marriage, between Mr Tho: Ledbroake of Portsmouth in New Hampshire, in New England & Deborah Booth of Winter Harbour in the prouince of Mayne in New England, yᵗ I Thomas Ledbroake do by these Pʳsents firmely Contract to & with the sd Deborah Booth, yᵗ I will not dispose off any part of yᵉ Estate, whither house land Marsh Cattle, household stuffe or any other Estate any wise to her Pertajneing, or belonging with out yᵉ free Consent of sd Deborah Booth, & Case it should please god yᵗ it should bee my portion to depart this life, before yʳ sd Deborah Booth my now promised wife, I do hereby firmely obleige my selfe, my heyres, & successors to leaue yᵉ sd Deborah in as good a Condition, in respect of an Estate, as now shee is at yᵉ day of her Marriage; It is further mutually agreed, that in Case the sayd

Book III, Fol. 108.

Deborah my now promissed wife, should depart this life before sd Thomas Ladbrooke then shee shall haue, & by these Presents haue full pouer & liberty to giue & dispose of all, or any part of y^t Estate which is now her own to any which shee shall see good/ In witness w^{r}unto I haue set my hand, the one & Twenteth of ffebru : 1681 :

Signed & Deliuer'd/   Tho : Ledbrwoke/
 in the Presence of us/   Mr Tho : Ledbrwoke did acknowl-
 Edw : Sargant/   edg this aboue Instrume^t to bee
 Jonathan Hammond/   his Act & Deede, this 21th of
            ffebru . 168½ before mee
            Samll Wheelewright Just : pe :

A true Coppy of this Contract or agreement aboue written, transcribed & Compard with originall this 8th day of Aprill 1682 : p Edw : Rishworth ReCor .

To all Christian people to whome these Presents shall come Joseph Storer sendeth greeteing/ Know yee y^t I Joseph Storer of Wells in the prouince of Mayne in New England, for seuerall good Causes & Considerations y^{r}unto moueing, & more espetially for and in Consideration of a Certen Tract of Land and Marsh, with a dwelling house and barne, now standing vpon sayd land, to mee in hand deliuered by Samll Austine which is to my satisfaction, and wheie with I am fully Contented, haue from mee my heyres, executors Administrators & Assigns, haue exchanged barganed sould granted Enfeoffed & Confirmed and by these Presents do exchange bargane sell Enfeoff & Confirme unto Samell Austine of the aforesayd Town and Prouince his heyrs executors administrators & Assignes for euer, my now dwelling house barne and all out houseing, with all my Land and March bounded as followeth, the vpland Contayneing about too hundred Acers, bounded on the North East side by that lott of Land which was formerly James Gouch his land, now in the Costody of Jonathan Hamonds, and bounded on the South West side by Jeremiah Storer, and so to runne vp into the Countrey till too hundred Acres bee Compleated, being one halfe of that Tract of Land which was between my selfe & my brother Benjamen, deceased, also one halfe of the Marsh belonging unto the sayd place bounded on the North East by James his Marsh, and so down from the vpland to the Harbors Mouth, and bounded on the South West side by Jeremiah Storer/ also all that vpland & Marsh which I bought of ffrancis Backehouse, at Drakes Ysland with all the profetts, priuiledges, Commans Commages, with all and singular the appurtenances and priuiledges, in any wise appertajneing or belonging, freely & quietly to haue and to hould, without any matter of Clajme or demand of mee the sayd Joseph Storer or any Person or Persons either from by or under mee my heyres executors administrators and Assignes for euer, hee the sayd Samell Austine his heyres executors administrators and Assignes I do hereby declare to bee truely and rightly possessed of each and euery part and prcell of houses land and Marsh abouesd And that hee the sayd Samuell Austine, his heyres executors administrators and assignes shall peaceably and quietly haue hould and Imoy euery part and Percell of the Premisses, granted and sould to him for euer, and do here promiss and Couenant to and with the sayd Samuell Austine, that all the Premisses granted and sould and euery part and Percill thereof are free and Cleare from all Gyfts grants bargans Dowrys Morgages Judgments, and all other Incomberances whatsoeuer, and do promisss to warrant and Defend the Title and Interest of the Premisses, from mee my heyres executors administrators and Assigns and from any Prson or Persons by mee or under mee or by my meanes or procurement/ In testimony where of I haue hereunto set too my hand and seale, this secund day of March one thousand six hundred eighty one, in the thirty third yeare of ye Reigne of our Soueraign Ld Charles the secund, by the gra   od of

England Scotland ffrance, & Ireland King, Defend[r] of the
ffaith &c 1681 : Joseph Storer (his seale)
Signed sealed & deliuered/

In the Presence of I Hannah Storer the wife
Testes Samuell Wheelewright/ of Jos: Storer do giue
          my free Consent to this
Joseph Storer & Hannah Storer with in written bill of
Came & acknowledged this In- sayle, & do freely de-
strument to bee y[r] act & Deed liuer vp my right of
the secund day of March 168½ Dowry witness my hand
before mee   this 2: day of March
Samuell Wheelewright Just pe 1681.
             Hannah Storer/

vera Copia of this Instrument aboue written transcribed, out of the originall & there with Compared this 11th day of Aprill 1682 p Edw · Rishworth ReCor

To all Christian people to whom these Presents shall Come, Samuell Austine sends Greeteing, Know yee that I Samuell Austine of Wells in the Prouince of Mayne in New England, for severall good Causes & Considerations mee there unto moueing & more esspetially, for & in Consideration of a Certen Tract of Land & Marsh with a dwelling house and barne now standing vpon sayd Land, and one hundred pounds to mee in hand deliuered, & sufficiently Assured to bee payd by Joseph Storer, which is to my satisfaction, & where with I am fully Contented, haue from mee my heyrs executors Administrators, haue exchanged barganed sould granted Enfeoffed & Confirmed, and by these Presents do exchange bargan sell Enfeoff & Confirme unto Joseph Storer of the aforesd Town and Prouince his heyres, executors, administrators & Assignes, for euer, my now dwelling house [109] barne and all out houseing with all my vpland, and Marsh bounded as followeth/ the vpland being in breadth about three scoore pooles, being bounded with John Barrett on the Norther side, and Joseph Bolls on the

Book III, Fol. 109.

South West side, and so to runn vp into the Countrey till three hundred Acres bee Compleated, and the Marsh to runn the whoole breadth of the vpland down to Webbhannet River, also foure acres of Marsh at the sea Wall too acres of it lyeth at the North est end of ffrancis Littlefejlds Island, and Joseph Bolls on the North East, side, & the other too acres lyes next the Harbours mouth by the sea Wall, with Joseph Bolls on the North West side, with all ye appurtenances & priuiledg^s there unto belonging with Commans & Commonidges, with all thejr Conueniencys, in any wise Partaineing and belonging, freely & quietly to haue & to hould, with out any matter of Clajme or demand, of mee the sayd Samell Austine or any Person, or Persons either from by or under mee, my heyres, executors, administrators or Assignes for euer: bee the sayd Joseph Storer, his heyrs executors administrators & Assignes I do hereby declare to bee truely & rightly possessed of each & euery part and Percell of land and Marsh abouesayd, and that hee the sd Joseph Storer, his heyrs executors administrators and Assignes shall peaceably & quietly haue hould and Imoy all & euery part and Percell of the Premisses granted and sould to them for euer/ And I do hereby promiss and Couenant to and with the sayd Joseph Storer, that all the Premisses granted & sould, and euery part there of are free and Cleare from all gyfts grants barganes, leases Dowrys, Morgages, Judgments and all other Incomberances whatsoeuer, and to promiss to warrant to defend ye title and Interest of the Premisses, from mee my heyres executors Administrators and Assignes, and from any Person or Persons under mee or by my meanes or procurement/ In testimony w^{r}of I haue set too my hand and seale, this secund day of March one thousand six hundred eighty one, and in the three an thirteth yeare of the Reigne of our soueraigne Lord Charles the secund, by the grace of

Book III, Fol. 109.

god of England Scotland ffrance and Ireland King, Defender of the faith &c :

Signed sealed & Deliuered/   Samuell Austine (his seale)
  In the Presence of/   I saraih the wife of Samuell Aus-
Samuell Wheelewright/   tine, do giue my free Consent
Jonathan Hamond/   to this with in written bill of
                              sale, & do freely deliuer vp my
                              right of Dowry/ witness my
                              hand y^s 2cund day of March
                              1681 :   Saraih Austine her
Samuell Austine & Saraih Austine Came &   marke/
acknowledged this Instrumcᵗ to bee yʳ
Act & Deed this 2cund day of March
1681 . before mee Samull Wheelewright
                    Jusṫ pe
A true Coppy of this Instrument transcribed out of yᵉ
originall & yʳ with Compared this 12th of March 1681 :
                   p Edw : Rishworth ReCor :

Witness these Presents, that I Antipas Mavericke of Kittery in Pischataqua Riuer in the County of yorke In New England do Confess my selfe to owe & iustly to stand indebted unto Moses Mauericke of Marblehead in the County of Essex New England atoresd the full & iust some of foure scoore & tenn pounds to bee payd unto Moses Mauericke his heyres executors, administrators or Assignes in Mʳchantble dry Cod refuge ffish board or barrell staues to bee payd at Marblehead, at money price, at or vpon the Twenty fourth day of June next after the Date here of, for the which payment well & truely to bee made & done I the sd Antipas Mauericke, bind mee my heyres executors Administrators & Assignes, firmely & for the further Confirmation of the true Prformance of the abouesd payment, I the sd Antipas

Book III, Fol. 109.

Mauericke do Assign & make ouer unto the aforesd Moses Manericke, to him & his heyres or Assignes for ever, my house & Land y{t} is scituate & being in Kittery in Pischataqua River, in the County of yorke aforesd/ And w{r}as I the sd Antipas Manericke haue formerly made a Deed, of bargane & sale of sd house & Land beareing date the eight of August one thousand six hundred sixty & one unto Thom{s} Booth for fiue hundred & Twenty pounds to bee payd according to y{e} expressions of y{e} Deed, y{t} If the sd Booth doth hould the sd house & land, then I the sayd Antipas Manericke do promiss to surrender the sd Deed vnto sd Moses Manericke, to him & his heyres & Assignes proper vsse, & behoofe, And It is also agreed between the aboue Partys, y{t} If it so falls out, that y{e} sd Moses Manericke do sell the sd house & Land, then y{e} sayd Moses is to pay him selfe all Damages & Charges & what remajnes the sayd Moses is to returne unto y{e} sd Antiphas his heyres or Assignes/ unto all which, I the sayd Antipas Manericke haue set too my hand & seale, this fineteenth of Decemb{r} 1663 :

Signed sealed & deliuered   Antipas Manericke ($_{seale}^{his}$)
 In the Presence of/   Antipas Manericke acknowledged
 Fran : Johnson/   this to bee his Act & Deed this
 Samll . Hind/   16 : th October 1663 .
          before mee William Hawthorne/

A true Coppy of this Instrument aboue written transcribed & Compared this 20{th} day of April 1682 :
       p Edw : Rishworth ReCor :

Receiued of my brother Antipas Manericke, on the Accompt of the writeing on the other side, & other Accopts between us, the some of Twenty seauen pounds, so y{r} doth remajn due to mee sixty three pounds on all Accompts to this day/ as witness my hand this 29{th} of June 1674 :
       p me Moses Manericke/

Book III, Fol. 109.

To receiued of my brother Antipas Mauericke more on the accomp.^t of the writeing on the other side six pounds fiue shillings & foure peence/ I say receiued this 13th day of August 1675 · Witness my hand/

Moses Mauericke/

I vnderwritten do Assigne & sett ouer vnto Major Nic: Shapleigh of Kittery, for & in Consideration of finety pounds in money already payd & secured vnto mee, the within mentioned Morgage or deed of sayle, that is to say all my right Title & Interest there in specifyd, & the abouesd some of fiuety pounds is in full satisfaction of all debts & demands whatsoeuer, from the Estate of my brother Antipas Mauericke deceas'd & If need bee I shall giue a Deed of sayle according to Law vnto the sd Shapleigh or his order, unto the acknowledgm.^t of all which true & faithfully to bee Pr formed, I do hereunto sett my hand & seale, this seauenth day of Octob.^r 1680 ·   Moses Mauericke (his seale)
Signed sealed & deliuered/

In the Presence of us/	Mr Moses Mauericke owned the
ffrancis Hooke/	aboue-d Assignation to bee his
Mary Hooke	Act & Deed this seauenth of
	October 1680 : before mee
	ffran · Hooke Just pe :

A true Coppy of the too receipts & ye Assignation here aboue written, transcribed out of the originall, & y.^r with compared this 20th day of Aprill 1682

p Edw: Rishworth ReCor.

·

This Indenture made the twelth day of July Anno Dom͞: one thousand six hundred eighty & one, Annoq̨ R: Re^s Caroli secundi xxxiij &c · between walter Gendall of Casco In the Prouince of Mayne In New England yeomon, & Joane his wife, on the one part, & Bartholmew Gydney of Salem in the County of Essex, in the Coloney of the Massatusetts, in New England Esq[r] on the other part, witnesseth, that y[e] said Walter Gendall & Joane his wife, for & in Consideration of the sume of one hundred [110] & tenn pounds of Current money of New England, to them in hand at or before the Ensealeing & deliuery of these Presents, by the sayd Bartholmew Gydney well & truely payd, the receipt where of they do hereby acknowledg, & them selues there with fully satisfyd & Contented, & there of & of euery part there of, do acquitt exonerate & discharge, the sd Bartholmew Gydney his heyres, executors administrators & Assignes, for euer by these Presents; haue given granted barganed sould, aliend Enfeoffed & Confirmed, & by these Presents do fully freely Clearely & absolutely giue grant bargane, sell aliene, Enfeoff & Confirme unto the sayd Bartholmew Gydney his heyres, & Assignes for euer : All that y[r] tract & Parcell of Land, Scituate lijng or being in Casco aforesd, on the North side of y[e] bay there ; the Front whereof next the sea, lijeth with in the Townshipe of North yarmouth in New England aforesd, as the same Land was formerly granted by seuerall Indean Sagamores to Thomas Steuens of Kenebecke yeamon, as by deede of sale under y[e] hands & seales of the sayd Indean Sachems, beareing date the nineteenth day of January 1673 : reference where unto being had more fully, & at large doth & may appeare, & one Moeity there of was granted by the sayd Thomas Steuenes vnto the sd Gydney as by Deed of sayle beareing date 12 day of Octob[r] 1674 more fully may appeare, & the other moeity y[r]of was granted by sd Thomas Steuenes unto Henery Sayword, & by him morgaged unto y[e] sayd Bartholmew Gydney, and afterwards the same became forfited into the hands of the sayd Gidney, & also one peece or Parcell of land scituate on Casco Bay aforesayd, on a Certen Poynt, there Commanly Called & known by the name of Ryalls Poynt Containeing by Estimation two Acres bee the same more or lesse, all which sayd

Book III, Fol. 110.

Premisses were since Conuajed by the sayd Gydney, vnto the sd walter Gyndall, togeather with all & singular the houses, oarchards buildings, Edifices gardens orchards, Lands, Meddows Marshes trees woods, vnder woods Swamps-waters, water courses ways Easements, profitts priuiledges rights, lybertys, Commoditys, hyreditaments, Emoluments, and appurtenances whatsoeuer, to the sayd Premisses, to any part, or Parcell there of, belonging or in any wise appertajne-ing, To haue & to hould the sayd Tract, or Parcell of Land with the too acres of land scituate lying and being as afore-sayd, with all the other aboue granted Premisses, with thejre appurtenances with euery part & parcell there of vnto the sayd Bartholmew Gidney his heyres & Assignes, & to the onely proper usse benefitt, & behoofe of the sd Barthol^w Gydney his heyres, & Assignes for euer/ And the walter Gyndall, and Joane his wife for hem them selues, there heyrs executors & administrators, do hereby Couenant Promiss & grant, to & with ye sayd Bartholmew Gydney his heyers & Assignes, in manner and forme following, that is to say that the sayd Bartholmew Gidney his heyres & Assignes shall & may by force, & uertue of these Presents, from tyme to tyme, & at all tymes for euer hereafter law-fully peaceably & quietly hould haue uss, occupy possess and Inioy the aboue granted premisses with thejr appurtenances and euery part y^{r}of, free & cleare, & Clearely acquitted & discharged, of and from all manner of former & other Gyfts Grants, bargans Sayles leases, Morgages ioynters, Dowers, Judgments executions Intailes forfitures, & of & from all other titles, troubles Charges & incomberances whatsoeuer, had made Committed done or suffered to bee done by them the sayd walter Gyndall & Joane his wife, or either of them there or either of thejr heyres or assignes at any tyme or tymes before the Ensealeing here of; And further that ye sayd walter Gyndall & Joane his wife, thejr heyres execu-tors administrators & Assignes shall & will from tyme to tyme, & at all tymes for euer here after warrant & Defend

the aboue granted Premisses with thejr appurtenances & euery part and Peicell thereof unto the sd Bartholmew Gydney his heyies & assignes, against all & euery peison & Persons whatsoeuer any ways lawfully clajming or demanding the same or any part there of, from by or vnder the sd Walter Gindall, & Joane his wife, oi either of them, thence or either of thejre heyres or assignes . Prouided always and It is neuer the less agreed & Concluded upon by & between the sayd partys to these presents, and It is the true intent & meaneing of these Presents, that if the aboue named Walter Gindall his heyres administrators, executors or Assignes or either of them, shall & do well & truely pay, or cause to bee payd vnto the sd Bartholmew Gydney his heyres executors, administrators or Assignes, the full and iust sume of one hundred and Tenn pounds of Current money of New England, in manner & forme following (that is to say) finety pounds there of on or before ye last day of July which shall bee Anno Dom̃ : one thousand six hundred eighty eighty too, and the full & iust some of sixty pounds more thereof, on or before the last day of July which shall bee Anno Dom̃ : 1683 · one thousand six hundred eighty & three, being the full remajnder of the sayd sume of one hundred tenn pounds, that then this Present Indenture sale & grant & euery Claime & particle there in, shall cease determine, bee uoyd and of none æffect, this Indenture, or any thing there in Contajned to the Contrary there of in any wise Notwithstanding/ In witness w^{r}of the sayd Walter Gyndall and Joane his wife, haue here unto set y^r hands & scales, the day & yeare first aboue wiitten/ Walter Gyndall (Locus Sigilli)
Signed sealed & deliuered by the
aboue named Walter Gyndall, Boston in New England/

In the Presence of us/   This Instrument was acknowl-
John Hayward/ Scrĩ   edged by the aboue named
Eliezer Moody Sci^{ty} Walter Gyndall as his Act
                                              & Deede the 12th of July
                                              1681 : before mee
                                              Tho : Damforth President :

BOOK III, FOL. 110, 111.

vera Copia of this Indenture aboue written transcribed out of the originall & there with Compared, this 24th day of May 1682: p Edw: Rishworth Re Cor

Lett all men know by these Presents, that I Nicholas Hodgsden of the Town of Kittery in the prouince of Mayne, togeather by & with the Consent of Elizabeth my now wife, as well for & in Consideration of the summe of Tenn pounds Cur- pay in new England, as also for diuerse other good causes & Considerations, the sd [111] Nicholas there unto espetially moueing, the sd tenn pounds in hand payd mee before the Insealeing here of, the receipt whereof I the sd Nicholas do hereby acknowledg to haue receiued, of Timothy Hodgsden my sonn, & yrof & of euery part yrof do hereby acquitt him the sd Tymothy, his heyres executors & Admini-strators for euer: Haue giuen, granted, sould, Infeoffed, & Confirmed, & by these Presents, do giue grant sell Infeoffe & Confirme unto the sd Tymothy Hodgsden my sonn, all them too tracts of Land that I heretofore purchased of one Peter Wittum of Kittery, being by Estimation the one fourty acres & the other two Acres bee It more or less, as by the too seuerall Deeds under his hand & seale beareing date the seauenteenth day of Septembr 1673 · more at large doth appeare, bounded butting upon the land of the sd Nicholas, & on Miles Tompsons Land on the West end, & runneth backe unto the rocky Hills on the East, & adiouneing unto John Morralls land on the North, & the Commans on the South, which parcell or Tract of Land being upland & swampe Contayning fourty two acres, as aboue with all ye benefitts, & priuiledges there unto belonging, hee the sd Tymothy Hodgsden is to haue & to' hould from the day of the date of these Presents, to & for him selfe, his heyres & Assignes for euer, for his & theire owne proper uss & behoofe: And sd chart. N l L Hodgsden for him selfe his heyres, executors, & Administrators, do further Couenant & promiss, to & with the sd Tymothy his heyres, executors, Administrators & Assignes, y^t hee ye sd Tymothy his heyres & Assignes shall or may quietly & peaceably haue hould & Inioy the sd Land as aforesd, with out the Lawfull Lett sujte or putting off him the sd Nicholas or Elizabeth his wife, his or theire heyres executors, administrators or Assignes, or any other person or Persons whatsoeuer, lawfully Claiming the sd Land, or any part or parcell thereof: In witness here of I the sd Nicholas Hodgsden, & Elizabeth my wife, haue hereunto set our hands & seales, euon ye Twenteth day of Febru : In the yeare of o^r Ld god sixteene hundred seauenty nine/ The marke of Nicolas

Sealed & deliuered in the   Hodgsden ⱧH (his seale)
p^rsence of us/
Bennonie Hodgsden/   The marke of Elizabeth
The marke of Nathan   Hodgsden E (his seale)
Lawde Junio^r X
Andrew Searle/   This Deed of sayle was acknowledgd by Nicholas Hodsden & Elizabeth his wife, to bee thejr free act & Deede this 10th day of March 1679 : in Kittery, before mee/ John Wincoll

           Assotiate/

vera Copia of y^s deede transcribed out of the originall, & there with Compard this 27th 1682 : as Attests/

           Edw : Rishworth Re : Cor :

Know all men by these Presents, that w^ras Nicholas Hodgsden of the Town of Kittery but now Called Barwicke In the Prouince of Mayne In New England, sould unto mee Tymothy Hodgsden his sonn, a Certen Tract of Land lijng & being in ye sd Town butted & bounded with the sd Nicholas Hodgsdens & Miles Tompsons lands, on the West & runneth backe to Rocky hill on y⁰ East, & adioyneing to John Morralls Land on the North, & to the Commans on the South, which land was formerly bought of Peter Wittum of the sd Town by sd Nicholas, & is by estimation fourty too Acres bee It more or less, as appeares by the sd Nicholas his Deede, to his sd sonn Thymothy bearcing date the Twēteth day of Febru. sixteen hundred seauenty nine. Now know all men by these p'sents, that I sd Tymothy Hodgsden, In Consideration of Twelue pounds tenn shillings payd, or secured to bee payd in Current Moneys of New England, before the signeing sealeing & deliuery here of, Haue absolutely giuen grāted bargained sould aliend Infeoffed & Confirmed, & by these Presents do absolutely giue grant bargane sell aliene Infeoff & Confirme, all the abouesd land butted & bounded as abouesd, unto my brother Bennouje Hodgsden of the sd Town, hee the sd Bennony Hodgsden from y⁰ day of the date here of; To haue & to hould all the Land beforesd, to him his heyres & Assignes for euer, togeather with all priuiledges giants, and appurtenances w'soeuer, there to belonging And hee y⁰ sd Tymothy Hodgsden doth hereby Couenant, & promiss y' at y⁰ signeing sealeing & deliuery here of, he is the true & proper owner of all the Land barganed & sould as aboue, & hee hath in him selfe full pouer right & authority to alienate y⁰ same from him selfe his heyres & Assignes to the sd Bennonje Hodgsden, his heyres executors administrators & Assignes for euer, & that y⁰ sd land is free from all Incomberances w'soeuer, & that y⁰ sd Bennome his heyres & assignes shall & may Inioy the Land as abouesd quietly & peaceably, with out any let or hinderance from the sd Tymothy, or any other P'son lawfully clajmeing y⁰ sd land or any part y'of, In witness w'of I the

Book III, Fol. 111.

sd Tymothy Hodgsden haue here unto set my hand & seale, this third day of Aprill 1682 :   Tymothy Hodgsden ($^{his}_{seale}$)
Signed sealed & deliuerd

 in the Presence of us/ Tymothy Hodgsden Came & ac-
 John Forgisson/   knowledged this aboue written
 Charles Frost/   Instrument to bee his act &
          deede, this 3d of Aprill : 1682 :
          before mee Charles Frost
              Just^s pe :
vera Copia of this Instrument transcribed & Compared with ye originall this 30th day of May 1682 .

        p Edw : Rishworth ReCor :

p these Presents, I Aylce Shapleigh of Kittery in the Prouince of Mayne in New England, Administratrix to the Estate of Major Nicho : Shapleigh her husband deceased, do acknowledg to haue receiued full satisfaction of y^t Morgage of Land, made by Antiphas Mauericke to Moses Mauericke, & Assined to my deceased husband, by sd Moses Mauericke aforesd, of Stephen Paul & Edw : Gillman Administrators & heyres to the sd Antipas Mauericks estate, of whome I haue receiued full satisfaction for the Premisses, & do fully acquitt & discharge the sd Persons from all matters w^{t}soeuer, which may or do Concerne sd Morgage, as witness my hand this 7th day of June 1682 :

          Ailce Shapleigh/

     Ailce Shapleigh came before mee this 7th of
The Morgage re- June : 1682 : & owned this Instre^t to bee her
lateing to y^t re-
ceipt Entred in Act & deede/ Edw : Rishworth Just^s pe :
this booke
pa 109. A true Coppy transcribed & Compared with originall this 20th of June 1682 :

       p Edw : Rishworth Re · Cor :

BOOK III, FOL. 111, 112.

Witnesseth these Presents that I Stephen Paul of Kittery in the Prouince of Mayne shippwright, & Catterine wife of Stephen, & Edw: Gillman of Ecceter in the Prouince of New Hampshyre yeamon, & Abigaile wife of sd Edward for & in Consideration of the some of fourty pounds New England money by Allexander Dennet in hand payd, before the signeing sealeing & deliuery here of well & truely payd, the receipt w^{r}of, Wee sayd Stephen & Catterine Paul, Edw · & Abigayle Gillman, & euery & each of us do acknowledg our selues to bee fully Contented & satisfyd, & payd, & y^{r}of & euery part & parcell y^{r}of, do fully Clearely & absolutely acquitt exonerate & discharge the sayd Allexander Dennitt his heyres executors & Administrators &c · Haue giuen barganed, sould, aliend Enfeoffed & Confirmed, & by these Presents do giue grant bargan sell aliene, enfeoffe & Confirme [112] unto sd Allexander his heyres executors administrators & Assignes for euer, forty ^{40} Acres of Land which was our deceased fathers Antipas Mauericke bought by sayd Mauericke of Edw Smale, & by sayd smale obtajned from Mr Thomas Gorges agent to Mr Thomas Gorges agent to Sir ffardinando Gorges marked & bounded as followth vid^t 30 rodd fronting to ye water side of the Riuer of Pischataqua Southwardly, with ye lands of sd Mauericke on ye Eastwardly part, & on the westwardly with the Land formerly were Ellinghams, & Majo^r Nicho^s Shapleighs, & so to runne backe by the sd thirty rodd breadth bounded on the Easterne, & westerne side as aforesd, into the woods, till sayd fourty Acres bee fully made up, & Compleated togeather, with all woods under woods. Emoluments, benefitts profitts, proceeds, & aduantages there off, & y^{r}from ariseing, growing accrewing, or happening, or which after shall arise, grow accrew & happen unto him ye sayd Allexander, his heyres & Assignes for euer. haue given granted barganed & sould, aliend Enfeoffed & Confirmed as aforesayd, to haue & to hould unto the sd

Book III, Fol. 112.

Allexander, his heyres, executors, administrators, & Assignes for euer, & to his & thejr onely uss benefitt & behoofe, all & singular the here in before granted Premisses with the appurtenances there of & there to belonging, or any wise apprtajneing togeather, with profitts pductions, reuennews increase & Improvements, hereby disclaimeing & acquitting all right, title Interest & Clajme in & unto ye Premisses, from us o^r heyrs & successors & any other Prson or Prsons wch Clajm^g by from or under us either or any of us, our heyrs or Assignes. And sayd Stephen Paul & Catterine his wife, Edw: Gillman & Abigaile his wife, for them selues euery & each of them, thejr euery & each of thejr heyres, & do Couenant & promiss that y^t sd Allexander, his heyres executors adminstrators & Assignes, shall peaceably & quietly haue hould occupy uss possess & Injoy all & singular the before mentioned Premisses, togeather with euery part & parcell there of, with out any lett, hinderance, disturbance, Controuersy sujte, action, or trouble, from by or under the sayd Stephen, & Catterine, Edw. & Abigaile, thejr heyres executors, adminstratois or Assignes or any other Prson or Persons Clajmeing p from or under them or either or any of them, thejr either or any of thejr meanes forfiturs or procurements And further the sd Stephen &c. do Assure & Mantajne they stand seized, & in a sure & firme & sound title in fee symple ye which they shall make good against all manner of Prsons lawfully lajng Clajme in or unto the Premisses, & shall make signe seale & deliuer being desired thereto, such further Assurance, or Assurances, as Councill learned in the law, shall reasonably demise aduise or require, at the Prticular Cost & Charges of him the sajd Allexand^r In witness where of, the Partys to these Presents, haue sett y^r hands &

seals this seauenth day of June in the yeare of our Lord, one thousand six hundred eighty too/ · 1682:

Signed sealed & Delineied,   Stephen Paul ($^{his}_{seale}$)
   in the Presence of/   Edw. Gillman ($^{his}_{seal}$)
   William Bickham/   Katherine Paul ($^{her}_{seal}$)
   John Shapleigh/
      Stephen Paul Edw: Gillman   her marke K
      Katherine Paul & Abigall
      Gillman Came before mee   Abigayl A Gillman
      this: 7th day of June 1682:   her marke ($^{her}_{seale}$)
      & did acknowledg this Instrument
      aboue written to bee y^r Act & Deed/
        Edw · Rishworth Just pe:

A true Coppy of this Instrument aboue written transcribed & with originall Compard this 20th day of June 1682:
           p Edw. Rishworth Re: Cor:

   To all Christen people to whom these Presents shall Come/ Know yee y^t I Jonathan Mendum now of Kittery, for Certen good Causes & ualewable Considerations moueing mee there unto, & for & in Consideration of too oxen & one Cow already receiued, of Nicholas weekes of the aforesd Town of Kittery, w^{r}of & where with I own my selfe togeather with my father Robert Mendum to bee fully satisfyd, & Contented for a Parcell of Land, which I togeather with the Consent of my father abouesd haue barganed sould, & deliuered unto the aforesd Weekes, which sd land is bounded as followeth, on the East side of Spruse Cricke begining in at Martyns Coue, at a stonny brooke runneing vp into the Woods so fare as the sd Mendums Land runneth East & by North, & more ouer to runn from the sd Martins Coue by the water side unto John Phœnix his bounds, & from thence to runne vp into the woods North East so fare as the sd phœnix his land runneth /

Book III, Fol. 112.

To haue & to hould the aforesd Land with its app'rtenances, & euery part y'rof unto y'e sayd Weekes, his heyres executors administratoıs & Assignes, freely peaceably & quietly as his & y'r own propeı land for euer: with out any lett or deniall of us, or heyres executors Administratоrs or Assignes or any of us, with warrantees against all people for euer by these Presents; unto the Confirmation of all which, wee do here unto set our hands & seales this one & twenteth day of May, one thousand six hundred eighty one/ 1681:

Signed sealed & deliuered   Jonathan Mendum (his seal)
in Presence of us/   Jonathan Mendum came and ac-
                   knowledged the aboue wıitten
                   Instrument or deede of sale to
                   bee his free act & Deed May:
                   21th 1681: before mee Richd
                   Maı tyn, of y'e Councill of New
                   Hampshire/

A tıue Coppy of this Instrument aboue written, transcribed & Compared with the originall this 20th day of June 1682·   p Edw. Rishworth Re. Coı.

James Grant w't Assistance Hene: Sayword doth want in drawing Tymber, do you further him in/ If hee do not pay you I will/ god Assisting with my loue remembred remayne/ Boston 30th of Septembr 1662/   your freind Tho: Clarke

A true Coppy transcribed & Compared with originall this 20th June 1682.   p Edw. Rishworth ReCor:

James Grant I haue sent you by Mary Donell three pounds sixteen shillings, full of your money part, as fare as I k... bee more due to you I will pay it wn

Boston. 6. of July· 62:   you
                          Tho.....

Book III, Fol. 112, 113.

A true Coppy so fare as was to bee read in this writeing wch I Conceiue was Capt: Clarkes letter wch was Torne part of it, transcribed & Compar'd this 20th of June 82
p Edw. Rishworth ReCor

Bee It known unto all men by these presents that I John Ross of the Town of Kittery Planter, for seuerall good Causes & Considerations with full satisfaction in hand receiued do acknowledg my selfe to haue sould unto John Bready his heyers & Assignes, for him or them peaceably to possess & inioy for euer, a Tract of Land granted to mee by the Select Towns men of the Town of Kittery lijng & being & adioyneing to Edw· Waymoths Land, neare to Mast Coue as appeareth by a Coppy of a Town record beareing date the Twenty three of Novem^br one thousand six hundred sixty fiue, 1665 I say sould to ye aforesayd Bready, his heyres & Assignes as aforesd, with my dwelling house, & all app'tenances belonging to the afore-ayd Tract of Land, as Woods, trees, waters, & water Courses, as also all fence or fences by mee [113] Erected & Improued, all which I do by these Presents acknowledg mee to haue deliuered to John Bready aforesd, in full & quiet possession, & as witness my hand & seale, this 20th day of June 1672

Signed sealed & deliuered/   The signe of John
In Presence of us/   Ross ┼┼ (his seale)
William Gowen/
Christopher Banfejld/   John Ross acknowledged this Deed, to bee his Act this 26th of June 1673 before mee Richd Waldern Commissio^r/

vera Copia of this Deed transcribed & Compar'd with ye originall this 26th day of June 1682:
p Edw. Rishworth ReCor:

Book III, Fol. 113.

December the 30th 1674:

Mesured & layd out vnto John Bready his grant of fiuety Acres of land, with eleauen acres as Addition to his house lott, being a hundred & two pooles in length East North East, from the Ledg of Rockes, & one hundred poole in breadth south South East, bounded on the North with the Land of Israell Hodgsdon, & on the East with the Commans at the third hill, & on the South & West with the other Comanes, as by the seuerall marked trees; the ouerplus allowed for high ways/   John Wincoll   } surayrs
                        Roger Plaistead }

vera Copia of this Measuration of John Breadys Grant transcribed out of ye originall & yrwith Compaid this 26th day of June 1682 ·   p Edw: Rishworth ReCor:

Articles of agreement made & Concluded, this eighteenth day of July, in the Nineteenth yeare of the Reigne of our most gratious Soueraigne Lord, Charles 2cund by the Grace of god, of England, Scotland, France & Ireland King, Defendr of faith &c: Between Daniell Paul of Kittery in prouince of Mayne in New England of ye one Party, & Stephen his sonn of the other party witnesseth; That ye sd Daniell Paul for & in Consideration of a Maraige forth with to bee solemnizd between the sd Stephen Paul & Cattorine the daughter of Antipas Manericke, haue giuen & granted vnto my sd sonn Stephen after my decease, all my lands, & houseing wrin I now liue, being & lijng & scituate with in the Town of Kittery, aforesd, as likewise all my housebould stuffe, & goods, Moueables & Immoueables wtsoeuer (excepting the Cattle which are, & their Increase to bee for the uss of the house, dureing the Naturall life of the sd Daniell Paul, & afterwards to the uss & behoofe of my sd sonn Stephen) & likewise I do except fiueteen Acres of land, I formerly gaue to my sonn in law Joseph Allcocke, next Adioyneing to the house w^rin hee now liueth In kittery aforesd/ & also I giue unto my sd sonn Stephen, all my other lands within the Town of Kittery aforesd, with the same latitude as aforesd, togeather with all ye priuiledges aduantages, immunitys hærīditaments, & app^rtenances, w^tsoeuer y^run belonging/ to haue & to hould to him the sd Stephen, his heyres, executors, administrators & Assignes for euer, with out any lett hinderance or Molestation, w^tsoeuer, as witness my hand & seale/ Dated in Kittery aforesd, the day & yeare first aboue written/

Memorandum/ It is agreed & Concluded, y^t in Case the sd Stephen do dy without Issew, then the sd Cattreine shall Inioy the sd P^rmisses dureing her naturall life, & then the whoole to bee at ye sd Daniell Pauls disposeing, & his Assignes/

Signed sealed & deliuered/   Daniell Paul (his seale)
  In the Presence of/   This aboue written was acknowl-
  ffrancis Champ^rnoown/   edged by Daniell Paul to bee
  John Shapleigh/   his Act & Deed with his hand
    The marke of   & seale set to it, this 22th of
  Joseph   ℸA   Allcocke/   August : 1672 : before mee
                                    John Wincoll Assōte/

A true Coppy of this instrument aboue written transcribed & Compared with the originall this 27th of June 1682 :
                 p Edw: Rishworth Re: Cor:

To all Christean people to whome this Prsent Deed shall Come/ Elizabeth Haruy Widdow, Relict to Michaell Mitton of Casco alias ffalmouth, in the prouince of Mayne in New England, sendeth Greeteing ; Know yee that ye sd Elizabeth Haruy, for the summe of Twenty shillings in hand receiued of Richard Powsland, now of Casco, alias Falmouth Panter within the sd prouince, of Mayne in New England, & do absolutely fully & freely for her my heyres, executors &

Book III, Fol. 113.

Assignes acquitt, & for euer discharge the sayd Richd Powsland, his heyres, executors administrators, & assignes: hath & do hereby fully freely clearely & absolutely giue grant bargan sell, aliene, Enfeoff Conuay, & Confirme unto Richd Powsland, his heyrs executors, administrators, & Assignes, foure Acres of vpland lijng on the North side of Cascoe riuer vpon that Necke of land, Comanly Called Mr Munioys Necke, being butted, & bounded on ye sd Riuer Southwardly, & adioyneing to ye Land of Leef^t Anthony Bracketts land Eastwardly, & butting of the Land of Elizabeth Clark & Spencers Westearly, & so to runne vp into the woods North West untill ye foure Acres bee fully Compleated. & ended, with all trees, woods, underwoods Mines Mineralls, profetts priuiledges, lybertys, easements & all other appurtenances to the p'misses belonging, or in any wise app'taineing, To haue & to hould to him sd Richd Powsland, his heyres executors administrators & Assigns, to his & y^r soole & proper uss, & behoofe, from henceforth & for euer : & the sd Elizabeth Haruy, for her selfe, her heyres, executors administrators & Assigns, do Couenant & Grant, to & with the sd Richard Powsland his heyres, executors Administrators & Assignes, that shee the sd Elizabeth Haruy is the true & proper owner of the aboue barganed Premisses, & haue in her selfe full pouer good right & lawfull authority the Premisses to giue grant, sell Convay & Confirme unto ye sd Richd Pousland, his heyres executors, administrators, & Assignes, in manner as aforesd, & that the sd Premisses, & appurtenances are at ye sealeing & deliuery hereof, are free & Cleare acquitted & discharged of & from all manner of former Gyfts Grants barganes sales, leases Morgages Joynters, Dowers, Judgm^{ts}, executions, will Intayles forfiturs, seizurs, titles, troubles, & all other Acts alienations incumberances w^tsoeuer had made or done, or suffered to bee done, by mee or any other Pison or Persons from by or under mee, & the sd Richd Powsland shall & may for euer hereafter for euer peaceably & quietly haue hould, vsse, occupy, possess, &

Book III, Fol. 113, 114.

Inioy all & singular the afore barganed Premisses, & appurtenances, with out the lett trouble hinderance, molestation or disturbance of mee the sd Elizabeth Haruy, my heyres executors, administrators & Assignes, or any of them or of any other Pison Clajmeing a right thereto or any part y^rof from by or under mee & ye P^rmisses against her selfe & euery other Prson lawfully Clajmeing a right y^rto unto the sayd Richard Powsland his heyres, executors Administrators & Assignes, shall warrant & euer defend by these Presents, & the sayd Elizabeth Haruy do further Couenant, & promiss that at any tyme hereafter vpon the reasonable request & demand, of the sd Richd Powsley to do [114] any further act, or other thing that may bee for the better secureing of the Premisses to him or his, according to the true meaneing & intent of the Premisses/

In witness w^runto I haue hereunto sett my hand & seale, this secund day of Decemb^r one thousand six hundred eighty one, & in the thirty third yeare of ye Reigne of our Soueraign Lord Charles the secund, by the Grace of god of England Scotland &c · King Defend^r of the faith 1681 :

Signed sealed & deliuered/   The marke (of
In the Presence of/   Elizabeth Harvy (her seale)

Taddeous *TC* Clarke/   Taddeous Clarke made oath y^t
his marke/   hee see Elizabeth Haruy,
George Pearson/   sign seale & deliuer the
with in Instrument unto
Richd Powsley, And Geo:
Ingersall & Taddeous
Clarke made oath y^t Elizabeth Haruy deliuered possession of the with in mentioned land by turff & Twig
to Richd Powsley/ taken
vpon oath this 24th of Decemb^r 1681 : before mee
Edw King Just of pe:

BOOK III, FOL. 114.

Elizabeth Harny owned the with in Instrument to bee her Act & Deed for the vss of Richd Powsley, this 30th of Decemb^r 1681 : before mee Edw : Tyng Just pe ·

A true Coppy of this Instrument aboue written transcribed, & with ye originall Compared this 29th June 1682.

p Edw . Rishworth Re : Cor :

Know all men by these Presents, that I Thomas Mayhew of Martins Vineyard M^{r}chant, & Jayne my wife, for & Consideration of the sume of thirty pounds Sterling, Money, to us in hand well & truely payd, by Peter Oliuer of Boston in New England M^{r}chant, the receipt w^{r}of wee acknowledg : Haue given granted, barganed sould Assign, set ouer Enfeoffed & Confirmed, & do by these Psents bargan, sell, Assign set ouer Enfeoff & Confirme unto him the sd Peter Oliuer, his heyres executors, administrators & Assignes for euer, one full quarter part of the greatest Ysland of Elizabeth Yslands, begining at the Western end, Called by the Indeans Katamiwick, being about eight Miles long, lijng Northward from Martynes Vineyard, & Southward from Monument Bay, being bought & purchased by us of Quajaceset Sachem of Monument, & also of Quaquaquijott a great Sachime vpon ye Mayne neare Pacanuakicke . To haue and to hould, the aforesd quarter part of the sd Ysland, with one full quarter part of all & singular the Meddows vplands, tymber trees, priuiledges benefitts & benefitts, & accommodations y^{r}unto belonging, or in any wise from thence to bee had made or raysed, unto him the sd Peter Oliuer his heyres executors, administrators & Assig̃ & to his & thejre proper uss & behoofe for euer : And I the sd Thomas Mayhew & Jayne my wife, do for us & either of us, our & either of o^r heyres executors & Administrators, Couenant, promiss, grant & agree, to & with the sd Peter Oliuer his heyres, executors, Administrators & Assigns, y^t Wee befor the En-

Book III, Fol. 114.

sealeing & deluery here of, are true owners & Proprietors of the afore barganed quarter part, of the sayd Ysland, & haue in our selues, full pouer, right, and authority, to sell & dispose of the same, & that ye afore barganed Premisses, are not onely free & Cleare, & freely & Clearly acquitted, exonerated, & discharged of for & from all former & other barganes, sales, gyts grants, titles. Dowrers Morgages, leases, or Incomberances w'soeuer but shall & will defend & mantaine, & keepe harmeless ye same against any Person or Persons whatsoeuer, clajmeing or demanding the same; or any part or percell there of, by from or under us/ In witness w^rof wee haue here unto sett our hands, & seales this Twenty seauenth day of Septem^br one thousand six hundred sixty & six, & in the eighteenth yeare of ye Reign of our Soueraign Ld Charles the secund, by the grace of god, of England, Scotland, France, & Ireland King: Defend^r of the faith/

Signed sealed & deliuered   Thomas Mayhew (his seale)
in Presence of Jonathan   This Deed acknowledged by
Krympton/ John Oluer/   Mr Thomas Mayhew: 28th
                               7th 66 · at Boston/
                               Richd Bellingham Gouer

vera Copia of this Instrument aboue written transcribed out of ye originall & y^rwith Compared this 5th day of July 1682.   p Edw: Rishworth ReCor

Know all men by these Presents, y^t I Abraham Conley of Kittery in the County of yorke for & in Consideration of fourty shillings to mee in hand payd, by Renold Genkens of ye aforesd Town & County, as also for diuerse other Causes & Considerations, mee y^runto moneing, haue granted, barganed, & sould, & by these Presents do grant bargane, sell & Confirme unto him the sd Renold Ginkens, his heyres or Assignes for euer, too Acres of upland bee it more or less, lijng & being on the North West side of Sturgeon Cricke,

BOOK III, FOL. 114.

being bounded by Capt ffrosts Sault Marsh on the North east side, & so runneing down the sd Cricke as sd Ginkens his fence now goeth/ always prouided y^t sd Ginkens, shall not debarr the sd Conley, or any other y^t shall imoy the sd Conleys Land, y^t is adioyneing y^runto, but shall keepe a peyre of barrs or a gate for conuenient passage to ye Cricke for a Teame of oxen To haue & to hould the sd Land with all ye benefitts y^runto belonging, to him the sd Ginkens his heyres or Assignes, from mee the sd Conley my heyres or assignes, with out any lett or hinderance from mee or any, from by or under mee/ In witness w^rof, I haue here unto set my hand & seale, this third day of March Anno Dom̃: one thousand six hundred seauenty & foure/

Signed sealed & deliuered,
  in Presence of/
  The marke of Adrian
    Fry   A F
  Jos : Hammond/

The marke ∫ of
Abra : Conley/ (his seale)
The aboue written Deed of Sale, was acknowledged by the within named Abra : Conley to bee his act & Deed, with his hand & seale to it, this 4th day of May 1675 . before mee
  John Wincoll Assot̃e .

vera Copia of this Instrument aboue written transcribed & with ye originall Compared this 6th day of July 1682 :
  p Edw : Rishworth Re : Cor :

To his loueing freind Mr Geo. Smyth {

Mr Smyth/ my loue remembred unto you/ you sent to mee If I would Come this Moenth to you, to reckon with you & ballance our Accompts, but my Occasions is so y^t I Can not yet Come, but I would Intreate you to forbeare, till the latter end of ye yeare & then I will come to you with the helpe of god, for

Book III, Fol. 114, 115.

I haue taken a hter to go in till Michellmass, & then I am Cleare of all Ingagements, & then I hope to bee with you, & in the meane tyme, for your security I will putt into yor hands. the house & ground I haue at Kittery, & tenn pounds y^t Thomas ffursonn oweth mee, to bee pd the 5th of June next Come Twelue Moenth, & if you Can Sell the house & ground, keepe the whoole, till I Come to you, or set It to any one whom you see fitting/ & I would Intreate you to make ye writeings for the Conuayances of it ouer to you, & send It to mee by the next that Cometh & I will put my hand to them/ I am to receiue tenn pounds this yeare of Thomas ffurson in pipe staues but I haue sould y^m & I am bound in tenn pounds bond for deliuering of them, which I would Intreat you not to desire them of mee/ as for the Accop^t of M^r JSill you know w^t It is as well as I do know, I had Caryed them all downe if I could haue had them, & I was much damnifyd. because I Could not haue them, but in ye meane tyme you know I was to haue tuety shillings [115] a thousand, & w^t I receiued you Can tell, for you receiued them. & so for y^t Accomp^t I would Intreat you to put it to rights. so I will referr my selfe to you & Capt Wiggins so I rest. desireing god to guide you in all your affavres. & giue you health & a long tyme to liue, remembering my loue to my Maister & Mistress/ with all ye rest, & the rent I haue payd to a penny/ all this Anthony & John Pickerine Can tell/ If they will not pay Nicholas, let y^m make too letters of Atturney & send to mee & I will put my hand to them/ so I remember my loue to Nicholas, & to you all in generall. & so I rest, your loueing friend

        John yougroufe/

 John Yewgroufs letter receiued 19th Aprill 1641:
 vera Copia of this letter aboue written transcribed & Compared with ye originall this 8th day of July 1682.

       p Edw: Rishworth ReCor:

Book III, Fol. 115.

To all people to whome these Presents shall Come/ I George Smyth of Douer sendeth Greeteing, in our Lord God euerlasting; Know yee y^t I the sayd George Smyth for & in Consideration of & for the summe of six pounds thirteen shillings & foure peence, Sterling, well & truely satisfyd & payd at & before the sealeing & deliuery hereof, by Dīness Downeing of Kittery haue barganed granted & sould, & by these Presents do bargane grant & sell unto ye sd Dīniss Downeing all y^t Messuage & tenement In Kittery, w^m the sayd Dinniss now dwelleth, & heretofore in the possession of one John Yougrofe, scituate & being neare to y^t Riuer of Pischataqua, between Watts fort & Frankes ffort, & also thirty Acres of vpland, lijng & being neare to ye sd Messuage or tenement togeather with all profetts Comoditys & priuiledges to ye Premisses belonging, with the appurtenances/ To haue & to hould the sayd Messuage or tenement thirty Acres of Land & other the Premisses, unto the sayd Dinness Downeing his heyres & Assigns for euer; to the uss & behoofe of ye sayd Dinness Downeing, his heyres executors administrators & Assignes for euermore/ In witness where of I haue here unto sett my hand & seale, the eighteenth day of Decemb^r in the yeare of o^r Lord God, one thousand six hundred & fiuety/ 1650 :

Sealed & Deliuered in   George Smyth (his seale)
the Presence of us/   this Deede or writeing is ReCorded
Nicholas Shapleigh/   in the Town booke of Kittery this
John Hall/   29 : December 1653 : by mee
George Branson his   Humphrey Chadborne
      marke 2   Town Clark/
                    A true Coppy of this Instrument
                    transcribed & Compared with y^e
                    originall this 8th day of July 1682 :
                    p Edw : Rishworth Re : Cor :

To all Christian people to whom this Present writeing shall Come, send Greteing/ Know yee y{t} I Dinniss Downeing, of the Town of Kittery in the Prouince of Mayne, in New England bla⁻: Smith, for diuerse good Causes & ualewable Consideiations mee hereunto moueing, & for & in Consideration of the naturall loue & affection which I ow haue & beare unto my onely & well beloued sonn Josua Dow̄ing, & more espetially in Consideration of a Mariage lately solemniz'd, between him & Patience Hatch single woman; Haue giuen & granted unto my sonn Josua, & by these Presents, do freely Clearely & absolutely giue & grant, unto him my sayd sonn, his heyres, executors, administrators, & Assignes, all & singular my goods, wares, househould stuffe, ready money, lands, leases, Chattles, swine, sheepe Implements, & all other things, aliue, or dead, whatsoeuer, as well Moueuables as Immoueables, both reall, & Prsonall whatsoeuer, they bee, & in whose hands & Custody & possession whatsoeuer, the same or any of them, or any part y{r}of, Can or may bee found, remajneing & being as well in the Messuage, & tenement with the app{r}tenances, wherein I now dwell, as in any other place, or house whatsoeuer, within the Dominions of our most gratious Soueraigne Lord, King Chailes; To haue & to hould all the sayd goods, wares, househould, stuffe, ready money, Lands, Leases, Chattles, Implements, & all other the Premisses, unto the sayd Josua Downeing to him, his heyres, or Assignes for euer, next & Immediately, after the decease of mee the sayd Dinniss, but for & dureing the Continewance of my naturall life, the afore mentioned Premisses, to bee possessed, Improued, Imployed, occupied in & for the necessary, & Conuenient Mantenace, sustenance & Accommodations by mee, as formerly, with out any Contradiction of my sayd sonn Josua, or any other from by or und{r} him, dureing my Naturall life, & after my decease, y{e} sd Josua to possess & quietly Inioy the aforesayd Premisses, with euery part & parcill there off: as freely giuen, & Granted by mee the sayd Dinniss/ prouided that my sayd sonn, do giue unto Joanna Downeing Daughter of John Downeing, a Cow & a Calfe, at the day of her Marriage/ to the faitfull acknowledgment & free Consent of ye Premisses, utterly renownceing & denijng any fradulent Instrument, in oposition to ye sd Premisses, or in the hands of whome soeuer: I set my hand & seale this sixteenth day January in the yeare of our Lord, Anno Dom̄ one thousand six hundred seauenty six/

Signed, sealed & Deliuered/   The signe of   ᴅ   (his seale)
   In the Presence of us/
   Phineas Hull/   Dinnis Downeing
   Joseph Hammond/   Dinnis Downeing owned the aboue written Deede of Gyft, with his hand & seale to It, to bee his free Act & Deede, this foureteenth day of June, 1679:
                     before mee John Wincoll
                             Assotiate/

A true Coppy of this Instrument aboue written transcribed & with originall Compared this 11th day of July 1682:
               p Edw: Rishworth Re: Cor:

The Deposition of John Coussons aged 86 yeares, & of Agnis Carter, alias Maddiuer of about 82 yeares, & of Richd Carter of about 37 yeares/

Being examined maketh oath, that to y^r knowledg & remembrance, Richd Carter Senjo^r, who liued in Cascoe Bay, at a place called westgostuggoe, who neare about thirty yeares agone, sould the Interest of his house & Land there, about ye quantity of sixty Acres, with garden fejlds fenced in, with all outlands belonging to it, whither of Land or Tymber, & all other app^{r}tenances, vnto John Mayne, which house & Land the sd Carter had diuerse yeares liued on & possessed, lijng vpon the Poynt on ye westerne side of y^t

Book III, Fol. 115, 116.

Riuer, Westgostuggo riuer being in the Middle of Casco Bay, where sd John Mayne afterwards hued & quietly possessed the sd house & Lands from y^t tyme hee first bought them of Carter abouesd, vntill him selfe & family, with many others were forced out by ye late warrs of the Indeans, about 6 or seauen years agone/ & further these Deponents do remember, that John Mayne had a bill of sale of Richd Carter for sd Land/

Dated 26 · June · 1682.

John Cossons, Agnis Carter, & Richd Carter, Came this day before mee, & did Attest vpon thejr oaths to ye treuth of y^r euidences aboue written/ Edw. Rishworth Just pe:

A true Coppy Coppy of these euidences aboue written, transcribed & with originall Compared this · 17th day of July 1682: p Edw: Rishworth ReCor:

[116] These Presents do witness, that I ffrancis Champernoown of Kittery, in the Prouince of Mayne Esqr, do by these Presents, grant & Confirme vnto Mis Ailce Shapleigh widdow, that if any of y^t Land belonging to y^t farme at or neare braue beate Harbour, which was formerly Mis Godfreys, & now belonging to the sd Mis Shapleigh, do fall with in my pattent, or y^t grant made to my father by Sir ffardi. Gorges. I the sayd ffrancis, do freely Consent & grant, that ye sd Aylce Shapleigh shall freely & peaceably Inioy the same to her, her heyres executors & Assignes for euer, with out the lett or Molestation of mee the sd ffrancis, my heyres, executors, administrators or Assignes for euer/ Witness my hand this nine & twenteth day of June one thousand six hundred eighty too/ 1682:   ffran: Champernoown/

Capt Francis Champernoown Came before mee, this 29th day of June: 1682. & did acknowledg this Instrument to bee his Act & Deede, John Dauess Dep^{ty} President/

Book III, Fol. 116.

A true Coppy of this Act or deed aboue written, transcribed & with originall Compared this 17th day of July 1682:
p Edw: Rishworth Re: Cor.

The testimony of Mr Edw: Johnson aged about 89 yeares/
Being examined, maketh oath, that about fourty too, or 43 years agone, hee remembereth that at that tyme, Mis Ann Messant, alias Godfrey. liued with Mr Geo: Burdett, then Minister of Agamenticus, now Called yorke In the Prouince of Mayne, & at that tyme keept sd Burdetts house, who had Occasion to borrow, of sd Ann Godfrey a certen Prcell of Money, amounting to the ualew of seauen scoore pounds, or y^r abouts, which money remajned in the sayd Burdetts hands, for some years before, the sd Burdet left ye Countrey, a little before which tyme, the sd Ann Godfrey began to Consider, how shee should haue her money, w^{t}vpon shee desired some Assurance for security y^{r}of, upon which hee gaue Ann Messant, alias Godfrey afterwards, a writeing Pretending It to bee a Deede for his farme, but had neither Date nor his hand affixed y^{r}unto, as Mr Vines tould her to whom shee shewed It, w^{t}vpon sd Ann Messant as then Calld, requested a better Assurance of the Land of ye sd Burdetts from him, where vpon hee Impoured this Deponent to deliuer unto the aforesd Ann Messant, the Legall possession of his farme, land & Meddows, lijng between Gorgeana as then Called, & braue boate Harbour, in lew of her money, for Which hee ye sd Johnson, by sayd Burdetts order deliuered to her by Turff & Twigg for her satisfaction, which accordingly this Deponent did, & further sayth not/

And Mis Præcilla Johnson aged 65 yeares sayth y^t shee remembreth, that Mr George Burdett sent for her husband, & shee heard him sd Burdet say y^t hee would deliuer his farme & Cattle into his Costody & possession for ye vss of

Book III, Fol. 116.

Ann Messant, in lew of satisfaction for that debt which y⁰ sd Burdet owed vnto her & further sayth not/

These testimonys taken vpon oath this 29th of June 1682:
before mee Edw: Rishworth Justˢ pe:

A true Coppy of these testimonys, transcribed & Compared with yᵉ originall this 17th July 1682

p Edw: Rishworth ReCor:

To all Christian people, to whom these Presents may or shall Come; Now know yee yᵗ I John Hoole, with the free Consent of Elizabeth my wife, now rescident at Spruse Cricke lyng in the Town shipp of Kittery, in the Prouince of Mayne in New England, for diuerse good Causes & Considerations yʳ vnto mee moueing, & more espetially for & in Consideration of the full & iust some of seauenteene pounds to mee in hand already payd, by Edmund Hamon now rescident in Kittery aforesd, ther receipt wʳof, & of euery part & Parcell thereof, I do own & acknowledg my selfe to haue receiued, & there with all, do acknowledg my selfe to bee fully payd, Contented and satisfyd; Do by by these Presents, In behalfe of my selfe, my heyres, executors, admnistrators & Assignes, giue grant, bargan, sell, Infeoffe, & Confirme, & by these Presents haue giuen, granted sould, barganed, Enfeoffed, & Confirmed, from mee, my heyres, executors, Administrators & Assigns, vnto the aforesayd Edmūd Hammons, his heyres, executors, administrators & Assignes for euer, a Certen Tract or Parcell of vpland lyng at Spruse Cricke in yᵉ Town of Kittery aforesd as bounded & layd out Contajneing the full quantity of thirty seauen Acres & an halfe, & about foureteen pooles, being bounded as followeth: vpon a South West lyne, next to Mr Thomas Withers his land, one hundred fiuety nine pooles, & vpon the North West side runneing next adiacent to the sd Withers his land, seauenty fiue pooles & an halfe, & next to my

own Land vidz't sayd John Hooles Land, lijng East & by East, sixty six pooles, & an halfe, & North East & by East one hundred pooles, & vpon an East lyne twenty pooles, all bounded next adioyneing to the sd Hooles lands, with all the profetts, priuiledges, & aduantages thereunto belonging, & or any wise app'rtajneing, from mee my heyres, namely sd John Hoole, my executors, administrators, & Assignes, unto ye before named Edm: Hammons, to haue, & to hould & for euer to inioy quietly, & peaceably, for his own Prticular benefit, & behoofe & vss, to sd Hammons, his heyrs executors administrators & Assigns foreuer; And I the sd John Hoole, do further Couenant & promiss to & with the sayd Hammons, that ye sd land is free & Cleare from all Morgag^s aicres, Intailes, Intanglements, Dowers, Judgm^{ts}, & executions, & all other Intanglements w^{t}soeuer, & do further promise to warrant & defend, the title & Interest of the Premis^s unto the sd Edmund Hamons, his heyres executors administrators & Assignes, from all Prson or Prsons w^{t}soeuer Clajmeing or Prtending any Clajme from, by, or under mee, or any by my procurement, the Lord Proprietors rent (onely excepted) to bee payd to him When Demanded/ In witness w^{r}of, I haue hereunto atixed my hand, & seale, this 26th of July Año: Dom: 1681: being in the Thirty third yeare of the Reigine of o^r soueraign Ld, of England Scotland, France, & Ireland King, Defend^r of the faith one thousand six hundred: 81:   John Hoole ($^{his}_{seale}$)
Signed, sealed, & Deliuer'd

  In Presence of/   John Hoole doth acknowledg this
  Edw: Rishworth   Instrument to bee his free act &
  John Saywoid/   Deede, this 15th day of Janu-
                            ary: 1681: before mee
                                Edw: Rishworth Just pe:

A true Coppy of this Deed or Instrument transcribed out of ye originall & y^{r}with Compar'd this 3d day of August, 1682:
                           p Edw: Rishworth ReCor:

Book III, Fol. 116, 117.

Let all men know by these Presents, that I John Green the Ellder, of the Town of Kittery, & parish of Vnity, In the County of yorke, for & in consideration of the sume of three pounds, Current pay of New England in hand payd, before ye sealeing & deluery hereof, by John Searle my sonn in law of the Town of Kittery afoiesd, & also for other good Causes & Considerations, mee thereunto espetially moueing, haue by & with the Consent & free will of Julian my now wife, giuen, granted, Enfeoffed, alienated, barganed, & sould unto ye sd John Seaile, one lott or tract of Land, which was granted to mee by the Town of Kittery, being by Estimation fiueteene acres, bee It more or less, which was granted by the sd Town as an Addition to a former Grant or lott of Land of mine, sd John Greens, & It is lijng & being between the Land of Thos Abbetts my sonn in law on ye East, & North, or there abouts, & the Land of Daniell Goodine, & my own home lott, on the South, & West, upon which aforesd fiueteen Acres, the sd John Seaile hath lately bujlt an house, & the sd lott is or at least should bee sixty rodds in length & fourty in breadth, bee It more or less, to Compleate the sd fiueteen Acres; To haue & to hould the sd lott, or Tract of Land, unto him the sd John Searle, or his Assign, from hence for euer, in as large & ample manner, to all Constructions, intents, & purposes, as I the sd John Green, & Julian my aforesd wife, Can or may Estate or sell the same: And I the sd John Green, for mee my heyres, executors, administrators, & Assignes, do hereby promiss, Couenant, & agree to & with the sd John Seaile his heyres, executors, administrators, & Assignes, & to & with euery & either of them & hee or they, & euery, & either of them, shall from tyme to tyme & at all tymes hereafter dureing the aforesd tearme, quietly, & peaceably, haue, hould, Occupy, possess, & [117] Inioy the aforesd Premisses, with the appurtenances, with out the lawfull lett, suite, Molestation, disturbance, trouble, Interruption, euiction, ... sd John G. . . . . . Julian my aforesd wife, my heyres, executors, administraters, or Assigns, or any other Prson or persons whatsoeuer lawfully Clajmeing the sd Lott of Land, or any Part or Parcell there of; In witness w^r of I the sd John Green, & Julian my wife, haue hereunto set our hands, & seales, euen the Twenteth day of Decemb^r in the Twenty seauenth yeare of the Reign of our Soueraign Ld Charles the second, by the grace of god, of England, Scotland, ffrance, & Ireland King, Defend^r of ye faith &c : In the yeare of our Lord (1675)

Signed, sealed & Deliuered/ John Greene (his seale)
 in the Presence of us/   (her seale)
Andrew Searle Senio^r/ The within named John Greene
The marke of ⟨H⟩ Senjo^r, did acknowledg ye with
Nicholas Jellison written Deed of Sale with
      his hand & seale to it, to bee
      his Act, & Deed, this 12th
      day of June 1676. before
      mee John Wincoll
        Assotiate/

The with in named Julian, wife to ye abouesd John Green did freely acknowledg her Consent to ye act of her sd husband in the Deede of sale, & did declare her willingness that ye with in named John Searle, should Inioy the Land y^r in sould to him/ Dated 12th June 1676 : before mee John Wincoll Assōte/

A true Coppy of this Deede, or Instrument aboue written transcribed & with originall Compared the 30th day of August 1682. p Edw: Rishworth Re· Cor·

This Instrument made the Twenty first of May, In the yeare of our Ld one thousand six hundred seauenty foure, between William Palmer of Kittery in the County of Yorke, planter on the one part, and Peter Glanefejld of Portsmo^th In the County of Portsmouth & Douer Taylo^r, on the other part, witnesseth, that the sd Palmer for & in Consideration of six the sume of pounds receiued, In lawfull money of New England, before the Insealeing, & deliuery of these Presents, well & truely payd the receipt w^r of the sd Palmer doth acknowledg, & him selfe to bee fully satisfyd Content, & payd, & there of, & of euery part & penny there of, do acquit exonerate & dischaige, sayd Glanefejld, his heyres, executors, administratois, & Assignes for euer by these Presents, as also for diuerse other good Causes & Considerations, him the sd Palmer there unto especially moueing, hath given, granted, barganed & sould, ahend Infeoffed, released, deliuered, & Confirmed, And by these Presents doth giue, grant bargan sell, aliene Infeoff, release, deliuer, & Confirme, unto the sd Glanefejld, a peece of Land lijng & being in Kittery, and bounded as followeth; on the Northward side, by the Land of the sayd Glanfejld, formerly bought of the sayd Palmer, runneing out of the woods from an Hemlocke, Cutt on foure sides, to the Riuer, to an ould Redd oake stumpe, fiuety two pooles or y^r abouts, which was the Southermost bounds of the sayd Glanfejlds formerly bought Land, and from the sayd maike at the Riuer side, Twenty foure pooles Southward vpon the side of Riuer to a little Poynt of Land marked with a Hemlocke cutt on too sides, standing vpon the sd Poynt next to ye Riuer, being the South side of a Rocke, called Bass Rocke, and from thence runneth backe agajne to the sd Hemlocke in the woods, Cutt on foure sides, the figure of It being trianguler, and Contajneing foure Acres or y^r abouts, togeather with all woods, underwoods, priuiledges, to and vpon the water, as all profetts & aduantages, benefitts & appurtenances, too & with in the sd boundary and peece of Land belonging: To haue & to hould, the before hereby granted & barganed Premisses, and euery part & Parcell there of with the appurtenances to the sayd Glanefejld, his heyres, executors, administratois & Assignes for euer: And the sayd Palmer for him se... his he... ... ...administrators & Assignes,

Book III, Fol. 117.

doth Couenant, promiss, & grant, to & with the sd Glanefejld his heyres, executors, administrators, & Assignes, and to & with euery of them by these Presents, that all & singular the sd Premisses, with all y^r pfetts benefitts, & aduautages, in & by these Presents, given, granted, barganed and sould, & euery part & Parcell y^{r}of, at the tyme of the Insealeing, & deliuery of these Presents, are & bee, & at all tymes hereafter, shall bee remajne, & Continew, Clearely acquitted, exonerated, discharged, from all manner of former & other barganes, sales, gyfts, grants, leases, Charges, Dowers, titles, troubles, & Incomberances, w^{t}soeuer made Committed suffered, or done, or to bee made, Committed suffered or done by the sd Palmer, his heyres executors, administrators, or Assignes, or by any of them or by any other Prson, or Prsons whatsoeuer, Clajmeing from by or under him, them, or any of them, & shall defend y^e title of the sd land/ In witness w^{r}of, hath to these Presents set his hand & seale the day & yeare first aboue written/

Signed, sealed &	William Palmer ($^{his}_{seale}$)
deliuered, in the	Great Ysland 23 · June 1674 : William
Presence of Elyas	Palmer Came & acknowledged this
Styleman John	Instrument to bee his free Act &
Pickerine/	Deede, before mee Elyas Styleman
	Commissio^r

A true Coppy of this Instrument transcribed, & with y^e Originall Compared this 11th of Septemb^r : 1682 :

p Edw : Rishworth ReCor :

To all Christian people to whome this Present writeing shall Come/ to bee seene. read, or heard; Know yee y^t I Samuell Knight, dwelling in Kittery, with in the prouince of Mayne In New England, & Am̃e my wife sendeth greeteing, in our Ld god Euerlasting : Know yee y^t Wee the sayd Sam̃uell & Ammie Knight, for & in Consideration of the summe of Eighteen pounds in hand payd, by Peter Glanefejld of Portsmouth [118] in the Prouince of New Hampshyre, in New England, w^rwith I acknowledg my selfe to bee fully satisfyd, of the whoole, & euery pait y^rof, Haue given, granted, baiganed, sould, enfeoffed, & Confirmed to Peter Glanefejld, to him, his heyres, executors, administrators, & Assignes for euer/ To haue and to hould a Prcell of vpland, Contajneing about Twelue Acres, scituate lijng & being, vpon Kittery side In the Riuei of Pischataqua, bounded with the Land of Thomas Spinney on the North, and ye Land of William Palmer formerly, now in the possession of Peter Glanefejld, on the South vpon a Cricke y^t runnes into Land on Kittery side, which Land is the halfe of about twenty foure Acres, which was sould by Joseph Allcocke formerly to Christopher Joyse, & Edw: Clarke deceased, which Land was diuided between sd Joyse, & Clarke, which Land of Joyses lyeth between the Land of the aforesd Spinnie on the North side, & this Land now premised, Which sd Land was settled by a Court held at Poitsmouth, And ye Court ordered, & settled vpon ye relict of the sd Edw: Clarke deceased, Now Mary Smyth, the wife of John Smyth, the sd Land being twelue poole bieadth, the one halfe faceing to ye sd Cricke, or y^r abouts, & is about eighteene score rodds backewards, being parted by a fiesh Cricke between the sd Palmer, & sd barganed premisses, which sd Premisses were given & granted to ye sd Joseph Allcocke by the Town of Kittery, as may bee made appeare by the sd Town ReCords reference y^runto being had, togeather with all the appurtenances, houses, ædifices, outhouses, oarchards, gardens backe sid^s ways, water Couises, Comans piiuiledges, profitts, Comoditys, easements and appurtenances, w^tsoeuer to the sd Land, Messuage, & Premisses belonging, or any wise app^rtajneing, & Wee do by these Presents Couenant giant & agree, to & with sd Peter Glanefejld, his heyres & Assignes, & y^t Wee are seized of a good Estate, lawfull & absolute, in fee symple, of & in the sd Land and p^rmisses; And haue full pouer good right, & lawfull authority, to grant bargan, sell, & Conuay the same to Peter Glanefejld, his heyres & Assignes in manner & forme as aforesd, from us, our heyres, executors & administrators, & from the heyres of Edw: Clarke, to him the sd Peter Glanefejld, his heyres, executors, administrators, & Assignes, to haue & to hould for euer, with quiett possession, & peaceable Inioyment: And do promiss & Ingage, to defend the title y^rof, to the sd Peter Glanefejld, hish eyres, executors, administrators & Assignes from any Prson or Prsons w^tsoeuer, laijng lawfull Clajme y^runto with out any let sujte, trouble, deniall, interruption, or disturbance, by us the sayd Samell Knight & Amie his wife, our heyres or Assignes, or of any other Person or Persons, lawfully Clajmeing from by or under us, our heyres or Assignes, or from by or under sd Edw: Clarke, & Mary Smith thejre heyres, or Assignes, or any of us, or them or by ours, or thejr meanes. Consent, act, or procurement; And y^t freely & Clearely haue acquitted, & discharged, or otherwise, from tyme to tyme well & sufficiently saued, & keept harmeless, from all former, & other Gyfts, grants, bargans, sales, leases, Morgages, Joyntures, dowers, Title of Dowers. Statutes, recogniscences, Judgm^ts, executions, vses, Intalements forfitures, fines, Issews of amercements, had made Committed, suffered, or omitted, or done by us the sd Samell Knight or Amie, his wife, our heyres, or Assignes, or any other Person or Persons/ In witness where of Wee the sd Samell Knight & Amie my wife, haue hereunto set our hands & seales, the eight of July one thousand six hundred eighty and too/ It is further agreed

Book III, Fol. 118.

before the Insealeing, & deliuery of these Presents, that Tenn Acres are sould Certen, and Twelue Acres uncerten/

Signed, Sealed & Deliuered	Sam^{ll} Knight ($_{seale}^{his}$)
in Presence of us	Ammie Knight ($_{seale}^{her}$)
Joseph Jewell his	her ✝ Marke
Marke 𝔉	Samell Knight, & Ammie his wife,
John Barsham/	Came before mee at y^e day &
Witness Joⁿ Diament/	date aboue written, & acknowl-
Humfrey Axell/	edged the aboue Instrument to
	bee y^r Act & Deed/
	Tho. Daniell of Councill of the
	prouince of New Hampshire/

A true Coppy of this Instrument aboue written transcribed, & with originall Compared this 12th day of Septemb^r 1682: p Edw: Rishworth ReCor.

Witnesseth these Presents. y^t I Waymouth Lyston of Kittery in the County of yorke, alias Prouince of Mayne, under ye Jurisdiction of ye Massatusetts in New England, fisherman, for diuerse good & ualewable Considerations y^runto mee moueing, & more espetially for seauenteen pounds to mee in hand payd, by Charles Nellson of the Town & County aforesd, fisherman, w^rwith I do acknowledg my selfe to bee fully payd Contented, & satisfyd, haue by these Presents, giuen, granted, sould, bargained Enfeoffed & Confirmed, & do hereby giue grant, sell, bargan Enfeoffe, & Confirme unto ye aforesd Charles Nellson, his heyres, executors administrators & Assigns for euer, a Certen Tract, or Prcell of Land being one moeity or halfe deale of a Certen Parcell of Land, formerly purchased of Joseph Allcocke, between my selfe & Gyllbard Lugg Jointly, whose right I stand now in a Capacity to dispose of, by uertue w^tof I do hereby dispose of, & do from my selfe, my heyres,

executors, administrators, & Assigns giue, grant, bargan
sell, aliene Infeoff & Confirme the one Moeity or the one
halfe of the aforesd Tract of Land, lijng between John
Symons his Lott, on the one side, & Stephen Pauls ground
on the other side, unto the aforesd Charles Nellson, his
heyres, executors, & Assigns for euer: To haue & to hould
the sd Land as bounded, with all the Lybertys, priuiledges,
proffetts, Immunitys, & other app'rtenances, belonging, or
in any wise app'rtajneing to the Premisses; And I do further
Couenant & promiss, to & with ye sd Charles Nellson, that
ye sd Land is free & Cleare from all titles Clajms, Morga^es
[119] Assignements, alienations intanglements, & all other
incomberances w'soeuer/ & further, I my selfe my heyres,
executors, administrators, & Assignes, do by these Presents
stand bound, to defend & warrant the Interest & Title y^rof
unto all Prson or Prsons w'soeuer, Clajmeing any right or title
y^runto, from by or under mee/ In witness w^rof, I haue hereunto set my hand & seale this eight day of July Anno Dom:
1675. & this is done by the free Consent of Martha the wife
of y^e aforesd Waymouth Lyston/

Signed sealed & deliuered/ Waymouth Lyston ($^{his}_{seale}$)
 in the Presence of/ Waymouth Lyston, & Martha his
 Edw: Rishworth/ wife, do acknowledg this Instru-
 Thomas Spinny/ ment to bee y^r Act & Deed, be-
      fore mee
        Edw: Rishworth Assote/

A true Coppy of this Instrument aboue written, transcribed & Compared with the originall this 28th day of September 1682: p Edw: Rishworth Re: Cor:

Know all men by these Presents, v^t I Allexand^r Maxwell
of yorke of the Prouince of Mayn In New England Planter,
with the free Consent of my wife Annis, vpon good & ualewable Considerations y vnto mee moueing, & more specially,

for & in Consideration of the full & Iust some of sixteen pounds to mee in hand payd, by Robert Junkines of yorke aforesd, the payment hereof I do hereby own & acknowledg, to haue receiued of sd Junkines, y^rwith, & euery part & Parcell y^rof, I do own my selfe to bee fully payd, Contented, & satisfyd; And I the sd Allexand^r Maxwell in the behalfe of my selfe my heyres, executors, administrators, & Assignes, do acquitt & discharge the sd Robert Junkines, his heyres, executors, administrators & Assigns for euer: Haue giuen, granted, barganed, sould, Enfeoffed, & Confirmed, & do by these Presents, giue, grant, bargan, sell, Enfeoff & Confirme from mee my heyres, executors, administrators, & Assignes, a Certen Tract & Parcell of vpland, the bounds w^rof begining at the Prtition fence, neare vnto James Grants Spring of Water, ljing & being twenty pooles in breadth, upon the vpper side of the path goeing to Newgewanacke, & runneing baCke into the woods in length so fare in distance as Allexanders Maxwells Land goeth, towards bass Coue brooke, & also a little shpp or Prcell of Land, w^r now the sd Junkines his Oarchard is plan . . . & his barne now standeth, running backe as high as a Certen Rocke: prouided always the sd Robert Junkines, is to mantaine a sufficient Prtition fence, between Allexand^r Maxwell & him selfe, dureing the full tearme of sd Maxwells life: To haue & to hould the sd Tracts of Land, as aboue bounded with all the profetts, libertys, priuiledges, Comans, Easem^ts Woods und^r-woods, with all & singular ye app^rtenances, in any wise belonging or app^rtajneing, from mee my heyres, executors Administrators & Assigns, to sd Robert Junkines his heyrs, administrators & Assigns for euer And sd Allexd^r Maxwell doth hereby own him selfe, to bee ye true & lawfull owner of the aboue named Premisses, & that hee hath in him selfe, full right, pouer & authority, to sell, & make good sale of sd Land, & that it is free & Cleare from all Morgages, Dowers, titles, troubles, Judgm^ts alienations, executions, & all other · · · · · aunt &

promiss In behalfe of my heyres & Assignes, to warrant, &
defend the Title & Interest of sd Land, vnto the aforenamed
Robert Junkines, his heyres & Assigns for euer: from all
Prson or Persons w'soeuer Clajmeing, or Pretending any
Clajme title or Interest y'unto, from by or under mee, or
any other by my procurement/ In testimony w'of, I haue
hereunto afixed my hand & Seale, this Thyrty secund yeare
of o' Souerigin Ld Charles the secund of England, Scotland,
France, & Ireland King, ffidei defensoris: the 24th of
March 168¾   Allexander Maxwell (his seale)
Signed sealed & deliuer'd   his **2** marke
in the Presence of/

Edw: Rishworth   Allexander Maxwell & Annas his wife
Tho Harriss his   do own this Instrument aboue writ-
   marke Q   ten to bee y' Act & Deed this 10th
              day of June 1681: before mee
              Edw: Rishworth Jus: pe·

A true Coppy of this Deed or Instrument aboue written,
transcribed out of y⁰ Originall & y'with Compared this 23th
of Octob' 1682.   p Edw: Rishworth Jus. pe:

Know all men by these Presents, y' I Thomas Onyon of
Portsmouth in New England fisherman, for & in Consideration of fiueteen pounds to mee in hand payd before the
Ensealeing & deliuery hereof, haue given granted, barganed
& sould, & do by these Presents, giue grant bargane & Sell,
unto Gabriell Tetherley of Kittery in Pischataqua Riuer, one
dwelling house with Twenty Acres of Land, bee It more or
less scituate & being, between the Land of Christean Ramacke
on the South, & the Land of Daniell Paul on the North, in
Kittery near unto the Boyleing Rocke, with all the priuiledges & appurtenances y'unto belonging, all which Premisses, I the sd Thomas Onyon do acknowledg to bee barganed & sold unto the sd Gabriell Tetherley his heyres

executors & Assigns for euer, & do hereby promiss, to defend ye title y^rof, against all manner of Prsons w^tsoeuer, from by or under mee, Laijng Clajme to the same: And hereunto I the sd Thomas Onyon, bind mee mine heyres, executors Administrators/ In witness w^rof haue here unto set my hand, & seale this first day of May, one thousand six hundred & sixty/
Sealed & deliuered/
in Presence of us
Witnesses/
this 8th of June 1660/
Phillip Babb/
his marke 𝒫
Richard Pomrey/

Thomas Onyon
his marke 𝐼 𝐸 (his seale)
The signe of Margerett
Onyon ⊖

A true Coppy of this Instrum^t transcribed & with the originall Compared this 6th day of Novemb^r 1682 ·
p Edw: Rishworth ReCor:

Know all men by these Presents that I Daniell King of Kittery In the Prouince of Mayne, In the County of Yorke shipp Carpenter, for & in Consideration of fiue pounds sterlg: receiued of Gabriell Tetherley of the same Town, to full Content & satisfaction, haue giuen, granted barganed sould, Enfeoffed & Confirmed, & I do by these Presents giue grant [120] Sell Enfeoff, & Confirme, unto the aforesd Gabriell Tetherley, a Certen Tract of Land scituate & being in the Town of Kittery, aforesd. Contayneing Thirty Too Rodds, in length, & sixteene Rodds in breadth, & bounded on the South East with land of ye sd Gabriell, & on the North West with the Land of sd Daniell King, & on the South West with the great River of Pischataqua, & on the North East with a small sault water Cricke, & the Land of the sd Daniell King Which Parcell of Land was formerly part of a grant of Land made by the Toun of Kittery unto ye sd Daniell .... sould into ye sayd Gabriell Tetherley; To haue & to hould all the aboue barganed Premisses, with all the appurtenances & priuiledges, with all the appurtenances & priuiledges, there unto belonging unto the sd Gabriell Tetherly, his heyrs, executors, administrators & Assigns for euer, the same to defend against all manner of Prsons w'soeuer, Clajmeing any lawfull right title or Interest, in the aboue barganed Premisses, or any part or Parcell thereof by from or under mee, & for Confirmation of the treuth here of, I the abouesd Daniell King, haue hereunto set my hand & seale this seauenth day of May, in the yeare of o'r Lord one thousand six hundred seauenty foure/   Daniell King (his seale)

Signed sealed, & deliuer'd,

in Presence of us/   The aboue written Deed of Sale was
John Wincoll/   acknowledged by ye within Named
Christean Remaih/   Daniell King to bee his free Act
                      & Deede, May 7th 1674: before
                      mee John Wincoll Assotiate

A true Coppy of this Deed aboue written transcribed & Compared with ye originall this 6th of Novembr 1682·

                            p Edw: Rishworth ReCor:

ffalmouth the 28th Septembr 1682:

Leeft Geo· Ingersoll & Deniss Moroth being Chosen apprisers of a Parcell of Land & Marsh, belonging formerly to Nath Mitten, Judg ye Land to bee foure scoore Ackers, & ye March three acres/ & the ualew of the land & Marsh to bee Thyrty too pounds/ Taken vpon oath the 28th of Septembr 1682: before mee Edw: Tyng Justs pe:

A true Coppy of this apprisall transcribed & Compared with originall this 6th of Novebr 1682:

                            p Edw: Rishworth ReCor:

BOOK III, FOL. 120.

Granted & giuen unto Nath^{ll} Maysterson Thyrty Acres of vpland, being a Prcell of Land which hee hath fenced in, adioyneing & neare to his house, part w^rof hee hath made vss of seuerall yeares/ In witness w^rof, Wee haue here unto sett our hands Janvary sixteenth one thousand six hundred
& seaventy/   Edw Rishworth/
vera Copia transcribed & Compared   Edw : Johnson/
  with ye origmall this 12th day of   John Allcocke/
  March 168⅔   John Dauess/
    p Edw : Rishworth ReCor :   Mathew Austine/

March 10th 1679 :

whereas there was some troubles like to arise between Major Clarke & Mr Rishworth, by reason of John Dauess the Smyths deniyng the Sale of a little Poynt of Land on Mr Gorges Cricke, Where the saw Mills standeth, & vpon Consideration to Preuent any further trouble, Wee the Select men of the Town of Yorke, do Confirme the sd Parcell of Land to Mr Edw : Rishworth, purded y^r bee no former Grant to any other Person/   John Dauess/
vera Copia, of this Confirmation or grant   Richd Bankes/
  transcribed & with originall Compared   John Twisden/
  this 12th day of March 168⅔
    p Edw : Rishworth ReCor :

      Certen Lands granted & layd out by us

These Presents bindeth mee John Smith Senjor, my heyres, executors, Administrators & Assignes, vpon good Considerations mee y^runto Moueing, & more espetially for y^t naturall loue & affection which I beare unto my beloued sonn John Smith Jujo^r do bargan giue & bequeath vnto ye sd John Smith my sonn his heyres & Assignes a Certen

BOOK III, FOL. 120.

Tract & Prcell of vpland, Contajneing the full quantity of six Acres, bounded on the South West side with my new fence, & on the Eastermost side with James Jackesons fence, & so from the little swampe, backe to ẙ great swamp till six Acres bee Compleated, vnto whom ye sd Land I haue barganed & sould & bequeathed the sd six Acres of Land, with all the appurtenances y^{r}vnto belonging to him & his heyres for euer/ as witness my hand & seale this 12th day of October 1674:

                          John Smith   (his seale)

John Smith Senjor owneth this Instru- his Marke J
ment to bee his free act,& Deed to
his sonn John Smith this 12th of October 1674 : before mee

            Edw: Rishworth Assote

A true Coppy of this Instrument transcribed out of ye originall & y^{r}with Compared this 12th day of March 168⅔

                 p Edw: Rishworth ReCor:

Bee It known vnto all men by these Presents, that I John Barrett of the Town of Wells in the Prouince of Mayne in New England, with ye free Consent of Elizabeth my wife, Senerall good Causes & Considerations y^{r}unto moueing & more espetially for & in Consideration of fineteen pounds to mee in hand pd by Samell Austine, Haue from mee my heyrs executors, Administrators & Assigns barganed granted, sould assign'd, Inffeoffed & Confirmed, & by these Presents do giue, grant, bargane sell, Assigne, Infeoff & Confirme, unto Samll Austine of the aforesd Town & prouince, in New England his heyres executors Administrators & Assignes, a Certen Prcell of Marsh, ljng in the Town of Wells, bounded as followeth; Begining at a Certen fence, which parts the sd Marsh from Mr Samll Wheelewrights Land, & so running down to ffran: Littlefejlds Marsh, & a Certen Prcell of Marsh of Will͞m: Webbs, ljing on ye South East side of Jos:

Booles & his on y̆ᵉ Nore West sid wᶜʰ Parcell of Marsh Contajnes about three Acres, with all the pfitts & priviledges yʳᵘⁿto belonging to him the sd Samuell Austine, to haue & to hould for euer/ & I the sd John Barrett do hereby declare, the sd Samell Austine to bee rightly & truely possessed of the sd Prcell of Marsh, & yᵗ yᵉ sd Marsh & euery part of it, is free & Cleare of all gifts, grants, barganes, leases, Dowers Morgages Judgmᵗˢ, or any other Incomberances wᵗsoeuer, & do hereby prmiss & Couenant to & with yᵉ sd Samell Austine, yᵗ I will warrant, & defend yᵉ Title & Interest of the Premisses granted & sould from any Prson or Prsons wᵗsouer, either from by or under mee, & the sd Samuell Austine, his heyrs & successors, shall quietly & peaceably hould & inoy, the sd Marsh & euery part of it, free & Cleare without any matter of Challeinge, Clajme, or Demand, from mee my heyres & successors for euer; In witness wʳᵘⁿto Wee haue set too oʳ hands & seals, this 15ᵗʰ day of Marsh in the yeare of oʳ Lᵈ 168½ :   John Barret (his seale)
Signed sealed & Deluerd/   Elizabeth Barret (her seale)
in Presence of us/   her Marke/ 𝒮
Joseph Storer/
Jonathan Hamonds/ John Barett & Elizabeth Barrett did
acknowledg this Instrument to
bee yʳ Act & Deede, this 15th :
of Marsh 168½ before mee
Samell Wheelewright Justˢ pc :

A true Coppy of this Instrument, transcribed with originall Compared this this 28th of March 168⅔

p Edw: Rishworth ReCor:

[121] Know all men by these Presents yᵗ I Samuell Austine haue made ouer sould & Assignd from mee my heyres & Successors, all my right title & Interest of this within Mentioned Marsh, vnto Emanuell Dauess his heyres & Successors for euer, peaceably & quietly to haue hould & inioy, with out any matter of Challenge, Claime or demand

Book III, Fol. 121.

from mee My heyres & successors for euer/ In witness w'unto, I haue set my hand this 15th day of March in y̆ yeare of o' Ld 168½/   Samuell Austin/
Sign'd & deliuer'd,
   in the Presence
   of us/ Jos. Storer/
   Jonathan Hamonds/

A true Coppy of this Assignement transcribed out of the originall & y'with Compared, this 28th day of March 168⅔
                 p Edw: Rishworth ReCor:

Bee It known unto all men by these Presents, y' I Samuell Austine of the Town of Wells in the prouince of Mayn, in New England, for seuerall good Causes & Considerations mee y'unto moueing & more espetially for and in Consideration of eleavn pounds to mee in hand payd & lawfully Assured to bee payd by Emanewell Dauis of y̆ aforesd Town & prouince, in New England, do from mee my heyres, executors & Administrators sell Assigne & make ouer, & by these Presents haue barganed, sould, Assignd & made ouer Infeoffed & Confirmed unto y̆ aboue named Emanuell Dauis his heyres & successors for euer all my right & interest of this wrth in mentioned Tract of Land, to mee granted & bound ouer by Abraham Collmes, to him y̆ sd Emanuell Dauis, his heyres executors administrators & Assignes, with all the appurtenances & priuiledges, y'unto belonging & any wise app'rtaineing, to haue & to hould & peaceably to inioy for euer. with out any matter of Challenge Claime or demand from mee the sd Samell Austine my heyres, & successors for euer, & do here by promiss & Couenant to & with y̆ sd Emanewell Dauess y' I will mantayne & Defend the title & Interest of y̆ aboue mentioned Premisses, from any Prson or Prsons w'souer either from by or under mee, & I do hereby declare the sd Emanuell Dauis, to bee truely & rightly possessed of each & euery part of y̆ Premisses aboue mentioned, & y' the sd Land & euery part of it, are free &

Book III, Fol. 121.

Cleare from all gifts grants barganes leases, dowrys morgages Judgm^ts, or any other Incomberances w^tsoeuer/ In testimony w^rof I the sd Sam̃ll Austine haue set my hand & scale this 15th day of March in the yeare of o^r Ld, Anno: Dom̃: 168¼   Samuell Austine/
In Prsence of us/

Jos. Storer/   Sam̃uell Austine Came before mee this
Jonathan Ham̃onds   26th day of March 1683 : & owned
        this Instrument to bee his Act &
        Deede/ Samuell Wheelewright
            Jus : pe :

A true Coppy of this Instrument aboue written transcribed & with the originall Compared this 28th day of March 1683
      p Edw Rishworth ReCor :

Know all men by these Presents, that I Roger Derent of Kittery, in the prouince of Mayn executor to ye Estate of my father Roger Derent deceased, for diuerse Causes y^runto mee moueing, but more especially the loue & affection I beare unto my loueing brother Clement Deareing, haue freely given & granted, & do by these Presents giue grant & Confirme vnto my sayd brother Clement Dearent, his heyres, executors, Administrators & Assignes, a tract of Land, Containeing Twelue rodd square, in the Town of Kittery, & is with in the bounds of that Land, which formerly did belong unto my father Deareing, deceased & is now in my possession, which Land aforesd is to begin at the further Corner of the Coue, next to John Pearce his Land, & so to runne vp by his bounds twelue rodd, &'from thence for an head line, Twelue Rodd, & then from thence South & by west to a Whitte Oake stumpe by the water side : the lower bounds to runn by the Coue side · To haue & to hould the aforesd Land with all the priuiledges y^runto belonging, to the onely uss & .... executors, Administrators & Assigns for euer: freely peaceably & quietly as his & y' own proper Land for euer, with out any lett or denyall, of mee my heyres, executors, administrators, & Assigns for euer, Onely if my brother or his heyrs shall hereafter thinke meete to dispose of y² abouesd Land, hee or they shall giue mee or mine the first tender of It: vnto which gyft as abouesd, I do hereunto set my hand & seale, this one & Twenteth day of June 1681:

Signed sealed, & deliuered,   Roger Deareing (his seale)
  in the Presence of us/   Roger Derent Came & owned
  Francis Hooke/   ' this Instrum^t to bee his Act &
  Mary Hooke/   Deede, this 21th day of June:
                            1682: before mee
                            Fran^s Hooke Just. peace

A true Coppy of this Instrum^t transcribed, & with the Originall Compared this 5th day of Aprill 1683:
                p Edw: Rishworth ReCor:

Know all men by these Presents y^t I John Bray shipwright liueing in Pischataqua River in the Prouince of Mayn, in New England do acknowledg y^t I haue freely given unto William Pepperell, my sonn in law for euer, one Acre of Land lijng & being, ioyneing to Thos: Langleys Land that now hee possesseth, & to begin from the Wharff at ye water side, giueing lyberty if y^r bee Occasion to make uss of ye Wharff, & so to runne backe leaueing the bujlding Yard, & to runne backe to ye high way, to a plajne place, neare the high way to place his house, & so from ye house backeward to ye Northwards till the acre of Land bee accomplished/

BOOK III, FOL. 121, 122.

In witness here of I haue here unto set my hand & seale, this seauenteenth day of Nouebr 1682 :   John Bray (his seale)
as witnesseth at ye sealing signeing John Bray Came before
  & deliuering, in Prsence of/   mee this 4th day of Aprill
  Dorothy Low/   1683 · & acknowledged
  Joane Derent/   this Instrumt to bee his
                      Act & Deed/ Edw:
                      Rishworth Jus . pe :

A true Coppy of this Instrument, transcribed, & with originall Compared, this 5th day of Aprill 1683

            p Edw . Rishworth ReCor :

Know all men by these Presents, yt I Edw · Rishworth of Yorke, in the prouince of Mayne in New England ReCor: for diuerse good Causes & Considerations yrunto mee moueing, & more espetially for yt tender loue & affection which I beare unto my beloued daughter Mary Sayword wife to John Sayword, togeather with the full & iust some of sixty pounds, & so much rent yearely besids, truely to bee payd to mee or my order, & assigns, according to the manner & Conditions specifyd in a bill & obligation vnder sd Jon Saywords hand made [122] vnto mee beareing date the seauenteenth of October, 1682 : by him sealed, & ye Contents wrof being accordingly dischaiged, wrwith I do acknowledg my selfe fully satisfyd Contented & payd, & hereby for euer acquitt, exonerate & discharge him ye sd John Sayword my sonn in law, his heyres, executors & administrators of all & euery part & Parcell yrof : Haue given, granted sould, alienated, Enfeoffed & Confirmed, & by these Presents, do giue grant bargan, sell aliene, Enfeoff & Confirme vnto sd John Sayword, his heyres, executors, administrators & Assigns, my dwelling house which I now liue in with Thirty foure Acres of vpland swampe & Pasture land, on part wrof the

BOOK III, FOL. 122.

sd house is bujlt, with a small Prcell of sault Marsh adioyneing to it, lijng on ye North East side of y^t Cricke, Called Comanly by ye name of the New Mill Cricke, w^r Hene : Sayword formerly lived, & bujlt those saw Mills yet in being; I do also giue unto my sayd sonn in Law John Sayword all those peeces, & Poynts, & Prcells of Marsh lijng & being on the South West side of that Cricke Comanly Called the ould Mill Cricke, with all the skirts & Coues of sault & bastard Marsh, grass & thatch lijng on ye south West side of ye sd Cricke, running along y^t branch Southwardly so fare as the head of y^t branch doth extend : Which Marsh & thatch, aboue ye parting of y^t Cricke on both sides of sd branch, with a small Prcell of vpland Contajneing about Twenty or 30 Acres bee It more or less, part w^rof was giuen mee by ye Town of Yorke, as by grant appeares Novem^{br} 6 : 1677 : I do further giue & grant unto my sonn in law John Sayword, fiuety Acres of vpland given & granted to mee, by the Select men of Yorke, as appeareth by y^r grant beareing date June 21th 1673 : lijng on ye other side of ye bridg, on ye North East branch of Yorke Riuer, vpon the South side of ye sd branch being part y^rof, a round Hill lijng neare to ye Westward of a Coue Called by ye name of ffrethys Coue/ Which house pasturs Medows, gardens, out houses, with all the profitts priuiledges, & Immunitys, or tymber woods, vnd^rwoods, & all other appurtenances y^runto app^rtajneing, or in any wise belonging, I do by these Presents, from mee my heyres, executors, & administrators giue, grant & Confirme, to sd John Sayword his heyres, executors Administrators & Assigns for euer ; And further ye sd Rishworth doth Couenant & agree to & with ye sd Sayword, y^t the Premisses aboue mentioned are free & Cleare from all barganes, sales, Claimes, Morgages, Dowrys, & all other Incomberances w^tsoeuer (except onely ye Cleareing of y^t Morgage made to John Cutt Esqr deceased) of fourty foure pounds 10^s in Coman pay, at Current prises, with w^t monys & otherwise, my sonn Sayword stands bound by his obligation to pay according to his bill, w^n I or any by my order shall demand it: & further do promiss to defend the Title y^rof, from all Prson or Prsons w'soeuer, Pretending any Title or Clajme, from by or under mee, or in any wise by my procurement: In testimony w^rof I haue here unto afixed my hand & seale, this 16th day of Octob^r 1682:

Signed, sealed & Deluered   Edw: Rishworth (locus sigilli)
  in Presence of/   Mr Edw: Rishworth Came before
  Lydia Euerest/   mee this 16th of Octob^r 1682: &
  her marke ┼   acknowledged this aboue written
  Jonathan Sayword/   Instrument to bee Act & Deede/
                         Samuell Wheelewright Jus: pe:

vera Copia of this Instrume^t aboue written, transcribed, & with Originall Compared this 19th day of Aprill 1683.

                     p Edw: Rishworth ReCor:

These Presents bindeth mee, my heyres & Assignes, Namely John Sayword of Yorke, in the Prouince of Mayn Millwright, y^t in consideration of an hous. vplands & Meddows, & y^r app^rtenances, by mee purchased ot my father in law Edw. Rishworth of sd prouince Re·Cor: according to certen Conditions mentioned, & quantitys & boundarys expressed, in a bill of saile beareing date the 16th of Octob^r 1682: do by these Presents stand Ingaged in the behalfe of my selfe & my Assignes, to pay or Cause to bee payd unto the sd Rishworth or his order, or Assignes, the Just sume of sixty pounds, fourty foure pounds tenn shillings to bee payd in ordinary speties, at Coman prise to ye Estate of John Cutt Esqr deceased, & fiueteene pounds tenn shillings to bee payd in Current New England Money, six or seauen pounds at or vpon demand, & the remajnder y^rof w^n the sd Rishworth or his Assignes hath Occasion for it, after the expiration of one yeare from this Present date; And further I *** selfe &

Book III, Fol. 122.

my Assignes, to pay unto father Rishworth or his order or Assignes, the iust some of six pounds p Ann͠. to bee payd in good M^rchañible pay, boards, prouissions, or such other goods, as his Occasions from tyme to tyme shall require, at Current money prise to bee Deliuered at yorke, at the house of the sd John Sayword which hee bought of ye sd Rishworth his father in law, who by thejr mutuall agreement is to haue ye free uss of ye lower rowme hee now liueth in, so long as his naturall life Contineweth, at his own soole disposeing, as also to haue his horse keept, by sd John Sayword at sd Saywords own proper Charge, for wch I am Ingaged to allow one Loade of English hay, & one loade of sault Marsh hay for his keepeing in ye winter, If hee require it, & It is to bee understood & Intended, y^t John Sayword is to mantajne sd Rishworth his father with Comfortable dyet so long as hee sees good to liue with him, but If hee see good to liue else Where, then so much of ye rent to bee abated as hee is absent from him; & in Case hee Continews with him, the whoole rent to bee acquitted, & is to prouide Convenient fire wood for his rowme as his necessity shall require/ In witness w^rof I haue hereunto sett my hand & seale, this seauenteenth day of Octob^r 1682 :   John Sayword (his seale)

Signed deliuer'd &   John Sayword came before mee this
 sealed in Presence, of   17th of October 1682. & acknowl-
 Jonathan Sayword/   edged this Instrume^t to bee his
 Lydea Euerest her   Act & Deede/
   marke ⊹   Samll Wheelewright Jus: pe:

A true Coppy of this Instrument transcribed & with originall Compared this 19th day of Aprill 1683 :

                    p Edw: Rishworth Re: Cor:

To all people whom this Deed of Gyft, or Instrument may Concerne, or shall Come/ Know yee, y^t I Geo: Parker with the free Consent of Hannah my wife, of the Towne of Yorke

BOOK III, FOL. 122, 123.

In the Prouince of Mayne in New England as well for & in Consideration of that loue Which Wee beare to Peter Bass our sonn in law, as of our own Present weakeness & decrepedness. by reason of our ould age, & daly infirmitys accompanijng the same, w^rby wee are altogeather made uncapable to mañage y^t little Estate Wee haue for our future luelihood The Premisses Considered, Wee haue hereby given, granted, & Confirmed, & do [123] by these Presents, giue grant & Confirme vnto Peter Bass aforesd, freely & absolutely, our soole right, title, & Interest of o^r house houseing & lands where wee now liue, vidz^t o^r home lott, & lotts at home & abroad, vplands meddows gardings, orchards, & Wood Lands, with o^r whoole stocke of Cattle being nine neat Cattle, with all other app^rtenances, y^runto belonging unto o^r sayd Estate, from us o^r heyrs, administrators & Assignes, to ye sd Peter Bass his heyrs executors administrators, & assignes for euer : To haue & to hould all & singular ye Premisses, togeather with all the priuiledges, Comanages & appurtenances, quietly & peaceably to Inioy from us o^r heyres & Assignes to the sd Peter Bass his heyres & Assigns for euer Prouided it is to bee understood, as always was & is intended to bee ye true & honest meaneing of these Presents, y^t vpon the Condition & Consideration of ye Premisses, the sd Peter Bass aboue mentioned, stands hereby firmely Ingag'd hence forward to take all effectuall, & all necessary Care, to make his best Improuem^t of sd Estate, for the Comfortable Mantenance of his father in law Geo. Parker & his mother in law sd Geo Parkers wife, prouideing for y^m necessary foode rayment lodging, sutable tendance & Conuemences. as there Crasie & weake Conditions may require, according to y^r Capacity as ordinarily Can bee expectd from ye frugall Mañagem^t of such an Estate, & this maintenance sd Peter Bass is to giue & allow them, dureing ye tearme of there naturall lifes/ In witness w^runto Wee haue hereunto sett our hands & seales Interchangably, this t   of the reigne, of o^r soueraign L^d of England, Scotland, France, & Ireland, King, fidej Defenso^{rs} Anno : Dom̃ : one thousand six hundred eighty three/ 1683 :

Signed sealed & deliuered/
in the Presence of/
 Richd Bankes his
  marke/ R
 Abia : Preble/

Geo : Parker his
 marke 4 (his seale)
Hannah Parker her
 marke/ H (her seale)
Peter Bass his
 marke P (his seale)

Geo : Parker & Hannah his wife, & Peter Bass do acknowledg this Instrume^t to bee y^r act & deed before mee this 18th of Aprill 1683 : Edw Rishworth

       Jus^t pe :

Peter Bass doth hereby Ingage him selfe to mantajne Elieazer Johnson as his own Child, till hee Come to 21 years of age, & then to giue him a Cow of three or foure years ould, as witness my hand this 18th day of Aprill 1683 :

Signed in ye Presence of/
 Richd Bankes his
  marke/ R
 Abra : Preble/

     Peter Bass his
      marke P

Peter Bass doth acknowledg this Instrument or Ingagem^t abouesd to Eleazer Johnson, to bee his act & Deed, this 18th of Aprill 1683 : before

     Edw Rishworth/ Jus : pe :

A true Coppy of this Instrument aboue written, & of this Ingagem^t made by Peter Bass underwritten, transcribed out of ye originall, & y^{r}with Compared, this 20th day of Aprill 1683 : p Edw . Rishworth Re . Cor

This Deed of gyft witnesseth, y^t I Thomas Spinny of Kittery in the County of Yorkeshire in New England, & Margery his wife, for & in Consideration of the naturall loue, & affection they beare unto John ffurnald, of the same

Town shoemaker, who maried Mary the daughter of the
sd Spinny, his sd wife, & for ye loue & affection, they beare
unto y^r sd daughter Mary, & to her Children, & for y^e
furtheran .. of thejr Comfortable subsistance, haue absolutely giuen, granted, alienated Enfeoffed & Confirmed, &
do by these Presents, for y^m selues, y^r heyrs, executors, &
administrators, absolutely giue, grant, alienate, Enfeoff, &
Confirm unto the aforesayd John ffurnald, a Certen parcell
of Land, scituate & lijng in the Town of Kittery aforesd, &
Contajneing too Acres & an halfe, as It is now fenced in &
bounded with an high way of eight foote wide, on the South
West side ioyneing to ye Land, of ye late Jos : Allcocke &
ye North West bounded with other Land of ye sd Joseph
Allcocke deceased, & bounded on ye North East, with y^e
Land of ye sd Thos Spinny, & bounded on ye South East
with ye house lott of ye sayd ffurnald ; To haue & to hould,
the sd too Acres & an halfe of Land, with all the app^rte-
nances, & priuiledges, y^rto belonging or in any wise app^r-
tajneing, to him ye sd John ffurnald, & to his heyres for
euer/ prouided always, y^t If the sd John ffurnald, or any of
his heyrs, shall at any tyme or tyms hereafter make saile
of ye Land on Which hee now dwelleth y^t then this Deed of
Gyft to bee of no force, & the sd too Acres & an halfe of
Land to returne to ye sd Spinny, or to his heyrs in ye same
state as it was before, & for Confirmation of ye treuth here of
the aforesd Thos Spinny & Margery his wife, haue set tow y^r
hands, & seales, the foure & twenteth day of Septem^{br} in the
yeare of o^r Lord one thousand six hundred seauenty nine/

Signed sealed & Deluerd   Thomas Spinny (_{seale}^{his})
 in Presence of us/   Margery Spinny (_{soule}^{her})
 Samell ffurnald his   her marke

  marke $\mathcal{SF}$ Thomas Spinny & Margery his wife,
 Samell Spinny/   acknowledg y^e aboue written deed of
        gift to bee y^r free act & Deed, this
        24th day of Septem^{br} 1679 :

        before mee John Wincoll Assote/

BOOK III, FOL. 123, 124.

A true Coppy of this Deede of Gift, transcribed, out of ye originall & y^r with Compard this 25th day of Aprill 1683 :
p Edw : Rishworth ReCor :

Know all men by these Presents, that I William Hearle, with ye Consent of my wife Beaton, of the Town of Portsmouth in the prouince of New Hampshyre in New England, for & in Consideration of a ualewable some of Money & goods to mee in hand payd, by John ffurnald of the Town of Kittery In the prouince of Mayn shoemaker, with which some I do hereby acknowledg my selfe to bee fully satisfyd, haue barganed, & sould, & do by these Presents bargan sell aliene, Enfeoff, Convay, & make ouer, all that Prcell of Land wch was formerly in the possession of Andrew Newcome, lijng & being in the Tow . of Kittery aforesd, neare unto, & butting vpon ye broad Coue, Comanly Called Spinnys Coue, Containeing Twenty Acres being fourty Rodds broad, butting vpon the Coue aforesd, & haueing the Land of Christian Ramix on the South side & the Land of John Saward on ye North side, & so runnes eighty rodds East into the Woods, Which sayd Land was sould by William Hilton vnto the sd Andrew Newcome ; To haue & to hould, vnto him ye sd John Furnald his heyres, executors, Administrators & Assignes, all ye aboue sd Prcell of Land so butted & bounded, as aforesd, with all the priuiledges, & app^rtenances y^runto belonging, for euer · & to defend the same for euer, from any former [124] barganes, sals, Morgages, Joynters, Dowrys, alienations, or Incomberances w^tsoeuer made by the sd Andrew Newcome, his heyrs, executors, or Assignes ; I do hereby further bind my selfe, my heyres, executors, & Administrators, to warrant & defend, all the aboue mentioned Premisses, & euery part & Prcell thereof, unto the sd John ffurnald his heyres, executors,

Book III, Fol. 124.

administrators & Assignes, from any Prson or Prsons w'soeuer, from by or under mee y' shall Pretend to lay any legall right vnto the same: In witness w'of I haue here vnto sett my hand & seale, eaven this first day of ffebru: In ye yeare of o^r Lord, one thousand six hundred & eighty/ 1680:

Signed, sealed, & deliuered,   The marke of
  in the Presence of us/   Will: Hearle ✝ (his seale)
Christein Remich/   The marke of
John Cotten/   Beaton Hearle ✗ (her seale)

William Hearle & his wife Beaton, came & acknowledged the aboue Instrum^t to bee y^r free Act & Deed, & shee renders vp her thirds or right of Dowry, in all ye aboue mentioned Premisses, ffebru: primo: 1680: before mee

    Richd Martine of the Councill of New Hampshyre/
vera Copia of this Instrum^t aboue written, transcribed & with originall Compared, this 26th day of Aprill 1683:
                p Edw: Rishworth Re: Cor:

Know all men by these pres^{ts} that Richard Vines of the River of Saco Gent. for diverse good Causes and Considerations him thereunto Mooveing, Doth give grant enfeoffe and confirme, and by this present Deed hath given granted enfeoffed and confirmed unto Thomas Williams of Saco affores^d all that one Messuage or tenement, scittuate lyeing and being at Winter harbor in Saco affores^d, Containing one hundred and twenty Acres of Land bounded on the Southwest with the Lands of Robert Sanky, lately Deceased, on the South East with the fllatts, on the North East with certaine trees marked for bounds by the s^d Richard Vines, and so by all the breadth affores^d to extend North West till one hundred and twenty Acres be accomplished and compleated, together with a Certaine percell of Marsh ground containeing by Estimation twelve Acres or thereabouts be it more or less Adjoyning to the East and to part of the North East of the p'misses, with free liberty of ffishing & ffowling in and upon the p'misses according to the Custome of this Country, To Have and to hold the s^d p'misses with the s^d Land and their appurtenances vnto the aboue named Thomas Williams his heires and Assignes for Ever Yeilding and paying to the abovenamed Richard Vines his heires or assignes one Acknowledgment or rent Charge of ffive shillings yearly on the ffeast of St Michael th' Archangell two dayes worke of one man at harvest, and One ffatt Goose on the ffive & twentieth day of Decemb^r yearly, And if it shall happen the s^d Rent or any part or percell thereof to be vnpayde being lawfully demanded, that it shall be Lawfull for the s^d Richard Vines his heires, or assignes to enter into any part of the p'misses and to take a distress and the same to detaine & keep till the affores^d Rent be p^d And the s^d Richard Vines doth Covenant and promiss for himselfe his heires and assignes that the s^d Thomas Williams his heires and assignes shall peaceably hold and Enjoy the saide demised p'misses with euery part and percell thereof, without any lett or disturbance of the s^d Richard Vines his heires or assig . . . or any other person by his or there meanes or procurement. In Wittness whereof the partyes affores^d haue Interchangeably sett to theire hands and seales the second day of Aprill in the Eighteenth yeare of the Reigne of o^r Soveraign Lord King Charles. Annoq^e Domi. 1642/.

Sealed Signed and Deliud   Richd Vines (his seale)
in the presence of us/
Richard Bonython   A true Coppy of this Instrument
John Lee   aboue written transcribed out of
Roger Garde   ye originall. & y^{r}with Compared
                           this 24th day of May 1683 ·
                               p Edw : Rishworth ReCor .

Book III, Fol. 124.

Know all men by these presents that I Thomas Williams of Saco River in the Province Of Mayne In New England for divers causes and Valueable Considerations, Butt more Espetially for and in Consideration of my Maintainance Dureing my Naturall Life from and by my Grandson in Law Phineas Hull of the s^d place and province, Have given, granted, bargained, and doe Alienate enfeoffed and confirmed unto the s^d Phineas Hull and his heires Lawfully begotten by his now marryed Wife Jerusha, All my houses & Lands, and Meadowes In Win . . . harbor or within the Towneship of Saco : with all the Appurtenance thereunto belonging, to bee the affores^d Phineas Hull and the s^d heires for Ever. And fo . the Confirmation of the premisses I haue Subscribed my hand & Seale this Seaventeenth day of Decemb̃, In the yeare of our Lord one thousand Six hundred Eighty & one /.

Signed Sealed & possession given to Phineas Hull In the presence of us/

Thomas his   Williams
marke
and Seale (seale)

John his U/ Sergant
marke
Henry Williams /.

Thomas Williams did acknowledge the aboue Instrument to be his Act and Deed Before mee this 4th of May 1682 ã John Daves Justice peace/

vera Copia of this Instrume^t transcribed, & with originall Compared, this 25th of May 1683 :

p Edw : Rishworth ReCor :

Know all men by these presents that I Thomas Haley Señ resident at Saco in th . province of Mayne In New England vpon diverse considerations mee thereunto moveing, and more espectially for that naturall affection which I beare unto m . . . . son Thomas Haley . . d the Rather for his

Love and care in providei . . for mee, and Liveing with mee now in my Old Age, And as hee is my only lega . heyre to my Estate doe give grant bargaine Sell Enffeoffe & confirme, and by these presents haue given granted, bargained, Sold Enfeoffed and confirmed in . sole Right title and Intrest, of All my houseing & lands Marshes Meadowes that . . Bankes, and all other appurtenances thereunto belonging or any wise appertain . . . Contayning the . . antity of ffiuety Acres of Vpland or thereabout where I n . . [125] live from mee my heires Exect^{rs} Adm^{rs} & assignes, vnto my affores^d son Thomas Haley his heires Exect^{rs} Adm^{rs} & assignes for ever, which vpland & meadow as above specifyed the s^d Thomas Haly my son is to haue & to hold after my Decease from mee and my heires to him and his heires for ever. And I Thomas Haly doe Covenant & promiss with my s^d Son Thomas that the s^d Lands are free and cleare from all Assignm^{ts} Mortgages, gifts graunts, and all other Intanglem^{ts} whatsoever. And doe hereby covenant with my s^d Son to defend the Intrest thereof from all persons from, by or vnder mee or any by my procurem^t. In testimony whereof I have herevnto sett my hand and seale this 21th day of May 1683 .a

Signed Sealed & Deliu^d
  in presence of/   Thomas Haly his ——/
Nathaniel Masterson   marke &   (Seale)
Phineas Hull   Thomas Haly Sen came before mee
                     this 21. day of May 1683 and Acknowledged this Instrum^t above written to bee his Act and Deed/
                     Edw : Rishworth Jus : pe ·

vera Copia of this Instrument transcribed & with originall Compared this 25th day of May 1683 :

                     p Edw · Rishworth ReCor :

Book III, Fol. 125.

Att a Generall Court held at Boston the 13th of Octob: 1680 ⁂

In Answer to the Petition of George & John Engersoll this Court confirmes to the Petitioners the Sixty Acres a peice granted them as they expresd in theire Petition and doe Referr it to the President of s^d Province on such equall Conditions as he shall see meet to grant them Accommodation of timber for theire Mill that this is a true Coppy taken out of the Courts Records, Attests/.

Edward Rawson Sec^t

In persuance hereof

Haueing perused the above written order Doe give and grant and it is hereby given and granted vnto George Ingersoll Juñ. & John Ingersoll there heyres Exect^{rs} or assignes for Ever the liberty & priviledge of the ffresh Water Streame where the old Mill stood for the building & Errecting of a New Saw Mill and a Grist Mill, as also the Liberty of cutting all such timber as may be brought downe conveniently on that streame for the Imploy of there Mill they paying to the Lord Proprietor or his order ffive pounds p Añ in good Merch^{tble} Boards at the usuall place of takeing aboard the vessells, & at the Curiant Merch^{tble} price, to be Deliu^d upon Demand of the Tress. of s^d Province. And noe persons whatsoever may by any meanes stop or alter the streame at any time to theire prejudice.

Mem^d the first paym^t to be made the first day of Aprill in the yeare of our Lord One thousand six hundred Eighty & ffoure & so Annually for the ffuture so long as the Mill there shall be Imployed & Improoved. Dated in Boston. 3. 1. 168½   Thomas Danforth President

vera Copia of this Instrument transcribed, & with originall Compared this 31th of May 1683:

p Edw: Rishworth Re: Cor:

Book III, Fol. 125.

Bee it known unto all men by these Presents, that I Collonell John Archdalle o . Wicham in the County of Buch[s] Esq[r], by pouer & authority from mee deriued . . Fardinando Gorges, the Ld Proprietor of the prouince of Mayne, in New England, h . . . Contracted & agreed with Cap[t] Walter Barefoote of Douer, in Consideration of one . . dred pounds, by mee already in hand receiued, before y[e] sealeing & dehuery here of, . . . fiue hundred Acres of Land, adioyneing in length vpon the backe, of y[t] Land whi . . . . bought of Cap[t] Fran[s] Champernoown, as will appeare by a deed under his hand, . . sd Barefoote, I do hereby Ingage y[t] the sd Barefoote, shall quietly & peaceably . . . . the same to him & his heyres & Assignes for euer, with out any molestation from y[e] date . . . . of, prouided y[t] If any part of the abouesd bee legally possest by any Prson, t . . . sd Barefoote, shall make vp his Complement of fiue hundred acres to y[e] nearest . . . most Conuenient Lands y[r]to adioyneing, hee paijng for his yearely acknowledgm[t] . . the Lord proprietor or his order, two Couple of Pulletts vpon Easter day next, . . . for euer, If lawfully demanded, puided also y[t] all Masts from 26 Inches t . . . . . & vpwards, shall bee reserued to y[e] Ld of the Prouince, & not to bee felld with o . . his Lycence/ In witness w[r]of, I haue here unto set my hand & seale, this . . . . teenth of Octob[r] in the yeare of o[r] Lord god, one thousand six hundred sixt . . . . .

Signed sealed & Deliūd   John Archedale
  in the Presence of/   Abra : Corbett one of the witnesses
  Abra : Corbett/   to these Prsents, doth Attest that
  Moses Gillman/   hee saw John Archedale aboue
                         Named, set his hand & seal . .
                         . liuer it as his Act & Deed, the
                         day of y[e] date aboue writt . .
                         before mee Edw : Rishworth
                                       Assotiate/

BOOK III, FOL. 125.

August 7 · 9th 1678 : Moses Gillman made oath hee saw John Archedale . . seale the aboue written as his Act & Deede, before mee Elyas Stylemā. Comis . . . .

A true Coppy of this Instrumt aboue written transcribed, & with ye originall . . . pared this 5th of June 1683 :
p Edw : Rishworth ReCor/

June 4th 1683 :

I Timothy Yeales do acquitt & discharge Charles Martine from all debts, dues & . . . . w'soeuer, from ye begining of the world, to ye day of the Date here of, as witn . . my hand, the day & yeare aboue written/

Timothy Yea . . .

A true Coppy transcribed out of the originall this 5th day of June . 1683 : p Edw . Rishworth ReCor .

The Deposition of Major John Dauess, aged 70 years, or y'abouts, & Capt Charles . aged 52 years or there abouts/ these Deponents respectiuely testify, & say yt Wilha . Hilton now resedent in yorke, in the prouince of Mayne, was Comanly known, & . . . led, to bee ye sonn of William Hilton Senjor deceased, & formerly liued in yorke abo . . . on yt Tract of Land, yt lyeth on the South, or South West side of ye Riuer . . yorke ouer against the fishing flakes, & next the Ferry, & further sayth no .

Taken vpon oath in Court this 30th of May 1683 .
p Edw : Rishw . . . . ReCor ·
vera Copia transcribed & Compar'd this 4th of June 1683 :
p Edw . Rishworth Re : Cor :

BOOK III, FOL. 125, 126.

To all whome these Presents may Conceine/ W^as^ John Hull, Roger Playstead, & J . . . Wincoll, did by Deede of sale absolutely bargane sell, giue, grant, aliene, Enfeoff, & . . . firme vnto George, & John Broughton, one fourth part of the Too saw Mills, bu . . . . the salmon ffalls on great Newgewanacke Riuer, in Pischataqua, togeather with one part of ye land ye sd Mills stand on, or was belonging to ye sd Mills, & one fourth pa . . . . the dwelling house, & outhouses, & Lands, which they stood vpon, or belonged to the . . . . ing scituated neare ye sd Salmon ffalls Mills, as also one fourth part of all the' runci . . geares & utellences, riuer, Dame, flewmes, boune peeres, Tymber grant, or w^t^ priuiledges . . tles soeuer, was belonging to the sd Mills, houses, land, Tymber grant, Riuer, to bee to y . . . & Inheritance of them, the sayd Geo · & Jo^n^ Broughton thejr heyres, executors, Admin . . . . & Assignes for euer, as may more apply appeare by a Deede of sajle giuen them by . . . aboue mentioned, Dated ye Twenty fourth day of Septem^br^ one thousand six hundred sea . . . . . three, & is recorded in the third booke of ReCords for the County of Yorke, pa: first July ye T . . 1676: Now know all by these Presents, that ye sd George Broughton, for & in Considera . . . . [126] of the sd John Hull his remitting a debt of fourty one pounds tenn shillings, which I haue owed him seuerall yeares, & in Consideration of the sd Johns Hulls bond giuen mee (beareing date with these Presents) for saueing mee harmeless from a bond which I the sd George Broughton & my brother John Broughton as principall Debters, & ye sd John Hull as our security stands bound ioyntly & seuerally for paijng one hundred pounds in money to Zachary Long of Charles Town, Mariner, the Twenty secund day of Decemb^r^ sixteene hundred eighty foure, & on the sd day Annually to pay eight pounds in moneys more to the sd Longe, for fiue yeares yet to Come; And finally in Consideration of sixty foure pounds Sterlg payd mee by ye sd John Hull at ye signeing & seal ing of these Prec ts, I

Book III, Fol. 126.

the sd Geo. Broughton haue absolutely given, granted, barganed, aliend Enfeoffed & Confirmed, & by these Presents do absolutely giue, grant, bargan, sell, aliene Enfeoff & Confirme, unto ye sd John Hull, his heyres, executors, administrators, & Assigns for euer, the whoole of w^t I bought of the sd John Hull, Roger Playstead, & John Wincoll, according to the Deed aboue mentioned, on record, being one halfe of y^t quar^{tr} part, of ye sd Mills, houseing land Timber grant, Riuer, & all other priuiledges, & appurtenances to them belonging, which they sould unto my brother John Broughton & my selfe; To haue & hould all the before barganed Premisses, to him the sd John Hull his heyres, executors, Administrators, & Assignes for euer, And ye sd George Broughton doth Couenant, pmiss, & grant, for him selfe his heyrs, executors, Administrators & Assignes to & with Joⁿ Hull his heyrs executors Administrators & Assigns that hee ye sd Geo. Broughton now is (at ye signeing & sealeing of these Presents, the true owner of all the sd Halfe of w^t was sould according to ye sd Deed, to his brother & him selfe) & y^t hee hath in him selfe full pouer, & lawfull authority, to sell & Alienate the same & euery part y^r of, according to y^t Deed of sale which hee receiued, from ye sd John Hull, Roger Playstead, John Wincoll, beforesd (the ruines of the bujldings by fyre & otherwise, since y^t deed aforesd was made, excepted. And the sd George Broughton doth for him selfe his heyres, executors, administrators & Assignes, hereby warrant the before barganed Premisses, & euery part of them, unto ye sd John Hull, heyres, executors, administrators & Assigns, y^t they now are, & for euer hereafter shall bee, free & Cleare of all other barganes, sales gifts, grants Morgages Joynters, Judgm^{ts}, wills, Entales, Wifes thirds, & all other Incomberances w'soeuer, had, made, done, or suffered to bee done, by him the sd George Broughton, or any other Person, by from or under him w^rby the sd John Hull his heyres or successors, may bee disturbed in ye peaceable possession of all, or any part of the before barganed Premisses, & y{t} his wife Pearne Broughton in order to a peaceable Imoyment of y{e} Premisses, shall acknowledg her Consent to this Deed of sale for Preuenting after Controuersys about her thirds/ In witness w{r}of I haue here unto set my hand & seale, this twelfth day of Janvary sixteen hundred seauenty nine/

Signed sealed, & Deliuer'd   George Broughton (locus sigilli)
in the Presence of/   Peerne Broughton (her seal)
Thomas Broughton/   This Deed was acknowledged by
Nathall Broughton/   Geo: Broughton to bee his Act & Deed this Twelfth day of January 1679 : before mee Edward Tynge Assist/

Mis Pearne Broughton Came before mee August 29 : 1682 : & acknowledged y{t} shee gaue her free Consent unto the aboue written Instrument/ Symon Bradstreete Gouer/

vera Copia of this Instrume{t} aboue written, transcribed out of y{e} originall, & y{r} with Compared this : 16{th} day of June : 1683 : p Edw : Rishworth ReCor :

.. ounce
.. Mayne

W{r}as, wee whose names are here subscribed, by pouer deligated unto us by the Court & Couicill of this Prouince, May 29 : 1683 : were Impoured to settle the Estate of Majo{r} Nicho{s} Shapleigh, deceased, & to secure the disposeing of one third part there of, into the hands of Mis Alice Shapleigh his relict & Administratrix y{r}unto/ And y{e} other too thirds into y{e} Costody of Mr John Shapleigh his kinesman for the Improuement y{r} of, & payment of debts, so as may Conduce most to Present & future aduantage, by makeing sale of such Lands as may bee thought necessary for y{t} end & settleing y{e} Widdows thirds as the law requireth; The Premisses Considered Wee y{e} subscribers, togeather with the free & mutuall Consent of Aylce

& John Shapleigh aforesd, do Order & Conclude the Present settleing of yᵉ Estate aforesd, as followeth/

1. That the sd Alyce Shapleigh shall haue the free & frequent uss of any such Moueables as do appʳtajne to her deceased husbands Estate, for her necessary Occasions from tyme to tyme, dureing the tearme of her naturall life/

2: The sd Alyce Shapleigh shall haue the free & soole disposeing of these Prticulars underwritten, as shee shall Judge meete dureing her life, & at her death shall haue pouer to dispose yʳof, to such Person or Persons as neare as shee Can, which may fullfill the Majors will & intentions Whilst hee liued/

3. Aylce Shapleigh is hereby Invested in one third part of the whoole estate of her deceased husband dureing the Continewance of her naturall life/

4. It is orderd yᵗ sd Alyce Shapleigh shall haue a bed, furniture, & wᵗ Conueniences are Needfull to her lodging rowme, for her necessary vss, & yᵉ vss of yᵉ parlour, & yᵗ part of the house shee now liueth in, & those too rowmes & the seller underneath, with the leantows adioyneing, & the other seller next to yᵉ Hall Chymney, & to haue yᵉ vss of a garding or gardings, wᵗ shee Can Improue, where they may bee most Conuenjent for her, & to haue the vss of all necessary Conueniencys for dressing of uictualls, as potts panns &c & of yᵉ brew house to brew, bake, wash, or dress uictualls in, as Occasion shall require/

Lastly The other too parts, or too thirds of sd Majoʳ Shapleighs Estate is hereby disposed of into the hands & Costody of John Shapleigh his Kinesman, for the satisfijng of yᵉ Majoʳˢ iust debts & obligations, & for Improuemᵗ yʳof to yᵉ best aduantage of the Estate, & for him selfe & his, & after the decease of his Aunt Alyce Shapleigh, the whoole of yᵉ Estate of Lands then remayneing, shall bee & remajne to bee the true & proper Estate of John Shapleigh to him

Book III, Fol. 126.

selfe his heyres & Assignes for euer ; And it is to bee understood w{t} debts are app{r}tajneing to y{e} s{d} Estate are free from thirds, & to belong to John Shapleigh, & that Mis Alyce Shapleigh is peaceably to Inioy her own proper Estate, with out any Incomberance or Molestation/

The Sedule of y{e} Piticulars dispos'd of to Mis Shapleigh are as followeth/

one large bible| Two peyre of Cotton sheets|
three doz of Napkines| one Cubbard Cloath|
Six towells 3 feather beds| 12 Table plates two butter plates|
with w{t} belongs to them| toure Sacers, one sault seller|
Too dosen of Osenbridg napkines| One Iron dripinpan|
three Chamberpotts| the Majors Chest|
Three Tramells| 2 peyre of pott hookes| Moore a Neger Called b{rā} Will to
one Copper Kettle bee Mis Shapleighs Dureing her life,
too peyre of Dowless sheets| & w{t} shee thinkes meete besids, be-
3 Table Cloaths| longing to her lodging Rowme|
26 pewter dishes| 5 peyr of Cannise sheetes|
one Copper Kettle| 3 peyre of pillow bears
Too spitts y{t} were Mis Godfreys| Two pewter Candlesticks|
Too Trunkes| one brass Candlesticke|
one siluer Tankerd given to Nicholas, Two Iron potts|
by his Aunt| one peyre of great Andirons|

& the M{r} yo{rs} Cloake is disposed of likewise to Nic Shapleigh sonn to John Shapleigh as his own Proper goods |

Moore to bee added y{t} was forgotten | Two great Chares | tenn siluer Spoones | one pewter bason |

ffrom this Present Date Mr John Shapleigh is to take notice that his Aunt is vpon her thirds for her own Mantenance, & y{t} according to this mutuall Agreement between y{m}, hee taketh Charge of y{e} other too thirds of y{e} Estate, &

At yorke this returne brought in & Presented to the Generall Assembly houlden for this Prouince, this 27th day of June 1683 who accepted thereof, & Declared their approbation of the Premisses | Edw Rishworth Secr

the Due Managem^t y^rof accordingly/ & ye family y^runto
belonging/ Alice Shapleigh/
   Dated 12th June 1683 : Jo^n Shapleigh/
John Dauess/
A true Coppy of this agreement aboue   Edw: Rishworth
written, transcribed out of ye origi-   Charles Frost/
nall, & y^rwith Compared this 16 :
day of June 1683 .
    p Edw · Rishworth ReCor :

To all Christian people, to whom these Presents shall
Come/ Thomas Withers of Kittery in the prouince of Mayn
sends Greeteing/ Now know yee, y^t I the aboue mentioned
Thomas Withers, for diuerse good Causes & Considerations
y^runto moueing, more espetially for in Consideration of y^e
sume of tenn pounds [127] In hand receined of James Johnson of Hampton, in the Prouince of New Hampshire, the
receipt where of I acknowledg, & of euery part & Prcell
there of, haue given, bargained, sould, aliend, granted, Infeoffed made ouer, & Confirmed, & by these Presents, for
my selfe, my heyres, executors, Administrators, & Assignes, do absolutely giue grant, bargane, sell, alliene,
Infeoffe, make ouer, & Confirme unto him ye sd James
Johnson his heyres, executors, Administrators, & Assigns
for euer, all my right, title, & Interest, of a peece or Prcell
of Land, scituate, & being on the North East side of Spruse
Cricke contayneing tenn Acres, begining eight rodd aboue y^e
saw Mill, which is there Erected & so to runne vp by the
side of ye sayd Cricke thirty rodd, vpon a North, North
West lyne, & from ye sd Cricke to runn backe vpon an
East, North East lyne, foure & fiuety Rodds : To haue & to
hould the aboue given & granted Premisses, with all the
priuiledges & app^rtenances y^runto belonging, or in any way

app'tajneing, to him y⁰ sd James Johnson, his heyres, executors, administrators & Assigns for euer, from mee y⁰ sd Thomas Withers, my heyres, executors, administrators, & Assigns, Conenanting & promissing, to & with y⁰ sd James Johnson, his heyrs executors, Administrators & Assignes, that I the aboue mentioned Thoˢ Withers, haue in my selfe good right, full pouer, & lawful authority, y⁰ aboue giuen & granted Premisses, to sell & dispose off, & yᵗ euery part & Prcell yʳof is free & cleare, & freely & Clearely acquitted exonerated & discharged, of & from all, & all manner of Wills, Entayles Judgmᵗˢ, executions, deeds of Gyft, pouer of thirds, & all other incomberances, of what kind or nature soeuer, And do by these Presents promiss & Ingage for mee my heyrs executors, administrators, & Assignes, the aboue giuen & granted Premisses for euer to defend/ In witness wʳof the sd Thoˢ Withers hath set too his hand, & seale this eight & twenteth day of May In y⁰ yeare of or Lord Anno Dom̃: one thousand six hundred eighty three/
Signed, sealed, & deliuered,   Thomas Withers (his sealc)

In Presence of/   Mr Thoˢ Withers Came before mee
Elizabeth Withers/   this 13ᵗʰ of June 1683 : & ac-
Joseph Hammonds/   knowledged the aboue written
                             Instrument, to bee his free act
                             & Deed/ Charles Frost/
                                           Jusᵗ pe :

A true Coppy of this Instrumeᵗ transcribed out of y⁰ originall, & yʳwith Compared this . 18ᵗʰ day of June 1683 ·
                     p Edw : Rishworth Re : Cor :

To all Christian people, vnto whome this Present bill of sale, or Instrument of writing shall Come/ Stephen Paul shippwright, & Inhabitant In y⁰ Town of Kittery, in the prouince of Mayne, in New England, send Greeteing : Know

Book III, Fol. 127.

yee yt I sd Stephen Paul, for & in Consideration of the sume of Twenty eight pounds, Current money of & in New England, to mee in hand payd by John Soaper, now in New England aforesd, the receipt wrof, I do hereby acknowledg, & from which & from euery part of which, I ye sayd Stephen Paul Confessing my selfe satisfyd, Contented & payd, at & before the Insealeing & deliuery of these Presents do acquitt, exonerate, & discharge the sayd John Sloper, his heyres, executors, & Administrators for euer, haue barganed & sould, & by these Presents, do fully Clearely & absolutely bargan, & sell, unto the sayd John Sloaper, in plajne & open manner with out fraude, one Certen Parcell of vpland Contajneing Twenty Acres more, or less, scituate, ljng & being, in the Townshipp of Kittery, Joyneing, & adiacent to Richd Cowells Land, on ye North side, & on mine the sd Stephen Pauls Land, on ye South side in the great Coue, neare the bovleing Rocke, bounded North, & South as aboue, & by an East & west lyne, as may appeare by seuerall marked trees into the Woods, untill yt sd Twenty Acres bee accomplished, or howsoeuer It is lade out & livery & seasin granted & given to the sd John Soaper, by these Presents by mee sayd Stephen Paul; To haue & to hould the sd Twenty Acres of vpland, togeather with all ye woods trees, priuiledges Conueniences ytunto belonging, unto him ye sd John Soaper, his heyrs executors, administrators, & Assignes for euer, & to his & yr usses, & behoofe for euer/ And I the sd Stephen Paul, & my wife Cattharine Paul, & our executors & Administrators, & euery of us, the sd demised Land according to law shall & will warrant acquitt & for euer defend by these Prsents, against all manner of Prsons/ In witness wrof Wee Stephen Paul, & Catterine Paul haue here unto putt or

hands & seales, this foureteenth day of Febru : in y⁰ yeare of
our Ld, one thousand six hundred seauenty nine, 1679 :
Signed, Sealed, & deliuered/   Stephen Paul (his seale)
   In Presence of us/   Catthcrine Paul
   Gowen Willson/   her Marke K (her seale)
   The ⱶ Marke of
   Ephraim Crockett/   Stephen Paul, & Cattherine his wife,
acknowledged this Instrument to
bee thejr Act & Deede, this foure-
teenth day of February 1679 : be-
fore mee Francis Hooke
                                        Comissio^r/
A true Coppy of this Instrument aboue written transcribed
out of y⁰ originall, & y^rwith Compared this thirteth day of
June 1683 : p Edw : Rishworth ReCor/

    Bee It known unto all men by these Presents, that I Har-
lakenden Symonds late of Wells In y⁰ County of yorke
Gentle : haue given & granted bargained & sould, & by these
Presents do giue grant, bargan sell & Confirme, unto my
sister Mis Martha Symonds, all y^t part of Land Meddow &
pasture, Contayneing by estimation fiue hundred Acres bee
It more or less, with the app^rtenances, set lijng & being on
the Wester side of my father Mr Samuell Symonds fiue hundred Acres reserued, which hee purchased of mee, being
part of y⁰ Tract of Land which I purchased of John Bush &
Peter Turbett, which Tract of Land lyeth next Cape Porpis
bounds, & in the sd County of Yorke, to haue & to hould
the sayd fiue hundred Acres, with all singular y⁰ app^rtenances
to her y⁰ sd Martha Symonds, her heyres, & Assigns for
euer/ In witness w^rof I the sd harlacenden Symonds, haue
hereunto set too my hand & seale the seauenteenth day of

Book III, Fol. 127, 128.

the secund Moenth Called Aprill. In y̎ᵉ yeare of oʳ Lord
God 1661 :　　　　　　　Harlacinden Symonds (ˡᵒᶜⁿˢ/ˢⁱᵍⁱˡⁱ)
Subscribed Sealed &
　Deluer̃d in the Pres-　This Deed was acknowledged by yᵉ
　ence of us/ vidzᵗ　　 sd Harlainden Symonds vpon the
　Samĩll Symonds Junjoʳ 18ᵗʰ day of Novemᵇʳ 1662 . before
　Samuell Epps/　　　　mee Samĩell Symonds/
vera Copia transcribed, & with originall Compared, this
6th day of July 1683 : p Edw : Rishworth ReCor :

To all Christian people, know yee yᵗ I John Shapleigh of
Kittery in the prouince of Mayne In New England Gentle :
heyre to Majoʳ Nicholas Shapleigh late of Kittery aforesd
deceased, for & in Consideration, & full satisfaction of the
sum̃e of Too hundred & eight pounds of New England money
due & payable from the Estate of yᵉ sd Nichoˢ Shapleigh
vnto Richard Wharton of Boston in the Coloney of the Massatusetts In New England, aforesd Mʳᶜhant & for other
good Causes & Considerations mee yʳunto Moueing ; haue
given, granted barganed sould demised aliend, Enfeoffed &
Confirmed, & by these Presents do giue grant, bargane sell
demise, aliene Enfeoff & Confirme, to the sd Richard Wharton, all yᵗ tract or Necke of Land Called Mereconege, lijng
ouer against an Ysland Called Sebasco, alias Sequasco Diggin
in Casco Bay [128] In the prouince of Mayne, And is
bounded at the head or upper end with yᵉ plaines, of pegip-
scott, or land late belonging to or clajmed by Mr Purchass,
& on all other parts & sides is Incompassed, & bounded
with, & by the sault water ; And also all that the aforesd
Ysland Called Sebascoa, alias Sequascoo Diggine, togeather
with all Isletts, rockes, shoares, beeches, Hauens, Crickes,
Coues, & all trees, woods under woods, pooles, ponds, waters, water Courses, & all Mineralls, & Mines, & all other

profitts, priuiledges, Aduantages, & Immoluments, to ye premisses, or any part y^rof, belonging, or any wise app^rtayncing :
To haue & to hould, to him the sd Richard Wharton his
heyres & Assignes for euer, all the aforesd Necke or tract of
Land Called Meraconeeg, bounded as aforesd, & the aforesd
Ysland Called Sebascoe, alias Sequascoe Diggine togeather
with all Isletts, Rocks, shoares, beeches, Hauens, Cricks,
Coues, & all woods, under woods, trees, pools, ponds, waters
water Courses, & all Mineralls, & Mines, & all other profitts,
priuiledges, aduantages, & Emoluments, to ye Premisses or
any part y^rof, belonging or any ways app^rtajneing, yejlding
y^rfore & paijng to our Soucraigne Ld King Charles the
secund, his heyres & successors the fifth part of all the Oare,
of gould & siluer that shall bee found and gott vpon any part
of the Premisses, & makeing & Prformeing such acknowledgments, & dutys as are reserued to, or do belong, & are
due unto ye Crown : And I the sd John Shapleigh do for mee
my heyres, Couenant & promiss to & with the sd Richard
Wharton his heyres & Assignes, y^t I am the true & proper
owner of the Premisses, & that I haue in my selfe good
right, & full pouer, & athority to alienate, & dispose the
same ; & the same now are & shall bee made & keept free &
Clere & freely & Clearely acquitted, & discharged off & from
all former & other Gyfts, grants Intailes, Joynters Dowers,
or rights of Dower, from all Morgages, Judgm^ts executions
& extents, & from all Incomberances w^tsoeuer · And y^t I
will warrant & defend the same to the sd Wharton his
heyres, & Assignes, against all & euery Prson or Prsons
that may Legally Clajme or Pretend to haue any right, title,
or Interest in ye Premises or any part y^rof · And y^t vpon y^e
reasonable request of ye sd Richard Wharton, his heyrs executors administrators, or Assigns, I will do Prforme execute,
& acknowledg such other Acts Deeds, & Instruments as y^e
learned in the Law shall Aduise necessary, firmely & æffec-
tually to demise & Convay the Premisses, & euery part y^rof

BOOK III, FOL. 128.

the sd Richard Wharton, his heyres & Assignes, according to ye true Intent & meaning of these Presents: prouided I bee not Compelled for ye Doing there of, to trauell or go with out ye bounds & lymitts of the prouince of Mayne; And I the sd John Shapleigh do hereby further Couenant & promiss, y^t I will Deliuer unto the sd Richd Wharton, or order fayre & uncanelled, all such Deeds, writeings, & euidences, relateing unto, or Concerneing the Premisses, or any part y^rof, as now are in my possession, or hereafter may Come to my hand, In witness w^rof I the sd John Shapleigh haue herevnto set my hand & seale this fourth day of July in ye yeare of o^r Lord, one thousand six hundred eighty & three, & In the Thyrty fifth yeare of the Reigne of our Soueraigne Lord Charles ye secund/

Sealed & deliuered,   John Shapleigh (locus sigilli)
In ye Presence of   Mr John Shapleigh came before mee
William Bickeham/ this fourth day of July 1683: &
Danjell Epps/   did acknowledg this Instrume^t to
                    bee his free Act & Deed/
                    And Mis Aycle Shapleigh then appeared like wise, & renowned all her Interest of Dowry or thirds relateing to ye Premisses aboue mentioned this fourth day of July 1683: Edw: Rishworth Jus pc:
                    In Prouince of Mayn/

This Instrument Entered into the third booke of ReCords for the prouince of Mayn, pages 127 & 8/ this 7th day of July: 1683 p Edw Rishworth ReCor

Book III, Fol. 128.

Prouince of
Mayne |

The Depositions of ffrancis Smale Senjo[r], aged about fifty six yeares, & Elizabeth Smale aged about fourty nine yeares/

Being examined make oath, y[t] about Twenty three or twenty foure years agone, this Deponent ffrancis Smale Senjo[r], was Imployed by Majo[r] Nicolas Shapleigh, to purchase a Certen great Ysland, which some Call Sebascoe Diggin, for Which this Deponent payd the Indeans a Considerable sume of Wampompeag, seuerall Gunnes, & a Parcell of Toba. for y[e] sd Ysland, lijng against a Necke of Land Called Mericaneeg/ Which y[e] Deponent purchased with y[e] sayd Ysland in Majo[r] Shapleighs behalfe; And further ffrancis Smale testifyeth y[t] hee built an house by order of Majo[r] Shapleigh, & possessed the sd Ysland In Majo[r] Shapleighs behalfe/ & further sayth not/ Taken vpon oath this tenth day of May 1683 · before mee Edw. Rishworth Just. pe:

A true Coppy of these testimonys aboue written transcribed & Compared with originall this 7th day of July 1683:

p Edw: Rishworth ReCor

Prouince of
Mayn

The testimony of John Cossons, aged about eighty seauen yeares/ Being examined maketh oath y[t] when this Deponent liued in Cascoe Bay seuerall years before the warrs, It was Comanly reported there & so vnderstood by many of the Inhabitants who then liued there, that y[e] great Ysland lijng at or neare the bottome of y[e] sd Bay Called Sequascoe Diggin, lijng Northwardly in from Whittes ysland, did belong to Majo[r] Nicho[s] Shapleigh, & was accompled his Ysland by diuerse of us y[t] liued there/ & further sayth not/

Taken vpon oath this 14th day of May 1683:

before mee Edw: Rishworth Just: pe:

A true Coppy of this testimony transcribed & with originall Compared this seauenth day of July 1683:

p Edw: Rishworth ReCor:

Book III, Fol. 128, 129.

To all Christean people to whome these Presents shall Come/ Know yee that Gylbard Endicott of Wells Weauer In the Prouince of Mayne, & in the County of yorke In New England In America sendeth Greeteing/ Know yee that the sd Gillbard Endicott for diuerse good causes & Considerations mee y^r unto moueing, but more espetially for a Tract or Tracts of Lands, lijng at Casco alias ffalmouth In ye Prouince as abouesd, all secured unto mee before ye Insealeing & deliuery here of according to law, & by these Presents of James Ross Cordwind^r of Wells aforesd, the receipt where of I do acknowledg, & y^r with to bee fully satisfyd Contented & payd, & do for my selfe my heyres, executors. Administrators, acquitt & discharge the aboue named James Ross, his heyres, executors Administrators from euery part & Prcell there of, haue given granted, & by these Presents do fully freely & absolutely giue grant bargan sell, aliene, Assigne, Confirme & set ouer unto James Ross, his heyres, executors, Administrators or Assignes, one saw Mill with all the Iron worke y^r unto belonging, standing in or vpon a little Riuer at Cape Porpus, with fiuety Acres of vpland, I bought of Majo^r Willham Phillips Adioyneing unto the sd Mill, & is bounded with a Cricke on the West side John Millers Land, & so runnes vp the Riuer on the Towns Land on the South side vntill fiuety Acres bee fully Compleated, & accomplished with all woods under woods, Tymber & Tymber Trees & all the Loggs that is now Cut that is now at the Mill neare her, or in the Woods with ye free lyberty & priuiledg of ye sd Riuer for water, & the like free lyberty & priuiledge for all Tymber or tymber trees on the Towns Land, or the Comanes, for the full supplijng of the sd Mill with loggs to saw, or any other priuiledg [129] there unto belonging, with all my right title & Interest, I now haue or out to haue at the tyme of the sealing of these Presents, in all & singular the Mill Iron worke, Loggs Tymber & Tymber trees, with all the Land aboue specifyd, with all the profitts priuiledges & appurtenances there unto belonging, To haue & to hould, all & singular aboue granted & barganed Premisses, to euery part & percell there of, with all & singular other priuiledges, & to euery part or Prcell y'of unto mee belonging, with all my right Title & Interests, y'of unto y° sd James Ross his heyres, executors, administrators or Assigns to his or y' owne proper uss benefitt & behoofe, for euer: And the sd Gillbard Endicott, do by these P'sents Couenant & promiss, for my selfe my heyres, executors, Administrators or Assignes, that at or Immediately, before the Insealeing of these Presents, was & is the true & lawfull owner, of all & singular the afore barganed Premisses: & that I haue good right & lawfull authority, In my owne name to giue grant, bargane, sell, aliene, Conuay & Confirme the same as aforesd; And that the sd James Ross his heyres, executors Administrators or Assignes, shall & may by uertue & force of these Presents, from tyme to tyme, & at all tymes, for euer hereafter lawfully, quietly, & peaceably, Haue hould, vsse, occupy, possess & Injoy the aboue granted Premisses, with y' appurtenances free & cleare & freely discarged, & Clearly accquitted of & from all mañer of former gyfts, Sales, leases, acknowledgm'', Morgages, Joynters, Dowers, Judgm'' executions forfiturs, rents, & Rerages, troubles, & Incomberances whasoeuer, had made done, or suffered to bee done by mee the sd Gillbert Endicott, or my heres, executors, Administrators & Assignes, at any tyme or tyms before the sealing & deliuery of these P'sents & I the sd Gillbard Endicot my heyres executors Administrators or Assigns, shall & will from tyme to tyme & at all tymes for euer hereafter, warrant & Defend, the aboue giuen & granted Premisses, with y' apurtenances & euery part & Parcell thereof unto y° aboue named James Ross, his heyrs executors administrators or Assigns against all & euery Prson or Persons laijng Clajme y'to, or any part y'of from by or under mee, my heyers, executors, Administrators or

Book III, Fol. 129.

Assignes/ In witness w^runto, I haue here to set my hand & seale, this sixth day of Aprill, one thousand six hundred eighty & three, Annoq, Regni Regis Carolj secundy thirty fifth 1683 ·

Signed sealed & Deliuered/   Gillbart Endicott (his scale)
In the Presence of
Samuell Barton his   his $\mathcal{B}$ marke/

marke/ $\mathcal{P}$ Gilbhard Endicott appeared before
                   mee this 16th day of Aprill 1683 ·
George Pearson/   & owned this Instrument to bee
                    his Act & Deede/
                    Samull Wheeleright Jus : pe :

This Instrument aboue written out of the originall transcribed into the 3d booke of ReCords of the prouince of Majne, pa. 129; & y^rwith Compared ye 29th day of July 1683   p Edw : Rishworth ReCor/

To all Christean People unto whome these Presents shall Come/ Israell Harding of Wells In the Prouince of Mayne In new England, blacke smyth, & Lydea his wife Sends Greeting/ Know yee, that I the aboue mentioned Israell Harding & Lydea my wife, for diuerse good Causes & Considerations us moueing y^runto, more espetially for & in Consideration of the some of fourty nine shillings in money in hand receeued, before the signeing & sealing here of, of Jos. Bolls of the same Town of Wells, & Prouince aforesd, Gentle : w^rwith Wee acknowledg o^rselues fully satisfyd, Contented & payd, & y^rof & euery part & Parcell y^rof, do acquitt, & for euer discharge the sd Joseph Bolls his heyres & Assignes by these Presents, haue absolutely given granted barganed sould aliend Infeffed & Confirmed, & by these Presents do absolutely giue, grant, bargane, sell alliene Enfeoff & Confirme unto ye abouenamed Joseph Boolls a

Book III, Fol. 129.

peece or Parcell of Meddow sault Marsh, being by measure too Acres, lijng & being in the Town of Wells & bounded as followeth/

vidz^t with the sea wall on the South East/ with a Cricke on the North West/ with ye Marsh of the sd Jos: Bolles on the North West/ & with the Marsh of Joseph Storer on the North East · To haue & to hould, the aboue mentioned peece of sault Marsh to him the sd Joseph Bolls his heyres & Assigns for euer, & to the onely proper uss benefitt & behoofe for euer: And the sd Israell Harding & Lydea his wife, for them selfes thejr heyres, executors, & Administrators, do Couenant promiss & grant, to & with Joseph Bolls his heyres, heyres, executors, Administrators & Assignes, that they ye sd Israell Harding, & Lydea his wife, haue in them selues good right, full pouer & lawfull authority ye aboue given & Granted Premisses to sell, & dispose of, & that ye same & euery part & Prcell y^rof are free & Cleare, & freely & Clearely acquitted exonerated & discharged, off & from all manner of former Gyfts, grants leases Morgages, wills, Intajles, Judgments, executions pouer of thirds, & all other Incomberances, of what nature & kind soeuer, had made done, acknowledged, Committed or suffered to bee done, or Committed w^rby the sd Joseph Boolls, his heyres, executors Administrators, or Assignes, shall or may any ways bee Molested in, Euicted, or Erected out of the aboue granted Premisses, or any part or Parcell thereof, by any Person or Persons whatsoeuer, haueing, Claimeing, or Pretending to haue, or Clajme any legall right, title, Interest, Clajme, or demannd of, in & to the aboue granted Premisses: And the sayd Israell Harding & Lydea his wife, do for them selues y^r heyres executors, & Administrators, Couenant, promiss & grant to & with the sayd Joseph Bolls his Heyres, & Assignes the aboue granted peece of sault Marsh to warrant & for euer defend by these' psents; In Witness whereof, the sd Israell Harding, & Lydea his wife,

haue here unto putt y^r hands & seales, the Twenty Ninth
day of Janv one Thousand six hundred eighty Two/

Signed sealed, & Deluerd, in   Israell Harding (his seale)
  the Presence of us/   Israell Harding owned this Instru-
  Jeremiah Storer/   ment to bee his Act & Deede,
  Edmund Littlefejld/   this 29th of Janvary 1682: be-
                    fore mee Samuell Wheelewright
                                Jus: pe:

A true Coppy of this Instrument aboue written, transcribed out of the originall & there with Compared, this
30th day of July 1683: p Edw. Rishworth ReCor:

[130] The bill bindeth mee Edm^d Sheare now rescident
at Boston to pay or Cause to bee payd to Mis Mary Sayword of yorke, the full & Just some of thirty shillings in
money at or before the last of August next Insewing, the
date here of & for the true Prformance there of, I bind mee
my heyres, executors Administrators, or Assignes to ye sd
Mary Sayword her heyres executors Administrators, or
Assignes, as witness my hand this 27th of May 1683:

Witness
  Hene · Williams/   Edmund Sheere
  Samull Wakefejld/   his Marke
      A true Coppy transcribed, & Compard with the
        originall this 30th July 1683.
                p Edw. Rishworth ReCor:

Bee It known unto all men by these Presents, y^t I Phynæs
Hull of Newgewamacke in ye Town of Kittery, & prouince
of Mayne, Carpenter, & Jerusea my now wife, for & in Consideration, of the full & iust sume of tenn pounds lawfull

money of New England, to mee in hand payd & secured to bee payd, before the sealeing & delivery hereof, by the hands of John Hearle, of the same Town & prouince, Husbandman the receipt w'of, I the sd Phineas Hull do hereby acknowledg & y'of & of euery part & pcell y'of do acquitt the sayd John Hearle, his heyres executors Administrators for euer, Haue & by these Presents do giue grant bargane sell Enfeoffe, & for euer Confirme unto him the sd John Hearle, his heyres executors Administrators & Assignes, a Certen Tract of Land which was granted unto mee by the Town of Kittery aforesd & Legally layd out, being by æstimation thirty Acres or y^r abouts bee it more or less, & It is ljing & being at a place Called the post wigwame In ye Town of Kittery aforesd, bounded on the North or y^{r}abouts, with ye Lands of one Thom^s Parke, & on the East, with a fresh Riuer Called ye little Riuer, & on the South or y^{r}abouts, with the Lands belonging to ye Lands of Mr Hutchinsons great workes saw Mill, & on the West with the Lands of Humfrey Chadborne, with all ye priuiledges, & appurtenances y^{r}to belonging, or in any wise app^{r}tajneing, & Member, part, or Prcell y^{r}of, & It is ljing & being neare the sd poast Wigwame In the Town of Kittery, aforesd/ To haue & to hould, the sd Tract of Land to him the sd John Hearle, his heyres executors, Administrators, & Assignes, with all the priuiledges, & appurtenances y^{r}unto belonging, from & Immediately after the date hereof, for euer, in as ample large a manner, to all Constructions, Intents, & purposes, as I the sd Phinæs Hull Can or may, bargane, sell giue, grant, or Estate the same, with Jerusea my wife/ And I the sd Phyneas Hull, do hereby for my selfe, my wife, my heyres, executors & Administrators, & for euery & either of them, Couenant promiss & agree to & with ye sd John Hearle his heyres, executors Administrators & Assignes, & to & with euery & either of them, by these Presents y^t hee ye sayd John Hearle, that hee ye sd John Hearle his heyres, execu-

tors Administrators & Assignes, & euery & either of them
shall & may from tyme to tyme, & at all tyms, here after
quietly, & peaceably haue hould, vss, possess, & Imoy the
sd Tract of Land, & Premisses aforesd, hereby granted,
with out the Lawfull lett, suite, euiction eiection, Molestation or disturbance of mee the sd Phineas Hull, Jeruseah
my wife, my heyres executors Administrators, or Assignes,
or of any other Person or Prsons w'soeuer, lawfully Claimeing the sd Tract of Land, or Premisses, or any part y^{r}of for
euer/ In witness hereof I ye sd Phineas Hull, & Jeruseah
my wife haue here unto sett our hands & seales, euon the
secund day of June In the one & Thirteth yeare of ye Reign
of o^r Soueraign Ld, King Charles the secund by the grace
of god of England, Scotland, ffrance, & Ireland, King,
Defend^r of ye faith &c . In ye yeare of o^r Ld one thousand
six hundred seauenty nine, 1679 :

Sealed & Delud in Presence	Phyneas Hull/ (his seale)
of us/	Jerusha Hull (her seale)
Thomas Hearle/	Phineas Hull, & Jerusha his wife
his marke	acknowledged this aboue written
Thomas Abbott/	Deed of Sale, to bee y^r free act & Deede, y^s 26 day of June 1679 · before mee
	John Wincoll Assotiate/

vera Copia of this Deed, transcribed & with originall
Compared this 31 : July 1683 : p Edw Rishworth ReCor :

To all Christean people to whom these Presents shall
Come/ John Hearle of Barwicke In the Prouince of Mayne,
in New England husbandman sends greeteing , Know yee y^t
I the aboue named John Hearle, for diuerse good Causes &
Considerations mee moueing there unto, more especially for
& in Considerations of Tenn Thousand foote of M^{r}chtble

pine boards in hand receiued before ye signeing & sealeing hereof, of Abraham Lord where with I acknowledg my selfe fully satisfyd, Contented & payd, & there of, & of euery part & Percell y^{r}of, do acquitt & for euer discharge the sd Abra. Lord his heyres, & Assigns by these Presents, haue absolutely giuen, granted, barganed, sould aliend, Infeoffed, & Confirmd & by these Presents, do absolutely giue, grant, bargane, sell aliene Infeoffe & Confirme unto the aboue named Abraham Lord his heyres, & his Assignes for euer, a Certen peece or Parcell of Land being fourty Acres, being & lijng in the vpper diuission of Kittery now Called Barwicke, being butted & bounded as followeth/

vidz^t On the North or y^{r}abouts, with ye Land of Thomas Parkes, & on the East with a fresh Riuer, called the little River, & on the South or y^{r}abouts with the Lands belonging to Mr Eliakime Hutchinson, Which do Joyne to the Great workes saw Mill, & on the West with the Lands of Humphrey Chadborne/ being in length one hundred & sixty pooles, South East & by South, & fourty seauen or fourty eight pooles in breadth bee It more or less Comanly Called post Wigwame In Barwicke aforesd: To haue & to hould the aboue mentioned peece or Prcell of Land, with the Wood & Tymber that is vpon It, & all the appurtenances & priuiledges thereto belonging or any wise appertaineing to him the sd Abra: Lord his heyres & Assignes, from the day of the date here of for euer · And to thejr onely proper uss, benefitt & behoofe for euer: And the sayd John Hearle doth for him selfe, his heyres executors Administrators & Assignes, Couenant promiss & grant to & with the sd Abra: Lord his heyres, & Assignes, that hee the sd John Hearle, hath in him selfe good right full pouer, & lawfull Authority, the aboue giuen & granted Premisses to sell & dispose of & y^t the same, & euery part & Parcell there of, are free & Cleare & are freely & Clearely acquitted exonerated & dischaiged of & from all and all manner of former Gyfts, grants, leases, Morgages, Wills, Intales, Judgm^ts executions pouer of thirds, & all other Incumberances, of w^t nature & kind soeuer, had made done acknowledged Comitted, or suffered to bee done Comitted, or Omitted by ye sayd John Hearle, or by his meanes or procurement/ w^rby the sd Abraham Lord his heyres or Assigns, shall or may bee Molested in, euicted or Eiected out of, the aboue granted Premisses, or any part or Parcell thereof, by any Prson or Prsons whatsoeuer, haueing, Clajmeing or Pretending to haue, or Clajme any Legall right, title Interest Clajm or demand, of in or two ye aboue granted Premisses [131] And the sayd John Hearle doth for him selfe, his heyres executors & Administratos, Couenant promiss & grant, to & with ye sd Abraham Lord his heyres & Assignes, the aboue granted peece or Prcell of Land, to warrant & for euer defend by these Presents (the proprietor, or high Lord of the soyle & prouince onely excepted) & foreprised, any thing in these Presents Contajned to ye contrary In any wise Notwithstanding, In witness w^rof the sd John Hearle hath hereunto sett his hand & seale this Twenty seauenth day of August, one thousand six hundred eighty & one, In the Thirty fourth yeare of the Reign of o^r Soueraign Ld Charles the secund, of England Scotland, ffrance & Ireland King, Defendor of the faith &c :

Signed sealed & Deliuerd/   The marke of
  In Presence of us/
  George Broughton/   ⁊ H   (his seale)
  Walter Allin/   John Hearle/

November 12th 1681 · Abraham Lord tooke Deliuery of this Land before us/
    James Playsted
    William Spencer/

This Deed of sale was acknowledged by the with in named John Hearle, to bee his free Act & Deede, the Eleuenth day May 1682. before mee
    John Wincoll Jus : pe :

Book III, Fol. 131.

A true Coppy of this Instrume^t aboue written transcribed out of the originall & y^rwith Compared this first day of August 1683: p Edw: Rishworth ReCor.

To all Christean people to whome this shall Come/ Know yee that I Phynæs Hull of Sacoe In the Prouince of Mayne In New England, for diuerse good Causes mee moueing there unto, especially for & in Consideration of fiue pounds in money receiued already of Henery Child of Barwicke, in the Town of Kittery & Prouince of Mayne, to full Content & satisfaction, haue, giuen granted, barganed sould Enfeoffed & Confirmed, And do by these Presents for my selfe my heyres executors & Administrators, giue, grant, bargane, sell, Infeoff & Confirme, vnto the sd Hen: Child a Certen Prcell of Land, scituate & being in the parish of Barwicke, & town of Kittery aforesd, Contajneing thirty Acres, being the one halfe of a Grant of sixty Acres of Land from ye Town of Kittery, & ljing in the Woods North Eastward, from Quamphegon, & bounded on the South West, with ye Land of sd Henery Child & on ye South East, North East, & North West, bounded with the Present Comans, & now by mee the sd Phynæs Hull sould unto the aforesd Henery Child, with all ye appurtenances, & priuiledges w^tsoeuer, y^runto belonging or in any wise app^rtajneing/ To haue & to hould to him the sd Henery Child his heyres, executors, administrators & Assignes for euer, freely & Clearely exonerated & discharged from all & all manner of Gyfts, grants barganes, sales, Morgages, or other Incomberances w^tsoeuer, had made done, or suffered to bee done by mee ye sd Phyneas Hull, or any other Prson or Prsons by, from, or und^r mee, the sd Phyneas Hull or any other Prson or Prsons w^tsoeuer, Clajmeing any Interest in ye Premisses, or any part or Prcell y^rof, from mee, or by

Book III, Fol. 131.

my Assignes, & for Confirmation of the treuth hereof, I the aforesd Phyneas Hull haue hereunto set my hand & seale, this twelfth day of July in y⁰ yeare of oʳ Lord one thousand six hundred eighty three, 1683:

Signed sealed & Deliuered   Phenis Hull (his seale)
 In Presence of us   Phyneas Hull owned yᵉ aboue
 Witness James Playstead/   written bill of sale to bee
 John Playstead/   this free Act & Deed, this
           twelth of July. 1683.
          John Wincoll Jus: pe:

A true Coppy of this Deed aboue written transcribed & with yᵉ originall Compared, this 7th day of August 1683:
       p Edwᵈ · Rishworth ReCor:

To all Christean people to whome these Presents shall Come/ Thomas Holms of Kittery in the County of yorke shire In the Prouince of Mayne In New England Yeamon, & Joanna his wife sends Greeteing. Now Know yee, that I Thomas Holms, & Joanna my wife, for diuerse good Causes & Considerations, us moueing here unto, more espetially for & In Consideration for the sume of fourty three thousand foote of Mʳchantable pine boards, in hand receiued & secured, to bee payd by Henery Child of Kittery, In the County of Yorke shyre in New England Yeamon, before yᵉ signeing & sealeing hereof, Where with Wee acknowledg oʳ selues to bee fully satisfyd Contented & payd, & of euery part, & Prcell thereof do acqnit exonerate & discharge the sayd Henery Child, & his heyres for euer by these Presents, Haue giuen granted, barganed, sould, aliend, Enfeoffed, & Confirmed, & by these Presents do absolutly giue, grant bargane, sell, aliene, Enfeoffe, & Confirme unto the aforesd Henery Child, his heyres executors administrators, & Assignes, a Certen Tract of Land in the Town of Kittery,

Contajneing fourty Acres with yᵉ dwelling house, & out houses, & fences, lijng & being on the East end of Mr Thomas Broughtons Land, on the south side of the Dirty Swampe & so to Wells path, with all the priuiledges, & appurtenances, Tymber, & all the Wood, & underwoods, there in, & there to belonging, or any ways app'tajneing; To haue and to hould, vnto him the sayd Henery Child his heyres, executors, Administrators & Assignes for euer all the aboue mentioned fourty Acres of Land, with the dwelling house out houses, fences, wood, Tymber, tymber trees, underwoods, & all the priuiledges, & appurtenances thereto belonging; And I the sd Thomas Holms, & Joanna my wife do Couenant promiss, & grant to & with the sayd Henery Child, his heyres & Assignes, that they haue in them selues good right, full pouer, & lawfull authority, the aboue mentioned Tract of fourty Acres of Land with the dwelling house, & out house, & out houses, wood, & Tymber, & all other priuiledges, there unto belonging, to sell, & dispose off & that the same & euery part & Parcell thereof, are free & Cleare, & freely & Clearely acquitted, exonerated & discharged of & from all & all manner of former Gifts, grants leases, Morgages, Wills Entajles Judgments, executions, pouer of thirds, & all other Incomberances of what Nature, & kind so euer, had made done, Comitted or suffered to bee done, or Comitted where by the sayd Henery Child, his heyrs executors, Administrators or Assignes, may bee any ways Molested in Euicted, or Eiected out of the aboue mentioned Tract of Land, or house or any part or Prcell there of, by any Prson or persons Whatsoeuer, haueing Clajmeing or pretending to haue, or Clajme any Legall right title, or Interest of, in & to the Premisses, or any part or Prcell thereof And the sayd Thomas Holms and Joannah his wife, doth for them selues, thejr heyres executors & Administrators, Couenant promiss & Grant, to & with the sayd Henery

Book III, Fol. 131, 132.

Child his heyres, executors Administrators & Assignes the aboue mentioned Tract of fourty Acres of Land, with the Dwelling house and out houses, & with all the priuiledges, and appurtenances there unto belonging, [132] or in any wise appertajneing, of what nature & kind soeuer, to warrant & for euer defend by these Presents/ In witness whereof the sayd Thomas Holms & Johannah his wife, haue here unto sett thejre hands & seales this Twenty sixth day of June, In the yeare of our Lord, one thousand six hundred seauenty and Nine, . 1679 :   Thomas Holms (his seale)
Signed sealed, & deliuered,
  In ye Presence of us/   his Marke 𝑇
George Broughton/
Thomas Abbott/   Joannah Holms
Jonathan Nason   her marke 𝐹 (her seale)

  his Marke 𝑇   Thomas Holmes & Joannah his Wife, acknowledged the aboue written Deed of Sale to bee yr free Act & Deede, this 25th day of June 1681 : before mee   John Wincoll Justs of pea :

A true Coppy of this Deed aboue written transcribed out of ye originall & there with Compared this Eight day of August 1683/   p Edw . Rishworth Re : Cor :

Book III, Fol. 132.

Possession was given according to law, by Turff & Twigg, unto Jon Smyth Junjor by the sd Weare, & Consent of his with in mentioned wife Mary, the 19th of July 1683 In Presence of Samell Bankes | John Spencer his marke +

Know all men by these Presents, that I Peter Weare Senior of Yorke, with my wife Mary, for & in Consideration of the Just sume of fiuetene pounds, of currant pay of New England, in hand payd by John Smyth Junjor of Yorke in the prouince of Mayne, In New England, w^r with I do acknowledg my selfe to bee fully satisfyd: do acknowledg to haue barganed & sould, & by these Presents do bargan sell Alliene, assigne & set ouer unto the sd Smyth, to him his heyres, executors, Administrators, & Assignes for euer, a Parcell of Land contajneing Twelue acres, Marsh & vpland, more or less, ljng on that side, & being on the Eastward side of Cape Nuttacke Riuer, the first North Eastward Cricke, from the Harbours Mouth extending from the sd Cricke, Compassing a small Poynt of Marsh unto a Small Coue, w^r at the vpper end there is a Stake stucke up, being the bound marke, & from thence to runne vpon a North East lyne, being part of the sd Weares Lott of Land, given & granted by Mr Edw: Godfrey owneing him selfe a Pattentee, & the sd lott of being & Improuement about Thirty yeares by the sd Weare, Which sd Vpland & Marsh with all the app^rtenances y^runto belonging or app^rtajneing, to bee to ye onely vss & behoofe of ye sd Smyth, to him his heyres, executors, Administrators & Assignes for euer, with out any lett Molestation or disturbance of vs, the sd Peter & Mary Weare & do hereby promiss to defend the title y^rof, against all manner of Prsons from by or under us, laijng Clajme unto the same, & here unto Wee bind us o^r heyeres, executors, Administrators & Assignes: The sd Smith his heyres, & Assigns is duely to pay or Cause to bee payd from tyme to tyme, & all tymes lawfully demanded such acknowledgment to ye proprietor, according to w^t by pportion the sd Weare

Book III, Fol. 132.

doth/ In witness w^rof haue here unto set o^r hands & seales, this eighteenth of July 1683 · Peter Weare (his seale)
Signed Sealed & Mary Weare (her seale)
Deliuered in the her marke
Presence of/
Samuell Bankes/ Peter Weare & his wife Mary, came
John Spencer before mee, this 10th day of August
his marke ┼ 1683 : & did own this Instrume^t to
bee y^r free Act & Deed
Edw. Rishworth Jus : pe :
vera Copia of this Deed aboue written transcribed out of the originall & there with Compared this seauenteenth of August : 1683 : p Edw. Rishworth Re . Cor .

Seizine & possession was given by ye with in named Peter Weare, unto ye sd Thomas Euerell this 11th of July 1683 by Turff and Twigg, In the Presence of Samuell Bankes | Silvester Stover

his marke

Know all men by these Presents, that I Peter Weare Senjor of Yorke, with in the prouince of Mayne In New England, with the Consent of his wife Mary, for & in Consideration of foureteen pounds In Current pay of the sd New England to mee In hand payd, before signeing, sealeing, & deliuering hereof by Thomas Euerell, sometyms of Wells with in the aforesd Prouince, In Consideration of a Tract of Land, lijng & being about one Mile on the Eastward side of Cape Nuddaeke Riuer, begining vpon the South side of a Small pond of Water, & from thence vpon a Streight Lyne unto a Percell of Low Land, know by the name of the burnt Marsh brooke, & so bounded by the sea, unto a Small Coue w^r the fresh water runnes into the sea · Being a Necke of Land Contajneing about Twenty seauen Acres, more or less, giuen & granted, by the Select men of ye aforesd Town of yorke, vnto the

Book III, Fol. 132.

aforesd Weare, fully ratifijng & Confirmeing, all the right, & title, & Interest, in the sd Land, togeather, with all the appurtenañs there vnto belonging, & app^rtajneing, & to bee to the onely uss, & behoofe of ye sayd Euerell, unto him his heyres, executors, Administrators or Assignes/ And I the sayd Weare with my sd wife, do hereby promiss to defend the Title y^rof against all manner of Prsons, from by or under us, laijng any Clajme unto the same, & here unto wee bind us our heyres, executors, Administrators, & Assignes/ In witness w^rof, haue here unto set our hands & scales this tenth of July 1683;

Signed, sealed, & Deliuered   Peter Weare (his seale)
    In the Presence of/   Mary Weare (her seale)
    Samell Bankes   her marke
    Siluester Stouer   Peter Weare Senjo^r & his wife Mary
    his marke   came before mee this 14th day of August 1683 : & owned this Instrument to be y^r free Act & Deed/ Edw: Rishworth Jus. pe.

A true Coppy of this Instrument transcribed, & Compared with the originall this 17th of August: 1683:
            p Edw · Rishworth ReCor

Prouince of Mayne | Whereas It doth appeare vpon record that y^r seuerall grants made & given by the Town of Kittery unto Richard & Geo: Leader of Certen Trats & portions of Lands & Tymber lijng & being in the Town of Barwicke alias Newgewanacke for the accomodations of those saw Mills, there bujlt by the sd Rich'd Leader as by the date of seuerall grants vidz^t

first/ one Grant of upland beareing date Aprill Twelth 1654. lijng on the East side of the little Riuer, lately lajde out & measured by Capt John Wincoll, to bee Two hundred thirty & six Acres/ & another grant of the same date, for all the pine trees being vp the little riuer, paijng fiueteene pounds yearely for Annuall rent/ & another grant of sixty Acres of Meddow Dated August 24th 1653 : Called by the name of Totnocke/ with another Grant of three Acres, of Meddow beareing the same date ;

Also measured & layd out by order of the Town, by Capt John Wincoll the suruayer to William Hutchinson a Pcell of Land Contayneing one hundred and Thirty Acres/ one hundred acres of the same being for the exchange of Twelue Acres for ye accomodation of the Ministrey, & the other thirty acres given in lew of an Allder Swampe, & seuerall other spotts of Marsh or Meddow ; And another Grant lijng on the Westerly side of the little Riuer according to Estimation three hundred Acres of Land Adiouncing to the Saw Mills/ which being measured by Capt Wincoll the suruayer is one hundred seauenty eight Acres/

[133] Wee the Select men of the Town of Barwicke, alias Newgewanacke, In Consideration of those greate disbursements, ouer & aboue ye purchase of sd Saw Mills of Mr Richard Leader by payment of a great rent, & carrijng on of the whoole worke, for more then Twenty years togeather, w^rby many hundreds, if not some thousands of pounds haue beene expended, as Wee haue Certenly beene by there agents Informed, & in a greate part do o^r selues know & understand & y^t by Mr Richd Hutchinson of London deceased, & since his decease by Eliakime Hutchinson & W^m : Hutchinson, & there agents, y^t haue alsoe beene at more then ordinary Charges for the new bujlding of the sd Mills, Rebuilding of the Dames at sundrey tymes , And w^ras y^r are seuerall Prticular Grants made as aboue specifyd in diuerse small papers, which may bee apt to mischarrage, for better Preuenting & security w^rof, Wee Judg meete to draw y^m into & Intyre wrighting, togeather, & do giue o^r free approbation, of what o^r Town in the whoole formerly haue

granted & done: unto the aforesd Eliakime Hutchinson as a full Confirmation of the Premisses/

Witness John
   Emerson/

As witness our hands this 28th day of August 1683:

These Select men which haue here subscribed do acknowledg in the behalfe of the Town this to bee y{r} Act & deed to Mr Eliakime Hutchinson/ before mee Edw. Rishworth Jus: pe:

John Wincoll/
James Emery/
Will Loue his Marke/ 𝓜
James Playstead
John Shapleigh/
John Bray/

} Select men of Kittery

vera Copia of this Instrument aboue written, transcribed out of the originall, & y{r} with Compared this 21th day of Septb{r} 1683: by Edw: Rishworth ReCor.

Know all men by these Presents, that I William Palmer of Yorke in the Prouince of Mayne yeoman, for & in Consideration of Twenty three pounds, In Current pay of New England In hand receined, before the Insealeing & Deliuery of these Presents, by Isaac Guttadge of Kittery lately from England, the receipt of hee doth hereby acknowledge, & him selfe y{r} with to bee freely satisfyd Content & payd, & doth for him selfe his heyres executors, administrators & Assignes, & for euery of them for euer, exonerate acquitt release, & discharge Isacc Gutridge, his heyres, executors, Administrators & Assigns of & from y{e} sd sume, & euery part & penny thereof, as also for diuerse other good Causes & Consideiations, Haue given granted barganed & sould, Enfeoffed, released & Confirmed, to Isacc Gutteridg abouesd his heyres, executors, Administrators or Assignes, all my right Title & Interest, vnto that his halfe part of a Certen Necke of Land, scituate & being in Cape Porpus, Comanly

Book III, Fol 133, 134.

known by the name of Batsons Necke, with all the halfe part of Marsh adioyneing & app'rtajneing to it, as It is now seuered, & diuided by seuerall marked trees, through the sayd Necke of Land sometyms in the possession of John Ellson, & afterwards in the possession of John Dauess Senjo^r, & now in the sayd Palmers possession, which was sometyms In the Teano^r of Fardinad^o Goft or his Assigns with all my right & Title to a Certen Parcell of Land, Comanly known & Called by the name of the grass plott: neare adioyneing together with all my right title & Interest unto, & in all Lands, whither vpland Marsh in ye sd Town of Cape Porpus

_{This Deed wholly Entered in pa 134}

[134] Wee whose names are here vnder written, being Chosen, & appoynted by the Select men, of the Townes of yorke & Wells, to runne the lyne between the aforesd Townes, from the marked red oake tree, that standeth in ye way, that goeth from yorke to Wells, wch are ye bounds between them, to the South West side of Tocnocke Marshes, did accordingly on the thirteenth day of Septemb^r one thousand six hundred eighty three begjne at ye aforesd Marked tree, & runne a lyne North West, & by west, & marked ye trees in the lyne as Wee went, to the South west side of Tockenocke Marshes, to an apple pine tree wch standeth in the lyne, y^t diuideth the Towns of yorke & Kittery, & Wells about one hundred & Twenty pooles, or pearch, from ye South West side of Totnocke Marshes, & marked the sd apple pine tree, on foure sides, & there made these too letters Y. W. It being in distance from ye abouesd marked tree, y^t standeth in ye way from Yorke to Wells, about six Miles & a quarter/ witness our hands/

    Joⁿ Littlefejld Abra · Preble
    John Cloyce   Arther Bragdon
    for Wells   for yorke /

Book III, Fol. 134.

A true Coppy of these boundarys between yorke & wells as bounded by Prsons appoy'd & chosen by both transcribed & Compared with the originall this 19th Octob^r 1683 :
Edw : Rishworth ReCor : p Edw . Rishworth ReCor :

These Presents bindeth mee William Ardell & my Assignes, to pay to Mathew Austine Junjo^r of yorke or his order, or Assignes, the iust sume of six pounds Current New England Money, for & in Consideration of an horse, that ye sd Austine hath sould unto him, & this day I haue receiued of him, which six pounds is to bee payd to him the sd Mathew Austine, at or before ye Twenteth day of Septemb^r next Insewing, the date hereof, as witness my hand this 21th day of August 1683 :

William Ardell

Mr. William Ardell came before mee, this 21th of August 1683 & acknowledged y^s bill aboue written to bee his Act & Deed/ Edw : Rishworth Jus · pe

A true Coppy of this bill transcribed & with the originall Compared this this 21th of Octob^r : 83 :

p Edw : Rishworth ReCor

This bill bindeth mee Edmund shore now resident at Boston to pay or cause to bee payd to Mis Mary Sayword of yorke ye full & iust some of thirty shillings, in money or goods æquiuolent to money at or before the last of Septemb^r next Insewing the date here of, & for the true payment thereof, I bind mee, my heyres, executors Administrators or Assigns, as witness my hand this 26 : May : 1683 :

Samll wakefejld/ Edw . Shoare his marke/
Hene : Williams/

BOOK III, FOL. 134.

A true Coppy of yᵗ bill tianscribed, & Compaied with yᵉ originall this 23 : Octobʳ 1683 : p Edw : Rishworth Re : Coi

Know all men by these Presents, yᵗ I William Palmer of Yoike. In the piouince of Mayne yeamon, for & in Consideiation of the sume of Twenty thiee poūds in Cuiient pay of New England, In hand receiued before the Ensealing & deliuery of these Prsents, by Isanac Gutteridg of Kittery lately fiom England, the receipt wʳof, hee doth hereby acknowledg, and him selfe to bee there with fully satisfyd, content, & payd, & doth for him selfe, his heyrs executors, administrators, & Assignes, & foi euery of them, do for euer exonerate, acquitt, release & discharge, sayd Isace Gutteridge, his heyres executors, administratois & Assignes, of & from the sd sume, & of euery part Paicell & penny there of, as also for diuerse other good Causes, & Considerations haue giuen gianted, barganed & sould, Enfeoffed released & Confirmed, to Isacae Gutteridg abouesd, his heyers, executors Administiatois, oi Assignes, all my iight title & Interest, unto that his halfe part of a Certen Necke of Land scituate & being in Cape Porpus, Commanly known by the name of Batsons Necke, with all the halfe part of Marsh adioyneing & appʳtajneing to It, as It is now severed, & diuided; by seuerall marked trees, through yᵉ sd Necke of Land, sometyme in yᵉ possession of John Ellson, & afterwards in yᵉ possession of John Dauess Senjoʳ, & now in the sayd Palmeis possession, Which was sometyme in the Tenoʳ of ffardinand Hoffe, as his Assignes; togeather with all my iight & Title to a Certen parcell of Land Called Commanly & known by the name of the grass plott, neier adioyneing togeather, with all my right Title & Interest unto, & in all Lands, whither vpland Marsh in our Town of Cape Porpus, whither layd out or not, which were giuen to John Dauis̄s abouesard; by the sayd T; yᵣ ci which at any tyme,

Book III, Fol. 134, 135.

I bought & purchased, or possessed by Town grant, & hath not beene otherwise disposed off, by selfe & sayd Dauiss, Senjo^r with all & euery dwelling house, or out houseing, or any part of all the Premisses, before barganed & sould, with all the right priuiledgges, & Imunitys, Tymber & Tymber trees, woods and underwoods, there with formerly used, or y^{r}unto belonging or app^{r}tajneing; To haue & to hould, the sayd Necke of Land, Marsh, Town grants, bought Lands, garden plott &c · unto him the sayd Isaac Gutteridg, his heyres, executors Administrators or Assignes for euer/ And sayd William Palmer, for him selfe, his heyres executors, Administrators, & Assignes, doth Couenant promiss & grant, to & with the sd Isaac Gutteridg, his heyers, executors Administrators & Assignes that all & singular the before giuen, & granted, & barganed Premisses are & shall bee remajne and Contmew, Clearly acquitted, exonerated discharged & keept harmeless, from all & all manner of former & other barganes, gyfts, grants Morgages, extents, Judgments, executions Dowers Title of Dowers, or Incomberances whatsoeuer, to bee had made, suffered or done by the sayd Palmer, his heyres executors Administrators, or Assignes, or any other Person, from by or under him them or any of them, as Witness my hand & seale, this one & Twenteth day of August, [135] In the yeare of o^r Lord, one thousand six hundred eighty & Three/

Signed sealed & Deliuered In   William Palmer ($_{\text{seale}}^{\text{his}}$)
    the Presence of us/   William Palmer came before mee
    Mary Partridge/   this 25th day of Septemb^r 1683:
    Anthony Stannion/   and owned this Instrument aboue
    John Bartsham/   written to bee his Act & Deede/
    George ffabine/   Edw · Rishworth Jus : pe :

A true Coppy of this Instrume^t aboue written, transcribed out of the originall, & there.with Compared this 29th day of Octob^r 1683:   p Edw: Rishworth ReCor:

Book III, Fol. 135.

To all Christean people, to whose these Presents shall Come, ffrancis Backhouse sends greeteing: Know yee that I ffran: Backehouse, with the free Consent of my wife Darcas, of Sacoe of the Prouince of Mayne In New England, for seuerall good Causes & Consideiations mee y^{r}unto moueing, & moie espetially, for & in consideration of seauenteen pounds receiued, in hand Deliuered & sufficiently payd, by Joseph Storer which is to my satisfaction, & w^{t}with I am fully Contented, haue from mee my heyres executors, Administrators, haue barganed sould granted Enfeoffed & Confirmed, & by these Presents do sell Enfeoffe, & Confirme unto Jos. Storer of Wells, & ye aforesd pıouince, his heyres executois, Administratois & Assignes, for euer my Land & Marsh, lijng at Drakes Ysland the Marsh being fiue acres moie oi less the sd Maish is bounded with Mr Nannys Maish on the West side, & John Gouches Maish on the East side, & one end bounded with a great Cıicke, & the other end with the ysland, & about one halfe of y^e vpland, which was formeıly John Crosses vpon y^e sd Ysland, with all y^e appurtenances & priuiledges y^{r}unto belonging, with all Conuenieney$_s$ in any wise app^{r}tayneing or belonging, freely & quietly to haue & to hould with out any matter of Clajme, or demand fıom mee y^e sd ffıancis Backehouse, or any Prson or Persons from by oi undeı mee my heyıes executors, Administıatoıs, & Assignes for euer, to hee the sd Jos: Storer his heyres, executoıs, administıatoıs & Assignes; I do hereby declare to bee truely & rightly possessed, of each & efiy part & Paicell of Land & Maish as abouesd; And y^t hee ye sd Jos Storer, his heyres executors, administrators & Assignes, shall peaceably & quietly haue hould & Inioy all ye abouesd Prıises granted & sould to them for euer: & I do heıeby promiss & Couenant to & with the sd Joseph Storeı, that all ye Premisses gıanted & sould are free & Cleare fıom all gyfts grants, bargans, leases Dowrys, Morgages, Judgm^{ts}, & all other Incomberances w^{t}soeuer, & do pıomiss to warrant & defend the Title & Inteıest of the Premisses, fıom mee my heyres, executors, Administrators & Assignes, & from any Prson under mee, or by my meanes, or procurement/ In testimony where of wee haue to our hands & seales sett, this thirteenth day of October 1683 :

Witnesses/   ffrancis Backehouse (his seal)
Edw. Rishworth/   Darcas Backehouse (her seale)
Elizabeth Scamon
her marke   her marke

ffrancis Backehouse & his wife Darcas came before mee this 13th day of Octob^r 1683 : & owned this Instrumet to bee y^i act & Deede/ Edw. Rishworth Jus : pc .

A true Coppy of this Instrum^t aboue written transcribed out of ye originall, & y^{r}with Compared this 30th day of October 1683 : p Edw. Rishworth

Know all men by these Presents, that I Edw : Rishworth of Yorke, in ye Prouince of Mayne In New England Re : Cor : for seuerall good Causes & Consideiations there unto mee moueing, & more especially for & in Consideration of the iust sume of Twenty one pounds tenn shillings, to mee in hand payd & secured to bee payd in good Current siluer of New England, by Capt Job Allcocke of Yorke aforesd, w^{r}with, & of euery part & Prcell y^{r}of, I do acknowledg my selfe to bee fully payd, Contented, & satisfyd, do by these Presents giue grant sell ; bargane, aliene, conuay, Enfeoff, & Confirme, And haue hereby given granted, sould, barganed, aliend, Conuayd, Infeoffed, & confirmed, from mee my heyrs executors, administrators, & Assignes, unto the aboue named Job Allcocke his heyres, executors, administrators, & Assignes, all or any of them, a Certen tract Messuage, or Parcell of Land, contajneing the quantity & proportion of about foure acres, of Pastour Land, vpland or y^r

abouts, bee It more or less, being & butting vpon yorke Riuer, ljng neare to the Harbours Mouth, ljng bounded by y^t acre of Land, which I the sd Rishworth formerly sould unto Job Allcocke, Adioyneing to the Land of John Brawn to ye South East, & a Parcell of Land of sd Allcocks own Land, ljng & being on the North West side of the sd Land, runneing backe Eastwardly, so fare as the high way, as also a Certen Landing place adioyneing to the sd vpland or pasture, being a poynt of Land, & beach runneing home to ye Riuer, on the South West end of the Land aforesd, next unto sd Allcocks house which landing place was formerly Richd Burgesses, & by him sould to ye sd Rishworth, as by his bill of sale appeareth, beareing Date the 14th day of Decemb^r 1660: which foure Acres of pasture Land, as aboue mentioned, & the Landing place as aboue expressed & bounded, with all ye prinledges, imunitys & appurtenances, unto ye sd vpland & Landing place, in any wise app'rtajneing & belonging, To haue & to hould all & euery part of the before recipted Premisses, from mee the sd Rishworth my heyres, executors, Administrators & Assignes, unto the aforesd Job Allcocke, his heyres, Administrators & Assignes for euer · And further I the sd Edw: Rishworth do Couenant & agree In the behalfe of my selfe, my heyrs, executors, Administrators & Assignes, with ye sd Job [136] Allcocke his heyres, executors, Administrators, & Assignes, that ye d Land & Landing place aboue mentioned, is free & Cleare from all, & all manner of Titles, Clajmes, troubles, leases barganes, morgages, & all other Incomberances w'soeuer: And further p these Presents, I bind my selfe my heyres, Administrators & Assignes, to warrant & Defend the sd Land aboue specifyd from all Prsons w'soeuer, Clajmeing or Pretending any right, title, Interest, from by or under mee, or by any way or meanes throg^h my procurement: In testimony w^rof, I haue hereunto afixed my hand & seale, the Twenty fourth day of ffebru: One thousand six hundred & eighty. Anno: Dom : 1680: in the Thyrty secund

Book III, Fol. 136.

yeare, of the Reign of o*ʳ* Soueraigne L*d* Charles the secund of England, Scottland, France, & Ireland, King, Fidej Defenso*ʳ* Edw : Rishworth (his scale)

Signed sealed & deliuered/   M*r* Edw Rishworth came & In the Presence of   made his acknowledgm*ᵗ* y*ᵗ* John Penwill/   the Instrument aboue written was his act & Deede/ acknowledged this 26*ᵗʰ* off ffebru : 1680 : before mee John Dauess/ Jus . pe ·

A true Coppy of this Instrument aboue written transcribed out of the originall, & there with Compared this 30*ᵗʰ* day of Octob*ʳ* 1683 ·   p Edw : Rishworth ReCor .

.

J vnderwritten do Ingage my selfe, my heyres & Assignes to pay to Mary Sayword or her order, the iust sume of fourty shillings in siluer at demand, as witness my hand, this 29th day of August 1683 :   John Price/
Testes/   A true Coppy of this bill transcribed & John Dauess/   Compared with originall this 6th of Noveb*ʳ* 1683 :

     p Edw : Rishworth Re :Cor :

Bee It known unto all men whom this may Concerne, that I Eliakime Hutchinson now rescident in the Town of Boston County of Suffocke of y*ᵉ* Coloney of ye Massatusetts In New England, M*ʳ*chant, for diuerse good Causes & Considerations there unto moueing & more espetially for the sume of Eleaven pounds fineteen shillings, in Current money of New England to mee in hand already payd by Daniell Goodine Senio*ʳ*, now rescident in Barwicke alias Newgewanacke, in the prouince of Mayne, for which sume, being by mee receiued of the sd Gooding, I do hereby acknowledg my selfe to bee fully satisfyd, Contented & payd, do by these Presents, giue grant sell alliene, make ouer & Confirme a Certen Tract of Land from mee my heyres executors Adminstrators & Assignes, & haue given granted sould aliend make ouer & Confirmed the Parcell of Land aforesd, Contayneing the full quantity of Eleauen Acres & three quarters of vpland, lijng & being next Adioyneing, to Humphry Spencers Land w^ron formerly hee liued, & his dwelling house standeth, unto ye sd Daniell Gooding his heyrs executors, Administrators & Assignes for euer/ to haue & to hould ye sd tract or parcell of Land, as before expressed according to these bounds as followeth/ Ninety pooles South East & by East being next vnto ye Land of Humfrey Spencer, & Eighty pooles East, next adioyneing to the Coman high way, & South fourty eight pooles, next to the sd Eliakime Hutchinson, to which portion or Parcell of Lands as thus aboue bounded, with all the Imunitys & appurtenances as aboue bounded y^runto belonging or any wise app^rtayneing; I the sd Eliakime Hutchinson make ouer & Confirme in behalfe of my selfe, my executors, Administrators & Assignes, to sd Daniell Gooding his heyres, executors, Administrators & Assignes for euer: And do further Conenant promiss y^t the sd part or portion of Land, is Cleare & free from all gifts, grants leases, Morgages, executions Dowries, & all other Incomberances W^tsoeuer, & do by these Presents promiss in behalfe of my selfe my heyres, executors, Administrators & Assignes to ye sd Daniell Gooding his heyres executors & assignes to defend & warrant the title, & Interest of the sd Land, from by or under mee, or any of us, & from all others, by us or any others by o^r procurement/ In testimony w^rof I haue here unto set my hand

Book III, Fol. 136.

& seale, this Twenty eighty day of August, 1683 :
Signed sealed & Deliuered/   Eliakim Hutchinson (locus sigilli)
 in the Presence of/   Mr Eliakime Hutchinson Came
 William Playstead   before mee this 29th day of
 Christopher Battersby/   August 1683 : & owned this
                              Instrument to bee his Act &
                              Deed Edw : Rishworth
                                          Jus : pe
A true Coppy of this Instrument transcribed & with ye originall Compared this 6th day of Decembr 1683 :
                              p Edw : Rishworth ReCor

These Presents witness, that wras Renold Jenkines by his Deed of gyft to his sonn Stephen Jenkines beareing date the tenth day of February sixteen hundred seauenty eight, hath giuen & granted to his sd sonn his whoole Estate both Prsonall & reall (except some Perticulars yrof, as are in the sd Deed expressly excepted) Now know all men by these Presents that I ye sd Stephen Jenkines for & in Consideration of fourty shillings In hand payd to mee by Capt Charles Frost, before ye signeing & sealeing hereof, haue absolutely given & granted, barganed sould, aliend Enfeoffed & Confirmed And by these Presents do absolutely giue grant, bargan sell aliene Enfeoff & Confirme vnto the sd Capt Charles Frost his heyres executors, administrators & Assigns for euer : a peece of sault Marsh Contayneing one Acre more or less, lijng & being at Sturgeon Cricke, ouer against the place called the Ceaders, or landing place, bounded with Sturgeon Cricke on the East, & North & North West, & on the South & South Wet, with the fence on the vpland, the sd Marsh being part of my fathers Gyft not excepted in his Deede of Gyft beforesd ; To haue & to haue & hould all the before barganed Premisses, to him ye sd Capt Charles Frost his

BOOK III, FOL. 136, 137.

heyrs executors Administrators & Assigns for euer; And the sd Stephen Jenkens doth further Couenant promiss & grant for him selfe, his heyrs executors administrators & Assignes, to & with ye sd Capt Charles Frost, his heyrs executors, Administrators & Assigns, y^t hee ye sd Steven Jenkins is now ye true owner of the abouesd Marsh, at the signeing & sealeing of these Presents: & y^t hee hath in him selfe, full pouer & lawfull authority to sell, & alienate ye same, & doth hereby warrant the same & euery part y^rof, unto the sd Capt Charles Frost his heyres executors Administrators & Assignes that it now is & euer shall bee free & Cleare of wifes Thirds, or any other Incomberances w'soeuer, had made done or suffered to bee done, by him ye sd Stephen Jenkins on any other Person by from or under him, w^rby the sd Capt Frost, his heyres or successors may bee disturbed, [137] in the peaceable possession of the whoole, or any part of the before purchased Premisses, & for auoyding of any after Controuersys, y^e wife of sd Stephen Jenkines, shall acknowledg her Consent to this Present deede, of sale aforesd/ In witness here of I haue here unto sett my hand & seale, this 20th of Nouember 1683:

Signed sealed & deliuered/   Stephen Jenkins
in the Presence of us/   his marke O ($^{his}_{seal}$)
Christopher Banefejld/   Stephen Jenkins & Elizabeth his
William Stacie/   wife came before mee this thirteenth day of Novemb^r one thousand six hundred eighty three, & they did both acknowledg this Instrum^t aboue written to bee y^r free Act & deed
    Edw: Rishworth Jus: pe:

A true Coppy of this Instrument aboue written, transcribed out of ye originall & y^rwith Compared this 6th day of Decemb^r 1683:   p Edw: Rishworth ReCor:

Book III, Fol. 137.

To all whome these Presents shall come, Renold Jenkines of Kittery in the County of yorke, In the Massatusetts Coloney In New England, sends greeting the Tenth day of February, in ye yeare of o^r Lord God Anno Dom̄: one thousand six hundred seaventy & eight, & in the Thirteth yeare of the Reigne of his Serene Majesty o^r Soueraigne Ld Charles the secund, by the Grace of God of England, Scotland, France & Ireland King, Defend^r of the faith &c: Now know yee, that I the aboue mentioned Renold Jenkins, for seuerall good causes & Considerations mee y^{r}unto moueing, & more espetially for ye reall loue & Intyre affection which I beare unto my Elldest sonn Stephen Jenkines I being lawfully possessed of seuerall Lands goods & Cattle, haue hereby freely & absolutely given, granted, Enfeoffed, made ouer & confirmed, & by these Presents do absolutely give, grant Enfeoffe make ouer & confirme vnto him the sd Stephen Jenkines his heyres, executors, Administrators & Assignes for euer, all my Lands, Meddows, Oarchards, houses buildings, Ediffesces, goods Chattles moneys wares, M^{r}chandises, with all & euery the priuilidges, appurtenances profitts benefitts, y^{r}unto belonging or any wise app^{r}tajneing, & to his own proper vss & benefitt, to dispose of any or any part, or Parcell y^{r}of, with what benefitt or Increase shall bee made y^{r}of to him & his heyres for euer : & for all such sum̄e or som̄s of money, as are now, & hereafter shall bee due to mee the sd Renold Jenkins, I do also giue unto my sd sonn Stephen, & do giue him full pouer & authority in his own name, to sue for arrest Imprison, acquit or giue acquittances for all or any such debts as hee shall thinke most fitt, & I the sd Renold Jenkins do hereby Ingage my selfe y^t my sd sonn Stephen shall any tyme, or tyms hereafter or hereafter at this Present tyme Seize or take into his own possession, all & euery the Perticulars abouesd (except the too lower peeces of Sault Marsh wch are lyng on Sturgeon Cricke, wch I haue given unto my sonn Jabez Jenkins as appeareth

Book III, Fol. 137.

by a writeing under my hand, always prouided y^t my sd sonn Stephen shall prouide for mee a Comfortable Mantenance both meate drinke, washing lodging, & apparell dureing the tyme of my naturall life, & imediately after my decease, my sonn Stephen shall pay unto my too younger daughters, namely Saraih, & Mary fiue pouds a peece or each of them a Cow/ I do further Ingage y^t I the sd Renold Jenkin, will at no tyme hinder Molest or Contradict, my sd son Stephen my selfe, or any other from by or under mee/ In witness w^rof I haue hereof I haue here unto sett my hand & seale the day & yeare first aboue written/

Signed sealed & deluered/   The marke of [mark] (his seale)
In the Presence of
Joseph Hamond/   Renold Jenkins
Kathern Leighton   Renold Jenkins appeared before mee this 20th day of March 167⅔ & did acknowledg the aboue written Deed of Gift to bee his act & Deed, with his hand & seale to it/

           John Wincoll Assotiate/

A true Coppy of ye Deed of Gyft transcribed, & with the Originall Compared this 7th of Decemb^r 1683:

           p Edw · Rishworth ReCor

Wee whose names are here vnderwritten, being appoynted a Comittee by the last Court of pleas held at yorke, May 29th 1683 · In order & in referrence to the settleing of the Estate of Thomas Rogers of Sacoe, Decesed/

Wee haue reuised the Accomp^t & do find all Legall debts being payd, y^t there is due to the children being fiue, the full sume of one hundred fiuety seauen pounds 157^{lb} 03 : 06 : out of which the Land & Marsh comes to one hundred &

foure pounds 10^s, which Land wee Judge meete to appoynt for ye too sonns, the Elldest son Richard Rogers, to haue a double portion, being fiuety too pounds 10^s 7^d, & ye rest of the children to haue thejr proportion, which is Twenty six pounds 3^s 11^d each Child, the youngest his sonn to haue his part out of ye Land, & as it was apprised at first, & the other children to haue y^r portions when they come to yeares payd them as the law directs by Richd Rogers who is to giue in security for the Performance hereof to the Court or Councill of this prouince as is aboue expressed; hee the sd Richd Rogers, possessing the Land & March, as abouesd for his own proper uss, & brothers as is aboue expressed, the Administrator being payd his disbursements, & other losses allowed to him which nineteene pounds fiue shillings 8^d, which with the sume due to the Children abouesd being one hundred fiuety seauen pounds 3^s 6^d is according to the Inventory one hundred seaventy six pounds 9^s 2^d, unto which Conclusion wee haue hereunto sett our hands, this one & Twenteth of July one thousand six hundred eighty three/

A true Coppy of this Instrume^t aboue written Compared & transcribed with the originall this 26th of November 1683 : p Edw: Rishworth Re: Cor:	ffrancis Champernown ffrancis Hooke/ Charles Frost/

[138] This bill bindeth mee Thomas Heath of Boston in New England, my heyres, executors Administrators or Assignes, to pay or Cause to bee payd unto Robert young of yorke, or his heyres or Assignes the full & iust some of fiueteen pounds Current money of New England, at or before the fifth day of November next Insewing, the date hereof/ & for the true Prformance hereof, I bind mee my

Book III, Fol. 138.

heyres, executors or Assignes unto the sd Robert young his heyres or Assignes as witness my hand this foureteenth day of December 1681.

Testes   Thomas Heath
John Penwill/   Thomas Heath came before mee this
The marke   first of Decemb^r 1681 · & acknowl-
of John Hoy *TH*   edged this Instrum^t of writeing to
                       bee his Act, & Deede,
                       John Dauess Dep^{ty} Presid^t

A true Coppy of this bill transcribed & Compared with the originall this 18th day of December 1683 · 83 ·

                 p Edw . Rishworth ReCor/

To all Christean people to whome these Presents shall come/ Know yee y^t I Nathll ffryer of Portsmouth, in Pischataq̊, riuer M^{r}chant, & Dorothy my wife, for & in Consideration of the sum̄e of one hundred thirty & fiue pounds in hand payd, Before the Ensealeing here of, by Rewben Hull of Portsmouth in Pischatq̊ riuer M^{r}chant, the receipt whereof Wee hereby acknowledg & y^{r}of & of euery part & Parcell thereof, do for us o^r heyres, executors, & Assigns acquitt & discharge the sd Rewben Hull, his heyers, executors, Administrators, Or Assignes & y^{r}with do acknowledg our selues to bee satisfyd, Contented & payd, haue barganed, sould, aliend, Assigned Sett ouer, & p these Presents do bargane Sell aliene Assigne & sett ouer unto the sayd Rewben Hull, all that Island being one of the Ysles of shoales com̄anly known by the name of Malligo Ysland togeather, with all the dwelling house ware houses fishing houses stage houses, stages, flakes, flakerowmes there on . with all the Chaynes, Ankers, & moreings & moreing places whatsoeuer, & all other profitts, and priuiledges to ye sd Ysland belonging or in any wise appertayneing, or here to fore p mee or my Assigns used & Inioyed, which sd Ysland of Malligo, is now in the possession of y⁰ sd Rewben Hull. To haue & to hould, unto him the sd Rewben Hull, his heyres, executors, administrators, or Assignes for euer, & the sd Nathall ffryer for him selfe his heyres, executors, & Administrators, & for euery of them do Couenant & promiss to & with the sd Rewben Hull, his heyres executors, Administrators, or Assignes, & with euery of them, that the Present, & before the Ensealeing hereof, hee standeth ceazed & possessed of all the aboue mentioned Premisses, in a good Estate of fee symple, & y' not barganed sould, giuen granted, aliened, Assigned sett ouer, or morgaged the aboue mentioned, nor any part thereof, to any Person whatsoeuer, & further the sd Nathaniell Fryer & Dorothy his wife, for them selues theire heyres, executors & Administrators & for euery of them, do Couenant & promiss, to & with the sd Rewben Hull, his heyres, executors Administrators Or Assignes, & with euery of them to defend the Title y'of, unto him the sd Rewben Hull his heyres executors, Administrators or Assignes, against all Prsons w'soeuer laijng Claime thereto from by or under mee/ In witness w'of I the sd Nathll ffryer & Dorothy my wife haue here unto sett our hands, & seales the Eleauenth of October, Anno Dom̄: one thousand Six hundred eighty & three, & in the Thirty fiue yeare of y⁰ Reign of our soueraigne Lord Charles the secund, King of England, Scottland ffrance, & Ireland, Defend' of the faith : 1683 : This Deed do not Include the Moreing place, Cheyne, & Anker bought of William Seauy, & sould to Phillip Odihorne, & now In sd Odihornes possession/   Nathaniell ffryer (his seal)

Signed Sealed, & Deliuered   Dorathy ffryer (her seale)

   In Presence of us/   Mr Nathll ffryer, & Dorathy his wife
   Elias Styleman/   Came before mee the 27th day of
   Samll Wentworth/   Decembr 1683 . & did both own this
   John Gillman/   Instrument aboue written, to bee
                        thejr free act, & deed
                            Edw : Rishworth Jus : pe :

BOOK III, FOL. 138, 139.

A true Coppy of this Instrument aboue written, transcribed out of the originall & there with Compared, this 28th day of Decembr 1683 : as Attests Edw : Rishworth ReCor :

These may satisfy whome It may Concerne, yt John Card at the day of his Marage to Widdow Winchester, being ye sixteenth day of Janv : 1683 : the sd John Card did relinquish, & doth disown & Ingage yt hee will not Meddle with any Estate of her former husbands, or any thing that belonged to her, but onely her Person/

owned before mee, & seuerall other Prsons the day & yeare aboue written/ John Dauess Jus : pe :

Will : Moore/
John Moore/

William Moore & John Moore Came before mee this 16th of Jañy 1683 : & made oath to ye treuth of wt is aboue Written/

Taken vpon oath before mee/ John Dauess Just : pe :

vera Copia of this aboue written, & of these oaths vnder written transcribed, & with originall Compard this 19th of Janvary 1683/ p Edw : Rishworth Re : Cor :

[139] Mis Katherine Nanny haueing a good & Legall Interest of a Certen Poynt or Necke of land, lijng at yorke In ye prouince of Mayne, comanly Called by ye name of Mis Gorges Poynt, Contajning about 12 : or 20 Acres of Land bee It more or less, as executrix to her first husband Mr Robt Nanny deceased, till a debt of Eleauen pounds Sterlg was fully satisfyd, as appeareth by a Judgt granted for ye same at a prouinciall Court houlden at Pischataq, poynt for sd Prouince Octobr 18th 1647 : which by sd Rishworth was

possessed & Improued seuerall years from ye right of ye sd Robert Nanny/

Edw: Rishworth in behalfe of ye sd Katherine Nanny alias Nayler, Enteres Cawtion to secure ye Interest of the sd Land according to ye aforesd Judgm^t & against the acknowledgm^t or Entering the ReCord of any Deede for any Person w'soeuer relateing y^runto, vntill the eleuen pounds Sterling as aboue sayd, bee duely satisfyd & payd/

Entered this 29th Janv: 1683: p Edw: Rishworth ReCor.

INDEX.

INDEX OF

Date.	Grantor	Grantee.	Instrument.
1675, Jan. 10	ABBET, Richard et ux.	Thomas Parkes	Deed
1677, May 31	ABBET, Richard et ux.	Thomas Holms	Deed
	ABUMHAMEN, Indian, see Robin-Hood		
1670, Jan, 6	ALLCOCKE, Job	Joseph Penwill	Deed
1679, Dec. 10	ALLCOCKE, Job	Abraham Parker	Deed
16$\frac{79}{80}$, Mar 4	ALLCOCKE, Job	Sylvester Stover	Assignment
1680, Sept 13	ALLCOCKE, Job et ux.	Sylvester Stover	Deed
1679, Feb. 18	ALLCOCKE, John, estate of	Job Allcocke	Award
1678, Nov. 18	ALLCOCKE, Joseph, estate of, by John Twisden, administrator	Shubael Dummer	Deed
1677, Dec. 7.	ALLARD, Hugh	Francis Wanewright	Mortgage
16$\frac{79}{80}$, Mar. 11	ALLDEN, John	George Pearson	Deposition
1678, Nov. 13	ALLEN, Edward	George Bramhall	Deed
1681, July 15	ALLEN, Edward et ux.	Andrew Mainenell	Deed
1678, Dec. 4	ANDREWS, John	Margery Bray	Deposition

GRANTORS.

Folio.	Description.
64	40 acres in *Kittery* on Newgewanacke river, near Post Wigwame, excepting Mr Leader's pine timber.
14	30 acres with house in *Kittery* near Quamphegan falls, north of the fort hill; and 6 acres marsh.
52	House, garden-plot and appurtenances in *York*, next Edward Rishworth's.
97	80 acres in *York* between York river, Piscataqua bounds and lots of Thomas Adams and Samuel Bragdon
107	Of a claim of 55 shillings against the estate of John Allcocke.
100	One fourth of the Cape Neck in *York*.
107	Assigning to Job the interest in the Cape Neck in *York*, conveyed by him to Sylvester Stover
60	One half of Farmer Allcock's Neck at mouth of York river and 4 acres marsh on the western branch, in *York*.
17	Land, house and personal property on the *Isles of Shoals*, to secure £70
66	As to payment by Pearson to Richard Bray of the consideration for Cousins island in *Casco Bay*.
69	Quitclaim to 400 acres [in *Falmouth*] conveyed by George Cleeve to Hope Allen, except 50 acres to Henry Kirke.
100	50 acres in *Casco* [*Falmouth*] formerly given to Henry Kirke, and by him forfeited
39	As to Joseph Pearce's disposition of his estate in her favor.

Index of Grantors.

Date.	Grantor.	Grantee.	Instrument.
1674, Feb. 25	ANGER, Samson	Richard Wood	Deed
1678, Oct. 26	ANGER, Samson et ux.	John Pullman	Deed
1683, Sept. 21	ARDELL, William	Matthew Austine, jun.	Bond
1679, Sept. 3	ARMITAGE, Joseph	—— Smyth	Letter
1672, April 4	ASHLY, William et ux.	Francis Littlefield, sen.	Deed
1681, Mar. 2	AUSTINE, Samuel et ux.	Joseph Storer	Deed
168½, Mar. 15	AUSTINE, Samuel et ux.	Emmanuel Davess	Deed
168½, Mar. 15	AUSTINE, Samuel et ux.	Emmanuel Davess	Deed
	AVERALL, see Everell		
1677, Jan. 14	BACKUS, Francis	John Cross, sen.'s estate	Receipt
1683, Oct. 13	BACKEHOUSE, Francis et ux.	Joseph Storer	Deed
Recorded, 1679, June 28	BANEFIELD, Christopher and James Emery	Nathan Lawd, sen.	Survey
1680, July 23	BAREFOOTE, Walter	John Jefford and John Sargent	Caution
1675, April 12	BARRETT, John	Francis Littlefield	Deed
1678, Sept. 19	BARRETT, John et ux.	Joseph Bools, sen.	Deed
168½, Mar. 15	BARRETT, John et ux.	Samuel Austine	Deed
1670, Sept. 14	BARRETT, Mary	John Barrett	Deed
1683, Apr. 1?	BASS, Peter	G. Parker et ux.	Mortgage

INDEX OF GRANTORS. 5

Folio.	Description.
12	40 acres on the sea wall next the long sands and the way to Cape Neddick, in *York*.
34	10 acres upland and marsh in *York*, on south-west side of York river, between Henry Donnell, Jasper Pullman and Edward Johnson.
134	To pay £6 for a horse purchased.
57	About satisfying Smyth's execution against him.
11	Marsh in the great marsh in *Wells*, formerly John Wadleigh, senior's.
108	300 acres land and house and marsh between John Barrett and Joseph Bolls, and down to Webhannet river, and 4 acres marsh, in *Wells*.
121	Quitclaim to 3 acres of marsh in *Wells* conveyed him by John Barrett et ux.
121	Quitclaim to marsh in *Wells* bonded for conveyance by Abraham Collins.
16	For his wife's portion.
135	Land and marsh at Drake's island in *Wells*.
44	Tract [in *Kittery*] sold by Abraham Conley to Nicholas Frost.
77	Concerning land and rental in *Saco*.
10	2 acres of marsh at Great river in *Wells*.
59	3 acres of marsh in *Wells*.
120	3 acres of marsh in *Wells*.
101	Land, house, meadow and personal property in *Wells*.
122	Of land in *York*, conditioned to maintain Parker and wife.

Index of Grantors.

Date.	Grantor.	Grantee.	Instrument.
1683, April 18	Bass, Peter	Eleazer Johnson	Agreement
1661, Aug. 12	Billine, John	Thomas Crocket	Deed
1642, July 22	Bleasdall, Ralph	Robert Knight	Deed
1679, July 29	Boaden, Ambrose	Nathan Bedford	Deed
	Bonighton, John, see James Gibbines		
1679, July 25	Botts, Isaac, estate of, by Moses Spencer, adm'r	Walter Alline	Deed
1661, July 29	Bragdon, Arthur, sen. et ux.	Thomas Mowlton	Deed
1680, May 4	Bragdon, Arthur et ux.	Philip Frost	Deed
1678, Jan. 8	Bray, Jane	George Pearson	Deed
1681, Sept. 29	Bray, John	Maine, Treas'r of	Receipt
1682, Nov. 17	Bray, John	Wm. Pepperrell	Deed
1676, July 25	Bray, Margery	Richard Roe	Deposition
1669, Dec. 24	Bray, Richard	John Bray	Deed
1678, Dec. 23	Bray, Richard	[George Pearson]	Deposition
1678, Jan. 1	Bray, Richard et ux.	George Pearson	Deed
1678, Jan. 1	Bray, Richard et ux.	George Pearson	Deed
	Bray, Richard, see John Cossons		
1679, Jan. 12	Broughton, George et ux.	John Hull	Deed
1678, Oct. 24	Broughton, John et ux.	Geo. Broughton	Deed

Index of Grantors.

Folio.	Description.
123	To support Johnson till he was 21 years of age.
73	Ratifying a former conveyance of house and lot on *Kittery* point, made when he was a minor.
42	House and lot in *Agamenticus* [York].
74	150 acres of upland and meadow on northwest of mouth of Spurwink river, at Black point in *Scarborough*.
48	20 acres of land and house between Salmon Falls brook and the road to Dirty swamp in *Kittery*.
24	3 acres marsh, called Gallows point, tract of marsh below the above and upland between, in *York*.
96	20 acres land between Bragdon's and Frost's lands adjoining Bass Cove river, in *York*, excepting the landing place.
41	Quitclaim to Cousins island in *Casco Bay*.
103	For £8 in full of all demands, &c.
121	One acre land [on *Kittery* point].
2	Relating to lost heifer bought of Diggory Jefferies.
52	One-fourth of Cousins, or Hog, islands in *Casco Bay*.
84	That he never consented that his son [John] Bray should marry Ann Lane.
35	One-half of Cousins island and of Long island in *Casco Bay*, and 5 acres of marsh on the mainland.
36	60 acres plantation between Richard Carter's and John Maine's at *Casco Bay*.
125	One-eighth of two saw mills and appurtenances at Salmon Falls on Great Negewanacke river in Piscataqua [*Berwick*]
49	Of one-half in common of three acres next the Salmon Falls mills [in *Berwick*].

Index of Grantors.

Date.	Grantor.	Grantee.	Instrument.
1679, June 7	BROUGHTON, John	John Hull	Mortgage
1676, Aug. 24	BROUGHTON, Thomas	Jacob Willett	Deed
1678, Nov. 30	BURRIN, George	Nic. Shapleigh	Deed
1677, Dec. 28	CAMER, Edward et ux.	Samuel Lynde	Deed
1683, Jan. 16	CARD, John	Widow Winchester	Contract
1680, Apr. 16	CARTER, John et ux.	Francis Backeus	Deed
	CARTER, Agnes, see John Coussons		
	CARTER, Richard, see John Coussons		
1649, Oct. 18	CHABINOCT (Cabinocke), Thomas, sagamore	John Wadleigh	Deed
1651, May 15	CHADBORNE, Humphrey	Hatevill Nutter	Deed
	CHADBORNE, Humphrey, see Willam Hutchinson		
1680, Feb. 2	CHADBORNE, James et ux.	Thomas Roads	Deed
	CHADBORNE, James, see Richard Otis		
1682, June 29	CHAMPERNOOWN, Francis	Alice Shapleigh	Deed
1662, July 6	[CLARKE], Tho[mas]	James Grant	Letter
1662, Sept. 30	CLARKE, Thomas	James Grant	Letter
1674, Apr. 3	CLARKE, Thomas and Thomas Lake	John Clarke	Deed

INDEX OF GRANTORS. 9

Folio.	Description.
47	One-eighth of the above two saw-mills, &c.
6	One-third part of Sturgeon creek swamp and the lands and farms about it, also one-third of Stephen Greenum's lot, all granted by and in *Kittery*.
37	House and 20 acres land on east side of Braveboat harbor in *York*.
80	Camer's formerly called Purchase's island in [Kennebeck] river, south of Merrymeeting bay.
138	Antenuptial contract.
82	140 acres south of Saco river between it and Smyth's brook, also a neck of land called Church point [in *Saco*].
65	Tract called Nischassett between Ogunquit and Kennebunk, the sea and Cape Porpoise falls [in *Wells*].
70	Two meadows on east side of Piscataqua river [in *Berwick*], one called Burcham point, the other on Black creek.
106	30 acres or one-half of Tomson point in *Kittery*, except John Ross's lot.
116	Quitclaim to any of that land near Braveboat harbor formerly [Ann] Godfrey's that falls within his patent or his father's [Arthur] in *Kittery*.
112	Covering remittance of £3 : 16.
112	Promising to pay for labor done for Henry Sayword.
66	A small island near mouth of Piscataqua river, purchased of Christopher Lawson.

INDEX OF GRANTORS.

Date.	Grantor.	Grantee.	Instrument.
Recorded 1679, Mar. 28	CLARKE, Thomas	Henry Sayword's estate	Caution
1660, May 31	CLEEVES, George	Hope Allen	Deed
1661, May 14	CLEEVES, George	John Bush	Certificate
1673, Feb. 23	CLOYCE, John et ux.	John Manning	Deed
1679, Apr. 7	CLOYCE, Peter et ux.	William Frost	Deed
1679, Mar. 6	COLLINES, Abraham et ux.	William Sawyer	Deed
1680, Dec. 28	COLLINES, Timothy et ux.	Duncan Stewart	Deed
1674, Mar. 3	CONLEY, Abraham	Renold Ginkens [Jenkins]	Deed
1676, July 27	CONLEY, Abraham	John Morrell	Deed
	CONLEY, Abraham, see John Heard		
1678, Dec. 23	COOLE, Nicholas and Eleanor Redding	George Pearson	Deposition
1650, Feb. 21	COSSONS, John	Richard Bray	Agreement
1682, June 26	COUSSONS, John and Agnes Carter *alias* Maddiver Richard Carter	John Mayne	Deposition
1683, May 14	COSSONS, John	Nic. Shapleigh	Deposition
1675, June 16	COWELL, Thomas et ux.	William Hubbard	Mortgage
1678, Jan. 4	COWELL, Thomas et ux.	Abel Porter	Deed

INDEX OF GRANTORS. 11

Folio.	Description.
40	Claiming two-thirds of the saw and other mills and land at Mill creek called York mills, in *York*.
68	400 acres on Casco river [*Falmouth*] between land of Ann Mittine and James Andrews.
87	That he granted Bush 400 acres near Little river, *Cape Porpoise*, as agent for Alexander Rigby.
11	6 acres fresh meadow at Totnucke in *Wells*.
59	House and land west of Webhannet river; two parcels of marsh; also 100 acres upon Maryland plain; all in *Wells*.
46	93 acres upland, 20 acres salt meadow, adjoining Mary Smyth and Thomas Wells, in *Wells*.
92	100 acres upland, meadow and marsh formerly his father Christopher's at Blue point [*Scarborough*] on the sea, between Giles Barge and Nathan Bedford.
114	2 acres northwest side of Sturgeon creek in *Kittery*.
19	Tract called Coole Harbor in *Kittery*, excepting two acres for Henry Kirke's house.
84	That John Bray was not legally married to Ann Lane.
37	As to payment for half of Cousins island, in *Casco Bay*, fencing, rental and trade with Indians.
115	As to John Mayne's purchase of Richard Carter, sen., at Wescustogo, Royal river, in *Casco Bay*.
128	As to ownership of *Sebascodegan Island*.
3	Land and house at Crooked lane in *Kittery* on Piscataqua river and Spruce creek, except 2 acres of Francis Trickey's, also Grantum's island in the creek.
39	25 acres on Spruce creek in *Kittery*, granted to William Seely.

Index of Grantors.

Date.	Grantor.	Grantee.	Instrument.
167¾, Mar. 23	Crafford, John et ux.	Isaac Botts	Deed
1676, Oct. 20	Crafford, John et ux.	Joseph Barnard	Deed
1676, Oct. 27	Crafford, John et ux.	Thomas Holms	Deed
1679, Jan. 27	Crockett, Ann	Elihu Gunnison Joseph Gunnisson	Deposition
Acknowledged 1679, July 21	Crockett, Ann Hugh Joseph Joshua	Ephraim Crocket	Deed
168⁰⁄₉, Mar. 8	Cut, John	Edw'd Rishworth	Receipt and partial discharge
	Cut, Robert, see Elizabeth Seely		
1673, Jan. 29	Davess, John and John Penwill	John Bray	Contract
1675, Nov. 24	Davess, John	John Bray	Contract
1683, May 30	Davess, John and Charles ——?	William Hilton	Deposition
1678, Aug. 2	Deane, Thomas	[Nath'l Fryer?]	Discharge
1681, June 21	Deareing, Roger estate of, by Roger Deareing, executor	Clement Deareing	Deed
	Dod, Mehitable, see John Ryal et ux.		
1680, July 12	Donell, Henry	Thomas Clarke	Deed
1676, Jan. 16	Downeing, Dinnis	Joshua Downing	Conditional deed
1679, June 21	Downeing, Dinnis	Joan Dyamont	Deed

Folio.	Description.
48	20 acres in *Kittery* southeast by way to Dirty swamp; southwest by Thos. Broughton; northwest by Salmon falls brook; northeast by land of grantor.
21	20 acres in *Kittery* southeast on Wells highway; Dirty swamp on northeast, between Isaac Botts and Mrs. Olive Playsted.
9	40 acres with house, &c., between Thomas Broughton's, south of Dirty swamp and Wells path, granted by and in *Kittery*.
107	As to Hugh Gunnison's disposition of the premises leased to Seely and Rogers.
73 74	Quitclaim to land conveyed to Ephraim by [Thomas] Crocket, [in *Kittery*.]
102	For £26 on account, and release of mortgage on 4 acres.
23	For building a vessel of 80 or more tons burthen.
23	For building the ship *John & Alice*.
125	That Hilton was son of William Hilton, sen., and formerly lived in *York*.
30	Of a mortgage [*Query*, of Book II, 157].
121	144 square rods of land in *Kittery*, adjoining John Pearce.
74	3 acres, more or less, of marsh on York river in *York*.
115	Messuage and all personal property in *Kittery*.
47	10 acres granted by and in *Kittery*, late in possession of William Dyamont, deceased.

Index of Grantors.

Date.	Grantor.	Grantee.	Instrument.
1679, June 21	Downeing, Joshua et ux.	Joane Dyamont	Deed
167⅘, Mar. 5	Dummer, Shubael	Joseph Raynkine	Contract
16⅔, Mar. 2	Duston, Thomas et ux.	John Cutt	Mortgage
166⅔, Mar. 19	Durston, Elizabeth	John Cutt	Deed
1680, June 9	Dyamont, Andrew and Michael Endle	Mary Mathews	Deposition
1679, Sept. 2	Elliet, Robert	John Davess	Letter
1660, May 12	Emery, Anthony et ux.	James Emery	Deed
1659, Oct. 21	Emery, James et ux.	Peter Grant	Deed
1662, Mar. 6	Emery, James et ux.	Peter Grant	Deed
1663, Dec. 4	Emery, James et ux.	Steph'n Robinson	Deed
1673, Nov. 27	Emery, James et ux.	Abraham Conley	Deed
1681, Aug. 2	Emery, James et ux.	Samuel Fernald	Deed
	Emery, James, see Christopher Banefield		
1683, Apr. 6	Endicott, Gilbert	James Ross	Deed
1678, Dec. 9	Endle, Michael	William Oliver Richard Oliver	Deed
	Endle, Michael, see Andrew Dyamont		
1670, July 12	Epps, Daniel	Henry Sayword	Conditional deed
1673, Feb. 23	Everell, Thomas	Fran. Littlefield, sen.	Deed

INDEX OF GRANTORS. 15

Folio.	Description
47	Quitclaim to land conveyed by Dennis Downeing, above.
73	To deliver a heifer for the use of his apprentice.
20	Messuage and all lands in *Kittery* to secure £17 17 : 11.
21	Quitclaim to all the above.
71	As to her deceased husband Walter's ownership of two lots, &c, on the *Isles of Shoals*.
57	Had never accepted his and Rishworth's joint bond.
38	House and all his lands and personal property at Cold harbor, Sturgeon creek, in *Kittery*.
14	Messuage and tract bought of John Lamb, 24 April, 1654, [in *Kittery*]
14	5 acres marsh near York pond in *Kittery*.
45	House and 50 acres near Frank's fort in *Kittery*, formerly Robert Waymouth's.
20	Cool Harbor point, 63 rods on river by 120 back, [at Sturgeon creek] in *Kittery*.
97	Quitclaim to town grant of 6 acres, the next point below Thomas Spinney's in *Kittery*.
128	Saw mill &c., and 50 acres land on Little river at *Cape Porpoise*.
71	Stage and flakes on Smuttynose island, *Isles of Shoals*.
33	Farms bought of Gooch, Austine and Mussy in *Wells*, also land bought of John and Robert Wadleigh between Cape Porpoise and Kennebunk rivers.
11	200 acres upland and 10 acres meadow at Meriyland in *Wells*.

Index of Grantors.

Date.	Grantor.	Grantee.	Instrument.
16$\frac{73}{74}$, Feb 23 Recorded	Everell, Thomas et ux.	Francis Littlefield senior	Deed
1681, Mar. 25	Everell, Thomas	John Bankes and others	Caution
1680, June 5	Everest, Andrew et ux.	Thomas Everell	Deed
168$\frac{9}{1}$, Mar. 18	Everest, Andrew et ux	Benjamin Curtis	Deed
1675, Feb. 5	Everest, Isaac et ux	John Wentworth	Deed
1679, Apr. 28	Everest, Isaac et ux	Jeremiah Mowlton	Deed
1680, June 23	Felt, George, sen.	Walter Gyndall	Deed
1675, Apr 12	Fenix, John et ux.	Peter Lewis	Deed
1677, Sept. 11	Forgison, John	William Smyth's children	Deposition
	Foxwell, Philip, see James Gibbines		
1671, June 10	Freathy, William et ux.	Thomas Holms et ux.	Deed
1681, Oct. 31	Freathy, William et ux.	John Freathy	Deed
1680, Mar. 24	Frost, Charles	Abraham Tilton	Deposition
1680, Apr. 13	Frost, Charles and John Frost Joseph Hammond	William Gowine alias Smyth	Partition
1678, Nov. 14	Frost, John, estate of by John Frost Philip Frost Alexander Maxell Rose Frost } adm'rs	Edw Rishworth John Davess	Reference

Index of Grantors. 17

Folio.	Description.
11	Quitclaim of above endorsed on deed to him from Jonathan Hammonds.
88	Against accepting or recording Andrew Everest's deed.
87	16 acres upland and marsh called Pond marsh, also 40 acres given by and in *York*.
89	40 acres on west side of northwest branch of York river in *York*.
15	House and 15 acres on the road from York to Henry Sayword's, also 20 acres given by and in *York*.
50	3 acres marsh on northwest branch of York river in *York*.
76	100 acres on *Casco Bay* west of Felt's old house, also two parcels of meadow.
81	House and land on east side of Spruce creek in *Kittery*.
16	As to Trustrum Harris' intended disposition of his estate.
81	40 acres on York river, between Edward Start and Henry Sayword, in *York*.
105	One-half his homestead in *York;* also other half after his own and wife's decease.
64	As to Tilton's purchase of building timber on Abraham Conley's land [in *Kittery*].
67	Of Nicholas Frost, junior's real estate [in *Kittery*].
33	Power to hear and determine differences.

Index of Grantors.

Date.	Grantor.	Grantee.	Instrument.
1678, Dec. 26	Frost, John, estate of, by Edward Rishworth and John Davess, referees	Philip Frost Rose Frost	Award
	Frost, John, see Charles Frost		
1677, June 16	Frost, Mary	William Smyth's children	Deposition
16$\frac{78}{88}$, Mar. 4	Frost, Philip	Shubael Dummer et ux.	Indenture
16$\frac{78}{88}$, Mar. 5	Frost, Philip	Joseph Raynkine	Contract
1679, Dec. 23	Frost, William et ux.	Fran. Littlefield	Deed
1683, Oct. 11	Fryer, Nathaniel et ux.	Reuben Hull	Deed
1680, Apr. 10	Gibbones, James et ux.	Benjamin Blackeman	Deed
1681, Sept. 23	Gibbines, James and John Bonighton John Harmon Philip Foxwell	To one another	Division
Recorded 1679, Mar. 28	Gibbs, Robert, estate of, by Elizabeth Corwin, administratrix	Henry Sayword and others	Caution
	Gilman, Edward et ux., see Stephen Paul		
1680, Jan. 5	Godfrey, Ann	William Moore	Deed
1653, May 10	Godfrey, Edward	Philip Addams	Deed
1655, Aug. 16	Godfrey, Edward	Philip Addams	Deed
1680, Aug. 18	Godfrey, Edward, by Edward Johnson, attorney	John Harmon	Lease

Index of Grantors.

Folio.	Description.
33	Chattels and leasehold [in *Kittery*].
16	As to Trustrum Harris's intended disposition of his estate.
73	Of apprenticeship of his step-son Joseph Raynkine.
73	To keep a heifer for said Raynkin "on halves."
60	Land, &c., in *Wells*, bought of Peter Cloyce.
138	Malaga island, *Isles of Shoals*.
94	100 acres east of and adjoining Saco river falls, part of Lewis and Bonighton's patent in *Saco*.
102	Of Lewis and Bonighton's patent in *Saco*.
40	Claiming saw mill and 300 acres at Cape Porpoise river falls.
86	The sunken marsh at Braveboat harbor in *York*.
37	Land in *York* between Scituate men's swamp, and the way to Mr. Gorges, John Parker and Henry Symson.
37	40 acres on west branch of river Agamenticus in *York*.
83	Of lands and meadows in *York*.

Index of Grantors.

Date.	Grantor.	Grantee.	Instrument.
1679, May 24	GOODIN, Daniel, sen.	Daniel Goodin, jr.	Deed
1679, May 24	GOODIN, Daniel, sen.	Daniel Stone	Deed
1636, Dec. 12	GORGES, Sir Ferdinando	Arthur Champernoown	Lease
1638, June 14	GORGES, Sir Ferdinando	Arthur Champernoown	Lease
1643, July 18	GORGES, Sir Ferdinando, by Thomas Gorges, deputy governor	John Smyth	Deed
1665, Oct. 20	GORGES, Ferdinando, by John Archdale, agent	Francis Champernowne	Deed
166-, Oct. —	GORGES, Ferdinando, by John Archdale, agent	Walter Barefoot	Covenant
	GOWINE, *alias* Smyth, William, see Charles Frost		
1677, June 20	GRANGER, John	William Smyth's children	Deposition
166⅞, Mar. 16	GRANT, James	John Pearce	Deed
1668, May 20	GREENE, John et ux.	Thomas Abbet et ux.	Deed
1675, Dec. 20	GREENE, John et ux.	John Searle	Deed
167⅔, Mar. 1	GREENE, John, sen. et ux.	Thomas Abbet	Deed
1679, June 16	GYDNEY, Bartholmew	Henry Sayword's estate	Caution

Index of Grantors. 21

Folio.	Description.
54	House and lot in *Kittery* bounded by the fowling marsh, the river, Daniel Stone, James Emery and grantor's lands.
54	5 acres in *Kittery* part of town grant, bounded by the river, James Emery's and grantor's lands.
97	500 acres of land between Piscataqua river and Braveboat harbor, to be called Dartington; also 500 acres marsh northeast of Braveboat harbor river to be called Godmorrocke, all in *Kittery*.
98	By the same description.
74	100 acres of land and an island opposite, at *Cape Porpoise*.
99	300 acres of land in *Kittery* between Capt. Champernowne's former house and Thomas Crockett.
125	For quiet possession of 500 acres bought of Francis Champernoown [see Book I, 77, 82].
16	As to Trustrum Harris's intended disposition of his estate.
22	10 acres on Mr. Gorges's neck, between the new mill creek and Bass cove in *York*.
6	20 acres of land in *Kittery* between grantor and Peter Grant.
116	15 acres land in *Kittery* between grantor's homestead, Thomas Abbet's and Daniel Goodin's lots.
63	Homestead, 54 acres on Great Newgewanacke river in *Kittery*.
43 44	Claiming one-half of *Casco* mills, lands, &c.

INDEX OF GRANTORS.

Date.	Grantor.	Grantee.	Instrument.
1681, July 12	GYDNEY, Bartholmew et ux.	Walter Gyndall	Deed
1681, July 12	GYNDALL, Walter	Bartholmew Gydney	Mortgage
1683, May 21	HALY, Thomas, sen.	Thomas Haley	Deed
1671, Oct. 22	HAMMOND, Jonathan	Thomas Everell	Deed
168 9/0, Mar. 23	HAMMOND, Jonathan	Wm. Hammond	Mortgage
	HAMMOND, Joseph, see Charles Frost		
168 9/0, Mar. 23	HAMMOND, William	Jonathan Hammond	Conditional deed
1682, Jan. 29	HARDING, Israel	Joseph Bolls	Deed
1670, June 24	HARDY, Clement	John Præsbery	Deed
	HARMON, John, see James Gibbines		
1681, Dec. 2	HARVY, Elizabeth	Richard Powsland	Deed
1648, June 12	HEARD [Hord], John	John Parker	Deed
1676, June 28	HEARD [Hord], John and Abraham Conley	Richard Nason James Emery Chris. Banefield Nic. Shapleigh	Reference
1678, June 24	HEARD [Hord], John, estate of	Abraham Conley	Award
1677, Nov. 5	HEARD [Hord], John, estate of by Nicholas Shapleigh John Shapleigh Jos. Hammonds William Spencer Abraham Conley } Trustees	Richard Otis Jas. Chadborne	Deed

Folio.	Description
95	The Stevens tract at *North Yarmouth*
109	The Stevens tract at *North Yarmouth*; also 2 acres on Ryall's point, to secure £110
124	Homestead, &c, in *Saco*.
11	200 acres upland and 10 acres meadow at Maryland in *Wells*.
89	Of property conveyed to secure maintenance of William and his wife.
89	Homestead of 400 acres and chattels in *Wells*.
129	2 acres at the sea wall in *Wells*
42	50 acres east of Saco river called Paige's plantation in *Saco*.
113	4 acres on the neck [*Falmouth*] between Anthony Bracket and Clark and Spencer.
71	House and all lands in *Gorgeana*.
54	To determine bounds at Sturgeon creek, [in *Kittery*].
55	Of arbitrators fixing above bounds.
17	Subrogation to the trust.

Index of Grantors.

Date.	Grantor.	Grantee.	Instrument.
1680, Nov. 5	HEARD [Hord], John	Sylvester Stover	Deed
1681, Aug. 27	HEARLE, John	Abraham Lord	Deed
1680, Feb. 1	HEARLE, William et ux.	John Furnald	Deed
1681, Dec. 14	HEATH, Thomas	Robert Young	Note
1679, Nov. 4	HENDERSON, John	William Down	Mortgage
1681, Oct. 20	HESKINS, Nicholas and Francis Tucker	Richard Bickeham & Co.	Deposition
1677, Mar. 30	HILL, Roger	Joseph Cross	Receipt
1674, Nov. 2	HILTON, Katherine	Samuel Trueworgye	Deed
1678, Dec. 9	HODGSDEN, Benoni	Nicholas Hodgsden	Agreement
1678, Oct. 22	HODGSDEN, Nicholas	Benoni Hodgsden	Deed
1679, Feb. 20	HODGSDEN, Nicholas et ux.	Timothy Hodgsden	Deed
1682, Apr. 3	HODGSDEN, Timothy	Benoni Hodgsden	Deed
1681, Apr. 16	HOLMES, Joseph	Joshua Scottow	Mortgage
1679, June 26	HOLMS, Thomas et ux.	Henry Child	Deed
1650, July 16	HOOKE, William	John Allcocke John Heard	Deed
1650, July 16	HOOKE, William	John Allcocke John Heard	Deed
1681, July 26	HOOLE, John	Edmund Hammons	Deed
1678, Feb. 13	HOWELL, John et ux.	John Morton	Deed
1673, Mar. 11	HOWLEY, John	George Pearson	Deposition

Index of Grantors. 25

Folio.	Description.
100	One fourth of Cape Neddick neck in *York*.
130	40 acres at Port Wigwam in *Berwick* on the Little river.
123	20 acres in *Kittery* adjoining Spinney's cove.
138	For £14.
79	40 acres at Winter harbor, [*Saco*] between Peter Henderson and Humphrey Case.
103	As to Elizabeth Cowell's, former widow of William Seely, livery of a lot at Spruce creek, *Kittery*, in satisfaction of a debt due them.
13	In part for his wife's portion.
9	Tomson's point above Sturgeon creek, in *Kittery*, bought of Rowles, sagamore.
41	Relative to carrying on a farm in *Kittery*.
31	Homestead of 40 acres, bought of John Wincoll; also, 56 acres town grant, except 7 acres to John Morrell, all in *Kittery*.
110	40 acres and 2 acres bought of Peter Wittum in *Kittery*.
111	The above two lots.
96	Land purchased of Francis Neale in *Casco* to secure £160.
131	House and 40 acres in *Kittery* between Dirty swamp and Wells path.
107	One-half of Cape Neddick neck in *York*.
107	One-half of Cape Neddick neck in *York*.
116	37½ acres at Spruce creek in *Kittery*.
42	100 acres on Black Point river, at Dunstan, in *Scarborough*.
66	As to payment for Cousins island in *Casco Bay*.

INDEX OF GRANTORS.

Date.	Grantor	Grantee	Instrument.
1676, July 5	HUBBARD, John, by William Hubbard, ag't	[Elizabeth Seely]	Receipt
	HULL, John, see John Wincoll		
1679, June 2	HULL, Phineas et ux	John Heaile	Deed
1683, July 12	HULL, Phineas	Henry Child	Deed
1683, Aug. 28	HUTCHINSON, Eliakim	Daniel Goodine, senior	Deed
1673, July 18	HUTCHINSON, William	Humphrey Chadborne	Agreement
1669, June 5	JEFFREYS, Diggory et ux	John Moore, sen.	Deed
1678, Feb. 10	JENKINS, Renold	Stephen Jenkins	Conditional deed
1683, Nov. 20	JENKINS, Stephen et ux	Charles Frost	Deed
1670, June 14	JOHNSON, Edward	John Pearce	Receipt
1676, July 11	JOHNSON, Edward and Robert Knight	Edw Rishworth	Deposition.
1680, Aug. 18	JOHNSON, Edward et ux.	John Harmon	Conditional deed
1682, June 29	JOHNSON, Edward	Ann Godfrey, *alias* Messant	Deposition
1682, June 29	JOHNSON, Priscilla	Ann Messant [*alias* Godfrey]	Deposition
167⅘, Mar 1	JOHNSON, William et ux.	Richard Wood	Deed
Recorded 1681, Sept. 22	JORDAN, Robert, estate of	Dominicus Jordan, by Joshua Scottow, att'y	Claim
1677, Jan. 25	JORDAN, John	Elizabeth Styleman	Marriage settlement

INDEX OF GRANTORS.

Folio.	Description.
3	In full.
130	30 acres at Post Wigwam in *Kittery* or *Berwick*.
131	30 acres in *Berwick*, north-east from Quamphegan.
136	11¾ acres in *Berwick*, adjoining Humphrey Spencer.
91	Establishing new bounds for their lands at Assabumbedicke falls in *Kittery*.
88	Two islands or necks, and 4 acres land adjoining, and houses in *Kittery* between John Bray and Roger Dearing.
137	All his estate, real and personal, in *Kittery*, except two pieces of marsh to Jabez Jenkins.
136	One acre at Sturgeon creek, opposite the Cedars, in *Kittery*.
23	£15 in full of all demands, &c.
2	That Mr. Richard Vines gave Henry Norton meadows along York river, now in Rishworth's possession, [in *York*].
83	Homestead of 10 acres on the creek opposite the meeting house in *York*; 5 acres woodland at Bass cove; 3 acres of marsh on the river, and 60 acres town grant.
116	Concerning a loan by her to George Burdett, and livery of his real estate to her.
116	As to Mr. George Burdett's livery of his estate to Mrs. Godfrey.
12	30 acres on the way to Cape Neddick in *York*.
101	To 1000 acres at the Great pond at Cape Elizabeth in *Falmouth*.
34	Richman's island, also 300 acres of land and marsh, opposite the island [in *Falmouth*].

Index of Grantors.

Date.	Grantor.	Grantee.	Instrument.
1675, Feb. 29	JORDAN, Robert et ux.	Robert Jordan, jr.	Deed
1678, Jan. 28	JORDAN, Robert	Sarah Jordan, wife, and 6 sons	Will
1679, July 14	JORDAN, Robert, jr.	Nathaniel Fryer	Deed
16$\frac{78}{80}$, Mar 5	KEMBLE, Thomas	George Pearson	Depositio
1674, May 7	KING, Daniel	Gabriel Tetherly	Deed
1678, Oct 13	KIRKE, Henry et ux	John Morrall	Deed
1653, Mar 16	KITTERY, town of	James Emery	Grant
1654, Apr 12	KITTERY, town of	Richard Leader	Grant
1654, Nov. 1	KITTERY, town of	James Emery	Survey
1654, Nov 1	KITTERY, town of	Anthony Emery	Survey
1655, Mar 20	KITTERY, town of	John Lamb	Grant
1656, July 15	KITTERY, town of	John Lamb	Survey
1656, July 15	KITTERY, town of	Alexander Maxell	Survey
Transcribed 1662, Nov. 25	KITTERY, town of	John Lamb	Grant
1666, July 17	KITTERY, town of	Francis Champernowne	Grant
166$\frac{8}{9}$, June —	KITTERY, town of	Stephen Robinson	Grant
1671, Apr. 13	KITTERY, town of	Alexander Cooper	Grant
1671, Apr 13	KITTERY, town of	George Gray	Grant
1671, Oct 5	KITTERY, town of	John Ball	Grant
1671, Feb. 20	KITTERY, town of	John Green, sen.	Survey

Index of Grantors. 29

Folio.	Description.
2	Tract called Cape Elizabeth [in *Falmouth*.]
44	Devising all his real estate about Spurwink [in *Falmouth*.]
69	One-half of Cape Elizabeth tract in *Falmouth*, also one-half of his share of marshes in common.
66	As to Richard Bray and wife's execution of two deeds.
119	Lot 32 by 16 rods on Piscataqua river in *Kittery*.
31	House and 20 acres land at Cold Harbor in *Kittery*.
97	6 acres, the next point below Thomas Spinny's.
64	All pine trees on Little river except Chadborne's and Spencer's.
38	50 acres by the water side adjoining Daniel Gooding's lot.
39	Land between said Emery and Henry Pounding.
20	20 acres meadow north of brook near William Love's bridge.
20	50 acres by the water side adjoining John Green's lot.
22	35 acres by the water side adjoining James Warren's lot.
14	20 acres meadow near William Love's bridge.
100	500 acres by water side towards Brave-boat harbor.
46	18 acres behind his dwelling.
22	60 acres.
22	60 acres.
44	10 acres adjoining his land at Spruce creek.
14	15 acres adjoining his house lot.

Index of Grantors.

Date.	Grantor.	Grantee.	Instrument.
1671, Feb. 27	KITTERY, town of	William Spencer	Survey
1671, Feb. 27	KITTERY, town of	Thomas Spencer	Survey
167½, Mar. 6	KITTERY, town of	Alexander Cooper	Survey
1673, Jan. 20	KITTERY, town of	Thomas Withers	Grant
1673, Mar. 4	KITTERY, town of	James Emery, senior	Survey
167¾, Mar. 2	KITTERY, town of	John Green, sen.	Survey
167¾, Mar. 4	KITTERY, town of	Peter Grant	Grant
1674, Dec. 15	KITTERY, town of	Thomas Abbett	Survey
1674, Dec. 16	KITTERY, town of	Thomas Abbett	Survey
[No date]	KITTERY, town of	Thomas Abbett	Survey
1674, Dec. 19	KITTERY, town of	Alexander Cooper	Survey
1674, Dec. 30	KITTERY, town of	John Bready	Survey
1683, Aug. 28	KITTERY, town of	Eliakim Hutchinson	Confirmation
	KITTERY, town of, see York county commissioners		
1677, Feb. 15	KNIGHT, Richard	Rowland Young	Deed
1673, Aug. 12	Knight Robert	Rowland Young	Deed
1676, June 23	KNIGHT, Robert	Richard Knight	Will
	KNIGHT, Robert, see Edward Johnson		
1682, July 8	KNIGHT, Samuel et ux.	Peter Glanefield	Deed

Index of Grantors.

Folio.	Description.
80	About 150 acres adjoining brook from Willcock's pond, as per grant of 1651.
80	100 acres adjoining the above.
22	60 acres by Willcock's pond and brook.
94	Land and meadow not described.
43	Eight lots, aggregating 315 acres.
14	60 acres near York pond
15	120 acres on west side of York pond.
21	110 acres at Slut's corner.
21	31 acres adjoining John Green.
21	19 acres adjoining his own land and John Green.
22	18¼ acres at the north of his lot, near White's marsh.
113	50 acres and 11 acres additional.
132	Of former grants to Leaders and Hutchinsons.
38	House and lands [in *York*] devised by his father Robert Knight.
25	4 acres in *York*, between grantor's land and a spring by a lot formerly Edward Start's.
37	Realty and chattels in *York*.
117	12 acres in *Kittery* on Piscataqua river, bounded north by Thomas Spinny, south by grantee's land.

INDEX OF GRANTORS.

Date.	Grantor.	Grantee.	Instrument.
1675, Apr. 5	KNOULTON, John,	Samuel Sayword	Letter and power of attorney
1678, Mar. 14	KNOULTON, John, by John Davess and Samuel Sayword, att'ys	John Parsons	Bond
1679, Oct. 5	KNOULTON, John, by Samuel Sayword and John Davess, att'ys	John Parsons	Bill of sale
	LAKE, Thomas, see Thomas Clarke		
1677, Dec. 7	LAWSON, Christopher	Samuel Lynde	Discharge
	LAWDE, see Lord		
1681, Feb. 21	LEDBRWOKE,[Ledbroake] Thomas	Deborah Booth	Contract
1678, June 28	LORD, Nathan et ux.	Thomas Abbett Jonathan Nayson	Deed
1678, June 28	LORD, Nathan et ux.	Thomas Abbett Jonathan Nason	Deed
	LORD, Nathan, see John Heard's estate		
1672, Dec. 27	LYDDEN, George et ux.	Edward Clarke	Deed
1677, Sept. 13	LITTEN [Lydden], George by Sarah Litten, att'y	Mary Clarke	Receipt
1679, June 10	LYNDE, Simon	Henry Sayword, estate of, and others	Caution
1679, June 12	LYNDE, Simon	Henry Sayword, estate of, and others	Caution
1675, July 8	LYSTON, Waymouth et	Charles Nellson	Deed

Folio.	Description.
56	Authorizing sale of his property in *York*, and other matters.
56	For a bill of sale of his house at *York*.
56	Dwelling house between houses of John Preble and Henry Symson in *York*.
80	Of mortgage by Edward Camer on Purchase's, or Camer's island in Kennebeck river.
108	Ante-nuptial contract.
25	10 acres called Abraham Conley's marsh at Sturgeon creek, in *Kittery*.
26	40 acres adjoining the above, excepting Peter Wittum's lot.
51	10 acres at Crooked lane in *Kittery*, between John Amerideth and Francis Tricky.
52	In full of a note of £4 of her husband's, Edward Clarke.
55	Claiming farms bought by Epps of Gouch, Austine and Mussy, also one half the Mousam mills in *Wells*.
44	Claiming one half the Mousam mills, &c., at *Wells*.
118	One half, in common with Gilbert Lugg, of lot in *Kittery*, bought of Joseph Allcocke.

INDEX OF GRANTORS.

Date.	Grantor.	Grantee.	Instrument.
1678, July 21	MACKYNTYRE, Micum	Thomas Traffton	Deed
	MADDIVER, Agnes, see Agnes Carter		
1680, Oct. 13	MASSACHUSETTS, General Court of	Geo. Ingersoll, jr. John Ingersoll	Grant
1663, Dec. 15	MAVERICKE, Antipas	Moses Mavericke	Mortgage
1678, June 16	MAVERICKE, Antipas	Nic. Shapleigh	Deed
1674, June 29 1675, Aug. 13	MAVERICKE, Moses	Antipas Mavericke	Receipts(2)
1680, Oct. 7	MAVERICKE, Moses	Nic. Shapleigh	Assignment
1678, Nov. 2	MAXELL, Alexander et ux.	John Frost	Conditional deed
1682, Mar. 24	MAXWELL, Alexander et ux.	Robert Junkines	Deed
1666, Sept. 27	MAYHEW, Thomas	Peter Oliver	Deed
1681, May 21	MENDUM, Jonathan	Nicholas Weekes	Deed
1676, Sept. 16	MIDDLETON, James	William Gowine *alias* Smyth	Deed
1681, Dec. 17	MILLS, Thomas	Nathaniel Cloyce	Deed
1681, July 12	MILLS, Thomas	John Cloyce	Deed
1662, Mar. 1	MITTON, Elizabeth	Thaddeus Clarke	Deed
1682, Sept. 28	MITTON, Nathaniel, estate of	Mitton's heirs	Appraisal
1677, Apr. 1	MORGAN, Francis	John Bray	Bond
1681, Sept. 10	MOORE, John et ux.	Thomas Andrews Anthony Farley John W[illegible]	Bond

Folio.	Description.
30	40 acres with marsh on York river, in *York*.
125	Confirming previous grants of 60 acres each, and granting mill privilege [in *Falmouth*].
109	House and land in *Kittery*, subject to conditional sale to Thomas Booth.
27	30 acres of land and house adjoining William Ellingham's in *Kittery*.
109	For payments on above mortgage.
109	Of above mortgage.
51	20 acres at Scotland, in *York*.
119	20 acres between the way to Newgewanacke and Bass cove brook, in *York*.
114	One quarter of Elizabeth islands north of Martyn's Vineyard.
112	Land at Martyn's cove in Spruce creek, *Kittery*.
67	Land on Kennebec river in common with Thomas Humfrys, also Small point.
105	One half in common of a neck of land in *Wells*, east of Mr. Wheelwright's neck.
105	The other half in common of the above tract in *Wells*.
76	Quitclaim to 100 acres on the point in Casco Bay [*Falmouth*].
120	Of 80 acres and 3 acres marsh [in *Falmouth*].
24	For payment of £11 : 8.
104	For a deed of house, stage, &c., on Star island, *Isles of Shoals*.

INDEX OF GRANTORS.

Date.	Grantor.	Grantee.	Instrument.
1676, July 28	MORRALL, John et ux.	Abraham Conley	Deed
1680, May 13	MORRALL, John	Thomas Roberts Hatevill Roberts	Deed
1674, July 9	MUNJOY, George	William Phillips	Deposition
Recorded 1683, Jan. 29	NANNY, Robert, estate of, Catherine Nayler, ex'x, by Edward Rishworth, attorney	All persons	Caution
1664, Feb. 4	NASON, Richard	Nathaniel Lord	Deed
	NASON, Richard, see Nicholas Shapleigh		
1662, Nov. 9	NEALE, John	Alexander Cooper	Deed
1680, June 9	OLIVER, William, and John Tetherly	Mary Mathews	Deposition
1660, May 1	ONYON, Thomas et ux.	Gabriel Tetherly	Deed
1677, Nov. 5	OTIS, Richard, and James Chadborne	John Heard's estate	Acceptance
1673, Oct. 25	PAINE, John	John Whitte Robert Brimsdon	Deed
1673, Dec. 10	PAINE, John	Daniel Stone Robert Brimsdon	Deed
1674, May 21	PALMER, William	Peter Glanefield	Deed
	PALMER, William	Isaac Gutteridge	Incomplete deed
1683, Aug. 21	PALMER, William	Isaac Gutteridge	Deed
1683, Apr. 10	PARKER, George et ux.	Peter Bass	Conditional deed
1661, Jun			

Index of Grantors.

Folio.	Description.
18	House and 7 acres, part of Hodgsden's former homestead; also, 70 acres as by three town grants, lying together, all in *Kittery*
70	Marsh and meadow called Burcham point on east side of Piscataqua river, in *Kittery*.
87	As to bounds of 4 miles, surveyed west from Saco river along the coast
139	Claiming mortgage on 20 acres on Gorges point in *York*.
27	9 acres at Newgewanacke [*Berwick*] adjoining grantee's land.
22	25 acres near White's marsh on Piscataqua river in *Kittery*.
71	As to her husband, Walter Mathews's ownership of two lots at the *Isles of Shoals*.
119	House and 20 acres near the Boiling rock in *Kittery*.
17	Of the trusteeship.
28	800 acres above *Wells* and *Cape Porpoise*, part of the tract sold by Sosowen sagamore. [See Book I. 1 107.]
29	150 acres in Wells township about 4 miles from the town; also two parcels of marsh.
117	4 acres near Bass rock in *Kittery*, adjoining land of grantee.
132	Re-recorded folio 134.
134	One half of Batson neck in *Cape Porpoise;* also the grass plot and marsh.
122	All realty and chattels in *York*.
23	Land on Kennebec river south of Winnegance creek.

Date.	Grantor.	Grantee.	Instrument.
16$\frac{79}{80}$, Mar. 20	PARSONS, John	William Vahan	Mortgage
1668, July 18	PAUL, Daniel	Stephen Paul	Deed
1679, Feb. 14	PAUL, Stephen et ux.	John Soaper	Deed
1682, June 7	PAUL, Stephen et ux., and Edward Gillman et ux.	Alexander Dennet	Deed
1676, Jan. 30	PEARCE, Joseph	John Bray	Bond
1681, June 11	PECKET, Christopher	Henry Williams	Mortgage
1680, July 3	PENDLETON, Bryan	Joseph Cross	Deed
1681, June 13	PENDLETON, James	William Vahan	Deed
	PENWILL, John, see John Davess		
1666, Oct. 11	PHILLIPS, William et ux.	Bryan Pendleton	Deed
1669, July 5	PHILLIPS, William	John Sargeant	Deed
1675, June 15	PHILLIPS, William	Rebecca Lord Robert Lord Samuel Phillips William Phillips Mary Field Martha Thirston Elizabeth Allden Sarah Turner Zachary Gyllum Peleg Santford John Sanford Elisha Sanford Eliphal Stratton John Jolliffe Jno. Woodmancy Elisha Hutchins'n Theo. Atkinson John Santford William Hutos'n	Deed

Folio.	Description.
66	House formerly John [K]noulton's and 12 acres granted by the town in *Kittery*.
113	House and all his realty in *Kittery*, except 15 acres to Joseph Allcocke.
127	20 acres near the Boiling rock in Great cove in *Kittery*.
111	40 acres by the water side in *Kittery*, formerly Antipas Maverick's.
12	To pay £12.
93	House and land at Black point, *Scarborough*, to secure a draft of £6: 15.
77	474 acres on Webhannet river in *Wells*.
93	300 acres of land and 3 islands at *Cape Porpoise*.
74	100 acres and an island at *Cape Porpoise* bought of John Smyth.
82	30 acres at Winter Harbor, *Saco*, between George Pearson and Ralph Trustrum, excepting Richard Randall's lot.
5	In common, 19,000 acres, 1000 acres apiece, west of Kennebunk river at the head of Wells township, in a tract 8 miles from the sea and 8 miles square, part of the tract bought of Flewellin.

Date.	Grantor.	Grantee.	Instrument.
1676, June 12	PHILLIPS, William	Edward Spragg $\frac{2}{8}$ Robert Lord $\frac{2}{8}$ John Allden $\frac{1}{8}$ Samuel Phillips $\frac{1}{8}$ William Phillips $\frac{1}{8}$	Deed
1676, July 8	PHILLIPS, William et ux.	Zachary Gyllum Ephraim Turner	Deed
1676, July 8	PHILLIPS, William et ux.	Ephraim Turner	Deed
1661, July 13	PICKEARD, Edmund	Nathaniel Fryer	Deed
1676, Aug. 17	PLAYSTEAD, Roger, estate of, by Olive Playstead William Playstead $\Big\}$ exrs. James Playstead	Eliakim Hutchinson Wm. Hutchinson	Account stated
1676, Oct. 5	PLAYCE, John	Richard Wood	Indenture
1650, May 31	PARMOT, Philemon and William Wardell	John [Wadlew] Wadleigh Robert Wadleigh	Deposition
16$\frac{78}{80}$, Mar. 22	PORTER, Abel et ux.	Michael Endle	Deed
1679, Sept. 27	PREBLE, Abraham	John Stover, sen.	Deed
1683, Aug. 29	PRICE, John	Mary Sayword	Prom. note
	RAWMEGON, see Robin-Hood		
167$\frac{3}{4}$, Mar. 10	REDDING, Eleanor	James Andrews	Mortgage
1680, Apr. 12	REDDING, Eleanor	Joshua Atwater's estate by Mary Higginson, administratrix.	Mortgage
	REDDING, Eleanor, see Nicholas Cole.		

Folio.	Description.
3	In common the said proportions to each of 32 square miles between Kennebunk river and Batson's river, bought of Mogheggine, sagamore.
7	500 acres on southwest side Saco river, and one eighth each of a mine above *Saco*. [Confirming deed, Book I. I. 134.]
8	400 acres adjoining the above.
58	House, stage, &c., and two shallops at Smuttynose island, *Isles of Shoals*.
13	120 M pine boards due William Hutchinson and 86½ M due Eliakim Hutchinson.
12	Of apprenticeship of his son Richard Playce.
65	As to livery of the tract called Nischassett between Ogunquit and Kennebunk rivers in *Wells*.
78	25 acres at Spruce creek in *Kittery*.
58	12 acres on south of York river between Little cove and Eddy's point in *York*.
136	40 shillings on demand.
93	Two thirds in common of her husband's estate [in *Wescustogo*] to secure £25.
94	200 acres upland and 16 acres meadow on east side of Wescustogo river, to secure £40 : 4 : 4.

Index of Grantors.

Date.	Grantor.	Grantee.	Instrument.
1678, Feb. 12	REDDING, John	Edward Budd.	Deed
1680, Nov. 19	REDDING, John	Joshua Atwater's estate by Mary Higginson, administratrix.	Deed
1681, Oct. 13 1681, Oct. 25	RENALDS, John, and John Turbet	[Richard Bickeham & Co. by Francis Tucker agent]	Deposition
1674, Feb. 12	RENALDS, William et ux.	John Renalds	Conditional deed
1680, June 28	RICE, Thomas et ux.	Richard [Monson] Munson	Deed
1646, Apr. 13	RIGBY, Alexander	William Ryall	Grant
1650, Jan. 1	RIGBY, Alexander, by George Cleeve, agent	Michael Mitton	Grant
1675, Apr. 12	RISHWORTH, Edward and John Wincoll	John Renalds	Certificate
1678, June 15	RISHWORTH, Edw. et ux.	Thomas Traffton	Deed
1679, July 22	RISHWORTH, Edward	John Cut	Mortgage
1680, Feb. 24	RISHWORTH, Edward	Job Allcocke	Deed
1682, Oct. 16	RISHWORTH, Edward	John Sayword	Deed
1680, Apr. 20	ROBERTS, John, senior	John Roberts, jr.	Deed

Folio.	Description.
53	60 acres on west side of Harriseket river.
94	Quitclaim to property on east side of Wescustogo river.
104	As to Mrs. Elizabeth Cowell's livery of land at Spruce creek, in *Kittery*, her former husband's, William Seely's, to satisfy a debt.
57	All estate at Kennebunk in *Cape Porpoise*.
90	32 acres near Ox point at Spruce creek, in *Kittery*.
61	Messuage of 30 acres, Ryall's island and neck of 250 acres between Wescustogo and Shushquissacke rivers.
74	100 acres on the Point in *Casco Bay* adjoining grantee's house.
57	That William Renalds made provision for his sons William and Job.
30	4 acres of marsh at head of the old mill creek in *York*.
50	House and 34 acres opposite Sayword's, also 50 acres west of York bridge, &c., all in *York*.
135	4 acres on York river near the harbor's mouth, also a landing place in *York*.
121	All his realty in *York*, subject to above mortgage to John Cut.
70	3 acres called the Fowling marsh above Birch point, in *Kittery*.

Index of Grantors.

Date.	Grantor.	Grantee.	Instrument.
1660, May 9	ROBIN-HOOD, *alias* Rawmegon, sagamore and Terrumquine, sagamore Weesomonascoe, sagamore Squawquee, Indian Abumhamen, Indian	Thomas Webber	Deed
1679, April 5	ROBINSON, Stephen	Jos. Hammonds	Deed
1679, Apr. 5	ROBINSON, Stephen	Jos. Hammonds	Assignment
1683, July 21	ROGERS, Thomas, estate of	Richard Rogers and four other children not named	Partition
1675, May 6	ROGERS, William	Elihu Gunnison	Deed
1650, Oct. 17	ROMANASCOH, Indian	John Wadleigh	Deed
1672, June 20	Ross, John	John Bready	Deed
1678, Oct. 1	Row, Richard	Margery Bray	Deposition
1651, Oct. 3	ROWLES, Mr., sagamore	Katherine Trueworgy	Deed
1680, June 21	RYALL, John et ux. and Mehitable Dod	Samuel Donell	Deed
1673, Mar. 28	RYALL, William, senior	William Ryall John Ryall	Conditional deed
1676, July 25	SARDEN, Timothy	Richard Roe	Deposition
1663, Apr. 16	SAVAGE, Thomas	Mary Hill	Award
1673, Sept. 3	SAYWORD, Henry	John Leverett	Mortgage
1682, Oct. 17	SAYWORD, John	Edw. Rishworth	Bond
1673, Feb. 2	SCARBOROUGH, town of	Henry Brookeing	Grant

Index of Grantors.   45

Folio.	Description.
23	Tract 3 miles broad on west side of Kennebec river, opposite Arrowsic island.
46	50 acres of land near Frank's fort in *Kittery*.
46	Of rights under town grant of 18 acres in *Kittery*.
137	Apportioning land at *Saco* to two sons, daughters to be paid from personal estate.
106	House and one half the neck of land on western side of Spruce creek, in *Kittery*.
65	Quitclaim to tract conveyed by her son, Thomas Chabinocke.
112	House and grant of land near Mast cove, in *Kittery*.
89	As to Joseph Pearce's disposition of his estate in her favor.
10	Tompson's point [in *Kittery*].
72	Two-thirds of Nicholas Davis's house and land near the way to the ferry, in *York*.
62	House and lands between Wescustogo and Chesquissicke rivers.
2	As to purchase of a lost heifer from Diggory Jefferys.
101	Securing her an annuity of 50 shillings on lands [at Winter Harbor.]
39	One-third of saw mill, grist mill, 600 acres of land, &c., at *York*.
122	To discharge a mortgage to John Cut [see folio 50], to maintain him and pay annuity of £6, &c.
17	Land adjoining his plantation and near his house.

INDEX OF GRANTORS.

Date.	Grantor.	Grantee.	Instrument.
1673, Feb. 2	SCARBOROUGH, town of	Henry Brookeing	Grant
Recorded 1679, Mar. 28	SCARBOROUGH, town of	John Foxwell	Grant
1681, Oct. 21	SCOTTOW, Joshua	Humphrey Scammon	Certificate
1674, May 9	SEELY, Elizabeth	Robert Cutt	Award
1683, June 12	SHAPLEIGH, Alice	John Shapleigh	Award and agreement
1683, July 4	SHAPLEIGH, John	Richard Wharton	Deed
1661, Sept. 28	SHAPLEIGH, Nicholas, by Richard White, agent	Abraham Brown	Receipt
1682, June 7	SHAPLEIGH, Nicholas, estate of, by Alice Shapleigh, administratrix	Antipas Mavericke's estate	Discharge
1683, June 12	SHAPLEIGH, Nicholas, estate of	Alice Shapleigh John Shapleigh	Award
1683, May 27	SHEARE, Edward	Mary Sayword	Prom. note
1683, May 26	SHORE, Edward	Mary Sayword	Prom. note
1677, June 16	SMALE, Francis, senior	William Smyth's children	Deposition
1683, July 7	SMALE, Francis, sen., and Elizabeth Smale	Nicholas Shapleigh's estate [Richard Wharton]	Deposition
1674, Oct. 12	SMYTH, John, senior	John Smith, jr.	Deed
	SMYTH, William, see William Gowine		
1679, Sept. 24	SPINNY, Thomas et ux.	John Furnald	Deed
	SQUAWQUEE, Indian, see Robin Hood		

Index of Grantors. 47

Folio.	Description.
17	6 acres marsh adjoining Beaver creek.
40	6 acres of marsh near Phippeny's plantation.
103	That Jane Waddocke's deed was made by his and Major Pendleton's consent.
104	Establishing dividing line at Spruce creek [in *Kittery*].
126	Apportioning Nicholas Shapleigh's estate.
127	Merriconeag neck and Sebascodegan island in *Casco Bay*.
31	For a shallop and appurtenances.
111	Of mortgage [folio 109]
126	Of arbitrators dividing the estate.
130	For 30 shillings due August 31.
134	For 30 shillings due September 30.
16	As to Trustrum Harris's intended disposition of his estate.
128	As to purchase and occupancy of Sebascodegan island in behalf of Major Shapleigh
120	6 acres between grantor and James Jackson [in *York*].
123	2¼ acres in *Kittery* between grantor's and grantee's and Joseph Allcock's lands.

Index of Grantors.

Date.	Grantor.	Grantee.	Instrument.
1678, Mar. 12	STEPHENS, Edward	Edward Budd	Deed
1681, Mar. 2	STORER, Joseph et ux.	Samuel Austine	Deed
1680, Jan. 28	STOVER, John, senior	Thomas Lee	Mortgage
1673, Aug. 27	SWADDEN, Philip	Nicholas Frost	Deposition
1661, April 17	SYMONDS, Harlakenden	Martha Symonds	Deed
1661, Apr. 17	SYMONDS, Samuel	Harlakenden Symonds	Trust deed
1640, Apr. 15	SYMSON, Henry	Geo. Puddington	Deed
1641, Mar. 3	SYMSON, Henry	Geo. Puddington	Deed
1675, Aug. 25	SYMSON, Henry	Roger Rosse	Bond
1680, Apr. 7	SYMSON, Henry	Edward Johnson	Deed
	TERRUMQUINE, sagamore, see Robin-Hood		
	TETHERLY, John, see William Oliver		
1672, April 3	TILLTON, Abraham	William Gowine, *alias* Smyth	Deed
1677, Sept. 11	TOMSON, John	William Smyth's children	Deposition
1678, June 15	TRAFFTON, Thomas	Joseph Coutch	Deed
1674, Nov. 6	TRUEWORGY, Sam'l et ux.	Richard Rich	Deed
	TUCKER, Francis, see Nicholas Heskines		
1680, A. . .	. . . . . .	. . . .	Bill of sale

Index of Grantors.

Folio.	Description.
53	House, plantation and 5 acres of marsh on Harriseket river.
108	House and 200 acres near harbor mouth in *Wells*, also land and marsh at Drake's island.
86	House, land, &c., in *York* to secure £4 13 4
13	As to Thomas Wannerton's gift to Frost, of land at Fort point in *Kittery*.
127	500 acres of the tract next *Cape Porpoise* bounds bought of Bush and Turbett.
91	250 acres in the above tract to be conveyed to Martha Symonds.
84	All the land conveyed by William Hooke to grantor at Agamenticus plain in *York*, except two acres sold Thomas Footeman.
85	All his planting field and other land in *York* between grantee's and Ralph Blaysdell.
15	To deliver 5,000 red oak pipe staves.
78	10 acres by Meeting-house creek, also 5 acres near Bass cove, in *York*.
64	Of growing timber on Abraham Conly's land at Spruce creek, *Kittery*.
16	As to Trustrum Harris's intended disposition of his estate.
24	2 acres marsh adjoining Christopher Mitchell [in *Kittery*].
10	Tomson's or Trueworgy's point at Sturgeon creek, in *Kittery*.
77	House on Smuttynose island, *Isles of Shoals*.

Index of Grantors.

Date.	Grantor.	Grantee.	Instrument.
	TURBET, John, see John Renalds		
1657, July 2	TURBET, Peter et ux.	William Renalds	Deed
1678, May 6	TWISDEN, John	John Preble	Deed
1642, Apr. 2	VINES, Richard	Thomas Williams	Deed
1679, Dec. 4	WADDOCKE, Jane	Humphrey Scammon	Deed
1680, Sept. 4	WALDRON, Isaac	Elihu Gunnisson	Receipt
	WARDELL, William, see Philemon Pormot		
1680, June 6	WATTS, Henry	Nathan Bedford	Deed
1683, July 10	WEARE, Peter et ux.	Thomas Everell	Deed
1683, July 18	WEARE, Peter et ux.	John Smyth, jr.	Deed
Recorded 1679, Mar. 28	WEBB, Henry's estate, by Margaret Thatcher, Elizabeth Corwine, Mehitable Sheath, exec's	Henry Sayword's estate and others	Caution
	WEESOMONASCOE, sagamore, see Robin-Hood		
1679, Aug. 28	WENTWORTH, John	Isaac Parker	Deed
1680, Oct. 20	WENTWORTH, John et ux.	John Harmon	Deed
1680, July 5	WHEELEWRIGHT, Samuel	Edward Rishworth	Agreement

Folio.	Description.
57	House and 200 acres at Kennebunk, in *Cape Porpoise.*
24	8 acres adjoining James Sharpe, in *York.*
124	120 acres upland adjoining Robert Sanky, and 12 acres marsh at Winter Harbor, *Saco.*
103	200 acres north of the river, and 20 acres marsh at Goosefair, in *Saco.*
107	In full of all demands, &c.
74	100 acres at Blue point, *Scarborough,* except some marsh; also marsh at Crooked lane on the east side of the river.
132	Neck containing 27 acres on east side Cape Neddick river, in *York.*
132	12 acres upland and marsh on east side Cape Neddick river, in *York.*
40	Claiming one-third of York mills, in *York.*
63	House and 15 acres northeast of the path to Henry Sayword's; also 20 acres in *York.*
84	100 acres upon the highway adjoining Samuel Wheelwright's, in *Wells.*
92	To part land in *York,* devised by John Wheelewright's will.

INDEX OF GRANTORS.

Date.	Grantor.	Grantee.	Instrument.
1648, Nov. 15	WHITTE, John	Anthony Emery	Deed
1650, Nov. 11	WHITTE, John	[Anthony Emery]	Receipt
1678, Nov. 1	WHITTE, (Whight) John	Robert Allen Hannah Allen Francis Allen	Deed
1679, June 29	WHITTE, Richard	Nicholas Shapleigh Francis Hooke	Mortgage
1678, Nov. 14	WHITTE, Samson	Margery Bray	Deposition
167⅔, Feb. 20	WIGGENS, James, sen.	Robert Elliott	Bill of sale
1664, Sept. 26	WIGGIN, Thomas	Micum Mackyntire	Order
1680, Oct. 12	WILLIAMS, Thomas	Lydia Playstead	Deed
1681, Dec. 17	WILLIAMS, Thomas	Phineas Hull	Deed
1673, Sept. 24	WINCOLL, John and John Hull Roger Playstead	Geo. Broughton John Broughton	Deed
	WINCOLL, John, see Edward Rishworth		
1677, Jan. 25	WINTER, John, estate of, by Robert Jordan, adm'r	John Jordan	Deed
1667, Apr. 26	WITHERS, Thomas	John Ball	Deed
1675, Apr. 10	WITHERS, Thomas et ux.	John Feanix	Deed
1675, Mar. 4	WITHERS, Thomas	Thomas Rice	Deed
1676, June 23	WITHERS, Thomas	John Waters	Deed
1679, Oct. 3	WITHERS, Thomas	Edmund Ham-	Deed

INDEX OF GRANTORS. 53

Folio.	Description.
51	House and field, the Great Barren marsh, Hereges marsh and other marsh at Sturgeon creek, in *Kittery*.
51	For £5, part of the consideration for above conveyance.
102	All his realty and personal estate in *Kittery*, life estate to first two, reversion to Francis.
78	House and land at head of Braveboat harbor, in *Kittery*, bought of Ephraim Crockett, to secure £210.
39	As to Joseph Pearce's disposition of his estate in her favor.
104	Horses, kine, &c.
16	For £26 on John Paine.
92	One-third of his house lot and 4 acres (one-half) of his marsh at Winter Harbor, *Saco*.
124	All his realty at Winter Harbor, *Saco*.
1	One-fourth of two saw mills and timber land, buildings, appurtenances, &c., at Salmon falls on Great Negewanacke river, in *Berwick*.
33	Quitclaim to Richman's island and 300 acres opposite [in *Falmouth*], devised to said John.
44	12 acres called Eagle point on Spruce creek, in *Kittery*.
81	22¼ acres on east side of Spruce creek, in *Kittery*.
90	32 acres and marsh at Ox point on Spruce creek, in *Kittery*.
102	8 acres on south side of Spruce creek in *Kittery*.
95	2 acres on east side of Spruce creek in *Kittery*.

Index of Grantors.

Date.	Grantor.	Grantee.	Instrument.
1681, Mar. 25	WITHERS, Thomas	Nic. Shapleigh John Shapleigh	Deed
1683, May 28	WITHERS, Thomas	James Johnson	Deed
1678/83, Mar. 24	WITTUM, Peter, junior	Abraham Tillton	Deposition
1677, April 21	WOOD, Richard et ux.	Joseph Preble	Deed
1683, June 4	YEALES, Timothy	Charles Martine	Receipt
1675, May 3	YORK, county of, by Peter Weare, treasurer	Francis Littlefield	Prom. note
1670, Oct. 22	YORK county commissioners	Kittery, town of York, town of	Report
1663, Oct. 12	YORK, town of	John Frost	Grant
1666, Sept. 21	YORK, town of	William Roanes, and his wife and children, not named	Survey
1667, Apr. 22	YORK, town of	William Johnson	Survey
1670, Dec. 15	YORK, town of	John Frost	Survey
1670, Mar. 12	YORK, town of	Nathaniel Maysterson	Grant
1674, May 1	YORK, town of	John Hoy	Grant
1677, Jan. 7	YORK, town of	Thomas Donell	Survey
1678, Oct. 9	YORK, town of	John Parsons	Survey
1678, Mar. 12	YORK, town of	Thomas Addams	Survey
1679, Mar. 10	YORK, town of	Edw. Rishworth	Grant
1680, May 6	YORK, town of	Silvester Stover	Survey

INDEX OF GRANTORS.   55

Folio.	Description
91	Sufficient land for saw mills at Oak point on Spruce creek, in *Kittery*.
126	10 acres on northeast side Spruce creek, near the saw-mill in *Kittery*.
65	As to sale to him of building timber on Abraham Conley's land in *Kittery*.
13	90 acres, house and 3 acres marsh toward Cape Neddick, in *York*.
125	In full of all demands, &c.
13	For £3.
58	Establishing the towns' dividing lines.
25	10 acres on the western point of the harbor's mouth.
72	12½ acres on the northeast of the path from Bass cove to the marsh.
72	30 acres west from the little highway bridge.
25	50 acres on further side of York bridge.
120	30 acres near his house.
9	30 acres near the way to Newgewanacke.
23	45 acres south of York river adjoining Rogers cove brook.
57	12 acres by the highway adjoining John Preble.
67	40 acres on south side of York river.
120	Point of land where the saw-mill stands on Mr. Gorges's creek.
88	100 acres between Stony neck and the brook that runs into his marsh at Cape Neddick neck.

Index of Grantors.

Date.	Grantor	Grantee.	Instrument.
Recorded, 1683, Oct. 19	YORK, town of	Wells, town of	Commis'rs report
	YORK, town of, see York county commissioners		
Endorsed "Received 19th Aprill, 1641"	YOUGROFE, John	[George] Smyth	Letter and power of attorney
1650, Dec. 18	YOUGROFE, John, by George Smyth, attorney	Dennis Downeing	Deed
	———, Charles, see John Davess.		

Folio.	Description.
134	Fixing bounds between the towns.
114	Authorizing sale of house, &c. [See Book I. 1 16]
115	House and 30 acres near the river, between Watts fort and Frank's fort, in *Kittery*.

INDEX OF

Date.	Grantee.	Grantor.	Instrument.
1668, May 20	ABBET, Thomas et ux.	John Greene et ux.	Deed
1674, Dec. 15	ABBET, Thomas	Town of Kittery	Survey
1674, Dec. 16	ABBET, Thomas	Town of Kittery	Survey
167⅝, Mar. 1	ABBET, Thomas	John Greene, sen. et ux.	Deed
[No date]	ABBET, Thomas	Town of Kittery	Survey
1678, June 28	ABBET, Thomas and Jonathan Nayson	Nathan Lord et ux.	Deed
1653, May 10	ADDAMS, Phillip	Edward Godfrey	Deed
1655, Aug. 16	ADDAMS, Phillip	Edward Godfrey	Deed
1678, Mar. 12	ADDAMS, Thomas	Town of York	Survey
1679, Feb. 18	ALLCOCKE, Job	John Allcocke's estate	Award
1680, Feb. 24	ALLCOCKE, Job	Edward Rishworth	Deed
1650, July 16	ALLCOCKE, John and John Heard	William Hooke	Deed
	ALLDEN, Elizabeth, see Rebecca Lord		
	ALLDEN, John, see Edward Spragg		
	ALLEN, Francis, see Robert Allen		

GRANTEES.

Folio.	Description.
6	20 acres of land in *Kittery* between grantor and Peter Grant.
21	110 acres at Slut's corner.
21	31 acres adjoining John Green.
63	Homestead, 54 acres on Great Newgewanacke river in *Kittery*.
21	19 acres adjoining his own land and John Green.
25	10 acres called Abraham Conley's marsh at Sturgeon creek, in *Kittery*
37	Land in *York* between Scituate men's swamp, and the way to Mr. Gorges, John Parker and Henry Symson.
37	40 acres on west branch of river Agamenticus in *York*.
67	40 acres on south side of York river.
107	Assigning to Job the interest in the Cape Neck in *York*, afterwards conveyed by him to Sylvester Stover.
135	4 acres on York river near the harbor's mouth, also a landing place in *York*.
107	One-half of Cape Neddick neck in *York*.

Index of Grantees.

Date.	Grantee.	Grantor.	Instrument.
	ALLEN, Hannah, see Robert Allen		
1660, May 31	ALLEN, Hope	George Cleeves	Deed
1678, Nov. 1	ALLEN, Robert, and Hannah Allen Francis Allen	John Whitte (Whight)	Deed
1679, July 25	ALLINE, Walter	Isaac Botts, estate of, by Moses Spencer, administrator	Deed
Recorded 1683, Jan. 29	All Persons	Robert Nanny's estate, Catherine Nayler, ex'x, by Edw'd Rishworth, attorney	Caution
167¾, Mar. 10	ANDREWS, James	Eleanor Redding	Mortgage
1681, Sept. 10	ANDREWS, Thomas, and Anthony Farley John Winslow, jr.	John Moore, et ux.	Bond
	ATKINSON, Theodore, see Rebecca Lord		
1680, Apr. 12	ATWATER, Joshua, estate of, by Mary Higginson, administratrix	Eleanor Redding	Mortgage
1680, Nov. 19	ATWATER, Joshua, estate of, by Mary Higginson, administratrix	John Redding	Deed
1683, Sept. 21	AUSTINE, Matthew, jun.	William Ardell	Bond
1681, Mar. 2	AUSTINE, Samuel	Joseph Storer et ux.	Deed
168½, Mar. 15	AUSTINE, Samuel	John Barrett et ux.	Deed

Index of Grantees.

Folio.	Description.
68	400 acres on Casco river [*Falmouth*] between land of Ann Mittine and James Andrews.
102	All his realty and personal estate in *Kittery*, life estate to first two, reversion to Francis.
48	20 acres of land and house between Salmon Falls brook and the road to Dirty swamp in *Kittery*.
139	Claiming mortgage on 20 acres on Gorges point in *York*.
93	Two thirds in common of her husband's estate [in *Wescustogo*] to secure £25.
104	For a deed of house, stage, &c., on Star island, *Isles of Shoals*.
94	200 acres upland and 16 acres meadow on east side of Wescustogo river, to secure £40: 4: 4.
94	Quitclaim to property on east side of Wescustogo river.
134	To pay £6 for a horse purchased.
108	House and 200 acres near harbor mouth in *Wells*, also land and marsh at Drake's island.
120	3 acres of marsh in *Wells*.

Index of Grantees.

Date.	Grantee.	Grantor.	Instrument.
1680, Apr. 16	BACKEUS, Francis	John Carter et ux.	Deed
1667, Apr. 26	BALL, John	Thomas Withers	Deed
1671, Oct. 5	BALL, John	Town of Kittery	Grant
	BANEFIELD, Christopher, see Richard Nason		
Recorded 1681, Mar. 25	BANKES, John and others	Thomas Everell	Caution
166-, Oct. —	BAREFOOTE, Walter	Ferdinando Gorges by John Archdale, ag't	Covenant
1676, Oct. 20	BARNARD, Joseph	John Crafford et ux.	Deed
1670, Sept. 14	BARRETT, John	Mary Barrett	Deed
1683, Apr. 10	BASS, Peter	George Parker et ux.	Conditional deed
1679, July 29	BEDFORD, Nathan	Ambrose Boaden	Deed
1680, June 6	BEDFORD, Nathan	Henry Watts	Deed
1681, Oct. 20	BICKEHAM, Richard & Co.	Nicholas Heskins Francis Tucker	Deposition
1681, Oct. 13 1681, Oct. 25	[BICKEHAM, Richard & Co.]	John Renalds John Turbet	Deposition
1680, Apr. 10	BLACKEMAN, Benjamin	James Gibbones et ux.	Deed
	BONIGHTON, John, see James Gibbines		
1678, Sept. 19	BOOLS, Joseph, sen.	John Barrett et ux	Deed
1682, Jan. 29	BOTTS, Joseph	Israel Harding	Deed

INDEX OF GRANTEES.   63

Folio.	Description.
82	140 acres south of Saco river between it and Smyth's brook, also a neck of land called Church point [in *Saco*].
44	12 acres called Eagle point on Spruce creek, in *Kittery*.
44	10 acres adjoining his land at Spruce creek.
88	Against accepting or recording Andrew Everest's deed.
125	For quiet possession of 500 acres bought of Francis Champernoown [see Book I, 77, 82].
21	20 acres in *Kittery* southeast on Wells highway; Dirty swamp on northeast, between Isaac Botts and Mrs. Olive Playsted.
101	Land, house, meadow and personal property in *Wells*.
122	All realty and chattels in *York*.
74	150 acres of upland and meadow on northwest of mouth of Spurwink river, at Black point in *Scarborough*.
74	100 acres at Blue point, *Scarborough*, except some marsh; also marsh at Crooked lane on the east side of the river.
103	As to Elizabeth Cowell's, former widow of William Seely, livery of a lot at Spruce creek, *Kittery*, in satisfaction of a debt due them.
104	As to Mrs. Elizabeth Cowell's livery of land at Spruce creek, in *Kittery*, her former husband's, William Seely's, to satisfy a debt.
94	100 acres east of and adjoining Saco river falls, part of Lewis and Bonighton's patent in *Saco*.
59	3 acres of marsh in *Wells*.
129	2 acres at the sea wall in *Wells*.

Index of Grantees.

Date.	Grantee.	Grantor.	Instrument.
1681, Feb. 21	BOOTH, Deborah	Thos. Ledbrowke, [Ledbroake]	Contract
167¾, Mar. 23	BOTTS, Isaac	John Crafford, et ux.	Deed
1678, Nov. 13	BRAMHALL, George	Edward Allen	Deed
1669, Dec. 24	BRAY, John	Richard Bray	Deed
1673, Jan. 29	BRAY, John	John Davess and John Penwill	Contract
1675, Nov. 24	BRAY, John	John Davess	Contract
1676, Jan. 30	BRAY, John	Joseph Pearce	Bond
1677, Apr. 1	BRAY, John	Francis Morgan	Bond
1678, Oct. 1	BRAY, Margery	Richard Row	Deposition
1678, Nov. 14	BRAY, Margery	Samson Whitte	Deposition
1678, Dec. 4	BRAY, Margery	John Andrews	Deposition
1650, Feb. 21	BRAY, Richard	John Cossons	Agreement
1672, June 20	BREADY, John	John Ross	Deed
1674, Dec. 30	BREADY, John	Town of Kittery	Survey
	BRIMSDON, Robert, see John Whitte		
	BRIMSDON, Robert, see Daniel Stone		
1673, Feb. 2	BROOKEING, Henry	Town of Scarborough	Grant
1673, Feb. 2	BROOKEING, Henry	Town of Scarborough	Grant
1678, Oct. 24	BROUGHTON, George	John Broughton et ux.	Deed

Folio.	Description.
108	Ante-nuptial contract.
48	20 acres in *Kittery* southeast by way to Dirty Swamp; southwest by Thos Broughton; northwest by Salmon falls brook, northeast by land of grantor
69	Quitclaim to 400 acres [*in Falmouth*] conveyed by George Cleeve to Hope Allen, except 50 acres to Henry Kirke.
52	One-fourth of Cousins, or Hog, islands in *Casco Bay*.
23	For building a vessel of 80 or more tons burthen.
23	For building the ship *John & Alice*.
12	To pay £12.
24	For payment of £11 . 8.
39	As to Joseph Pearce's disposition of his estate in her favor.
39	As to Joseph Pearce's disposition of his estate in her favor.
39	As to Joseph Pearce's disposition of his estate in her favor.
37	As to payment for half of Cousins island, in *Casco Bay*, fencing, rental and trade with Indians.
112	House and grant of land near Mast cove, in *Kittery*
113	50 acres and 11 acres additional.
17	Land adjoining his plantation and near his house.
17	6 acres marsh adjoining Beaver creek.
49	Of one-half in common of three acres next the Salmon Falls mills [in *Berwick*].

Index of Grantees.

Date.	Grantee.	Grantor.	Instrument.
1673, Sept. 24	BROUGHTON, George and John	John Wincoll, John Hull, Roger Playstead	Deed
	BROUGHTON, John, see George Broughton		
1661, Sept. 28	BROWN, Abraham	Nic. Shapleigh, by Richard White, agent	Receipt
1678, Feb. 12	BUDD, Edward	John Redding	Deed
1678, Mar. 12	BUDD, Edward	Edward Stephens	Deed
1661, May 14	BUSH, John	George Cleeves	Certificate
1673, July 18	CHADBORNE, Humphrey	William Hutchinson	Agreement
	CHADBORNE, James, see Richard Otis		
1636, Dec. 12	CHAMPERNOOWN, Arthur	Sir Ferdinando Gorges	Lease
1638, June 14	CHAMPERNOOWN, Arthur	Sir Ferdinando Gorges	Lease
1665, Oct. 20	CHAMPERNOWNE, Francis	Ferdinando Gorges, by John Archdale, ag't	Deed
1666, July 17	CHAMPERNOWNE, Francis	Town of Kittery	Grant
1679, June 26	CHILD, Henry	Thomas Holmes, et ux.	Deed
1683, July 12	CHILD, Henry	Phineas Hull	Deed
1672, Dec. 27	CLARKE, Edward	George Lydden et ux.	Deed
1674, Apr. 3	CLARKE, John	Thomas Clarke, Thomas Lake	Deed

Index of Grantees. 67

Folio.	Description.
1	One-fourth of two saw mills and timber land, buildings, appurtenances, &c , at Salmon falls on Great Negewauacke river, in *Berwick*.
31	For a shallop and appurtenances
53	60 acres on west side of Harriseket river.
53	House, plantation and 5 acres of marsh on Harriseket river.
87	That he granted Bush 400 acres near Little river, *Cape Porpoise*, as agent for Alexander Rigby
91	Establishing new bounds for their lands at Assabumbedicke falls in *Kittery*.
97	500 acres of land between Piscataqua river and Braveboat harbor, to be called Dartington; also 500 acres marsh northeast of Braveboat harbor river to be called Godmorrocke, all in *Kittery*.
98	By the same description.
99	300 acres of land in *Kittery* between Capt. Champernowne's former house and Thomas Crockett.
100	500 acres by water side towards Braveboat harbor.
131	House and 40 acres in *Kittery* between Dirty swamp and Wells path.
131	30 acres in *Berwick*, north-east from Quamphegan.
51	10 acres at Crooked lane in *Kittery*, between John Amerideth and Francis Tricky.
66	A small island near mouth of Piscataqua river, purchased of Christopher Lawson.

INDEX OF GRANTEES.

Date.	Grantee.	Grantor.	Instrument.
1677, Sept. 13	CLARKE, Mary	George Litten [Lydden], by Sarah Litten, attorney	Receipt
1662, Mar. 1	CLARKE, Thaddeus	Elizabeth Mitton	Deed
1680, July 12	CLARKE, Thomas	Henry Donnell	Deed
1681, July 12	CLOYCE, John	Thomas Mills	Deed
1681, Dec. 17	CLOYCE, Nathaniel	Thomas Mills	Deed
1673, Nov. 27	CONLEY, Abraham	James Emery et ux.	Deed
1676, July 28	CONLEY, Abraham	John Morrall et ux.	Deed
1678, June 24	CONLEY, Abraham	John Heard's [Hord's] estate	Award
1662, Nov. 9	COOPER, Alexander	John Neale	Deed
1671, Apr. 13	COOPER, Alexander	Town of Kittery	Grant
167½, Mar. 6	COOPER, Alexander	Town of Kittery	Survey
1674, Dec. 19	COOPER, Alexander	Town of Kittery	Survey
1678, June 15	COUTCH, Joseph	Thomas Traffton	Deed
Acknowledged 1679, July 21	CROCKET, Ephraim	Ann Crockett Hugh Crockett Joseph Crockett Joshua Crockett	Deed
1661, Aug. 12	CROCKET, Thomas	John Billine	Deed
1677, Jan. 14	CROSS, John, sen.'s estate	Francis Backus	Receipt

Index of Grantees.

Folio.	Description.
52	In full of a note of £4 of her husband, Edward Clarke's.
76	Quitclaim to 100 acres on the point in Casco Bay [*Falmouth*].
74	3 acres, more or less, of marsh on York river in *York*.
105	The other half in common of the tract, next below, in *Wells*.
105	One half in common of a neck of land in *Wells*, east of Mr. Wheelwright's neck.
20	Cool Harbor point, 63 rods on river by 120 back, [at Sturgeon creek] in *Kittery*.
18	House and 7 acres, part of Hodgsden's former homestead; also, 70 acres as by three town grants, lying together, all in *Kittery*.
55	Of arbitrators fixing bounds at Sturgeon creek, in *Kittery*.
22	25 acres near White's marsh on Piscataqua river in *Kittery*
22	60 acres.
22	60 acres by Willcock's pond and brook.
22	18¾ acres at the north of his lot, near White's marsh.
24	2 acres marsh adjoining Christopher Mitchell [in *Kittery*].
73 74	Quitclaim to land conveyed to Ephraim by [Thomas] Crocket, [in *Kittery*.]
73	Ratifying a former conveyance of house and lot on *Kittery* point, made when he was a minor.
16	For his wife's portion.

Index of Grantees.

Date.	Grantee.	Grantor.	Instrument.
1677, Mar. 30	Cross, Joseph	Roger Hill	Receipt
1680, July 3	Cross, Joseph	Bryan Pendleton	Deed
168$\frac{2}{3}$, Mar. 18	Curtis, Benjamin	Andrew Everest et ux.	Deed
16$\frac{58}{59}$, Mar. 2	Cutt, John	Thomas Duston et ux.	Mortgage
166$\frac{3}{4}$, Mar. 19	Cutt, John	Elizabeth Durston	Deed
1679, July 22	Cutt, John	Edward Rishworth	Mortgage
1674, May 9	Cutt, Robert	Elizabeth Seely	Award
168$\frac{1}{2}$, Mar. 15	Davess, Emmanuel	Samuel Austine et ux.	Deed
168$\frac{1}{2}$, Mar. 15	Davess, Emmanuel	Samuel Austine et ux.	Deed
1679, Sept. 2	Davess, John	Robert Elliet	Letter
	Davess, John, see Ed- Rishworth		
1681, June 21	Deareing, Clement	Roger Deareing, estate of, by Roger Deareing, executor	Deed
1682, June 7	Dennett, Alexander	Stephen Paul et ux. Edward Gilman et ux.	Deed
1680, June 21	Donell, Samuel	John Ryall et ux. Mehetabel Dod	Deed
1677, Jan. 7	Donell, Thomas	Town of York	Survey
1679, Nov. 4	Down. William	John Henderson	Mortgage

Index of Grantees.

Folio.	Description.
13	In part for his wife's portion.
77	474 acres on Webhannet river in *Wells*.
89	40 acres on west side of northwest branch of York river in *York*.
20	Messuage and all lands in *Kittery* to secure £17 : 17 : 11.
21	Quitclaim to all the above.
50	House and 34 acres opposite Sayword's, also 50 acres west of York bridge, &c, all in *York*.
104	Establishing dividing line at Spruce creek [in *Kittery*].
121	Quitclaim to 3 acres of marsh in *Wells* conveyed him by John Barrett et ux.
121	Quitclaim to marsh in *Wells* bonded for conveyance by Abraham Collines.
57	Had never accepted his and Rishworth's joint bond.
121	144 square rods of land in *Kittery*, adjoining John Pearce.
111	40 acres by the water side in *Kittery*, formerly Antipas Maverick's.
72	Two-thirds of Nicholas Davis's house and land near the way to the ferry, in *York*
23	45 acres south of York river adjoining Rogers cove brook.
79	40 acres at Winter harbor, [*Saco*] between Peter Henderson and Humphrey Case.

Index of Grantees.

Date.	Grantee.	Grantor.	Instrument.
1650, Dec. 18	Downeing, Dennis	John Yougrofe, by George Smyth, att'y	Deed
1676, Jan. 16	Downing, Joshua	Dennis Downeing	Conditional deed
1678, Nov. 18	Dummer, Shubael	Joseph Alleocke, estate of, by John Twisden, administrator	Deed
16$\frac{78}{80}$, Mar. 4	Dummer, Shubael, et ux.	Philip Frost	Indenture
1679, June 21	Dyamont, Joan	Dennis Downeing	Deed
1679, June 21	Dyamont, Joan	Joshua Downeing et ux.	Deed
167$\frac{2}{3}$, Feb. 20	Elliott, Robert	James Wiggens, sen.	Bill of sale
1648, Nov. 15	Emery, Anthony	John Whitte	Deed
1650, Nov. 11	[Emery, Anthony]	John Whitte	Receipt
1654, Nov. 1	Emery, Anthony	Town of Kittery	Survey
1653, Mar. 16	Emery, James	Town of Kittery	Grant
1654, Nov. 1	Emery, James	Town of Kittery	Survey
1660, May 12	Emery, James	Anthony Emery et ux.	Deed
	Emery, James, see Richard Nason		
1673, Mar. 4	Emery, James, senior	Town of Kittery	Survey
16$\frac{78}{80}$, Mar. 22	Endle, Michael	Porter, Abel et ux.	Deed
1671, Oct. 22	Everell, Thomas	Jonathan Hammond	Deed

Folio.	Description
115	House and 30 acres near the river, between Watts fort and Frank's fort, in *Kittery*.
115	Messuage and all personal property in *Kittery*.
60	One half of Farmer Allcock's Neck at mouth of York river and 4 acres marsh on the western branch, in *York*.
73	Of apprenticeship of his step-son, Joseph Raynkine.
47	10 acres granted by and in *Kittery*, late in possession of William Dyamont, deceased
47	Quitclaim to land conveyed by Dennis Downeing, above.
104	Horses, kine, etc.
51	House and field, the Great Barren marsh, Herges marsh and other marsh at Sturgeon creek, in *Kittery*.
51	For £5, part of the consideration for above conveyance.
39	Land between said Emery and Henry Pounding.
97	6 acres, the next point below Thomas Spinny's.
38	50 acres by the water side adjoining Daniel Gooding's lot.
38	House and all his lands and personal property at Cold harbor, Sturgeon creek, in *Kittery*.
43	Eight lots, aggregating 315 acres.
78	25 acres at Spruce creek in *Kittery*.
11	200 acres upland and 10 acres meadow at Maryland in *Wells*.

INDEX OF GRANTEES.

Date.	Grantee.	Grantor	Instrument.
1680, June 5	EVERELL, Thomas	Andrew Everest et ux.	Deed
1683, July 10	EVERELL, Thomas	Peter Weare et ux.	Deed
	FARLEY, Anthony, see Thomas Andrews		
1675, Apr. 10	FEANIX, John	Thomas Withers et ux.	Deed
1681, Aug 2	FERNALD, Samuel,	James Emery et ux	Deed
	FERNALD, see Furnald		
	FIELD, Mary, see Rebecca Lord		
Recorded 1679, Mar. 28	FOXWELL, John	Town of Scarborough	Grant
	FOXWELL, Philip, see James Gibbines		
1681, Oct 31	FREATHY, John	William Freathy et ux	Deed
1683, Nov. 20	FROST, Charles	Stephen Jenkins et ux.	Deed
1663, Oct 12	FROST, John	Town of York	Grant
1670, Dec. 15	FROST, John	Town of York	Survey
1678, Nov. 2	FROST, John	Alexander Maxell et ux.	Conditional deed
1673, Aug 27	FROST, Nicholas	Phillip Swadden	Deposition
1680, May 4	FROST, Philip	Arthur Bragdon et ux.	Deed
1678, Dec. 26	FROST, Philip, and Rose Frost	John Frost, estate of, by Edward Rishworth and John Davess.	Award

Index of Grantees.

Folio.	Description.
87	16 acres upland and marsh called Pond marsh, also 40 acres given by and in *York*.
132	Neck containing 27 acres on east side Cape Neddick river, in *York*.
81	22½ acres on east side of Spruce creek in *Kittery*.
97	Quitclaim to town grant of 6 acres, the next point below Thomas Spinney's in *Kittery*.
40	6 acres of marsh near Phippeny's plantation.
105	One-half his homestead in *York;* also other half after his own and wife's decease.
136	One acre at Sturgeon creek, opposite the Cedars, in *Kittery*.
25	10 acres on the western point of the harbor's mouth.
25	50 acres on further side of York bridge.
51	20 acres at Scotland, in *York*.
13	As to Thomas Wannerton's gift to Frost, of land at Fort point in *Kittery*.
96	20 acres land between Bragdon's and Frost's lands adjoining Bass Cove river, in *York*, excepting the landing place.
33	Chattels and leasehold [in *Kittery*].

Index of Grantees.

Date.	Grantee.	Grantor.	Instrument.
1679, Apr. 7	Frost, William	Peter Cloyce et ux.	Deed
1661, July 13	Fryer, Nathaniel	Edmund Pickeard	Deed
1678, Aug 2	[Fryer, Nathaniel?]	Thomas Deane	Discharge
1679, July 14	Fryer, Nathaniel	Robert Jordan, jr.	Deed
1679, Sept 24	Furnald, John	Thomas Spinny et ux	Deed
1680, Feb. 1	Furnald, John	Wm. Hearle et ux.	Deed
	Furnald, see Fernald		
1681, Sept. 23	Gibbines, James and John Boughton, John Harmon, Philip Foxwell	From one another	Division
1674, Mar. 3	Ginkens [Jenkins], Renold	Abraham Conley	Deed
1674, May 21	Glanefield, Peter	William Palmer	Deed
1682, July 8	Glanefield, Peter	Samuel Knight et ux.	Deed
1682, June 29	Godfrey, Ann, *alias* Messant	Edward Johnson	Deposition
1682, June 29	Godfrey, Ann, *alias* Messant	Priscilla Johnson	Deposition
1679, May 24	Goodin, Daniel, jr.	Daniel Goodin, sen.	Deed
1683, Aug. 28	Goodine, Daniel, sen.	Eliakim Hutchinson	Deed
1672, Apr. 3	Gowine, William, *alias* Smyth	Abraham Tilton	Deed
1676, Sept. 16	Gowine, William, *alias* Smyth	James Middleton	Deed

Index of Grantees.

Folio.	Description.
59	House and land west of Webhannet river; two parcels of marsh; also 100 acres upon Maryland plain; all in *Wells*.
58	House, stage, &c., and two shallops at Smuttynose island, *Isles of Shoals*.
30	Of a mortgage [*Query*, of Book II, 157].
69	One half of Cape Elizabeth tract in *Falmouth*, also one half of his share of marshes in common.
123	2½ acres in *Kittery* between grantor's and grantee's and Joseph Allcock's lands.
123	20 acres in *Kittery* adjoining Spinney's cove.
102	Of Lewis and Bonighton's patent in *Saco*.
114	2 acres northwest side of Sturgeon creek in *Kittery*.
117	4 acres near Bass rock in *Kittery*, adjoining land of grantee.
117	12 acres in *Kittery* on Piscataqua river, bounded north by Thomas Spinny, south by grantee's land.
116	Concerning a loan by her to George Burdett, and livery of his real estate to her.
116	As to Mr. George Burdett's livery of his estate to Mrs. Godfrey.
54	House and lot in *Kittery* bounded by the fowling marsh, the river, Daniel Stone, James Emery and grantor's lands.
136	11¾ acres in *Berwick*, adjoining Humphrey Spencer.
64	Of growing timber on Abraham Conly's land at Spruce creek, *Kittery*.
67	Land on Kennebec river in common with Thomas Humfrys, also Small point.

INDEX OF GRANTEES.

Date.	Grantee.	Grantor.	Instrument.
1680, Apr. 13	GOWINE, William, *alias* Smyth	Charles Frost John Frost Joseph Hammond	Partition
1662, July 6	GRANT, James	Tho[mas] [Clarke]	Letter
1662, Sept. 30	GRANT, James	Thomas Clarke	Letter
1659, Oct. 21	GRANT, Peter	James Emery et ux.	Deed
1662, Mar. 6	GRANT, Peter	James Emery et ux.	Deed
167¾, Mar. 4	GRANT, Peter	Town of Kittery	Grant
1671, Apr. 13	GRAY, George	Town of Kittery	Grant
1671, Feb. 20	GREEN, John senior	Town of Kittery	Survey
167¾, Mar. 2	GREEN, John, senior	Town of Kittery	Survey
1675, May 6	GUNNISON, Elihu	William Rogers	Deed
1680, Sept. 4	GUNNISON, Elihu	Isaac Waldron	Receipt
1679, Jan. 27	GUNNISON, Elihu, and Joseph Gunnison	Ann Crockett	Deposition
	GUTTERIDGE, Isaac	William Palmer	Incomplete deed
1683, Aug. 21	GUTTERIDGE, Isaac	William Palmer	Deed
1681, July 12	GYDNEY, Bartholomew	Walter Gyndall	Mortgage
1680, June 23	GYNDALL, Walter	George Felt, sen.	Deed
1681, July 12	GYNDALL, Walter	Bartholomew Gydney et ux.	Deed

Folio.	Description.
67	Of Nicholas Frost, junior's real estate [in *Kittery*].
112	Covering remittance of £3 . 16.
112	Promising to pay for labor done for Henry Sayword.
14	Messuage and tract bought of John Lamb, 24 April, 1654, [in *Kittery*].
14	5 acres marsh near York pond in *Kittery*.
15	120 acres on west side of York pond.
22	60 acres.
14	15 acres adjoining his house lot.
14	60 acres near York pond
106	House and one half the neck of land on western side of Spruce creek, in *Kittery*.
107	In full of all demands, &c.
107	As to Hugh Gunnison's disposition of the premises leased to Seely and Rogers.
132	Re-recorded folio 134.
134	One half of Batson's neck in *Cape Porpoise;* also the grass plot and marsh.
109	The Stevens tract at *North Yarmouth;* also 2 acres on Ryall's point, to secure £110
76	100 acres on *Casco Bay* west of Felt's old house, also two parcels of meadow.
95	The Stevens tract at *North Yarmouth*.

Index of Grantees.

Date.	Grantee.	Grantor.	Instrument.
	Gyllum, Zachary, see Rebecca Lord		
1676, July 8	Gyllum, Zachary and Ephraim Turner	William Philhps et ux.	Deed
1683, May 21	Haley, Thomas	Thos Haly, sen.	Deed
168?, Mar. 23	Hammond, Jonathan	Wm Hammond	Conditional deed
168?, Mar. 23	Hammond, William	Jona. Hammond	Mortgage
1679, April 5	Hammonds, Joseph	Steph'n Robinson	Deed
1679, April 5	Hammonds, Joseph	Steph'n Robinson	Assignment
1679, Oct. 3	Hammon, Edmund	Thomas Withers	Deed
1681, July 26	Hammons, Edmund	John Hoole	Deed
1680, Aug 18	Harmon, John	Edward Godfrey, by Edward Johnson, att'y	Lease
1680, Aug 18	Harmon, John	Edward Johnson et ux.	Conditional deed
1680, Oct 20	Harmon, John	John Wentworth et ux.	Deed
	Harmon, John, see James Gibbines		
	Heard, John, see John Allcocke		
1677, Nov 5	Heard, John, estate of,	Richard Otis James Chadborne	Acceptance
1679, June 2	Hearle, John	Phineas Hull et ux.	Deed
1663, Apr. 16	Hill, Mary	Thomas Savage	Award

Folio.	Description.
7	500 acres on southwest side Saco river, and one eighth each of a mine above *Saco*. [Confirming deed, Book I. i. 134.]
124	Homestead, &c., in *Saco*.
89	Homestead of 400 acres and chattels in *Wells*.
89	Of property conveyed to secure maintenance of William and his wife.
46	50 acres of land near Frank's fort in *Kittery*.
46	Of rights under town grant of 18 acres in *Kittery*.
95	2 acres on east side of Spruce creek in *Kittery*.
116	37½ acres at Spruce creek in *Kittery*.
83	Of lands and meadows in *York*.
83	Homestead of 10 acres on the creek opposite the meeting house in *York*; 5 acres woodland at Bass cove; 3 acres of marsh on the river, and 60 acres town grant.
84	100 acres upon the highway adjoining Samuel Wheelwright's, in *Wells*.
17	Of the trusteeship.
130	30 acres at Post Wigwam in *Kittery* or *Berwick*.
101	Securing her an annuity of 50 shillings on lands [at Winter Harbor.]

Index of Grantees.

Date.	Grantee.	Grantor.	Instrument.
1683, May 30	HILTON, William	John Davess Charles ——?	Deposition
1678, Oct. 22	HODGSDEN, Benoni	Nic. Hodgsden	Deed
1682, Apr. 3	HODGSDEN, Benoni	Timothy Hodgsden	Deed
1678, Dec. 9	HODGSDEN, Nicholas	Benoni Hodgsden	Agreement
1679, Feb. 20	HODGSDEN, Timothy	Nicholas Hodgsden et ux.	Deed
1671, June 10	HOLMS, Thomas et ux.	William Freathy et ux.	Deed
1676, Oct. 27	HOLMES, Thomas	John Crafford et ux.	Deed
1677, May 31	HOLMS, Thomas	Richard Abbet et ux.	Deed
	HOOKE, Francis, see Nicholas Shapleigh		
1674, May 1	HOY, John	Town of York	Grant
1675, June 16	HUBBARD, William	Thomas Cowell et ux.	Mortgage
	HUDSON, William, see Rebecca Lord		
1679, June 7	HULL, John	John Broughton	Mortgage
1679, Jan. 12	HULL, John	George Broughton et ux.	Deed
1681, Dec. 17	HULL, Phineas	Thomas Williams	Deed
1683, Oct. 11	HULL, Reuben	Nathaniel Fryer et ux.	Deed
1683, Aug. 28	HUTCHINSON, Eliakim	Town of Kittery	Confirmation

	Description.
125	That Hilton was son of William Hilton, sen., and formerly lived in *York*.
31	Homestead of 40 acres, bought of John Wincoll; also, 56 acres town grant, except 7 acres to John Morrell, all in *Kittery*.
111	The two lots described second below.
41	Relative to carrying on a farm in *Kittery*.
110	40 acres and 2 acres bought of Peter Wittum in *Kittery*.
81	40 acres on York river, between Edward Start and Henry Sayword, in *York*.
9	40 acres with house, &c., between Thomas Broughton's, south of Dirty swamp and Wells path, granted by and in *Kittery*.
14	30 acres with house in *Kittery* near Quamphegan falls, north of the fort hill; and 6 acres marsh.
9	30 acres near the way to Newgewanacke.
3	Land and house at Crooked lane in *Kittery* on Piscataqua river and Spruce creek, except 2 acres of Francis Trickey's, also Grantum's island in the creek.
47	One-eighth of the following two saw-mills, &c.
125	One-eighth of two saw mills and appurtenances at Salmon Falls on Great Newgewanacke river in Piscataqua [*Berwick*].
124	All his realty at Winter Harbor, *Saco*.
138	Malaga island, *Isles of Shoals*.
132	Of former grants to Leaders and Hutchinsons.

Date.	Grantee.	Grantor.	Instrument.
1676, Aug. 17	HUTCHINSON, Eliakim and William Hutchinson	Roger Playstead's estate by Olive Playstead Wm. Playstead James Playstead executors	Account stated
	HUTCHINSON, Elisha, see Rebecca Lord		
	HUTCHINSON, William, see Eliakim Hutchinson		
1680, Oct. 13	INGERSOLL, George, jr. and John Ingersoll	General Court of Massachusetts	Grant
	INGERSOLL, John, see George Ingersoll, jr.		
1680, July 23	JEFFORD, John and John Sargent	Walter Barefoote	Caution
1678, Feb. 10	JENKINS, Stephen	Renold Jenkins	Conditional deed
	JENKINS, see Ginkens		
1680, Apr. 7	JOHNSON, Edward	Henry Symson	Deed
1683, Apr. 18	JOHNSON, Eleazer	Peter Bass	Agreement
1683, May 28	JOHNSON, James	Thomas Withers	Deed
1667, Apr. 22	JOHNSON, William	Town of York	Survey
	JOLLIFFE, John, see Rebecca Lord		
Recorded 1681, Sept. 22	JORDAN, Dominicus, by Joshua Scottow, att'y	Robert Jordan's estate	Claim
1677, Jan. 25	JORDAN, John	John Winter's estate by Robert Jordan, adm'r	Deed

Index of Grantees.

Folio.	Description.
13	120 M pine boards due William Hutchinson and 86½ M due Eliakim Hutchinson.
125	Confirming previous grants of 60 acres each, and granting mill privilege [in *Falmouth*].
77	Concerning land and rental in *Saco*.
137	All his estate, real and personal, in *Kittery*, except two pieces of marsh to Jabez Jenkins.
78	10 acres by Meeting-house creek, also 5 acres near Bass cove, in *York*.
123	To support Johnson till he was 21 years of age.
126	10 acres on northeast side Spruce creek, near the saw-mill in *Kittery*.
72	30 acres west from the little highway bridge.
101	To 1000 acres at the Great pond at Cape Elizabeth in *Falmouth*.
33	Quitclaim to Richman's island and 300 acres opposite [in *Falmouth*], devised to said John.

Index of Grantees.

Date.	Grantee.	Grantor.	Instrument.
1675, Feb. 29	Jordan, Robert, jr.	Robert Jordan et ux.	Deed
1678, Jan. 28	Jordan, Sarah, wife, and 6 sons	Robert Jordan	Will
168?, Mar. 24	Junkines, Robert	Alexander Maxwell et ux.	Deed
1680, Apr. 5	Kelley, Roger	Lewis Tucker	Bill of sale
1679, Oct. 22	Kittery, town of, and York, town of	York county commissioners	Report
1676, June 23	Knight, Richard	Robert Knight	Will
1642, July 22	Knight, Robert	Ralph Bleasdall	Deed
1655, Mar. 20	Lamb, John	Town of Kittery	Grant
1656, July 15	Lamb, John	Town of Kittery	Survey
Transcribed 1662, Nov. 25	Lamb, John	Town of Kittery	Grant
Recorded 1679, June 28	Lawd, Nathan, sen.	Christopher Banefield James Emery	Survey
	Lawd, see Lord		
1654, Apr. 12	Leader, Richard	Town of Kittery	Grant
1680, Jan. 28	Lee, Thomas	John Stover, sen.	Mortgage
1673, Sept. 3	Leverett, John	Henry Sayword	Mortgage
1675, Apr. 12	Lewis, Peter	John Fenix et ux	Deed
1675, April 12	Littlefield, Francis	John Barrett	Deed
1675, May 3	Littlefield, Francis	York county, by Peter Weare, treasurer	Prom. note

Folio.	Description.
2	Tract called Cape Elizabeth [in *Falmouth*.]
44	Devising all his real estate about Spurwink [in *Falmouth*.]
119	20 acres between the way to Newgewanacke and Bass cove brook, in *York*.
77	House on Smuttynose island, *Isles of Shoals*.
58	Establishing the towns' dividing lines.
37	Realty and chattels in *York*.
42	House and lot in *Agamenticus* [York].
20	20 acres meadow north of brook near William Love's bridge.
20	50 acres by the water side adjoining John Green's lot.
14	20 acres meadow near William Love's bridge.
44	Tract [in *Kittery*] sold by Abraham Conley to Nicholas Frost.
64	All pine trees on Little river except Chadborne's and Spencer's.
86	House, land, &c., in *York* to secure £4: 13: 4.
39	One-third of saw mill, grist mill, 600 acres of land, &c., at *York*.
81	House and land on east side of Spruce creek in *Kittery*.
10	2 acres of marsh at Great river in *Wells*.
13	For £8.

Date.	Grantee.	Grantor.	Instrument.
1679, Dec. 23	LITTLEFIELD, Francis	William Frost et ux.	Deed
1672, Apr. 4	LITTLEFIELD, Francis, sr.	William Ashley et ux.	Deed
1673, Feb. 23	LITTLEFIELD, Francis, sr.	Thomas Everell	Deed
167¾, Feb. 23	LITTLEFIELD, Francis, sr.	Thomas Everell et ux.	Deed
1681, Aug. 27	LORD, Abraham	John Hearle	Deed
1664, Feb. 4	LORD, Nathaniel	Richard Nason	Deed
1675, June 15	LORD, Rebecca and Robert Lord Samuel Phillips William Phillips Mary Field Martha Thirston Elizabeth Allden Sarah Turner Zachary Gyllum Peleg Santford John Sanford Elisha Sanford Eliphal Stratton John Jolliffe John Woodmancy Elisha Hutchinson Theodore Atkinson John Santford William Hudson	William Phillips	Deed
	LORD, Robert, see Rebecca Lord		
	LORD, Robert, see Edward Spragg		
	LORD, see Lawd		
1677, Dec. 7	LYNDE, Samuel	Christopher Lawson	Discharge
1677, Dec. 28	LYNDE, Samuel	Edward Camer et ux.	Deed

Index of Grantees.

Folio.	Description.
60	Land, &c., in *Wells*, bought of Peter Cloyce.
11	Marsh in the great marsh in *Wells*, formerly John Wadleigh, senior's.
11	200 acres upland and 10 acres meadow at Merryland in *Wells*.
11	Quitclaim of above endorsed on deed to him from Jonathan Hammonds.
130	40 acres at Post Wigwam in *Berwick* on the Little river.
27	9 acres at Newgewanacke [*Berwick*] adjoining grantee's land.
5	In common, 19,000 acres, 1000 acres apiece, west of Kennebunk river at the head of Wells township, in a tract 8 miles from the sea and 8 miles square, part of the tract bought of Flewellin.
80	Of mortgage by Edward Camer on Purchase's, or Camer's island in Kennebeck river.
80	Camer's formerly called Purchase's island in [Kennebeck] river, south of Merrymeeting bay.

Index of Grantees.

Date.	Grantee.	Grantor.	Instrument.
1664, Sept. 26	MACKYNTIRE, Micum	Thomas Wiggin	Order
1681, Sept. 29	MAINE, Treasurer of	John Bray	Receipt
1673, Feb. 23	MANNING, John	John Cloyce et ux.	Deed
1681, July 15	MARENELL, Andrew	Edward Allen et ux.	Deed
1683, June 4	MARTINE, Charles	Timothy Yeales	Receipt
1680, June 9	MATHEWS, Mary	Andrew Dyamont Michael Endle	Deposition
1680, June 9	MATHEWS, Mary	William Oliver John Tetherly	Deposition
1674, June 29 1675, Aug. 13	MAVERICKE, Antipas	Moses Mavericke	Receipts(2)
1682, June 7	MAVERICKE, Antipas, estate of	Nicholas Shapleigh's estate, by Alice Shapleigh, adm'x	Discharge
1663, Dec. 15	MAVERICKE, Moses	Antipas Mavericke	Mortgage
1656, July 15	MAXELL, Alexander	Town of Kittery	Survey
1682, June 26	MAYNE, John	John Coussons Agnes Carter *alias* Maddiver Richard Carter	Deposition
1670, Mar. 12	MAYSTERSON, Nathaniel	Town of York	Grant
	MESSANT, Ann, see Ann Godfrey		
1650, Jan. 1	MITTON, Michael	Alexander Rigby by Geo. Cleeve, agent	Grant
1682, Sept. 28	MITTON, Nathaniel, heirs	Nathaniel Mitton's estate	Appraisal

Index of Grantees.

Folio.	Description.
16	For £26 on John Paine.
103	For £8 in full of all demands, &c.
11	6 acres fresh meadow at Totnucke in *Wells*.
100	50 acres in *Casco* [*Falmouth*] formerly given to Henry Kirke, and by him forfeited.
125	In full of all demands, &c.
71	As to her deceased husband Walter's ownership of two lots, &c., on the *Isles of Shoals*.
71	As to her husband, Walter Mathews's ownership of two lots at the *Isles of Shoals*.
109	For payments on mortgage, second below.
111	Of mortgage [folio 109].
109	House and land in *Kittery*, subject to conditional sale to Thomas Booth.
22	35 acres by the water side adjoining James Warren's lot.
115	As to John Mayne's purchase of Richard Carter, sen., at Wescustogo, Royal river, in *Casco Bay*.
120	30 acres near his house.
74	100 acres on the Point in *Casco Bay* adjoining grantee's house.
120	Of 80 acres and 3 acres marsh [in *Falmouth*].

INDEX OF GRANTEES.

Date.	Grantee.	Grantor.	Instrument.
1669, June 5	MOORE, John, sen.	Diggory Jeffreys et ux.	Deed
1680, Jan. 5	MOORE, William	Ann Godfrey	Deed
1676, July 27	MORRELL, John	Abraham Conley	Deed
1678, Oct. 13	MORRALL, John	Henry Kirke et ux.	Deed
1678, Feb. 13	MORTON, John	John Howell et ux.	Deed
1679, Apr. 28	MOWLTON, Jeremiah	Isaac Everest et ux.	Deed
1661, July 29	MOWLTON, Thomas	Arthur Bragdon, sen. et ux.	Deed
1680, June 28	MUNSON, [Monson] Richard	Thomas Rice et ux.	Deed
1676, June 28	NASON, Richard and James Emery Christopher Banefield Nicholas Shapleigh	John Heard [Hord] Abraham Conley	Reference
	NAYSON, Jonathan, see Thomas Abbett		
1675, July 8	NELLSON, Charles	Waymouth Lyston et ux.	Deed
1651, May 15	NUTTER, Hatevill	Humphrey Chadborne	Deed
1666, Sept. 27	OLIVER, Peter	Thomas Mayhew	Deed
1678, Dec. 9	OLIVER, Richard and William Oliver	Michael Endle	Deed

Folio.	Description.
88	Two islands or necks, and 4 acres land adjoining, and houses in *Kittery* between John Bray and Roger Dearing.
86	The sunken marsh at Braveboat harbor in *York*.
19	Tract called Coole Harbor in *Kittery*, excepting two acres for Henry Kirke's house.
31	House and 20 acres land at Cold Harbor in *Kittery*.
42	100 acres on Black Point river, at Dunstan, in *Scarborough*.
50	3 acres marsh on northwest branch of York river in *York*.
24	3 acres marsh, called Gallows point, tract of marsh below the above and upland between, in *York*.
90	32 acres near Ox point at Spruce creek, in *Kittery*.
54	To determine bounds at Sturgeon creek, [in *Kittery*].
118	One half, in common with Gilbert Lugg, of lot in *Kittery*, bought of Joseph Allcocke.
70	Two meadows on east side of Piscataqua river [in *Berwick*], one called Burcham point, the other on Black creek.
114	One quarter of Elizabeth islands north of Martyn's Vineyard.
71	Stage and flakes on Smuttynose island, *Isles of Shoals*.

INDEX OF GRANTEES.

Date.	Grantee.	Grantor.	Instrument.
1677, Nov. 5	OTIS, Richard, and James Chadborne	John Heard's [Hord's] estate, by Nic. Shapleigh Jno. Shapleigh Jos. Hammonds Wm. Spencer Abra. Conley Trustees	Deed
1679, Dec. 10	PARKER, Abraham	Job Allcocke	Deed
1683, Apr. 10	PARKER, George et ux.	Peter Bass	Mortgage
1679, Aug. 28	PARKER, Isaac	John Wentworth	Deed
1648, June 12	PARKER, John	John Heard [Hord]	Deed
1675, Jan. 10	PARKES, Thomas	Richard Abbet et ux.	Deed
1678, Oct. 9	PARSONS, John	Town of York	Survey
1678, Mar. 14	PARSONS, John	John Knoulton, by John Davess and Sam'l Sayword, att'ys	Bond
1679, Oct. 5	PARSONS, John	John Knoulton, by Sam'l Sayword and John Davess, att'ys	Bill of sale
1668, July 18	PAUL, Stephen	Daniel Paul	Deed
166⅔, Mar. 16	PEARCE, John	James Grant	Deed
1670, June 14	PEARCE, John	Edward Johnson	Receipt
1678, Jan. 1	PEARSON, George	Richard Bray et ux.	Deed

INDEX OF GRANTEES.

Folio.	Description.
17	Subrogation to the trust.
97	80 acres in *York* between York river, Piscataqua bounds and lots of Thomas Adams and Samuel Bragdon.
122	Of land in *York*, conditioned to maintain Parker and wife.
63	House and 15 acres northeast of the path to Henry Sayword's; also 20 acres in *York*.
71	House and all lands in *Gorgeana*.
64	40 acres in *Kittery* on Newgewanacke river, near Post Wigwame, excepting Mr. Leader's pine timber.
57	12 acres by the highway adjoining John Preble.
56	For a bill of sale of his house at *York*.
56	Dwelling house between houses of John Preble and Henry Symson in *York*.
113	House and all his realty in *Kittery*, except 15 acres to Joseph Allcocke.
22	10 acres on Mr. Gorges's neck, between the new mill creek and Bass cove in *York*.
23	£15 in full of all demands, &c.
35	One-half of Cousins island and of Long island in *Casco Bay*, and 5 acres of marsh on the mainland.

Date.	Grantee.	Grantor.	Instrument.
1678, Jan. 1	PEARSON, George	Richard Bray et ux.	Deed
1678, Jan. 8	PEARSON, George	Jane Bray	Deed
1678, Dec. 23	[PEARSON, George]	Richard Bray	Deposition
1678, Dec. 23	PEARSON, George	Nicholas Coole Eleanor Redding	Deposition
167$\frac{8}{9}$, Mar. 5	PEARSON, George	Thomas Kemble	Deposition
167$\frac{8}{9}$, Mar. 11	PEARSON, George	John Allden	Deposition
167$\frac{8}{9}$, Mar. 11	PEARSON, George	John Howman	Deposition
1666, Oct. 11	PENDLETON, Bryan	William Phillips et ux.	Deed
1670, Jan. 6	PENWILL, Joseph	Job Allcocke	Deed
1682, Nov. 17	PEPPERRELL, William	John Bray	Deed
	PHILLIPS, Samuel, see Rebecca Lord		
	PHILLIPS, Samuel, see Edward Spragg		
1674, July 9	PHILLIPS, William	George Munjoy	Deposition
	PHILLIPS, William, see Rebecca Lord		
	PHILLIPS, William, see Edward Spragg		
1680, Oct. 12	PLAYSTEAD, Lydia	Thomas Williams	Deed
1678, Jan. 4	PORTER, Abel	Thomas Cowell et ux.	Deed
1681, Dec. 2	POWSLAND, Richard	Elizabeth Harvy	Deed

Index of Grantees.

Folio.	Description.
36	60 acres plantation between Richard Carter's and John Maine's at *Casco Bay*.
41	Quitclaim to Cousins island in *Casco Bay*.
84	That he never consented that his son [John] Bray should marry Ann Lane.
84	That John Bray was not legally married to Ann Lane.
66	As to Richard Bray and wife's execution of two deeds.
66	As to payment by Pearson to Richard Bray of the consideration for Cousins island in *Casco Bay*.
66	As to payment for Cousins island in *Casco Bay*.
74	100 acres and an island at *Cape Porpoise* bought of John Smyth.
52	House, garden-plot and appurtenances in *York*, next Edward Rishworth's.
121	One acre land [on *Kittery* point].
87	As to bounds of 4 miles, surveyed west from Saco river along the coast.
92	One-third of his house lot and 4 acres (one-half) of his marsh at Winter Harbor, *Saco*
39	25 acres on Spruce creek in *Kittery*, granted to William Seely.
113	4 acres on the neck [*Falmouth*] between Anthony Bracket and Clark and Spencer.

98 Index of Grantees.

Date.	Grantee.	Grantor.	Instrument.
1670, June 24	PRÆSBERY, John	Clement Hardy	Deed
1678, May 6	PREBLE, John	John Twisden	Deed
1677, Apr. 21	PREBLE, Joseph	Richard Wood et ux.	Deed
1640, April 15	PUDDINGTON, George	Henry Symson	Deed
1641, Mar. 3	PUDDINGTON, George	Henry Symson	Deed
1678, Oct. 26	PULLMAN, John	Samson Anger et ux.	Deed
16$\frac{48}{49}$, Mar. 5	RAYNKINE, Joseph	Shubael Dummer	Contract
16$\frac{79}{80}$, Mar. 5	RAYNKINE, Joseph	Philip Frost	Contract
1674, Feb. 12	RENALDS, John	William Renalds et ux.	Conditional deed
1675, April 12	RENALDS, John	Edw'd Rishworth John Wincoll	Certificate
1657, July 2	RENALDS, William	Peter Turbet et ux.	Deed
1675, Mar. 4	RICE, Thomas	Thomas Withers	Deed
1674, Nov. 6	RICH, Richard	Samuel Truworgy et ux.	Deed
1676, July 11	RISHWORTH, Edward	Edward Johnson Robert Knight	Deposition
1679, Mar. 10	RISHWORTH, Edward	Town of York	Grant
1680, July 5	RISHWORTH, Edward	Samuel Wheelewright	Agreement
168$\frac{0}{1}$, Mar. 8	RISHWORTH, Edward	John Cut	Receipt and partial discharge

INDEX OF GRANTEES.

Folio.	Description.
42	50 acres east of Saco river called Paige's plantation in *Saco*.
24	8 acres adjoining James Sharpe, in *York*.
13	90 acres, house and 3 acres marsh toward Cape Neddick, in *York*.
84	All the land conveyed by William Hooke to grantor at Agamenticus plain in *York*, except two acres sold Thomas Footeman.
85	All his planting field and other land in *York* between grantee's and Ralph Blaysdell.
34	10 acres upland and marsh in *York*, on south-west side of York river, between Henry Donnell, Jasper Pullman and Edward Johnson.
73	To deliver a heifer for the use of his apprentice.
73	To keep a heifer for said Raynkin "on halves."
57	All estate at Kennebunk in *Cape Porpoise*.
57	That William Renalds made provision for his sons William and Job.
57	House and 200 acres at Kennebunk, in *Cape Porpoise*.
90	32 acres and marsh at Ox point on Spruce creek, in *Kittery*.
10	Tomson's or Trueworgy's point at Sturgeon creek, in *Kittery*.
2	That Mr. Richard Vines gave Henry Norton meadows along York river, now in Rishworth's possession [in *York*].
120	Point of land where the saw-mill stands on Mr. Gorges's creek.
92	To part land in *York*, devised by John Wheelewright's will.
102	For £26 on account, and release of mortgage on 4 acres.

Index of Grantees.

Date.	Grantee.	Grantor.	Instrument.
1682, Oct. 17	Rishworth, Edward	John Sayword	Bond
1678, Nov. 14	Rishworth, Edward and John Davess	John Frost's estate, by John Frost, Philip Frost, Alex. Maxell, Rose Frost, admurs	Reference
1680, Feb. 2	Roads, Thomas	James Chadborne et ux.	Deed
1666, Sept. 21	Roanes, William, and his wife, and children not named	Town of York	Survey
1680, Apr. 20	Roberts, John, jr.	John Roberts, sr.	Deed
	Roberts, Hatevill, see Thomas Roberts		
1680, May 13	Roberts, Thomas, and Hatevill Roberts	John Morrall	Deed
1663, Dec. 4	Robinson, Stephen	James Emery et ux.	Deed
166⅔, June —	Robinson, Stephen	Town of Kittery	Grant
1676, July 25	Roe, Richard	Margery Bray	Deposition
1676, July 25	Roe, Richard	Timothy Sarden	Deposition
1683, July 21	Rogers, Richard, and four other children not named	Thomas Rogers's estate	Partition
1683, Apr. 6	Ross, James	Gilbert Endicott	Deed
1675, Aug. 25	Rosse, Roger	Henry Symson	Bond
	Ryall, John, see William Ryall		
1646, April 13	Ryall, William	Alexander Rigby	Grant

Index of Grantees. 101

Folio.	Description.
122	To discharge a mortgage to John Cut [see folio 50], to maintain him and pay annuity of £6, &c.
33	Power to hear and determine differences.
106	30 acres or one-half of Tomson point in *Kittery*, except John Ross's lot.
72	12½ acres on the northeast of the path from Bass cove to the marsh.
70	3 acres called the Fowling marsh above Birch point, in *Kittery*.
70	Marsh and meadow called Burcham point on east side of Piscataqua river, in *Kittery*.
45	House and 50 acres near Frank's fort in *Kittery*, formerly Robert Waymouth's.
46	18 acres behind his dwelling.
2	Relating to lost heifer bought of Diggory Jefferies.
2	As to purchase of a lost heifer from Diggory Jefferys.
137	Apportioning land at *Saco* to two sons, daughters to be paid from personal estate.
128	Saw mill &c., and 50 acres land on Little river at *Cape Porpoise*.
15	To deliver 5,000 red oak pipe staves.
61	Messuage of 30 acres, Ryall's island and neck of 250 acres between Wescustogo and Shushquissacke rivers.

Date.	Grantee.	Grantor	Instrument.
1673, Mar. 28	RYALL, William, and John Ryall	William Ryall, senior	Conditional deed
	SANFORD, Elisha, see Rebecca Lord		
	SANFORD, John, see Rebecca Lord		
	SANTFORD, John, see Rebecca Lord		
	SANTFORD, Peleg, see Rebecca Lord		
1669, July 5	SARGEANT, John	William Phillips	Deed
	SARGENT, John, see John Jefford		
1679, Mar. 6	SAWYER, William	Abraham Collines et ux.	Deed
1670, July 12	SAYWORD, Henry	Daniel Epps	Conditional deed
Recorded 1679, Mar. 28	SAYWORD, Henry, estate of	Thomas Clarke	Caution
1679, June 10	SAYWORD, Henry, estate of	Simon Lynde	Caution
1679, June 12	SAYWORD, Henry, estate of	Simon Lynde	Caution
1679, June 16	SAYWORD, Henry, estate of	Bartholmew Gydney	Caution
Recorded 1679, Mar. 28	SAYWORD, Henry and others	Robert Gibbs's estate, by Elizabeth Corwin, administratrix	Caution

Index of Grantees. 103

Folio.	Description.
62	House and lands between Wescustogo and Chesquissicke rivers
82	30 acres at Winter Harbor, *Saco*, between George Pearson and Ralph Trustrum, excepting Richard Randall's lot.
46	93 acres upland, 20 acres salt meadow, adjoining Mary Smyth and Thomas Wells, in *Wells*
33	Farms bought of Gooch, Austine and Mussy in *Wells*, also land bought of John and Robert Wadleigh between Cape Porpoise and Kennebunk rivers.
40	Claiming two-thirds of the saw and other mills and land at Mill creek called York mills, in *York*.
55	Claiming farms bought by Epps of Gouch, Austine and Mussy, also one half the Mousam mills in *Wells*.
44	Claiming one half the Mousam mills, &c., at *Wells*.
43 44	Claiming one-half of *Casco* mills, lands, &c.
40	Claiming saw mill and 300 acres at Cape Porpoise river falls.

Index of Grantees.

Date.	Grantee.	Grantor.	Instrument.
Recorded, 1679, Mar. 28	SAYWORD, Henry, estate of, and others	Henry Webb's estate, by Marga't Thatcher Elizab'th Corwine Mehitable Sheath exec's	Caution
1682, Oct. 16	SAYWORD, John	Edw'd Rishworth	Deed
1683, May 26	SAYWORD, Mary	Edward Shore	Prom. note
1683, May 27	SAYWORD, Mary	Edward Sheare	Prom. note
1683, Aug. 29	SAYWORD, Mary	John Price	Prom. note
1675, Apr. 5	SAYWORD, Samuel	John Knoulton	Letter and power of attorney
1679, Dec. 4	SCAMMON, Humphrey	Jane Waddocke	Deed
1681, Oct. 21	SCAMMON, Humphrey	Joshua Scottow	Certificate
1681, Apr. 16	SCOTTOW, Joshua	Joseph Holmes	Mortgage
1675, Dec. 20	SEARLE, John	John Greene et ux.	Deed
1676, July 5	[SEELY, Elizabeth]	John Hubbard by William Hubbard, ag't	Receipt
1682, June 29	SHAPLEIGH, Alice	Francis Champernoown	Deed
1683, June 12	SHAPLEIGH, Alice, and John Shapleigh	Nicholas Shapleigh's estate	Award
1683, June 12	SHAPLEIGH, John	Alice Shapleigh	Award and agreement
	SHAPLEIGH, John, see Alice Shapleigh		
	SHAPLEIGH, John, see Nicholas Shapleigh		

Index of Grantees. 105

Folio.	Description.
40	Claiming one-third of York mills, in *York*.
121	All his realty in *York*, subject to mortgage to John Cut.
134	For 30 shillings due September 30.
130	For 30 shillings due August 31.
136	40 shillings on demand.
56	Authorizing sale of his property in *York*, and other matters.
103	200 acres north of the river, and 20 acres marsh at Goosefair, in *Saco*.
103	That Jane Waddocke's deed was made by his and Major Pendleton's consent.
96	Land purchased of Francis Neale in *Casco* to secure £160.
116	15 acres land in *Kittery* between grantor's homestead, Thomas Abbet's and Daniel Goodin's lots.
3	In full.
116	Quitclaim to any of that land near Braveboat harbor formerly [Ann] Godfrey's that falls within his patent or his father's [Arthur] in *Kittery*.
126	Of arbitrators dividing the estate.
126	Apportioning Nicholas Shapleigh's estate.

Date.	Grantee.	Grantor.	Instrument.
1678, June 16	SHAPLEIGH, Nicholas	Antipas Mavericke	Deed
1678, Nov. 30	SHAPLEIGH, Nicholas	George Burrin	Deed
1680, Oct. 7	SHAPLEIGH, Nicholas	Moses Mavericke	Assignment
1683, May 14	SHAPLEIGH, Nicholas	John Cossons	Deposition
1683, July 7	SHAPLEIGH, Nicholas, estate of	Francis Smale, sr. Elizabeth Smale	Deposition
	SHAPLEIGH, Nicholas, see Richard Nason		
1679, June 29	SHAPLEIGH, Nicholas, and Francis Hooke	Richard Whitte	Mortgage
1681, Mar. 25	SHAPLEIGH, Nicholas, and John Shapleigh	Thomas Withers	Deed
1679, Sept. 3	SMYTH, ——	Joseph Armitage	Letter
Endorsed "Received 19th Aprill, 1641"	SMYTH, [George]	John Yougrofe	Letter and power of attorney
1643, July 18	SMYTH, John	Sir Ferdinando Gorges by Thos. Gorges, dep. governor	Deed
1674, Oct. 12	SMYTH, John, jr.	John Smyth, sen.	Deed
1683, July 18	SMYTH, John, jr.	Peter Weare et ux.	Deed
1677, June 16	SMYTH, Wm., children of	Mary Frost	Deposition
1677, June 16	SMYTH, Wm., children of	Francis Smale, sr.	Deposition
1677, June 20	SMYTH, Wm., children of	John Granger	Deposition
1677, Sept. 11	SMYTH, Wm., children of	John Forgison	Deposition
1677, Sept. 11	SMYTH, Wm., children of	John Tomson	Deposition

Folio.	Description.
27	30 acres of land and house adjoining William Ellingham's in *Kittery*.
37	House and 20 acres land on east side of Braveboat harbor in *York*.
109	Of mortgage of house and land in *Kittery*.
128	As to ownership of Sebascodegan Island.
128	As to purchase and occupancy of Sebascodegan island in behalf of Major Shapleigh.
78	House and land at head of Braveboat harbor, in *Kittery*, bought of Ephraim Crockett, to secure £210.
91	Sufficient land for saw mills at Oak point on Spruce creek, in *Kittery*.
57	About satisfying Smyth's execution against him.
114	Authorizing sale of house, &c. [See Book I. i. 16.]
74	100 acres of land and an island opposite, at *Cape Porpoise*.
120	6 acres between grantor and James Jackson [in *York*].
132	12 acres upland and marsh on east side Cape Neddick river, in *York*.
16	As to Trustrum Harris's intended disposition of his estate.
16	As to Trustrum Harris's intended disposition of his estate.
16	As to Trustrum Harris's intended disposition of his estate.
16	As to Trustrum Harris's intended disposition of his estate.
16	As to Trustrum Harris's intended disposition of his estate.

Index of Grantees.

Date.	Grantee.	Grantor.	Instrument.
	SMYTH, William, see William Gowine		
1679, Feb. 14	SOAPER, John	Stephen Paul et ux.	Deed
1671, Feb. 27	SPENCER, Thomas	Town of Kittery	Survey
1671, Feb. 27	SPENCER, William	Town of Kittery	Survey
1676, June 12	SPRAGG, Edward ⅜ and Robert Lord ⅛ John Allden ⅛ Samuel Phillips ⅛ Wm. Phillips ⅛	William Phillips	Deed
1680, Dec. 28	STEWART, Duncan	Timothy Collines et ux.	Deed
1679, May 24	STONE, Daniel	Daniel Goodin, senior	Deed
1673, Dec. 10	STONE, Daniel, and Robert Brinsdon	John Paine	Deed
1681, Mar. 2	STORER, Joseph	Samuel Austine et ux.	Deed
1683, Oct. 13	STORER, Joseph	Fr. Backehouse et ux.	Deed
1679, Sept. 27	STOVER, John, sen.	Abraham Preble	Deed
16⅞⁸, Mar. 4	STOVER, Sylvester	Job Allcocke	Assignment
1680, May 6	STOVER, Sylvester	Town of York	Survey
1680, Sept. 13	STOVER, Sylvester	Job Allcocke et ux.	Deed
1680, Nov. 5	STOVER, Sylvester	John Heard [Hord]	Deed

Folio.	Description.
127	20 acres near the Boiling rock in Great cove in *Kittery*.
80	100 acres adjoining the following.
80	About 150 acres adjoining brook from Willcock's pond, as per grant of 1651.
3	In common the said proportions to each of 32 square miles between Kennebunk river and Batson's river, bought of Mogheggine, sagamore.
92	100 acres upland, meadow and marsh formerly his father Christopher's at Blue point [*Scarborough*] on the sea, between Giles Barge and Nathan Bedford.
54	5 acres in *Kittery*, part of town grant, bounded by the river James Emery's and grantor's lands.
29	150 acres in Wells township about 4 miles from the town; also two parcels of marsh.
108	300 acres land and house and marsh between John Barrett and Joseph Bolls, and down to Webhannet river, and 4 acres marsh, in *Wells*.
135	Land and marsh at Drake's island in *Wells*.
58	12 acres on south of York river between Little cove and Eddy's point in *York*.
107	Of a claim of 55 shillings against the estate of John Allcocke.
88	100 acres between Stony neck and the brook that runs into his marsh at Cape Neddick neck.
100	One fourth of the Cape Neck in *York*.
100	One fourth of Cape Neddick neck in *York*.

Date.	Grantee.	Grantor.	Instrument.
	STRATTON, Eliphal, see Rebecca Lord		
1677, Jan. 25	STYLEMAN, Elizabeth	John Jordan	Marriage settlement
1661, Apr. 17	SYMONDS, Harlakenden	Samuel Symonds	Trust deed
1661, Apr. 17	SYMONDS, Martha	Harlakenden Symonds	Deed
1660, May 1	TETHERLY, Gabriel	Thomas Onyon et ux.	Deed
1674, May 7	TETHERLY, Gabriel	Daniel King	Deed
	THIRSTON, Martha, see Rebecca Lord		
1680, Mar. 24	TILTON, Abraham	Charles Frost	Deposition
167⅞, Mar. 24	TILTON, Abraham	Peter Wittum, jr.	Deposition
1678, June 15	TRAFFTON, Thomas	Edw. Rishworth et ux.	Deed
1678, July 21	TRAFFTON, Thomas	Micum Mackyntyre	Deed
1651, Oct. 3	TRUEWORGYE, Katherine	Mr. Rowles, sagamore	Deed
1674, Nov. 2	TRUEWORGYE, Samuel	Katherine Hilton	Deed
1676, July 8	TURNER, Ephraim	William Phillips et ux.	Deed
	TURNER, Ephraim, see Zachary Gyllum		
	TURNER, Sarah, see Rebecca Lord		

Folio.	Description.
34	Richman's island, also 300 acres of land and marsh, opposite the island [in *Falmouth*].
91	250 acres in the following tract to be conveyed to Martha Symonds.
127	500 acres of the tract next *Cape Porpoise* bounds bought of Bush and Turbett.
119	House and 20 acres near the Boiling rock in *Kittery*.
119	Lot 32 by 16 rods on Piscataqua river in *Kittery*.
64	As to Tilton's purchase of building timber on Abraham Conley's land [in *Kittery*].
65	As to sale to him of building timber on Abraham Conley's land in *Kittery*.
30	4 acres of marsh at head of the old mill creek in *York*.
30	40 acres with marsh on York river, in *York*.
10	Tomson's point [in *Kittery*].
9	Tomson's point above Sturgeon creek, in *Kittery*, bought of Rowles, sagamore.
8	400 acres adjoining tract sold Turner and Zachary Gyllum, whom see.

Index of Grantees.

Date.	Grantee.	Grantor.	Instrument.
16$\frac{79}{80}$, Mar. 20	VAHAN, William	John Parsons	Mortgage
1681, June 13	VAHAN, William	James Pendleton	Deed
1649, Oct. 18	WADLEIGH, John	Thos. Chabinoct (Cabinocke) sagamore	Deed
1650, Oct. 17	WADLEIGH, John	Romanascoh, Indian	Deed
1650, May 31	WADLEIGH, John, and Robert Wadleigh	Philemon Parmot Wm. Wardell	Deposition
	WADLEIGH, Robert, see John Wadleigh		
1677, Dec. 7	WANEWRIGHT, Francis	Hugh Allard	Mortgage
1676, June 23	WATERS, John	Thomas Withers	Deed
1661, June 3	WEBBER, Mary	John Parker et ux.	Deed
1660, May 9	WEBBER, Thomas	Robin-Hood, *alias* Rawmegon, sagamore Terrumquine, sagamore Weesomonascoe, sagamore Squawquee, Indian Abumhamen, Indian	Deed
1681, May 21	WEEKES, Nicholas	Jona. Mendum	Deed
Recorded 1683, Oct. 19	WELLS, town of	Town of York	Commis'rs report
1675, Feb. 5	WENTWORTH, John	Isaac Everest et ux.	Deed
1683, July 4	WHARTON, Richard	John Shapleigh	Deed

Index of Grantees. 113

Folio.	Description.
66	House formerly John [K]noulton's and 12 acres granted by the town in *Kittery*.
93	300 acres of land and 3 islands at *Cape Porpoise*.
65	Tract called Nischassett between Ogunquit and Kennebunk, the sea and Cape Porpoise falls [in *Wells*].
65	Quitclaim to tract conveyed by her son, Thomas Chabinocke.
65	As to livery of the tract called Nischassett between Ogunquit and Kennebunk rivers in *Wells*.
17	Land, house and personal property on the *Isles of Shoals*, to secure £70
102	8 acres on south side of Spruce creek in *Kittery*.
23	Land on Kennebec river south of Winnegance creek.
23	Tract 3 miles broad on west side of Kennebec river, opposite Arrowsic island.
112	Land at Martyn's cove in Spruce creek, *Kittery*.
134	Fixing bounds between the towns.
15	House and 15 acres on the road from York to Henry Sayword's, also 20 acres given by and in *York*.
127	Merriconeag neck and Sebascodegan island in *Casco Bay*.

Date.	Grantee.	Grantor.	Instrument.
1683, July 7	[WHARTON, Richard]	Francis Smale, sr. Elizabeth Smale	Deposition
1673, Oct. 25	WHITTE, John, and Robert Brimsdon	John Paine	Deed
1676, Aug. 24	WILLETT, Jacob	Thos. Broughton	Deed
1681, June 11	WILLIAMS, Henry	Christo. Pecket	Mortgage
1642, Apr. 2	WILLIAMS, Thomas	Richard Vines	Deed
1683, Jan. 16	WINCHESTER, widow	John Card	Contract
	WINSLOW, John, jr., see Thomas Andrews		
1673, Jan. 20	WITHERS, Thomas	Town of Kittery	Grant
1674, Feb. 25	WOOD, Richard	Samson Anger	Deed
167⅘, Mar. 1	WOOD, Richard	Wm. Johnson et ux.	Deed
1676, Oct. 5	WOOD, Richard	John Playce	Indenture
	WOODMANCY, John, see Rebecca Lord		
	YORK, town of, see Kittery		
1681, Dec. 14	YOUNG, Robert	Thomas Heath	Note
1673, Aug. 12	YOUNG, Rowland	Robert Knight	Deed
1677, Feb. 15	YOUNG, Rowland	Richard Knight	Deed

Folio.	Description.
128	As to purchase and occupancy of Sebascodegan island in behalf of Major Shapleigh.
28	800 acres above *Wells* and *Cape Porpoise*, part of the tract sold by Sosowen sagamore. [See Book I. I. 107.]
6	One-third part of Sturgeon creek swamp and the lands and farms about it, also one-third of Stephen Greenum's lot, all granted by and in *Kittery*.
93	House and land at Black Point, *Scarborough*, to secure a draft of £6: 15.
124	120 acres upland adjoining Robert Sanky, and 12 acres marsh at Winter Harbor, *Saco*.
138	Antenuptial contract.
94	Land and meadow not described.
12	40 acres on the sea wall next the long sands and the way to Cape Neddick, in *York*.
12	30 acres on the way to Cape Neddick in *York*.
12	Of apprenticeship of his son Richard Playce.
138	For £14.
25	4 acres in *York*, between grantor's land and a spring by a lot formerly Edward Start's.
38	House and lands [in *York*] devised by his father Robert Knight.

INDEX OF OTHER PERSONS.

Abbett, Abbott,
  Elizabeth, 9.
  Richard, 9.
  Thomas, 15, 54, 117, 130, 132.
Adams, 37.
  Nathaniel, junior, 93
  Philip, 24.
  Thomas, 97.
Addington, Isaac, 30, 38, 40.
Allcocke,
  Job, 23, 85, 38, 57, 67, 72, 102, 107.
  John, 25, 52, 72, 86, 120
  Joseph, 113, 118, 123
  Lieutenant, 50.
Allen,
  Edward, 71, 102
  Hope, 101.
  children of Robert and Hannah, not named, 102.
Alline,
  Arnold, 61.
  Edward, 72.
  Walter, 131.
Amendeth, John, 44, 51.
Andrews,
  James, 68, 101
  John, 39.
Anger, Samson, 12, 13.
Archdeale, John, 99, 100, 125.
Ashley, William, 90.
Atherton, Humphrey, 87
Atwater, Mary, 94.
Austine, 33, 55,
  goodman, 59
  Matthew, 25, 120
  Matthew, senior, 30.
  Samuel, 101
  Thomas, 70.
Axell, Humphrey, 118.

Babb, Philip, 119
Backeho

Bane, Beane,
  Lewis, 15, 63.
Banfield, Banefield,
  Christopher, 44, 48, 54, 55, 113, 137
Bankes,
  John, 88.
  Richard, 78, 120, 123
  Samuel, 132.
Barge, Giles, 92.
Barnard,
  Benjamin, 50
  Joseph, 48.
Barnett, Bartholomew, 74.
Barrett, John, 109.
Barsham, Bartsham, Batsham,
  John, 31, 69, 91, 118, 135.
Bartholmew, William, 38
Bartlett, Nicholas, 69
Barton, Samuel, 129
Biston, Thomas, 59, 65.
Bates, John, 89.
Batsham, see Barsham,
Batson,
  Richard, 98.
  Stephen, 65
Battersby, Christopher, 136.
Beames, Joseph, 22
Bedford, Nathan, 40, 92.
Beeson, Thomas, 30, 37.
Belcher,
  Jeremiah, senior, 71.
  Samuel, 71, 77.
Bellingham, Richard, 114.
Benmore, Philip, 68.
Bennicke, Mary, 27.
Berry, Ambrose, 86.
Berrye, Joseph, 82.
Bickum,
  Richard & Co, 103, 104
  William, 17, 45, 112, 128.
Bickton, Waymouth, 93.

INDEX OF OTHER PERSONS. 117

Blackeman, Mr., 102, 103.
Black Will, a negro, 126.
Blaysdell, Ralph, 85.
Boaden, 74.
 John, 103.
Bolls, Booles,
 Joseph, 11, 57, 65, 78, 109, 120.
 Mary, 78
Bonighton, Bonython,
 captain, 95.
 John, 86, 87
 Richard, 102, 87, 124.
 William, 42.
Boodridge, Benjamin, 92.
Booth, Thomas, 109.
Botts,
 Elizabeth, 48.
 Isaac, 21.
Bowey, John, 103.
Brackett, Anthony, 69, 113.
Bradstreet, Broadstreet,
 Simon, 41, 54, 84, 126.
Bragdon,
 Arthur, 12, 51, 97, 134.
 Arthur, senior, 23.
 Samuel, 78, 97
Branson, George, 115,
Brawn, John, 35, 72, 135.
Bray,
 John, 39, 44, 66, 84, 88, 133.
 John, illegitimate daughter of, 84.
 Nathaniel, 53, 66
 Richard, 41, 53, 62, 66, 76, 84
 Rebella, or Sabella, 37, 66, 84
 Samuel, 41.
 William, 105
Breathy, John. 106
Brocke, John, 37.
Broughton,
 George, 15, 46, 47, 49, 63, 131, 132.
 John, 47, 125, 126.
 Mary, 6.
 Mr, 14, 20.
 Nathaniel, 126.
 Thomas, 1, 8, 14, 47, 48, 50, 58. 126, 131
Brown,
 Abraham, 52.

Brown, continued,
 Andrew, 40, 43, 96.
 John, 36.
Bugg, John, 52
Bullgar, Richard, 42
Burdett, George, 85, 116.
Burgess, Richard, 37, 135.
Bush,
 Grace, 93.
 John, 28, 57, 127.

Cæsar, Indian, 65.
Came, Arthur, 22.
Camer,
 Edward, 80.
 [Mary], 80.
Canny, Thomas, 70.
Cardon, (see Sarden)
 Timothy, 12.
Carle, 104.
Carmichael, see Cirmihill.
Carter,
 Richard, 36.
 Richard, senior, 115.
Carwine, Corwin,
 Jonathan, 40
Case, Humphrey, 79.
Chabinocke, Thomas, sagamore, 65.
Chadborne,
 Alice, 17
 Humphrey, 10, 14, 20, 22, 64, 70, 80, 97, 115, 130.
 Humphrey, senior, 91, 92.
Chamberlain, Richard, 91
Champernoown
 [Arthur], 116.
 captain, 99.
 Francis, 98, 99, 113, 125, 137
Chase, Aquila, 21.
Checkley, Anthony, 30, 82.
Child, Henry, 26, 27.
Cirmihill, John, 30.
Clarke,
 Edward, 52, 118.
 Elizabeth. 76, 113.
 major, 120.
 Mary, 118.
 Matthew, 103.
 Richard, 98.
 Thaddeus, 114.

118   Index of Other Persons.

Clarke, continued,
  Thomas, 1, 6, 7, 87.
Cleeve, Cleeves,
  George, 52, 61, 62, 74, 86, 87, 101.
  Joanna, 69.
  Mr., 37.
Clemons, Clements,
  Job, 70, 71, 101.
Cloyce, Cloyse,
  John, 11, 89, 92, 100, 105, 134.
  Nathaniel, 60.
  Peter 84.
Cobbett, Thomas, 70.
Cocks, William, 23.
Collines,
  Abraham, 121.
  Christopher, 921.
Conley,
  Abraham, 25, 26, 31, 44, 64, 65.
  old, 55.
  Sarah, 19. –
Coole,
  Jane, 47.
  Nicholas, 29.
  Peter, 6.
  William, junior, 65.
Copp, David, 6.
Corbett, Abraham, 100, 125.
Cossons, Cussons,
  Isaac, 53, 54, 84.
  John, 35, 52, 53.
Cotten, John, 124.
Couch, Coutch,
  Joanna, 24.
  Joseph, 30.
Cowell,
  Elizabeth, 103.
  Mrs. 104, 106.
  Richard, 127.
  Thomas, 103, 104.
Crockett,
  Ephraim, 37, 79, 127.
  [Thomas], 73, 99, 107.
Cromewell, Philip, 10.
Cross, John, 135.
Cummines, Richard, 87.
Curtis,
  Hannah, 42.
  Thomas, 24.

Cutt,
  John, estate of, 122.
  John, junior, 20, 102.
  Mary, 39, 78.
  Richard, 20, 39, 81.
  Robert, 100, 103, 104.

Dadiver, Dodiver, 56.
Dale, John, 104.
Damforth, Danforth,
  Thomas, 26, 67, 84, 96, 110, 125.
Daniell, Thomas, 118.
Davess, Davis,
  captain, 56, 66.
  Daniel, 51.
  Isaac, 77.
  John, 9, 25, 31, 33, 37, 38, 57, 59, 66, 72, 73, 74, 78, 84, 86, 88, 93, 95, 96, 97, 100, 116, 120, 124, 126, 134, 136, 138.
  John, senior, 133, 134.
  Mary, 61.
  Nicholas, 72.
  Samuel, 73.
  Sylvanus, 23.
  William, 101.
Davie,
  Humphrey, 65, 78.
  Mr. 65.
Dawlton, Samuel, 9.
Dearcing, Derent,
  Joan, 121.
  Roger, 88.
Denison, Daniel, 18, 38, 65, 92.
Denmarke, Patrick, 67.
Derumcin, sagamore, 80.
Derumcin's kindred, 80.
Devine, John, 23.
Dixon, goodwife, 52.
Dod,
  Elizabeth, 72.
  Mary, 72.
Donell,
  Henry, 13, 23, 24, 35, 37, 57, 67, 72, 86.
  Joseph, 94.
  Mary, 112.
  Ruth, 94.
  Thomas, 78, 83.
Downe, Richard, 20.

Downing,
  Joanna, 115.
  John, 115.
  Joshua, 100.
Drake, Thomas, 36.
Dudley, Joseph, 38, 45.
Dummer,
  Richard, 92.
  Shubael, 79, 107.
Durston, Thomas, 21.
Diament, Dyamont,
  John, 47, 118.
  William, 47.
Dynham, Henry, 99.

Edgscome,
  John, 95.
  Nicholas, 43.
Ellingham, 112.
  William, 27
Elliott, Robert, 23, 39, 93, 100.
Ellson, John, 133, 134.
Emerson, John, 133.
Emery,
  Anthony, 19, 20, 31.
  Elizabeth, 19.
  James, 7, 15, 18, 19, 44, 54, 55, 70, 100, 133
  John, senior, 38.
  John, junior, 38
Endecutt, John, 69.
Epps,
  Daniel, 91, 128.
  Daniel, jun , 33.
  Daniel, senior, 55.
  Samuel, 127
Everell, Thomas, 11.
Everest,
  Andrew, 23, 58, 74.
  Isaac, 63.
  Job, 88.
  Lydia, 122.
Evens, Evines,
  John, 55.

Fabine, Fabines,
  George, 135.
  John, 104.
Farnum, Joseph, 66
Fennicke, (see Phœnix),
  John, 92.

Fernald, see Furnald.
Fletcher,
  John, 102.
  Pendleton, 93.
  Seth, 11, 77.
Flewelline, Fluelline,
  sagamore, 5, 28.
Footeman, Thomas, 85.
Ford, Stephen, 58.
Forgisson,
  Daniel, 38.
  John, 111.
Fox,
  Jabez, 1.
  Mr , 21.
Foxwell, Richard, 40, 86, 87.
Freathy,
  Samuel, 105.
  William, 74, 78.
Frissell, Alexander, 23.
Frost,
  captain, 16, 114.
  Charles, 22, 44, 59, 64, 94, 100, 106, 111, 126, 127, 137.
  Elizabeth, 68.
  John, 77.
  Katherine, 68.
  Nicholas, 38, 44, 55.
  Nicholas, junior, 67, 68.
  William, 105.
Fry, Adrian, 114.
Fryer, Nathaniel, 2, 45, 74, 104.
Furnald,
  Mary, 123.
  Samuel, 123.
Furson, Thomas, 114.

Garde, Roger, 24, 74, 85, 86, 124.
Gibbons, Judith, 42.
Gillman,
  Edward, 65, 111.
  John, 9, 27, 77, 138.
  Moses, 125.
Godfrey,
  Edward, 78, 83, 85, 132.
  Mrs , 116, 126
Goft, error for Hoff, q. v.
Gooch, Gouch, 33, 55.
  James, 11, 108.
  John, 135.

120 INDEX OF OTHER PERSONS.

Gooding, Goodwin,
  Daniel, 21, 38, 54, 63, 70 117.
Gorges,
  Ferdinando, esq , 4, 5.
  Mr , 37, 120.
  Sir Ferdinando, 4, 5, 68, 70, 112, 116
  Thomas, 70, 93, 112
Goutch,
  John, 23.
  Robert, 23.
Gowen, Gowein,
  William, 48, 113.
Grant,
  James, 30, 97, 112, 119.
  Peter, 6, 14, 22, 43, 63.
Graves, John, 77.
Gray, George, 14.
Green,
  John, 20, 21, 45, 81.
  John, senior, 21, 54.
  Richard, senior, 45.
Greenham, Greenum,
  Stephen, 6, 54, 55
Gunnisson,
  Elihu, 107.
  Hugh, 3, 106, 107.
  Joseph, 107.
  mistress, 57.
  Sarah, 3
Gydney,
  Eleazer, 94.
  Hannah, 95, 96
Gyllbard, William, 94.
Gyllum, Zachariah, 8
Gyndall,
  Joane, 109, 110
  Walter, 74.
Gynkens [Jenkins], Jabez, 102

Haines, William, 53.
Hale, John, 33.
Haley, 102
Hall, John, 115
Hammond,
  Elizabeth, 80
  Jonathan, 10, 11, 101, 108, 109, 120, 121.
  Joseph, 47, 91, 114, 115, 127, 137
  Joseph, register, 91, 100.

Hammond, continued,
  William, 77, 101.
  William's wife, 90.
Harding,
  Israel, 11.
  Lydia, 129.
Harker, John, 107.
Harlo, Thomas, 76.
Harmon,
  Deborah, 83.
  John, 103.
Harris,
  Thomas, 119.
  Trustrum, 16.
Hart, John, 99.
Hartopp, Hartupp,
  Richard, 1, 47.
Harvy, Peter, 76.
Hatch, Patience, 115.
Hathorne, Ele[anor], 60
Hawthorne, William, 4, 5, 7, 8, 60, 94, 109.
Haward, Hayward,
  John, junior, 94, 96, 110.
Hays, Edward, 27, 43
Heard (see Hord),
  Elizabeth, 106.
  Isabel, 17
  James, 17, 22, 46, 106.
  James, children of, 17.
  John, 17, 55, 106.
  Mary, 106
  Sarah, 17.
Heale, Thomas, 130.
Henderson,
  John, 87.
  Peter, 79.
Heskines, Nicholas, 70, 74, 104
Hichcock, Hitchcock,
  Lucretia, 92.
  Mr., 86
Hickes, Richard, 57
Higginson,
  John, senior, 94.
  Mary, 94
Hill (see Isill),
  Joseph, 101.
  wife of Roger, 13.
  [Peter ?] 101.
  Valentine, 37.

INDEX OF OTHER PERSONS. 121

Hilton,
  Katherine, 10
  William, 123.
  William, senior, 125.
Hind, Samuel, 109.
Hodgsden,
  Benoni, 111
  Elizabeth, 18, 31
  Joseph, 10, 67
  Nicholas, 18, 19, 111.
Hoff, Ferdinand, 133, 134.
Holman, John, 53
Holms, Thomas, 64.
Hooke,
  Francis, 55, 64, 65, 73, 74, 77, 89, 94, 97, 104, 107, 109, 121, 127, 137.
  Mary, 104, 109, 121.
  William, 84, 85.
Hoole,
  Elizabeth, 116.
  John, 95.
Hord (see Heard),
  John, 44, 64, 70.
Hoskines,
  Christian, 34.
  William, 34
Howard,
  John, 43.
  Robert, 69.
  William, 29, 30.
Howell,
  John, 96.
  Rice, 81.
Hoy, John, 138
Hubbard, John, 3
Hudson, William, 4.
Hull,
  Jerusha, 124
  John, 7, 47, 80, 125, 126.
  Mr., 37.
  Phineas, 64, 95, 115, 125.
  Reuben, 77.
Humfrys, Thomas, 67.
Hunnell, Richard, 89.
Hutchinson,
  Eliakim, 130, 133.
  Mr., 130.
  Richard, 133.
  William, 7, 8, 132, 133.

Indians, 16, 95 [see Book II, 191], 110 See Cæsar, Chabinocke, Derumcin, Flewelline, Jone Junkssquaw, Mogheggine, Nell, Quajacesett, Qnaquaquijott, Romanasco, Rowles, Saguawah, Sasagihuah, Sosowen.
Ingersall, Ingersoll,
  George, 114, 120
Isill (perhaps Hill?), Mr., 114

Jackeson, James, 120.
Jaffaray, George, 46.
Jefferys,
  Diggory, 2, 37.
  Gregory, 93.
Jellison, Nicholas, 117.
Jenkins (see Gynkens),
  Jabez, 26, 27, 137
  Mary, 137.
  Renald, 51, 136.
  Sarah, 137.
  Stephen, 54.
Jewell,
  Joseph, 118.
  Mary, 107.
Joans,
  Alexander, 102.
  Thomas, 53.
Johnson,
  Benjamin, 24.
  Edward, 25, 35, 50, 87, 120.
  Francis, 61, 74, 109
  James, 91
  John, 46
  William, 13.
Jone Junkssquaw, Indian, 65.
Jordan, 69
  John, 2, 34, 69.
  Robert, 34, 74, 76, 101.
  Robert, senior, 69.
  Sarah, 34, 69.
Joy, Ephraim, 63
Joyse, Christopher, 118

Kemble, Thomas, 6, 23, 27, 36.
King, father of Daniel, 120.
Kirke, 103.
  Henry, 19, 69, 101.

Knight,
  Ezekiel, 57, 65, 84.
  Robert, 2, 25, 30, 38.
Knoulton, see Nowlton.
Krympton, Jonathan, 114.

Lake, Thomas, 1, 101.
Lamb, John, 14, 92.
Lane, Layne,
  Ann, 84
  James, 84, 93, 94
  James, junior, 53.
Langley, Thomas, 121.
Lawd, see Lord
Laws, John, 58.
Lawson, Christopher, 66
Leader,
  George, 132.
  Mr., 64.
  Richard, 91, 92, 132, 133.
Lee, John, 124.
Leigh, Thomas, 62.
Leighton,
  goodman, 86.
  Katherine, 137.
  Mary, 68
Levitt, James, 50.
Lewis,
  George, 69.
  Mr., 102.
  Peter, 81
  Thomas, 87, 94, 95.
Littlefield, 11.
  Edmund, 59, 129
  Francis, 13, 59, 109, 120.
  Francis, junior, 11.
  Francis, senior, 59.
  James, 10, 92, 100.
  John, 134
  Meribah, 59
  Thomas, 59, 105.
Lockewood, captain, 100.
Long, Zachary, 47, 126.
Lord,
  Nathaniel, 31, 55.
  Nathan, junior, 42, 111.
Love, William, 14, 20, 133.
Low, Dorothy, 121.
Lugg, Gilbert, 118

Lusherland, William, 4.
Lynn, 107
Lyscomb, 7, 8.

Maisters, Nathaniel, 84.
Mare, Walter, 82.
Martine, Martyne,
  John, 71.
  Richard, 15, 31, 46, 52, 69, 112, 124
Mathews, Walter, 58, 71.
Mattocks, Samuel, 53, 54.
Mavericke,
  Antipas, 109, 113.
  Catherine, 113.
  Moses, 9, 111.
  Samuel, 37.
Maxell, Maxwell,
  Alexander, 22, 24, 97.
Mayhew, Jane, 114
Mayne, John, 36.
Maysterson, Masterson,
  Nathaniel, 15, 22, 125.
Mellcher, Edward, 21.
Mendum,
  Mr., 100.
  Robert, 44, 94, 112.
Miller,
  John, 128.
  Joseph, 42.
Mills, Thomas, 89
Mitchell, Christopher, 24.
Mittine, Mitton,
  Ann, 68, 101.
  Elizabeth, 76
  Michael, 61, 62, 76, 113.
Mogheggine, sagamore, 4
Moody,
  Eleazer, 43, 94, 96, 110.
  Joshua, 20, 93.
Moore,
  John, 138
  William, 25, 37, 138.
Moroth, Dennis, 120.
Moriall, Morrell,
  John, 32, 111.
  Sarah, 19, 32.
Morse, Joseph, 78.
Mosear, John, 93.

INDEX OF OTHER PERSONS. 123

Mowle, Edward, 79.
Mowlton,
   Jeremiah, 30
   Mary, *alias* Young, 25.
Munjoy,
   George, 69, 76.
   Mr., 113.
Munson, Richard, junior, 91.
Mussy, 33, 55.

Nanny,
   Mr, 135
   Robert, 139.
Nason, Nayson,
   Jonathan, 7, 132.
   Richard, 21, 39, 44, 54, 55, 91, 92, 100.
Neale,
   Francis, 42, 62, 76, 93, 96.
   Joan, 106
Needum, William, 1.
Negro, see Black Will.
Nell, Indian, 65.
Newcome, Andrew, 123.
Nicolls, Mr, 84
Norton, 57
   Henry, 2, 37, 72, 78, 83
Nowlton, John, 66.
Nutter,
   Anthony, 50, 55.
   Hatevill, 70.

Oakman,
   Elias, 42.
   Samuel 17, 40.
Odihorne, Philip, 138.
Oliver,
   James, 40.
   John, 114.
Ope, Nicholas, 31.
Ormesby, Richard, 58.
Oulted, William, 81.

Page, 42.
Paine, Payn,
   Edward, 41.
   John, 16, 37
   William, 80.
Palmer, William, 44, 118.

Parker,
   Basil, 107.
   John, 37.
   John, senior, 78, 83.
   Thomas, 92.
Parkes,
   Thomas, 130.
   William, 101
Parrott, Sarah, 3.
Partridg,
   John, 31.
   Mary, 135.
   William, 12.
Paul,
   Daniel, 119.
   Stephen, 111, 118.
Pearce,
   John, 30, 121.
   Joseph, 39.
Pearson, George, 13, 37, 47, 57, 58, 77, 82, 114, 129.
Pendleton,
   Bryan, 7, 8, 11, 46, 82, 84, 93.
   Eleanor, 93.
   Hannah, 93.
   James, 11.
   major, 103.
   Mary, 82.
Penwill, John, 74, 86, 102, 103, 136, 138.
Pheelps, James, 73.
Phillips,
   Bridget, 5.
   lieutenant, 86.
   Nathaniel, 3.
   William, 86, 87, 93, 128.
Phippeny, 40
Phoenix (see Fennicke),
   John, 112.
Pickering,
   Anthony, 115
   Benjamin, 96.
   John, 107, 115, 117.
Playce, Richard, 12.
Playstead,
   James, 92, 131, 133.
   John, 131.
   lieutenant, 32.
   Mr., 43
   Olive, 18, 21.

Index of Other Persons.

Playstead, continued,
  Roger, 7, 11, 14, 15, 21, 22, 47, 49, 67, 94, 113, 125, 126
  Roger, senior, 49
  William, 49, 92, 136.
Pomrey, Richard, 119.
Pormot, Philemon, 65.
Pott, John, 24.
Pounding, Henry, 39.
Preble,
  Abraham, 38, 50, 57, 59, 72, 74, 78, 83, 88, 102, 103, 107, 123, 134
  John, 56, 57.
  Mr, 87.
  Nathaniel, 12, 13, 57, 97.
Puddington, John, 86.
Pullman, Jasper, 35.
Purchass, Mr., 128
Purrington, John, 91.
Pynchon, John, 1.

Quajacesett, sagamore, 114.
Quaquaquijott, sagamore, 114.

Ramacke, Ramix,
  Christian, 44, 94, 119, 120, 123, 124.
Randall,
  Edward, 103.
  Richard, 82.
Randolph, Edward, 84
Ranger, Edmund, 80.
Rawson, Edward, 1, 22, 87, 125.
Rayn, Joseph, 91
Raynkine,
  Andrew, 96.
  Joseph, 73
Rayns, Francis, 25.
Readman, John, 57.
Redding,
  Eleanor, 53
  Thomas, 93, 94
Reed, Stephen, 12, 24.
Remaih, Remick, see Ramacke.
Renalds,
  John, 103
  Nicholas, 23
  William, 103, 104
Rice, Ryce,
  Mary, 102

Rice, Ryce, continued,
  Thomas, 81, 95
Richards, John, 93.
Rigby,
  Alexander, 62, 87.
  baron, 68.
  Edward, 62.
Rishworth,
  Edward, 2, 3, 10, 11, 12, 13, 14, 16, 17, 19, 22, 23, 24, 25, 28, 30, 31, 33, 38, 49, 50, 51, 52, 56, 57, 58, 63, 64, 67, 71, 73, 77, 83, 84, 86, 88, 89, 90, 91, 93, 97, 103, 105, 107, 111, 112, 115, 116, 118, 119, 120, 121, 122, 123, 125, 126, 128, 132, 133, 134, 135, 136, 137, 138, 139.
  Edward, recorder, 1—139.
  Edward, secretary, 126.
Roberts,
  John, 71.
  John, junior, 71.
  Thomas, 101
Robinson, Francis, 74.
Rogers,
  Francis, 98.
  George, 70.
  Richard, 45.
  Thomas, 102
  William, 3
  [William], 107.
Romanasco, Romanascoe, Indian, 65.
Ross, John, 54, 106.
Row, Richard, 39.
Rowles, Mr., Indian, 9, 10.
Rucke, Thomas, 57
Ryall, Phœbe, 62.

Sagnawah, Indian, 65.
Sanders, John, 28, 93
Sands, John, 93
Sanky, Robert, 124.
Sarden (see Cardon),
  Timothy, 24
Sargant, Sargeant,
  Edward, 108.
  John, 74, 124.
  William, 78

INDEX OF OTHER PERSONS. 125

Sasagihnah, Sasogihowah,
   Indian, 65.
Savage,
   Ephraim, 5, 7, 8.
   Thomas, 87, 94.
Sayword,
   Henry, 15, 16, 30, 50, 63, 72, 81,
     95, 110, 122
   John, 116, 123.
   Jonathan, 122.
   Mary, 81, 121.
   mistress, 56.
   Samuel, 66.
   Samuel's uncle and aunt, 56.
Scadlocke, William, 57.
Scammon, Elizabeth, 135
Scottow, Joshua, 1, 101, 103.
Scrivine, William, 39, 78.
Searle,
   Andrew, 7, 19, 26, 27, 28, 32,
     42, 81, 106, 111.
   Andrew, senior, 117.
   John, 63.
Seavy,
   William, 138
Seely,—
   Elizabeth, 3, 39, 104, 106.
   William, 3, 39, 78, 103, 104, 106.
   [William], 107.
Shapleigh, 126
   Alice, 111, 128
   John, 112, 113, 133.
   major, 73, 100, 126, 128.
   Nicholas, 10, 13, 25, 45, 54, 55,
     70, 86, 91, 92, 100, 112, 115,
     126, 127, 128
Sharpe, James, 24.
Sheath, Sampson, 40.
Sheeres, Jeremiah, 88
Smale, Edward, 16, 112.
Smyth, 120
   Francis, 57
   John, 16, 74, 93, 118.
   John, senior, 88.
   Mary, 46, 118.
   Nicholas, 16.
   William, 16, 55.
   William, *alias* Gowine, 55.
Snell, Hannah, 79.
Sosowen, sagamore, 28.

Spencer, 113
   Humphrey, 15, 64, 136.
   John, 132.
   Roger, 86, 87.
   Thomas, 64, 80.
   William, 14, 15, 22, 80, 131.
Spinny,
   Mary, 123
   Samuel, 123.
   Thomas, 97, 118.
Stacie, William, 137.
Stachfield, William, 99.
Stannion, Anthony, 135.
Start, Edward, 25, 81.
Stephens, Stevens,
   Thomas, 95, 110.
Stillson, William, 101.
Stoddard, Anthony, 66.
Stoone,
   Daniel, 29, 54, 63.
   wife of Daniel, 54.
Storer,
   Benjamin, 108.
   Jeremiah, 108, 129.
   Joseph, 13, 120, 121, 129.
Stover,
   Richard, 41.
   Silvester, 132
Stowton, William, 1.
Stileman, Styleman,
   Elias, 2, 10, 22, 34, 39, 45, 47,
     58, 67, 70, 74, 82, 104, 107,
     117, 125, 138.
   Mary, 89.
   Richard, 9, 20, 34, 46, 67, 89.
Symons, John, 118.
Symonds,
   Harlakenden, 28
   Martha, 91.
   Samuel, 29, 30, 127.
   Samuel, junior, 91, 127.
   William, 13, 30, 59
Symson,
   Henry, 37, 56, 78, 100.
   Henry, senior, 83.
   Henry, junior, 83.
   Thomas, 56.

Tapping, Joseph, 5, 7, 8.
Tayer, John, 107.

Index of Other Persons.

Taylor, Taylour,
  Edward, 9.
  John, 21, 46, 94.
Thaythes, Rebecca, 58.
Thwayt, Alexander, 23.
Tommass,
  Elizabeth, 73.
  Rice, 73.
Tomson, Miles, 19, 32, 111.
Tookie, Job, 53.
Tooser, Job, 82.
Towltwood, Henry, 100.
Traffton, Thomas, 23.
Trelany, Robert, 34.
Trewiss, Richard, 93.
Treworgy, Trueworgye,
  James, 10.
  Samuel, 28.
Trickie, Tricky,
  Francis, 3, 51.
  Sarah, 8.
  Thomas, 3.
Trustrum, Ralph, 82.
Tucker,
  Francis, 104.
  John, 38.
  Nathaniel, 18.
Turbett,
  John, 103.
  Peter, 28, 127.
Turner, Ephraim, 8.
Tuttle, John, 101.
Twisden, Twysden,
  John, 12, 15, 24, 25, 38, 50, 63,
    67, 72, 107, 120.
Tyding, Benjamin, 69.
Tyng,
  Edward, 1, 30, 36, 38, 40, 41, 53,
    66, 80, 114, 120, 126.
  Edward, senior, 7.
  Mr., 66.
Tynny, John, 17, 40.

Veren, Verin,
  Hilliard, senior, 60, 79, 94.
  Hilliard, junior, 60.
Vines,
  Mr., 92, 116.
  Richard, 2, 52, 87, 97, 98, 99.

Waddocke, Henry, 103.
Wadleigh, Wadlow, 105.
  John, 33, 55.
  John, senior, 11.
  Robert, 33, 55, 65, 77.
  William, 42.
Wakefield,
  Henry, 13.
  Samuel, 130, 134.
Walden,
  Richard, 20, 32, 67, 100, 113.
  Richard, jun., 32.
Walker, Isaac, 40.
Wallis, Margaret, 103.
Wally, John, 66.
Wanerton, Thomas, 13.
Wanewright, John, 18.
Wardell, William, 65.
Warren, James, 22.
Waymouth,
  Edward, 43, 112.
  James, 104.
  Robert, 45.
Watson, John, 62.
Weare,
  Peter, 9, 12, 67, 72, 86.
  Peter, senior, 23, 38, 64, 88.
  Peter, junior, 64.
Webb,
  Henry, 37.
  William, 120.
Weden, Joseph, 86.
Wells,
  Thomas, 46.
  William, 52.
Wentworth,
  Martha, 63.
  Samuel, 82, 107, 138.
West, John, 77.
Wheeler, David, 20.
Wheelwright,
  John, 84, 105.
  [John], 92, 100.
  Mr., 59, 105.
  Samuel, 11, 13, 30, 35, 47, 59,
    60, 73, 84, 90, 100, 105, 107,
    108, 109, 120, 121, 122, 129.
Whidden, Samuel, 107.
White,
  Mary, 37, 50, 63, 73.

INDEX OF OTHER PERSONS.

White, continued,
  Richard, 25, 31.
  Samson, 39, 79.
Wiggens, Wiggin,
  captain, 115
  James, junior, 79.
  Thomas, 21.
Williams, Henry, 17, 40, 124, 130, 134.
Willkines, John, 22.
Willmott, Nicholas, 38.
Wills,
  Mr., 14.
  Thomas, 22, 50
Willson, Gowen, 127.
Wincoll,
  captain, 44, 78, 132.
  Elizabeth, 1.
  John, 9, 14, 15, 16, 21, 22, 31, 32, 37, 39, 42, 43, 47, 48, 50, 54, 57, 59, 63, 64, 67, 68, 78, 79, 81, 92, 94, 95, 100, 102, 103, 104, 111, 113, 114, 115, 117, 120, 123, 125, 126, 130, 131, 132, 133, 137
Winnington, John, 98.
Wittum,
  Peter, 18, 54, 111.
  Peter, senior, 26.
Withers,
  Elizabeth, 127
  Mr., 100
  Thomas, 116
Woddy, Richard, 57.
Wollcocke, Edward, 35.
Wollcott, Edward, 100.
Wood, wife of Richard, 12.
Woodbridge, John, 101.
Woster, William, 37.
Wright, Captain, 66.

Young,
  Joan, 25
  Mary, 25, see Mary Mowlton.
  Rowland, senior, 25.
  Thomas, 102.

INDEX OF PLACES.

Agamenticus, afterwards York, 42, 57, 84, 85, 116.
Agamenticus river, York, 37.
Allcock's neck, York, 60, 61.
Alewife cove, Cape Elizabeth, 2, 69
Arrowsic island, Kennebec river, 23
Ashton Phillips, Somerset county, England, 97, 98.
Assabumbedicke falls, Newgewanacke, 91.

Barberry marsh, York, 12, 13
Bass cove, York, 22, 72, 78, 83.
  brook, 119
Bass rock, Kittery, 117.
Batson's neck, Cape Porpoise, 133.
Batson's river, Cape Porpoise, 3, 4
Beaver creek, Scarborough, 17.
Berwick, 111, 130, 131, 132, 133, 136 See Newgewanacke.
  called the Upper Division of Kittery, 130.
  Commons, 14, 131
  Little river, 130, 132.
  Ministry lands, 132.
  Quamphegan, 131.
Bideford, Devon county, England, 58
Birch point, Kittery, 18, 70.
  brook, 18.
Blackberry marsh, Kittery, 14.
Black creek, Newgewanacke, 70.
Blackman's mill, Saco, 102, 103
Black Point, Scarborough, 42, 74, 93, 94, 96, 103
  river, 74, 87.
Blue Point, Scarborough, 74, 87, 92, 102.
Boiling rock, Kittery, 117, 127

Boston, Massachusetts, 1, 3, 5, 6, 15, 28, 29, 33, 35, 36, 38, 39, 40, 41, 42, 44, 47, 53, 55, 57, 65, 66, 68, 74, 78, 79, 80, 82, 86, 87, 93, 94, 96, 110, 112, 114, 125, 127, 130, 134, 136, 138
Braveboat harbor, Kittery, 15, 58, 78, 79, 97, 98, 100, 116
  York, 37, 58, 86, 116.
  bridge landing place, 15.
Bricksome, Kittery, 33
Bucks county, England, 99, 125.
Burcham point, Newgewanacke, 70
Burnt marsh brook, York, 132.

Camel's island, Kennebec river, 80
Cape Elizabeth, 2, 34, 69. See Falmouth.
  Alewife cove, 2, 69.
  Great marsh, 101.
  Great pond, 2, 69, 101.
  island not named, 69
  Long sands, 2, 34, 69.
Cape Nuttacke, York, 13, 87, 88, 107
  neck, York, 100, 107.
  river, York, 132.
Cape Porpoise, 28, 57, 74, 86, 87, 93, 103, 127, 128, 133.
  by description, 3.
  Batson's neck, 133.
  Batson's river, 3, 4.
  Little river, 87, 128
  islands not named between Batson's river, and Kennebunk river, 4, 74
Cape Porpoise river, 28, 33, 40, 44, 55.
  falls, 65
Casco, 23, 36, 43, 44, 61, 72, 93, 95, 96, 107, 109, 110, 113, 128.

Index of Places.

Casco Bay, 12, 35, 36, 37, 41, 52, 53, 66, 68, 74, 76, 84, 94, 95, 110, 115, 127, 128.
  Cussons's island, 35, 37, 41, 52, 66.
  Long island, 35, 37, 52.
  town of, 53.
Casco,
  mills, 43, 44.
  river, 68, 74, 76, 101, 113.
Cedars, the, Kittery, 44, 55, 136.
Charlestown, Massachusetts, 47, 126.
Chief island, Kennebec river, 23.
Church point, Saco, 82
Chusquissacke, Shushqnisacke, river, North Yarmouth, 35, 37, 61, 62
Cleves, George's, grants or patents, Falmouth, 87.
Cold (Coole) harbor, Kittery, 18, 19, 38, 102.
  point, 20, 31
Connecticut, Stonington, 93.
Coxhall, by description, afterward Lyman, 5, 28, 127.
Craggy hills, Kittery, 21
Crooked lane, Kittery, 3, 51, 103.
  Scarborough, 74.
Cussons's island, Casco bay, 35, 37, 41, 52, 66
Cutchechah, (Cocheco, afterward Dover) New Hampshire, 15, 100.

Darrington, Dartington, Devonshire county, England, 97, 98
Devon county, England, 58, 61, 97, 98
Dirty swamp, Kittery, 21, 48, 131.
  Negewanacke, 9
Dover, New Hampshire, 6, 10, 55, 69, 70, 71, 100, 115, 125.
Dover and Portsmouth, county of, New Hampshire, 14, 21, 31, 69, 117
Drake's island, Wells, 108, 135.
Duck pond, Saco, 86.
Dunstan, Scarborough, 42, 96.

Eagle point, Kittery, 44.
East York, 81.

Eastern parts of New England, 2, 69.
Eddy point, York, 58.
Elizabeth islands, Mass., 114.
England, 4, 5, 133.
  Ashton Phillips, 97, 98.
  Biddeford, 58.
  Bucks county, 99, 125.
  Dartington, 97, 98.
  Devon county, 58, 61, 97, 98.
  Lancaster county, 61.
  London, 3, 5, 6, 133.
  Northam, 58.
  Plymouth, 34, 61.
  Rigby, 61
  Somerset county, 97, 98.
  Wickham, 99, 125.
Essex county, Massachusetts, 17, 59, 79, 91, 95, 109.
Exeter, New Hampshire, 9, 27, 111.

Falmouth, 68, 87, 93, 101, 113, 120, 128. See Cape Elizabeth.
  Cleves, George's, grants or patents, 87
  Munjoy's neck, 113.
  Nonesuch, 45.
  Richman's or Richmond's island, 2, 34, 69.
  Spurwink, 33, 44, 45, 76.
Fort hill, Kittery. 14.
Fort point, Kittery, 13
Fowling marsh, Kittery, 54, 70.
France, island of Oleron, 42.
Frank's fort, Kittery, 45, 115.
Frethy's cove, York, 122.

Gallows point, York, 24.
Godmorrocke, Kittery, 97, 98.
Goosefare, Saco, 103.
Gorgeana, afterward York, 58, 71, 72, 107, 116.
Gorges, Mr's creek, York, 120.
  neck, York, 22.
Gorges, Mis, (error for Mr., see Book IV, 43,) point, York, 139.
Grantums island, Kittery, 3.
Great cove, North Yarmouth, 76.
Great island, New Hampshire, 2, 9, 10, 22, 34, 44, 45, 47, 57, 67, 74, 103, 104, 117.

Index of Places.

Great pond, Cape Elizabeth, 2, 69.
Great river, Wells, 10.
Great Works, saw mills, Newgewanacke, or Berwick, 130.

Haly's gut, Saco, 102.
Hampton, New Hampshire, 57, 127.
Harricisseeke, Henry Sickett, (Harraseket) river, North Yarmouth, 53.
Hereges marsh, Kittery, 51.
Hogg, or Cussons island, Casco bay, 52.
Hull's creek, York, 37.

Ipswich, Massachusetts, 3, 17, 33, 56, 66, 91.
Ireland, 67.
Islands, not named,
  between Kennebunk river and Batson's river.
  Cape Porpoise, 4.
  Cape Elizabeth, 2, 69.
  Cape Porpoise, 74, 93.
  Kittery, 107.
  Piscataqua river, 66.
Isles of Shoals, 3, 17, 18, 51, 58, 71, 77, 81, 104, 138.
  Malaga island, 71, 138.
  Smuttynose island, 58, 71, 77.
  meeting house, 58.
  Star island, 88, 104.

Katamiwick island, Massachusetts, 114.
Kennebec, 67, 80, 95, 110.
Kennebec river, 23, 67.
  Camers island, 80.
  Purchas's island, 80.
  Whiskeag, 80.
  Winnegance creek, 80.
Kennebunk, 57, 65.
Kennebunk river, 3, 4, 5, 33, 55, 80.
Kittery, 1, 3, 6, 9, 10, 12, 13, 14, 16, 17, 18, 19, 20, 21, 22, 24, 25, 26, 27, 28, 31, 32, 37, 38, 39, 41, 44, 45, 46, 47, 48, 49, 51, 54, 60, 66, 64, 67, 76, 77, 78, 81, 84, 86, 88, 90, 91, 92, 95, 99, 102, 104, 106, 109, 110, 111, 112, 113, 114, 115, 116, 117, 118, 119, 120, 121, 123, 126, 127, 130, 131, 132, 133, 134, 137. See Piscataqua.
Barren marsh, the great, 51.
Bass rock, 117.
Birch point, 18, 70.
Birch point brook, 18.
Blackberry marsh, 14.
Boiling rock, 119, 127.
Braveboat harbor, 15, 58, 78, 79, 86, 97, 98, 100, 116.
Bridge landing place, 15.
Brickesome, 33.
Cedars, the, 44, 55, 136.
Cold, Coole, harbor, 18, 19, 38, 102.
Cold, Coole, harbor point, 20, 31.
Common and common lands, 14, 21, 27, 64, 111, 113.
Craggy hills, 21.
Crooked lane, 3, 51, 103.
Dirty swamp, 21, 48, 131.
Eagle point, 44.
Fort hill, 14.
Fort point, 13.
Fowling marsh, 54, 70.
Frank's fort, 45, 115.
Godmorrocke, 97, 98.
Grantum's island, 3.
Great Newgewanacke river, 1.
Harbor mouth, 73.
Hereges marsh, 51.
Highway to Wells, 21.
Highway to Dirty Swamp, 48.
Ledge of rocks, 113.
Long point, 103, 104.
Mantill tree, 13.
Martyn's cove, 112.
Mast cove, [upper, 6] 112.
Mast creek, 38.
Oak point, 91.
Ox point, 90.
Point, 73.
Quamphegan falls, 14.
Rocky hills, 21, 43, 111.
Shapleigh's store house, 73.
Shot's corner, 21.

INDEX OF PLACES. 131

Kittery, continued.
  Spinny's cove, 123.
  Spruce creek, 3, 39, 44, 78, 81, 90, 91, 95, 102, 103, 104, 106, 112, 116, 127.
  Sturgeon creek, 6, 9, 10, 16, 20, 25, 26, 38, 51, 54, 55, 64, [65], 68, 106, 114, 136, 137.
  Sturgeon creek swamp, 6.
  Third hill, 113.
  Tomson's point, 9, 10, 106.
  Treworgy's point, 9, 10.
  Unity parish, 22, 116.
  Watt's fort, 115.
  Wells path, 131.
  White's marsh, 22.
  Willcock's pond, 22.
  William Love's bridge, 14, 20.
  York marshes, 58.
  York path, 21.
  York pond, 14, 15, 43, 58.

Lewis and Bonighton's patent, Saco, 87, 94, 102, 103.
Little cove, York, 58.
Little river, branch of Newgewanacke, 14, 130, 132.
  between Saco and Cape Porpoise, 87, 128.
London, England, 3, 5, 6, 133.
  Bishopsgate, 3.
Long island, Casco bay, 35, 37, 52.
Long point, Kittery, 103, 104.
Long point, Wells, 46.
Long sands, Cape Elizabeth, 2, 34, 60.
Long sands, York, 12, 13.
Love's bridge, Kittery, 14, 20.
Lygonia, 61, 65, 74, 87.
Lyman, see Coxhall.
Lynn, Massachusetts, 57.

Maine, province of, 70, 74, 103, 125, 127.
  Surrey county, 74.
Malaga island, Isles of Shoals, 71, 138.
Manor, place not named, 98, 99.
Mantill tree, Kittery, 13.
Marblehead, Massachusetts, 18, 71, 109.

Martin's cove, Kittery, 112.
Martin's [Martha's] Vineyard, Massachusetts, 114.
Maryland, Wells, 11, 59, 60.
Massachusetts,
  Boston, 1, 3, 5, 6, 15, 28, 29, 33, 35, 36, 38, 39, 40, 41, 42, 44, 47, 53, 55, 57, 65, 66, 68, 74, 78, 79, 80, 82, 86, 87, 93, 94, 96, 110, 112, 114, 125, 127, 130, 134, 136, 138.
  Charlestown, 47, 126.
  Elizabeth islands, 114.
  Essex county, 17, 59, 79, 91, 95, 109.
  Ipswich, 3, 17, 33, 56, 66, 91.
  Katamiwick island, 114.
  Lynn, 57.
  Marblehead, 18, 71, 109.
  Martin's [Martha's] Vineyard, 114.
  Middlesex county, 21.
  Monument bay, 114.
  Muddy river, 93.
  Newbury, 92.
  Norfolk county, 9, 42.
  Pacannakicke, 114.
  Salem, 43, 44, 59, 79, 94, 95, 109.
  Salisbury, 42, 107.
  Suffolk county, 6, 38, 68, 79, 136.
  Waymouth, 53, 94.
Mast cove, upper, Kittery, 6.
Mast cove, Kittery, 112.
Mast creek, Kittery, 38.
Merriconeag, afterward Harpswell, 127, 128.
Merry Meeting bay, 80.
Middlesex county, Massachusetts, 21.
Mill creek, (old), York, 2, 30, 122.
Mill creek, (new), York, 22, 40, 122.
Monument bay, Massachusetts, 114.
Mousam, Wells, 44.
Mousam mills, Wells, 44, 55.
Muddy river, Massachusetts, 93.
Munjoy's neck, Falmouth, 113.

Newbury, Massachusetts, 92.
Newgewanacke, afterwards Berwick, 9, 13, 16, 27, 70, 92, 119, 130, 132, 133, 136.

Index of Places.

Newgewanacke, continued.
  Assabumbedicke falls, 91.
  Black creek, 70.
  Burcham point, 70.
  Dirty swamp, 9.
  Great Swamp, 80.
  Great Works saw mills, 130.
  highway to the Salmon falls mills, 49.
  Pipe Stave point, 13.
  Post Wigwam, 64, 130.
  Salmon falls, 1, 16, 47, 125.
  Salmon falls brook, 48.
  Salmon falls mills, 49, 125.
  Salmon falls river, 49.
  Tom Tinker's swamp, 64.
  Wells path, 9.
  White hill, 91.
Newgewanacke [Great] river, 1, 63, 64, 91, 92, 125.
  Little river, 64, 130.
New Hampshire, 90, 100, 101, 112, 123. See Norfolk county.
  county of, 70.
  Cutcheechah (Dover), 15, 100.
  Dover, 6, 10, 55, 69, 70, 71, 100, 102, 115, 118, 125.
  Dover and Portsmouth county, 14, 21, 31, 69, 117.
  Exeter, 9, 27, 111.
  Great island, 2, 9, 10, 22, 34, 44, 45, 47, 57, 67, 74, 103, 104, 117
  Hampton, 57, 127.
  Ossaby (Ossipee), 16.
  Oyster river, 45, 46.
  Portsmouth, 9, 10, 14, 20, 21, 31, 33, 34, 44, 46, 50, 58, 66, 67, 69, 81, 88, 90, 93, 104, 108, 117, 118, 119, 123, 138
  Strawberry bank (Portsmouth), 67, 102.
Newscossecke, Indian name of Wells, 65.
New Somerset, afterwards Maine, province of, 97, 98, 99
Nimschassett, Nischassett, Indian name of Wells, 65.
Nonesuch, Falmouth, 45.
Norfolk county, Massachusetts, 9, 42

Northam, Devon county, England, 58.
North Yarmouth, 95, 110. See Wescustogo.
  called town of Casco Bay, 53.
  Chusquissacke or Shushquisacke river, 35, 37, 61.
  Commons, 53.
  Great cove, 76.
  Harricissecke, Henry Sickett, river, 53.
  Ryall's island, 61.
  Ryall's point, 110.
  Wescustogo river, 53, 61, 62, 94, 115.

Oak point, Kittery, 91.
Ogunquit, Wells, 65.
  river, 92, 100.
Oleron, island of France, 42.
Ossaby (Ossipee), New Hampshire, 16.
Ox point, Kittery, 90.
Oyster river, New Hampshire, 45, 46.

Pacaunakicke, Massachusetts, 114.
Parker's neck, Saco, 86.
Pejepscot plains [now Brunswick], 128
Piscataqua, Pischataqua, Kittery, 10, 13, 66, 77, 78, 97, 125.
  point, 139.
  river, 3, 6, 9, 10, 13, 17, 20, 22, 32, 33, 34, 45, 46, 54, 66, 67, 70, 78, 80, 88, 93, 97, 98, 109, 112, 115, 117, 118, 119, 120, 121, 138.
  called Fore river, 70
Plymouth, Devon county, England, 34, 61.
Portsmouth, New Hampshire, 9, 10, 14, 20, 21, 31, 33, 34, 44, 46, 50, 58, 66, 67, 69, 81, 88, 90, 93, 104, 108, 117, 118, 119, 123, 138.
  Strawberry bank, 67, 102
Portsmouth and Dover county, see Dover and Portsmouth county.
Post Wigwam, Newgewanacke, 64, 130
Pickles creek, York, 57

INDEX OF PLACES. 133

Preston, Wells, 65.
Purchase's island, Kennebec river, 80.

Quamphegan falls, Berwick, 14, 131.

Richman's, or Richmond's island, Falmouth, 2, 34, 69.
Rigby, Lancaster county, England, 61
Rocky hills, Kittery, 21, 43, 111
Rogers's cove brook, York, 23.
Ryall's island, North Yarmouth, 61.
  point, 110.

Saco, 3, 5, 7, 8, 42, 74, 77, 82, 86, 87, 92, 94, 96, 103, 124, 131, 135, 137.
  Blackman's mill, 102, 103.
  Church point, 82.
  Common lands, 79, 86.
  Duck pond, 86.
  Goosefare, 103.
  Haly's gut, 102
  Lewis and Bonighton's patent, 87, 94, 102, 103
  Ministry lands, 77.
  Page's plantation, 42.
  Parker's neck, 86
  Sea wall, 86, 87.
  Smyth's brook, 82.
  Trustrum's, Ralph, brook, 82.
  Vines' patent, 87
  West's brook, 7, 8
  Winter harbor, 8, 42, 79, 82, 86, 92, 108, 124.
Saco river, 7, 8, 42, 79, 82, 86, 87, 94, 102, 103, 124.
  falls, 94
  little brook, emptying into, 94, 95
  lower falls, 95
Salem, Massachusetts, 43, 44, 59, 79, 94, 95, 109.
Salisbury, Massachusetts, 42, 107.
Salmon Falls, Newgewanacke, 1, 16, 47, 125.
  brook, 48.
  mills, 49, 125.

Scarborough, 74, 87, 93.
  Beaver creek, 17.
  Black Point, 42, 74, 93, 94, 96, 103.
  [Black Point] river, 74, 87.
  Black Point river, 40, 42
  Blue Point, 74, 87, 92, 102.
  Crooked lane, 74.
  Dunstan, 42, 96.
  Phippenny's plantation, 40.
Scituate men's swamp, York, 37.
Scotland, York, 51.
Sebascodegan, or Sequasco Diggin island, Harpswell, 127, 128.
Shapleigh's store house, Kittery, 73.
Shushquisacke, see Chusquissacke.
Six Acre marsh, Wells, 11.
Slut's corner, Kittery, 21.
Small point, afterwards Phipsburg, 67
Smuttynose island, Isles of Shoals, 58, 71, 77.
Smyth's brook, Saco, 82.
Somerset county, England, 97, 98.
Spinny's cove, Kittery, 123.
Spruce creek, Kittery, 3, 39, 44, 78, 81, 90, 91, 95, 102, 103, 104, 106, 112, 116, 127
Spurwink, Falmouth, 33, 44, 45, 76.
  river, 34, 45, 69, 74, 101
Star island, Isles of Shoals, 88, 104.
Stonington, Connecticut, 93.
Stony neck, York, 88.
Strawberry bank, Portsmouth, N. H., 67, 102
Sturgeon creek, Kittery, 6, 9, 10, 16, 20, 25 26, 38, 51, 54, 55, 64, [65], 68, 106, 114, 136, 137.
  swamp, 6
Suffolk, county of, Massachusetts, 6, 38, 68, 79, 136
Sunken marsh, York, 72, 86.
Surrey county, 74.

Tomson's point, Kittery, 9, 10, 106.
Tocnocke, Totnucke, Wells, 11, 132.
  marshes, between Wells and York, 59, 134.
Treworgy's point, Kittery, 9, 10
Trustrum, Ralph's, brook, Saco, 82.

Index of Places.

Unity parish, Kittery, 22, 110.

Vines's patent, Saco, 87.

Watertown, Massachusetts, 21.
Watts fort, Kittery, 115.
Waymouth, Massachusetts, 53, 94.
Webhannet river, Wells, 59, 77, 105, 109.
Wells, 5, 10, 11, 13, 16, 21, 28, 29, 33, 40, 44, 46, 55, 59, 60, 64, 65, 77, 82, 84, 87, 89, 101, 105, 108, 120, 121, 127, 128, 129, 132, 134, 135.
  bridge, 59.
  commons, 46, 77.
  Drake's island, 108, 135.
  Great marsh, 11.
  Great river, 10.
  Harbor mouth, 109.
  Long point, 46.
  Maryland, 11, 59, 60.
  Ministry land, 77.
  Mousam, 44.
  Mousam mills, 44, 55.
  Newscossecke, Ninschasset, Nischassett, Indian names of Wells, 65.
  Ogunquit, 65.
    river, 92, 100.
  Preston, 65.
  river, 11.
  sea wall, 11, 89, 90, 100, 109, 129.
  Six acre marsh, 11.
  Totnucke, 11, 132.
    marshes, 59, 134.
  Town's land, 128.
  Webhannet river, 59, 77, 105, 109.
  Wheelwright's neck, 105.
Wescustogo, Westgostuggo, Westquatogoe, afterward North Yarmouth, 52, 62, 115.
West's brook, Saco, 7, 8.
Wheelwright's neck, Wells, 105.
White hill, Newgewanacke, 91.
White's island, Casco bay, 128.
White's marsh, Kittery, 22.
Wickham, Bucks county, England, 99, 125.

Willcock's pond, Kittery, 22, 80.
  brook, 80.
Winneganee creek, Kennebec river, 23.
Winter harbor, Saco, 8, 42, 79, 82, 86, 92, 108, 124.
Whiskeag, Kennebec river, 80.

York, 9, 12, 13, 15, 22, 23, 24, 25, 30, 33, 34, 37, 39, 40, 43, 50, 51, 52, 55, 56, 57, 58, 60, 63, 66, 67, 72, 73, 74, 78, 83, 84, 86, 87, 88, 89, 96, 97, 100, 102, 105, 116, 119, 120, 121, 122, 125, 130, 132, 133, 134, 135, 139. See Agamenticus and Gorgeana.
  Agamenticus river, 37.
  Allcock's neck, 60, 61.
  Barberry marsh, 12, 13.
  Burnt marsh brook, 132.
  Bass cove, 22, 72, 78, 83.
    river, 96.
    brook, 119.
  Braveboat harbor, 37, 58, 116.
  bridge, 25, 50, 74, 83, 122.
  Cape neck, or Cape Nuttacke neck, 100.
  Cape Nuttacke, 13, 87, 88, 107.
    river, 132.
    way, 12, 13, 87.
  church, 73.
  commons, 81.
  common path, 78.
  East York, 81.
  Eddy point, 58.
  ferry, 72, 125.
  Frethy's cove, 122.
  Gallows point, 24.
  Gorges, Mr.'s creek, 120.
    neck, 22.
  Gorges, Mis, (error for Mr. See Book IV, 43), point, 139.
  Harbor mouth, 25, 132, 135.
  highway, 57.
  Hull's creek, 37.
  landing place, 96.
  ledge of rocks, 12, 13.
  Little cove, 58.
  Little Highway bridge, 72.
  Long sands, 12, 13.

INDEX OF PLACES. 135

York, continued.
  marshes, 58, 74.
  Meeting house creek, 78, 83.
  Mill creek, (old), 2, 30, 122.
    (new), 22, 40, 122
  path from the town to Henry Sayword's, 15, 68.
  Pond marsh, 87.
  Preble's creek, 37, 50.
  Roger's cove brook, 23.
  Sandy beach, 107.
  saw mills, Gorges' creek, 120.
  Scituate men's swamp, 37.
  Scotland, 51.
  sea wall, 13.
  Stony neck, 88.
  Sunken marsh, 72, 86.

York, continued.
  Tocnocke marshes, 134.
  the plain, 84.
  tree bridge, 78.
  way to Newgewanacke, 9, 119.
    from Cape Nuttacke to Wells, 87.
    to Wells, 134.
York marshes, Kittery, 58, 74.
York mills, 40.
York path, Kittery, 21.
York pond, Kittery, 14, 15, 43.
  York, 58.
York river, 2, 23, 24, 25, 30, 34, 35, 39, 50, 58, 60, 67, 74, 81, 83, 86, 89, 96, 97, 122, 125.

GENERAL INDEX.

Abatement in price for shortness of measurement of land, 9.
Acceptance of trust, 17.
Accompt, for inventory, 137.
Accounts to balance, 114, 115.
Account stated, 13.
Acknowledgment omitted, 7.
 before authority, 18.
 fealty, 61, 98, 99
 to the lord proprietor, 11, 93, 116, 125.
 of one farthing per acre, 87.
 day's work, 37, 44, 124.
 a couple of hens, 99.
 a fat goose, 124.
 four pullets, 125.
 "the usual," 37.
 annual rent, 68, 74, 76, 97, 98, 99, 124, 125
 rents, 85
 covenants and conditions, 85.
 to the Crown, 128
Acre, measurement of defined, 61
Act of a town, for town vote, 22.
Act of Massachusetts general court explanatory of the Act of 20 Nov., 1652 (see Book I, 26), relating to priority of land grants, 87.
 for solemnizing marriages, 84.
Acts of trade cited, 84
Administration, 44
Administrators, 13, 16, 33, 34, 39, 40, 48, 60, 111, 126, 137
Admiralty, special court of, convened, 84.
Agents, attorneys, 74, 87, 99, 112, 133.
Agreements, see under Contracts.
Agriculture. See Husbandry.
Anchors, 58, 138.
Andirons, 41, 126.
Apple trees, 20

Apple-pine tree, 134.
Apprenticeship. See under Contracts.
Apprentices, 12, 42, 73.
Appraisal, 120.
Arbitrators, 33, 55, 62, 67.
Assignee, 58.
Assignments, 107, 109.
Assistants, members of the Governor's council in Massachusetts, 1, 4, 5, 6, 7, 8, 13, 26, 30, 36, 38, 40, 41, 53, 60, 65, 66, 78, 80, 87, 93, 94, 126
 in New Hampshire, 45.
Associates, Yorkshire magistrates, 2, 3, 7, 9, 10, 11, 12, 13, 14, 16, 19, 22, 23, 24, 25, 30, 37, 39, 42, 47, 48, 49, 50, 52, 54, 56, 57, 59, 60, 63, 64, 73, 76, 79, 81, 90, 95, 102, 107, 111, 113, 114, 115, 117, 119, 120, 123, 125, 130, 133, 137.
Attorneys, 13, 47, 52, 56, 62, 66, 73, 74, 83, 87, 88, 98, 99, 101, 112, 125, 128, 139. See also Powers of attorney.
Authority, those in, 18, 84
Award, see also under Reference, 33, 55, 67, 91, 101, 104, 107, 126.

Bait, 2, 69.
Baking, 126
Barren marsh, 38.
Bastard marsh, 122
Bars, pair of, 114.
Bartys, recorder's error for bairns, 36
Basin, pewter, 126.
Bass trees, 92.
Beaches, conveyed, 128.
Berwick, see Index of Places.
 town meeting (of Unity parish), 22

General Index. 137

Berwick, continued.
  grants recorded, see Index of Grantors, under names following:
    Broughton, George, 125.
    Broughton, John, 47, 49.
    Chadborne, Humphrey, 70.
    Hearle, John, 130.
    Hull, Phineas, 130, 131.
    Hutchinson, Eliakim, 136.
    Nason, Richard, 27.
    Wincoll, John, 1.
Bestow, expend, 41.
Bible, 126
Bill of Sale, 14, 56, 64, 65, 66, 77, 91, 104, 138
  for deed, 103.
Bills of Sale referred to,
  Abraham Conley to Abraham Tilton, 64.
  Kittery, town of, to Thomas Withers, 91.
  William Seavy to Nathaniel Fryer, 138.
  Nathaniel Fryer to Philip Odihorne, 138.
Blacksmith, 14, 42, 47, 115, 129.
Boards, 91. See also under Pay.
Boat, 23.
  boat-room, anchorage, 34.
Bolsters, 45.
Bonds, 1, 12, 15, 21, 24, 33, 56, 57, 104, 122, 123, 126, 134
Boom-piers, 125.
Bownes, booms, 1.
Bread-corn, 61.
Brew-house, 126.
Brewing, 19, 24, 126.
Bricklayer, 19, 24.

Cable, 58
Cap, 66.
Cape Porpoise See Index of Places
  grants recorded See Index of Grantors, under the names following:
    Endicott, Gilbert, 128.
    Gorges, Sir Ferdinando, 97.
    Phillips, William, 74.

Cape Porpoise, continued.
  grants referred to:
    Town to Bryan Pendleton, 93.
    Grace Bush to Bryan Pendleton, 93.
    Gregory Jefferys to Bryan Pendleton, 93.
    Moghegin to William Phillips, 4.
    William Phillips to Gilbert Endicott, 128.
    John Sanders to Bryan Pendleton, 93.
    John Smyth to William Phillips, 74, 93.
  records, or town book, 93.
  town line between and Saco, 86.
Captain, 1, 9, 16, 23, 31, 33, 47, 56, 57, 64, 66, 77, 78, 80, 87, 93, 95, 96, 99, 100, 101, 102, 115, 116, 125, 132, 135
Carpenter, 45, 64, 71, 74, 88, 130.
Carter, 42.
Carver, 53.
Case pending in Court
  Richard Otis vs. Nicholas Frost, 55.
Cattle. See under Domestic Animals.
Caution, caveat, 40, 43, 44, 55, 77, 88, 139.
  claim, 101.
  used for costs of court, 84.
Cellar, 126.
Certificate, by a magistrate in nature of a deposition, not requiring verification by oath, 87.
Chains, 138.
Charcoal burning, 92.
Charges, 41.
Chattels, 115. See also movables.
Chest, 126.
Chimney, 126.
Chirurgeon, surgeon, 29.
Christmas day, 124.
Claim to lands, 101.
Cleat, 23.
Cloak, 126.
Cloth-making, 41.

General Index.

Cloths,
  cotton, 41.
  linen, 41, 126.
  napkins, 126.
  sheets, 126.
  towels, 126.
  weaver, 28.
  woolen, 41.
Clothing,
  cap, 66.
  cloak, 126.
  double-suit, 73.
Colonel, 74, 99, 125.
Commission to justices, special for a Court of Admiralty, 84
Commissioners, inferior magistrates
  of Yorkshire, 38, 46, 57, 65, 74, 76, 84, 101, 103, 107, 127
  of Massachusetts, 13, 37, 66
  in New Hampshire, 2, 9, 10, 15, 20, 22, 27, 31, 32, 34, 39, 45, 46, 47, 52, 58, 67, 69, 70, 71, 74, 81, 82, 104, 112, 117, 125
  appointed by the court, 58, 59, 126, 137.
  appointed by towns, 59, 88, 134.
Committee, commissioners, special, 87
Commonage in wood cutting, 27.
Compass, 17, 18, 81
Complaint, petition, 87.
Composition, satisfaction, 87
Confirmation, 68, 73.
Consideration, see also under Pay.
  affection and love, 2, 3, 5, 8, 9, 16, 52, 54, 62, 70, 81, 83, 89, 92, 99, 102, 105, 115, 120, 121, 122, 123, 124, 137.
  bond for maintenance, 63
  bond to save harmless, 126
  debts due, 79, 86, 92, 126.
  dowry, 105.
  faithful service, 99.
  gifts, 65.
  labor, 2
  land in exchange, 11, 18, 48, 128
  liquor, 10.
  support and maintenance, 124.
Consent of parents to marriage, 84.
Constables, 84.
Continent, continuing,

Contracts, 23, 73, 77, 87, 112, 138.
  agreements, 13, 37, 41, 54, 55, 68, 91, 92, 101, 102, 103, 107, 123, 126.
  antenuptial and marriage settlement, 18, 19, 34, 54, 105, 108, 113, 115, 138.
  apprenticeship, indenture of, 12, 42, 73
  order, 16
Coparceners See Partnerships.
Coplement, complement, 14.
Cordwainer, 59, 66, 128.
Corn,
  field, 14, 63
  ground, 10.
  Indian, 16.
  mills at Falmouth, 125.
  at York, 39.
Costs, deposit for required, 84.
Council for New England at Plymouth, 61.
Council of the Province of Maine, 126, 137.
Councillors of New Hampshire, 65, 77, 100, 101, 107, 112, 118, 124.
Counterpart, of an indenture, 98.
Country's service, 16.
Course of law, action at, 87.
Court of Associates, 55.
Courts,
  county. 61, 126, 137.
    at Kittery, 139.
    at Wells, 60, 61.
    at York, 55, 58, 67, 126, 137.
  of admiralty, convened, 84.
    travel, disbursement and entertainment of, 84.
  of pleas, 76, 137.
  of New Hampshire, as probate court, 45, 118.
Covenant, 125.
  for a year and a day, 42
  for further and better assurance, 34, 85, 94, 98, 99, 112, 113, 128, and elsewhere.
Coxhall, afterward Lyman,
  grants recorded. See Index of Grantors under
  Paine, John, 28
  Symonds, Harlakenden, 197.

General Index. 139

Coxhall, continued.
    Symonds, Samuel, 91.
    grants referred to:
        Fluelline to William Phillips, 5.
        Fluelline to Peter Turbet, John Sanders and John Bush, 28.
        Sosowen to Peter Turbet, John Sanders and John Bush, 28.
        Peter Turbet, John Sanders and John Bush to Harlakenden Symonds, 28.
Cupboard-cloth, 126
Currier, 31, 68.
Curtilages, 61.
Custom of the country, 82, 124
    as to apprentices, 73.
Custom of England, 98.

Dame, 12.
Dams, 1, 95, 133.
Deconancy, discrepancy, 91.
Deeds,
    drawing of, 66, 114.
    execution of, 66, 114.
    imperfect, 116.
    incomplete, 133.
    lost, 80, 86
    of gift, 69, 101, 136.
Depositions. See Index of Grantors, under the names following.
    Allden, John, 66
    Andrews, John, 39.
    Bray, Margery, 2.
    Bray, Richard, 84.
    Carter, *alias* Maddiver, Agnes, 115.
    Carter, Richard, 115.
    Coussons, John, 115, 128.
    Crocket, Ann, 107.
    Coole, Nicholas, 84.
    Davess, John, 125.
    Dyamont, Andrew, 71.
    Endle, Michael, 71.
    Forgison, John, 16.
    Frost, Charles, 64.
    Frost, Mary, 16.
    Granger, John, 16.
    Heskines, Nicholas, 103.
    Howman, John, 66.

Depositions, continued.
    Johnson, Edward, 2, 116.
    Johnson, Priscilla, 116.
    Kemble, Thomas, 66.
    Knight, Robert, 2.
    Maddiver, *alias* Carter, Agnes, 115.
    Munjoy, George, 87.
    Oliver, William, 71.
    Pormot, Philemon, 65.
    Redding, Eleanor, 84.
    Renalds, John, 104.
    Row, Richard, 39.
    Sarden, Timothy, 2
    Smale, Elizabeth, 128
    Smale, Francis, sen., 16, 128
    Swadden, Philip, 13.
    Tetherly, John, 71.
    Tomson, John, 16
    Tucker, Francis, 103.
    Turbet, John, 104.
    Wardell, William, 65.
    Whitte, Samson, 39.
    Wittum, Peter, jr., 65.
    ———, Charles, 125.
Deputy governor of the province of Maine, 74.
Deputy governor of Massachusetts, 29, 30, 41, 54, 84.
Deputy president of the province of Maine, 82, 95, 116, 138.
Deputy president of New Hampshire, 100, 104.
Detinue, 37.
Dinner, at noon time, 16.
Discharges (see also Receipts), 30, 80, 102, 111, 125.
    of a mortgage upon the record thereof, 30.
Dishes, 41.
Distraint, 61, 68, 98, 124.
Division lines, 88, 91, 104.
Divident, part divided, 37.
Domestic animals,
    bull, 37.
    calves, 79, 115.
    cattle, 33, 38, 57, 79, 89, 104, 107, 108, 113, 116, 123.
    increase of, 113.
    neat, 41, 63, 123.

Domestic animals, continued.
  cattle,
    yearlings, 104.
    cows, 37, 41, 63, 79, 104, 112, 115, 123, 137.
  fowls, 41
    goose, 124.
    hens, 99.
    pullets, 125.
  heifer, 2, 102.
    yearling, 73.
  hogs, 41, 79, 104.
    swine, 41, 63, 115.
  horses, 27, 41, 79, 104, 122, 134.
    mare, 79, 104.
  oxen, 41, 112, 114.
  sheep, 115
  steers, 41, 79, 104.
Domestic uses. See Domestic animals and Furniture.
  baking, 126.
  bread corn, 61.
  brew-house, 126.
  brewing, 19, 24, 126.
  Indian corn, 16, 72.
  fire wood, 51, 122.
    cutting, 27, 104.
  spinning, 41.
  washing, 126.
  victuals, dressing, 126
Double suit, supply with two suits, 73
Dowless sheets, Dowlas, a coarse linen cloth, 126.

Easter day, 125
Eastern parts of New England, 2, 69.
Egress, see under Ingress.
Eldest son's double portion, 137.
Enemies, Indian, 16.
England, great seal of, 4, 5.
English measure, square measure, 97.
Enrollment in the court of pleas, 76.
Equity, 40.
Escript, a writing or schedule, 85.
Esquire, 3, 4, 5, 39, 40, 61, 66, 84, 93, 97, 98, 99, 102, 109, 116.
Estate, to convey, 19, 20, 32.

Execution, 57.
Executors, 34, 40, 45, 94, 121, 139.

Falmouth. See Index of Places.
  selectmen, 87.
  grants recorded. See Index of Grantors under the names following.
    Allen, Edward, 69, 100.
    Cleeves, George, 68.
    Harvy, Elizabeth, 113
    Holms, Joseph, 96.
    Jordan, John, 34.
    Jordan, Robert, 2, 69.
    Massachusetts General Court, 125.
    Mitton, Elizabeth, 76.
    Rigby, Alexander, 74.
    Winter, John's estate, 33
  grants referred to
    Edward Allen to Henry Kirke, 101.
    Sir Ferdinando Gorges to George Cleeves, 68.
    Robert Jordan to John Jordan. 45.
    Baron [Alexander] Rigby to George Cleeves, 68.
    [Gorges and Rigby] to George Cleeves, 87.
Farmer, 60.
Farming. See Husbandry.
Feather bed, 45.
Fealty, 61, 98, 99.
Fees of magistrates, jurors and court officials, 84.
Fee simple, 3, 9, 10, 28, 29, 88, 95.
Fee tail, 34, 45, 52, 102.
Felt-maker, 5
Fences, 14, 25, 37, 38, 42, 59, 95, 107, 120, 136.
Fence, log, 3
  partition, 119.
Fencing, 14.
Filial portion, meaning dowry, 105.
Fire-wood, 51, 122.
Fish, 8, 23, 24, 79.
  dry cod fish, 18, 109.
  mackerel, 24
  refuse, 93, 109.

General Index.   141

Fisherman, 12, 17, 23, 24, 25, 30, 34, 42, 51, 71, 74, 77, 78, 79, 88, 90, 102, 105, 118, 119.
Fishing, liberty of, 4, 5, 23, 53, 82, 95, 97, 98, 124.
Fishing houses, 138.
Fishmonger, 74.
Fishing uses, 2, 69.
   bait, 2, 69
   flake room, 58, 71, 104, 138.
   flakes, to dry fish upon, 17, 58, 71, 125, 138
   lying room, to spread fish, 71.
   salt-house, 104.
   shallops, fishing boats, 17, 31, 58
   stages, fishing, 17, 34, 58, 71, 104, 138
   houses, 138.
   room, 58.
Flats, 80, 124
Flumes, 1, 125.
Fodder, food for cattle, 41
Forfeiture of the conditions of a deed of gift, 101.
   mortgage, 110.
Forks, 56
Fowling, liberty of, 4, 5, 23, 53, 82, 95, 124.
Fowls, 41
Frame, of a house, 51.
Franchises, 98, 99.
Fretchett, freshet, brook, 23.
Funeral charges, 16.
Furniture, 126
   andirons, 41, 126.
   basin, pewter, 126.
   bed, 126.
   bolsters, 45.
   candle sticks,
      brass, 126.
      pewter, 126.
   chairs, 126.
   chamber-pots, 126
   chest, 126.
   dishes, 41.
   dripping pan, iron, 126.
   feather beds, 126.
   forks, 56.
   kettle, copper, 126.
   napkins, 126.
   pans, 126.

Furniture, continued.
   pillow-bears, 126.
   plates, 126.
   porridge-pot, 17.
   pot-hooks, 41.
   pots, 126.
   salt-cellars, 126.
   saucers, 126.
   sheets, 126.
   spits, 41, 126
   spoons, 41, 126.
   table-cloths, 126.
   tankard, 126.
   towels, 126.
   trammels, 41, 126.
   trunks, 126.

Gardens, 36, 38, 41, 42, 50, 61, 77, 83, 95, 102, 110, 118, 122, 126.
Garden-plot, 52, 71
Gear, running, for mill, 1, 47, 125.
General Assembly of the province of Maine, 126.
General Court of Massachusetts, 44, 86, 87
   order of, concerning bounds of Saco, 86.
   order for settling differences between individuals, 86, 87.
   order referring petition of Geo. and John Ingersoll for a grant, to the determination of the President of the Province of Maine, 125.
   report to, of commissioners, 86.
Gentleman, 33, 44, 49, 59, 61, 68, 74, 91, 98, 124, 127, 129.
Goodman, 59, 86.
Goodwife, 52.
Governor of Massachusetts, 69, 114, 126.
Grants, oldest to have precedence, 87.
Grants referred to. See Patents.
Grantors.
   Allcocke, Joseph, 118
   Allen, Edward, 101.
   Billine, John, 73
   Botts, Isaac, 48.
   Burdett, George, 116.
   Burgess, Richard, 135.

Grants referred to, continued.
  Bush, Grace, 93.
    John, 28, 127.
  Canny, Thomas, 70.
  Cape Porpoise, town of, 93.
  Carter, Richard, 115.
  Champernoon, Francis, 125.
  Cleeves, George, 37, 52, 74.
  Cloyce, Peter, 59.
  Collines, Abraham, 121.
  Conley, Abraham, 26, 31.
  Cossons, John, 35, 52.
  Crocket, Ephraim, 79.
  Denmark, Patrick, 67.
  Derumein et als., 80.
  Donell, Henry, 13.
  Drake, Thomas, 36.
  Everest, Isaac, 63.
    Job, 88.
  Fletcher, Seth, 77.
  Fluelline, 28.
  Godfrey, Edward, 37, 132.
  Gorges, Sir Ferdinando, 68, 70, 87, 112.
  Grant, James, 30.
  Greene, John, 45.
  Gunnison, Hugh, 3.
    Sarah, 3.
  Hammond, William, 77.
  Harvy, Elizabeth, 113.
  Hodgsden, Nicholas, 18.
  Hooke, William, 84.
  Howell, Rice, 81.
  Indian sagamores, 95, 110.
  Jefferys, Gregory, 93.
  Jordan, Robert, 45.
  Kittery, town of, 1, 6, 9, 14, 18, 19, 26, 28, 31, 39, 47, 51, 54, 64, 78, 104, 112, 118, 120, 130, 131, 132.
  Knights, Ezekiel, 84.
  Lawson, Christopher, 80.
  Littlefield, James, 11, 59.
  Mass. General Court, 44.
  Mavericke, Antipas, 109.
  Maxell, Alexander, 22.
  Moghegine, 4.
  North Yarmouth, town of, 53.
  Norton, Henry, 78, 83.
  Nutter, Hatevill, 70.
  Phillips, William, 5, 126.

Grants referred to, continued.
  Playstead, Roger, 49.
  Rigby, Alexander, 68, 87.
  Sanders, John, 28, 93.
  Smale, Edward, 112.
  Smyth, John, 74, 93.
  Sosowen, 28.
  Stephens, Thomas, 95, 110.
  Symonds, Harlakenden, 127.
  Sympson, Henry, 85.
  Turbet, Peter, 28, 127.
  Vines, Richard, 2, 52.
  Wadleigh, 105.
  Walker, Isaac, 40.
  Wannerton, Thomas, 13.
  Wells, town of, 29, 44, 59, 89.
  West, John, 77.
  Wincoll, John, 31.
  Wittum, Peter, 111.
  York, town of, 12, 15, 21, 23, 37, 63, 83, 87, 88, 89, 122, 134.
Grantees:
  Abbet, Richard, 14.
  Abbett, Thomas, 21.
  Adams, Philip, 37.
  Allcocke, Joseph, 118.
  Anger, Samson, 12.
  Ashly, William, 11.
  Austine, Samuel, 121.
  Barefoote, Walter, 125.
  Baston, Thomas, 59.
  Bedford, Nathan, 40.
  Booth, Thomas, 109.
  Bragdon, Arthur, sen., 23.
  Bray, Richard, 35, 36, 52.
  Broughton, George, 49.
    John, 49.
    Thomas, 6.
  Bush, John, 28.
  Camer, Edward, 80.
  Canny, Thomas, 70.
  Chadborne, Humphrey, 64.
  Clarke, Edward, 118.
    Thomas, 66.
  Cleeves, George, 68, 87.
  Cloyce, Peter, 59.
  Conley, Abraham, 26, 54.
  Coole, Nicholas, 29.
  Cossons, John, 37, 52.
  Crawford, John, 9, 48.

General Index.

Grants referred to, continued
  Crocket, Thomas, 73.
  Davess, John, 134
  Downeing, Dennis, 47.
  Emery, James, 14
  Endicott Gilbert, 128.
  Everell, Thomas, 88
  Everest, Andrew, 87, 88.
    Isaac, 15, 63
  Footeman, Thomas, 85.
  Freathy, William, 81.
  Frost, Nicholas, 13
  Godfrey, Ann, 116
  Goodin, Daniel, senior, 54
  Gydney, Bartholomew, 95, 110.
  Gyllum, Zachary, 7, 8.
  Hammond, Jonathan, 89
  Hodgsden, Nicholas, 31, 111.
  Hord, John, 54.
  Hull, Phineas, 130, 131.
  Jordan, John, 45
  Joyce, Christopher, 118.
  King [William], 120
  Kirke, Henry, 31, 101.
  Lake, Thomas, 66.
  Lawson, Christopher, 80.
  Leader, George, 132.
    Richard, 132.
  Lugg, Gilbert, 118.
  [Lydden, George] 51.
  Lyston, Waymouth, 118.
  Mackemtyre, Micum, 30.
  Mavericke, Antipas, 112.
  Mayne, John, 115.
  Messant, Ann, 116.
  Middleton, James, 67.
  Mills, Thomas, 105.
  Moore, William, 37.
  Morrall, John, 18, 19, 70.
  Nason, Richard, 28.
  Neale, John, 22.
  Norton, Henry, 2.
  Nutter, Hatevill, 70.
  Palmer, William, 134.
  Pendleton, Bryan, 77, 93.
  Phillips, William, 4, 5, 74, 93.
  Redding, John, 53.
  Rishworth, Edward, 122, 135
  Roberts, John, 70.
  Rogers, William, 3.
  Ross, John, 112.

Grants referred to, continued.
  Sanders, John, 28.
  Sayword, Henry, 44, 95, 110.
  Seely, William, 3, 39, 78, 104.
  Sheeres, Jeremiah, 88.
  Smale, Edward, 112.
  Stephens, Thomas, 95, 110.
  Symonds, Harlakenden, 28, 127.
    Samuel, 127
  Sympson, Henry, 37, 78, 83, 84.
  Tommass, Rice, 73.
  Tricky, Thomas, 3.
  Turbet, Peter, 28
  Turner, Ephraim, 7, 8.
  Watts, Henry, 74.
  Waymouth, Robert, 45.
  Weare, Peter, 132, 134
  Wentworth, John, 63, 84.
  White, Richard, 79.
  Wincoll, John, 1
  Wittum, Peter, sen., 26.
  Wood, Richard, 13.
Grapnel, 31.
Grappers, grapnels, 17.
Grist mills. See Corn mills.
Guns, 12, 128.
Gut, gully, 53, 69, 74, 102.

Halfendeale, halfe and deale, half part, half share, 41, 69, 106.
Harvest (time), 124.
Havens, 97, 99, 128.
Hawking, liberty of, 4, 5, 23, 53.
Hay, 35, 41.
  English, 122.
  salt marsh, 122.
Head-wears, 95.
Heifer, 2, 102.
Heir or heiress, by descent, 13, 16, 73, 74, 83, 92, 120, 127.
  by devise, 38, 72, 92, 93, 101, 106.
High-water mark, 54, 88.
Highways, 6, 43, 51, 55, 57, 59, 76, 121, 123, 136.
Home farm, 32.
Home lot, 15, 43, 63, 116.
Homestall, homestead, 105.
Horse, keep of, 122.

House upon leased land, 56, 116.
Household goods, see Furniture.
Houses and appurtenances. See Gardens, Messuages, Tenements.
  cellar, 126.
  chimney, 126.
  curtilages, 61.
  frame, 51.
  on leased land, 56, 116.
  hinges, 56.
  homestead, 56, 116.
  lean-tos, 71, 126.
  nails, 56.
  store-houses, 71, 73.
  wells, 52.
Howle, hold, 23.
Hunting, liberty of, 4, 5, 23, 53.
Husbandman, 25, 26, 31, 41, 80, 82, 102, 130. See Farmer, Yeoman.
Husbandry, appurtenances of, etc. See Domestic animals, Fences, Orchards.
  apple trees, 20.
  apple-pine tree, 134.
  barren marsh, 38.
  bastard marsh, 122.
  bars, pair of, 114.
  barns, 36.
  corn ground, 10.
    field, 14, 63.
  fodder, 41.
  harvest, 124.
    Indian, 16.
  hay, 35, 41, 122.
  home farm, 32.
  horse-keep, 122.
  implements and furniture, 41, 115.
  keep of a heifer, 73.
  manuring, 41.
  team of oxen, 114.
  tillage, conversion into, 98, 99.

Illegal trading, 84.
Illegitimacy, 84.
Imbesseling, impairing, 41.
Imbessill, waste, 73.
Immoveables, see Unmoveables.
Implements of husbandry, 41, 115.

Indian corn, 16.
Indian harvest, 16.
Indians, 23, 65, 114, 128. See Sagamores.
  called heathen, 37.
  war, 80, 115.
  warfare, 16.
Ingress, regress, egress, 2, 52, 69.
Inlet, mouth, 8.
Interest, rate of, 93.
Inventoring, appraising, 44, 55.
Inventory, 73.
  called accompt, 137.
Iron-work of a saw mill, 128.
Isles of Shoals. See Index of Places.
  grants recorded. See Index of Grantors under the names following:
    Allard, Hugh, 17.
    Endle, Michael, 71.
    Fryer, Nathaniel, 138.
    Pickeard, Edmund, 58.
Issue, determination, final ending, 87.

Joiner, 28, 106.
Joiner's work, 23.
Joint tenants, 54, 62, 65, 69, 72, 106, 118.
Judgment of Court, 139.
Jurisdiction, 91,
  regal, of Maine, 3, 5.
  his majesty's immediate government (of New Hampshire), 100.
  Massachusetts, 21, 48, 56, 58, 64, 87, 97, 118.
Jury summoned, 84.
Justices of the peace appointed under President Danforth, 1680:
  John Davess, 74, 78, 86, 88, 96, 97, 100, 124, 136, 138.
  Charles Frost, 106, 111, 127.
  Francis Hooke, 64, 65, 77, 89, 91, 97, 104, 107, 109, 121.
  Edward Rishworth, 71, 73, 83, 84, 86, 89, 90, 91, 93, 97, 103, 105, 111, 112, 115, 116, 119, 121, 123, 125, 128, 132, 133, 134, 135, 136, 137, 138.
  Joshua Scottow, 103.

Justices of the peace, continued.
　Edward Tyng, 114, 120.
　Samuel Wheelwright, 90, 105, 108, 109, 120, 121, 122, 129
　John Wincoll, 68, 78, 92, 103, 131, 132.
　under the second charter in 1701: Joseph Hammond, 91.

Keep of a horse, 122.
Keeping (a heifer) upon halves, 73
Kennebec See Index of Places.
　grants recorded See Index of Grantors, under the names following:
　　Camer, Edward, 80
　　Middleton, James, 67.
　　Parker, John, 23.
　　Robin-Hood, 23.
　grants referred to
　　Edward Camer to Christopher Lawson, 80.
　　Patrick Denmark to James Middleton, 67.
　　Derumcin et als. to Christopher Lawson, 80.
　　Christopher Lawson to Edward Camer, 80.
Kennebunk, then a district of Wels.
　grants recorded. See Index of Grantors under the names following.
　　Chabinoct. Thomas, 65.
　　Renalds, William, 57,
　　Romanascoh, 65.
　　Turbet, Peter, 57.
Ketch, a two masted vessel, 84.
Kettle, copper, 126.
King's royalty of a fifth of gold and silver ore, 61, 98, 99, 128.
Kittery See Index of Places
　bounds of the town, 64.
　constable, 84
　records or town book, 9, 14, 19, 44, 80, 118.
　selectmen, 6, 14, 20, 22, 54, 64, 91, 94, 97, 100, 104, 133
　town clerk, 14, 20, 22, 44, 46, 64, 115.
　town line between and York, 58.

Kittery, continued.
　town meetings, 6, 18, 22.
　town grants, 14, 15, 20, 21, 22, 38, 39, 43, 44, 46, 64, 80, 94, 97, 100, 113, 132.
　other grants recorded. See Index of Grantors, under the names following:
　　Abbett, Richard, 14, 64.
　　Billine, John, 73
　　Botts, Isaac's estate, 48.
　　Bray, John, 121
　　Broughton, Thomas, 6.
　　Chadborne, James, 106
　　Champernoown Francis, 116.
　　Clarke, Thomas, 66.
　　Conley, Abraham, 19, 114.
　　Cowell, Thomas, 3, 39.
　　Crafford, John, 9, 21, 48.
　　Crockett, Ann, 73, 74.
　　Dearing, Roger's estate, 121.
　　Downeing, Dennis. 47, 115.
　　Durston, Elizabeth, 21.
　　Duston, Thomas, 20.
　　Emery, Anthony, 38.
　　　James, 14, 20, 45, 97.
　　Fenix, John, 81.
　　Frost, Charles, 67.
　　　John's estate, 33.
　　Goodin, Daniel, 54.
　　Gorges, Sir Ferdinando, 97, 98, 99, 125.
　　Greene, John, 6, 63, 116.
　　Heard, John, 17.
　　Hearle, William, 123.
　　Hilton, Katherine, 9.
　　Hodgsden, Nicholas, 31, 100.
　　　Timothy, 111.
　　Holms, Thomas, 131.
　　Hoole, John, 116.
　　Jefferys, Diggory, 88.
　　Jenkins, Renold, 137.
　　　Stephen, 136.
　　King, Daniel, 119.
　　Kirke, Henry, 31
　　Knight, Samuel, 117.
　　Lord, Nathan, 25, 26.
　　Lydden, George, 51.
　　Lyston, Waymouth, 118.
　　Mavericke, Antipas, 27, 109.
　　Mendum, Jonathan, 112.

Kittery, continued.
  Morrall, John, 18, 70.
  Neale, John, 22.
  Onyon, Thomas, 119.
  Palmer, William, 117, 132, 134.
  Parsons, John, 66.
  Paul, Daniel, 113.
  Stephen, 111, 127.
  Porter, Abel, 78.
  Rice, Thomas, 90.
  Roberts, John, 70.
  Robinson, Stephen, 46,
  Rogers, William, 106.
  Ross, John, 112.
  Rowles, sagamore, 10.
  Spinny, Thomas, 123.
  Tilton, Abraham, 64.
  Traffton, Thomas, 24.
  Trueworgy, Samuel, 10.
  Whitte, John, 51, 102.
  Richard, 78.
  Withers, John, 44, 81, 90, 91, 95, 102, 126.
  Yougrofe, John, 115.
  grants referred to:
    town to Richard Abbett, 14.
    Joseph Allcocke, 118.
    Thomas Broughton, 6.
    Humphrey Chadborne, 64.
    Abraham Conley, 26.
    Abraham Conley and John Hord, 54.
    John Crafford, 9.
    Dennis Downeing, 47.
    Daniel Goodin, sen., 54.
    Nicholas Hodgsden, 31.
    Phineas Hull, 130, 131.
    [William] King, 120.
    George and Richard Leader, 132.
    [George Lydden], 51.
    John Morrall, 18, 19.
    Richard Nason, 28.
    John Ross, 112.
    William Seely, 39, 78, 104.
    John Wincoll, 1.
  Joseph Allcocke to Christopher Joyce and Edward Clarke, 118

Kittery, continued.
  Jos. Allcocke to Waymouth Lyston and Gil. Lugg, 118.
  John Billine to Thomas Crocket and Rice Tommass, 73.
  Isaac Botts to John Crafford, 48.
  Thomas Canny to Hatevill Nutter, 70.
  Fran. Champernoown to Walter Barefoote, 125.
  Abraham Conley to Henry Kirke, 31.
  Abraham Conley to Peter Wittum, sen., 26.
  Ephraim Crocket to Richard White, 79.
  Sir Ferdinando Gorges to Thomas Canny, 70.
  Sir Ferdinando Gorges to Edward Smale, 112.
  John Greene to Robert Waymouth, 45.
  Hugh Gunnisson to Thomas Trickey, 3.
  Sarah Gunnisson to William Rogers and William Seely, 3.
  Nicholas Hodgsden to John Morrall et ux., 18.
  John Lamb to Jas. Emery, 14.
  Christopher Lawson to Thos. Clarke and Thos. Lake, 66.
  Antipas Mavericke to Thomas Booth, 109.
  Alexander Maxell to John Neale, 22.
  Hatevill Nutter to John Roberts, sen., 70.
  Hatevill Nutter to John Morrall, 70.
  Roger Playsted, sen., to Geo. and John Broughton, 49.
  Edward Smale to Antipas Mavericke, 112.
  Thomas Wannerton to Nicholas Frost, 13.
  John Wincoll to Nic. Hodgsden, 31.
  Peter Wittum to Nic. Hodgsden, 111.

Land Titles. Act of Massachusetts General Court, explanatory of the act of 20 Nov., 1652, (see Book I, 26), relating to priority of land grants, 87.
Landing places, 78, 92, 96, 136.
Late troubles, Indian war of 1676, 80.
Laws of England, 98.
Law of Oleron, 42.
Law, national, of our king of England, 74.
Laws of this jurisdiction (Maine), 8.
  here established, 57.
Leantos, 71, 126.
Leases, 33, 71, 83, 97, 98, 107.
  referred to, Hugh Gunnisson, to William Rogers and William Seely, in Kittery, 3.
Legacy, 34, 72.
Letters,
  Joseph Armitage to Smyth, 57.
  Thomas Clarke to James Grant, 112.
  [Thomas] Clarke to James Grant, 112.
  Robert Elliot to John Davess, 57.
  John Knoulton to Samuel Sayword, 56.
  John Yougrofe to [George] Smyth, 114.
  a torn letter, 112.
Libel, maritime, 84.
Lieutenant, 52, 86, 97, 107, 113, 120.
Life estates and reservation of estates for life, 33, 34, 45, 62, 65, 92, 102, 105, 106, 113, 115, 122, 126.
Liter, lighter, a large open boat, 114.
Limited warranty, 101.
Liquor, 10
Livery and seizin, 1, 12, 13, 21, 26, 35, 39, 62, 65, 69, 74, 79, 88, 91, 93, 98, 103, 104, 107, 114, 116, 131, 132.
Log fence, 3.
Logging, 30, 65.
Log house, 30.

Logs, 1, 91, 128.
Lord proprietor of Maine, 4, 5, 11, 28, 74, 99, 125.
Lord of the fee or soil, 85, 106, 131.
Low water mark, 7, 80.
Lumbering. See Pay, Prices, Timber.
  booms, 1.
  boom-piers, 125.
  logging, 30, 65
  logs, 1, 91, 128.
  lumber, 91.
  pine trees, 91, 104, 132.
Lying room, to spread fish, 71.
Lygonia, Alexander Rigby, president, and lord proprietor of, 74.
Lyman, see Coxhall.

Magistrates of York county, 84.
Main, main land, 34.
Maine. See Lygonia, New Somerset, York county.
  Council of the province, 126, 137.
  counties, see Surrey, Index of Places.
  courts,
    admiralty, 84.
    associates, 55.
    county, held at Kittery, 139.
    Wells, 60, 61.
    York, 55, 58, 67, 126, 137.
    of pleas, 76, 137.
    orders of as probate court, 17, 67.
  general assembly of the province, 126.
  jurisdiction, regal, while under government of the king's commissioners, 3, 5.
  laws of the jurisdiction, 8, 57.
    here established, 8, 57.
  lord proprietor of, (Sir Ferdinando Gorges), 4, 5, 11, 28, 70, 74, 85, 93, 99, 106, 116, 125, 131.
  magistrates, see President, Deputy president, Deputy governor, Assistants, Associates,

Maine, continued.
  Commissioners, Justices of the peace, Magistrates of York county, 84, Recorders, Registers, Steward general.
  Thomas Danforth, president of, 67, 84, 96, 110. 125.
  Bryan Pendleton, deputy president of, 82
  John Davess, deputy president of, 95, 116, 138.
  Thomas Gorges, deputy governor of, 74.
  Richard Vines, steward general of, 97, 98
  records, public, 4, 7. See also York county.
Major, 3, 5, 7, 8, 13, 17, 27, 31, 37, 45, 67, 74, 78, 79, 82, 84, 86. 87, 91, 93, 100, 103, 109, 111, 112, 120, 126, 127, 128
Manners and Customs See Contracts Marriage settlements, Occupations, Partnerships, Support, Titles.
  custom of the country, 73, 82, 124.
  custom of England, 98
  Christmas, 124
  day's labor, 2, 37, 44, 124.
  dinner at noon, 16.
  interest, 93.
  liquor, 10.
  man and wife, 84
  Michaelmas, 51, 114, 124.
  minority, 73, 137
  overseers of wills, 17, 45
  pressed men, 16.
  publishing intentions of marriage, 84.
  rates, taxes, 37, 41.
  salary of minister, 107.
  tree bridge, 83.
Mantill tree, 13.
Manuring, a farm, 41.
Mariner, 3, 5, 9, 10, 47, 52, 58, 82, 104, 126
Marked trees, 11, 21, 22, 24, 25, 27, 28, 32, 39, 43, 44, 55, 57, 59, 76, 78, 80, 81, 87, 90, 91, 92, 113, 117, 124, 127, 134.

Marriage settlements, 18, 19, 34, 54, 105, 108, 113, 115, 138.
Marriage questioned, or requisites to a legal, 84.
Marshal of Agamenticus, 57.
  deputy, 57
Mason, 31, 42.
Massachusetts :
  act of General Court relative to land titles, 87.
  assistants. See under for members of the Governor's council.
  commissioners of, 13, 37, 66.
  deputy governors of,
    Simon Bradstreet, 41, 54, 84.
    Samuel Symonds, 29, 30.
  general court of,
    order concerning bounds of Saco, 86
    order for settling differences between individuals, 86, 87.
    order on petition of George and John Ingersoll, 125.
    report to, of commissioners, 86.
  governors of,
    Richard Bellingham, 114.
    Simon Bradstreet, 126.
    John Endicott, 69.
  jurisdiction of, 21, 48, 56, 58, 64, 87, 97, 118.
  secretaries of,
    John Haward, 43, 94, 110.
    Edward Rawson, 87
  Suffolk county court, clerk of, 38
Master, 12.
Masts, upwards of 26 inches, reserved by the lord proprietor, 125.
Merchants, 1, 5, 6, 17, 20, 27, 28, 29, 35, 41, 44, 45, 50, 58, 66, 67, 69, 79, 80, 93, 94, 107, 114, 127, 136, 138.
Messuage, 20, 39, 61, 78, 115, 124.
Michael-mass, 51, 114, 124.
Milline, a mill and its appurtenances, 59.
Mills. See Corn mills, Saw mills.
  at Casco, 43, 44.
  at Mousam, Wells, 44, 55.
  at Newgewanacke, 13.

GENERAL INDEX. 149

Mills, continued.
  at Saco, 82, 86, 102, 103.
  at Wells, 82.
  at York, 22, 40.
Mills, appurtenances and products.
  See Water-right.
  boards, 91.
  booms, 1
  boom-piers, 125.
  dams, 1, 95, 133.
  gear, running, 1, 47, 125.
  head-wears, 95.
  iron-work, 128.
  lumbering, see under.
  milline, 59.
  tools, 1, 39, 41, 125.
Mill-wright, 33, 39, 122.
Minerals, 61, 76, 97, 113, 128.
Mines, 7, 61, 76, 113, 128.
  royal, gold and silver, 97, 99, 128.
Ministers, 84, 116.
  salary of, 107.
  presbyter, 33.
Ministry lands, Wells, 77.
Minority, 73, 137.
Mis, Mrs, 3, 10, 21, 72, 78, 86, 101, 104, 116, 127, 130, 134, 139.
Mistress, 106
Moorings, 104, 138
Mooring-cables, 58.
  place, anchorage, 58, 71, 104, 138.
Moveables, chattels, 17, 33, 41, 89, 101, 102, 113, 126.
Mr., 1, 2, 7, 9, 10, 11, 13, 14, 20, 21, 22, 23, 24, 25, 33, 34, 35, 37, 38, 39, 40, 41, 45, 48, 49, 50, 55, 57, 59, 60, 64, 65, 66, 69, 70, 72, 74, 76, 77, 78, 79, 83, 84, 86, 87, 92, 93, 94, 96, 100, 101, 102, 103, 104, 105, 106, 107, 108, 113, 114, 116, 120, 122, 127, 128, 130, 131, 133, 139.
Muniments of title, 19, 20, 28, 85, 88, 94, 96, 128.

Napkins, 126.
  Ossenbridg, 126.
Navr, perhaps *alias*, 65. Compare Book I, 129.
Negro, 126.

New England Council, rents received to, 61.
New Hampshire,
  commissioners of, 2, 9, 10, 15, 20, 22, 27, 31, 32, 34, 39, 45, 46, 47, 52, 58, 67, 69, 70, 71, 74, 81, 82, 104, 112, 117, 125.
  councillors of, 65, 77, 100, 101, 107, 112, 118, 124.
  court of, as a probate court, 45, 118.
  deputy presidents of,
    Elias Styleman, 104.
    Richard Walden, 100.
  government, under his Majesty's immediate, 100.
  president of, John Cut, 102
  secretary of, Richard Styleman, 9, 67.
New Somerset, province of, 97, 98.
Noble, 6s, 8d, 37.
North Yarmouth. See Index of Places.
  selectmen, (called of Casco Bay), 53.
  grants recorded. See Index of Grantors under the names following
    Bray, Jane 41.
    Bray, Richard, 35, 36, 52
    Felt, George, 76
    Gyndall Walter, 109
    Redding, Eleanor, 93, 94.
    Redding, John, 53, 94.
    Rigby, Alexander, 61.
    Ryall, William, 62.
    Shapleigh, John, 127.
    Stephens, Edward, 53.
  grants referred to :
    Town to John Redding, 53.
    Richard Carter to John Mayne, 115.
    Mr. [George] Cleeves to John Cossons, 37, 52.
    John Cossons to Richard Bray, 35, 52.
    Thos. Drake to Richard Bray, 36.
    Indian sagamores to Thomas Stephens, 95, 110.

150   GENERAL INDEX.

North Yarmouth, continued.
  Thomas Stephens to Bartholomew Gydney, 95, 110.
  Henry Saywoid to Bartholomew Gydney, 44, 95, 110.
  Thomas Stephens to Henry Saywoid, 95, 110.
  Thos Redding to John Sands, 93.
  Mr [Richard] Vines to John Cossons, 52.
Notary public, 69.
Notes of hand. See Promissory notes

Ocum, oakum, 23.
Oars, 17.
Occupations,
  blacksmith, 14, 42, 47, 115, 129.
  bricklayer, 19, 24.
  carpenter, 45, 64, 71, 74, 88, 130
  carter, 42
  carver, 53.
  charcoal-burner, 92
  chirurgeon, surgeon, 29.
  clark, minister, 2
  cordwainer, 59, 66, 128.
  currier, 31, 68.
  farmer, 60
  felt maker, 5
  fisherman, 12, 17, 23, 24, 25, 30, 34, 42, 51, 71, 74, 77, 78, 79, 88, 90, 102, 105, 118, 119
  fishmonger, 74.
  husbandman, 25, 26, 31, 41, 80, 82, 102, 130
  joiner, 28, 106
  logging, 30.
  mariner, 3, 5, 9, 10, 47, 52, 58, 82, 104
  mason, 31, 42.
  merchant, 1, 5, 6, 17, 20, 27, 28, 29, 35, 41, 44, 45, 50, 58, 66, 67, 69, 79, 80, 93, 94, 107, 114, 127, 136, 138
  mill-wright, 33, 39, 122.
  notary public, 69.
  packer, 3.
  planter, 2, 10, 13, 22, 24, 27, 30, 34, 37, 45, 46, 50, 51, 52, 54,

Occupations, continued.
  59, 62, 63, 73, 76, 84, 89, 96, 100, 107, 112, 113, 117, 119.
  presbyter, clergyman, 33, 34.
  scrivener, 20, 110.
  seaman, 51, 53.
  servant, 31.
  ship carpenter, 119.
  shipwright, 12, 23, 24, 39, 111, 121, 127.
  shoemaker, 24, 42, 123.
  shop-keeper, 93.
  smith, 120.
  soldier, 16.
  surveyors, 14, 15, 21, 22, 43, 55, 92, 100, 113.
  tailor, 36, 41, 42, 53, 117.
  vintner, 5.
  weaver, 128
  wood-cutter, 104.
  writing school master, 5.
  yeoman, 9, 14, 46, 58, 59, 67, 74, 76, 91, 95, 109, 111, 131, 134.
Orchards, 36, 38, 41, 63, 83, 95, 110, 118, 119, 137.
Ossenbridg napkins, Osnaburg, a coarse linen cloth, 126.
Overseers of will, 17, 45.

Packer, 3.
Pans, 126.
Parchment, a deed, 86.
Parlor, 126
Partnerships, 7, 41, 49, 103, 104.
Partitions, 62, 67, 102, 107, 118.
Patents, 87.
  at Falmouth, Cleeves's, 87.
  Gorgeana, (William Hooke), 107.
  of Maine, 4, 5.
  Saco, (Lewis and Bonighton's) 87, 94, 102, 103
  Saco, (William Phillips's), 5, 8.
  Vines, 87.
  (Francis Champernowne's) at Kittery, 116.
  at York, 37, 132.
Pay See Consideration.
Barbadoes goods, 23.
barrel staves, 109.
beaver, 37.

Pay, continued.
  beef, 37.
  boards, 13, 24, 33, 40, 72, 109, 122, 125.
  bond, note, 66, 102.
  cattle, 112
  clothing, 101.
  common, 102, 122.
  corn, 72.
  current of New England, 3, 9, 23, 26, 29, 31, 39, 58, 103, 104, 110, 116, 122, 132, 133, 134.
  current money, 14, 31, 35, 36, 46, 79, 87, 90, 95, 110, 111, 117, 127, 136, 137.
  day's work, 2.
  dry cod fish, 18, 109.
  English goods, 23, 95.
  fish, 23, 24, 79.
  goods, 23, 123, 134.
  guns, 128.
  hogshead staves, 97.
  horse, 27.
  land, 11, 18, 48, 108, 128.
  lawful money, 39, 42, 94, 130
  lawful pay of New England, 99
  liquor, 10.
  lumber, 91.
  mackerel, 24.
  merchantable fish, 3.
  merchantable provision, 3, 96.
  money, 28, 37, 46, 47, 49, 53, 64, 66, 68, 72, 76, 86, 92, 96, 103, 111, 114, 123, 129, 130, 131, 134.
  money's worth, 92.
  neat hides, 67.
  New England money, 111, 127
  pay, lawful of New England, 44, 106.
  pine boards, 9, 13, 21, 49, 64, 130, 131
  pipe staves, 15, 29, (red oak, 93, 97), 114.
  plank, 40.
  pork, 37.
  provisions, 23, 101, 122
  refuge (refuse) fish, 93, 109.
  saddles and pillion, 100.
  shoes, 56, 67.
  silver, 13, 50, 136.

Pay, continued.
  silver, current New England, 102, 135
  sole and upper leather, 66.
  specie, 93, 122.
  staves, 13, 24, 86
  tobacco, 128.
  wampompeig, wampum, 128.
Penalty for breach of covenants, 10, 42, 54
Perch, defined to be 5½ yards, 61.
Petitions, 86, 87, 125.
Physic, medicine, 62
Pillion, a lady's saddle, 100.
Pillow-bears, pillow cases, 126.
Pine trees, 91, 104, 132
Pipe of tobacco, 16.
Plantations, 17, 80, 96, 101.
Planter, 2, 10, 13, 22, 24, 27, 30, 34, 37, 45, 46, 50, 51, 52, 54, 59, 62, 63, 72, 73, 76, 84, 89, 96, 100, 107, 112, 113, 117, 119
Plymouth Council. See Council for New England.
Porridge-pot, 17.
Post-mortem disposition of estate, 16, 39.
Pot, iron, 126.
Pot-hooks, 41.
Pots, 126.
Powers of attorney, 56, 66, 74, 98, 99, 114, 115, 137. See also under Attorneys
Presbyter, clergyman, 33, 34.
Precious stones, 98, 99.
Pressed men, 16
President of the province of Maine, 67, 84, 96, 110, 125.
  New Hampshire, 102
President and proprietor of the province of Lygonia, 74.
Prices,
  boards, 33.
  forks, 56.
  hinges, 56
  horse, 134.
  land, per acre, 102.
  mattock, a sort of pick axe, 56.
  nails, 56.
  neat hides, 67.
  pine boards, 13, 64.

Prices, continued
  pipe staves, 114
  rapier, 57.
  shoes, 57, 67.
  shovel, 56
  spade, 56
  tons burthen, 23
Promissory notes, 13, 52, 56, 130, 134, 136, 138.
Proprietor of the province of Maine, 70, 74. See also under Lord proprietor
Publication of intention of marriage, 84
Punctilios, formalities, 7.

Quarries, 98, 99
Quick goods, chattels, 41.

Rates, taxes, 37.
Receipts (see also Discharges), 3, 13, 16, 23, 27, 31, 51, 52, 102, 103, 107, 109, 125
Recorder, 30, 33, 50, 56, 102, 121, 135
  Edward Rishworth, 1—139.
  Joseph Hammond, 91, 100.
Records, public of Maine, or Yorkshire, 4, 7
Redown, revert, 45
References, 33, 54, 91. see also under Award
Register, 91, 100.
  York, 9
Regress, see under Ingress.
Release, 44.
Remittance, 112
Rent, 13, 20, 61, 63, 68, 74, 76, 77, 85, 87, 107, 115, 121, 122
  charge, 101.
  service to the Lord proprietor, 11, 37, 85
  of one farthing per acre, 87.
Renowned, renounced, 128.
Reports, 58, 86, 134
Reservations, 57, 82, 91, 95, 106, 113, 122, 125, 137.
  the fifth of gold and silver, 61, 98, 99
Reverend Mr , 73.

Reversions, 25, 33, 45, 53, 57, 62, 66, 101, 113, 123.
Ridge, of a plain, 29
Right of way, 2, 6, 52, 69, 78, 96, 114.
Road, hawser, 17, 31.
Royalties, 98, 99.

Sachem, sagamore, q. v. 114.
Saco, see Index of Places.
  bounds of, established by order of General Court, 86.
  town line between and Cape Porpoise, 86.
  townsmen, selectmen, 86.
  width of, surveyed along the sea side, 87.
  grants recorded, see Index of Grantors under the names following.
    Carter, John, 82.
    Collines, Timothy, 92.
    Gibbines, James, 94, 102.
    Haly, Thomas, 124.
    Hardy, Clement, 42.
    Henderson, John, 79.
    Phillips, William, 7, 8, 82.
    Vines, Richard, 124.
    Waddocke, Jane, 103
    Williams, Thomas, 92, 124.
  grant referred to:
    Wm Phillips et ux. to Zachary Gyllum and Ephraim Turner, 7, 8.
Sagamores,
  of Cape Porpoise, 4.
  Kennebec, 23, 80.
  Sanford, 5
  Lyman, &c., 28
  Monument bay, 114.
  near Pacannakicke, 114.
  Nimschasett, Wells, 65.
  Piscataqua, 9, 10
Salary of a minister, 107.
Saw mill, recorder's error for saw mill, 1.
Salt-house, 104.
Sanford, tract of eight miles square set apart for a township, afterwards called Phillipstown, 5.

Sanford, continued.
  former dwellers rights reserved, 5.
  grant recorded, see Index of Grantors, under,
  Phillips, William, 3, 5.
Saw Mills,
  at Cape Porpoise, 40, 128.
  Casco, 43, 44.
  Falmouth, 125.
  Kittery, 91, 127.
  Newgewanacke, 1, 47, 64, 125, 126, 130, 132, 133.
  Wells, 10, 44, 59.
  York, 39, 40, 120, 122.
Scarborough, see Index of Places.
  selectmen, 17, 40.
  town meetings, 40.
  town grants, 17, 40.
  other grants recorded see Index of Grantors under the names following:
    Bedford, Nathan, 74.
    Howell, John, 42.
    Pecket, Christopher, 93.
    Watts, Henry, 74.
  grants referred to:
    Geo. Cleeves to Henry Watts, 74.
    Isaac Walker to Nathan Bedford, 40.
Scotchman, in Kittery, 14.
Scrivener, public writer, 20, 43, 110.
Seaman, 51, 53.
Secretary,
  of the general assembly of the province of Maine, 126.
  of Massachusetts, 43, 87, 94, 110.
  of New Hampshire, 9, 67.
  of the special admiralty court, 84.
Sedule, schedule, 38, 126.
Seizin, see under Livery and Seizin.
Selectmen,
  Casco Bay, i. e. North Yarmouth, 53.
  Falmouth, 87.
  Kittery, 6, 14, 20, 22, 54, 64, 91, 94, 97, 100, 104, 134.
  Saco, 86.

Selectmen, continued.
  Scarborough, 17, 40.
  Wells, 133.
  York, 12, 15, 23, 25, 56, 57, 67, 72, 120, 134.
Sergeant, 15, 63.
Servant, 12, 31, 73.
  apprentice, 12, 73.
  Servt, recorder's error for Scrv^r, scrivener, 43.
Set, let, 114.
Shallop, fishing boat, 17, 31, 58.
Sheep-pasturage, 34.
Sheets, canvas, 126.
  cotton, 126.
Ship "John & Aylce," 23.
Ship-carpenter, 119.
Shipwright, 12, 23, 24, 39, 111, 121, 127.
Shoemaker, 24, 42, 123.
Shop-keeper, 93.
Shores, conveyed, 128.
Skirts, strips, 122.
Slipps, strips, 2.
Smith, 120.
Soldiers, 16.
  company of, 16.
Spetie, species, like kind, 93.
  specie, 40.
Spinning, 41.
Spit, 4, 126.
Spoons, 41, silver, 126.
Springs, 79, 102, 107, 119.
Stage, fishing, 17, 34, 58, 71, 104, 138.
  houses, 138.
  room, 58.
Steward general, 97, 98.
St. Michael's day, 124.
Stock, cattle, 41.
Store-house, 71, 73.
Suffolk county court, clerk of, 38.
Support and maintenance, 17, 31, 33, 57, 62, 63, 73, 83, 90, 122, 123, 124, 126, 137.
Surveyors, 14, 15, 19, 21, 22, 43, 55, 92, 100, 113.
Survivors, successors, 55.

Tailor, 36, 41, 42, 53, 117.
Tankard, silver, 126.

154　General Index.

Tar, 23.
Taxes, 37, 41.
Team, of oxen, 114.
Tenants, in common, 37, 67, 92, 93, 100, 101, 108, 118, 133
Tenement, house, 13, 15, 115.
Tenure,
　free and common soccage, 61, 98, 99.
　as of the manor of ——, 98, 99.
Thwart, across, 59.
Tillage, conversion into, 98, 99
Timber, grant of, 1, 14, 39, 43, 44, 47, 62, 63, 64, 87, 91, 125, 128, 132, 134.
　building, 64, 65.
　lying, felled, 1, 21, 48
　standing, 1, 21, 48, 51, 64, 65, 68, 91, 128.
　standing, for masts upwards of 26 inches, reserved, 125.
　drawing, 112.
Titles,
　captain, 1, 9, 16, 23, 31, 33, 47, 56, 57, 64, 66, 77, 78, 80, 87, 93, 95, 96, 99, 100, 101, 102, 115, 116, 125, 132, 135, 136.
　colonel, 74, 99, 125
　dame, 12
　esquire, 3, 4, 5, 39, 40, 61, 66, 84, 93, 97, 98, 99, 102, 109, 116, 122.
　farmer, 60.
　gentleman, 33, 44, 49, 59, 61, 68, 74, 91, 98, 124, 127, 129.
　goodman, 59, 86.
　goodwife, 52.
　lieutenant, 52, 86, 97, 107, 113, 120.
　major, 3, 5, 7, 8, 13, 17, 27, 31, 37, 45, 67, 74, 78, 79, 82, 84, 86, 87, 91, 93, 100, 103, 109, 111, 112, 120, 126, 127, 128
　master, 12
　Mis, Mrs, 3, 10, 21, 73, 78, 86, 101, 104, 116, 127, 130, 134, 139
　mistress, 106
　Mr. 1, 2, 7, 9, 10, 11, 13, 14, 20, 21, 22, 23, 24, 25, 33, 34, 35, 37, 38

Titles, continued
　50, 55, 57, 59, 60, 64, 65, 66, 69, 70, 72, 74, 76, 77, 78, 79, 83, 84, 86, 87, 92, 93, 94, 96, 100, 101, 102, 103, 104, 105, 106, 107, 108, 113, 114, 116, 120, 122, 127, 128, 130, 131, 133, 139.
　reverend Mr., 73.
　sergeant, 15, 63.
Tobacco, 16, 128
Tons burthen, 23
Tools, mill, 1, 39, iron, 41.
Towels, 126.
Town lines,
　between Kittery and York, 58.
　Saco and Cape Porpoise, 86.
　York and Wells, 134.
Townsmen, selectmen, 86, 87, 91
Trades, trading, see under Occupations, Pay and Prices.
Trammels, iron hooks, for suspending pots over fire, 41, 126.
Traynefatt, train vat, 17.
Treasurer, of the province of Maine, 103, 125
Tree-bridge, 83.
Trunks, 126
Trustees, 17, 91
Turf and twig, livery by, 21, 26, 35, 39, 93, 103, 116, 132.

Under-trade, under bid or undersell, 37.
Unmoveables, fixtures, 89, 101, 113.
Utellences, utensils, 125
Utensils, mill, 1, 125.

Vessels, and appurtenances, 23.
　anchors, 58, 138.
　boat, 23
　　room, anchorage, 34.
　cable, 58
　chains, 138.
　cleat, 23.
　compass, 17, 18, 81
　hold, 23
　grapnels, grappers, 17, 31.
　joiner's work, 23.
　ketch, 84.

Vessels, continued.
  lighter, 114.
  masts, 125.
  moorings, 104, 138.
    cables, 58.
    places, 58, 71.
  oakum, 23.
  oars, 17.
  road, hawser, 17, 31.
  shallops, 17, 31, 58.
  ship "John & Aylce," 23.
  tar, 23.
  tons burthen, 23.
Victuals, dressing, 126.
Vintner, 5.

Wages, servant's, 41.
Wampumpeag, wampum, 128.
Warehouses, 138.
Warrants, 84.
Washing, 126.
Water, right to, appurtenant to mills, 1, 91, 95, 125, 128.
  right to draw, 52.
  courses, 1, 61, 81, 95, 110, 112, 118, 125, 128, and elsewhere.
Weaver, 128.
Well, 52.
Wells See Index of Places. See Kennebunk.
  constable, 84.
  selectmen, 133
  town line between and York, 134.
  grants recorded. See Index of Grantors, under the names following:
    Ashly, William, 11
    Austine, Samuel, 108, 121.
    Backehouse, Francis, 135
    Barrett, John, 10, 59, 120.
    Barrett, Mary, 101.
    Cloyce, John, 11.
      Peter, 59.
    Collines, Abraham, 46.
    Epps, Daniel, 33.
    Everell, Thomas, 11.
    Frost, William, 60
    Hammond, Jonathan, 11.
      William, 89.
    Harding, Israel, 129.

Wells, continued.
  Mills, Thomas, 105.
  Paine, John, 29.
  Pendleton, Bryan, 77.
    James, 93.
  Storer, Joseph, 108.
  Wentworth, John, 84.
  grants referred to:
    town to Peter Cloyce, 59.
    Nicholas Coole, 29.
    Jonathan Hammond, 89.
    Henry Saywoid, 44.
    John Bush and Peter Turbet to Harlakenden Symonds, 127
    Peter Cloyce to Thomas Baston, 59.
    Abraham Collines to Samuel Austine, 121.
    Seth Fletcher to Bryan Pendleton, 77.
    William Hammond to Bryan Pendleton, 77.
    Ezekiel Knights to John Wentworth, 84.
    Francis Littlefield to William Ashly, 11.
    Francis Littlefield to Peter Cloyce, 59
    Massachusetts General Court to Henry Sayword, 44.
    Henry Sayword to Simon Lynde, 44, 55
    Harlakenden Symonds to Samuel Symonds, 127
    ——— Wadleigh to Thomas Mills, 105.
    John West to Bryan Pendleton, 77.
Wharves, 33, 121.
Whole, hold, 23.
Wigwam, 64.
Wills,
  Robert Jordan, 44.
  Robert Knight, 37.
  referred to,
    Thomas Chabinoct, sagamore, 65.
    Nicholas Davis, 72.
    John Heard, 17, 106.
    Robert Jordan, 69, 101.

Wills referred to, continued.
　Bryan Pendleton, 93.
　[John] Wheelwright, 92, 100.
　John Winter, 34
Winchester measure, 61.
Wood-cutters, 104.
Wood-cutting, commonage in, 27.
Writing-school master, 5.

Yeoman, 9, 14. 16, 58, 59, 67, 74, 76, 91, 95, 109, 111, 131, 133, 134.
York. See Index of Places.
　constable, 84.
　records, 9, 72.
　selectmen, 12, 15, 23, 25, 56, 57, 67, 72, 120, 134.
　town book of, 72.
　town line between and Kittery, 58.
　town line between and Wells, 134
　town meetings, 9, 88.
　town grants, 9, 23, 25, 67, 72, 88, 120.
　other grants recorded. See Index of Grantors, under the names following
　　Allcocke, Job, 52, 97, 100.
　　　John's estate, 107.
　　　Joseph's estate, 60
　　Anger, Samson, 12, 34.
　　Bass, Peter, 122.
　　Bleasdall, Ralph, 42
　　Bragdon, Arthur, 24, 96.
　　Burrin, George, 37.
　　Donell, Henry, 74
　　Everest, Andrew, 87, 89.
　　　Isaac, 15, 50.
　　Freathy, William, 81, 105.
　　Godfrey, Ann, 86.
　　　Edward, 37, 83.
　　Grant, James, 22.
　　Heard, John, 71, 100.
　　Hooke, William, 107.
　　Johnson, Edward, 83.
　　　William, 12
　　Knight, Richard, 38.
　　　Robert, 25
　　Mackyntyre Micum (Malcolm), 30.

York, continued
　Maxwell, Alexander, 51, 119.
　Parker, George, 122.
　Preble, Abraham, 58.
　Rishworth, Edward, 30, 50, 121, 135.
　Ryall, John, 72.
　Sayword, Henry, 39.
　Smyth, John, 120.
　Stover, John, 86.
　Symson, Henry, 78, 84, 85.
　Twisden, John, 24.
　Weare, Peter, 132.
　Wentworth, John, 63.
　Wood, Richard, 13.
　grants referred to :
　　town to Thomas Abbett, 21.
　　Samson Anger, 12.
　　Arthur Bragdon, sen., 23.
　　John Davess, 134.
　　Andrew Everest, 87, 89.
　　Isaac Everest, 15, 63.
　　William Palmer, 134.
　　Edward Rishworth, 122.
　　Jeremiah Sheeres, 88
　　Henry Sympson, 37, 83.
　　Peter Weare, 134.
　　George Burdett to Ann Messant, *alias* Godfrey, 116.
　　Richard Burgess to Edward Rishworth, 135
　　Henry Donell to Rich'd Wood, 13.
　　Isaac Everest to John Wentworth, 63.
　　Job Everest (by attorney) to Thomas Everell, 88.
　　Edward Godfrey to William Moore and Philip Adams, 37.
　　Edward Godfrey to Peter Weare, 132
　　James Grant to Micum Mackcintyre, 30.
　　Wm. Hooke to Henry Sympson, 84.
　　Rice Howell to William Freathy, 81.
　　Henry Norton to Henry Sympson, 78, 83.
　　Henry Sympson to Thomas Footeman, 85.

York, continued
    Richard Vines to Henry Norton, 2.
York county   See also Maine.
    magistrates, 84.

York county, continued.
    records, 4, 7, 47, 55, 66, 70, 86, 88, 91, 93, 101, 102, 129.
    treasurer, 103.
Ysland, inland, 5.

CPSIA information can be obtained
at www.ICGtesting.com
Printed in the USA
LVHW081948070521
686793LV00002B/80